Neobaroque in the Americas

New World Studies

J. Michael Dash, *Editor*

Frank Moya Pons and
Sandra Pouchet Paquet,
Associate Editors

Neobaroque in the Americas

Alternative Modernities in Literature, Visual Art, and Film

MONIKA KAUP

University of Virginia Press
Charlottesville and London

University of Virginia Press

Printed in the United States of America on acid-free paper

First published 2012

9 8 7 6 5 4 3 2 1

Library of Congress Cataloging-in-Publication Data
Kaup, Monika.
Neobaroque in the Americas : alternative modernities in literature, visual art, and film / Monika Kaup.
p. cm. — (New world studies)
Includes bibliographical references and index.
ISBN 978-0-8139-3313-9 (pbk. : alk. paper) — ISBN 978-0-8139-3312-2 (cloth : alk. paper) — ISBN 978-0-8139-3314-6 (e-book)
1. Latin America—Civilization—21st century. 2. United States—Civilization—21st century. 3. Baroque literature—Influence. 4. Art, Baroque—Influence. I. Title.
F1408.3K385 2012
980.04—dc23

2012019470

For my parents

CONTENTS

ILLUSTRATIONS

ACKNOWLEDGMENTS

Over the years that went into the making of this book, large debts of gratitude have accumulated to many colleagues and friends who offered advice and encouragement at various stages.

I would like to acknowledge and thank Eric Ames, Herb Blau, Marshall Brown, Laura Chrisman, Ruth Little, Christopher Johnson, Adrian Martin, Geoffrey McCafferty, Brian Reed, Jacobo Sefamí, and James Tweedie. I am indebted to Patrick Blaine, Eric Ames, and the staff at the University of Washington's Center for Digital Arts and Experimental Media for technical assistance in acquiring screen captures. Mary Brisson of the Peterson Automotive Museum offered generous help. Special thanks are due to Lois Parkinson Zamora, who provided crucial encouragement and instruction at the beginning of my engagement with the myriad forms of the Baroque. In addition, I would like to extend warm thanks to the "Neobarockers" of the Hispanic Baroque research project, funded by the Social Sciences and Humanities Research Council of Canada, for providing me with a sounding board for my ideas as my work progressed. At the University of Virginia Press, I am grateful to my editor Cathie Brettschreider, to my in-house editor Morgan Myers, and to the two anonymous readers who offered helpful comments. Finally, throughout I have been fortunate to count on the companionship of Robert Mugerauer for insights, inspiration, and boundless support.

There are also institutions to thank: a grant from the Royalty Research Fund at the University of Washington supported initial research for this project, and a sabbatical leave allowed me to complete the manuscript. My college and department at the University of Washington provided financial support for production costs, and *Modern Language Quarterly* contributed support for conference travel related to this project.

Finally, I would like to thank the publishers of journals in which earlier versions of certain chapters appeared:

The introduction includes revised versions of material originally published in "Neobaroque: Latin America's Alternative Modernity," *Comparative Literature* 58, no. 2 (Spring 2006), and "'The Future Is Entirely Fabulous': The Baroque Genealogy of Latin America's Modernity," *Modern Language Quarterly* 68, no. 2 (June 2007).

Chapter 2, on Djuna Barnes, is a revised and significantly expanded version of "The Neobaroque in Djuna Barnes," published in *Modernism/Modernity* 12, no. 1 (2005).

The section in chapter 3 on José Donoso is a revised version of "Postdictatorship Allegory and Neobaroque Disillusionment in José Donoso's *Casa de campo,*" *Chasqui* 34, no. 2 (November 2005).

Chapter 5 incorporates revised portions of "Becoming-Baroque: Folding European Forms into the New World Baroque with Alejo Carpentier," *CR: The New Centennial Review* 5, no. 2 (2005).

Neobaroque in the Americas

Introduction

Neobaroque Alternative Modernities

THIS BOOK opens with a portrait of neobaroque T. S. Eliot and closes with contemporary baroques in Chicano lowrider art and the hip-hop baroque in Cuban American art. In between, it ranges over vastly diverse territory: the major works of Djuna Barnes, contemporary antidictatorship literature and film from Chile and Argentina by Diamela Eltit, José Donoso, Raúl Ruiz, and María Luisa Bemberg, and Latin American and Caribbean postcolonial theory outlining the emergence of a decolonizing New World baroque in the seventeenth and eighteenth centuries. It encompasses Spanish-language and English-language works, focusing mainly on the United States and the Southern Cone (the region of Latin America comprising Argentina, Chile, Paraguay, Uruguay, and Southern Brazil), and juxtaposes long-neglected Anglo-American neobaroque expression with the more familiar (or at least more predictable) Latin American and Latino varieties. *Neobaroque in the Americas* is an interartistic study that spans literature, film, architecture, and the visual arts and also incorporates the twentieth-century philosophy and cultural theory of Walter Benjamin, Gilles Deleuze, Michel Foucault, Irlemar Chiampi, Bolívar Echeverría, and Christine Buci-Glucksmann. Few literary and cultural phenomena allow the researcher to roam this far in pursuit of her topic, looking both high and low in the arts, ranging from modernist experimentalism (Eliot and Barnes) to postmodern and contemporary developments such as post-Boom antidictatorship literature and film from the Southern Cone; traveling north and south across the American hemisphere; tracing parallel but distinct European and American mestizo genealogies of the same artistic expression (the European baroque and the transculturated mestizo New World baroque); and consequently being forced to make difficult choices along the way in balancing equally compelling word-based and image-based varieties.

The baroque is an exceptional and fascinating phenomenon, in no small part because of the prolific afterlife it has had in generating "new" baroques, both in the seventeenth and eighteenth centuries and again in the twentieth and twenty-first centuries. Baroque (of the European sort), New World baroque, and neobaroque are the terms that designate the milestones of this idiosyncratic, nonlinear trajectory. The baroque first arose in the capitals of the new centralizing nation-states and regional provinces of the seventeenth century—in Rome, Versailles, Vienna, Madrid—as the grand, monumental style of European absolutism (the state form succeeding feudalism in early modern Europe, founded on the centralization of power and the absolute sovereignty of the monarch unchecked by any other agency) and the Counter-Reformation. From the very beginning, the baroque has been an interartistic expression, emerging in a variety of media but predominantly in the visual arts because of the Counter-Reformation's emphasis on image-based religious pedagogy to indoctrinate the illiterate masses in Europe and the European colonies.[1] But even though the baroque began as a conservative style, in the official arts sponsored by the Catholic Church and the absolutist state, many of the new baroques that arose subsequently deviated diametrically from these social origins. The wayward, rich afterlife of the historical baroque has vastly expanded baroque expression along two paradigmatic coordinates, time and space—or history, as found in the twentieth- and twenty-first-century neobaroque, and geographic and cultural location, as found in the seventeenth- and eighteenth-century New World baroque, which has continuities with contemporary postcolonial and ethnic neobaroques.

Like the baroque before it, the neobaroque spread in nonlinear fashion across multiple boundaries among languages, nations (and continents), ethnic groups, and disciplines. Reflecting this rich transhistorical and transcultural genealogy of expression, the baroque today is one of the poster children of interdisciplinary arts and culture. The comparative nature of this study is perfectly suited to its subject: no narrow, disciplinary—nation-based, genre-based, ethnocentric or otherwise noncomparative—inquiry can ever hope to capture the uniqueness and complexity of the baroque. *Neobaroque in the Americas* examines the neobaroque—the twentieth- and twenty-first-century recovery of the baroque in modern and postmodern literature, film, the visual arts, and theory—within a hemispheric American framework. As such, it is broadly aligned with Roland Greene's suggestion that "the neobaroque in spirit is a decisively American phenomenon, probably because this hemisphere provides a distance and delay from the original baroque that allows it to be critically refashioned. *Baroque* and *neobaroque* should be among the first nouns in a common language between the early modern past and the inter-American present."[2]

This study is devoted to retheorizing the continuities of the baroque and the neobaroque as it traveled from Europe to the Americas and from the seventeenth to the twentieth (and twenty-first) century, and more narrowly to mapping a specific and understudied portion of this complex, transnational process, the hemispheric American dynamics of the neobaroque. The intent is to contribute to a fuller picture of the ongoing phenomenon of the neobaroque (such as the neobaroque's presence in Anglo-American modernism) and to correct some long-standing misperceptions (such as that the baroque stops south of the Rio Grande and that it is inherently conservative). The unusual breadth of material, which brings T. S. Eliot and Chicano lowriders together between the covers of the same book, is precisely the point: the argument I make here is that the baroque refuses to regard culture as a fixed, "self-contained system," the property of discrete, segregated social groups. Rather, the baroque is an "antiproprietary" expression that brings together seemingly disparate writers and artists; few artistic and representational phenomena are so good at bending so many different ways as the baroque.[3]

Both a historical period and a transhistorical, transcultural artistic sensibility and style, the baroque is a chameleon-like phenomenon that never coalesces into an integrated pattern.[4] An explanation for this definitional confusion of what constitutes the baroque can be found in the history of the concept. It was not until the nineteenth century that the art of the long seventeenth century, or the period between the Renaissance and eighteenth-century neoclassicism, came to be classified as baroque. The seventeenth century, in other words, did not view itself as "baroque."[5] "Baroque" first appeared in France in the eighteenth century as a pejorative term for nonclassicist art and architecture of the seventeenth century such as Bernini's—or rather, for its nonclassicist *use* of classical forms.[6] The origins of "baroque" are in a polemic on the part of neoclassicism against what it thought of as the undisciplined and capricious expression of the previous century that departed from strict classicist norms. From the outset, a rigid opposition between classicism and baroque has underpinned the use of this term, an opposition that has been as problematic as illuminating, for it has obscured the actual stylistic heterogeneity of the period pejoratively labeled baroque. Late sixteenth-century mannerism, for example, contrasts with Renaissance classicism as much as with the baroque. And there was a seventeenth-century classicism—a baroque classicism—in French art and architecture that is erased by this simple baroque-classic polarity. (Twentieth-century social historians of the baroque such as Arnold Hauser also draw careful distinctions between the Catholic state baroque and the bourgeois Dutch baroque.[7])

What is more, the etymology of the term *baroque* is suitably quixotic, matching its meaning. Three competing etymologies are usually given; they are: a neologism (*baroco*) coined to help remember the logical structure of a particular scholastic syllogism; a Portuguese word (*barrôco*), a jeweler's term, first documented in 1531, that designates an irregularly or oddly shaped pearl; and an Italian term from Tuscany (*barocco, baroccolo,* or *barocchio*) that refers to a usurer's contract.[8] Over time, the specific link between the pearl and baroque is dissolved, yielding to an abstract association between baroque and the irregular or bizarre as such. Some critics name the scholastic syllogism as the authoritative source, although that term appears to have survived as a distinct entity; no one prefers the usurer's term, which in any case was defunct by the eighteenth century. The development of the adjective "baroque" as a negative label meaning "eccentric," "bizarre," "illogical" took place in France, where it was first applied to Italian architecture in 1739. From there, the disparaging term "baroque" was translated into other European languages, and extended to seventeenth-century sculpture, painting, and literature as the neoclassicist polemic spread. The prejudice against the baroque persisted to the end of the nineteenth century. For two centuries, most seventeenth-century artists and writers were neglected, dismissed, and forgotten; their works went out of print.

The baroque has been maligned, and the concept of the baroque remains today a controversial if resilient critical term in seventeenth-century art (and literary) history.[9] Yet I began this introduction by stressing the lasting popularity of the baroque, and its astonishingly prolific afterlife. How is this possible? How, if the baroque had been pronounced dead for centuries, could it come back to life in the twentieth century and reproduce itself so vigorously? The purpose of this study is to offer an answer to this question. Overall, the baroque's modern appeal, and the countless twentieth-century revivals of the baroque (continuing into the twenty-first century), have as much to do with its intrinsic formal and structural qualities as with the social and historical forces that backed its detractors. Furthermore, as the discussion of the contemporary Latin American antidictatorship baroque will show, the baroque's own authoritarian social origins in the European state baroque have also had some remarkable contemporary effects. At this point, and before I proceed to discussing the transnational and transcultural as well as transhistorical dimensions of the baroque's trajectory, I emphasize the baroque's stigmatization and its effective extirpation from artistic canons in the eighteenth and nineteenth centuries, the nonlinear trajectory of its survival, and the antagonism between the antithetical terms *classic* and *baroque* that, for better or worse, remains inscribed in later developments, even as the meaning of the term changes and the baroque becomes a stylistic sensibility, a traveling culture (James Clifford), cut loose from the period and place where it arose.[10]

Originally, the baroque's transnational reach was impelled by European imperialism. As Alejo Carpentier has observed, the baroque first arrived in the Americas on the ships of the Spanish and Portuguese (and French) conquistadors.[11] Consonant with the conservative baroque of the Catholic courts, the baroque imported into the Iberian and French colonies of the New World was a repressive instrument of the colonial state. As the Uruguayan critic Ángel Rama contends, "The American continent became the experimental field for the formulation of a new Baroque culture. The first methodical application of Baroque ideas was carried out by absolute monarchies in their New World empires, applying rigid principles—abstraction, rationalization, and systematization—and opposing all local expressions of particularity, imagination, or invention."[12] Indeed, until the mid-twentieth century, a majority of historians and critics saw in the colonial American baroque nothing but a tool of European imperialism and inquisitorial repression. Then a postwar generation of Latin American intellectuals, foremost among them the Cuban writers José Lezama Lima and Carpentier, popularized the notion of an "anticolonial" New World baroque. Did the widespread evidence of idiosyncratic mestizo and local adaptations of the Iberian baroque, both in the colonial art and architecture produced by indigenous artisans and in the colonial literature authored by *criollos* (Americans of Iberian descent), not contradict the familiar repressive thesis? Lezama Lima and Carpentier argued that New World artists had stolen the colonizer's art and turned it into an expression of their own: in Lezama Lima's formulation, the American baroque was an instrument not of the Counter-Reformation but of *contraconquista* (counterconquest). During the seventeenth and eighteenth centuries a new, rebellious baroque emerged that was an early expression of what José Martí would later call "Our America." When indigenous artisans inserted pre-Columbian symbols into the iconography of the Catholic baroque, they undid the colonial negation of their world and at the same time deformed and re-created the European expression that had been imposed on them. At issue in the New World baroque is, in short, "the survival of Otherness piggybacking on the unsuspecting signs of Empire."[13] Carpentier offers an emblematic formulation of the anticolonial New World baroque:

> And why is Latin America the chosen territory of the Baroque? Because all symbiosis, all *mestizaje,* engenders the baroque. The American baroque develops along with *criollo* culture, . . . with the self-awareness of the American man, be he the son of a white European, the son of a black African or an Indian born on the continent . . . : the awareness of being Other, of being new, of being symbiotic, of being a *criollo;* and the *criollo* spirit is itself a baroque spirit. (100)

I use Deleuze and Guattari's notion of the "becoming-minor" of a major (official) expressive form, as well as the theory of articulation (Stuart Hall, Ernesto Laclau), to explain how the baroque came to be used against the grain of its origins in the institutionalized, authoritarian European state baroque. An articulation is a hookup, a historically and socially contingent linkage between disparate phenomena, that is temporarily forged and broken over time and across cultures. Like all cultural expressions, the baroque has been subject to never-ending flows of appropriation, resignification, and subversion that link it to new ideologies and political subjects. Pried loose from its original social setting, the baroque has become raw material for new articulations, such as alternative, critical baroque modernities (in Europe as well as in the Americas) and a decolonizing baroque of the Americas (the New World baroque). These concepts of baroque alternative modernities and of decolonizing, anti-institutional "minor" baroques constitute the dual theoretical lenses I bring to the study of my primary texts and visual art.

A few words regarding the notion of the baroque as an alternative modernity, which encapsulates the intellectual history behind the return of the baroque in the twentieth century. When the baroque became anathema in the eighteenth century, it fell victim to the principles of Enlightenment rationalism and neoclassicism, which vilified the expression of Europe's first modernity (predominantly Catholic and Southern), placing the baroque in a purgatory that would last for more than two centuries. Against Enlightenment modernity and scientific rationalism's grand narrative of linear progress by way of a radical rupture with the past and nonrationalist modes of thought, the baroque affirms the impure, hybrid coexistence of the disjunctive (modern and premodern, global and local, faith and reason, science and wonder). The twentieth-century crisis of Enlightenment modernity opened the way for the rediscovery of the alternative modernity of the baroque and its unique, nondissociative response to the upheavals of the modern age, religious and scientific. In the West—Europe and North America—the neobaroque has informed modernist (Walter Benjamin, Eugenio d'Ors) and contemporary poststructuralist (Gilles Deleuze, Michel Foucault, Christine Buci-Glucksmann) thinkers and writers who critique the reductive epistemology of scientific reason. On the West's periphery, Latin America and the Caribbean, the crisis of Enlightenment modernity triggered a radical decolonization of knowledge and cultural history: it cleared the way for the recuperation of Latin America's site-specific, dissonant modernity, which—as has been claimed in several recent studies by Irlemar Chiampi, Bolívar Echeverría, and others—is baroque, and which is characterized by the complex interplay of Western and indigenous elements and by the persistence of the "obsolete" in the contemporary.[14] My project contributes to the new global modernity studies through its analysis of baroque alternative modernities that deviate from the notion of a single, universal modernity modeled on European history in general, and Enlightenment ideology in particular.

Recent global modernity studies have challenged the notion of a singular, universal modernity modeled on Europe.[15] "How would one write of forms of modernity that have deviated from all canonical understandings of the term? . . . The old imperial option of looking down on them through sc version of the idea of *backwardness* has lost its appeal" (Chakrabarty, *Hat tations* xx). How, in other words, would one think about the hybrid culture of García Canclini's Latin America, where many premodern practices and beliefs persist, "where traditions have not yet disappeared and modernity has not completely arrived" (García Canclini 1)? Scholars are unanimous that the main obstacle to understanding modern India or Latin America is the absolute opposition between the traditional and the modern in the grand narrative of European "development"—a linear, teleological paradigm according to which cultures "advance" or "progress" by replacing traditional doctrines, social institutions, and everyday practices with their "modern" counterparts. Scientific and instrumental reason, the disenchantment of the lifeworld, the secular outlook, individualism, democracy, and industrialization are all said to displace premodern formations following a quasi-natural law: in Charles Taylor's analogy, "modernity is like a wave, flowing over and engulfing one traditional culture after another" (Taylor 182). It is this essentialist construct of evolutionism and its "transition" narratives—that modernity is something arrived at via the "transition to"—that needs to be dismantled: according to Chakrabarty, a "critique of historicism therefore goes to the heart of the question of political modernity in non-Western societies" (*Provincializing Europe* 9). The various negative scenarios of "deficient," "incomplete," or "belated" modernity ascribed to contemporary Third World societies all derive from the Eurocentric paradigm of a singular, universal temporality and history. In response, "subverting the historicist canon of the modern" that has been "constructed in the hegemonic centers of the Western world" is the central strategy of the postcolonial revision of modernity (Chiampi, "Baroque" 522, 508).

How, then, to "provincialize Europe"—to cite the title of Chakrabarty's felicitously named project—and to think in a constructive way about the impure, hybrid coexistence of the premodern and the modern characteristic of the global south? The first step, following Taylor, is that "instead of speaking of modernity in the singular, we should better speak of 'alternative modernities'" (182). Replacing linear historicism, in his landmark *Hybrid Cultures: Strategies for Entering and Leaving Modernity,* García Canclini proposed a spatial model of "entering" and "exiting" modernity through synchronic migrations, as in "a city, which one enters via the path of the cultured, of the popular, or of the massified. . . . The migrants cross the city in many directions and, precisely at the intersections, install their baroque stands of regional candies and contraband radios, medicinal herbs and videocassettes" (3). Instead of separating them on opposite sides of the historical watershed of "modernization," García Canclini's spatial model joins together the indigenous and the European, the baroque and the modern through linkages and passages that are unique to their cultural conditions. While Latin America's alternative modernity is not identical with contemporary India's, both societies share the common complex articulation of the premodern with the modern, of traditions with modernities, deconstructing the premodern's rupture and displacement by the modern. At the same time, the hybridity of global modernities also forecloses a solution via the opposite purism—nativism or indigenism—the affirmation of precolonial, indigenous origins and cultural autonomy at the expense of the complete dismissal of imported European modernity. It is important to realize that, in Chakrabarty's formulation, "provincializing Europe is not a project of rejecting or discarding European thought. . . . European thought is at once both indispensable and inadequate in helping us to think through the experiences of political modernity in non-Western nations" (*Provincializing Europe* 16).

The baroque constitutes Latin America's alternative modernity. In one of several recent studies that map the baroque genealogy of Latin America's modernity, *Barroco y modernidad,* Irlemar Chiampi states that the twentieth-century recovery of the baroque in Latin America enables "an archaeology of the modern, one that allows us to reinterpret Latin American experience as a dissonant modernity" ("Baroque" 508):

> The Baroque, crossroads of signs and temporalities, aesthetic logic of mourning and melancholy, luxuriousness and pleasure, erotic convulsion and allegorical pathos, reappears to bear witness to the crisis or end of modernity and to the very condition of a continent that could not be assimilated by the project of the Enlightenment. (ibid.)

> It is no accident, then, that the Baroque—pre-Enlightenment, premodern, prebourgeois, pre-Hegelian—should be reappropriated from this periphery (which enjoyed only the leftovers of modernization) as a strategy for subverting the historicist canon of the modern. The recovery of the Baroque is both an aesthetics and a politics of literature, an authentic paradigmatic shift in poetic forms that implies, among other consequences, the abandonment of the silent presence of the eighteenth century in our mentality. (522)

The transhistorical and transcultural intersections by which the baroque is articulated with the modern on the same synchronic plane in Latin America are one piece in the emerging puzzle of global modernities—or, as some scholars prefer, "modernity at large" (Arjun Appadurai), or "transmodernity" (Enrique Dussel).[16] Like Chakrabarty, García Canclini, and others, I propose that modernity should be conceived as having multiple, alternative forms resulting from the complex interplay of colonial and indigenous elements. The New World baroque and the Latin American neobaroque constitute such a site-specific, hybrid modernity from the global periphery, where imported European and native, modern and premodern forms are joined to generate an eccentric New World modernity that deviates from the metropolitan prototype.

But the twentieth-century rehabilitation and revival of the baroque was also a transatlantic phenomenon. Hence, we need to distinguish two distinct versions of neobaroque alternative modernities, one from Latin America, the other from Europe and North America. Like the Latin American variety, the European part of this story is nonlinear and complexly mediated through different historical moments, genres and disciplines, and geographic and social locations. I offer only a brief synopsis.

In Europe, the recovery of the baroque began with the sober, formalist analyses of Swiss art historian Heinrich Wölfflin in his influential studies of baroque art, culminating in *Principles of Art History* (1915), a landmark study that, more than any other, initiated the twentieth-century rehabilitation and recovery of the baroque.[17] Wölfflin argued that the strict norms of Renaissance classicism gave way to a freer conception of art in the baroque, replacing closed, self-contained compositions with decentered, dynamic ones. He made his case by analyzing underlying stylistic principles, grouped into five sets, in which a quality of Renaissance classicism was opposed to a characteristic of the baroque: (1) linear versus painterly, (2) planar versus recessive perspective, (3) closed versus open form, (4) multiplicity versus unity, and (5) absolute versus relative clarity. As the "tactile" (tangibility) gave way to the "visual" (appearance) and the focus shifted from essence to appearances, from "being" to "seeming," theatricality and subjectivism newly came to dominate. Nevertheless, Wölfflin claimed, objectivist classicism and subjectivist baroque are simply mutually incompatible styles. The baroque is not, as had previously been argued, a decadent art inferior to classicism.

Following Wölfflin, several literary and cultural historians, including Oswald Spengler, Wilhelm Worringer, Henri Focillon, and Eugenio d'Ors, reformulated the baroque as a typological concept, a timeless phenomenon recurring cyclically across the ages.[18] Wölfflin had prepared the ground for this development when he proposed the baroque as the unified style of a period in which no such unity existed (mannerism, baroque classicism in France). Now the baroque was completely detached from its seventeenth-century origins to become a constant of the human spirit: a late, exhausted phase of a once vital style and culture (Spengler), a late version of Gothicism (Worringer), the final of four successive states of a style (Focillon), and, most extravagantly, a timeless phenomenon found across millennia of Indo-European culture (d'Ors). Problematic from a scholarly perspective, these claims make the baroque so vague as to render it virtually meaningless (Wellek 92). But by severing the link between the baroque and a specific period, class, and ideology (seventeenth-century European Counter-Reformation and absolutist courts), speculations about a baroque spirit that was present across cultures and ages performed an important task. By producing a free-floating baroque sensibility available to anyone, they created a precedent and legitimation for subsequent twentieth-century rearticulations, recyclings and re-creations of the baroque, many of which are not only indifferent to but run directly against the grain of the "major" European state baroque.

In literature, the arts, and philosophy, the twentieth century produced a series of baroque revivals and neobaroques on the part of avant-garde, modernist, and postmodernist or poststructuralist writers. The recovery of the Spanish baroque poet Luis de Góngora by the avant-garde poets of the Spanish Generation of '27 is perhaps the best-known literary instance. T. S. Eliot's recuperation of John Donne and the English metaphysical poets is a seldom acknowledged Anglo-American counterpart to Hispanic neobaroque modernism. The modernist novelists Djuna Barnes and William Faulkner both employed ornate, neobaroque prose; German Expressionism was thought to be akin to the baroque and fed into the early twentieth-century German enthusiasm for the baroque that also produced Walter Benjamin's *The Origin of German Tragic Drama* (1928; *Ursprung des deutschen Trauerspiels*), which shed light on baroque allegory's demystification of modernity's master narrative of progress. Indeed, Benjamin's neobaroque critique of modernity, which writes modern history from the wasteland of ruins left behind by what is called progress, occupies a key position in this study. Postmodernists followed suit: proposing the concept of the "open work" for modern art, the Italian critic Umberto Eco traced its origins to the baroque, and the U.S. writer John Barth's notion of the "literature of exhaustion" invokes the baroque. The French philosophers Michel Foucault, Gilles Deleuze, Roland Barthes, and Christine Buci-Glucksmann worked out poststructuralist turns of the baroque.[19] Yet—and as will become clear at various points in this study—while Deleuze and Buci-Glucksmann in particular theorize the baroque as a transgression of seventeenth-century scientific reason, they remain Eurocentric in motivation and scope. Unlike the Latin American theorists of the New World baroque, they fail to turn the baroque alternative toward a postcolonial critique of the civilizing myth of Enlightenment modernity.

Indeed, the "postmodern" moment when the universal paradigm of Enlightenment rationality fully comes under attack marks a bifurcation between parallel critiques of modernity in Europe, on the one hand, and Latin America and other non-Western regions on the other. Europe works out the critique of Enlightenment reason through postmodern attacks on the authority of positivistic science, representation, and rational knowledge as such by Lyotard, Baudrillard, and others. In contrast, Third World critics such as Dussel, Chakrabarty, and García Canclini have since charged that the postmodern critique of the violence of modernity, with its totalizing grand narratives of rational knowledge, is nothing but a "provincial" European analysis that has only limited validity in the global periphery. There, the postmodern critique of universalism opened the door for a new and independent project: a critical genealogy of the legacy of modernity outside of Europe. Rather than once again mimic Europe as it undergoes yet another (now postmodern) cycle of modernity's development, Third World intellectuals seize the postmodern crisis as the occasion to challenge the Eurocentric narrative of modernity.

Notwithstanding their divergence, these two versions of neobaroque alternative modernities, the Latin American and the European, overlap by linking their critique of reductive rationalisms and Enlightenment modernity to a nonlinear genealogy connecting the baroque and the modern. Thus, the notion of alternative modernities offers a conceptual framework for the continuity of neobaroque expression across the twentieth and twenty-first centuries. It justifies my subsequent analysis of writers frequently considered modernist (such as the U.S. expatriate writers Eliot and Barnes) and postmodernist (the Chileans Donoso and Eltit) as part of a coherent neobaroque movement. Along the same lines, the idea of neobaroque alternative modernities establishes a common project among writers and artists who are not connected by any documented transmissions or causal links, such as U.S. modernists, contemporary U.S. Latino visual artists, and contemporary Latin American writers and filmmakers from Chile and Argentina. This is not to say, however, that no such links exist among any of them, as is, of course, the case with Eliot and Barnes, as well as with several other authors, such as the triumvirate of Cuban writers, José Lezama Lima, Alejo Carpentier, and Severo Sarduy, who articulated the Latin American theory of the New World baroque and neobaroque. Indeed, Eliot's and Barnes's common affinity for the neobaroque sheds fresh light on their much-discussed (and unequal) friendship.

My comparison of works selected here employs what the Cuban critic Gustavo Pérez Firmat calls the "mediative" approach in hemispheric American studies.[20] Mediative refers to a dimension that is "internal to the works themselves," already "embedded" in them (4). Among methods in comparative literature, it differs both from what Pérez Firmat calls the "generic" approach, which takes a common theme or widely applicable notion as the point of departure, and the "genetic" approach, perhaps the most conservative and traditional of all comparative methods, which limits itself to cases of documented transmission and influence (3). Looser than the genetic approach and stricter than the generic, the mediative approach to literary (as well as interartistic) comparison constructs its set by identifying its members as carriers of the same, common symptom, even though (to use a rough medical analogy) they may not have caught the virus from one another. For the twentieth- and twenty-first-century works participating in baroque revivals, the neobaroque is a more fitting term than its twinned counterparts, the modern and postmodern, because the latter posit an antagonistic relationship between modernism and the historical avant-garde and contemporary literature, obscuring the continuity of neobaroque expression across the twentieth century, whereas the former names the transhistorical aspect of these alternative modernities that recuperate residual expression from the early modern baroque. For Latin American works in particular, the neobaroque constitutes an important corrective optic to modern and postmodern discourses regularly imported from Europe: unlike the latter, the neobaroque is historically rooted in Latin America.

Whether implicitly or explicitly, recent scholarship on the baroque, the New World baroque, and the neobaroque is premised on the recognition of a variety of baroques, articulated from distinct historical, social, and ideological locations. Book-length studies by Omar Calabrese, Stephen Calloway, Gregg Lambert, and Angela Ndalianis have contributed to illuminating the transhistorical continuities connecting the baroque and the neobaroque. Further studies by Armstrong and Zamudio-Taylor, Irlemar Chiampi, Roberto González Echevarría, Robert Harbison, Arabella Pauly, and Lois Parkinson Zamora have complicated this configuration by drawing attention to the transcultural dynamics by which the New World baroque emerged by way of the rebellious consumption of the European baroque.[21] From their different angles, these critics have jointly overturned a doctrine of previous scholarship that identified the baroque with a specific period, class, and ideology (seventeenth-century European Counter-Reformation and absolutism), a reductive reading that long obstructed the recognition of alternative baroques, both in the seventeenth century and in the twentieth. This study, then, is part of a growing synthetic critical literature on the baroque, the neobaroque, and the New World baroque that began emerging in the 1990s. Along with these recent critics, I argue that we need to replace the notion of a single baroque with that of multiple baroques. For baroque aesthetics is an open and contested field. Even though it may originally have been co-opted by conservative ideology (as Maravall shows), it has subsequently been appropriated and resignified for decolonizing and other anti-institutional purposes.

The story of how the antimodern thesis of the baroque was modified, and how a recognition of the alternative modernity of the baroque slowly asserted itself, is complicated and can be told in various ways. In the remainder of this introduction I focus on two particular episodes that shed further light on my hemispheric American archive of neobaroque works. The first narrative goes as follows: For much of the twentieth century, and amid the appearance of ever-new cycles of neobaroque art and literature that presented live testimony to the modernity of the baroque, the historical baroque remained synonymous with political conservatism. Landmark instances range from Werner Weisbach's 1921 thesis of the baroque as the art of the Counter-Reformation to José Antonio Maravall's 1975 thesis of the *dirigismo* ("guided culture") of the baroque (which Ángel Rama seconds from a Latin American perspective in the passage quoted above).[22] The baroque was ideologically conservative—even reactionary—even as it was profoundly modern aesthetically. The baroque's reduction to an ornament of style and an escapist function in a conservative culture rejecting modernity was particularly common for the Spanish baroque. The following 1944 assessment by Latin American cultural historian Mariano Picón-Salas is representative: "In form this Spanish expression displayed a bold modernism, whereas in content it favored an extreme orthodoxy."[23] Literary and cultural critics tended to separate baroque ideology from baroque aesthetics to account for the undeniable modernity of the baroque. While acknowledging the baroque's beginnings as an instrument of absolutism and the Counter-Reformation, I follow Jeremy Robbins in cautioning against monolithic readings that deny the presence of any criticism of state control in baroque art, even in Spain.[24]

Such a cross-eyed view juxtaposing opposite tendencies in baroque ideology and aesthetics was but a makeshift formula that did little to reconcile the authoritarian state baroque with mounting twentieth-century evidence of the baroque's persistent modern appeal. Critical assessment of the baroque's ideological and cultural orientation needed further elaboration and refinement, which was furnished in a series of neobaroque poetics published by contemporary neobaroque writers and poets after World War II, both in Europe and in the Americas. In parallel but independent interventions in the 1950s, Umberto Eco and the Brazilian poet and critic Haroldo de Campos argued that in the seventeenth century, a distinctly modern style emerged that acknowledged the active role of the recipient (the reader, the spectator) and her creativity in completing the art work. Eco and de Campos proposed the same concept for this modern form—"the open work of art."[25] It is instructive that here thc initiative passed from professional critics to creative writers and artists. While creative writers and artists certainly do not have a monopoly on insight regarding the arts, they have consistently been on the front lines of innovation regarding the revival of the baroque in the twentieth century. Indeed, as will become evident in the first chapter, on T. S. Eliot's recovery of metaphysical poetry, or in the last chapter, on the recovery of the anticolonial New World baroque by the contemporary U.S. Latino/a artists Rubén Ortiz Torres, Luis Gispert, and Amalia Mesa-Bains, much of neobaroque theory and criticism belongs to poets and artists rather than critics. Significantly, it was practicing poets—the avant-garde poets of the Spanish Generation of '27—who first impelled the rehabilitation of the ultrabaroque Spanish poet Luis de Góngora y Argote (1561–1627) in Spain and Latin America, against the formidable resistance of professional literary critics.

According to Eco and de Campos, a new type of structural organization appears in modern works of art, across literature, the visual arts, and music. In contrast to static, enclosed compositions, modern works possess porous or mobile structures (both critics evoke the example of a mobile by Calder) that are literally unfinished and depend on the recipient to complete them. In the open work, the subjective element, Eco argues, the moment of indeterminacy that is a feature of all artistic reception, distinguishing it from non-art, comes to prevail. Recognizing "'openness' as an inescapable element of artistic interpretation," the modern artist "subsumes it into a positive aspect of his production" by incorporating "openness" into the very organization of the work of art (5). Violating the rules of Renaissance classicism, the open work first appears in the baroque:

> Here it is precisely the static and unquestionable definitiveness of the classical Renaissance form which is denied: the canons of space extended round a central axis, closed in by symmetrical lines and shut angles which cajole the eye toward the center in such a way as to suggest an idea of "essential" eternity rather than movement. Baroque form is dynamic; it tends to an indeterminacy of effect (in its play of solid and void, light and darkness, with its curvature, its broken surfaces, its widely diversified angles of inclination); it conveys the idea of space being progressively dilated. Its search for kinetic excitement and illusory effect leads to a situation where the plastic mass in the Baroque work of art never allows a privileged, definitive, frontal view; rather, it induces the spectator to shift his position continuously in order to see the work in constantly new aspects, as if it were in state of perpetual transformation. (7)

Nevertheless, Eco cautions, "it would be rash to interpret Baroque poetics as a conscious theory of the 'open work'" (ibid.). The seventeenth-century baroque only *practices* the open work; it is not yet able (or willing) to theorize it. Broadly concurring with Eco's differentiation, Christopher Braider argues that the baroque possessed an unsettling awareness of its own "belatedness" or "secondness," an ironic consciousness of the "historical contingency of the choices, conventions, and motives embodied in their works" that the Renaissance did not have (12, 13). But "its protagonists cannot reduce their experience to formal concepts" (15), mainly because this requires "a conceptual vocabulary unavailable until the development of a thoroughgoing *philosophy* of history by the German Romantics, and in particular Hegel and Marx" (13). Braider's point amplifies the notion that the seventeenth century did not know how baroque (in the sense of the baroque's original meaning of an unrestrained and eccentric impulse violating classicist norms) it actually was. There is a discrepancy between classicizing baroque poetic theory and baroque artistic practice: as Braider notes, the few extant baroque poetics are classicizing in orientation (stressing the *imitatio* of the classical tradition), seemingly out of touch with baroque artistic practice.[26]

Eco's (and de Campos's) stylistic categories of open versus closed form and their particular configuration of the antithetical opposition of classic and baroque derive from Heinrich Wölfflin's influential classification. In light of subsequent chapters, especially the discussion of Eliot's idiosyncratic neobaroque literary and cultural history in *The Varieties of Metaphysical Poetry,* Eco's interartistic genealogy of the baroque and the neobaroque will seem familiar. For Eco names late nineteenth-century symbolism (as practiced by, for example, Mallarmé) as "the first occasion when a conscious poetics of the open work appears" (8). Eco's twin figuration of the baroque as unconscious practice of the open work and symbolism as the first in a series of modern artistic movements that supplies a conscious poetics is paradigmatic for the kinship neobaroque artists construct between the seventeenth and twentieth centuries. The baroque prefigures modern and contemporary art; many twentieth- and twenty-first-century artists invoke baroque precedent to launch, justify, or illustrate their contemporary experiments. As Haroldo de Campos phrases it, "*the open work of art* [is] . . . a kind of modern baroque" (*Novas* 222). These elective affinities have been constructed against the grain of chronology, linking contemporary poetics and aesthetics to a distant period of early modern history.

The theory of the open work also underpins baroque allegory, especially in Walter Benjamin's neobaroque reconfiguration of allegory as a self-consciously artificial montage of fragments. Diamela Eltit's neo-avant-garde narrative *Lumpérica* (1983), Eliot's modernist poem *The Waste Land,* and Raúl Ruiz's antirealist film *Mémoire des apparences* (*Memory of Appearances*), also known as *Life Is a Dream* (1986), represent extreme instances of open works that employ the neobaroque aesthetics of fragmentation and allegory. Peter Bürger founds his concept of the avant-garde "nonorganic work of art" on Benjamin's notion of allegory.[27] According to Benjamin's analysis of baroque plays in his *Trauerspiel* study, allegory dismantles the false semblance of organic unity, exposing the actual historical state of destruction and decay. Baroque works are "consciously constructed ruins" that flaunt the seams of their arbitrary construction (*Origin* 182). This study features a series of neobaroque open works structured as decentered, broken wholes organized around the principles of discontinuity, artifice, antirealism, and the recycling and montage of materials outside their original, organic settings. (Eliot's erudite allusions in *The Waste Land* derive from this impulse, as do the Chicano popular baroque in lowrider cars and Barnes's and Eltit's quotations of the iconography of the Counter-Reformation baroque and its spectacles of sanctified suffering.)

The indeterminacy of the open work reflects the modern sensibility of crisis and instability that pervades the baroque and that results from the cumulative intellectual, political, and religious upheavals of the sixteenth and seventeenth centuries—Reformation and Counter-Reformation, the scientific revolution, the "discovery" of America, and colonial, civil, and religious wars. In electing the subjectivist, impressionistic, and theatrical baroque style as its preferred instrument of propaganda, the post-Tridentine Catholic Church consciously embraced an anti-objectivist representation perfectly suited to the deep schisms that divided Europe. Despite Rome's protestations, the one, universal, "Catholic" Church had ceased to exist, and its former eternal spiritual truths had become but one sectarian position in a bitterly fought and unresolved religious battle. The quintessential theatricality and illusionism of the baroque, which saw the world as a stage, is perfectly adapted to this self-consciously partisan view of reality—an efficient rhetorical tool available to spokespersons of opposite ideologies, be it the centralizing absolutist states, the Church, or modern science. In this way, the conservative religious dogma and orthodoxies of the Counter-Reformation baroque participate in modernity and its revolutions that decentered and displaced the traditional, static medieval outlook. In the baroque all parties, progressive and reactionary, have become players on a rapidly globalizing field of modern culture where timeless truths have ceased to exist, and they have retooled to modern communication strategies to rise to the occasion. For example, Descartes employed baroque strategies of hyperbolic doubt—reality may only be a dream—to make the case for refounding modern knowledge exclusively on reason. Sense evidence is questioned; a rational resolution of doubt is proposed: "Cogito, ergo sum."[28]

Discussing the specific impact of modern science, Eco speaks for many when he argues that the "openness and dynamism of the Baroque . . . reflects the rising interest in a psychology of impression and sensation, in short—an empiricism which converts the Aristotelian concept of real substance into a series of subjective perceptions by the viewer. On the other hand, by giving up the essential focus of the composition and the prescribed point of view for its viewer, aesthetic innovations were in fact mirroring the Copernican vision of the universe. This definitively eliminated the notion of geocentricity and its allied metaphysical constructs" (13–14). Eco points to "*structural homologies,*" or "striking analogies" between the arts and science, in which poetical systems develop "in harmony with modern science" (17, 18).[29] In this way, early modern upheavals produced the baroque, and twentieth-century scientific developments such as Einsteinian physics and Heisenberg's uncertainty principle registered in the emergence of the neobaroque revival of baroque expression. Over time, the historical trajectory is toward the intensification of modern centrifugal forces of decentering, the loss of organic wholes, the disintegration of the stable, self-enclosed universe—that is to say, toward the open form.

This idea of interdisciplinary homologies between baroque art and science also figures at the center of the Cuban neobaroque novelist and critic Severo Sarduy's theories of the baroque and the neobaroque. Exiled to France in 1961 and influenced by the Tel Quel circle (Roland Barthes, Julia Kristeva, others), Sarduy adopted a poststructuralist approach that sought to elucidate the structural laws governing baroque and neobaroque expression. In his 1974 collection of essays, *Barroco,* Sarduy proposes the notion of *retombée,* "the epistemological solidarity" (solidaridad epistemológica) between cosmology and art, in both the seventeenth and the twentieth centuries.[30] In the chapter "La cosmología barroca: Kepler" ("Baroque Cosmology: Kepler"), Sarduy's argument hinges on the geometry of ellipses, which is as fundamental to baroque art and architecture (Bernini, Borromini) and astronomy (Kepler) as the geometry of the circle is to the art and architecture of the Renaissance and pre-Keplerian cosmology.[31] The ellipse can be understood as a deformation and decentering of the circle, the symbol of classical perfection: displacing the circle's single center, it is generated by rotation around two centers. Sarduy points out that when Kepler applied the geometry of ellipses to planetary orbits, the potential of geometry for political subversion became explosive because of the social connotations of the single center, the sun, symbol of God and king. Sarduy goes on to compare the geometric *ellipse* to rhetorical *ellipsis,* the centerpiece of Góngora's poetics, where the single center is similarly elided through the constant displacement of meaning in linguistic circumlocution and periphrasis. Like Eco, Sarduy argues that decentering and destabilization intensify in the twentieth century: "As we have seen, the European Baroque and the early Latin American colonial Baroque present themselves as images of a mobile and decentered but still harmonious universe. . . . On the contrary, the contemporary Baroque, the Neobaroque, reflects structurally the disharmony, the rupture of homogeneity, of the logos as an absolute, the lack that constitutes our epistemic foundation."[32] The cosmological equivalent of the "neobarroco del desequilibrio" (neobaroque of disequilibrium), according to Sarduy, is the Big Bang theory.[33] The Big Bang theory posits that the universe is constantly expanding and has been ever since its creation in the explosion of the primeval atom. Galaxies fleeing each other are the fragments of this lost primeval atom. The center of the cosmos is truly empty; the open form has reached its final stage.

The second narrative makes another point that merits advance discussion, which is the following: for Anglo-American audiences, the neobaroque is a variety of postmodernism. Perhaps the most familiar passages that have shaped this perception are Umberto Eco's essay on the open work, John Barth's essay "The Literature of Exhaustion," Michel Foucault's discussion of the baroque at the beginning of *The Order of Things,* and Jorge Luis Borges's characterization of the baroque in the preface to the 1954 edition of *A Universal History of Iniquity.*[34] In *Neo-Baroque: A Sign of the Times,* the Italian critic Omar Calabrese consolidates this equation of the neobaroque with postmodernism, though by suggesting that the neobaroque should replace the postmodern as a concept for contemporary culture. But let me begin with the earliest instance of the postmodern neobaroque. In 1954, Borges affirmed, "I would define the baroque as that style that deliberately exhausts (or tries to exhaust) its own possibilities, and that borders on self-caricature. . . . I would venture to say that the baroque is the final stage in all art, when art flaunts and squanders its resources. The baroque is intellectual, and Bernard Shaw has said that all intellectual labor is inherently humorous" (*Collected Fictions* 4). According to Borges's definition, the baroque is a late, exhausted style that is self-reflexive and ironic. Borges's reading is not original. A century earlier, Nietzsche had made a similar claim: "The Baroque always arises with the decline of great art, when the demands of classical expression become too great."[35] Nietzsche here anticipated Wölfflin's better-known definition of Renaissance classicism and the baroque as opposite yet independent and equally valuable art historical styles. In Nietzsche's definition, the baroque appears as the second term of the classical-baroque binary that underwrites—whether explicitly or implicitly—virtually all of subsequent twentieth-century neobaroque theory. In Borges's interpretation, the classical pole of this opposition is elided, but it is nevertheless implicit in his notion of the baroque as a "final" stage phenomenon that follows an unstated previous order. Borges offers a useful reminder that the pairing also implies a temporal succession of "early" and "late." In this sequence, the baroque always follows the classical, never the other way around: the baroque is a rebellious postscript to classicism that deforms classical norms, setting them into variation. Belatedness connotes exhaustion, which in turn suggests parody, irony, cerebral linguistic tricks, and self-conscious stylization.

We can appreciate how well the Borgesian baroque is suited to the concept of postmodernism, the contemporary trend that the work of this Argentine writer embodied *avant la lettre.* An afterword to modernism, Borges's neobaroque postmodernism constitutes modernism's antithesis, not by offering yet another novelty but through a strategy of wayward repetition that destratifies existing artistic norms (including modernist aesthetic doctrines). In this postmodern neobaroque, to create is not to create from scratch but to re-create, to refashion existing works. This is precisely the argument Calabrese advances for abandoning the notion of postmodern for neobaroque: instead of the prefix "post," suggesting a rupture with modernism, the prefix "'neo' might induce the idea of repetition, return, or recycling" of exhausted modernist and other aesthetics (15). Similarly, in his influential 1967 essay, "The Literature of Exhaustion," John Barth builds his notion of the postmodern literature "of the exhaustion, or attempted exhaustion, of possibilities" on his reading of Borges, and in particular on Borges's definition of the baroque cited above:

> Borges defines the Baroque as 'that style which deliberately exhausts (or tries to exhaust) its possibilities and borders upon its own caricature.' While his own work is *not* Baroque, except intellectually (the Baroque was never so terse, laconic, economical), it suggests the view that intellectual and literary history has been Baroque, and has pretty well exhausted the possibilities of novelty. His *ficciones* are not only footnotes to imaginary texts, but postscripts to the real corpus of literature. (73–74)

According to Barth, "Pierre Menard, Author of the *Quixote,*" Borges's tongue-in-cheek tale about a nineteenth-century French symbolist who composes chapters from *Don Quijote,* is an exemplary postmodern work in the sense Barth intends. Its originality consists in outlining a blueprint for a contemporary poetics confronting the fact of the "used-upness" of literary possibilities (Barth 69). Given the impasse of literature's used-upness, "Pierre Menard" relinquishes the quest for absolute originality, having found a way of saying something new by revisiting canonical works ironically (64). Indeed, Borges's famous tale constitutes a contemporary instance of the "humorous, intellectual Baroque" outlined by Borges in the passage quoted above. Playfully parodic and replete with historicizing references to Cervantes's seventeenth-century masterpiece, "Pierre Menard" also encapsulates the postmodern neobaroque whose paradigm Borges's work, with its cerebral parody, erudite allusion, and intellectual games, helped shape for Barth and other readers in North America and Europe.[36]

In its dialogue with American literary studies in the United States, one of the goals of my study is to dismantle this reductive equation of the neobaroque with postmodernism. There is much more to the neobaroque than the contemporary crisis of representation that this association normally suggests. For example, Foucault takes his contemporary allusion to one of Borges's tales, "The Analytical Language of John Wilkins," at the outset of

The Order of Things in this direction when he cites the bizarre taxonomy in an apocryphal Chinese encyclopedia featured in it. Foucault quotes Borges to invoke the epistemic breaks in the Western orders of representation that are the subject of his study, which ends with the famous prediction of the impending ruin of the modern epistemic order of the study of "Man" in the human sciences, in the somber spirit of baroque vanitas: "man would be erased, like a face drawn in sand at the edge of the sea" (387). Yet no matter how limiting, the postmodern neobaroque also helps illustrate a larger and crucial point. The rebellious consumption of tradition underpinning Barth's postmodern literature of exhaustion (and Borges's "Menard") is nothing but a specific application of the widely used Baroque and neobaroque strategy. If the baroque can be characterized as what Christopher Johnson dubs "a period marked by contradictory feelings of novelty and belatedness" (5), this paradoxical quality derives from its signature strategy of the disruptive revisiting of established forms. Different neobaroque varieties of this strategy of rebellious rearticulation also appear in Anglo-American modernism (Eliot, Barnes), in the Latin American and Caribbean postcolonial theory of the New World baroque and its affiliated seventeenth- and eighteenth-century art historical archive, and in contemporary neobaroque U.S. Latino/a visual culture.

Like the baroque, the neobaroque arises from the differential refraction of preexisting literary and artistic expression. Sarduy has argued that the baroque is a deformation or disfigurement of a previous work (framed through his central concept of parody). But parody, emphasizing extraneous commentary, is only a partial understanding of this phenomenon; another view is existential and names the ontological re-creation that results from this procedure. To be sure, this claim cannot be reversed: because neobaroque expression is rooted in an aesthetics of recycling, it does not follow that any expression that recycles is neobaroque. Some lack baroque stylization, which consists in the reversal of functionalism's (or classicism's) prioritizing of order and restraint: not "less is more," as in the maxim of the International Style (that modernist avatar of classicism), but "more is not less," or "more is more." To invoke Sarduy, the preeminent contemporary spokesperson of this anti-utilitarian baroque aesthetic of artifice and stylistic excess: "Baroque space is superabundant and wasteful. In contrast to language that is communicative, economic, austere, and reduced to its function as a vehicle for information, Baroque language delights in surplus, in excess" ("Baroque and Neobaroque" 287).

The reason for the remarkable popularity of this seventeenth-century style in the twentieth and twenty-first centuries, as evidenced by countless baroque revivals, is precisely the fact that the baroque constitutes one successful blueprint for secondhand creation, a proven model for saying something new by remaking old forms. The original meaning of baroque as bizarre—the nonclassicist use of classical forms—already encapsulates this sense, though cast in a pejorative mold. For the various reasons I have sketched here, it took a couple of centuries for other artists, writers, and intellectuals to rediscover the baroque's generative and creative potential. An alternative modernity that eschews breaking with the past for re-creating the past, in the neobaroque, to create means to re-create: not to make from scratch but to remake by transposing, adapting, and resignifying existing expression. Perhaps the best explanation for why the neobaroque spirit has become so pervasive comes from Haroldo de Campos. In his landmark essay, "Anthropophagous Reason," de Campos demonstrates the baroque and neobaroque as the central instrument of the Brazilian anti- and postcolonial tradition of anthropophagy. While "anthropophagous reason" originally describes the "critical devouring of universal cultural heritage" as a way of becoming authentically Brazilian and American,[37] de Campos concludes by proclaiming that today it epitomizes our global contemporary condition: "To write, today, in both Europe and Latin America will mean, more and more, to rewrite, to rechew" (177).

All in all, it is evident that the nonlinear genealogy of the baroque and the neobaroque entails a new kind of temporality deviating from the conventional sense of the modern. In reflecting on the alternative temporality of the baroque and neobaroque, I follow the direction of thinkers such as Reinhart Koselleck, whose study *Futures Past: On the Semantics of Historical Time* demonstrates how in the early modern period a new time called modernity emerged that radically reconfigured the relation between past, present and future.[38] In "differentiating past and future, or (in anthropological terms) experience and expectation," Koselleck argues, "it is possible to grasp something like historical time" (xxiii). Until the end of the sixteenth century, Europe lived in the temporality of Christian eschatology, which is to say it lived in constant anticipation of an apocalyptic future, even as the expected end of the world was constantly deferred (6). The Reformation, the religious and civil wars of the sixteenth and seventeenth centuries, the scientific revolution, and the rise of the absolutist states delegitimized the temporality of Christian eschatology. Specifically, the prophesied future of the apocalypse, familiar in all its details from scripture, was replaced with a new and secular future, defined by its unknown (indeed, unknowable) quality, and by the increasing speed with which it was approaching (17). Thus, modernity arises from an inaugural rupture between past and future. According to Koselleck, the temporality of modernity is defined by an increasing difference between past and future: the distance between the space of experience and the horizon of expectations expands constantly (276). Columbus affords a memorable instance of this development: expecting to find Asia, he "discovered" America. Reflecting on the cumulative experiences of the previous three centuries that had constantly exceeded and annihilated expectations, Enlightenment Europe demonstrated its awareness of inhabiting a new temporality by conceptualizing this widening gap through a coinage: the notion of "progress" (279).

Against this foil, the alternative temporality unfolding through the interplay of baroque and neobaroque stands out clearly: a modernity without an irreversible break with the past. The idea of reviving, recycling, and re-creating the expression of a distant historical period for contemporary purposes shows that the neobaroque moves both forward and backward at once, suturing futures to pasts rather than expanding the distance between them. The neobaroque's alternative modernity beyond the logic of rupture is appropriately conveyed through the connective prefix *neo,* contrasting with the dissociative *post.* "Ubiquitous in contemporary critical discourse," the latter "underscores our troubled relationship to the past."[39] In contrast, *neo* accurately conveys the neobaroque's continuity across the twentieth century and into the twenty-first, and thus across putative ruptures between so-called modern and postmodern expression. Furthermore, Braider's point that the seventeenth-century baroque already felt an ironic sense of belatedness that it was unable to conceptualize abstractly indicates that an unsettling of established temporalities is at the core of baroque expression, then and now. As Enrique Dussel, Bolívar Echeverría, and others remind us, the early modern period saw the formation of not one but two modernities: it was Europe's first modernity, primarily Southern European and Catholic, that produced the baroque. But it wasn't until Enlightenment modernity, the modernity of the age of the industrial and political revolutions (primarily Northern European and Protestant), that the temporality of the modern age was understood as qualitatively new, oriented toward an unknown utopian future and severed from the past (Koselleck). It was the latter modernity that would become hegemonic and in turn delegitimize and vilify the Catholic and mercantile modernity of the baroque, effectively consigning it to an oblivion encompassing two centuries. The crisis of this hegemonic, futurist modernity in the early twentieth century triggers the revival and recuperation of the alternative modernity of the baroque. The exhaustion of the utopian temporality of rupture with the past and the critique of the reductivist rhetoric of scientific progress are key forces marking this epochal threshold and the rise of the neobaroque. How is the modern call to arms, "Make it new!," inflected in the crucible of the Janus-faced neobaroque, gazing both backward and forward? The following chapters answer this question through a comparative exploration of five distinct artistic solutions.

My study of the neobaroque in the Americas begins with two chapters about Anglo-American literature, then develops the Latin American alternatives in two more chapters, and concludes with a chapter on contemporary baroques in U.S. Latino/a visual culture and art that explores their grounding in the transhistorical genealogy of the New World baroque. Among the recent synthetic studies on the baroque, the New World baroque, and the neobaroque, no other study exists that attends to the complexities of the trans-American debate, mapping links between Latin American, Caribbean, and North American artistic and theoretical practices and their complex relationships with traditional (and postmodern) Eurocentric studies of the baroque and neobaroque.

Chapters 1 and 2 focus on the baroque revival in Anglo-American modernism, largely ignored because of anglophone culture's ingrained wariness of the baroque. As Christopher Braider, René Wellek, and other critics have noted, with a few exceptions, chiefly studies published decades ago by Wylie Sypher and Mario Praz, English and Anglo-American scholars for the most part have simply ignored the baroque.[40] As late as 2007, the Renaissance scholar Peter Davidson offered the following strong censure of British insularity and its anti-baroque prejudices:

> Britain has never been enthusiastic about describing its cultural production as part of an international movement, an unease which extends to Modernism almost as thoroughly as it does to Baroque. However, the early modern arts defy categorisation by nation. The language of visual symbol, emblem and *impresa* is as supra-national as the Latin tongue itself. British determination to see Baroque as the style of the enemy has wrongly stereotyped the baroque mode in all the arts as the sad, empty, enforced style of religious and political absolutism, rather than acknowledging the flexibility and diversity (indeed, the sheer, *permeability*) of baroque cultural production worldwide.[41]

From the British viewpoint, the baroque represented those continental cultural trends that were the most inimical to England and to English core values (liberalism and Protestantism)—absolutism, the Counter-Reformation, and the dynastic culture of Catholic Southern Europe. In 1649 the British beheaded the monarch, Charles I, who had threatened to bring England back into the fold of continental absolutism and Catholicism, and they exiled another monarch, James II, in the Glorious Revolution of 1688 for the same reason. English literary history substitutes local and political categories—Elizabethan, metaphysical, Jacobean, Caroline, Restoration—for "baroque" in its classification of seventeenth-century expression. Anglo-American scholarship in the main inherited these attitudes. This situation led to the neglect of existing baroque trends in seventeenth-century English literature, as well as anglophone contributions to twentieth-century baroque revivals and neobaroques.

In chapter 1, "Neobaroque Eliot: Antidissociationism and the Allegorical Method," the long-awaited 1993 publication of Eliot's 1926 and 1933 lectures, *The Varieties of Metaphysical Poetry,* enables me to reconstitute the work of the early Eliot as a seldom acknowledged Anglo-American equivalent of the Hispanic avant-garde poets of the Generation of '27, who rehabilitated the ultrabaroque Spanish poet Góngora to promote their own neobaroque vanguardist poetics. Eliot's lectures similarly recover seventeenth-century English metaphysical poets, especially Donne, Crashaw, and Cowley, in order to elaborate one of Eliot's most influential concepts, the "dissociation of sensibility" in the (late) seventeenth century. Eliot promoted metaphysical poetry as a rich, undissociated expression that eschewed the splitting of conceptual thought from feeling that, he contended, had vitiated poetry (and European culture in general) in the wake of Enlightenment rationalism. He outlines an idiosyncratic, neobaroque literary and cultural history that dismisses more than two centuries of literature to present the English metaphysicals as direct precursors of his own modernist poetry (latter-day metaphysical). Like the Hispanic avant-garde, Eliot points out striking affinities between seventeenth-century baroque and modernist poetics: in both, "ideas are felt, and feelings are transformed by ideas," though only in artificial (nonorganic) wholes possible under modern dissociationism—the fragmented unity of the metaphysical conceit and related forms of allegory and montage. These features shed new light on Eliot's revival of the metaphysical conceit and the montage structure of *The Waste Land,* as well as its panorama of modern civilization in ruins.

Chapter 2, "The Neobaroque in Djuna Barnes: Melancholia and the Language of Abundance and Insufficiency," demonstrates that the baroque offers a coherent framework to explain key features of Barnes's major works: her extravagantly ornate prose; the use of circumlocution, outlandish conceits, and a deliberately antiquarian style; the melancholia that afflicts her protagonists and increasingly darkens the atmosphere of her works; the use of the baroque iconography of martyrdom and its grand spectacles of sanctified suffering; and, last but not least, Barnes's affinity with Eliot as well as with Robert Burton's *Anatomy of Melancholy,* which occupies the place in her thinking and writing that metaphysical poetry does in Eliot's. Like Eliot, Barnes leverages the wastefulness of baroque circumlocution ("more is not less") against the reductive scientific outlook conveyed in the spare, economical language of scientific realism ("less is more"). But Barnes is a lesbian (or bisexual) writer trying to articulate transgender identities in the face of their pathologization by modern sexology and psychiatry. A self-professed melancholic, Barnes explores the baroque "language of abundance" as the "language of insufficiency" (a phrase I borrow from Carlos Fuentes's essay on Faulkner). Indeed, Barnes's *Nightwood* displays the same nonefficient relation between events (few and traumatic) and narration (superabundant) as Faulkner's *Absalom, Absalom!* Her lavish, melancholic language is a traumatized, wounded language of lamentation that, unlike the crisp language of science, is impotent before reality and the actuality of loss: *Nightwood*'s language is melancholia's abject symptom, not medicine's master signifier. Because of its extensive borrowings from the Catholic iconography of saints and the genre of hagiography so popular in the baroque, *Ladies Almanack* is best described as a queer parodic hagiography.

Chapters 3 and 4 discuss the antidictatorship neobaroque, a variety of the post-Boom literature of defeat and disillusionment that emerged in response to the right-wing military regimes that engulfed Latin America in the 1970s. In the wake of political catastrophe, new strategies for writing history were called for that would destroy the false harmonies of the post-coup regimes, which justified human rights abuses as the necessary collateral of having saved the nation from socialism. To unmask the dictatorships' official narrative of progress, the antidictatorship neobaroque uses the Benjaminian strategies of brushing history against the grain and writing history under the sign of melancholia and the untimely, thus exposing Latin American civilization under the dictatorships as a wasteland of ruins, strewn with the rubble of the discarded cultural residues of the violently destroyed past. I use the term antidictatorship (rather than another current term, postdictatorship) not only because three of my four selected works appeared before the formal end of the Chilean (in 1989) and Argentine dictatorships (in 1983) and these countries' return to democracy but also to underline their protest against the authoritarian state from a contemporary rather than a retrospective point of view.

Chapter 3, "The Latin American Antidictatorship Neobaroque," examines two antidictatorship novels from Chile that were published during the seventeen-year tenure of Pinochet's dictatorship. Comparing a novel published in the interior, Diamela Eltit's *Lumpérica,* to one published in exile, José Donoso's *Casa de campo,* this chapter straddles the cultural divide between Chilean literature at home and abroad (caused by this most violent of contemporary Latin American military regimes) to offer evidence for the broad relevance of neobaroque strategies for antidictatorship expression. Both Donoso and Eltit employ the great baroque theme of the slippage between truth and appearance, the baroque's ironic awareness of the kinship—as Wölfflin famously put it—between things "as they are" and "things as they seem to be," to expose the military regime's official rhetoric as a charade. Like Benjamin's famous angel of history (and Eliot's *Waste Land*), Donoso's neobaroque historical novel *Casa de campo* (1978;

A House in the Country) portrays Latin American history as a sequence of social orders imposed violently and subsequently overthrown, thereby exposing the discontinuities of history as Benjamin's proverbial heap of rubble. In *Lumpérica* (1983), Eltit, like Barnes, appropriates the iconography of the Counter-Reformation baroque and its grand spectacles of sanctified suffering to create a secular mythology of the collective agony of the Chilean people under Pinochet. Both Donoso and Eltit affirm Lezama Lima's thesis of the baroque as the anti-institutional art of counterconquest: their works belong to a literature of resistance written to reconquer the civil society destroyed by the military regimes.

Latin American antidictatorship neobaroque expression also includes films. Chapter 4, "Antidictatorship Neobaroque Cinema," examines two films that forge elaborate parallels between state terror in the twentieth and seventeenth centuries. Raúl Ruiz's *Mémoire des apparences* and María Luisa Bemberg's *Yo, la peor de todas* are cinematic adaptations of canonical seventeenth-century works and figures—Calderón's play *Life Is a Dream* (Ruiz) and the Mexican baroque poet Sor Juana Inés de la Cruz (Bemberg)—which stage seventeenth-century protagonists as counterparts of twentieth-century political prisoners and victims of state terror. They both combine a neobaroque aesthetics—hyperrealist mise-en-scène, lavish cinematography, and discontinuous or theatrically visible editing—with a critique of the authoritarian state baroque. Ruiz's *Mémoire des apparences* (1986; *Memory of Appearances*) deploys Calderón's baroque play about kingship and allegory to allegorize totalitarian repression under Pinochet. The theme of tyrannical rule and the oedipal struggle between a dictator-father and his disinherited, deceived, and imprisoned son in Calderón comes to allegorize Chile under totalitarian rule. Calderón's melancholy prince, Segismundo, becomes the counterpart of Ruiz's protagonist, the Chilean dissident Vega. But Ruiz also attacks Calderón's uncritical support of Spanish absolutism: turning the Calderonian image of a mountaintop tower-prison into a nomadic image that floats through the film, Ruiz refashions it into an allegorical image of antidictatorship resistance. Bemberg's *Yo, la peor de todas* (1990; *I, the Worst of All*) similarly adapts her cinematic biography of Sor Juana—one of the outstanding writers of the Hispanic baroque, who penned a famous autobiographical and feminist self-defense unique for her times—to the contemporary Argentine postdictatorship condition. Bemberg crafted her film's mise-en-scène and cinematography (high angles, grand traveling shots, protofascist architecture) to emphasize analogies between the colonial state baroque and fascism. Narrating the last fifteen years of Sor Juana's life, Bemberg traces her trajectory from literary triumph and public acclaim to her silencing and formal self-denunciation before a Church tribunal, portraying the feminist poet-intellectual as an archetypal victim of state terror.

Chapter 5, "Hemispheric Genealogies of the New World Baroque," turns from literature and film to visual culture and the visual arts. This chapter discusses popular baroques in U.S. Latino/a visual culture and art by placing them within the genealogy of the New World baroque. I argue that the anticolonial New World baroque conceptualized by Lezama Lima and Carpentier (and other Latin American and Caribbean intellectuals such as the Martiniquan Édouard Glissant and de Campos) after World War II, has survived intact into the contemporary period, and can also be observed north of the border, in the contemporary Chicano folk baroque of home altars and lowriders. What Indians did to the imperial Spanish baroque then, Chicano lowriders do to the American car today: the anticolonial, mestizo folk baroque that emerged in the colonial period when tribute and slave artisans Indianized and Africanized the imported colonial state baroque has become a border-crossing, transhistorical sensibility in Latin American folk arts and visual culture. One such instance is Chicano *rasquachismo,* a secondhand mode of production favoring flamboyant display and delirious ornamentation that operates through the rebellious consumption of consumer objects and all-American icons, such as the automobile. Just as Lezama Lima and Carpentier framed the New World baroque within processes of creative remaking and minoritizing appropriation where the colonized left their mark on the imperial European style imposed on them, so the Mexican American artists Rubén Ortiz Torres and Amalia Mesa-Bains today conceptualize their neobaroque art through Chicano *rasquache* strategies of the rebellious remaking and stylization of mainstream American culture. Similarly, the Cuban American artist Luis Gispert's mongrel lowbrow-highbrow art blends hip-hop's counterculture of luxury epitomized by bling with references to the iconography of the Catholic baroque.

Neobaroque Eliot

Antidissociationism and the Allegorical Method

NEOBAROQUE ELIOT? This chapter is written to claim for T. S. Eliot an unusual denominator, foreign-sounding not only within Eliot studies but also within studies of Anglo-American poetry and modernism. For decades, Eliot's persona has been stable: everyone recognizes the U.S.-born, English-convert poet-critic who developed from youthful vanguardist to cultural conservative, declaring himself "classicist in literature, royalist in politics, and anglo-catholic in religion."[1] Even as Eliot was first deified by the New Critics, then demonized by the next generation of poststructuralist and postmodernist critics reacting against New Criticism and the hegemony of high modernism, his attributes remained the same. In the 1990s, however, and partly responding to an accelerated publication of unpublished Eliot manuscripts, a third generation of Eliot critics entered the picture, expanding the frame of reference beyond the familiar and worn antagonisms deriving from Eliot's once canonical status.[2] New and "unofficial" Eliots are being recovered, such as Charles Pollard's "New World Eliot," claimed by the Afro-Caribbean poets Kamau Brathwaite and Derek Walcott as a precursor who offers a viable method for creatively overcoming the fragmentation of tradition in a postcolonial setting.[3]

My own project joins this general trend. Specifically, the "neobaroque Eliot" whose portrait I draw here emerges as a response to the 1993 publication, long awaited and long overdue, of Eliot's unpublished Clark and Turnbull lectures on metaphysical poetry.[4] In 1926, Eliot delivered eight lectures at Trinity College, Cambridge, titled "Lectures on the Metaphysical Poetry of the Seventeenth Century, with special reference to Donne, Crashaw and Cowley."[5] The earliest opportunity to turn the lectures into a book was missed; by 1933, when Eliot revised and consolidated them into three lectures titled "The Varieties of Metaphysical Poetry," presented as the Turnbull Lectures at Johns Hopkins University, he had abandoned the idea of ever publishing them.[6] The monographic length of the Clark Lectures alone makes them stand out against much of the critical work Eliot published during his lifetime, which typically took the form of short exploratory essays. In his introduction to *The Varieties of Metaphysical Poetry,* editor Ronald Schuchard suggests that their publication "will have as much impact on our revaluation of [Eliot's] critical mind as did the facsimile edition of *The Waste Land* (1971) on our comprehension of his poetic mind" ("Clark Introduction" 2). A bold claim, and one to whose fulfillment this chapter is dedicated.

The Clark and Turnbull lectures elaborate one of Eliot's most influential critical concepts, the dissociation of sensibility.[7] Eliot first presented this idea in a short essay, "The Metaphysical Poets," written as a preface for an anthology of early seventeenth-century verse, Herbert Grierson's *Metaphysical Lyrics and Poems of the Seventeenth Century: Donne to Butler* (1921).[8] There, Eliot famously claimed, "In the seventeenth century, a dissociation of sensibility set in, from which we have never recovered; and this dissociation . . . was aggravated by the influence of the two most powerful poets of the century, Milton and Dryden" (64). For Eliot, the dissociation of sensibility was nothing less than a cultural catastrophe caused by the rise of modernity and the dominance of science and rationalism. It was a historical rupture that split the unified, holistic Western mind (what Eliot called "sensibility") into separate, disconnected parts; conceptual, abstract thought was emancipated from, and elevated above, symbolic and supernatural modes of thought. Eliot dated it from the religious, political, and intellectual schisms of the seventeenth century that erupted into England's Civil War and parallel conflicts on the continent.[9] "The later Elizabethan and early Jacobean poets . . . incorporated their erudition into their sensibility: their mode of feeling was directly and freshly altered by their reading and thought. In Chapman especially there is a direct sensuous apprehension of thought, or a recreation of thought into feeling, which is exactly what we find in Donne" (63). According to Eliot, the disastrous consequences of the dissociation appear in the poets of the eighteenth and nineteenth centuries, who wrote either reflective (conceptual) or sentimental (emotional) poetry: "they thought and felt by fits, unbalanced; they reflected" (65). A good polemicist, Eliot quipped that the eighteenth century "developed a petty intellect uncriticised by feeling, and an exuberant feeling uncriticised by thought. The nineteenth century paid for this debauch of Rousseau and the encyclopaedists" (Clark Lectures 221).

The Twentieth-Century Critique of Dissociationism

The Clark Lectures revised the concept of metaphysical poetry beyond the standard meaning as period reference, forging it and the fledgling historical schema of dissociated and undissociated periods outlined in the 1921 essay ("Metaphysical Poets") into Eliot's own idiosyncratic literary and cultural history spanning seven centuries from Dante to Eliot's time. In all stages of its development, from nascent formulations in early reviews after 1917,[10] through the programmatic "Metaphysical Poets," to the final elaboration in the Clark Lectures and the retrospective coda in the Turnbull Lectures, Eliot's idiosyncratic literary history of the dissociation of sensibility manifests a twentieth-century neobaroque, a recuperation of baroque expression in cultural and literary theory as well as literary and artistic practice. As such, it is a seldom acknowledged Anglo-American thread in the twentieth-century neobaroque critique of Enlightenment rationalism. Eliot's neobaroque theories have occasioned little comparative discussion, in part because of an ingrained prejudice against the baroque in Anglo-Protestant culture as "the style of the enemy,"[11] in part because the 1926 and 1933 lectures in which he fully elaborated them were not published until recently.

The twentieth-century crisis of Enlightenment rationality opens the way for the recuperation of an earlier modernity, the baroque, which had been vilified as illogical and decadent by the newly ascendant Enlightenment and the formally stricter neoclassicism beginning in the eighteenth century and continuing through the nineteenth. But the twentieth century reversed the rationalist hierarchy between classicism and the baroque. Around 1900, intellectuals in Europe and the Americas rediscovered the *alternative modernity of the Baroque,* newly appreciating the baroque's idiosyncratic, nondualistic, and nondissociative response to the scientific and religious upheavals of the modern age. Dissociationism is the operative term here: narratives of modernity typically hinge on the related concepts of (multiple) breaks and new beginnings. In William Egginton's words, "dissociationism is perhaps the fundamental characteristic of a European modernity dating to more or less the beginning of the seventeenth century—to the period, in other words, known as the Baroque."[12] It is also a concept that Eliot made the centerpiece of his neobaroque cultural history of the dissociation of sensibility. The twentieth-century revival of the baroque sheds retrospective light on the internal heterogeneity of modernity and recalls the dividing line the Enlightenment placed between itself and Europe's first modernity (primarily Southern European and Catholic) that culminated in the baroque.

But what exactly is intended by the alternative, nondissociative modernity of the baroque invoked by Eliot and other writers and cultural theorists in the early twentieth century? The baroque and the Enlightenment (neoclassicism) part ways regarding the treatment of the conflict between the new mechanical science and the older symbolic or sacred outlooks. Descartes (1596–1650), the seventeenth-century progenitor of Enlightenment reason, offered epistemological justification for modern scientific dualism in his foundational separation of subject from object, mind (*res cogitans*) from matter (*res extensa*). In Cartesian philosophy there is a "sharp dualism" between the spiritual and the corporeal, mind and body, elevating the subject of knowledge above the physical world (as well as above its own body) and empowering it to inspect the world from afar.[13] Descartes' rationalist definition of man by way of his famous affirmation, *Cogito, ergo sum,* establishes that the essence of man is thought, and that the body, which does not think, does not belong to man's essence (Copleston 220). Although Descartes denied it, it is hard not to conclude that the body is a mere vehicle or instrument of the mind, which the mind controls without forming an organic unity with it. The interaction between mental and corporeal realms, between thought and non-thought, is a major problem for Cartesian philosophy and forms a cornerstone of the legacy of dissociationism in modern culture against which Eliot revolted.

Enlightenment reason divided mind and body, reason and faith, science and wonder, as well as principally distilling the premodern from the modern, which could still be found in hybrid forms of articulation in the previous baroque century. Enlightenment rationalism was different from and more radical than rationalist philosophies of the seventeenth century: by reason, the writers of the Enlightenment generally meant "a reason unhampered by belief in revelation, by submission to authority, by deference to established customs and institutions" (Copleston 34). In contrast, the German philosopher Gottfried Leibniz (1646–1716) may serve as an emblematic example of the undissociated baroque: along with Descartes, Leibniz was not only one of Europe's leading rationalists and mathematicians—the co-inventor (with Newton) of the differential calculus—he was also the author of a theodicy, in which he claimed that "God . . . has chosen [to create that world which is] the most perfect."[14] The posthumous notoriety of Leibniz's theological doctrine is mainly due to Voltaire's biting caricature of Leibniz through the figure of the foolishly optimistic philosopher Doctor Pangloss, whose infamous dictum, "this is the best of all possible worlds," flies in the face of all evidence to the contrary.[15] Voltaire's satire, however, misses the mark of Leibniz's thought, simplifying it and erasing the context of Leibniz's (admittedly ethereal) speculation about the relation between possible and actual worlds in which this remark appears.[16] The point here is that Voltaire's ridicule of Leibniz is paradigmatic for the dismissal and stigmatization of the baroque by Enlightenment reason, which put the baroque in a limbo of disgrace that would last until the late nineteenth century.

Responding to the crisis of Enlightenment modernity, the twentieth century overturned Enlightenment verdicts. The baroque's alternative, nondissociative thought (sensibility, Eliot would say) was revindicated as a newly valid alternative to the Enlightenment paradigm. The Cartesian subject/object dissociation in particular became a major target of ceaseless attacks from various intellectual and artistic movements, including French symbolism, phenomenology (including Heidegger), and poststructuralism, such as in the feminist poststructuralist critique of Western binary thought by Hélène Cixous.[17] The neobaroque—the twentieth-century recuperation of seventeenth-century baroque expression—takes its place within this broader search, ongoing since the late nineteenth century, for alternatives to scientific dualisms. For example, the celebration of baroque nondissociationism constitutes one of the core dimensions of Deleuze's 1988 study of Leibniz, *The Fold: Leibniz and the Baroque.* In a chapter discussing the same Leibnizian analysis of God's actualization of the best of all possible worlds that occasioned Voltaire's censure, Deleuze observes,

> That is where the Baroque assumes its position: Is there some way of saving the theological ideal at a moment when it is being contested on all sides, and when the world cannot stop accumulating its "proofs" against it, ravages and miseries, at a time when the earth will soon shake and tremble . . . ? The Baroque solution is the following: we shall multiply principles—we can always slip a new one out from under our cuffs—and in this way we will change their use. We will not have to ask what available object corresponds to a given luminous principle, but what hidden principle responds to whatever object is given, that is to say, to this or that "perplexing case." . . . A case being given, we shall invent its principle.[18]

We shall multiply principles: this passage proposes the inclusive baroque position of "both/and" as an alternative to the exclusive "either/or." Facing the modern epistemological crisis, the baroque opts for the strategy of abundance, excess, and contiguity of the dissimilar, which is also expressed in the baroque topos of *horror vacui,* the horror of the void. Against the Enlightenment program of rupture with "the obsolete" in the battle between science and faith (or any of the other schisms of modernity), the baroque—in Deleuze's words—is "just that, at a time just before the world loses its principles. It is the splendid moment when Some Thing is kept rather than nothing, and where response to the world's misery is made through an excess of principles, a hubris of principles" (*Fold* 68).

Indeed, Leibniz engaged in a calculated polemic against Cartesian dualism. Attacking the Cartesian notion of physical matter as "pure extension" and the resultant dualism of mind and body/world, interiority and exteriority, Leibniz proposed the notion of the unitary monad, living substance, which is indivisible.[19] Monads are the simple elements of which all things are composed, but unlike atoms, or Cartesian matter, monads are "metaphysical points" without extension, like minds or souls (Copleston 297). Moreover, like minds or souls, monads possess agency and an inner tendency to self-development. Indeed, Leibniz "trie[d] to combine mechanical causality with teleology. Each monad unfolds and develops according to an inner law of change, but the whole system of changes is directed, in virtue of pre-established harmony, to the attainment of an end" (35). In his study of Leibniz's philosophy, Deleuze develops Leibniz's nondissociative baroque principle of the fold: "The Baroque refers not to an essence but rather to an operative function, to a trait. It endlessly produces folds. . . . The Baroque fold unfurls all the way to infinity" (*Fold* 3). In the place of the Cartesian split between subject and object, and based on Leibniz's unitary monad, Deleuze posits the inclusive principle of the fold, imagining an endless process of doubling, unfolding, unfurling that connects body and soul, interior and exterior, subject and world. According to Tom Conley, Deleuze's fold "allows world to be placed within the subject (as monad) so that the subject can be in and of the world at large."[20]

1890 and 1920: Two Cycles of Neobaroque Artistic Practice

This struggle between Enlightenment dissociationism and neobaroque anti-dissociationism also plays itself out in the field of modern art. Eliot participated in a massive recuperation of the baroque by transnational modernisms and avant-gardes that began in nineteenth-century French symbolism and culminated in the avant-gardes of the 1920s. The proximity between symbolism and the neobaroque in general is well established: the symbolist spokesperson Rémy de Gourmont wrote a pathbreaking essay, "Góngora et le gongorisme," in 1911, thus preparing the way for the renewed appreciation of the Spanish poet Luis de Góngora (1561–1627), whose obscure, Latinate style, known as *culteranismo* (or simply Gongorism), had been reviled as exhibiting the baroque's worst excesses for centuries.[21] The aesthetic recovery of Góngora began with Mallarmé. As Irlemar Chiampi reminds us, "the 'discovery' of the Gongorine metaphor is tied to the postsymbolist critical context in Europe, where the aesthetic revalidation of Góngora begins through the parallel with Mallarmé, following the former's three centuries in purgatory."[22] Eliot, in turn, identified as a neosymbolist and was to celebrate French symbolist poets and critics as his immediate precursors.[23] Eliot would recall his initial encounter with the work of the symbolist poet Jules Laforgue as a "personal enlightenment"; he also borrowed the concept of dissociation from Rémy de Gourmont—the dominant inspiration behind his first collection of critical essays, *The Sacred Wood* (1920)—although he would resignify it to refer to the epochal disintegration of sensibility that made his use of this term famous.[24] While "replac[ing] romantic inspiration with deliberate craftsmanship," symbolism continued the postromantic cultivation of poetic language as a nonconceptual, nondualistic alternative to positivism—a richer, suggestive, unified language (such as the symbol) in which abstract and concrete, subjective interiority and exteriority, were inseparable.[25] Like "dissociation of sensibility," Eliot's other famous critical term, "objective correlative," derived from the symbolist tradition of synthetic sensibility: mediating between subjective interiority and exteriority, Eliot defined the latter as "a set of objects, a situation, a chain of events which shall be the formula of that *particular* emotion; such that when the external facts . . . are given, the emotion is immediately evoked."[26]

Following the Brazilian critic Irlemar Chiampi, I take neobaroque transnational modernisms and avant-gardes to encompass two distinct historical "cycles" of baroque recuperation: the first is the moment of 1890, which encompasses symbolism and Hispanic *modernismo,* initiated by the Nicaraguan poet Rubén Darío, who was inspired by symbolism (Chiampi, "Baroque" 509).[27] Chiampi's second emblematic moment is 1920, referring to the various historical avant-gardes in Latin America and Europe: the 1920s saw the peak of baroque enthusiasm in poetic practice as well as in literary criticism. At this moment, as John Beverley also notes, the neobaroque "is joined to the emergent problematic of the avant-garde."[28] The Spanish Generation of '27, named for the tercentenary of the death of Góngora, is emblematic: "It is only after the fin de siècle revolution in poetic language that Góngora becomes legible to modernity and can thus be definitively recovered, through a synchronic reading, by the generation that created contemporary poetry" (Chiampi, "Baroque" 510). Its members, the vanguardist poets Dámaso Alonso, Federico García Lorca, Gerardo Diego, and others, took inspiration from Góngora's baroque. Fellow neobaroque avant-gardes include, in Mexico, the Contemporáneos Group (Salvador Novo, Agustín Lazo, Xavier Villaurrutia), whose baroque revival focused on the idiosyncratic New World baroque produced in seventeenth-century Mexico, especially the work of the poet and nun Sor Juana Inés de la Cruz.[29] In Spain and Argentina, the ultraist movement (which included Borges's neobaroque phase of the 1920s, which he would later disavow),[30] as well as several Hispanic modernist poets not closely affiliated with any movement, created landmark experimentalist *neobarroco* poetry; notable writers here are the Mexican Octavio Paz and the Cuban José Lezama Lima. In criticism, the prize for the most intense baroque revival may go to Germany, the setting of Benjamin's study of the German baroque, *The Origin of German Tragic Drama* (1928).[31] Thus, both Herbert Grierson's 1921 anthology of seventeenth-century poetry and the programmatic essay Eliot wrote for it as a preface, "The Metaphysical Poets," are symptomatic expressions of a contemporaneous transnational vogue, in Europe as well as the New World, for the neobaroque.

It is instructive that these early twentieth-century literary revivals of the baroque owed much to practicing poets, whereas the official literary critical establishment put up some formidable resistance almost everywhere except in Germany. In Italy, the eminent critic Benedetto Croce upheld the entrenched classicist condemnation of the baroque.[32] In Spain, the institutionalized anti-baroque voice belonged to literary critic Marcelino Menéndez y Pelayo, editor of the first comprehensive anthology of Latin American poetry (the four-volume *Antología de poetas hispano-americanos,* 1893–95). Menéndez y Pelayo equated the baroque with an "epidemic" that had disastrous effects on Hispanic letters (and especially on Latin American literature) by extinguishing meaning under heavy layers of verbosity. If the ornate, difficult poetry of Góngora had represented the epitome of baroque decadence in Hispanic letters, it was precisely Góngora who was rehabilitated and elevated to the status of heroic precursor by the poets of the Generation of '27. For the tercentenary celebrations of Góngora's death in 1927, a baroque festival of sorts was staged that featured spectacular and much commented-upon happenings, including a mock auto-da-fé of the writings of Góngora's detractors, first and foremost those of Menéndez y Pelayo. (Alonso, García Lorca, and Diego constituted the tribunal that condemned them, but so as not to follow bad example, they burned cigarette paper in lieu of books.) More substantially, the group also coordinated new editions and studies of Góngora's works, as well as anthologies of modern poetry in his honor.[33] Among these, Alonso's celebrated prose translation of and commentary on Góngora's poem *Soledades* is the most famous: Alonso furnished proof that Góngora's infamous obscurity was soluble and based on a perfect poetic logic that, while hermetic, could be decoded into clear and unambiguous prose. Alonso's proposition is conveyed in the title of one of his essays, "Claridad y belleza de las *Soledades*" (The clarity and beauty of the *Solitudes*).[34] Converting disdain for Góngora into admiration, Alonso revolutionized the reception history of baroque literature by newly presenting Góngora as a cerebral logician-poet who is principally clear and accessible (even if the threshold of understanding is set extremely high). This does not mean that Góngora suddenly stopped being baroque and was reclassified as classicist. Rather, it staked out and legitimized the license poetic ingenuity and creative experimentation may take with established forms and still be intelligible.

It is important not to underestimate symbolism's and the avant-garde's successive returns to the seventeenth-century baroque. An integral part of their project of modernizing poetry, the baroque aided in the creation of modern poetic language as much as modern poetic language illuminated the hermetic rhetoric of baroque poetry. For if, as Hugo Friedrich noted in his influential study, *The Structure of Modern Poetry* (1956), "modern poetry is deromanticized Romanticism," the baroque renaissance must be recognized as one essential ingredient fueling the process of said deromanticization, or modernization, of poetry.[35] Baroque revivalism thus modifies the linear genealogy of modern poetry as canonized by Friedrich and his successors, which has been deconstructed many times, although without overturning the canonical trajectory of modern poetry's genesis as a postromantic phenomenon:[36] with roots in Rousseau and Diderot, and influenced by Poe and Novalis—following Friedrich—modern poetry was forged in France by three successive poets, Baudelaire, Rimbaud, and Mallarmé. From France it passed to the international avant-garde, where it proliferated in various national literatures, such as the Spanish Generation of '27, Valéry and Saint-John Perse, Eliot and Pound, Benn, Ungaretti, and others. Friedrich's teleological genealogy of formalist innovation assumes a steady progression, following internal structural laws, toward what he calls *Entpersönlichung* (loss of personal identity) and *Entrealisierung* (loss of external reality), along the way to the limits of absolute language. To his credit, Friedrich acknowledges the Spanish avant-garde's recourse to Góngora, as well as a systematic kinship between modern and baroque poetry. Indeed, his account of modern poetry is exemplary (and merits rereading) for his familiarity with seventeenth-century poetry.[37] Yet it does not alter (as it should) his strict linear schema. With the emergence of parallel twentieth-century baroque revivals (such as Eliot's), however, the Hispanic neobaroque appears less like a regional oddity and more like the rule.

In retrospect, and placed next to these two cycles of baroque revival associated with the emblematic moments of 1890 and 1920, Eliot's neobaroque trajectory seems paradigmatic: from symbolism to his own neobaroque vanguardist practice and criticism, necessarily accompanied by a metaphysical revival. Notably, reconnecting with late nineteenth-century symbolism (which other subsequent vanguards, such as futurism and surrealism, had broken with) was a crucial step.[38] Eliot's contribution to neobaroque modernism is double. As a poet and a critic, Eliot mediated between poetic practice and intellectual history. In modern art, dissociationism's emblematic representative is the International Style, whose engineering rationalism and minimalism is summed up by the slogan, "Less is more." In contrast, the appeal through which neobaroque modernisms asserted their integrative hybridism can be stated as "More is not less," or "More is more."

So Close to the Baroque, So Far from the Enlightenment and Its Aftermath

One staple of neobaroque discourse is the assertion of a close kinship between the respective theorist's twentieth-century present and the seventeenth century. For example, Eliot introduces the 1926 Clark Lectures with the claim that "our own mentality and feelings are better expressed by the seventeenth century than by the nineteenth or even eighteenth" (Clark Lectures 43). Parallels are easily found in Federico García Lorca's landmark 1928 lecture on Góngora, "La imagen poética de Don Luis de Góngora" (The poetic image in Don Luis de Góngora), the Spanish counterpart of Eliot's lectures on metaphysical poetry. On the tercentenary of Góngora's death, García Lorca called the seventeenth-century Cordoban poet the "poet-father of our language." He continued, "Góngora has been furiously abused and ardently defended. Today his work is as alive as though it had been created recently."[39] It is illuminating to savor the bizarre step Eliot (like García Lorca) took to offer his claim: the eighteenth and nineteenth centuries, that is to say, two hundred years of immediate past, first need to be dismissed as irrelevant for his assertion to become valid. Why would anyone want to disclaim the obvious, the powerful impact of one's immediate past, to claim instead a close affiliation with the distant past? Is there really something like continuity in the tradition that Eliot prized so much, the topic of his single most famous essay, "Tradition and the Individual Talent"? At the outset, we note that the continuity Eliot constructed in his idiosyncratic literary and cultural history of metaphysical poetry is of an extremely strained kind, shot through with large temporal gaps. And its internal gaps expose it as a fundamentally modern brand of tradition, reconstituted retrospectively and only after first performing one paradigmatic modern gesture: a rupture with the immediate past.

In 1957, Frank Kermode showed how symbolist doctrine taught Eliot specifically to appreciate metaphysical poetry, thus preparing him to participate in the baroque revival of the 1920s.[40] The symbolist doctrine of correspondences (linking the visible and the invisible) led to the recognition of parallel quests for cosmic analogies—destroyed by modern science—in the seventeenth century, as in the emblem and the ambitious conceits of metaphysical poetry. My aim is to connect Eliot, and Eliot studies, with the larger picture of the twentieth-century recuperation of the baroque. In so doing, I hope to reevaluate Kermode's verdict that Eliot's theory of a dissociation of sensibility in the seventeenth century is essentially a symbolist myth that is "quite useless historically" (Kermode 146). Kermode affirms, "The theory of the dissociation of sensibility is, in fact, the most successful version of a Symbolist attempt to explain why the modern world resists works of art that testify to the poet's special, anti-intellectual way of knowing. . . . And this attempt obviously involves the hypothesis of an age that was different, an age in which the Image was more readily accessible and knowable" (143).

It is certainly true that question marks remain around the dating of what we might call the "Great Dissociation"—to echo Foucault's parallel proposal of a rupture in the early seventeenth century. In *The Order of Things,* Foucault posits the baroque as an epistemic discontinuity that ends the premodern regime of "similitude" and inaugurates the modern age of "classical representation," when "things and words were to be separated from one another" (43). In a much-quoted passage, Foucault observes,

> At the beginning of the seventeenth century, during the period that has been termed, rightly or wrongly, the Baroque, thought ceases to move in the element of resemblance. Similitude is no longer the form of knowledge but rather the occasion of error, the danger to which one exposes oneself when one does not examine the obscure region of confusions. "It is a frequent habit," says Descartes, in the first lines of his *Regulae,* "when we discover several resemblances between two things, to attribute to both equally, even on points in which they are in reality different, that which we have recognized to be true only of one of them." The age of resemblance is drawing to a close. It leaves nothing behind but games. Games whose power of enchantment grow out of the new kinship between resemblance and illusion; the chimeras of similitude loom up on all sides, but they are recognized as chimeras; it is the privileged age of *trompe-l'oeil* painting, of the comic illusion, of the play that duplicates itself by representing another play, of the *quid pro quo,* of dreams and visions; it is the age of the deceiving senses. (51)

For Foucault, the baroque is situated at (and is the symptom of) an epochal rupture. Hence, the baroque is not a historical period but the break between historical periods. And as with Eliot's metaphysical theory, Foucault's observations are put forward in the context of readings of two baroque works of art, Velázquez's *Las Meninas* (1656) and Cervantes's *Don Quijote* (1605, 1615).[41] Indeed, we could easily use Eliot's concepts of unified and dissociated language to describe the epochal transition that confuses Foucault's Don Quijote: he cannot understand that the old world of resemblances—where signs are iconic, and signifiers look like their signifieds—has come to an end and has been replaced by the new world of representation, where signs are arbitrary. For Don Quijote, knowledge comes from appearance and analogy. "His whole journey is a quest for similitudes" (47) organized by the principle of "kinship of language with the world" (43): words from his beloved chivalric romances *must* belong to the same, single order as the world of his experience. Windmills, inns, and traveling merchants *must* resemble giants, castles, and errant knights, despite persistent evidence to the contrary.

That Don Quijote is also mad and deluded is confirmation of the fact that an epochal epistemic change has occurred that has alienated and uprooted him. The founding irony of *Don Quijote* revolves around the illusion harbored by the protagonist, who cannot understand why everyone else doesn't perceive the world the way he does, and the persistent disillusionment that follows him at every step, succeeding (much to the reader's amusement) to undeceive everyone but him. Don Quijote, the madman, "is the man who is *alienated* in analogy" (49). Indeed, the engine of *Don Quijote*'s plot is fueled by epistemic discontinuity: if there were no gulf between the outdated chivalric ethos and modern reality, there would be no adventures, or rather, there would be no quixotic adventures arising from the clash of premodern and modern codes. Here, Foucault's theory of the baroque as epistemic rupture intersects his previous work on the history of madness as the "history of the Other—of that which, for a given culture, is at once interior and foreign, therefore to be excluded . . . by being shut away" (xxiv).[42] Madness, the Other of knowledge for Foucault, constitutes the excluded negative within the intellectual history of Western epistemes outlined in *The Order of Things,* reminding the latter of its historical contingency. Likewise, like a monstrous remnant of once familiar but now disavowed magical beliefs, the literary figure of Don Quijote uncannily subverts the certainties the modern reader holds as self-evident, in an ironic reversal so typical of the baroque. Because it straddles modernity's first epistemic break, Foucault asserts, "*Don Quixote* is the first modern work of literature" (48). It is worth noting that the baroque inception of modern literature with Cervantes hinges on what Jerome Robbins calls the "culture of uncertainty," which involves the destabilization of narrative frames for describing reality.[43] From a twentieth-century vantage point, this ironic and self-reflexive baroque "culture of doubt" (Robbins) indeed seems more modern and contemporary than the realisms dominating eighteenth- and nineteenth-century literature.

Fredric Jameson has drawn attention to Foucault's strategic use of literature to narrate the discontinuities of his intellectual history of modernity: "in Foucault such breaks or transitions are neither conceptualized nor are they represented: a general scheme is laid in place, namely that the old system breaks up, and among its ruin (as in Piranesi's eighteenth-century views of classical Rome) a new system forms which has nothing to do with its predecessor."[44] Another important observation concerns Foucault's distinction between two successive modernities, each inaugurated by its own epistemic break: following the first modernity of the seventeenth and eighteenth centuries (Foucault's classical moment of modernity), inaugurated by the baroque crisis, there arises the second modernity of the nineteenth and twentieth centuries (Foucault's humanist or historicist moment of modernity), inaugurated by a second crisis around 1800, coinciding with the romantic revolt against classicism (Jameson 59–75). Foucault's notion of two breaks and two modernities roughly parallels (if one takes into account the idiosyncrasies of French history on which it is based) the difference between earlier (scientific and religious) and later (industrial) revolutions, which respectively produced what Enrique Dussel and others have called Europe's two modernities. By the same token, Foucault's intellectual history is one of many that explore the paradoxes of what Octavio Paz calls the modern "tradition of rupture."[45] If the modern is synonymous with "making it new," Paz asks, how can this discontinuity consolidate into its opposite by definition, "tradition"? Second, breaks multiply: there is more than one break. A series of ruptures gives rise to the paradox of a continuity—Paz's "tradition of rupture"—that consists in nothing but endless repetition of ruptures.

Perhaps the most useful element of Jameson's revisionary theory of modernity for our purposes is his critique of modern periodization via what he characterizes as the modern "dialectic of continuity and rupture" (23). Far from being reliable, the modern concept of rupture, which claims to establish a linear progression by imposing a qualitative hierarchy between the backward past and the progressive future, turns out to be slippery in the dialectic of the break and the period, for the break tends to expand "into a period of its own right" (24). For example, the "dark" Middle Ages came into being as a result of the Renaissance break with its premodernity; the Renaissance, in turn, was invented by nineteenth-century liberalism to deal a blow to the romantics and their nostalgic evocation of medieval culture.[46] Denouncing periodization while at the same time recognizing its inevitability, Jameson proposes the first of his four maxims on modernity: "We cannot not periodize" (29).[47] These observations are even more pertinent to so-called transitional periods such as the period "termed, rightly or wrongly, the Baroque" (Foucault 51): they shed fresh light on the baroque's quixotic trajectory from seventeenth-century popularity to eighteenth- and nineteenth-century oblivion, and on to twentieth-century revivals. Moreover, Jameson's dialectic of continuity and rupture again underscores the importance of the baroque's antithetical relationship with classicism. The twentieth century sponsored a series of baroque revivals under the auspices of a corresponding break with Enlightenment modernity because, as Jameson demonstrates, discontinuities transform into continuities, and vice versa.

Jameson's dialectic of the break and the period is essential to understanding nonlinear cultural genealogies such as the baroque and neobaroque, including Eliot's own. It shows that the pursuit of the new is not simply predicated on the destruction of the past but actually implies a more complex operation that also involves returning to the past. This is precisely how Eliot's notion of the dissociation of sensibility operates when it is elaborated into the idiosyncratic literary historical narrative of dissociated and undissociated periods in the Clark and Turnbull lectures.

If we now reconsider Kermode's dismissal of Eliot's theory of the dissociation of sensibility as a veridical description of seventeenth-century poetry, we can rejoin by pointing to the Jamesonian dialectic of break and rupture: Eliot's hypothesis should not be classified in terms of seamless, organic continuity (kinship-like filiation) but reframed instead as resulting from the vicissitudes of this dialectic of modern temporality that generates ever new constellations of periods with their own pasts and futures. In this sense, Eliot's neobaroque revival of the English metaphysicals is a narrative construction, an adoptive kinship-like affiliation. Incidentally, this point is also made by Octavio Paz: "This coincidence between the baroque and avant-garde poetics is not a question of influences but rather a question of an affinity operating as much in the sphere of the intellect as in sensibilities" (*Sor Juana* 53).

With the mention of Octavio Paz, we move from temporal continuities to the geographic (transnational) continuities underpinning Eliot's neobaroque work. Once again, our analysis has to contend with perceived ruptures that cover up hidden continuities: if "neobaroque Eliot" is an obscure figure in English-language criticism, he is not in Spanish-language criticism. As was noted earlier, the baroque and the neobaroque are acknowledged as key expressions of transatlantic Hispanic cultures' alternative modernities. There, Eliot is familiar as the Anglo-American equivalent of the Góngorist Generation of '27. Paz affirms, "It is anything but coincidence that Eliot's influence should have stimulated a reevaluation of Donne; neither was it by chance that the Spanish poets of the Generation of 1927, especially Gerardo Diego and Dámaso Alonso, inspired the revival of Góngora" (ibid., 52). In contrast, it is instructive to envision how different the situation was in Britain. Inserted as he was into English culture, Eliot was hamstrung by a cultural climate hostile to acknowledging such transnational continuities with Europe, and with Catholic Southern Europe in particular. As Peter Davidson charges, Grierson's introduction to the influential 1921 anthology *Metaphysical Lyrics and Poems of the Seventeenth Century* was strongly isolationist, presenting seventeenth-century British poetry "as if it existed in a kind of intellectual void," "immune" to foreign and continental influence (Davidson 54).[48] For British literary scholars, then, the revival of the term metaphysical was a way of *not* saying baroque, and thereby of asserting British cultural autonomy from Europe (29, 53, 65).

Further illuminating the dynamic of cultural and temporal continuities and disconnections, it is worth observing that the early seventeenth century—the period leading up to the English Civil War—also stands out as a turning point engendering the ideology of modern anglophone exceptionalism. As Laura Doyle argues in *Freedom's Empire,* a study on the rise of a transatlantic ideology of freedom as the birthright of Protestant Anglo-Saxons, first in Britain and subsequently in North America, the 1640s gave rise to a modern rhetoric of liberty against tyrannical foreign and absolutist rulers that was racialized and therefore exclusionary.[49] Liberty was legitimized as ancient rights the English could claim as their inheritance from the freedom-loving Saxons, undefeated by the invading Normans. As such, it was powerfully leveraged against the absolutism of James II and Charles I and their overtures to Roman Catholicism. Without a doubt, this heroic mythology the English fashioned about themselves during the very period of the baroque, as natives of a free nation who threw off the yoke of foreign tyranny, goes a long way toward explaining the ingrained British denial of the common European culture of the baroque. Symptomatic of this denial is Grierson's recovery of the notion of the metaphysical as an exceptionalist label for English seventeenth-century poetry, which is accordingly condemned by Davidson.

In his magisterial study of the Mexican baroque poet Sor Juana Inés de la Cruz, *Sor Juana; or, The Traps of Faith* (1988), Paz offers a compelling account of affinities between the seventeenth-century baroque and twentieth-century vanguardist poetics:

> The similarities between the aesthetic doctrine of the baroque, as expressed in the seventeenth century by a Gracián or a Pellegrini, and the ideas of the avant-garde are striking. For Gracián, "a conceit is an act of comprehension that expresses the correspondences that exist among objects." The cleverness will be all the greater the less visible the correspondence. Pierre Reverdy's well-known definition of the poetic image is nothing more than a variation of Gracián's formula: "The image is born not of comparison but of the bringing together of two realities. . . . The greater the distance between the objects and the greater the necessity to establish relations between them, the stronger and more effective the image will be." It is difficult to believe that Reverdy had read Gracián. This coincidence between baroque and avant-garde poetics is not a question of influences but rather a question of an affinity operating as much in the sphere of the intellect as in sensibilities. The baroque poet hoped to astonish and astound; Apollinaire proposed exactly the same thing when he extolled surprise as one of the basic elements of poetry. The baroque poet attempts to discover the secret relationships among things, exactly as affirmed and practiced by Eliot and Wallace Stevens. These similarities are all the more remarkable when one considers that the Baroque and the avant-garde spring from totally different origins, one from mannerism, the other from romanticism. The solution to this small mystery is perhaps to be found in the role played by form in both Baroque and avant-garde aesthetics. Baroque and avant-garde are both formalisms. (53)

"Transgressive formalism" is the formula that Paz offers in answer to the question, posed by Eliot, of why seventeenth-century poetry felt so close to Eliot's own. The baroque conceit, the yoking of the dissimilar (*coincidentia oppositorum*) into elaborately wrought, fragmentary assemblages, reappears in the striking comparison of the sunset with "a patient etherised upon a table" and the thickening fog with a cat in "Prufrock." It also resonates with the montage structure of *The Waste Land,* as well as Eliot's "mythical method," a concept he coined to analyze the structure of Joyce's *Ulysses* but which also explains that of his own long poem, similarly the product of "manipulating a continuous parallel between contemporaneity and antiquity."[50]

Hidden baroque affinities also explain another notorious aspect of Eliot's early aesthetic: his so-called objectivist doctrine of the poet's impersonality.[51] Adopting a combative anti-Romanticist, antisubjectivist stance, Eliot advocated a radical objectivism, expressed in the famous dictum that "poetry is not a turning loose of emotion, but an escape from emotion; it is not the expression of personality, but an escape from personality."[52] Although Eliot—according to the critics—had no more than a superficial understanding of science, his programmatic objectivism prompted the provocative analogy between a catalyst and the poet's creative mind. Like the neutral catalyst that triggers a chemical reaction, the poet's mind merely stimulates the conversion of raw material into poetry while itself "remain[ing] inert, neutral, and unchanged. The mind of the poet is the shred of platinum" ("Tradition" 41). But Eliot's related dictum that great poetry must offer an "objective correlative" to express any given subjective emotion shows that, for all his blustering dismissal of romantic subjectivism, his own modernist objectivism is really an attempt to integrate the subjective and the objective, mind and world. In short, it is an attempt to achieve the expression of "undissociated sensibility." Substantiating Friedrich's dictum that modern poetry is "deromanticized Romanticism," criticism since the 1950s, as Sanford Schwartz reminds us, has recovered the continuities between romanticism and Eliot's modernism, modifying the claim to revolt against romanticism that Eliot's poetry seemed to constitute from his own point of view.[53] In the Clark and Turnbull lectures, the chemical analogy is nothing but a metaphor for Eliot's conception of poetry's function as "integrating thought into life" (Clark Lectures 224). In near-identical phrases, the first lectures of both cycles single out as Eliot's subject "poetical work of the first intensity, work in which the thought is so to speak *fused* into poetry at a very high temperature" (Clark Lectures 50; see also Turnbull Lectures 252).[54] Far from rejecting poetry for science, Eliot merely resignifies concepts from scientific discourse for his own aesthetic, to convey the notion of exact expression in poetry of equivalents of intellect and feeling. For Eliot's delicate neosymbolist tightrope walk between the personal and the impersonal, feeling and thought, the following further observations by Octavio Paz are illuminating. Having outlined their parallel rebellion against classicist norms through formalist transgression, Paz goes on to elucidate differences between romantic and baroque anticlassicisms (this passage directly follows the passage from Paz quoted above):

> While the romantic transgression centers on the subject, the baroque transgression focuses on the object. Romanticism liberates the subject; the baroque is the art of the metamorphosis of the object. Romanticism is passionate and passive; the baroque is intellectual and active. Romantic transgression culminates

> in the apotheosis of the subject or in its fall; baroque transgressions lead to the appearances of an unheard-of object. Romantic poetics is the negation of the object through passion or irony; the subject disappears in the baroque object. Romanticism is explosion; the baroque is implosion. . . . The words "wit" (cleverness, ingenuity) and "conceit" define Baroque poetry; "sensibility" and "inspiration," the romantic. Wit *invents;* inspiration *reveals.* The inventions of wit are conceits—metaphors and paradoxes—that discover the secret correspondences that unite beings and things among and with themselves; inspiration is condemned to dissipate its revelations—unless a form can be found to contain them. *That is, romanticism is condemned to rediscover the baroque. This is precisely what Baudelaire, before anyone, did in modern times.* Passionate, romantic mannerism evolved into formalism: first symbolism and then the avant-garde. Like classic art, the baroque aspires to dominate the object—not by balance, however, but by the irritation of contradictions. Thus, like the avant-garde, it is at once romantic and classic. It is vertigo and stasis; congealed movement. (*Sor Juana* 54; emphasis mine)

Like the avant-garde, the baroque is at once romantic and classic. And, we might add, so is Eliot. Paz's comments show an uncanny if indirect grasp of Eliot's neobaroque trajectory through symbolism to the avant-garde, necessarily accompanied by a metaphysical revival tutoring this Anglo-American modernist poet in the baroque art of "the metamorphosis of the object."

Eliot was always quite frank about the tight linkage between his criticism and poetic practice, in attitudes veering between arrogance (practicing poets know best) and humility (I am a mere "craftsman").[55] Indeed, the canonization of modern art (including his own) was one underlying motive of the revised notion of tradition as "simultaneous order" that Eliot proposed in his classic essay "Tradition and the Individual Talent" (1919). In Eliot's words, "The existing monuments form an ideal order among themselves, which is modified by the introduction of the new (the really new) work of art among them. The existing order is complete before the new work arrives; for order to persist after the supervention of novelty, the *whole* existing order must be, if ever so slightly, altered" (38). In his quest for tradition—that is to say, by asserting the need to connect the present with a *living* past—Eliot departs from dominant modernity's discourse of an absolute break with the past. Instead, Eliot's tradition appears more like the premodern affirmation of the past's normative authority over the present, by which today's novelty has to satisfy yesterday's standards. But in point of fact, Eliot takes a third position: "the past . . . [is] altered by the present as much as the present is directed by the past" (39). Old and new, tradition and the individual talent are equals because the innovative talent also has the authority to retroactively alter the existing tradition. In short, Eliot's conception of the tradition "as a living whole of all the poetry that has ever been written" (40) is an open—not closed—canon always ready to admit new members and rearrange the furniture for them. Critics have tended to exaggerate the closure of Eliot's canon, in part responding to his well-publicized preferences for some writers and his dismissal of others.[56] Yet in "Tradition and the Individual Talent," Eliot proposes a complementary relation between continuity and change, canon and avant-garde, a democratic power-sharing arrangement of sorts in which each influences the other. The living past in "Tradition and the Individual Talent" belongs not to the establishment (a position Eliot would come to occupy much later) but to the young, vanguardist outsider.

In recovering neglected aspects of the young Eliot (while distinguishing the living Eliot from the statuesque figure produced by his New Critical successors), I join forces with recent work by Marjorie Perloff, who has recuperated the "avant-garde Eliot," and Jean-Michel Rabaté, who has recovered the young Eliot-as-recent migrant who referred to himself as a "metic" in the metropolis, an American foreigner self-consciously aware that his claim to European civilization was tenuous.[57] Eliot never really embraced avant-gardism as such. But, according to Perloff, it is arguable to claim the early Eliot of "Prufrock" (1915) and the radical modernist of the prewar years, who embarked on a "poetic revolution" whose "brilliant culmination" appears in *The Waste Land,* under the banner of the avant-garde (Perloff 39). Eliot expresses his feeling of dislocation and exclusion in a 1919 letter to a British friend, Mary Hutchinson: "But remember that I am a *metic*—a foreigner, and that I *want* to understand you, and all the background and tradition of you. I shall try to be frank—because the attempt is so very much worthwhile with you—it is very difficult with me—both by inheritance and because my very suspicious and cowardly disposition. But I may simply prove to be a savage" (quoted in Rabaté 212). Rabaté explains that "the term 'metic' looks more adequate as a self-description than 'savage,' for it designates not a total foreigner, but a stranger who is admitted to the city (originally of Athens) because of his utility: he pays certain taxes . . . and is granted rights and franchises although rarely admitted fully into the communal mysteries" (212).

Avant-garde, "metic" Eliot believes that his invention is not a negation of tradition, but that his rebellious work can be accepted into the existing republic of letters—and, what is more, that it can influence the existing classics. In point of fact, Eliot's Janus-faced stance toward innovation, looking forward and backward at once, is characteristic of a group of Anglo-American modernists "presided over by Pound and Eliot" and including H.D., Barnes, Joyce, and others.[58] As Peter Nicholls observes, "In contrast to Futurism and its derivatives, this modernism sought to correct the apparently amnesiac tendencies of modernity by reconnecting it to a valued cultural tradition. Here the avant-garde conception of a rupture between past and present was supplanted by a concern with figures of anachrony and temporal disjunction which put questions of narrative back on the agenda. This version of modernism ascribed fantasies of an absolute present to a decadent romantic tradition deluded by notions of originality" (Nicholls 164). For Eliot and his associates, then, "writing becomes a re-writing" (276), a re-creation of tradition. And Pound's "Make It New!" actually has tradition as its referent.[59] This is seen in the citational method of Eliot's *The Waste Land,* which begins with an invocation of regeneration, of new life springing from the buried corpse of the past. Its atmosphere of sterility in turn derives from the breakdown of regeneration, of the once fertile source of the past having dried up. Nothing innovative can emerge once the continuity to the past has been broken: modernity is a world laid waste (not liberated) by rupture.

Rabaté reminds us of the subversive impact of Eliot's "something that happens" to all past works on the arrival of the new: a "considerable modification . . . [of] the concept of 'influence'" to the extent that modern "re-readings" permanently change our perception of classical works (Rabaté 210). Jorge Luis Borges, fellow vanguardist *aficionado* of the neobaroque as a young artist, has immortalized this concept of modern reading as creative revision of historical works in his provocative tale, "Pierre Menard, Author of the *Quixote.*"[60] Eliot similarly aims to permanently co-opt the literary establishment for his brand of modernism by becoming an insider. As we know, he succeeded in changing the Anglo-American literature curriculum.

"The Varieties of Metaphysical Poetry": The Clark and Turnbull Lectures

I now turn to the Clark and Turnbull Lectures. By 1926, Eliot's concept of metaphysical poetry had expanded into an idiosyncratic literary and cultural history spanning seven centuries from Dante to the present. Originally a coinage of the neoclassicist critics John Dryden and Samuel Johnson, "metaphysical" loses all traces of the stigma intended by Johnson's disqualifying phrase, "the most heterogeneous ideas are yoked by violence together." Because of the modern dialectic of the break and the period, overturning anti-baroque Enlightenment doctrine is the precondition for the twentieth-century recuperation of the baroque: Benjamin's goal in the *Trauerspiel* study was to revindicate German baroque plays (all by Protestant writers from Silesia) from neoclassicist dismissal as failed classical tragedies.[61] Similarly, Federico García Lorca's discovery of Góngora's modernity was intended to restore one of the most difficult Spanish poets to canonical status. In the same way, the rediscovery of the metaphysicals in England rehabilitated writers such as Donne, Marvell, Crashaw, and Vaughan, who had virtually disappeared from the English literature canon since Johnson's time for their deviation from classicist taste.[62]

The title of the Clark Lectures—"On the Metaphysical Poetry of the Seventeenth Century with Special Reference to Donne, Crashaw and Cowley"—classifies metaphysical poetry with the seventeenth century. The title of the 1933 Turnbull Lectures, "The Varieties of Metaphysical Poetry," in contrast, refers to metaphysical poetry as a genre or type not specific to any period. In fact, the later—and striking—title better reflects the orientation of both lectures. In both the Clark and Turnbull lectures, "metaphysical poetry" stops operating as the standard textbook period term that refers to early seventeenth-century poetry. By 1926 there are three "metaphysical periods" of "undissociated sensibility" in poetry for Eliot: the thirteenth century (*trecento*) in Italy (Dante and his contemporaries), the early seventeenth century in England (Donne and Crashaw as main prototypes, Cowley as the last practitioner), and the late nineteenth century in France (symbolism: Jules Laforgue and Tristan Corbière). Departing from the 1921 foundational essay, where "metaphysical" still referred to poetry of the early seventeenth century, Eliot performs a new operation that makes his cultural and literary history possible: he severs the term "metaphysical" from its original reference to a specific historical period, the early seventeenth century. "Metaphysical poetry" has now become a transhistorical genre or style, reappearing at specific moments throughout European history, most recently in symbolist poetry in late nineteenth-century France. Initial traces of this redefinition are found even in the 1921 essay. There, Eliot concludes by pointing out that Laforgue and Corbière "are nearer to the 'school of Donne' than any modern English poet" ("Metaphysical Poets" 66). By 1926, Eliot's reinvention of metaphysical poetry as a universal type structures the argument in the Clark Lectures, even though the main focus of attention is on the seventeenth-century metaphysicals proper, with six of the eight lectures anchored in this period. The Turnbull Lectures, in contrast, are organized around Eliot's appropriation of the term. It is announced in the changed title ("The Varieties of . . ."); the first lecture begins with a warning not to expect a period study and justifies having to "invent" or "impose" a new meaning for "metaphysical poetry."[63] The three Turnbull Lectures attend to the three varieties of metaphysical poetry almost equally.

Detached from its fixed period setting, metaphysical poetry has become a sort of abstract ideal of expression, a creative impulse and universal constant of the human spirit. This is how the Catalan art critic Eugenio d'Ors also describes the baroque in his 1935 study *Lo barroco*. Paralleling Eliot's reinvention of metaphysical poetry, *Lo barroco* reinvents the baroque as a timeless phenomenon recurring cyclically in all ages and cultures. Taking up

Heinrich Wölfflin's proposal of the classic and the baroque as antithetical but twinned concepts, d'Ors reconfigures Wölfflin's art historical categories by abstracting them into opposing universal sensibilities of the human spirit—"eons" (from the Greek for "age"), as he calls them—that transcend any particular historical or cultural setting. D'Ors links the two styles to reason and nature, form and life, respectively. According to d'Ors, the baroque is "broken, *absurd,* like nature . . . not logical and unitary, like reason." Whereas the classical "transforms a tree into a column, a living form into a geometrical figure," in the baroque, "a column becomes a tree, as in Bernini's or Churriguera's works."[64] The two types have always contended with each other: the classical always narrowing human expression to the intellectual, the static, rationalist norms and dualisms, the baroque always opening human expression to the vitalist, the dynamic, heterogeneous expression more complex than objectivist, scientific language. D'Ors maintains that there is "a tendency toward singularity [*unidad*] and a demand for discontinuity: these characteristics mark the formal repertory of the rational spirit, the classical spirit. Inversely, the Baroque spirit can be recognized by its adoption of multinuclear patterns that exclude reason's dual demand: multinuclear patterns rather than single-centered ones, their elements merged and continuous rather than discontinuous and separate" ("Debate on the Baroque" 87).

The parallels between the d'Orsian undissociated baroque (the antithesis of the dissociative classical) and the Eliotic unified, rich expression of metaphysical poetry (the antithesis of reductive scientific language) are striking. Both thinkers go back to a seventeenth-century style to locate alternatives to scientific knowledge, sever it from its period- and culture-specific setting, and elevate it to the status of an abstract ideal available anywhere and anytime, including, of course, in Eliot's and d'Ors's twentieth-century present. By proposing a *universal* baroque that returns in the twentieth century in their respective neobaroque theories, d'Ors and Eliot reconnect with what the "Great Dissociations" of the scientific and industrial revolutions have severed. D'Ors famously counts twenty-two distinct "Baroques," evolving from "pristine" and "archaic" baroques through Macedonian, Alexandrian, Roman, Buddhist, and Gothic incarnations, all the way to Nordic, romantic, and fin de siècle baroques (the list is incomplete).[65] By comparison, Eliot's three varieties of metaphysical poetry, in the ages of Dante, Donne, and Laforgue, respectively, appear as a modest version of the dizzying d'Orsian proliferation of new baroques.

Likewise, both theories have been controversial for much the same reasons. Kermode's criticism that Eliot's theory of the dissociation of sensibility is a neo-symbolist myth, useless for the study of seventeenth-century poetry, corresponds to René Wellek's verdict that in d'Ors, the baroque "has become so broad and vague when cut off from its period moorings that it loses all usefulness for concrete literary study."[66] By 1960 even Mario Praz, an Italian critic of comparative literature and a strong supporter of Eliot, had admitted that Eliot's theory must be considered as "discredited nowadays." Praz concurred with the then recently published critiques by Kermode and others that the theory of dissociation of sensibility is a "projection on the past" of a post-Romantic theory of the poetic image.[67] Among the many virtues of Schuchard's meticulous edition and introduction of the lectures is the reconstruction of the close interactions between Praz's criticism and Eliot's theories (Schuchard, "Clark Introduction" 10–11, 19–21). Indeed, along with Eliot's, Praz's scholarship is an indispensable part of the revival of the English metaphysicals; both contributed essays on the occasion of one of its landmark events, the tercentenary of Donne's death, in 1931 (only four years after the 1927 Góngora tercentenary).[68] In 1925, Praz published a study of the English literary baroque in Donne and Crashaw, which Eliot reviewed enthusiastically and would later say stimulated his thinking as he was composing the Clark Lectures.[69] Clearly, Eliot's dual focus on Donne and Crashaw derives from Praz. In 1927, Praz read the Clark Lectures for potential publication at Eliot's request. In his initial review of the typescript of the Clark Lectures, Praz offered some criticism of Eliot's claims that seems to have discouraged Eliot from pursuing revisions for immediate publication.[70] In 1931, however, just when Eliot had publicly abandoned any publication plans for the lectures, Praz cited Eliot's claims as authoritative scholarship.[71]

My point is that in their focus on historicity, the critiques of Kermode and Wellek miss the generative potential of Eliot's and d'Ors's baroque typologies.[72] However suspect their scholarship, Eliot's and d'Ors's disarticulations of the baroque from a seventeenth-century period style were essential to subsequent twentieth-century rearticulations of alternative baroques of all varieties—including postcolonial ones (which I discuss in chapter 5). To break the link between the baroque and its historical period, culture, and class was the precondition for different historical subjects to reconceive the meaning of the baroque as a subversive, transgressive force. As Charles Pollard convincingly argues in his study of the "New World Eliot," Eliot's example—his modernist reconfiguration of tradition—taught West Indian poets after World War II how to deal with the fragmentation of tradition in their different—postcolonial—context. Eliot's lesson is that despite its cult of the new, tradition—the *living* past—remains vital for modern literature, and that tradition, even after it has been broken by modernity and colonialism, can be recreated and revived—indeed, must be fabricated where needed—to fit the needs of modern and contemporary poetic practice.[73] Like Rabaté's metic Eliot, Pollard links his argument to the recovery of the young emigré Eliot, self-conscious about his inferior status when facing European high culture: "As an American, Eliot stands out of the direct line of descent under the logic of tradition as cultural legacy. So he shifts from the metaphor of inheritance to that of labor, and tradition becomes property that a poet acquires not by blood but by hard work" (Pollard 46). The positive reception of Eliot by Caribbean writers, argues Pollard, has taught us contemporary metropolitan critics, fixated on the figure of Eliot the mandarin and cultural elitist, to rediscover this Eliot who devised a concept of tradition that empowers cultural outsiders who want to write themselves into a tradition from which they are excluded.

Similarly, d'Ors's disarticulation of the baroque from a seventeenth-century period style paved the way, if unintentionally, for Latin American postcolonial writers to counter the official "state baroque" associated with Spain, with the seventeenth century, with the ruling elite of Counter-Reformation Catholicism, and with the absolutist state. This insurgent, decolonizing New World baroque appears most dramatically in the work of Alejo Carpentier. It was none other than d'Ors whom Carpentier adapted to generate his postcolonial version of the "unified sensibility"—the notion of the mestizo New World baroque: "America, a continent of symbiosis, mutations, vibrations, *mestizaje*, has always been baroque."[74]

As Ronald Schuchard notes, subsequent to the three varieties of metaphysical poetry in the thirteenth, early seventeenth, and late nineteenth centuries, a fourth variety must be added by implication: that of the early twentieth century—none other than Eliot's own brand of modernist poetry.[75] The presentist dimension of Eliot's literary critical enterprise is plain: clearly—as critics have noted, and as Eliot does not deny—the deeper function of Eliot's criticism is to legitimize his modernist poetic practice. Indeed, the task of the Clark and Turnbull lectures on metaphysical poetry is to create a retrospective lineage for Eliot's own neobaroque avant-garde art, a kind of living past for the poetry of the future. In the third Turnbull Lecture, Eliot admits his partial stance vis-à-vis the metaphysical tradition in wording that—in today's language—belongs to a "situated" (rather than traditional) critic:

> I perhaps am of all critics the most disqualified from judging. For I know that when I first came across these French poets, some twenty-three years ago, it was a personal enlightenment such as I can hardly communicate. I felt for the first time in contact with a tradition, for the first time, that I had, so to speak, some backing by the dead, and at the same time that I had something to say that might be new and relevant. I doubt whether, without the men I have mentioned—Baudelaire, Corbière, Verlaine, Laforgue, Mallarmé, Rimbaud—I should have been able to write poetry at all. This fact alone renders me unsuitable to be a critic of them. Without them, the Elizabethan and Jacobean poets would have been too remote

> and quaint, and Shakespeare and Dante too remote and great, to have helped me. I cannot but be aware, therefore, that in emphasising their importance for the present, I may be only defending myself. (Turnbull Lectures 287)

For the first time . . . I had . . . some backing by the dead. . . . I may only be defending myself. Here, we have Eliot in 1933 recalling the anxieties of the vanguardist "metic" and talented American outsider, who, lacking the birthright of the European native, understands that tradition cannot be inherited, but "must [be] obtain[ed] . . . by great labour" ("Tradition" 38). We should be warned that, like the *Quixote* of Borges's "Menard," Eliot's Clark and Turnbull lectures subject the past to the retrospective influence of the present: they are a creative reinvention, not a faithful imitation, of European literary history. Along with their fellow hemispheric Americans Walcott and Braithwaite, Borges and Eliot share, to invoke the Brazilian postcolonial theory of anthropophagy, a cannibalistic relation to the European canon.[76]

Indeed, the three varieties of metaphysical poetry epitomized by Dante, Donne, and Laforgue congeal into a continuous tradition only from the particular viewpoint of the implicit fourth variety, Eliot's own. Eliot's eccentric, cosmopolitan literary and cultural genealogy linking works from three European languages and distant centuries to the immediate past and present is premised on the peculiar modern dialectic of the rupture and the period: Eliot first had to dismiss the two most recent centuries of English-language literature. He liked to point out that there was no "no poet, in either [Britain or the United States], who could have been of use to a beginner in 1908. The only recourse was to poetry of another age and to poetry of another language."[77] Having learned to write modern poetry by reading the French symbolists, Eliot worked his way backward in history from there to find further models in writers he came to call "varieties" of "metaphysical literature." Eliot's Clark and Turnbull lectures trace a continuity premised on multiple breaks. Like pearls on a string, the varieties of metaphysical poetry become what they are only by virtue of being torn from their original contexts, to be arranged within neobaroque literary history.

For Eliot, metaphysical poetry is a unique type of expression in which thought becomes poetry. In the first Clark Lecture, Eliot defines it as "that which occurs when an idea, or what is only ordinarily apprehensible as an intellectual statement, is translated in sensible form; so that the world of sense is actually enlarged" (Clark Lectures 53–54). Or, to quote a parallel definition, "I take as metaphysical poetry that in which what is ordinarily apprehensible only by thought is brought within the grasp of feeling, or that in which what is ordinarily only felt is transformed into thought without ceasing to be feeling" (Clark Lectures 220). Distinct from philosophical poetry, which merely expounds a philosophical system, in metaphysical poetry "ideas are felt, and feelings are transformed by ideas" (Turnbull Lectures 257). The double articulation of thought and feeling, the impulse to offer conceptual equivalents for emotions and "emotional equivalent[s]" (Clark Lectures 203) for ideas, is its unique characteristic. The articulation of "unified sensibility," metaphysical poetry is a development of Eliot's notion of the objective correlative. In a striking religious analogy that stresses the antithesis to reductive, conceptual discourse, Eliot explains, "this type of thought [is] the *Word made Flesh*" (Clark Lectures 54).

> Now, there is a great deal of good poetry in the world that is not metaphysical. Indeed, some of the greatest. You only have metaphysical poetry, as I understand it, when you have a philosophy exerting its influence, not directly through belief, but indirectly through feeling and behaviour, upon the minute particulars of a poet's daily life, his quotidian mind, perhaps his way of love-making, but also any activity. . . . Metaphysical poetry is highly civilised, and humanity is only civilised by fits and starts. Furthermore, the metaphysical poet must be subjective, or at least have a subjective side to him. . . . This tincture of human emotions by philosophy . . . is essential to metaphysical poetry as I conceive it. (Clark Lectures 294–95)

Jewel Spears Brooker has recently traced Eliot's critique of dissociationism back to his 1916 doctoral dissertation on the philosopher F. H. Bradley.[78] "Eliot's dissertation springs to life when it is understood in the context of the revolt against dualism" (Brooker 178). According to Brooker, Bradley's thought contains a historical and dialectical schema outlining a development in three stages, from unified to dualistic to reunified experience; it is also from Bradley that Eliot borrows the rhetoric of "felt thought" and "thought feeling" (189). The common reference to Bradley as an "idealist" philosopher has prevented an appropriate understanding of what should instead be considered Bradley's hybrid, "idealist-empiricist" epistemology. Bradley's thought is a reaction against the strong bias in Anglo-American philosophy for an analytic and empirical orientation, but one made from within this tradition (177). "Analytical thinking," according to Bradley, "shatters the unity between knowing and feeling" (188). Brooker identifies the twentieth-century revolt against Cartesianism as the context for Bradley's and Eliot's thought (173): modern discourse has become one-sided, reductively analytical and quantitative, resulting in what the Clark Lectures call a "disintegration of the intellect" (Clark Lectures 223, 227). The task of the modern poet—which Eliot defines by translating Bradley's epistemology into artistic practice—is, then, to reintegrate what scientific and technological progress have separated: "The thinking of the poet should be no more than transposing into poetry the thought of the time which he selects as important to him.

Neither Dante nor Donne nor Laforgue did more. They were no prophets; they merely performed the work of integrating thought into life" (Clark Lectures 223–24).

But the question remains, why choose the early seventeenth century as the moment after which massive degeneration and decline sets in? Why elect the metaphysical poets—rather than another literary movement—as the last frontier of integrated sensibility before what Eliot calls the "separation, [and] . . . consequent waste, of thought and feeling" in English literature of the eighteenth and nineteenth centuries (Clark Lectures 204)? Eliot devotes an entire lecture, the seventh Clark Lecture ("Cowley and the Transition"), to a poet whom he considers much inferior to Donne and Crashaw simply because his work constitutes the last of the line, after which the catastrophe—the great dissociation—occurs. The chapter mainly serves to make the point encapsulated in the following statement: "And with [Abraham] Cowley this enigmatic seventeenth century of the first Charles fades into the modern intelligibility of Dryden, Swift, Pope, Gay, and Bolingbroke, whose mental and emotional structure, I imagine, was very much like our own" (Clark Lectures 183). As M. A. R. Habib has recently shown, Eliot's antipathy toward the Enlightenment is consistent throughout his early critical and philosophical writings.[79] As Habib and Brooker both demonstrate, Eliot joins forces with a pervasive twentieth-century critique of Enlightenment rationalism and the scientific paradigm. In English literature, the neoclassical period begins with the Restoration (1660) that ends the Civil War of 1640–60, spanning the late seventeenth century and the entire eighteenth century up to the French Revolution and the beginning of Romanticism. Neoclassicist and Enlightenment discourse sponsor the condemnation of baroque expression as undisciplined, bizarre, and therefore degenerate; Eliot's dismissal of eighteenth- and nineteenth-century literature is simply the negation of the negation. Neoclassicism, endowed with "a petty intellect uncriticised by feeling" (Clark Lectures 221), chides Eliot, applies rigid conceptual criteria of decorum and genre to literature. It discourages poetic invention and produces blandly conventional poetry: "Instead of poetry, you get *genres* of poetry" (Clark Lectures 201).

By recuperating metaphysical poetry from long-term oblivion and embracing it as a model of unified expression balancing thought and feeling, Eliot dismisses subsequent neoclassicism as formulaic and doctrinaire and Romanticism as uncritically subjective and exuberant (see the passage quoted at the beginning of this chapter): both are one-sided. But in addition to abstracting metaphysical poetry from its period setting and reinventing it as a transhistorical ideal, Eliot performs an even odder operation: he elevates Dante, the late medieval (or early Renaissance humanist) poet,[80] to the status of ideal metaphysical poet while declaring the *original* seventeenth-century metaphysicals to be lesser variations thereof! Less perfect than Dante, the original metaphysicals are merely "conceited" metaphysicals (Clark Lectures 124, 266, and passim), that is, utilizing extended and ingenious similes known as *concetti,* or metaphysical conceits. Whereas Dante's similes and metaphors "have a rational necessity" (Clark Lectures 121), the conceit is defined as a hyperbolic, nonfunctionalist image employed "for its own sake, and not to make clearer an idea or more definite an emotion" (Clark Lectures 138). From a purely technical aspect, Eliot's emphasis on the hyperbolic character of the conceit, a figure forging improbable "likenesses in naturally dissimilar and unrelated phenomena," concurs with standard scholarship on the topic.[81] A figure of speech whose doubleness in meaning (between the literal and figurative, concrete and abstract) is strongly accented—Eliot discusses Donne's famous conceit of lovers' souls as the twin legs of a compass from "A Valediction: Forbidding Mourning"—the conceit constitutes a particular type of undissociated sensibility. Differentiating what it also yokes with violence together—to echo Johnson's phrase—the conceit presents a forced likeness, one that is not organic but artificial. It is a way of "sensualising thought" (Clark Lectures 134), but one that occurs after the breakdown of similitude—to invoke Foucault's schema of epistemic discontinuities, which is extremely apt in the present context. The unities constructed in the conceit are fragmented, broken, not organic wholes—undissociating rather than unified sensibility in a strict sense. The perfect harmony of analysis and lived experience, still present in Dante and the trecento, Eliot claims, has become impossible by the seventeenth century. In this way, Eliot traces a long decline of metaphysical poetry from its ideal expression (unified sensibility in Dante) to imperfect and "conceited" expressions of undissociating and undissociated sensibility in the seventeenth and nineteenth centuries.

In Eliot's words, while the "conceit is apt for the expression of the metaphysicality of the seventeenth century" (Clark Lectures 182), it is important "to distinguish the conceited clearly from the metaphysical, and to conclude how far the whole generation may be called metaphysical and how far merely conceited" (Clark Lectures 138). Even though "any poet who is conceited is likely to be more or less metaphysical" (Clark Lectures 138), this is not true of—surprisingly—Giambattista Marino (1569–1625) and Góngora (Clark Lectures 182): "I consider the Italian poetry of the age to be conceited without being metaphysical" (Clark Lectures 225). Why does Eliot exclude Góngora and Marino—the respective Spanish and Italian masters of the continental extravagant baroque—from his Anglo-American baroque revival? Paradoxically, he counts Crashaw, a Catholic convert who was exiled and died in Italy—the English metaphysical poet closest to the continental baroque and directly influenced by Marino—as the second paradigmatic seventeenth-century metaphysical, after Donne. What is more, the dismissal of Góngora and Marino occurs in the sixth Clark Lecture, on Crashaw, which discusses Crashaw's strong links to Marino and the Spanish mysticism of St. Theresa. The decisive impulse behind Eliot's incongruous recognition of Crashaw is clearly Praz's 1925 study, which shaped the Clark Lectures. There, Praz dubbed Crashaw's poetry the "literary counterpart . . . to Rubens's apotheoses, Murillo's languors and El Greco's ecstasies" (*Flaming Heart* 253). Yet overall, one cannot but conclude that Eliot's dismissal of the continental baroque is an affirmation of English exceptionalism: "the metaphysical at this moment flourished only in England" (Clark Lectures 225). It is motivated by the same ingrained Protestant and anglophone resistance to Catholic and continental influences that, as Wellek and Davidson have noted, has long obscured the recognition of a baroque literature and art made in England.[82]

The arch-representative of this nativist position is Grierson, who treats Crashaw and Donne as opposites, juxtaposing Crashaw's conceits "after the confectionary manner of the Italians" to "the scholastic or homely manner" of Donne and his followers (66). Sadly, Eliot does not extend the same generosity to the Hispanic-Italian and Catholic neobaroque tradition that the latter extended to him, via Octavio Paz's comments recognizing Eliot's contribution that I quoted above. Davidson conjectures that Eliot was "clearly aware of a contrary or internationalist position" to British cultural isolationism and its hostility to the baroque, but was "unwilling . . . to challenge" it, recognizing that a "radical wrench of perspective would have been too much at that cultural moment" given the investment of the "English establishment" in these views and attitudes (52).

The three varieties of metaphysical poetry in the thirteenth, seventeenth, and nineteenth centuries are arranged within a hierarchical system of disintegration and decline, specifically "a progressive deterioration of poetry" (Clark Lectures 227) beginning after Dante. This structure is the most polished aspect of the Clark and Turnbull lectures, and it is best presented by quoting several of Eliot's varying comparative and triangulated formulations:

> The acceptance of one orderly system of thought and feeling results, in Dante and his friends, in a simple, direct and even austere manner of speech, while the maintenance in suspension of a number of philosophies, attitudes and partial theories which are enjoyed rather than believed, results, in Donne and some of our contemporaries, in an affected, torturous, and often over-elaborate and ingenious manner of speech. (Clark Lectures 120)

> Donne might be called a voluptuary of thought; Crashaw could be called a voluptuary of religious emotion. . . . With Donne the thought is split up into thoughts, each inspected and tasted, so with Crashaw the emotion is split up into emotions;

> instead of one emotion informing the whole poem, you have emotion piled on emotion, as a man drinks when he is afraid of becoming sober. (Clark Lectures 168–69)
>
> In Dante . . . you get a system of thought and feeling; every part of the system felt and thought in its place, and the whole system felt and thought; and you cannot say that it is primarily "intellectual" or primarily "emotional," for the thought and the emotion are reverse sides of the same thing. In Donne you get a sequence of thoughts which are felt; in Crashaw you might say, by slightly straining the antithesis, that you have a sequence of feelings which are thought. In neither do you find a perfect balance. (Clark Lectures 182–83)
>
> The disintegration of the intellect, in Laforgue, had reached a much more advanced stage than with Donne: for Laforgue, life was *consciously* divided into thought and feeling; but his feelings were such as required an intellectual completion, a *beatitude,* and the philosophical systems which he embraced were so much *felt* as to require a sensuous completion. They did not fit. Hence the metaphysicality of Laforgue reaches in two directions: the intellectualising of the feeling and the emotionalising of the idea. (Clark Lectures 212–13; see the near-identical repetition in Turnbull Lectures 282)
>
> The *trecento* had an exact statement of intellectual order; the *seicento* had an exact statement of intellectual disorder; the nineteenth century had a vague statement of intellectual disorder. (Turnbull Lectures 278)

Given the radical dissociation between analytic and poetic language, the modern conceit—the self-consciously artificial construction of likeness from the dissimilar—offers the only way in which modern poetry can be metaphysical. For, as is Eliot's premise, a perfect fusion of philosophical thought and poetic sensibility is impossible in modernity. Eliot thus recognizes Laforgue and Corbière for presenting "as near as possible a modern analogy to the conceited metaphysical" (Clark Lectures 219). It is no accident that Eliot's own poetry—the implicit fourth variety of metaphysical poetry—is known for a revival of the metaphysical conceit. And here we also find the deeper reason why Eliot overcame his modernist condition of literary orphanhood only by leaping three centuries backward to affiliate himself with early seventeenth-century poetry as his adoptive ancestors. From Eliot's neosymbolist point of view, the transhistorical kinship between the early twentieth century and the early seventeenth century consists in the determination to bridge the dualisms that modernity is progressively sharpening—under adverse conditions more conducive to failure than success. The romantic symbol, a "metaphor in reverse" where "the vehicle has been expanded and put in place of the tenor, while the tenor is left to implication" (the cross in Christianity),[83] is an organic figure founded on fusion, or similitude, as

Foucault might say. In Eliotic theory, the symbol is eclipsed by the metaphysical conceit (the evening sky as etherized patient in "Prufrock"), an artificial figure of fragmented unity, bordering on allegory and montage, whose coherence is strained because forged against the grain of probability. We will test this hypothesis in the following section on *The Waste Land*. Eliot's notion of metaphysical poetry, in other words, embodies what the Italian critic Umberto Eco and the Brazilian critic Haroldo de Campos both call the "open work of art."[84] A paradigm of modernity, the open work is a decentered, broken whole, energized by centrifugal, dissociative forces that break up the self-enclosed, harmonious structures of tradition.

The Waste Land: Dissociationism's Counterpoetics and the Allegorical Method

The three varieties of metaphysical poetry discussed in the Clark and Turnbull lectures are followed by an implicit fourth variety, Eliot's own modernist verse. This fourth variety is a spectral presence in the lectures, never discussed but nonetheless generative, since Eliot's modernist verse produced Eliot's neobaroque literary genealogy, and vice versa. Indeed, it was the indirect light the theory of metaphysical poetry shed on Eliot's poetry that drew many readers to it in the first place.[85] This section is intended to extend Eliot's lectures with reflections on this spectral fourth "variety" of metaphysical poetry. What does it mean to read Eliot as a metaphysical poet? What new light does his neobaroque literary theory cast on his poetic practice? What aspects come to the fore when we consider Eliot's poetry through a neobaroque lens? I turn now to *The Waste Land* (1922), published four years before the delivery of the Clark Lectures.[86]

To begin with, the lectures' interpretation of metaphysical poetry as a specific type of philosophical poetry speaks directly to the enormous amount of learning stored in the poem. As Richard Shusterman, Jewel Spears Brooker, and other recent Eliot critics remind us, Eliot spent years training to become a professional philosopher, completing a doctoral thesis on the philosopher F. H. Bradley at the same time as he was also forming himself as an avant-garde poet.[87] Certainly, *The Waste Land* is intellectual poetry that translates thought into feeling, finding images or sensuous equivalents for abstract ideas. Oswald Spengler's notion of the decline of Western civilization, the most obvious example, is rendered via a succession of concrete and vivid images evoking the dominant wasteland theme:[88] the hellish landscape of "stony rubbish . . . / . . . where the sun beats, / And the dead tree gives no shelter, the cricket no relief" (ll. 20–23); the urban crowd of the living dead "flow[ing] over London Bridge" (ll. 60ff.); the emotional sterility of modern relationships in the twentieth-century upper-class Cleopatra and her lover and the lower-class couple Lil and Albert in "A Game of Chess," to name a few. Herman Hesse's corresponding 1922 discussion of the downfall of Europe inspired Eliot's nightmarish images of "hooded hordes swarming/Over endless plains" (ll. 368–69) and the urban apocalypse of "Falling towers/Jerusalem Athens Alexandria/Vienna London" (ll. 373–76). *The Waste Land* furnishes the modern "metaphysical poetry" that Eliot's neobaroque theory envisions: it is a counterpoetics to modern dissociationism. Eliot has reinserted analysis and ideas into poetry. It is true that *The Waste Land* is a poem that cannot simply be read, it must be studied. It sends the reader into the library. On the other hand, by presenting an intensely naturalist surface via a series of dramatic scenes and colorful pictures, many of them surreal, it lures the reader out of the library, back into life, or at least the vicarious living offered by an imaginary journey of exploration.

The scholarship in *The Waste Land* leads to a second feature characteristic of the neobaroque, especially in Latin America—montage. A montage of borrowed phrases extracted from world literature ranging from the Bible (and the Upanishads) to Baudelaire, Eliot's poem is not original in the usual sense. Much of its speech is secondhand. *The Waste Land*'s originality belongs to its procedure, its unique method of appropriating and recycling sources, which Eliot defined as the "mythic method" in his 1923 review of *Ulysses.* Resulting in the poem's famed polyphony, Eliot's allusive technique consists in the "theft" of phrases from one context (the works of dead artists: Ovid, St. Augustine, Chaucer, Dante, Spenser, Shakespeare, Marvell, Wagner—the list goes on) and their transfer to another (Eliot-the-individual-talent's new poem), where they acquire "new and powerful" meanings.[89] Thus, into the realistic description of a contemporary London street scene ("Under the brown fog of a winter dawn,/A crowd flowed over London Bridge, so many" [ll. 61–62]) there suddenly erupts a voice from the dead: Dante's sober "I had not thought death had undone so many./Sighs, short and infrequent, were exhaled" (ll. 63–64). Eliot's notes interrupt our reading and send us to study the original context in which these phrases occur. They are Dante's reactions to the sight of souls of the dead at the beginning of his descent into Hell in the *Inferno,* in the Vestibule (Ante-Hell) and first circle of Hell.[90] Prepared by the epithet "Unreal City" (l. 60), the superposition of a citation from Dante transforms the familiar twentieth-century urban reality into a surrealist world of the living dead, the eponymous "wasteland." Second, and throughout, human identities blend into each other as the subject position of the first-person speaker comes to be occupied by a succession of historical and fictional personae. The speaking "I" slides from an Austrian countess ("Marie") to Huxley's fortune-teller Madame Sosostris to Jessie Weston's fisher king, "fishing in the dull canal" (l. 189), to Ovid's Tiresias (l. 218) to Augustine as youthful rake in "To Carthage then I came" (l.307)—an arbitrary selection.[91] Eliot highlighted this polyphony in his famous note commenting that characters in the poem all “melt into” each other, that “all the women are one woman” and that “the two sexes meet in Tiresias” (*Waste Land* 23n218). Eliot’s mythic method creates an unstable oscillation between realism and surrealism, resulting from the citation and collage of diverse time-spaces from “contemporary reality” and “antiquity” that this method imports into the poem.

This secondary, derivative mode of production, via the transformative ingestion of the alien word, is identified by the Mexican critic Gonzalo Celorio as the type of originality characteristic of the postcolonial Americas. Analyzing the impure, baroque modernity of Latin America, Celorio writes, “In light of our Spanish, colonial, and therefore eccentric past, our American originality is to adopt ideas that are, in principle, alien to us but that we have made our own by virtue of the fact that we neither had them nor can have them. Herein lies our originality. We do not have a critical tradition in the European style; we have a critical tradition in the American style. And what is the American critical tradition? It is the tradition generated by the superposition of an Enlightenment and a Baroque system, which is to say, neither a displacement of one by the other nor a rupture between them, but rather a conjoining of supposedly universal European ideas and a supposedly eccentric American culture.”[92] *The Waste Land*’s cannibalistic relation to the European canon is another symptom of its hemispheric Americanness. All the learning in the poem is imported, (Indo-)European.[93] Just as significant, however, is the creative deformation and revision of these metropolitan sources. Eliot’s montage method should be understood as a process of articulation in Stuart Hall’s sense—as a subversive method with which the empire writes back to the center, to borrow Rushdie’s phrase. Confronting the legacy of European colonialism in the Americas, to write means to rewrite, to re-create by devouring the imported learning that the ex-colonial subject cannot help but consume. The “New World Eliot,” the critical anthropophagist who steals the alien European word and rearticulates it as his own, was the author of *The Waste Land*. Indeed, Haroldo de Campos explicitly hails Eliot in this way in his programmatic essay “Anthropophagous Reason,” in which he outlines the neobaroque as a rebellious mode of reinventing tradition: “Pound and Eliot ‘discovered’ Laforgue’s French and fed on it, on his ironic ‘logopoeia,’ to renew poetry in English.”[94] Eliot’s famous quip, “Immature poets imitate; mature poets steal,”[95] identifies this critical difference between a derivative and a rebellious and independent attitude to the European canon. (This is something that, as Charles Pollard points out, was not lost on Eliot’s post–World War II West Indian readers Brathwaite and Walcott).

Everything in this reading, however, depends on the exact nature of the relation between the words of the dead and Eliot’s own—to be precise, on a critical distance and antagonism (rather than reconciliation and fusion) between them. If it is fusion, then *The Waste Land* suggests a nostalgic return to the distant and past places, cultures, and people it summons. Is this the case, as conservative commentators have suggested (and leftist critics have charged)? Does Eliot's poem contrast secular modernity and religious past as inferior and superior, arguing that modernity should be transcended by conversion to Buddhism or Christianity? How to interpret the organic sterility/fertility symbolism pervading the poem? Drawing on Eliot's two anthropological sources, Frazer's *The Golden Bough* and Weston's study of the Grail legend, wasteland and water are the two antithetical master symbols giving rise to what little plot (sequence of events) there is in this predominantly static poem. Whereas wasteland scenarios suggest the suffering and sterility of the living dead, water symbolizes the desired rebirth through death of pagan vegetation myths (a symbolism that also underlies Christian baptismal and resurrection rites). After a long series of drought scenarios in the first three movements ("The Burial of the Dead," "A Game of Chess," "The Fire Sermon"), the fourth movement, "Death by Water," takes one step forward, portraying the drowned sailor drifting underwater, although this drowning appears to be neutral, stripped of any salvational symbolism.[96] Midway through the fifth movement ("What the Thunder Said") change finally comes: "Then a damp gust/Bringing rain" (ll. 393–94). What follows however, is enigmatic: when the thunder speaks, it is in Sanskrit; the fisher king reappears only to ask the question, "Shall I at least set my lands in order?" (l. 425). The poem then concludes with a jumble of quotations more incoherent than anything before.

Eliot speaks about "*manipulating* a continuous parallel between contemporaneity and antiquity" and "*a way of controlling, of ordering,* of giving a shape and a significance to the immense panorama of futility and anarchy which is contemporary history" ("*Ulysses*" 177; my emphases). My claim is that, despite Eliot's use of archetypal symbolism, the way it is deployed via *The Waste Land*'s mythic method is allegorical rather than symbolic. Eliot might have used the term "conceited" to point to the fragmentary, imperfect state of its system of correspondences. I will draw on Walter Benjamin's neobaroque theory of allegory to substantiate this claim. Across differences in genre, Benjamin's *The Origin of German Tragic Drama* and Eliot's *The Waste Land* share the same compositional method, the montage of fragments. As Bernd Witte has shown, Benjamin ostentatiously used an allegorical method in assembling his *Trauerspiel* study. In letters, Benjamin pointed out that the first draft of the *Trauerspiel* study "was almost entirely composed of quotations. The craziest mosaic technique one can imagine, which for works of this kind is likely to appear so strange that I will probably retouch it here and there in the final draft."[97] In point of fact, Benjamin composed the second part of *Origins*, "Allegory and *Trauerspiel*," in the manner of allegory, or emblems (kindred art forms Benjamin does not differentiate). Quotations from baroque plays serve in the place of the vehicle of the allegorical image and are collated with Benjamin's own analyses, which function as its tenor. One might say that in the place of traditional analytic concepts, Benjamin produces critical conceits—allegorical collages of literary quotations and criticism, which are intellectual but also literary. They are acts of interpretation that do not conceal their fabricated, arbitrary quality.

Taking up the opposition between symbol and allegory, one key target of the *Trauerspiel* study is the Romantic condemnation of allegory's artificiality and didacticism in favor of the symbol's supposed organic unity. As Harold Steinhagen has observed, Benjamin's critique of the Romantic symbol was primarily aimed at its "aura" (the key concept from Benjamin's "The Work of Art in the Age of Mechanical Reproduction"), its false reconciliation of the conflict between past and present, individual and archetype.[98] Attacking Goethe's generative distinction between antithetical semiotic procedures in allegory ("a poet's seeking the particular from the general . . . where the particular serves only as an instance or example of the general") and symbol ("his seeing the general in the particular . . . is the true nature of poetry") (*Origin* 161), Benjamin counters sharply:

> Whereas in the symbol destruction is idealized and the transfigured face of nature is fleetingly revealed in the light of redemption, in allegory the observer is confronted with the *facies hippocratica* of history as a petrified, primordial landscape. Everything about history that, from the very beginning, has been untimely, sorrowful, unsuccessful, is expressed in a face—or rather in a death's head. (166)

He continues:

> In the field of allegorical intuition the image is a fragment, a rune. Its beauty as a symbol evaporates when the light of divine learning falls upon it. The false appearance of totality is extinguished. . . . The dry rebuses which remain contain an insight, . . . the lack of freedom, the imperfection, the collapse of the physical, beautiful nature. . . . Beneath its extravagant pomp, this is precisely what baroque allegory proclaims, with unprecedented emphasis. (176)

Contrary to Romantic doctrine, the symbol's ideal, organic totality is unmasked as an appearance, an escapist delusion. And far from being inferior, allegory's artificial combination of disparate parts is celebrated as a strategy for radical, undeceived criticism. Here it should be noted that allegory differs from the symbol through a cerebral trait ("divine learning," "insight"), a feature that recalls Eliot's emphasis on the conceptual in poetic language. Both symbol and allegory are poetics of correspondences, or double-voiced discourses (to tweak Bakhtin's formula), but they treat their duality in opposite ways, as the Greek etymology of these terms indicates: the symbol (from the Greek verb *symballein,* "to put together") fuses the literal and figurative senses, whereas allegory ("to speak otherwise," from the Greek *allos,* "other," and *agoreuein,* "to speak") differentiates them.[99] The symbol presents its correspondences as organic analogy, with the second, abstract meaning implicit in the concrete image. Allegory in turn presents its correspondences as artificial montage, the work of a sovereign act of the allegorist, who projects a second, arbitrary meaning onto the concrete image. The allegorist, Benjamin insists, "must not conceal the fact that his activity is one of arranging" but rather should flaunt the "obviously constructed quality" of his work (*Origin* 179). In contrast to the symbol's organic mystifications, Benjamin claims, allegory is demystifying analysis. It unmasks the ruinous effects of time on nature. As he brilliantly states in his famous critical conceit of the angel of history (from the 1940 essay "Theses on the Philosophy of History"), modern history is not progress but destruction, catastrophe. In his subsequent work on nineteenth-century commodity culture, Benjamin developed his theory of baroque allegory into a critique of capitalism's destructiveness. "Emblems return as commodities" when capitalism accelerates the natural cycles of obsolescence.[100] For Benjamin, writes Theresa Kelley, "the past has no organic, natural connective to the present; it is always 'other' and thus under the sign of allegory."[101]

Given *The Waste Land*'s signature use of anthropological myths and symbols, these reflections are crucial. To amplify my claim stated above: Eliot's "mythic method" in his 1922 poem is an allegorical, demystifying method in Benjamin's sense. *The Waste Land* is intellectual poetry of disenchantment, not organic reenchantment. For Eliot, the late medieval and Renaissance cosmos of analogy, Foucault's episteme of "similitude," has given way to dissociated modernity in the seventeenth century. As the old order of correspondences is broken, all subsequent literature, including *The Waste Land,* cannot but *forge* and *fabricate* new orders of meaning allegorically, though discontinuous, "open works." Allies by virtue of their respective anti-Romantic campaigns as well as their baroque revivalism, neither the author of *The Waste Land* nor Benjamin believes there is a modern return to organicism.[102] To both, the only relation moderns can have with the past is a fragmented relation—or, in Eliotic idiom, the only undissociated expression available to moderns is a fragmentary one that does not dissimulate its extreme artifice, or "conceitedness," as he put it in the Clark and Turnbull lectures. Here I concur with Peter Bürger, who argues that Benjamin's theory of allegory "finds its adequate object" "in the avant-gardist (nonorganic) work of art," although it was first developed in the context of his study of the seventeenth-century baroque.[103] *The*

Waste Land's method of first disarticulating its material into fragments and then rearticulating these as a disunified assemblage runs directly counter to any organic and nostalgic treatment. For this reason, interpretations of *The Waste Land* that impute a conservative desire for the remythification and re-enchantment of the secular modern world are misguided. The best example is Cleanth Brooks's 1937 essay—a tour de force of close reading—which nevertheless suggests that Eliot reanimates the reproductive cycle of ancient vegetation myths as an indirect way of reviving Christian faith.[104] Brooks succumbs to the biographical fallacy. No matter Eliot's 1927 conversion to the Anglican Church, or the reactionary tone of his thirties criticism in *After Strange Gods*—everything Eliot says in the Clark and Turnbull lectures indicates that the back door to past organic unity is forever closed to moderns.[105] Eliot's poem *manipulates* parallels between alternative meanings and time-spaces, in particular twentieth-century urban life and archetypal myths, that flaunt the seams of their making. His only materials are scattered fragments, the detritus and ruins of myths of the past, which are recycled into an artificial assemblage of discontinuous parts.

This, I would argue, is the meaning of the *Waste Land*'s speaker's final statement at the brink of the close of the poem: "These fragments I have shored against my ruins" (l. 430). It is no accident that, immediately preceding and following what amounts to the maxim of *The Waste Land*'s allegorical method, the poem ends on a note of total textual and linguistic fragmentation:

> London Bridge is falling down falling down falling down
> *Poi s'ascose nel foco che gli affina*
> *Quando fiam uti chelidon*—O swallow swallow
> *Le Prince d'Aquitaine à la tour abolie*
> These fragments I have shored against my ruins
> Why then Ile fit you. Hieronymo's mad againe.
> Datta. Dayadhvam. Damyata.
> Shantih Shantih Shantih
>
> (ll. 426–33)

These last lines constitute but a mosaic of quotations, "stolen" words juxtaposed without any editorial links. Sanskrit, Latin, and three modern European languages collide without translation. The content of these allusions has been discussed exhaustively and needs no further elucidation. Here the important point is their discontinuous arrangement: a children's nursery rhyme acquires new apocalyptic overtones before it is displaced by another scene from Dante's visionary journey through hell and purgatory, which in turn yields to a Latin verse from late antiquity sounding again the Philomela theme, succeeded by an allusion to another figure of tragic isolation, the Prince of Aquitaine. Next, the staged madness of a Hamlet-like avenger figure (Hieronymo) brushes up against three divine injunctions (self-control, giving, compassion) from the Upanishads, whose ending formula, "Shantih," meaning "peace," also closes Eliot's poem.[106]

Much has been written about the theme of ruins, and cities in ruins, in *The Waste Land* as the literal and metaphorical state of modern Western civilization.[107] I want to close with a famous passage from Benjamin's *Trauerspiel* study that reveals the structural link between *The Waste Land*'s compositional method and its somber imagery and thematics. "Allegories are, in the realm of thoughts, what ruins are in the realm of things. This explains the baroque cult of the ruin" (*Origin* 178). *The Waste Land* stages a procession of corpses and scenes of physical and psychological martyrdom that rivals those of baroque tragedies, which, Benjamin says, "are resplendent with pale corpses" (*Origin* 219). The "drowned Phoenician sailor" is also the Hanged Man from the Tarot pack (l. 55), who in turn blends into the "corpse . . . planted" in the garden, which seems about to be dug up by a "Dog . . . that's friend to men" (ll.71, 74). The corpse of "Phlebas the Phoenician" reappears in "Death by Water" in an advanced stage of decomposition, as a sea current "picked his bones in whispers" (ll. 315–16). Ovid's Philomela, raped and mutilated by Tereus and changed into a nightingale, accuses Tereus in her song, "Jug jug jug jug jug jug/. . ./Tereu" (ll. 204–06). The gruesome story of Philomela and Tereus appears at least three times. Thirty-one-year-old Lil has lost her teeth after an abortion. Between contemporary Cleopatra and her estranged husband pass fiery words and "savage" silence (l. 110) while they press "lidless eyes" (l. 138). The passion of Christ is alluded to in the first stanza of "What the Thunder Said" (ll. 322–30). This has been operative since the beginning of the poem, which stages the foundational act of taking the life of nature. In the manner of Donne, Eliot's poem opens abruptly with a dramatic image: "April is the cruellest month" (l. 1). It establishes an atmosphere of universal suffering, due to a disaster that is the breakdown of the seasonal cycle of the reproduction of life. Negating Chaucer's fertile "Aprille with his shoures soote," which pictures the springtime reawakening of life that fuels the pilgrimages the *Canterbury Tales* narrate, *The Waste Land* performs the opposite gesture at its outset—the extinction of life.[108] In one fell swoop, the entire organic material and human world, shortly to appear in the poem, shrivels up, coagulates, freezes, and becomes stone. The poem goes on to parade nothing but its pale corpses and specters, fragments and residues—a land laid waste. Now that the lifeworld has been killed, its ruins can function as vehicles for the thoughts Eliot proposes to convey poetically. This act bears the signature of the dictatorial imagination of the baroque allegorist, which Benjamin describes as follows: "If the object becomes allegorical under the gaze of melancholy, if melancholy causes life to flow out of it and it remains behind dead, but eternally secure, then it is exposed to the allegorist, it is unconditionally in his power. That is to say that it is now quite incapable of emanating any meaning or significance on its own; such significance as it has, it acquires from the allegorist" (*Origin* 183–84). *The Waste Land* is a neobaroque poem in which artifice and anti-organicism rule in the realm of things, as in the realm of thoughts.

In the *Trauerspiele,* according to Benjamin, "the corpse becomes . . . the pre-eminent emblematic property" (*Origin* 218). This is because it is only in their devalued and discarded state as waste, corpses, wrecks, bones, debris, and so forth that the material world of things and bodies reveals the destructive work time wreaks on them (and which capitalist commodification compounds). Benjamin's thought here is very close to Eliot's. Allegory's demystifying analysis depends on avoiding pictures of life, beauty, harmony, because organicism is auratic, uncritical, illusive, deceptive. Only in a discarded, dismembered, degraded, ruined state does the real, material world enter allegory, for it is only when things have become broken or worthless, isolated from the organic lifeworld where they thrive, that the authentic structure of this lifeworld becomes visible for analysis.[109] In the words of the *Trauerspiel* study: "Criticism means the mortification of the works . . . : not then—as the romantics have it—awakening of the consciousness in living works, but the settlement of knowledge in dead ones" (*Origin* 182). Or, more to the point: "The objects of allegorical intention are severed from its living contexts: they are shattered and conserved at the same time. Allegory clings to its ruins" (Benjamin, "Zentralpark" 235–36). Far from gratuitous necrophilia, in Eliot's neobaroque poem the cult of the ruin serves the purpose of disillusionment. Or, to echo Bürger, the avant-garde nonorganic work of art "rejects all false reconciliation with what exists" (88). As in Benjamin, the shock strategy in *The Waste Land* is intentional, but really didactic. We might say that it serves to open the reader's eyes to what Benjamin's angel of history sees: "Where we perceive a chain of events, he sees one single catastrophe which keeps piling wreckage upon wreckage and hurls it in front of his feet" ("Theses" 257). Perhaps this is similar to what Eliot intended with his cryptic reference to Tiresias in the *Waste Land* notes: it takes Tiresias's aloof, inhuman perspective, like that of the Angel of History, to assess in contemporary history the full scale of the destruction that has already taken place: "What Tiresias *sees,* in fact, is the substance of the poem" (*Waste Land* 23n218).

The Neobaroque in Djuna Barnes

Melancholia and the Language of Abundance and Insufficiency

THE MOST salient features of Djuna Barnes's literary work are its obscurity and its hyperbolic style. In all her major works, Barnes flaunts an ornate, circular, rambling, extravagant prose. In this way, her work radically counters the engineering principles of efficiency canonized by modernist writers of the machine age who proposed to cleanse language of redundant, wasteful material, such as the imagists, Hemingway, and Stein. The early William Carlos Williams and Ezra Pound, for example, invoked technology as a model for modernist writing; Williams called the modern poem a "machine made of words."[1] In so doing, they emulated the battle cry of modern architecture, the art medium whose conversion to the engineering aesthetic was conducted in the most visible and public manner of all: according to modernism's founding father Le Corbusier, "The house is a machine for living in."[2] Tight control, precision, directness, no superfluous words, few and simple adjectives—through principles such as these, one particular strand of modernist literature joined the International Style in adopting engineering and technology as models of modern design.[3] If the International Style's slogan is "less is more," the reverse principle, "more is not less," inspires Barnes's prose. Neobaroque style is the precise antithesis of the spare, austere, economical style of modernist functionalism. It champions the same ornamentation and excess that functionalism condemns, and for the same reason—because it is superabundant and wasteful, and because it is language that encodes loss rather than seamless productivity and communication.

The case I want to make here is that Barnes's work participates in the twentieth-century recovery of the baroque that is the subject of this book. Along with Eliot's recuperation of metaphysical poetry, Barnes's work represents a cornerstone of the neobaroque in Anglo-American modernism. My conception of the neobaroque sheds new light on key features of Barnes's work, suggesting a common denominator for a range of seemingly disparate characteristics, such as her use of circumlocution, outlandish conceits, and allegorical combinations of images and concepts; the mannered artificiality of the diction, settings, and characters; the fragmentary, digressive organization of the works; the "impersonal," detached narration and the striking absence of stream-of-consciousness technique; the melancholia that afflicts Barnes's protagonists and increasingly darkens the atmosphere of her works; and, last but not least, Barnes's affinity with Eliot, as well as with Robert Burton's *Anatomy of Melancholy* (1621).[4] It is certainly true that Barnes's work, unlike Eliot's, has always been associated with the baroque. Reviewing Barnes scholarship since its beginnings with Joseph Frank's formalist reading of *Nightwood* (1936) as an example of spatial form, one can make a long list of references to seventeenth-century and baroque expression.[5] These references, however, are typically casual asides, and the important assumptions and implications of Barnes's use of the baroque are never unpacked. While frustratingly superficial, these casual observations are illuminating to compile. Collectively, they offer a glimpse of the rich variety of neobaroque phenomena in Barnes's works.

Not surprisingly, the first reference to a historical situatedness comes in T. S. Eliot's introduction to the first edition of *Nightwood*. Eliot praises "the great achievement of a style, the beauty of phrasing, the brilliance of wit and characterization, and a quality of horror and doom very nearly related to that of Elizabethan tragedy."[6] Following Eliot's lead, Joseph Frank compares the tone of the Doctor's monologues in *Nightwood* to that of "the religious sonnets of John Donne."[7] In *Djuna: The Life and Work of Djuna Barnes,* Barnes's biographer Philip Herring writes of Barnes's 1958 blank-verse play *The Antiphon* that "the play's idiom suggests Jacobean tragedy" and is written "in vaguely Jacobean verse form, strongly flavored with Shakespearean drama."[8] *The Antiphon* is a family revenge play in which the dead and absent father's sins fester like an open wound in present relations between mother and children, leading to the tragic murder of the daughter by the mother. *The Antiphon*'s idiom resembles *Nightwood*'s in its violent images of pain and ostentatious lamentation. Because their theatrical lamentation contrasts with what Walter Benjamin calls the silences of Greek tragedy, both works have much in common with the "unclassical" seventeenth-century German tragedies Benjamin discusses in his study of the baroque in *The Origin of German Tragic Drama.*[9] The baroque appeal to the emotions and the shift from absolute clarity to dramatic movement and subjective impressionism are traits that may also be found in Barnes's later works. In her introduction to *Silence and Power,* the landmark collection that marked the feminist reevaluation of Barnes's work, Mary Lynn Broe writes that "*Nightwood* has been called surrealistic, Eliotic, Dantesque, elegiac, fugal, Elizabethan, baroque, even Gothic."[10] Indeed, as Broe notes, until recently the term "baroque" was only one among many that critics resorted to as they were casting about for a way to describe Barnes's deliberately antiquarian and outlandish style.[11] For, as Louis F. Kannenstine reminds us, "*Nightwood* is steeped in the literary-historical past as thoroughly as it is grounded in its concrete present."[12] Among these observations, Dianne Chisholm's recent comment on "a darkness in *Nightwood*" via "Barnes' affection for Burton's *Anatomy of Melancholia* [*sic*]"[13] stands out as a concrete lead that enables us to explore the most immediately productive link between Barnes and the baroque.

One commonplace of Barnes criticism is that Barnes's favorite book was Robert Burton's famous seventeenth-century English study of melancholy.[14] Surpassing general gestures toward Elizabethan tragedy, Donne, and Jacobean drama, the mention of Burton is an important and specific clue that offers deeper insights into the kinship between Barnes's work and baroque expression. For Barnes, *The Anatomy of Melancholy* occupies the place metaphysical poetry does for Eliot—the melancholic scholarly voice of Burton's speaker persona, Democritus Jr., appears throughout Barnes's major works. As Panofsky, Saxl, and Klibansky note in their classic study of the Renaissance reinvention of melancholy, *Saturn and Melancholy* (1964), Burton's encyclopedic, nine-hundred-page tome is a monument to the modern invention of the melancholic man of genius.[15] In antiquity and the Middle Ages, melancholia for the most part was a pathological dejection whose causes were explained by the theory of the humors as an excess of black bile. In the Renaissance, Jennifer Radden points out, melancholia became linked to "some kind of compensatory quality of brilliance, intellectual refinement, genius, or creative energy."[16] No longer something exclusively negative, melancholia became the double-edged gift of the creative man of genius. Written at the end of the Renaissance "glorification of melancholia" (Klibansky, Panofsky, and Saxl 241), Burton's *Anatomy of Melancholy* offers a baroque scholarly retrospective of this phenomenon first initiated by the fifteenth-century Florentine philosopher Marsilio Ficino.[17] Then, after the first golden age of melancholia in the Renaissance, melancholia underwent a second renaissance in the twentieth century when it was taken up by Freud, and psychoanalysis after him. As Juliana Schiesari explains, scholarship on melancholia today "remain[s] divided into two camps," which mutually neglect each other: "in one are contemporary theorists of melancholia largely informed by psychoanalysis; in the other, Renaissance scholars interested in . . . iconographical and historical issues."[18] Focusing on the gendering of melancholia, Schiesari's feminist analysis exposes a common tendency in both the early modern and the psychoanalytic traditions—a systematic exclusion of women from the canon of reinvented modern melancholy and its privileges. From Ficino to Tasso to Hamlet to Burton to Freud, the "great melancholics" have all been men (Schiesari 3). If Barnes's neobaroque art is anchored in her creative recuperation of Burton's *Anatomy of Melancholy,* gender was clearly the major challenge she had to confront in her appropriation of melancholia. How did Barnes negotiate the gender gap between the melancholia of the "tortured but creative male genius" and its female counterpart, abject and "unproductive" depression (Schiesari 16)? How did she intervene in the androcentric modern canon of melancholia? Given the rebellious antipatriarchal and feminist edge of Barnes's writings, this will be a major point of interest in the following discussion.

In her recent analysis of *Nightwood,* Victoria Smith writes that "one explanation of the Renaissance 'tragic idiom' of *Nightwood* lies within the psychoanalytic discourse of melancholia."[19] Along with Deborah Parsons and Esther Sánchez-Pardo, Smith is one of several recent feminist and new historicist critics who take melancholia as their point of entry into Barnes's work.[20] As is well known, Barnes criticism has seen two broad phases or orientations: first, Barnes's early and formalist critics, following her publisher and long-time friend T. S. Eliot's lead, developed the importance of style and, in keeping with New Critical readings of modernism as experimental formalism, stressed the technical design of Barnes's work. Because of its organization into static symbol patterns reminiscent of poetry, *Nightwood* was proclaimed the paradigm of the modernist novel's spatial form by critic Joseph Frank.[21] Since the seventies, a new wave of feminist and new historicist critics has emphasized the political and subversive aspects of Barnes's work—her gendered modernism, critique of women's subjection in the patriarchal family, portrayal of lesbian culture, and subversive parody of the theories of modern sexology (in particular the notion of homosexuality as sexual "inversion").[22] While formalist readings of Barnes tended to focus exclusively on her magnum opus, *Nightwood,* recent criticism has brought all of Barnes's work into visibility, from her New York journalism and her short stories, plays, and poetry to her 1958 play *The Antiphon* and her late writings. As a result, the Barnes canon is now considered to comprise four major works: the autobiographical novel about Barnes's childhood and family, *Ryder* (1928); her allegorical portrait of Paris's lesbian expatriate counterculture, *Ladies Almanack* (also 1928); the novel *Nightwood,* which immortalizes Barnes's tumultuous relationship with Thelma Wood; and her verse play and family tragedy, *The Antiphon.*[23]

Reviewing the shift in interest from formal considerations to content in Barnes criticism, Smith observes that "while some of these latter critics have negotiated the twin difficulties of Barnes' obscure yet beautiful language and her radical insights into the nature of history and sexuality, few have attempted to show the content of Barnes' form—that is, what her radical narrative style might be in the service of" (195). Smith decodes Barnes's indirect and trope-laden style as the language of melancholia. Building on the work of Smith and Parsons, I identify Barnes's idiosyncratic style with the neobaroque, fusing formal as well as historical and ideological considerations. To insist on the centrality of style in Barnes's work seems pertinent given that, as more than one commentator has noted, it is style more than content that lends unity to her work.[24] Furthermore, the neobaroque can establish a conversation between and among formalist, feminist, and new historicist readings of Barnes. It can address the question of Barnes's experimental style as well as, in Smith's phrasing, the content of Barnes's form.

Among the four works mentioned above, my primary focus is on Barnes's two "queer" texts, *Ladies Almanack* and *Nightwood,* which are set in nonnormative sociosexual subcultures. They form the affiliative counterparts to Barnes's two fables of filiation, *Ryder* and *The Antiphon,* the plots and characters of which are allegorical representations of Barnes's own biological family. Critics have noted the complementary pairing of the filiative and the affiliative, heterosexual and homosexual worlds, in all four texts.[25] The result is a bifocal structure that is further developed by the simultaneous "darkening" of both the world of the patriarchal and birth family and that of the affiliative homosexual community. Between the earlier 1928 texts and the later works, the mood darkens from ironic playfulness and, especially in *Ladies Almanack,* witty and bawdy exuberance to utter tragedy. All four works end with the death or destruction of a major protagonist (Dame Evangeline Musset in *Ladies Almanack,* the grandmother figure Sophia in *Ryder,* the lover Robin in *Nightwood,* and the daughter and mother figures Miranda and Augusta in *The Antiphon*). An absence or loss at the center of each narrative forms the basis of a decentralizing structure of signification.

Melancholia, Loss, and the Neobaroque Language of Abundance and Insufficiency

In her late poem, "The Walking-Mort" (1971), which Djuna Barnes wrote when almost eighty years old, language that is at once obscure and studded with jarring images harks back to Donne and metaphysical poetry:

Call her the walking-mort; say where she goes
She squalls her bush with blood. I slam a gate
Report her axis bone it gigs the rose.
What say of mine? It turns a grinning grate.
Impugn her that she baits time with an awl.
What do my sessions then? They task a grave.[26]

Who or what is a "walking-mort"? In connection with the poem's theme of physical injury and impending death, the "walking-mort" appears to be one of the living dead, someone with one foot in the grave, whose smallest physical movements are painful. One can hear the walking-mort's bones grate as she moves, and almost feel her physical and spiritual pain in the harsh alliterations ("bush/blood"; "grinning grate"), which are reinforced by violent acts ("slam a gate," "bait time with an awl"). As in metaphysical poetry and its modernist revival in Eliot's early poetry, "The Walking-Mort" uses self-consciously artificial images that are obviously "yoked by violence together." In the image of time baited with an awl, for example, words referring to tools (bait, awl) are joined to a word from an unrelated realm, "time." Barnes's image is conceited, as Eliot would put it, a hyperbolic image that forges likenesses from the dissimilar. As such, it remains a fragmentary assemblage, flaunting the seams of its conscious construction. As in modern poetry in general, Barnes's farfetched analogies are private and do not derive from familiar mythological material as do their seventeenth-century baroque counterparts; their obscurity therefore cannot be fully resolved.[27] The picture of someone chipping away at time with a sharp object like a pick-axe as one would at ice could suggest either trying to gain more time or shortening one's life span—what is certain is only that this image suggests a forced deviation of time's natural progress. Other, even more startling images are completely obscure: what happens when the walking-mort "squalls her bush with blood"? What is an "axis bone"? How does one "gig" a rose? Furthermore, one cannot avoid noticing the breathless pace in which these arcane conceits are piled on top of each other. Images rush by in a torrent, each one more striking than the next. But because of the obscurity of their meaning, this abundance of language has an adverse effect, leaving the reader with contradictory feelings of stimulation and frustration rather than satisfaction.

"The Walking-Mort" marks the end point of development of Djuna Barnes's "poetic prose," prose whose dense figural ornamentation approximates poetry, as Eliot was the first to note (introduction to *Nightwood* xii). Its dominant characteristics are flamboyant and allegorical images that are suggestive rather than clarifying, ornamental rather than functional. They adorn ever more tragic sequences of events and actions set in an atmosphere conveying psychological as well as physical torment. Although concrete reasons are given as the cause of suffering (such as the loss of Robin Vote as love object in *Nightwood*), the suffering reaches such magnitudes of excess that it seems pathological, without adequate cause. Since antiquity, sadness without sufficient cause has been named one of the core features of melancholia (Radden, "Introduction" 10–12). I concur with Smith that melancholia, in the specific Freudian sense of the self constituted by loss, seems superbly suited to Barnes's work: Barnes's superabundant prose enacts a "memorial to loss" (Smith 196). Yet, given the early modern sources of Barnes's deliberately antiquarian style, as well as her profession as artist, the Renaissance sense of melancholia as the chronic disease of creative genius is equally important. In unfolding the links between melancholia, loss, and Barnes's neobaroque language, I begin with a brief outline of Barnes's life, a move necessitated by the autobiographical subject matter of all of Barnes's major works.

Scarred by a childhood and youth of emotional trauma and sexual abuse, Barnes was, in Herring's words, an "incorrigible pessimist" (Herring 50).[28] Born in Cornwall-on-Hudson, New Jersey, in 1892, the second of five children of Wald Barnes and his English wife, Elizabeth Chappell, Djuna grew up in a polygamous household comprising her ne'er-do-well father, her mother, and her father's second, common-law wife, Elizabeth Faulkner Clark (Fanny); the parents' two sets of children; and Wald's mother, Zadel Barnes. The matriarchal head of the household (Zadel's matronym is the family name), Zadel was a formidable and magnetic personality. Twice married and twice divorced and separated, she was a successful feminist journalist and writer connected to famous intellectuals and radical circles in Boston, New York, and London. She willingly struggled to provide for her son's ever-growing family and to mother his children through her old age even as her son blithely shirked the role of material provider. Zadel and Wald Barnes were close, sharing the bohemian, free-love philosophy that Zadel had passed on to her son. "Indulged by Zadel since childhood," for whom he "could do no wrong," Herring reports, with the exception of one three-week stint, Wald never worked in regular employment until after his mother's death, when he was fifty-three (26, 19). Instead, Wald pursued sexual escapades, dabbled in multiple trades and art, and distracted himself with numerous visionary but unrealistic schemes. One savage anecdote about Wald's promiscuity—exalted by his private philosophy, a cross of Thoreau and Brigham Young, about which he wrote a treatise subsequently destroyed for fear of legal consequences (Herring 25)—comes from Barnes's autobiographical novel *Ryder*. An illustration prefacing the novel depicts the Wald-figure Wendell Ryder, a self-declared patriarch whose ambition is to found a "race that shall be Ryder" (*Ryder* 210), riding around the neighborhood on his horse Hisodalgus seducing women, aided by a sponge attached to his saddle with which he wipes his private parts. Djuna grew up isolated on the family farm, where she was home-schooled (for fear of the school board's intervention into Wald's lifestyle) but immersed in a rich culture of home entertainment that included concerts, performances, and collective reading and learning (Herring 38). Resenting her mother's rival, who moved in with the family when she was five, and distant from both her father and mother, Djuna was passionately attached to her grandmother: "I loved [Zadel] as a child usually loves its mother—I cared little or nothing for the rest of the family" (quoted in Herring 52). In Djuna's teens, the family creed of sexual freedom traumatized her severely when Djuna was subjected to a humiliating sexual initiation arranged by Wald, followed by a private "marriage" at age seventeen, also arranged by Wald and Zadel, to a fifty-two-year-old family friend. There are also hints of consensual incest with her grandmother, traces of which reappear in *Nightwood,* through Nora's description of her love for Robin as incest (*Nightwood* 156), and through the resemblance between Zadel and Thelma Wood (Robin), which Barnes once mentioned as the reason why she fell in love with Wood (quoted in Herring 59).

One wonders what Freud would have thought about the psychodynamics of Barnes's polygamous family, a family in which the taboo against sexual play (and perhaps incest) was at a significantly lowered threshold. On the topic of Barnes's fascination with incest as a component of sex, Herring relates how Barnes's best friend, Emily Holmes Coleman, came to understand this connection: "Why did you say he [Scudder, one of Barnes's lovers in the 1930s] was a relative; does relative mean *sex?*" Coleman asks in a letter to Barnes. "If not why should you have felt such a sex-passion for Scudder, and also for Thelma, who was also 'your family.' Family means *sex.* I suddenly knew it" (quoted in Herring 269). According to one psychiatrist, "the psychological profile of Djuna Barnes was that of the sexually abused child" (Herring 269). Patriarchy (as Barnes makes clear in *Ryder*) was by no means abolished by sexual freedom—to the contrary. Motherhood reduces women to breeding machines whose duty is to sacrifice themselves in order to realize Wendell Ryder's dynastic ambitions. In *Ryder* and *The Antiphon,* Barnes systematically avenged herself for the psychological injuries sustained at the hands of her family. While *Ryder*'s target was her father, Wald, *The Antiphon* attacks her mother, Elizabeth, for failing to prevent Djuna's sexual violation as a teenager. Curiously, as Herring notes, Barnes's grandmother Zadel, who had much more authority over Wald than her mother and therefore could have intervened much more easily, is spared from all blame in *The Antiphon,* as she was for most of Barnes's life (Herring 269).[29] It appears that Barnes dealt with what must have been an enormous emotional ambivalence toward the maternal figure in her life by splitting the "good mother" from the "bad mother" and keeping them separated by projecting her love of the former onto her grandmother Zadel while fixating her hatred of the latter on her biological mother, Elizabeth. Indeed, Zadel Barnes remained the model Barnes would follow as an adult and as a professional, as it was Zadel's successful career as a journalist and writer that Barnes emulated, not to mention her independent, bohemian love life, outside the constraints of mainstream conventions. If women talk about becoming their mothers, Barnes talked about becoming her grandmother: "I always thought I was my grandmother, and *now* I am almost right," Barnes wrote in 1935 (quoted in Herring 54).

Another catastrophe—which occurred in 1912, when financial problems led to her parents' divorce, obliging Elizabeth and her children to strike out on their own and move to New York City—turned out to give Barnes her unexpected launch toward success. By helping to support her destitute mother and younger brothers with freelance journalism, she was able to start a successful career as a journalist, which culminated in her garnering a well-paying post as foreign correspondent for *McCall's Magazine* (the same magazine that had sent Zadel to London in 1880). The job brought Djuna to Paris in 1921. Until then, there could have been no better place in the United States for Barnes to apprentice herself to her dream occupation of artist and writer than New York City in the 1910s, the city that then hosted the so-called "New York Dada," or what Marjorie Perloff identifies as the "avant-garde phase of American modernism."[30] Attending art school for brief periods, Barnes participated in the modernism blossoming in New York by publishing in New York's flourishing avant-garde literary journals while living independently in its physical center, Greenwich Village. Socially, aided by her journalism, Barnes knew almost all the leading modernists then active in New York: the writers William Carlos Williams, Mina Loy, and Carl Van Vechten; the playwright Eugene O'Neill; the artists Marsden Hartley and Marcel Duchamp; the photographers Alfred Stieglitz and Berenice Abbott; and Margaret Anderson and Jane Heap, editors of *The Little Review,* which published Barnes's best work at the time.[31] With the exception of the traumatic death of her grandmother in 1917, for Barnes, the 1910s were a promising prelude to the 1920s, the happiest and most productive period of her life, which Barnes spent in the company of modernist artists and American expatriates in Paris. During her tempestuous relationship with the love of her life, the silverpoint artist Thelma Wood, between 1921 and 1929, Barnes produced her first major works, her best short stories (the Paris stories), as well as a bestseller (*Ryder*) and *Ladies Almanack.*[32]

The breakup with Wood in 1929 was the turning point, after which Barnes's world began to shrink instead of expand. Even as pain produced a jewel, *Nightwood,* which was laboriously composed and finally published in 1936, the 1930s marked a decisive downturn: a series of brief love affairs, an illegal abortion (performed by her friend Dan Mahoney, the model for Doctor O'Connor in *Nightwood*), and Djuna's descent into alcoholism, which resulted in her forced hospitalization in 1940 and from which she did not free herself until 1950. In 1940, Barnes made her permanent return to New York and Greenwich Village, where she spent the remaining forty-two years of her life in increasing self-isolation in a tiny flat, cultivating her misanthropy and wit and nurturing old grievances. Supported mainly by her friends even as she continued to alienate them, she produced only *The Antiphon,* in 1958, as well as some poetry.

Barnes was, in Deborah Parson's apt phrase, "a self-professed melancholic" ("Melancholic Modernism" 168). Reflecting on her mood after the publication of *Nightwood,* Barnes wrote to Coleman, "Melancholia, melancholia, it rides me like a bucking mare" (quoted in Herring 236). In a 1923 letter to her mother, Barnes wrote, "Having life is the greatest horror. . . . I cannot think of it as a 'merry, gay & joyous thing, just to be alive'—it seems to me monstrous, obscene & still with the most obscene trick at the end" (quoted in Parsons 168). She twice unsuccessfully tried to kill herself, in 1939 and again in the late 1970s; according to friends, her favorite aphorisms were "Our first mistake was being born" and "The wish to be good is the wish to be destroyed" (Herring 295). Considering her family background, one might concur that she had very good reasons for her chronic negativity.

Because it conceptualizes how early injury becomes formative of identity, shaping the self and its idiosyncratic mode of expression, Freud's psychoanalytic theory of melancholia, to which I turn now, provides a key to Barnes's work: it explains the curious, rare link between autobiographical content and the extreme artificiality and stylization of form in Barnes. Indeed, Barnes makes the personal impersonal and obscure—very few writers as autobiographical as Barnes stray this far from realism. Before moving on to an in-depth reading of *Nightwood,* Barnes's paradigmatic melancholic text in a subsequent section, I first offer some general observations on how Barnes's neobaroque language derives from her melancholic celebration of grief.

In his celebrated essay "Mourning and Melancholia" (1917), Freud presents an original interpretation of melancholia, which has remained foundational for clinical psychiatry, psychoanalysis after Freud, and literary and cultural analysis until this day.[33] Comparing melancholia's pathological condition to ordinary mourning, Freud writes that it shares with mourning the same symptoms of deep dejection, lethargy, and a lapse of interest in the outside world resulting from loss, either of a loved person through death or of an abstraction such as an ideal or belief. But unlike mourning, in melancholia the nature of this loss is not only mysterious, it is also accompanied by an incongruous loss of self-esteem, as well as by theatrical self-abasement: "In mourning it is the world which has become poor and empty; in melancholia it is the ego itself" (Freud, "Mourning" 246). The melancholic's characteristic inordinate self-criticism, including his suicidal tendencies, as well as the enigmatic nature of his loss (the masculine pronouns are Freud's), led Freud to come up with a sophisticated theory linking melancholia not just to mourning but also to narcissism and the process of ego development via the *incorporation* of the love object into the self. Instead of loosening, with time as in normal mourning, in melancholia the libido cathexis is not withdrawn from the lost object and eventually displaced onto a new person. Freud explains, "the free libido was not displaced on to another object; it was withdrawn into the ego. There, however, it was not employed in any unspecified way, but served to establish an *identification* of the ego with the abandoned object" (249). An image of the lost object is set up inside the ego, transforming the ego through identification with the object. The cause triggering this deviant course is, Freud surmises, that the original "object-choice has been effected on a narcissistic basis" (249), as he explains in this celebrated observation: "Melancholia, therefore, borrows some of its features from mourning, and the others from the process of regression from narcissistic object-choice to narcissism. It is on the one hand, like mourning, a reaction to the real loss of a loved object; but over and above this, it is marked by a determinant which is absent in normal mourning or which, if it is present, transforms the latter into pathological mourning" (250).

One key effect of this incorporation or introjection of the lost object into the self is that it forestalls the inevitable ending of mourning with the passage of time: in this way, love, and sorrow over its loss, are given endless life. As Freud poetically words it, "by taking flight into the ego love escapes extinction" (257). Melancholia does not want to know a future beyond grief. It abolishes time, locking the subject into his emotional state at the moment of trauma. The temporality of melancholia is the cannibalistic past that blots out the future, as Sartre notes in an essay on one of Faulkner's melancholic protagonists, Quentin Compson: Quentin's impending suicide is a "fatality," which he symbolizes by breaking off the hands of his watch.[34] Or, in Freud's equally evocative image, melancholia functions like "an open wound," a void that absorbs all psychic energies, and that refuses to close ("Mourning" 253).

The melancholic incorporation of the lost love object becomes even more complex through a third factor: ambivalence between feelings of love and hate. The three preconditions of melancholia according to Freud are "loss of the object, ambivalence, and regression of libido into the ego" (258). "The self-tormenting in melancholia, which is without doubt enjoyable," can be traced back to "a satisfaction of trends of sadism and hate which relate to an object, and which have been turned round upon the subject's own self" (251). As melancholia blurs the boundaries between self and other, it also projects the ambivalent feelings of love and hatred first felt for the love object onto the self. What was originally an external conflict between the self and the beloved other is therefore converted into an internal conflict *within* the self: "Thus the shadow of the object fell upon the ego, and the latter could henceforth be judged by a special agency, as though it were an object, the forsaken object. In this way an object-loss was transformed into an ego-loss and the conflict between the ego and the loved person into a cleavage between the critical activity of the ego and the ego as altered by identification" (249). As James Strachey observes in his editorial note to Freud's essay, the importance of "Mourning and Melancholia," above and beyond its immediate subject, rests on Freud's discovery, during his work on melancholia, of a "critical agency" within the self, which "in turn led on to the hypothesis of the super-ego in *The Ego and the Id* (1923) and to a fresh assessment of the sense of guilt."[35] It is this critical instance within the ego that is the representative of the loved person, incorporated within the self. This process also explains how, as Freud admits, many of the melancholic's outlandish complaints turn out to be truthful rather than imaginary. Radden notes that Freud is also adapting Renaissance melancholia's theme of compensatory brilliance when he states, "It is merely that he has a keener eye for the truth than other people who are not melancholic" (Freud 246).[36]

In short, the dialectic between the self and its love object, exacerbated by ambivalence, produces, by way of the melancholic psychic process, an internal division of the psyche, the split between the ego and the ego ideal (superego). Whereas Freud had contrasted normal mourning and pathological melancholia in the 1917 essay, this opposition disappeared as he developed the notion of the superego further in *The Ego and the Id*. It gives way to the thesis that identity as such (including the normal psyche) is melancholically constituted through loss: "We succeeded in explaining the painful disorder of melancholia by supposing that [in those suffering from it] an object which was lost has been set up again inside the ego—that is, that an object-cathexis has been replaced by an identification. At that time, however, we did not appreciate the full significance of this process and did not know how common and how typical it is. Since then we have come to understand that this kind of substitution has a great share in determining the form taken by the ego and that it makes an essential contribution towards building up what is called its 'character.'"[37] Identity in general derives from loss; as Freud puts it, "the character of the ego is a precipitate of abandoned object-cathexes and . . . contains the history of those object choices" (*Ego and Id* 44). He surmises that it "may be that by this introjection, which is a kind of regression to the mechanism of the oral phase, the ego makes it easier for the object to be given up or renders that process possible. It may be that this identification is the sole condition under which the id can give up its objects. At any rate the process, especially in the early phases of development, is a very frequent one" (44).

Freud's insights offer invaluable clues to some of *Nightwood*'s most brilliant and moving passages describing the violent grief that afflicts Nora (the novel's Djuna figure):

> In Nora's heart lay the fossil of Robin, intaglio of her identity, and about it for its maintenance ran Nora's blood. Thus the body of Robin could never be unloved, corrupt or put away. (56)

> As an amputated hand cannot be disowned because it is experiencing a futurity, of which the victim is its forebear, so Robin was an amputation that Nora could not renounce. As the wrist longs, so her heart longed. (59)

> [Nora] said: "She is myself. What am I to do?" (127)

> "I thought I loved her for her sake, and I found it was for my own." (151)

The emotional core of *Nightwood* is the melancholic dejection that Nora Flood (Barnes) experiences after her separation from Robin Vote (Thelma Wood). Did Barnes know Freud's theory of melancholia as she knew the Renaissance tradition of melancholia through Burton? In reading *Nightwood*'s Doctor O'Connor as a parody of either the Freudian psychoanalyst or the turn-of-the-century sexologist (Krafft-Ebing and Havelock Ellis), or both, and arguing that Barnes lampooned the scientific authority of these medical theories for their misogyny and homophobia, feminist and new historicist critics have assumed a substantial working knowledge of both sexology and psychoanalysis for Barnes.[38] Whatever the case may be for Barnes's familiarity with psychoanalysis—specialized knowledge beyond the Freudianisms that would have filtered down into the common knowledge of artistic and intellectual circles such as Barnes's Greenwich Village and feminist-lesbian Left Bank communities has not been documented—the overlap between certain Freudian concepts, such as melancholia, and Barnes's literary psychology is striking.[39] (In contrast, Barnes's knowledge of sexology's theory of homosexuality as inversion is documented, at least indirectly, through her use of the term, and through intertextual references in *Ladies Almanack* to Radclyffe Hall's literary portrait of lesbianism as inversion in *The Well of Loneliness*.) It is helpful to recall the enormous influence Freud's ideas in general (along with those of other intellectual giants such as Marx) exercised on the culture, literature, and art of the early twentieth century.[40] In particular, and as Foucault has shown, Freud stands at the end of a sexological revolution, beginning in the nineteenth century, in which sexual desire was acknowledged as foundational to identity.[41] Thus, Barnes's playful reflections on an identity and culture specific to lesbians in *Ladies Almanack,* and on the melancholic constitution of identity through desire and loss in *Nightwood,* are part and parcel of the modern approach to identity as the subject of desire.

Building on these existing studies, let me outline my approach to Barnes's literary psychoanalysis: what makes *Nightwood* truly exceptional are not the two direct statements cited above, Nora's confession that "[Robin] is myself" and her disillusioning insight that her love for Robin had been selfish. Granted, it is noteworthy that Nora's observations confirm two key Freudian claims, that of the narcissistic introjection of the love-object into the ego in melancholia, and that the melancholic's original object-choice must have been "effected on a narcissistic basis." What makes *Nightwood* unique is the characteristic *indirection,* the opaque, allegorical (rather than straightforward) manner in which this "second anatomy of melancholy" (as Barnes's friend John Holms dubbed the novel, comparing it to Burton's *Anatomy*) proceeds (see Herring 204). "In Nora's heart lay the fossil of Robin, intaglio of her identity, and about it for its maintenance ran Nora's blood" is another way of saying "she is myself." Again, "the fossil of Robin" is a hyperbolic image, a conceit fashioned from the strained correspondence between the petrification of organic matter and human love's stubborn persistence beyond separation and death. Such mannered juxtapositions of death and decay with human desire were baroque favorites: Barnes's image is reminiscent of the famous closing conceit from Francisco de Quevedo's sonnet "Amor constante más allá de la muerte" ("Love Constant beyond Death"): "polvo serán, mas polvo enamorado" ("they will be dust, but dust in love").[42]

Thus, what matters is the predominance of this allegorical mode of "saying otherwise," in which an abstract idea, Nora's melancholic incorporation of her lost lover, is presented indirectly, through a concrete sensuous equivalent. *Nightwood* does not communicate Nora's suffering through the scientific language of psychoanalysis but rather through the baroque iconography of martyrdom and its characteristic images of tears, hearts, blood, and severed limbs. Barnes would have been able to study the visual culture of the Counter-Reformation baroque in Paris and other European cities that she visited in 1931, such as Munich and, especially, Vienna.[43] The dramatic naturalism of one of the passages quoted above, the gory description of Nora's amputated hand, its analogy with Robin, from whom she has been separated, amplified by the statement that this is an amputation that Nora could not "renounce," and culminating in the horrific sight of Nora's amputated "wrist long[ing]" as "her heart longed," affords a tormented vision whose bloodthirstiness could rival any of the paintings of martyred saints so popular in the Catholic baroque of Southern Europe. This portrait of Nora agonizing under love melancholy is the verbal analogue of what John Rupert Martin calls the "furious martyrdoms" of the Counter-Reformation baroque (112). A good example is Tiepolo's depiction of the martyrdom of St. Agatha, whose breasts were cut off (fig. 1). The image replays standard iconography in depicting the saint's severed breasts on a platter. Like the spectacle of St. Agatha's agony, Nora's suffering the amputation of her hand is a picture intended to draw tears.

To a considerable degree, the emotional appeal of *Nightwood*'s style is due to the fact that Djuna Barnes, like Frida Kahlo (as Lois Parkinson Zamora has recently shown), "routinely engaged the Baroque iconography of sanctified suffering."[44] Neither Barnes nor Kahlo was religious. But like Kahlo, Barnes appropriated the iconography of the Catholic baroque to create an autobiographical and secular mythology for her personal suffering. Like Kahlo's art, Barnes's writings center on her own life, and both women's lives were defined by pain. Zamora points to Kahlo's "many surgeries and miscarriages" and "her two marriages to Diego [Rivera], a double disaster" (192), which are matched by Barnes's sexual abuse and emotional trauma and her troubled lesbian marriage to Thelma Wood. The subject of Kahlo's 1949 self-portrait, *Diego and I*, for example, is Kahlo's melancholic

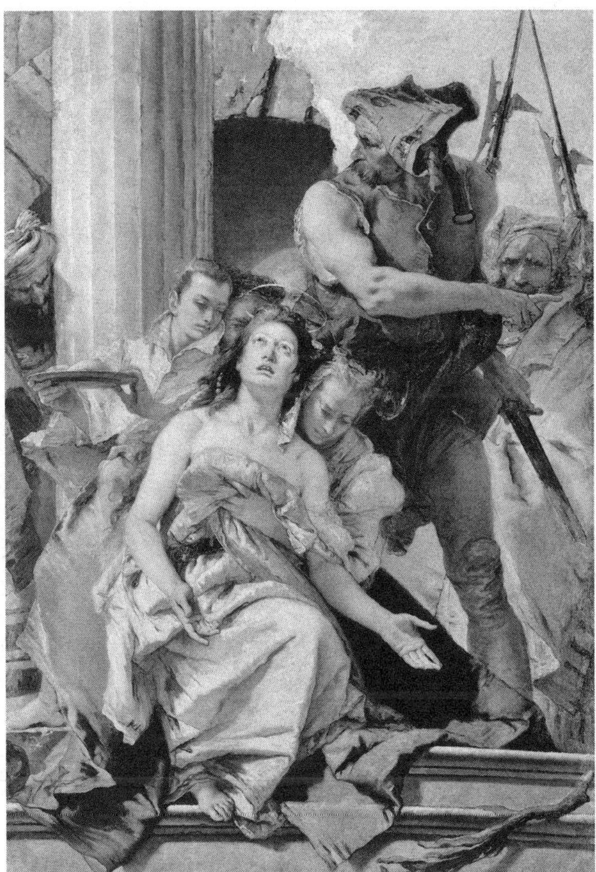

Fig. 1. Giambattista Tiepolo, *The Martyrdom of St. Agatha*, c. 1745–50. (Gemäldegalerie, Staatliche Museen, Berlin, Germany. Photograph: Jörg P. Anders, Berlin/Art Resource, New York)

incorporation of her husband, Diego, whom she had married in 1929, divorced in 1939, and remarried in 1941 in a second marriage that was no less turbulent than the failed first. Marked by streaming tears and and a portrait of Diego tattooed on her forehead, Kahlo's self-portrait depicts

Fig. 2. Frida Kahlo, *Diego and I,* 1949. (Banco de México Diego Rivera Frida Kahlo Museums Trust, Mexico/Instituto Nacional de Bellas Artes, Mexico/Artists Rights Society (ARS), New York)

a wounded, melancholic self (fig. 2). Had Kahlo been a writer instead of a painter, she might have found words similar to Barnes's: in Frida's heart lay the fossil of Diego, and about it for its maintenance ran Frida's blood. Thus the body of Diego could never be unloved, corrupt, or put away. Again, it was their agony from which both Kahlo and Barnes fashioned their art, which in each case was also a specifically female art (though of very different kinds) through which they both contributed to the formation of gendered modernisms. For both modernist women artists, then, various baroque styles and genres, both religious and secular, including but not limited to hagiography and its iconography of heroic suffering, enabled them to create glamorous, stylized representations of their personal torment that foregrounded the compensations of sorrow. It is here that we should also look for the sources of the Christian themes of damnation, sin, and redemption in *Nightwood,* whose tragic finale, in a chapter titled "The Possessed," takes place in Nora's chapel, in front of an altar featuring an uncharacteristic (for Nora's Protestantism) Catholic devotional object, a "Madonna" (*Nightwood* 169). As Georgette Fleischer has noted, the religious theme was discussed by Barnes's early formalist critics but has tended to be ignored by more recent feminist and new historicist interpretations.[45]

Indeed, the pictorial representation of the heroism of Christian saints suffering for the true faith was a staple of Counter-Reformation propaganda. Within the European reach of baroque expression, which straddled the religious battle lines between the Protestant North and the Catholic South, the cult of the saints, often in the form of the pictorial representation of their martyrdom, was a partisan affair of the Catholic South. As Arnold Hauser observes, "The works of the Dutch painters are to be seen everywhere except in churches; and the devotional picture is non-existent in the Protestant milieu."[46] The struggle over the status of holy images was at the center of the religious schism of the sixteenth century. As Margaret Miles points out in her study of visuality in the Christian tradition, differences between the Protestant Reformation and Counter-Reformation have tended to obscure that both parties, not just the Protestants, were engaged in reforming Christian doctrine and rituals in the sixteenth century.[47] The Protestant Reformation was iconoclastic and centered on the spoken word of God (Luther's maxim was *sola scriptura*). Churches in Protestant territories, especially in Calvinist Switzerland, were methodically stripped of religious art and decoration, leaving them with bare, white-washed walls.[48] Countering the Protestant campaign to eradicate devotional images, the Council of Trent (1545–63), which reformed Roman Catholic doctrine in response to the Protestant challenge, gave special emphasis to visual images as a medium of worship. This policy resulted in the Church of Rome's reinforced patronage of the visual arts—architecture, sculpture, and painting—whose legacy in stone and canvas Barnes (like any visitor) was able to admire in cities such as Vienna and Munich.[49] In addition to affirming the value of images in worship, among traditional Catholic doctrines upheld by the Catholic Reformation were the cult of saints and of the Virgin Mary as intermediaries between God and living believers. Indeed, the two were linked, for the Council of Trent's affirmation of image-based worship would come to focus on dramatic scenes from the exemplary lives of saints, the Virgin, and, of course, Christ's passion as core pedagogical tools of reformed Catholic worship (see Miles 121).

At the core of the holy image is a contradiction that was systematically exploited by the Counter-Reformation.[50] The sacred image makes the marvelous things of the faith accessible to the senses, visible and palpable, like the things of the everyday world. Images of Christ's resurrection, the Annunciation, the Holy Trinity, or purgatory, for example, all perform this act of visualizing the invisible. An early modern and Christian manifestation of what Alejo Carpentier would much later come to call marvelous realism, the holy image naturalizes the supernatural.[51] Embracing the pedagogical power of images, Counter-Reformation policy in the late sixteenth century began to promote a reinforced naturalism in sacred art designed to make the things of the spirit vivid and accessible to direct experience. This resulted in a baroque religious art in which the spiritual and the physical, the immaterial and the material were blended as never before. Bernini's sculpture *The Ecstasy of Saint Teresa* (1645–52) (fig. 3) may be one of the most famous examples of this new, hypersensualistic baroque religious art: in the depiction of the saint's mystical vision of God, writes John Rupert Martin, "divine love, as the baroque artist interprets it, shares something (at least in its outward manifestation) with its earthly counterpart, and it is an inevitable consequence that many representations of ecstatic visions contain more than a suggestion of a sublimated erotic experience" (102).

A perfect realization of the Counter-Reformation's goal of the direct sensual address of the believer through the sacred image, Bernini's Corona chapel, which houses the sculpture, also features spectators in marble along the sides who, mirroring the actual spectator, are watching the spectacle of the divine become marble pretending to be flesh. It is no accident, therefore, that, centuries later, Lacan would invoke Bernini's representation of the saint's spiritual passion as an illustration of his concept of female *jouissance*.[52] The same voluptuous naturalism was applied to the representation of pleasure's opposite, pain. Baroque visual representations of martyrdoms reach excesses of grisliness heretofore unknown. According to Miles, the Jesuits especially sponsored the painting of scenes of martyrdom, in part to train their own novices for their self-sacrificial lives of action in often dangerous missionary posts around the world (121–22). As exemplary

Christians, saints are first and foremost heroes and heroines, model subjects the worshipper is encouraged to emulate. Their steadfastness in faith, even under extreme pressure and to the point of torture, is what matters, and so the point of the representation of a martyr's death agony is to demonstrate the ability to transcend the suffering of the flesh in this world and find solace in the "marvelous reality" of the divine.[53] The *cause* for which the saint is suffering makes the suffering glamorous. It is precisely this dimension of idealization and glorification in representing the subject in pain, as it were, that attracted Barnes (and Kahlo, as Zamora would have it) to the opulent iconography of Catholic baroque art.

Fig. 3. Gian Lorenzo Bernini, *The Ecstasy of Saint Teresa,* c. 1645–52. (Cornaro Chapel, S. Maria della Vittoria, Rome, Italy. Photograph: Scala/Art Resource, New York)

Let me now return to the issue of the indirection of Barnes's prose, which motivated this exploration of *Nightwood*'s neobaroque iconography of melancholia, and approach it from another angle. In addition to the pictorial naturalism exemplified by the flamboyant conceits mentioned earlier (fossil of Robin, Robin as amputation), indirection also functions in another, opposite mode, to produce deliberate denaturalization and artificialization. These two distinct—sensual-naturalist and artificializing—modes of "saying otherwise" share the same larger goal: delegitimizing the authority of the scientific discourses of psychoanalysis and sexology and legitimizing literature's unique way of thinking passionately, as Eliot would put it. But in contrast to the first, illusionist mode that conceals its de facto constructedness, the second mode is openly allegorical, emphasizing the difference (rather than fusion) between the signifier and the signified, medium and message. (In fact, the lines between them are fluid, as we shall see.) It is this second mode I turn to now, the notorious circumlocution and redundancy of Barnes's language. Its most quoted instances are found in *Nightwood,* but it is also present in *Ladies Almanack,* and developed to extremes in *The Antiphon.* Losing his patience over Nora's ceaseless lamentation, Doctor O'Connor exclaims:

> A broken heart have you! I have falling arches, flying dandruff, a floating kidney, shattered nerves *and* a broken heart! But do I scream that an eagle has me by the balls or has dropped his oyster on my heart? Am I going forward screaming that it hurts, that my mind goes back, or holding my guts as if they were a coil of knives? . . . Isn't everyone in the world peculiarly swung and me the craziest of the lot? (*Nightwood* 154–55)

Or to cite the celebrated passage depicting Robin Vote's initial appearance in *Nightwood,*

> The woman who presents herself to the spectator as a "picture" forever arranged is, for the contemplative mind, the chiefest danger. Sometimes one meets a woman who is beast turning human. Such a person's every movement will reduce to an image of a forgotten experience; a mirage of an eternal wedding cast on the racial memory; as insupportable a joy as would be the vision of an eland coming down an aisle of trees, chapleted with orange blossoms and bridal veil, a hoof raised in the economy of fear, stepping in the trepidation of flesh that will become myth; as the unicorn is neither man nor beast deprived, but human hunger pressing its breast to its prey. Such a woman is the infected carrier of the past: before her the structure of our head and jaws ache—we feel that we could eat her, she who is eaten death returning. (37)

Both passages do more than present a strained, conceited analogy, they layer conceit over conceit, without ever reaching a convincing stopping point. In the first example, the Doctor matches his own melancholia against Nora's, by taking Nora's refrain, "broken heart," and echoing it back to her by way of a proliferation of parallel conditions (falling arches, flying dandruff, floating kidney, shattered nerves). Many meanings are at play here. First, the reference to "floating kidney" evokes the ancient humoral theory of melancholia (which Barnes knew through Burton) as an imbalance of black bile, the cold, dry and black element.[54] The organ associated with black bile is not the kidney but the spleen, however, and therefore this reference is parodical. In addition to his affliction with black bile, the Doctor's loquaciousness and his philosophical, learned monologues identify him as a paragon of the Renaissance melancholic, the man of genius, whose dejection is the dark side of his gendered privilege, as Schiesari argues—his intellectual gift. We will return to the Doctor in the last section of this chapter on *Nightwood*. My present point concerns the technique of displacement by which circumlocution avoids a simple, direct statement in the speech quoted above.

The same technique is at work in the second passage. Its subject is Robin, the irresistible but elusive object of love and desire, who is pursued by three characters successively. Possessing a primal vitality that casts a spell on everyone she meets, Robin, the femme fatale, is a quasi-supernatural character, someone "outside the 'human type'—a wild thing caught in a woman's skin" (146). When we first encounter Robin, she is lying unconscious on a bed, surrounded by proliferating plants, before she is brought back to life by the Doctor's magical but dubious ministrations. There the phrase "a woman who is beast turning human" evokes Robin's enigmatic nature, which conserves primitive features other adults have abandoned. But as in the previous passage, this initial description is displaced by a series of synonyms: "the beast turning human" yields to "image of a forgotten experience," which in turn is succeeded by "mirage of an eternal wedding," "vision of an eland," "unicorn," "the infected carrier of the past," and "eaten death returning." Eschewing direct definition, the effect of this circumlocution is the characteristic obscurity and opaqueness of Barnes's neobaroque discourse.

The Cuban novelist and theorist Severo Sarduy's theory of the baroque, which centers on baroque circumlocution and its programmatic imprecision, offers important insights into Barnes's technique. In the 1972 essay "The Baroque and the Neobaroque," Sarduy presents his poststructuralist reading of baroque and neobaroque art and literature as programmatic antirealism. According to Sarduy, the essence of baroque style is not naturalism, as one might expect; to the contrary, the semblance of naturalism is exposed as illusionistic, achieved through *"artificialization"*: the baroque is "the apotheosis of artifice, [and] the irony and mockery of nature."[55] Technically, artificialization is the result of metonymic displacement, as exemplified by José Lezama Lima's famous Gongorine conceit in *Paradiso* (1966), where he "calls a male organ 'the stinger of the leptosomatic macrogenitome'" (Sarduy, "Baroque and Neobaroque" 272). Of Sarduy's three mechanisms of artificialization—substitution, proliferation, and condensation—the second is the most useful for our purposes. More radical than substitution, which replaces one signifier (literal) by another (figural), proliferation describes a (theoretically) infinite "chain of signifiers that progresses metonymically and that ends by circumscribing the absent signifier, tracing an orbit around it" (273). In this sketch, it is easy to recognize Barnes's proliferating synonyms. Sarduy calls this process a "radial reading" (273), for the circularity of the baroque signifying process that orbits around an absent signified, not to mention a referent in the outside world. For Sarduy, baroque artificialization exposes the contingent nature of language as such, uncovering the arbitrary relation between signifier and signified and thereby exposing the fabrication of language's mimetic-realist claims. But most centrally, the wastefulness of baroque circumlocution is a rebellion against functionalism: baroque language is language at anarchic play, not language at work in the service of an external purpose (for example, science or religion). According to Sarduy, the baroque,

> superabundance, brimming cornucopia, prodigality, and wastefulness—hence the *moral* resistance it has provoked in certain cultures of economy and moderation, like the French—a mockery of all functionality, of all sobriety, is also the solution to this verbal saturation, the *trop plein* of the word, the abundance of nouns in relation to what is named, what can be enumerated, the flooding of things by words. Hence also its mechanism of periphrasis, of digression and detour, of duplication and even tautology. The Word, squandered forms, *language that because of its excessive abundance no longer designates things but only other designators of things, signifiers enveloping other signifiers in a mechanism of signification that ends up designating itself,* revealing its own grammar, the models of that grammar and its generation in the universe of words. . . . A language that speaks of language, Baroque superabundance is generated by the synonymic supplement, the initial "doubling," the overflow of the signifiers that the Baroque artwork, Baroque opera, catalogues. ("Baroque and Neobaroque" 281; emphasis added)

The following analyses of *Ladies' Almanack* and *Nightwood* argue that Barnes employs the baroque strategy Sarduy calls artificialization and its characteristic techniques of redundant circumlocution to escape the realist claims—and undermine the authority—of the several medical and scientific theories she is engaging in her creative works. These include, first and foremost, turn-of-the-century sexology, as well as psychoanalysis, but also the humoral theory of melancholia. For example, the proliferation of metaphors for an excess of black bile in the Doctor's speech quoted above denaturalizes humoral medicine's diagnosis of melancholia: now that it must compete with rival terms, such as "falling arches" and "flying dandruff," it has lost its privilege of naming and interpreting the Doctor's malady. Science and medicine depend on clarity of expression and the *mot juste*—economical, precise language. The baroque proliferation of signifiers works to obscure rather than clarify meaning, thereby delegitimizing the privileged status of the scientific language it appropriates. This is particularly effective in Barnes's resignification of the sexological theory of homosexuality as the pathological inversion of sexual desire in both *Ladies Almanack* and *Nightwood*. That Barnes's indirect, ornate style goes against the grain of machine age modernism's "less is more" to embrace the neobaroque principle of "more is not less" can be traced back to her anarchic rebellion against functionalist, instrumentalized, and institutionalized language also celebrated by Sarduy.

Sarduy's thesis connecting baroque ornamentation to antirealism and anti-utilitarianism explains the negative motives behind Barnes's stylistic choices (in other words, what they shun). I want to close this section with an alternative account that explores potential positive reasons: what could impel Barnes's stylistic mix of extravagance and indirection? This key force, I suggest, is melancholia. *Nightwood*'s dynamic, restless discourse, which proliferates indefinitely the process of naming things, is predicated on lack and loss.[56] In an essay on William Faulkner that identifies this Southern U.S. writer as yet another Anglo-American modernist whose work belongs in the ambit of the neobaroque, Mexican novelist Carlos Fuentes affirms: "The Baroque, language of abundance, is also the language of insufficiency. Only those who possess nothing can include everything. The *horror vacui* of the Baroque is not gratuitous—it is because the vacuum exists that nothing is certain. The verbal abundance of . . . Faulkner's *Absalom, Absalom!* represents a desperate invocation of language to fill the absences left by the banishment of reason and faith."[57] Fuentes's claim is paradoxical: verbal abundance is causally linked to epistemological uncertainty. His reference to the baroque topos, *horror vacui,* which describes the baroque habit of leaving no empty spaces, is important. It summons the vivid image of the thickly decorated walls of Catholic Reformation churches, contrasted to their diametrical opposite, the whitewashed walls of Protestant Reform churches.[58] But Fuentes points to a dimension of the baroque that seems belied by its extravagant surface—fear, even *horror.* This fearful dimension evokes the troubled political and cultural background from which the baroque emerged: the religious schisms and the cosmological, scientific, and epistemological revolutions of the sixteenth century. The baroque, Christopher Braider notes, "is in the main the inheritor of these things." It "marks the moment when Europeans begin to digest the far-reaching implications of the accumulated social, intellectual, religious and geographic upheavals of the preceding age." Thus, the opulence of Catholic baroque art conceals the fact that "faith itself . . . [has become] a field of corrosively sectarian perspectives and interests."[59]

Taking up an unnamed American critic's dismissal of Faulkner's language as "Dixie Gongorism," Fuentes's essay investigates the relation between the historical trauma of the U.S. South depicted in Faulkner and his obscure and extravagant language (543). According to Fuentes, the tragic element in Faulkner arises from a traumatic past of racial slavery and civil war *that is not past,* and that continues to haunt the present. In this living, traumatic past characteristic of Faulkner's works Fuentes discovers parallels between the work of this North American Southerner and Latin American writers similarly suffering from the burden of a violent past that cannot, as in the optimistic North American myth, simply be forgotten and remade.[60] The baroque poetics of tragic defeat in Faulkner, Fuentes proposes, is "why we Latin Americans feel the work of Faulkner lies so close to us. In North American literature, . . . Faulkner stands apart from that closed world of optimism and success and offers us instead . . . the image of defeat, separation, doubt—the image of tragedy" (543). Fuentes's example, *Absalom, Absalom!* (1936), consists of the interminable, meandering narration of memories and speculations that rehearse the same few events (violent and long past), over and over again. My point is that its language, which Fuentes calls "a desperate invocation to fill the absences," is melancholic. As we have seen, Freud claims that melancholia behaves like an "open wound," monopolizing all psychic energies, so that absence comes to shape identity and expression. In Schiesari's apt summary of Freud, the melancholic ego "is dependent on loss as a means through which it can represent itself" (43). In short: it is by virtue of being a traumatized, wounded language that *Absalom, Absalom!*'s language of abundance ends up being the language of insufficiency.

This description of language in *Absalom, Absalom!* equally characterizes Barnes's late work, *Nightwood* and *The Antiphon.* There is the same non-efficient, wasteful and unbalanced relation between events (few and traumatic) and narration (superabundant). As in Faulkner's novel, narration in Barnes's melancholic late works circles the all-absorbing "open wound" of trauma and mobilizes an inordinate amount of verbal material trying to fill this void. Here we encounter the alternate rationale motivating Barnes's neobaroque circumlocution, which proceeds by way of the technique of "radial reading" described by Sarduy. In her essay on *Nightwood,* Smith usefully describes Barnes's lavish melancholic narration as "the style of lamentation," as "keen[ing] a loss" (195)—that is to say, as a way of using language closer to crying or weeping than speaking. Indeed, lapsing from speech into weeping is precisely what Barnes reportedly used to do during many evenings at Hayford Hall during the summers of 1932 and 1933, when she was reading to her friends Peggy Guggenheim, Emily Coleman, and John Holms from the first draft of *Nightwood* she was composing at the time (Herring 203–4). The difference is crucial: as Schiesari reminds us, wailing is an uncontrolled, noisy style of mourning particularly associated with women. Indeed, Schiesari shows how the Renaissance glorification of melancholia "as an elite male affliction" coincided historically with the "assault on mourning, and most particularly on mourning insofar as it took place as a collective women's ritual."[61]

One of the most significant insights of feminist scholarship on the genealogy of melancholia is this gendered contrast, as Jennifer Radden formulates, between "loquacious male melancholy and the mute suffering . . . of women" (34) or, following Schiesari, "(female) mourning and (male) melancholia" (12). In *Nightwood,* the Doctor, who—as critics since Eliot have noted—presides over the novel as the central authority of knowledge and who (for this and other reasons) is the embodiment of the loquacious Renaissance melancholic genius, falls silent at the end. At the end of the penultimate chapter named for this decisive incident, "Go Down, Matthew," the Doctor collapses (although the immediate cause is excessive alcohol consumption). Nevertheless, he breaks off his interminable monologues with the solemn exclamation, "Now . . . the end—mark my words—now *nothing, but wrath and weeping*" (166). This disintegration of the Doctor in the chapter before the novel's (in)famous catastrophic ending contains *Nightwood*'s central message about the relationship between language and loss. The Doctor ceases to speak and begins to weep like Nora, the woman abjectly mourning her lost love. As his language too yields to helpless and inarticulate grief, he comes to occupy Nora's position of "keening" loss (as Smith has it), thereby losing his privileged masculine voice of intellectual mastery. As in Fuentes's description of *Absalom, Absalom!,* the baroque language of abundance in *Nightwood* is unmasked as the language of insufficiency. As speech finally disintegrates into weeping after the failure of words, it becomes clear that language is impotent before reality, and the reality of loss. Language cannot cure loss (the ambition of Freud's talking cure, which is lampooned in the conversations between Nora and the Doctor). Language cannot diagnose, control, or compensate for loss. Eliot (without whose ambivalent support *Nightwood* would most likely never have been published) viewed *Nightwood*'s "great achievement of a style" as an antidote and compensation for its "psychopathic" content, about which he expressed his discomfort (introduction xv, xvi). I would argue that

Eliot was mistaken: not just *Nightwood*'s content but also its form is melancholic. *Nightwood*'s language and form are melancholia's abject symptom, not medicine's master signifier.

Ladies Almanack: Parodic Queer Hagiography

Barnes criticism has firmly situated *Ladies Almanack* (1928) in the lesbian expatriate counterculture of Left Bank Paris: the little calendar book, with text and drawings by Barnes, is a biographical roman-à-clef. It portrays the members of Barnes's lesbian circle, of which her best friend, Mina Loy ("Patience Scalpel"), was the token heterosexual member.[62] Apparently beloved by the women it features (such as Natalie Barney, Uma Troubridge, and Janet Flanner) (Lanser 167), but only reluctantly acknowledged by Barnes herself (who published the treatise anonymously, attributing authorship to the pseudonym "Lady of Fashion," and who also does not appear in it as a character), this short text poses severe stylistic obstacles to the reader that are only partially explained by the in-group character of the biographical allegory. Even after the identities of the historical personages are revealed (Dame Musset is Natalie Barney; Lady Buck-and-Balk and Tilly-Tweed-In-Blood are Uma Troubridge and Radclyffe Hall, respectively; Nip and Tuck are Janet Flanner and Solita Solano, to mention only a few of its more than a dozen characters), the meaning of the text remains relatively inaccessible. This inaccessibility is the effect of Barnes's signature neobaroque style, hyperbolically ornate and indirect. One obvious and often advanced reason for its use is censorship: Barnes's subject matter, lesbian identity, sexuality, and culture, remained under threat of publishing bans throughout the 1920s.[63] While self-censorship may explain pseudonymous publication, the virtual absence of the term "lesbian" (only used once, in the phrase "Lesbian Eye" [*Ladies Almanack* 35]) and a good deal of circumlocution around the details of lesbian sexuality, it does not explain the persistent stylistic exaggeration, the use of outlandish conceits, of archaisms, of capitalization, of narrative chapter titles.[64] Susan Lanser vividly describes the book's bawdy illustrations as "baroque cherubs, medieval grotesques, parodic iconography, feminized zodiacs, sexual caricature, and other emblems archaic and arcane" (157).

I contend that *Ladies Almanack* employs Sarduy's neobaroque strategies of "artificialization" to escape the realist truth claims of turn-of-the-century sexological discourse and challenge the scientific authority of its delineation of homosexual identities as pathological and degenerative. Foucault describes the emergence of the Western *sciencia sexualis,* the multiple modern sciences of sex whose "will to know" newly defined human identity as sexualized identity. Of the modern discourse of sexuality's four figures enumerated by Foucault ("the hysterical woman, the masturbating child, the

Malthusian couple, and the perverse adult"), the fourth element, the "psychiatrization of perverse pleasure" is Barnes's target (Foucault, *History of Sexuality* 105). It is these discourses of scientific inquiry into "deviant" and "perverse" sexualities that *Ladies Almanack* targets—nineteenth-century sexology and psychiatry, as well as psychoanalysis, whose respective diagnostic profiles of homosexuals and women are cited by Barnes, but only to be stripped of their scientific authority. *Nightwood,* as Dana Seitler observes (and this is true for *Ladies Almanack* as well), "relies on, even as it perverts, medical and evolutionary tropes for sexual alterity informed by a conception of the mannish lesbian. . . . In fact, Barnes takes much pleasure in ironically redeploying early twentieth-century sexual politics, sometimes through a series of hilarious gender inversions" (544). Many characters, major and minor, in both of Barnes's queer texts (I use "queer" merely as a neutral and descriptive term for their setting in nonheterosexual subcultures) are parodic clones of the so-called "invert," the scientific figure of the "third sex," which, writes Esther Newton, became "an article of faith in Anglo-American culture."[65] Among them are Robin Vote, "the girl who resembles a boy" (*Nightwood* 136), the cross-dressing Doctor O'Connor, who cherishes "in [his] heart . . . the wish for children and knitting" (*Nightwood* 91), and the main protagonist of *Ladies Almanack,* Dame Evangeline Musset, whom the frontispiece describes as "carrying a pole and a muff" (ii). Canonized by sexologist Richard von Krafft-Ebing in 1886 and developed further by his British colleague Havelock Ellis after 1895, inversion was the dominant turn-of-the-century medical paradigm for homosexuality—a reversal of "normal" sexuality and gender identity that produces "mannish women" and "effeminate men."[66] As Foucault points out, the scientific "persecution of peripheral sexualities" posed a dystopian threat because of its thorough and minute regulation of the soul by way of an analysis of the body and its sexual acts: "The nineteenth-century homosexual became a personage, a past, a case history, and a childhood, in addition to being a type of life, a life form, and a morphology. . . . Nothing that went into his total composition was unaffected by his sexuality. It was everywhere present in him: . . . written immodestly on his face and body because it was a secret that always gave itself away" (*History of Sexuality* 43). On the other hand, sexology also offered a novelty with some potential—a fully developed delineation of a homosexual subject position, which some lesbian and gay writers appropriated to various degrees, most famously Radclyffe Hall in *The Well of Loneliness* (1928).[67] This positive resonance was mainly due to Ellis's revisionary account of inversion as congenital but not pathological or degenerative.

Ladies Almanack, however, distances itself from *The Well of Loneliness* and its tragic figure of the invert. Recounting the birth and childhood of

Dame Evangeline Musset, the preface to *Ladies Almanack* is a point-by-point parody of that of Hall's aristocratic lesbian heroine, Stephen Gordon.[68] Of "lofty Lineage," Evangeline Musset "had been developed in the Womb of her most gentle Mother to be a Boy, when therefore, she came forth an Inch or so less than this, she paid no Heed to the Error, but donned a Vest of a superb Blister and Tooling, a Belcher for tippet and a pair of hip-boots with a scarlet channel (for it was a most wet wading) she took her Whip in hand, calling her Pups about her, and so set out upon the Road of Destiny" (*Ladies Almanack* 7). Rejecting women's clothing and marriage, Evangeline leaves her biological family to found an alternative family, a community of what Barnes evasively calls "ladies," "women," "modern girls" or "girl's girls" (22 and passim). When her father recognizes her inversion, Evangeline is neither ashamed nor unhappy, telling him that rather than "be so mortal wounded," he should be happy to see that his daughter is fulfilling his desire for a son "without the Tools for the Trade, and yet nothing complain" (8).

Gifted with sexual prowess and expert in the arts of seduction, Dame Evangeline is an ironic female counterpart to Wendell Ryder, advocating free—if nonprocreative—love, which offers women the pleasures of sex while liberating them from the drudgery of marriage and childbirth—a real sexual revolution.[69] While there is some ambivalence about Evangeline's promiscuity (in the "March" chapter she leaves one lover in the midst of lovemaking to pursue another woman), the dominant tone is that of celebration: unlike Ryder, Dame Evangeline Musset is a female saint who is sanctified for dedicating her life to her adoptive (if secular) cause—the missionary dissemination of lesbian sexuality and culture. Indeed, *Ladies Almanack* is best described as a queer parodic hagiography. In different ways, it recuperates the medieval and Counter-Reformation genre of hagiography and its religious iconography to combat the stigmatization of "perverse" sexualities in modern scientific discourse. As always, Barnes's signature archaisms are profoundly political: religion is played off against secular science to create an insurgent and secular mythology celebrating the lesbian urban counterculture of the 1920s.[70] In contrast to *Nightwood,* however, *Ladies Almanack* is about sanctified *pleasure,* not pain: it carefully avoids one key feature of hagiography Barnes would later explore in *Nightwood,* the representation of martyrdom and its agonies.

Here, I think, lies one major explanation for Barnes's neobaroque circumlocutions with regard to the subject of lesbianism. The Sarduyan substitution of terms such as "Ladies," "modern Girl" (*Ladies Almanack* 22) or "first Woman born with a Difference" (26) for "female homosexual" fashions an artificialization that distances the fictional world of *Ladies Almanack* from referential realism. The proliferation of metaphors for lesbian sexuality and the lesbian body ("nook, path, keyhole, whorl, crevice, conch shell") describes a Sarduyan "radial reading" around the absent signified (lesbianism), which enables the text to elude reduction to denotative communication.[71] The baroquely spiraling language of *Ladies Almanack* takes pleasure in its prodigality and transgression of medical realism. In this way, Barnes appropriates sexology's authoritative diagnosis—"Evangeline is a mannish lesbian" and an "invert"—only to strip it of its official authorizing context and hence all its social power. The wasteful superabundance of synonyms into which sexology's medical jargon has been inserted disarms it. As Sarduy contends, the neobaroque is "language that because of its excessive abundance no longer designates things but only other designators of things" ("Baroque and Neobaroque" 281). Or, to use Roman Jakobson's schema, the baroque and neobaroque language of redundancy dismantles the communicative function of language and instead emphasizes other dimensions of language, especially what Jakobson refers to as its poetic function.[72] Uprooted from its proper institutional context in which a speaker, authorized by a medical degree, lectures in clear and precise language, and inserted into Barnes's parodic literary text, the notion of sexual and gender inversion loses its referential function of signifying abnormality. Instead, the image underlying the sexological term's original coinage—the extravagant "spatial metaphors of 'backwards-to-forwards,' . . . 'upside down,'" as well as "against the grain"[73]—gain new life. As we shall see, this becomes even more pronounced in *Nightwood.*

Some critics have claimed that Barnes's indiscriminate use of gender referents conflates female homosexuality and heterosexuality along the lines of what Adrienne Rich would later call the lesbian continuum (Lanser 163). I would argue that Barnes appropriates the female universal ("woman," "ladies") to make the point that lesbian women are no less feminine—a strategy that would complement her dismantling of inversion's referential function to pathologize anomalous desires. The "April" chapter of *Ladies Almanack* presents the following parody of the medical classification of the symptoms of the unnamed "distemper":

> Acute Melancholy is noticeable in those who have gone a long Way into this Matter, whereas a light giggling, dancing Fancy seems to support those in the very first Stages; brief of Thought; cut of Concentration; a Tendency to hop, skip, and jump, and to misplace the Eye at every single or several Manifestation of Girl in like Distemper. Chill succeeds, and Restlessness at Night, or unaccountable Tabulation of unimportant Objects, such as Flagstones (Busbys an [*sic*] she be in London!) Steeples, Mulberries in Baskets, Tabs to Dresses, Hooves to Horses, and Stars in the Sky. This gives place, in from six to eight Weeks, to a Sobriety that includes thoughts of Transmigration, Levitation, Myopia and Blight. The

> Eye trickles, the Breath is short, the Spleen is distended, and the Epiglottis rises and falls like the continual swallowing of the Heart. Whereupon the Veins are seen to lift themselves, the Nerves twitch, the Palms become moist, the Feet lose their activity, the Bowels contract, and, as in the old Days when a Person in the last stages of Hydrophobia sometimes found small Whelps in the Urine, in the Waters of such is seen the fully Robed on-marching Figure of Venus no larger than a Caraway Seed, a Trident in one Hand and a Gos-Wasp on the Left Fist. (27–28)

Clues such as "melancholy" and "spleen" reveal the target of parodic resignification in this chapter as the humoral medical theory of melancholia presented in Burton's *Anatomy of Melancholy.* A comparison with Burton's text reveals the parallels. In the section "Symptoms, or Signs of Melancholy in the Body," Burton (quoting from the writings of Hippocrates, Galen, Avicenna, and other ancient and medieval authors) affirms that melancholics

> are "lean, withered, hollow-eyed, look old, wrinkled, harsh, much troubled with wind and a griping in their bellies, or belly-ache, belch often, dry bellies and hard, dejected looks, flaggy beards, singing of the ears, vertigo, light headed, little or no sleep, and that interrupt, terrible and fearful dreams." . . . Some add palpitation of the heart, cold sweat, as usual symptoms, and a leaping in many parts of the body, . . . a kind of itching, saith Laurentius, on the superficies of the skin, like a flea-biting sometimes. Montaltus, *cap. 21,* puts fixed eyes and much twinkling of their eyes for a sign . . . . To some too, if they are far gone, mimical gestures are too familiar, laughing, grinning, fleering, murmuring, talking to themselves, with strange mouths and faces, inarticulate voices, exclamations, etc. . . . Their urine is most part pale, and low coloured . . . . If the heart, brain, liver, spleen, be misaffected, as usually they are, many inconveniences proceed from them, many diseases accompany, as incubus, apoplexy, epilepsy, vertigo, those frequent wakings and terrible dreams, intempestive laughing, weeping, sighing, sobbing, bashfulness, blushing, trembling, sweating, swooning, etc. (Part I, 383–84)

As is clear, Barnes matches Burton's hyperbolic catalog of symptoms with her own, noting similar signs from heart murmurs to discolored urine. Barnes's invocation of the baroque science of Burton's time, which mixes the modern empirical and experimental method with the citation of speculative medical theories such as humoral medicine, also serves to undercut the scientific authority of modern sexology and psychoanalysis. Along these lines of mixing science and speculation, one striking feature of the passage from *Ladies Almanack* just quoted is the juxtaposition of two distinct logics, the supernatural and the natural, the marvelous and ordinary reality. The melancholic "Lady" who has reached an advanced level of lesbian practice experiences "thoughts of Transmigration" and "Levitation." And her urine contains small objects that turn out to be miniature lesbians: "the fully Robed on-marching Figure of Venus no larger than a Caraway Seed, a Trident in one Hand and a Gos-Wasp on the Left Fist."[74]

The incorporation of the marvelous in ordinary reality is a defining feature of hagiography, which offers a personal portrait of the saint and narrates the legendary miracles that he or she performed on behalf of living Christians during life and after death, such as healings and clairvoyance, including levitating.[75] The marvelous in *Ladies Almanack*—along with the genre from which it arises, hagiography—has not been given its due in existing critical analyses.[76] This also applies to a recent article by Daniela Caselli, which takes its title from Barnes's foreword to the 1972 reprint of *Ladies Almanack*. "Neap-tide to the Proustian chronicle, gleanings from the shores of Mytilene [city on Lesbos]," Barnes writes, there are "glimpses of its novitiates, its rising 'saints' and 'priestesses.'"[77] As Barnes's wording suggests, *Ladies Almanack* queers hagiography; or, otherwise put, it celebrates lesbian sexuality and culture by playfully sanctifying it. Saints' days and festivals link the cult of saints to the ritual calendar of church liturgy; indeed, one of the criteria of a notable cult is the saint's presence in an important calendar, such as the Roman calendar and the calendar of the Book of Common Prayer.[78] Hence the almanac structure of Barnes's book, which follows the months of one year, marking seasonal festivals. A second temporality—not cyclical but historical time—traces a linear narrative from Dame Musset's birth (told in a preface before the annual cycle begins) to her death at the age of ninety-nine years in the month of December.

Originating in late antiquity, the cult of saints comprises distinct groups: after the martyrs of the early Christian Church who gave their lives in the battle against heathen religions, new saints that have emerged since the Middle Ages have tended to be founders, reformers, or simply members of religious orders (nuns and monks such as Hildegard of Bingen, St. Francis of Assisi, St. Teresa of Avila, and St. Ignatius of Loyola), who typically died a natural death. This later concept of sainthood, which reflects the "channelling of sanctity into specialized ecclesiastical institutions" (Wilson 5), underlies Barnes's figure of Saint Evangeline, who single-handedly founds a new if secular "order" of women devotees who similarly live together in self-imposed quasi-seclusion, forming a private countersociety apart from the general public. And here we discover another source of the much-discussed cliquish nature of *Ladies Almanack*—also exemplified by its private printing, hand distribution, and coded address of a self-selected audience of the already converted. Barnes ingeniously associates the elitism of Natalie Barney's Left Bank salon with the religious countersocieties of the past. In "March," the location of Evangeline's lesbian community is referred to as "the Temple of the Good Dame Musset" (18–19), evoking the local shrines that habitually spring up with saints' cults in the village or rural location (desert, mountain) where they lived and died. Like a Catholic saint, Dame Evangeline—a pun on "evangelist" (Benstock 250)—Musset works miracles as a missionary, but she is a saint with a difference, a queer saint.

The reasons for Barnes's recourse to Catholic (rather than Protestant) iconography are fairly obvious. To begin with, Protestant iconoclasm and rejection of the cult of saints and of the Virgin Mary as intermediaries between God and living Christians erased all feminine figures from Christian religion. Although saints are predominantly male (historian Stephen Wilson reports that the proportion of women among the Roman Catholic canon of saints "never rose above 20 per cent until [the twentieth] century," a significant imbalance since "women seem always to have participated fully in saints' cults"), saints seem largely to escape the normative binary gender system (37). Once canonized, female saints command as much reverence and power as male saints (the Virgin Mary being most powerful of all). Since saints are commonly known for their cures and their miraculous intercession on behalf of humans (thus, fulfilling stereotypically "feminine" caretaking functions), gender characteristics do not affect the election of female as opposed to male saints—in one sense, all saints are feminine. Being highly "specialized," furthermore, saints give protection and patronage to various groups and issues, such as toothache, specific countries and towns, firefighters, lost and stolen objects, and pregnant women. Dictionaries of saints offer long lists of the principal patronages of saints and their iconographical emblems, which reveal an astonishingly exotic taxonomy that seems to be principally infinite and nonexclusionary.[79] Each and every place, group, or person on earth can potentially have their patron saint; what can prevent Left Bank expatriate women writers from having theirs? In short, here we discover one major reason why Barnes chose the genre of hagiography and the saint as a parodic model of modern lesbian identity: it is a way of escaping the all-encompassing dichotomies of gender and sex that enforce constructions of lesbian sexuality and identity as abnormal.

There is an anarchic element in saints' cults: they spring up locally, as part of popular religion; the organized Church and the clergy, on the other hand, can only partially control this spontaneous process through canonization procedures. There is a transgressive excess in the cult of saints that seems to escape the panoptic power of the Foucauldian disciplinary confessional: believers in need may go on a pilgrimage instead of seeing a priest, thereby escaping ecclesiastic power. In fact, saints' cults have long served as vehicles of political opposition within the Church.[80] "As saints are persons possessed of a charisma that is potentially dangerous and anarchic," Wilson explains, "so pilgrimage cuts across geographical and social boundaries, takes people out of their established places, mixes social strata and the sexes, allows individuals to wander like vagabonds. . . . The pilgrimage route . . . became a regular vehicle for cultural exchange" (14). The apocryphal legend of Dame Evangeline Musset, narrated anonymously by "a Lady of Fashion," simulates the popular creation of a heroine outside official institutions and history. In *Nightwood,* Doctor O'Connor explains the difference between history and legend, the history of the dispossessed: "think of the stories that do not amount to much! That is, that are forgotten in spite of all man remembers . . . merely because they befell him without distinction of office or title—that's what we call legend and it's the best a poor man may do with his fate; the other . . . we call history, the best the high and mighty can do with theirs" (15). The Doctor's insurgent genre of legend, resignified by Barnes in *Ladies Almanack,* offers a fresh explanation for the book's pseudonymous publication and Barnes's self-erasure from her fictional representation of the Barney circle. This perspective takes some pressure off "all the questions" that Karla Jay urges us to "ask about Barnes' absence" as a fictional character from the artificial world of Dame Musset (Jay 193). Less than an "author" or a "known contemporary," Barnes merely assumes the anonymous persona of a popular follower of her heroine who records rather than invents a collective oral legend.

Patron saints are venerated by their devotees; by analogy, Dame Musset's queer sainthood implies the existence of a community, a lesbian community. The preface addresses this community, introducing *Ladies Almanack* as the book "which all Ladies should carry about with them, as the Priest his Breviary, as the Cook his Recipes, as the Doctor his Physic, as the Bride her Fears, and as the Lion his Roar!" (9). The cult of saints thus constructs a collective, public subjectivity defined independently of the Freudian family and its known polymorphous perversions. The recourse to hagiography allows Barnes to draft a narrative of physical and spiritual love that steers clear of the script of modern scientific psychoanalytic and sexological discourse. In other words, premodern and early modern narrative is resuscitated to deflect the panoptic gaze of modern science. *Ladies Almanack* thus mixes premodern and scientific knowledge, juxtaposing the veneration of saints to sexology's stigmatized invert. In this respect, it resembles the works of some seventeenth-century scholars, such as Burton, or the Mexican savant Carlos de Sigüenza y Góngora, or the German philosopher Gottfried Leibniz, who, as discussed in chapter 1, sought to reconcile scholasticism (the doctrine of revealed authority) and modern science, or faith and reason.[81] Similarly, Dame Evangeline's devotees worship their "wonder worker" saint (depicted in the frontispiece) in a way that modern science would condemn as superstition. On the death of Dame Musset, Barnes's narrator reports, "First forty Women shaved their Heads (all but Señorita Fly-About who for no Woman, quick or dead, would alter her Charm) and carried her through the City on a monstrous Catafalque, and then in forty different Heights these Women went down upon their knees in the darkness of the Catholic Church, and then she was sealed in a Tomb for many days, and the Women twittered about the Tomb like Birds about the Border of a Storm" (*Ladies Almanack* 82–83). The funeral cortege, on its way to Evangeline's final resting place, is greeted by wild animals, which join the human chorus of mourning, testifying to the cosmic repercussions of the saint's death: "a Bird came, and in passing, crowed lamentably," followed by a "Mountain Goat," which also "lamented bitterly," which in turn is followed by a "Night-owl," which said, "Oh! God!" (83). The list goes on, drifting once again into the hyperbolic. To be sure, the naive faiths of popular Catholicism and animism Barnes incorporates here are slanted parodically, but this is not the same as invalidating the Evangeline legend as "irrational."

As in medieval and early modern hagiographies and in twentieth-century magic realist fiction in part inspired by them, in the fictional world of *Ladies Almanack,* the marvelous is as natural and real as everyday reality. Barnes's narrative incorporates the fantastic and the miraculous to critique the reductive materialism of modern science. In *Ladies Almanack,* the miraculous aspects of Dame Evangeline's life are treated as seriously, or as nonseriously, as the myths of modern sexology—both are subjected to neobaroque procedures of artificialization and exposed as fictions, or constructions. Christopher Warnes distinguishes between two trends in magic realism, a faith-based fiction that affirms the authority of popular and non-Western outlooks, in which things of the visible and the invisible worlds share the same ontological plane (Carpentier and García Márquez), and an irreverent, skeptical fiction, closer to the postmodern, that employs the fantastic mainly to undermine the legitimacy of modern scientific rationalism (Borges).[82] The first type seeks to reenchant twentieth-century literature by naturalizing the supernatural, while the second type utilizes the supernatural strategically to denaturalize the rationalist realism of modern science. We may add *Ladies Almanack* to the latter: like Borges's, Barnes's attitude is epistemological skepticism. She proposes to ridicule the homophobic and misogynist myths of modern science.

In fact, *Ladies Almanack* offers two "creation myths" of lesbianism, one scientific, the other fantastic. As we have seen, the first presents Evangeline Musset as the congenital invert of turn-of-the-century sexology, the paradigm Newton calls "the mythic mannish lesbian." Evangeline accepts this innate condition but rejects the stigma attached to it by leaving mainstream society, and her biological family from which it originates, to found this alternative community of women like herself whose history and customs the *Almanack* narrates and to whom it is dedicated. The second origin myth, narrated in "March," tells of the miraculous birth of the first lesbian from an egg hatched, in less than nine months, by a gathering of angels: "This is the part about Heaven that has never been told. After the Fall of Satan (and as he fell, Lucifer uttered a loud Cry, heard from one End of Forever-and-no-end to the other), all the Angels, Aries, Taurus, Gemini, Cancer, Leo, Virgo, Libra, Scorpio, Sagittarius, Capricornus, Aquarius, Pisces, all, all gathered together, so close that they were not recognizable, one from the other. And not nine Months later, there was heard under the Dome of Heaven a great Crowing, and from the Midst, an Egg, as incredible as a thing forgotten, fell to Earth, and striking, split and hatched, and from out of it stepped one saying, 'Pardon me, I must be going!' And this was the first Woman born with a Difference" (25–26). This "angelic parthenogenesis" (Lanser 163) appropriates biblical narrative to invent a countermyth to sexology's social Darwinist account of degenerate sexuality: God created man, woman, *and* women "with a difference." The first creation story negates the second as much as the second invalidates the first: both stories are exposed as fictions, or myths.[83] *Ladies Almanack*'s opulent fabulations critique the reductive and mechanistic rationality of modern science, echoing Deleuze's description of the baroque thought of Leibniz. Such apocryphal tales multiply rather than reduce principles of understanding, highlighting the creative principle underpinning philosophy and science.

Like all saints, Saint Evangeline is a legendary heroine. Endowed with exceptional powers, she dedicates her life to a higher cause. The story of her life is the story of her conversion, by seduction, of new members to her secular movement. The "February" chapter lists Evangeline's "saints days" (14), one for each month, detailing the miraculous works for which she was canonized during her life : "When well thirty," we learn, "she, like all Men before her, made a Harlot a good Woman, by making her Mistress" (15–17). (This particular "miracle cure" can be traced to a definite episode in the life of the young Natalie Barney, who had indeed seduced a "known courtesan"—but only by expert readers who are familiar with the biographies of the historical figures portrayed, many of whom were unable to identify themselves.[84]) Borrowing from the baroque iconography of saints, the chapter is illustrated with a full-sized portrait of Musset as Saint Evangeline, crowned and cloaked, standing on a pillow and holding a rose in one hand and a heart in the other (fig. 4). Her head is surrounded by a halo and an outer ring of winged cherubs; devotees kneel at her feet. In the visual code of Catholic holy images that developed over two millennia of artistic representation, saints are recognized by their "attributes"—emblematic objects such as clothing, animals, or objects or physical postures and gestures that refer to key episodes in the saint's personal life. For example, St. Teresa is always represented in the cloak of the Carmelites (the order to which she

Fig. 4. Djuna Barnes, Evangeline Musset as Saint Evangeline. (Reproduced by permission of the Dalkey Archive Press)

belonged) (see fig. 3). Her other attributes are the arrow pointing at her heart and the clouds bearing her aloft, visible signs of the saint's ecstatic union with God.[85] Similarly, we are meant to recognize Saint Evangeline's cloak as the "habit" of her modern, queer "order." The heart and the rose are her "attributes," referring to her missionary service on behalf of earthly same-sex love.

Along the same lines, the frontispiece bears the following inscription: "Now as a wonder worker, Dame Musset was perhaps at her very best when, carrying a pole and muff, and sporting an endearing tippet, she stepped out upon that exceedingly thin ice to which it has pleased God, more and more, to call frail woman, there so conducting herself that none were put to the chagrin of sinking for the third time." We should see Dame Musset's pole and muff within the premodern and early modern hagiographic convention of constructing subjectivity, as well as within the psychoanalytic tradition.

In this light, the charged pole is not just what it seems to be for the post-Freudian reader, a phallic substitute; it is also, and simply, Musset's attribute, just as Mary Magdalen's attributes are discarded pearls (a reference to her former life of luxury). The post-Freudian sign is psychological and interiorized, whereas saint's attributes refer to external acts—in Musset's case, they allude to her miraculous conversions. In one sense, then, Barnes is reversing the shift of focus made by the new modern sciences of sexuality—in Foucault's famous observation—from perverse acts (such as sodomy) to perverse identities (the invert) (Foucault 43). Oscillating between all these various meanings, the pole's ambiguous status is another instance of the Sarduyan procedure of artificialization, as well as Deleuze's process of the multiplication of principles: one signifier has been superimposed on another, introducing a gap between sign and meaning whose effect is the dismantling of the referential function of language.

As Barnes avoids the paradigm of holy martyrdom to eschew the tragic script of lesbian identity, she adapts instead the persona of legendary founders of religious communities as well as the narrative of conversion, the story of sinner become saint. Here, her hagiographic sources run into a curious inconsistency: Evangeline herself was never converted but was born into the condition (twice, as we recall, in one natural and one supernatural birth). Most of her followers, on the other hand, are the products of Evangeline's conversion-seduction. Consequently, *Ladies Almanack* suggests that homosexuality is neither exclusively innate nor a choice, but can be either.

Ladies Almanack, then, subverts modern scientific discourses of phallic insufficiency and abnormal sexualities by parodically recuperating religious iconography. The book ends with another of Barnes's hilariously bawdy episodes, in which Dame Musset's famed "tongue," with which she has converted and seduced women during life, becomes her relic after her death. As Dame Musset is cremated for burial in the "December" chapter, her tongue does not burn, but "flamed, and would not suffer Ash, and it played about" (84), giving pleasure after her death. Here, Barnes heretically appropriates the Pentecostal imagery of holy tongues given to the apostles to inspire their work of conversion. Similarly, Musset's tongue comes on the mourners at her funeral who honor her life and work. Typically, the cult of saints is a cult of the dead; saints' cults are oriented around their tombs and relics. Their healing power is posthumous, and saints' cults contain a great deal of necrophilia (Wilson 9–10). In part, Barnes has resignified the conventions of popular Catholicism by shifting the accent from death to life, and canonized her fictional saint during her lifetime. On the other hand, Dame Musset's bodily remains yield a relic, one that, like so many saints' bones, is coveted by devotees. The final illustration in the book is a drawing of Evangeline's tomb, the shrine at which her devotees continue to worship.

Nightwood: Melancholia and the Inversion of Modern Scientific and Aesthetic Myths of Language and Knowledge as Instruments of Domination

Like *Ladies Almanack, Nightwood* is set in a world on the margins of official society: its protagonists, including its minor characters, are social outsiders—homosexuals, Jews, artists, and circus people. As if to emphasize the non-normative character of its social world, almost all of the episodes are set at night or in dark interiors. However, what Barnes's friend John Holms dubbed *Nightwood*'s "anatomy of the nightworld" (Herring 204) reaches beyond its confines: more ambitious than *Ladies Almanack, Nightwood* aims to deconstruct the social and discursive authority that, in the metaphoric language of the novel's symbol patterns, divides "night" from "day"—or rationality, consciousness, domesticity, order, and bourgeois normalcy from its Others: madness, desire, grief, dreams, perversity. In *Nightwood,* Barnes denaturalizes and dismantles the disciplinary authorities of language and society. My claim is that hyperbolic neobaroque signification, or the procedure Sarduy calls artificialization, accomplishes this decomposition.

In pursuing this aim, Barnes also joins Eliot in attacking the principle of dissociationism connected to the rise of modern rationalism and science. To be sure, Barnes's opposition to the "dissociation of sensibility" is more socially radical than Eliot's, coming as it does from a lesbian (or bisexual) writer attempting to articulate transgender identities against their pathologization by modern psychiatry, sexology, and psychoanalysis. But across the chasm of their divergent lifestyles and social locations, Barnes and Eliot share a modernist neobaroque poetics, one they leverage against the prevailing, reductive scientific outlook. Both writers revolt against the crisp language of the machine age, the language of functionalism and efficiency and its confident posture of mastery and control in the representation of reality. To uncover a neobaroque poetics common to their works is to offer confirmation that Eliot and Barnes were fundamental allies both intellectually and artistically. Despite the lingering conflicts that feminist criticism has foregrounded in the unequal relationship between the bohemian woman writer and her male editor, who by the time of *Nightwood*'s publication had become a figurehead of the modernist literary establishment, Barnes's and Eliot's long-term friendship was based on sound judgment on both sides, even if differences (especially during the torturous editing of *The Antiphon* between 1955 and 1958) would obscure these deeper agreements.

Recent research has vindicated Eliot of charges of pressuring Barnes into excessive editorial purging of *Nightwood;* as it turns out, most major cuts and revisions were made by Barnes herself, in collaboration with her friend

Emily Holmes Coleman, before Eliot ever saw the manuscript.[86] Earlier formalist criticism had established parallels between Eliot and Barnes by assimilating *Nightwood* to a pseudo-Eliotic aesthetics of impersonal, abstract design and by pointing out rough analogies between *Nightwood* and *The Waste Land* as modernist masterpieces arising from a cesarean birth performed by another famous poet-as-midwife, who administered the radical textual surgery needed for perfection. Subsequent feminist analyses challenged these parallels by highlighting autobiographical elements and gender and sexual subversion in Barnes's work. Such parallels now resurface in light of our present concerns, which foreground the self-consciously antiquarian neobaroque in both Eliot and Barnes. As discussed in the previous chapter, Eliot's allegorical method in *The Waste Land* derives from a melancholic contemplation of an outside world that is meaningless, sterile, and ravaged by destruction. As Maud Ellman observes, *The Waste Land* "is one of the most abject texts in English literature."[87] Like Barnes, Eliot listened to the baroque muse of melancholia: *The Waste Land* borrows a line from the poem "El Desdichado" ("The Disinherited") by Gérard de Nerval, to whom Kristeva dedicates a chapter in her study of melancholia, *Black Sun;* the poem is also the source of the phrase "black sun of melancholia" appearing in Kristeva's title.[88]

As most of *Nightwood*'s commentators have noted, the novel offers only a minimal plot and sketchy character development: set in the United States and in the European capitals of Paris, Berlin, and Vienna during the 1920s, *Nightwood*'s spare plot is propelled forward by Robin Vote's promiscuity, centering on her tormented relationships with her lovers. The Jewish convert to Catholicism and false baron Felix Volkbein meets the unlicensed gynecologist and scholar Doctor O'Connor, who introduces him to Robin Vote, a young American. They marry and have a child, but Robin soon abandons Felix and goes to America, where she meets the artist Nora Flood. Nora and Robin settle in Paris, but Robin soon takes to wandering again and meets Jenny Petherbridge, with whom she leaves for America. Nora, disconsolate, seeks out the Doctor in his quarters in Paris for advice and comfort. Before moving to Vienna with his mentally disabled son Guido, Felix does the same. Three of the final chapters are driven by the interminable talk of the Doctor, who, however, falls silent in the end before the magnitude of pain. In the last chapter, Robin, adrift once again, turns up in an abandoned chapel on Nora's property in the United States. In an enigmatic and disturbing scene the novel describes as "obscene and touching" (170), she falls to barking and running with Nora's dog. Here, the arc of collapse that the plot has been charting through its symbol pattern of "descent" and through the spiritual defeats of all the major characters culminates in Robin's regression to an animal state.

This scene of human becoming animal harks back to an earlier complementary scene of animal becoming human, Robin's "awakening" by the Doctor. *Nightwood* traces a circular trajectory for Robin that shows her to first appear, and then finally disappear, at the boundary of the primitive, the mythic, the archaic. Robin is said to be "outside the 'human type,'" a "wild thing caught in a woman's skin" (146). As Felix puts it, "The Baronin had an undefinable disorder, a sort of 'odour of memory,' like a person who has come from some place that we have forgotten and would give our life to recall" (118). Robin is a supernatural character even more marginal than the others because she is the embodiment of everything that is alien and deviant in the human social order: an emblem of the female Other in Western culture, Robin represents the empty center of *Nightwood*'s tragic narrative, the traumatic void that fuels its melancholic language. *Nightwood* mourns the loss of Robin as the love object that cannot be domesticated; at the same time, grief in *Nightwood* is larger than what could have been caused by Robin.[89] The nebulous nature of loss in *Nightwood* recalls melancholia's ancient definition as sadness without sufficient cause, as well as Freud's observation that the loss in melancholia has a narcissistic dimension and is "withdrawn from consciousness" ("Mourning" 245). As Nora tells the Doctor, "Have you ever loved someone and it became yourself?" (*Nightwood* 152). The biographical association of Robin-Thelma with Barnes's grandmother Zadel suggests that Robin's loss brought to the surface earlier childhood losses, reinjuring the wounded self that is Nora-Djuna. Whatever the case may be, investigating this issue exceeds the scope of this study, as the published version of *Nightwood* focuses its inordinate grief entirely on Robin.[90] Robin is both the paradigmatic object of the characters' desire and the focal object of the novel's neobaroque ornate, proliferating discourse. Robin possesses a primal vitality that makes her irresistible to humans, but driven by anarchic desires for nomadic wandering and promiscuous sexuality, she cannot be domesticated by her lovers. Neither does the Doctor's considerable erudition and volubility succeed in imposing discursive order on the chaos Robin leaves in her wake.

In part, Robin's status as the enigmatic object of representation is the result of a subtle management of narrative technique and devices of distancing and closeness. Barnes refuses to focalize the story through Robin's mind, although she grants an inside view of Felix, the Doctor, and especially Nora.[91] Robin does not speak more than a few phrases and expresses herself through silent gestures, as when, after giving birth to her son, she screams, "I didn't want him!" (49), or, on meeting Nora in the circus, she exclaims, "Let's get out of here!" and "I don't want to be here" (54–55). Spoken for by others and seen through the consciousness of others, Robin is never represented through psychological realism, one of the achievements of modernist experimentation. In general, *Nightwood*'s narration is unabashedly authorial, deviating from modernism's psychological dominant in its refusal to abandon omniscient narration to portray consciousness. Even free indirect speech, the nineteenth-century hybrid invention combining objective report with the subjective idiosyncrasies of character thought and phrasing, is difficult to find in *Nightwood,* not to mention actual modernist innovations such as interior monologue. Typically, Barnes's narrator describes her characters from the outside, speaking from a position aloof from the world of narrated fictional events and focalizing character thoughts, perceptions, memories (save Robin's, which are bracketed altogether) externally, from the viewpoint of an extra- and heterodiegetic narrator.[92] *Nightwood*'s distinctive lack of interiority is a baroque feature, as Octavio Paz explains in a discussion, quoted at length in the previous chapter, that contrasts Romantic subjectivism to the baroque "art of the metamorphosis of the object" (*Sor Juana* 54). *Nightwood*'s impersonality and its formal abstraction and difficulty (which its formalist critics responded to by subsuming it under concepts such as spatial form), like Eliot's, are neobaroque features.

When we first encounter Robin in the chapter named for her hybrid being, "La Somnambule," she is awakened from unconsciousness by the Doctor. In the passage describing her awakening, neobaroque discourse layers conceit over conceit without ever reaching a conclusion. The reader witnesses, as Paz phrases it, the metamorphosis of the object; Robin's subjectivity has "imploded" into her objecthood as the archetypal Other and object of desire and representation. The metonymic succession of signifiers referring to Robin in this episode ("born somnambule," "meet of child and desperado," "eland," "unicorn" [*Nightwood* 35, 37]) conducts the "radial reading" Sarduy describes: the dynamic movement of language circles the "absent signifier, tracing an orbit around it" (Sarduy, "Baroque and Neobaroque" 273). Such baroque proliferation of signifiers works to obscure meaning rather than clarify it, for, as Sarduy explains, the substitution of metaphors by other metaphors amplifies the distance between signifier and signified, thus highlighting the gap between them—"signifiers enveloping other signifiers in a mechanism of signification that ends up designating itself" (281). To link Robin, a young woman the Doctor treats as a patient, to such mythic creatures as "an eland coming down the aisle of trees" is to bury literal reference under thick layers of artifice.

Much of the effort of reading *Nightwood* is spent in the attempt to sort and order the multiplying descriptions of Robin's mysterious being. In one of her first appearances, Robin's sleeping figure is compared to "a painting by the *douanier* Rousseau," as she seems "to lie in a jungle trapped in a drawing room . . . thrown in among the carnivorous flowers as their ration" (35). Robin's first meeting with Nora (who later remarks that "Robin is incest too; that is one of her powers" [156]) at a circus performance again associates her with the primitive: a "powerful lioness came to the turn of the bars, exactly opposite the girl [Robin], she turned her furious great head with its yellow eyes afire and went down, her paws thrust through the bars and, as she regarded the girl, . . . her eyes flowed in tears that never reached the surface" (54). The caged lioness weeps tears of pity for Robin, recognizing a bond stemming from their common imprisonment. Robin's supposed primitive nature, the essence of her desirability and "damnation," generates a chain of signifiers that links Robin to ever more surreal instances of primitivism and perversity. The final stage of what Dana Seitler calls *Nightwood*'s "degeneration narrative" is the infamous episode of becoming-animal in the last chapter, "The Possessed." Robin is making her terminal escape from her captivity in civilization, domesticity, and human ties of love: wandering the countryside, she speaks "in a low voice to the animals. Those that came near, she grasped, straining their fur back until their eyes were narrowed and their teeth bare, her own teeth showing as if her hand were upon her own neck" (168). Abandoning her new lover Jenny like a domestic animal gone wild, she "circle[s] closer and closer" (168) toward Nora's property in New York State. It appears that Robin is finding the "scent of home" (56) she had lost earlier despite Nora's best efforts, and thus returning to Nora. As it turns out, the scent she has recognized isn't that of Nora's home, but of Nora's dog. It is with Nora's dog that Robin reunites in Nora's chapel, "going down" (169) on all fours. Romping with the dog, Robin abandons human speech for an abject duet with the dog of barking and howling, laughing and crying.

Robin's primitive nature links her to a favorite theme in Barnes, mixtures and metamorphoses of beasts and human. Robin's sensuality and promiscuity also connect her to a genealogy of Barnes characters associated with the acting out of their animal natures, such as Wendell Ryder.[93] The crucial difference is that, unlike Wendell, the free-roaming "stud" mating with fertile females in the neighborhood (Parsons), Robin is a caged animal—a lioness behind bars, but also a vampire ("eaten death returning" [37]). Her "desperate anonymity" (169), her passivity and lack of "volition" (43, 76), her inarticulate estrangement from language all associate her with the position of the abject woman as archetypal victim. And whereas Saint Evangeline is the phallic mother (as it were) of her alternative community of lesbians, founder of a nonheterosexual sociosymbolic order, Robin barely speaks and appears to forget her proper name. Robin's abjection is a symptom of the darkening of the theme of human-beast hybridism in Barnes's major works published after 1928.

What is the source of this darkening? One reason can be found in *Nightwood*'s fuller engagement with sexological and eugenicist discourses of perversity and degeneration, which has been investigated in recent new historicist readings by Seitler, Dianne Chisholm, Andrea Harris, and Leigh Gilmour. Whereas *Ladies Almanack* grafts inversion onto its comic-heroic plot of queer hagiography, *Nightwood* also explores the stigmatization of the perverse and obscene in human sexualities by fin-de-siècle science. Indeed, Robin's animal nature and the recuperation of *Nightwood*'s sexual and social transgression had also been the focus of early feminist readings of Barnes. These probed *Nightwood*'s formalist facade, praised by T. S. Eliot for its "great achievement of a style," even as he cautioned that to "regard this group of people as a horrid sideshow of freaks is . . . to miss the point" (introduction xvi). Reacting against the earlier formalist emphasis on style, feminist critics saw *Nightwood* as a novel that, although in an indirect way mediated by modernist design, brought to visibility various countercultures, not just the lesbian. They celebrated *Nightwood*'s carnivalesque articulation of the deviant desires of, in Jane Marcus's words, "the body of the Other—the black, lesbian, transvestite, or Jew."[94] In contrast, recent assessments are much more skeptical than optimistic, especially of the claim that *Nightwood* is a lesbian novel: the novel "frustrate[s] identitarian notions of sexuality," contends Seitler, echoing Chisholm's statement that Barnes's "narration does not voice the struggle of an emerging subculture. . . . Instead of speaking out on lesbianism in cryptic modernism, *Nightwood* seriously challenges the epistemological and ontological claims of sexual discourse in general and the category of 'inversion' in particular" (Seitler 549; Chisholm 172). *Nightwood* is seen to offer but a negative "queer antidiscourse" constructed out of "a heterogeneous figure of abjection" that is deployed against dominant sexological discourse (Chisholm 186, 195).

Published in the wake of Foucault's disciplinary construction of sociosexual identities, such new historicist analyses of *Nightwood* struggle to salvage a measure of the avant-garde and social transgression of which earlier feminist readings were more certain. My contribution to this debate is to suggest that Sarduy's theory of the neobaroque as the denaturalization of language's utilitarian function as a medium of communication provides the missing key that explains *Nightwood*'s subversion of sexological and eugenicist jargon. Searching for a critical framework to account for the novel's undeniable resistance to official homophobic discourses, Seitler and Chisholm steer clear of terms such as aesthetics or stylization to avoid contamination with the ideology of the high modernist style of Eliot's 1936 introduction to *Nightwood*. Critics agree that the main purpose of Eliot's introduction was to save *Nightwood* from publishing bans, censorship, and trials for obscenity—after all, as editor, Eliot also had to protect a financial risk for Faber and Faber.[95] But even as the prestige of Eliot's endorsement succeeded in keeping *Nightwood* off the index, his winning strategy at that time, which played off the novel's accomplished style as an antidote against its perverse content, would later come back to haunt the work. Eliot defended *Nightwood* by arguing that its "astonishing language" whose prose approximates poetry, the "brilliance" of the Doctor's monologues, and the "overall pattern" formed by the characters together (note the parallels with the compositional method of *The Waste Land*) all elevate the novel above its troubling, "psychopathic" content (xii–xv). But his politic deployment of the high modernist doctrine of mastery through design and form would set in place an antithesis between *Nightwood*'s language and content, which runs counter to way the novel actually operates. Not only has it frozen Barnes criticism into a false opposition between formalist (but apolitical) readings, on the one hand, and sociosexual realist (but antiformalist) readings on the other, it has also blocked insight into precisely how, as Seitler and Chisholm overcautiously formulate, *Nightwood* "redeploys" the scientific discourses of sexual and social degeneration (Seitler 555).

As I have noted throughout, the key to *Nightwood*'s style is its neobaroque indirection and wasteful redundancy. In Fuentes's wording, *Nightwood*'s language of abundance is a language of insufficiency, which is to say, a language undermining any single authoritative truth, especially that of science. As an example, we may consider the passage of Robin's awakening, quoted above, and the narrative's subsequent obsessive dwelling on her person: the more links there are in the chain of signifiers surrounding Robin, the more unlikely it is that any of these metaphors will be taken literally, referentially, in the authoritative way that sexological science would use them. Thus, when the Doctor finally refers to Robin as an "invert" (136), this sexological term loses its scientific authority simply by being inserted into the galaxy of surreal metaphors already orbiting Robin. In short, its antirealist neobaroque *style* provides the strategy by which *Nightwood* dismantles the functionalist-scientific discourse it appropriates, by undermining the official power of naming through singular, exclusive analytical concepts. Indeed, mirroring the fictional world of its characters, plot and setting, *Nightwood*'s aesthetics is transgressive, antinatural: this is an insight that has been missed by formalist, feminist, and new historicist critics of Barnes, who, in various ways, have misattributed the novel's form to categories of discipline and order rather than rebellion.

However, it is *Nightwood*'s neobaroque "apotheosis of artifice" (Sarduy) that produces the "hilarious gender inversions" (Seitler) and "rhetorical figures for the invert" (Harris 242) that critics have described. Further examples from *Nightwood*'s procession of "third sex" types will demonstrate how the figures of the "mannish woman" and "effeminate man" lose their referential function within medicine's precise, analytical discourse to acquire a poetic (Jakobson) or ornamental function, stripping them of all remnants of their former panoptic social power. The acrobat Frau Mann ("Mrs. Male/Man") is one of the circus characters. In the description of her body, nature yields to artifice—flesh becomes wood and skin becomes cloth: "She seemed to have a skin that was the pattern of her costume . . . and the bulge in the groin where she took the bar . . . was as solid, specialized and as polished as oak. The stuff of the tights was no longer a covering, it was herself; the span of the tightly stitched crotch was so much her own flesh that she was as unsexed as a doll" (*Nightwood* 13). Robin Vote, the tall girl in "boy's trousers" (169), and the voluble gynecologist with the baroque name, Matthew grain-of-salt-Dante O'Connor, who sometimes thinks he is "a bride" (33), dresses in women's clothes, and claims that he is "the woman God forgot" (90), form yet another third-sex couple, with a special twist—doctor and patient. Matthew, the "theoretician of sex as bearded lady" (Harris), has been read as a parody of the sexologist as well as the Freudian psychoanalyst.[96]

A clever parody, the Doctor is a medical expert on female sexuality and the female body who studies women because he really wants to *be* a woman—again, Matthew's theatrical transvestism cancels his scientific authority. If the doctor's scientific inquiry into deviant sexualities and perverse desires is also fueled by those same desires, and science itself becomes infected with sexuality, science's autonomous domain of "power-knowledge" (Foucault) over sexuality disappears. Even though it is unclear if another circus performer, "Nikka, the Nigger," is also an invert, the description of his body, "tattooed from head to heel with all the *ameublement* of depravity" (16), enacts the same exaggerated denaturalization of scientific analysis. Parodying sexology's axiom that (in Foucault's formulation) perverse sexuality is "written immodestly on [the patient's] face and body because it was a secret that always gave itself away" (*History of Sexuality* 43), Nikka's body is inscribed with an inordinate number of signs so as to blind the gaze of science. The "angel from Chartres" on his stomach; quotations from "the book of magic" and "Jansenist theory" on his buttocks; the "beautiful caravel in full sail" on his chest; "on each bosom an arrow-speared heart, each with different initials but with equal drops of blood"; the delicate "vine work" on his legs (*Nightwood* 16–17)—this welter of hilarious emblems is not a set of medical symptoms but ornaments, squandered in anarchic play so as to leave no empty spaces on the wrestler's skin.

This analysis of the subversive function of *Nightwood*'s neobaroque style can by amplified by investigating another strategy, Barnes's recourse to Freudian and Renaissance melancholia. As discussed earlier, melancholia, the language of loss, and its tragic construction of identity through suffering, is perhaps the chief cause of *Nightwood*'s gloomy atmosphere. Melancholia returns us to the autobiographical and emotional core of *Nightwood*,

Nora-Djuna's depression after her separation from Robin-Thelma. But by pairing Nora, the depressed woman "patient," with the Doctor in the novel's plotless, conversational chapters, Barnes performs another ingenious feminist act of discursive subversion. As noted earlier, the Doctor and Nora are both melancholics, and in their parodic pairing as female patient and male doctor Barnes highlights the gendered privilege of male melancholia. Whereas the Doctor embodies the Renaissance archetype of the melancholic genius, Nora's interminable grief is abject and unproductive—the precise contrast between "loquacious male melancholy and the mute suffering . . . of women" (Radden 34).

Indeed, the most distinctive characteristic of Doctor O'Connor is his learning and his intellect. A "middle-aged 'medical student'" with an interest in gynecology (*Nightwood* 14), the Doctor speculates about Enlightenment philosophy ("We may all be nature's noblemen" [15]), biblical legend (Sodom and Gomorrah [86]), and many other topics in both high and low culture. Known as a "liar, but a valuable liar" (30), Doctor O'Connor explains the connection between melancholic moods and the intellectual life: "Do you know what has made me the greatest liar this side of the moon, telling my stories to people like you, to take the mortal agony out of their guts" (135). But the link is not just between the suffering of others and the Doctor's torrential, mock learned narrative. The Doctor is a scholar as well as a melancholic: "The scalpel and the Scriptures have taught me that little I did not already know" (153), he claims, yet his brilliant discourse is marred by melancholic gloom. The Doctor's self-diagnosed "floating kidney"—a parodic evocation of the humoral theory of melancholia—and his "falling arches" and "flying dandruff" (154) are only the beginning of a long list of symptoms of his medical condition that, as in *Nightwood*'s elusive description of Robin's mysterious and primitive nature, keep deferring meaning.

The Doctor's incarnation of the Renaissance melancholic scholar, depicted in Burton as well as in Dürer's famous engraving *Melencolia I* (1514) (fig. 5), sheds new light on a much-discussed scene at the beginning of the chapter "Watchman, What of the Night?" When Nora seeks out the Doctor in his tiny quarters in the middle of the night, she finds him in bed, wigged, made up, "dressed in a women's flannel nightgown," and "extremely put out, having expected someone else" (79). Having been invited in, she hesitates at the door, "so incredible was the disorder that met her eyes. . . . A pile of medical books, and volumes of a miscellaneous order, reached almost to the ceiling, water-stained and covered with dust. . . . On a maple dresser, certainly not of European make, lay a rusty pair of forceps, a broken scalpel, half a dozen odd instruments that she could not place, a catheter, some twenty perfume bottles, almost empty, pomades, creams, rouges, powder boxes and puffs" (78). Perhaps the Doctor's dazzling multiple identities—devout

Catholic, unlicensed gynecologist, garrulous Irishman, and "bistro philosopher" (Herring 210)—to which this scene adds the drag queen, has kept critics from noticing yet another persona that is also presented here. This is the unhappy man of genius portrayed in Dürer's engraving. Dürer's allegorical Melancholia has lapsed into a gloomy state of inactivity and brooding. (Panofsky makes it clear that Melancholia's femininity is a symbolic attribute of the condition portrayed, part of the allegorical figure; there is

Fig. 5. Albrecht Dürer, *Melencolia I,* 1514. (Kupferstichkabinett, Staatliche Museen, Berlin, Germany. Photograph: Jörg P. Anders, Berlin/Art Resource, New York)

no realist intention to portray a woman as melancholic genius.) Although winged and crowned with laurels, she is crouching, a closed book in her lap, resting her drooping head on one hand, a compass dangling in the other. The ground at her feet, writes Panofsky, is littered "with tools and objects mostly pertaining to the crafts of architecture and carpentry . . . : a plane, a saw, a ruler, a pair of pincers, some crooked nails, a molder's form, a hammer, a small melting pot (perhaps for melting lead) with a pair of tongs to hold burning coals, an inkpot with a penbox; and, half hidden beneath the skirt . . . an instrument which can be identified . . . as the mouth of a pair of bellows."[97] The abandoned scholar's tools at her feet associate her with scientific and intellectual pursuits, from which she is temporarily alienated by her melancholic mood, which is also encoded in her swarthy complexion (colored by black bile).

The unused medical tools strewn about the Doctor's bedroom and abortion chamber, I suggest, similarly point to the Doctor's scholarly pursuits, picturing his gloomy inertia (not from sleepiness) as a melancholic loss of energy suffered by the gifted man of genius. Rather than proving the Doctor's misogyny (as Harris suggests in a literal reading, since they are "sure to maim" any woman patient [239]), the broken medical tools are more usefully read as part of the allegorical iconography of Renaissance melancholia. They are the instruments neglected by the despondent Renaissance thinker agonizing under the genius's malady. Not surprisingly, in response to Nora's question, "What of the night?," the Doctor quickly composes himself, seizing the chance to display his learning about "his favorite topic," swiftly launching into a long monologue which confidently begins, "Well I, Dr. Matthew-Mighty-grain-of-salt-Dante-O'Connor, will tell you how the day and night are related by their division" (*Nightwood* 80). Doctor O'Connor's recognition that "to think is to be sick" (158), furthermore, explicitly cites the early modern theory that learned pursuits cause melancholy. In an early section of *The Anatomy of Melancholy*, Burton discusses "*Love of Learning, or overmuch Study. With a Digression of the Misery of Scholars, and why the Muses Are Melancholy.*" "Many men," Burton elaborates, "come to this malady by continual study, and night-waking, and of all other men, scholars are most subject to it" (Part I, 301). Citing various authorities including Marsilio Ficino, who "puts melancholy amongst one of those five principal plagues of students," Burton offers "two main reasons . . . why students should be more subject to this malady than others. The one is, they live a sedentary, solitary life, . . . free from bodily exercise, and those ordinary disports which other men use; and many times if discontent and idleness concur with it, which is too frequent, they are precipitated into this gulf on a sudden; but the common cause is overmuch study: 'Too much learning . . . hath made thee mad; . . . only scholars neglect that instrument (their brain and spirits I mean) which they daily use, and by which they range over all the world'" (Part I, 301–2). Barnes echoes, nearly verbatim, Burton's formulation of the intellect by which scholars "range all over the world" in her description of Dr. O'Connor's "interest in gynecology [which] had driven him half around the world" (*Nightwood* 14).

In keeping with Barnes's source for the Doctor's speeches, the baroque rhetoric of Burton's *Anatomy* (blended, to be sure, with Barnes's notes on the speeches of Dan Mahoney, the Doctor's real-life model [Herring 210]), the Doctor rapidly lapses from clear analysis into obscure, digressive, ornate rhetoric: "The very constitution of twilight is a fabulous reconstruction of fear, fear bottom-out and wrong side up. Every day is thought upon and calculated, but the night is not premeditated. The Bible lies the one way, but the night-gown the other. The night, 'Beware of that dark door!'" (*Nightwood* 80). The Doctor's outlandish "anatomy of the night" matches the incongruous taxonomy of Burton's anatomy of melancholy, resulting from a patchwork of quotations from ancient, medieval, and Renaissance authorities: some authors, writes Burton, "make two kinds" of melancholy, some "make four or five kinds," others yet "will have that melancholy of nuns, widows, and more ancient maids to be a peculiar species of melancholy differing from the rest: some will reduce enthusiasts, ecstatical and demoniacal persons to this rank, adding love-melancholy to the first, and lycanthropia" (Part I, 175). (Burton famously remarked that "The tower of Babel never yielded such confusion of tongues, as the chaos of melancholy doth variety of symptoms" [Part I, 397].) The Doctor's lectures are also adorned with stunning hyperbolic conceits: "Our bones ache only while the flesh is on them. Stretch it as thin as the temple flesh of an ailing woman and still it serves to ache the bone and to move the bone about; and in like manner the night is a skin pulled over the head of day that the day may be in a torment. We will find no comfort until the night melts away; until the fury of the night rots out its fire" (*Nightwood* 85). Here, the analogy forged between skull and skin on the one hand, and day and night on the other is compounded with the baroque iconography of holy martyrdom (flaying the skin) and heroic suffering. It recalls the gory conceits of Nora's wounded, melancholic self discussed above, and also refers back to the grotesque and gruesome anecdote Matthew tells earlier of Mademoiselle Basquette, the legless amputee who used to "wheel herself through the Pyrenees on a board" (26). Violated by a stranger, who abandons her far from home, she sets out on the herculean task of rolling herself back home, "weeping something fearful to see, because one is accustomed to see tears falling down to the feet" (26). The moral, according to the Doctor, comes dressed in yet another hypersensualistic baroque image of ecstatic suffering: "if one gave birth to a heart on a plate, it would say 'Love' and twitch like the lopped leg of a frog" (26–27).

Finally, reading the Doctor as Burton's (and Dürer's) melancholic Renaissance genius freshly justifies his unique, elevated position in *Nightwood.* He presides over the story as a commentator, as *Nightwood*'s central discursive authority and source of knowledge and comfort.[98] In this tragic romance, whose main protagonists are either abandoned lovers (Felix, Nora, Jenny) or their common and elusive beloved (Robin), the Doctor, who is neither a lover nor a love object, stands aloof from the action as detached observer, interpreting its meaning. The Doctor's profuse and rambling disquisitions have the quality of a dream, but his is a *rational* delirium. To this I would add that José Lezama Lima's description of the American baroque as "Baroque curiosity," a baroque that was friendly toward, rather than hostile to, the Enlightenment, sheds light on the paradoxical fusion of the rational and the irrational in the Doctor's discourses.[99] The "night," both the setting and the subject of the Doctor's lectures in "Watchman, What of the Night?," is a hallucinatory world. But unlike the night of surrealism, the medium of escape from rationality, *Nightwood*'s is a profoundly intellectual night.[100] Tellingly, the doctor's speculative and analytical mind classifies and systematizes distinct philosophical, geographic, and phenomenological dimensions of the "night."

For all these reasons, the collapse of social and narrative authority enacted in the novel, whose final episode is Robin's shocking degeneration in the closing scene, is all the more dramatic. As I have argued, the collapse is double, for just as Robin's lovers must "bow down" before their failure to possess Robin, so the Doctor finally realizes that he cannot "speak" Robin. As pointed out earlier, *Nightwood*'s religious theme exalts its tragic dénouement, sanctifying suffering: Robin converts to Catholicism during her marriage to Felix, and even though her religious quest cannot save her, it elevates her struggle. Conversely, Nora is an American Protestant whose agony is nonetheless depicted in the hypersensuous iconography of Counter-Reformation martyrdom. Felix and his son Guido are drawn to the Catholic Church and make Vienna their final home in hopes of Guido's entering the Church. The Doctor observes Catholic rituals, such as mass and funerals. In addition, many of *Nightwood*'s grieving characters seek out Catholic worship for the creaturely comfort it offers by addressing the senses—the murmuring of prayers, the rattling of rosaries, the chanting, the flickering of candles, the incense, the rich vestments of the priest, and, last but not least, the luxurious sensuality of divine passions depicted in holy images.[101]

Nightwood's deconstruction of discursive authority becomes emblematic in the moment when the Doctor falls silent, breaking off his prolific monologues; his last words are "now *nothing, but wrath and weeping*" (166). In addition to bringing down the social order of domesticated love, Robin, the femme fatale, also causes the breakdown of the symbolic order of representation. As discussed earlier, this moment occurs when the Doctor lapses from learned speech into inarticulate weeping. To put it differently, the melancholic Renaissance scholar-genius is stripped of poetic melancholia's privileges and compensations and reduced to the abjection of his sorrow. His male creative melancholy implodes into Nora's female condition of unproductive melancholia—plain and unmitigated despair. Matthew O'Connor's initial intellectual confidence, displayed in his philosophical monologues on "woman" and "the night," full of learned allusions, gives way to bitter resignation as he realizes that knowledge is nothing but a dress and a lie: "You have dressed the unknowable in the garments of the known" (136). Here is yet another dazzling neobaroque conceit that thinks feelingly, as Eliot put it, incarnating abstract thought in sensuous reality. Again, the disintegration of the doctor's epistemological mastery exemplifies baroque *desengaño,* disillusionment. In their resigned tone, Matthew's late, melancholic insights into life's meaninglessness, "I've not only lived my life for nothing, but I've told it for nothing" (165), begin to approximate Nora's lamentations, which, in Smith's apt phrase, "keen" loss, in a use of language blurring the categories of weeping and speech. "I'll never understand her—I'll always be miserable—just like this," says Nora, before "tears" begin to "run down [her] face" (85, 93). Misery without the illumination of knowledge, black night without insight prevail at *Nightwood*'s close. Language and knowledge, including modern science and medicine (to recall the Doctor's role as sexologist), are exposed as impotent vis-à-vis the reality they claim to represent.

In affirming the failure of language and representation, *Nightwood*'s melancholic discourse inverts the high modernist doctrine of mastery through technique and narrative design. Because Eliot deployed it in his politic introduction intended to steer Barnes's novel past the censors, it is useful to recall his influential 1923 definition of the "mythic method": "It is simply a way of controlling, of ordering, of giving a shape and a significance to the immense panorama of futility and anarchy which is contemporary history."[102] For Eliot's own early work—as we have seen in the previous chapter—the control of modernist experimental form over its anarchic content was tenuous, with the seams of the poet's manipulation of his materials in plain sight. In *Nightwood,* however—and contrary to Eliot's affirmation regarding its "achievement of style" compensating for its "psychopathic" content—style and form neither redeem nor contain, neither order nor cure the "futility and anarchy" of the traumatic events they represent. Barnes's neobaroque lamentation is language squandered in the futile attempt to close melancholia's open wound. Instead of healing and scarring over as a result of the

Doctor's talking cure, Nora's psychic wound explodes into a full-scale hemorrhage in the final chapter, when, after the failure of knowledge and speech, the injured patient (Nora)—so to speak—bleeds to death. After Nora loses consciousness, "[striking] the wood" (169), no one alive is left to witness and comment upon the grueling conclusion of the tragedy—Robin's degeneration. As Fuentes suggests and as Sarduy recognizes, *Nightwood*'s hyperbolic, ornate language is a language of insufficiency. *Nightwood*'s narration is powerless to exert symbolic discipline over reality: ceaselessly dwelling on the disturbing reality (Robin's promiscuity and the "night," or the larger trauma Robin represents), it circles a grief that will not cease and a wound that will not close.

I want to close by contrasting *Nightwood* with another modernist novel that, much better than Eliot does, articulates the modernist doctrine of technical mastery and control, by way of subscribing to the engineering aesthetic's maxim "less is more": Ernest Hemingway's *The Sun Also Rises* (1926).[103] There are such close parallels between Barnes's and Hemingway's novels that their antithetical politics of language and form—including *Nightwood*'s insurgency—stand out even more clearly. Set in Paris and Europe of the 1920s among the American expatriate community, both novels deal with modern gender anxieties and rising gender tensions, the result of the modern breakdown of traditional distinctions between the sexes (as well as race and class, in Hemingway's case).[104] Both novels feature characters who personify deviant genders and sexualities—masculine women who dress in men's clothes (Brett Ashley and Robin Vote), effeminate or physically emasculated men (Jake Barnes, Robert Cohn, and the Doctor), homosexuality (Brett's Parisian male friends, all major characters in *Nightwood* except Felix), and promiscuity (Brett and Robin). Both *Nightwood* and *The Sun Also Rises* are about disastrous love and the path of destruction an alluring femme fatale leaves in her wake, featuring a "modern girl" who appropriates the traditionally male prerogative of promiscuity, on her own terms. Both Brett and Robin are nomadic and restless; they are antidomestic women, whose unbridled sexuality will not be contained in monogamous relationships. Brett, like Robin, is shown to destroy her lovers; both women's promiscuity poses a serious threat to social peace in the community. Even more interestingly, the psychic wound or trauma of an abandoned lover is at the center of the narrative in both novels: Jake, hopelessly enamored of Brett, cannot consummate his love for her because of a war wound that has emasculated him physically. Like Nora, Jake is suffering from melancholic dejection and its characteristic "loss of interest in the outside world" (Freud).

Against the foil of these parallels, the differences in resolution of psychic trauma and melancholia are all the more striking. Under the surface of its fast-paced plot, Hemingway's novel performs a ritual of social catharsis, cultural purification and renewal, which restores the traditional status quo and reinforces traditional differences of gender (and race and class) threatened by the permissive Parisian ambience. Hemingway's revolutionary, lean prose style conveys a culturally conservative message: on a trip to Spain during the bullfighting season in Pamplona, the main protagonists undergo various trials in a rural, traditional setting, which results in the purging of gender (and social) deviance. Brett, the aggressive femme fatale who collects men and their hats, is finally vanquished by a bullfighter, a "masculine man," who breaks her spirit and teaches her that, after all, she is only a woman and a "lady." (Having previously referred to herself as "chap"—an androgynous attribute—at the close, Brett pointedly asks Jake, "*Would* you like to buy a lady a drink?" [*Sun* 244].) Jake, on the other hand, proves his manliness by way of his *afición* for bullfighting and his stoic acceptance of his tragic condition (his physical and psychic injury), showing moral courage and thus overcoming his despair. Jake's wealthy Jewish rival, Cohn, in contrast, has lost face as a blunderer and a fool. Brett, after all, is only a woman; Cohn, despite his success, is only a Jew; but Jake, despite his war wound, is his own man. Through the traditional Spanish fiesta and various other cleansing rituals in nature, *The Sun Also Rises* purges the unnatural social excesses of expatriate American urbanites and their friends. This ending on an optimistic note is symbolically underlined by an epigraph from Ecclesiastes, from which *The Sun Also Rises* takes its title: even if the post–World War I "lost generation" may be beyond redemption, there is hope because of nature's eternal cycle of rebirth and regeneration—"one generation passeth away, and another cometh, but the earth abideth forever" (*Sun* vi).

Hemingway's novel conveys its disciplining of gender and sexual deviance through hypermodern, spare, precise and controlled prose. *The Sun Also Rises* is a "machine made of words" written according to principles of engineering efficiency—directness, simplicity, clarity, and conciseness—which its author absorbed when working as a reporter for the *Kansas City Star.* The principle of "one phrase to mean everything" is exemplified by the word "nice," which Hemingway famously utilizes "like fuel" to yield multiple meanings (Tichi, "Technology" 478). Similarly, the final social catharsis is conveyed in clipped words and phrases, such as Brett's self-reference as "lady," or Jake's final, composed observation, "Isn't it pretty to think so?" (*Sun* 247). In contrast, *Nightwood* is the antithesis of the idea that technical mastery can restore a semblance of order to the anarchy and chaos that was contemporary history—for both Hemingway *and* Barnes. For Barnes, there is no narrative or aesthetic cure for biographical or historical trauma—neither for Nora's melancholia nor for Robin's sexual promiscuity, the cause of all the pain. The cathartic ending of *The Sun Also Rises* breaks Brett's magic spell and affirms Jake's symbolic power as exorcist, as it were. At the catastrophic ending of *Nightwood,* in contrast, Robin's Circe-like allure is unbroken, and all attempts to reform her or exorcise her charms have failed. For its bleakness, *Nightwood*'s alternative title could be "The Sun Does Not Rise Again," as if to affirm, contra Hemingway, the stubborn reality of antinatural human sexualities outside the cycles of organic reproduction. It is useful to recall that, like Hemingway, Barnes had a long and successful career as a journalist; there is no reason to believe that she would not have been subjected to the same stylistic influences of machine-age syntax. Yet *Nightwood* inverts the modernist doctrine of style as discipline and order, exposing instead language's insufficiency—or rather language's inefficiency as an instrument of domination. As I have shown, Barnes's motivation is twofold, her rebellion against the disciplinary power of the fin-de-siècle medical sciences, and her listening to the baroque muse of melancholia.

The Latin American Antidictatorship Neobaroque

Allegories of History as Catastrophe and Performances of the Wounded Self in Diamela Eltit's *Lumpérica* and José Donoso's *Casa de campo*

Bajo la matas
En los pajonales
Sobre los puentes
En los canales
Hay Cadáveres

—Néstor Perlongher, "Cadáveres"

To articulate the past historically does not mean to recognize it "the way it really was." It means to seize hold of a memory as it flashes up at a moment of danger.

—Walter Benjamin, "Theses on the Philosophy of History"

THIS CHAPTER and the following turn to a new cycle of the neobaroque in the Americas, which I call the antidictatorship neobaroque. Crossing multiple borders of time and space, this shift takes us from Eliot's and Barnes's Anglo-American modernism to a unique Latin American variety of postmodernism. Across Latin America, the core period associated with postmodernism in the United States and Europe, from the late 1960s into the 1980s, saw a staggering number of right-wing military dictatorships, which conducted state-sponsored "dirty wars" against political opponents. Among them were the dictatorships in Chile (1973–89), Argentina (1976–84), Brazil (1964–84), and Uruguay (1973–85). During the same decades, Central American states such as El Salvador, Guatemala, and Nicaragua were racked by protracted civil wars between insurgent Marxist guerilla forces and counterinsurgent armed forces, trained and financed by the United States. According to the historian Edwin Williamson, the darkest period was the mid-1970s, when "only Colombia, Venezuela and Costa Rica had elected governments."[1] Not surprisingly, this violent political climate introduced dramatic, across-the-board changes into Latin American cultural, artistic, and literary scenes. In literature, it led to the termination of the optimistic spirit of departure characterizing the Boom of the 1960s and the inauguration of a post-Boom literature of crisis, defeat, and disillusionment.[2] In contrast to the United States, the postmodern in Latin America was thus forged in the shadow of political authoritarianism and a renewed eruption of political violence, both of which had vitiated the fates of Latin American republics since independence in the early nineteenth century. In this climate, the neobaroque became one key, symptomatic expression of the reigning social and political situation of crisis and catastrophe. In the postmodern late twentieth century, many Latin American writers once again looked back to the baroque as a congenial expression of historical discontinuity, political disillusionment, conflict between state authoritarianism and popular resistance, and a correspondingly somber mood—melancholia and mourning.

Surpassing the limited focus of this and the following chapters on the antidictatorship neobaroque, *neobarroco* also constitutes a major trend in twentieth-century Latin American fiction and poetry. Much has been written about its major exemplars, especially in fiction. Among them are such works as José Lezama Lima's *Paradiso* (1966; *Paradiso*); Alejo Carpentier's *Concierto barroco* (1974); Severo Sarduy's fiction, *De donde son los cantantes* (1967; *From Cuba with a Song*), *Cobra* (1972), and *Maitreya* (1978); Fernando del Paso's *Noticias del Imperio* (1987; *News from the Empire*) and *Palinuro de México* (1976; *Palinurus of Mexico*); Guillermo Cabrera Infante's *Tres tristes tigres* (1965; *Three Trapped Tigers*); Reinaldo Arenas's *El mundo alucinante* (1969; *The Ill-Fated Peregrinations of Fray Servando*); Gabriel García Márquez's *El otoño del patriarca* (1975; *The Autumn of the Patriarch*); and Carlos Fuentes's *Terra Nostra* (1975).[3] Hyperbole and antirealist strategies of artificialization characterize all these texts. Affinities with seventeenth-century expression in modern and contemporary Latin American literature can be traced to the formative impact of the baroque in Latin America; the baroque constitutes, as Irlemar Chiampi and Bolívar Echeverría point out, Latin America's alternative modernity. The antidictatorship neobaroque that I investigate here represents an understudied aspect of this familiar and important *neobarroco* tendency in twentieth-century Latin American literature.

In its somber refrain "hay cadáveres" (there are corpses), Argentine Néstor Perlongher's 1987 poem "Cadáveres" (Corpses) identifies the emblematic object of Latin American reality under the late twentieth-century dictatorships: corpses.

Bajo la matas
En los pajonales
Sobre los puentes
En los canales
Hay Cadáveres

En la trilla de un tren que nunca se detiene
En la estela de un barco que naufraga
En una olilla, que se desvanece
En los muelles los apeaderos los trampolines los malecones
Hay Cadáveres

(Under shrubs
In the undergrowth
On bridges
In canals
There are corpses

In the throb of a train that never stops
In the wake of a boat that is shipwrecked
In a tiny wave that is disappearing
On wharfs railway stations diving boards seawalls
There are corpses)[4]

A neobaroque poet in the filiation of the historical avant-gardes of the 1920s, Perlongher in his poetry participates in the dismantling of language's function as communication and reference to external reality, which is theorized by Sarduy in his essay "The Baroque and the Neobaroque." At one level, the corpses in Perlongher's poem are literal, real corpses—the anonymous human remains savagely left behind by the death squads, military coups, and aborted coup attempts, torture and disappearances, lawless violence, state terror, and guerrilla counterterror, which for two long decades were the order of the day in Latin America. Yet by its application to a principally limitless panorama extending beyond the real to the fantastic, the phrase "hay cadáveres" is expanded in meaning beyond literal reference. Cut loose from its immediate referent, "hay cadáveres" comes to represent a nameless haunting, a traumatic residue that clings to every place and every human transaction, serving as a reminder of the recent cataclysm that, in Perlongher's Argentina of 1987, had just been left behind (though it threatened to return via a series of aborted coup attempts after the formal restoration of democracy in 1984).

According to Benjamin, the corpse, like the ruin and the skull, is a paradigmatic object of the baroque imagination, which features nations laid waste by wars and other disastrous events, presenting a world whose life has been extinguished: the *Trauerspiel* study affirms that seventeenth-century baroque tragedies "are resplendent with pale corpses."[5] As in Benjamin, in Perlongher corpses are not merely realistic but also allegorical, in the sense intended by Benjamin in *The Origin of German Tragic Drama,* which we had occasion to consider earlier in connection with Eliot's *The Waste Land:* "Allegories are, in the realm of thoughts, what ruins are in the realm of things. This explains the baroque cult of the ruin" (178). The cult of the ruin (as emblematic object of mourning and loss) is similarly definitive of the antidictatorship neobaroque. For this reason, the analysis in this and the following chapters will draw on Benjamin's theory of the baroque, and of baroque allegory in particular, for its characteristic mode of writing history in a situation of crisis and catastrophe. "To articulate the past historically does not mean to recognize it 'the way it really was.' It means to seize hold of a memory as it flashes up at a moment of danger"[6]: Benjamin's celebrated proposition is also a maxim of the antidictatorship neobaroque. As we shall see, Benjamin's invective against false continuities in official historiography as the oppressive history of the victors in his 1940 essay "Theses on the Philosophy of History" articulates the core motives underpinning the allegorical and neo-avant-garde strategies of the antidictatorship neobaroque. The political parallels are unmistakable: both Benjamin and late twentieth-century Latin American antidictatorship writers were formed in the shadow of fascisms and dictatorships, the demise of liberal democracies, and the catastrophic collapse of what was thought to be civilization into barbarism.

Supporting Benjamin's claims, Perlongher's neobaroque procedure in his paradigmatic postdictatorship poem furnishes evidence that, contrary to what is often asserted, neo-avant-garde strategies of derealization are compatible with a commitment to social justice. What is more, antidictatorship neobaroque aesthetics of fragmentation and allegory are capable of offering unique insight into the comprehensive social damage wrought by state violence beneath the surface of material realism, in the areas of ideology, public language, and collective identity. My reading of the antidictatorship neobaroque is indebted to the writings of Chile's foremost theoreticians of the post-1973 arts and literary scene, Nelly Richard and Eugenia Brito, and to more recent work by Idelber Avelar.[7] My addition to their analyses of the postdictatorship literature and arts scene is to foreground neobaroque texts and investigate their particular strategies of demystification of official state narratives.

A few words concerning terminology and the related issue of selection of texts are in order at this point. Limiting my examples to writing produced *during* the period of the dictatorships, I examine what is technically *anti*dictatorship (rather than *post*dictatorship) writing. (When using this term, however, I take the prefix "post" to mean "after the onset" of the dictatorships, not "after their end.") Specifically, I compare two Chilean novels published during the seventeen-year tenure of Pinochet's military regime, a novel published in exile, José Donoso's *Casa de campo* (1978; *A House in the Country*), and a novel written and published in the interior, Diamela Eltit's *Lumpérica* (1983; *E. Luminata*).[8] Eltit's first novel, whose genesis (according to the author) goes back to 1976,[9] was conceived at the height of the Pinochet dictatorship, during the dirty war of the 1970s leading up to the first, tightly controlled Chilean plebiscite in September 1980, which approved Pinochet's rule, extending it until 1989. Discussions of Latin American literature and arts produced in the wake of the dictatorships frequently blur the distinction I make here between works produced *during* the tenure of the dictatorships proper (in the case of Chile, the period between Pinochet's coup on September 11, 1973, and the presidential elections in December 1989, which ended his regime) and works produced *after* the formal end of the dictatorships and the return to democracy (Chile in transition to democracy since 1989). Thus, Idelber Avelar puts equal emphasis on work produced during *and* after the tenure of the dictatorships in Chile, Argentina, and Brazil. There are very good reasons for doing so: the decisive turning points are the impositions of military rule, which resulted in catastrophic attacks on civil society and the public sphere, via censorship, the exile of intellectuals, and the defunding of state publication and fellowship outlets.[10]

Indeed, with the problematics of anti- and (especially) postdictatorship expression we are again in the throes of Frederic Jameson's dialectic of continuity and rupture. We "cannot not periodize," that is to say, we cannot escape the periodizing logic, although we know that ruptures, and the periods they organize, have a tendency to blend and morph into each other as time passes and new historical narratives are scripted.[11] The term "postdictatorship" is animated by much periodizing confidence: placing the break firmly on September 11, 1973 (in the case of Chile), it founds the period it conceptualizes on this radical historical beginning. The formal return to democracy in 1989 pales in comparison. Although it ended the dictatorship years, it failed to assert itself as a break comparable to that of the coup: the coalition for democracy that dominated Chilean politics for two decades until 2010 is known by the tentative denominator *transición* (transition to democracy). This, of course, is a result of the legal and political vise grip that the generals had on post-1990 democratic regimes: there were amnesties for the military, failures to prosecute the dictatorship's human rights abuses, and legal authoritarian enclaves in government owing to Pinochet's 1980 constitution, which continues in force today. It wasn't until an external event, Pinochet's 1998 arrest in London, that the military's stranglehold loosened (again, gradually), leading to Pinochet's trial after 2000, and to the

2005 reforms of the 1980 constitution. Recent studies by Francine Masiello, Nelly Richard and Alberto Moreiras, and Willy Thayer (published in 2001 and 2006) confirm that the memory of the violent mutilation of the public spheres by the military regimes remains the cardinal reference point for arts and literary scenes flourishing under the restored democracies in Latin America of the late 1980s and 1990s.[12]

Latin American historians and sociologists agree that the military dictatorships had an economic purpose—the integration of their nations into global markets and the imposition of reigning neoliberal policies. The dictatorships thus continued the project of economic modernization by violent means; the military stepped in when it became clear that the democratic state was unable to defeat (indeed, was in serious threat of being taken over by) substantial popular and socialist constituencies that opposed globalization, free market economic policies, and the reduction of the state sector of the economy.[13] Citing recent work by Chilean sociologist José Joaquín Brunner, Avelar affirms that the dictatorships ushered in "the transition from State to Market," that is to say, the "transit from the modern national state to the trans-national post-state market," completing (especially in the case of Chile and Brazil) a "capitalist refoundation" of Latin American states that "could not be accomplished under a democratic regime" (*Untimely* 55, 58–59, 56). The neoliberal technocrats appointed by Pinochet and other strongmen to restructure the economy were derisively known as the "Chicago Boys" for their adherence to the economic creed of Milton Friedman of the University of Chicago. In Chile, the redirection of production from high-wage national to low-wage global markets resulted in substantial income cuts. "By 1975 Chile had 30 percent unemployment, and wages had dropped by 30–50 percent, leaving a huge proportion of the population destitute. . . . 'Pinochet's job was to offer a cheap workforce to the world.'"[14] In the shantytowns of Santiago, unemployment remained at 40 percent throughout the 1970s (Williamson 507). The concerted attack on organized labor necessary to redirect the economy from national to global markets is also evident in Argentina: 37 percent of the *desaparecidos* in the so-called Argentine *proceso* (as the Argentine dictatorship was known, after the self-designation of the military government headed by General Jorge Videla: Proceso de Reorganización, or Process of National Reorganization) were "shop stewards or trade-union officials" (ibid. 477).

The economic roots of the recent Latin American dictatorships shed a special (and chilling) light on Jameson's dictum that postmodernism is the cultural logic of late capitalism.[15] They point to a fundamental contrast between North America and Latin America. In Latin America, globalization could not be imposed peacefully as it was in the United States. Or, as Uruguayan writer Eduardo Galeano put it incisively, "in Uruguay, people were being tortured so that prices could be free" (quoted in Avelar, *Untimely* 79). The military justified its human rights violations through a fascist rhetoric of social surgery and analogizing the nation to the human body: as surgeons must amputate infected limbs or organs to save the life of the patient, so the military had to surgically extirpate diseased parts of the social body to safeguard the economic prosperity of the nation. The "central role of the military regimes" was to "purge the social body of all elements that could offer some resistance to a generalized opening to multinational capital" (ibid. 36).

It is against the foil of this official, fascist language of social surgery that we need to place the performances of self-mutilation and the rhetoric of the wounded body and the wounded self that are prominent characteristics of antidictatorship expression. This is especially true in the case of Chile, in what Richard has called Chile's *escena de avanzada* (new arts scene), which took off in the late 1970s in the interior, after the sepulchral silence of the initial, most repressive phase of military rule. Its foremost practitioners are the Chilean writers Raúl Zurita and Diamela Eltit, who staged "the mutilated, sacrificed body" in their early works of the 1970s (Brito 17). Most flamboyantly, in 1975, Raúl Zurita burned his cheek with an iron, then wrote his first volume of poetry, *Purgatorio* (1979; *Purgatorio*), about it; in 1980 he tried (unsuccessfully) to blind himself by throwing ammonia at his face, which became the theme of his second volume of poetry, *Anteparaíso* (1982; *Anteparadise*). In 1980, Diamela Eltit inflicted incisions and burns on her arms in preparation for a reading of the manuscript of her first novel, *Lumpérica*, at a brothel in Santiago; her photograph (by collaborator Lotty Rosenfeld) with her arms bandaged and bearing the stigmata of her wounds later became a key element in the published work. The borrowings from the Christian discourse of holy martyrdom are unmistakable. According to Richard, it is through the enactment of self-sacrifice that antidictatorship artists construct an alliance between themselves and the silenced collective suffering they endeavor to give voice to: "The very notion of the wounded body refers to that of the community; all the tearing of flesh is a token of the broken texture of a whole collectivity" (*Margins* 32). This rhetoric of physical self-injury is not restricted to Chile, however: Jill Kuhnheim examines the "metaphor of writing as a kind of wounding" in literature engendered or published under dictatorship, such as the Argentine poet Liliana Lukin's *Cortar por lo sano* (1987; Cut to the Quick).[16] My contribution to the critical debate on "the image of the polis as *wounded body*" (Avelar, *Untimely* 168) in antidictatorship writing will be to demonstrate that these strategies are also specific borrowings from the iconography of the Counter-Reformation baroque and its grand spectacles of sanctified suffering.

Antidictatorship writing is very conscious of the economic motivation of the recent Latin American dictatorships and highlights their contradictory mix of political authoritarianism and economic neoliberalism. It underscores the paradoxical contrast between the freedom of the market and the imprisonment of citizens. A schizoid world is presented in which domestic repression under sadistic patriarchal figures is yoked to heightened commercial activity. In Donoso's allegory of Pinochet's Chile in *Casa de campo,* the "parents," representatives of the oligarchy, are eager to sell off the family residence—the Chilean nation—to wealthy "foreigners" (global capital) after they have violently repressed a domestic rebellion with the help of the Mayordomo (Pinochet) and the "servants" (the military). The events presented in Eltit's *Lumpérica* are similarly overshadowed by authoritarian power. Its embodiment is a flashing neon sign—ominously referred to as "El luminoso" (the illuminated sign; literally "the luminous one")—which is personified (and gendered masculine) as if it were endowed with human attributes. Set in a public square in Santiago on a single winter night during the curfew, *Lumpérica*'s events and their human agents are bathed in the flickering electric light of the neon sign mounted on top of a building in the square. Nothing escapes the purview of this commercial sign, the allegorical eye of state power, which is at the same time a landmark of Pinochet's capitalist restructuring of Chile. Ricardo Piglia's postdictatorship science fiction novel *La cuidad ausente* (1992; *The Absent City*)—to offer an Argentine example—is similarly set in a dystopian city (Buenos Aires) under military siege.[17] The city's sepulchral silence clashes strangely with its hypermodern infrastructure. Here, too, technological and economic modernity coexists with antidemocratic rule.

The dramatic social effects of the dictatorships cannot be overstated: their regimes produced traumatic historical discontinuities, rupturing and fracturing existing social, cultural, and artistic institutions and movements. Most spectacularly, Pinochet's bloody overthrow of Allende's democratically elected socialist government inflicted a "zero hour" on the cultural scene—a total cultural blackout (*apagón cultural*) and a complete destruction of the existing lively cultural scene under Allende's Popular Unity government (a coalition of communists, socialists, and other radical splinter groups).[18] In her aptly titled study of the new post-1973 "scene of writing," *Campos minados* (Minefields), Eugenia Brito writes that "the military coup produced a silence and a horizontal and vertical cut across all cultural systems, including literature in particular" (11). In her history of the same new post-1973 scene in the visual arts, *Margins and Institutions,* Richard concurs that the coup "that shattered the preceding framework of social and political experiences, also destroyed all the language and models of signification by which those experiences could be named, a language thereafter powerless to designate or symbolise what was, after all, a real crisis of intelligibility" (17). Richard points to more subtle, immaterial effects of the regime's social surgery that were perhaps more devastating in the long term: as the dictatorship abducted public language and placed it under a penal system of surveillance and discipline, Chileans faced the complete disintegration of existing frameworks of meaning, ideology, and collective identity. Any artists or writer who continued to work inside the dictatorship regimes had to confront what Eltit's close collaborator, the Chilean poet Raúl Zurita, identifies as "the hierarchization of language" and "the appearance of the unstated as the ordering axis of language."[19] "The Chilean experience after the military coup of 1973 would show us a language which reaches a maximum degree of disconnection among its components; signifiers see their signifieds changed, and the entire regime of conversation becomes a parody of itself. Language becomes pre-understood as precarious, insofar as the truth that it represents has taken refuge in other areas of experience: the unstated, the non-verbalizable" (Zurita, "Chile" 306).

Eltit was one of the founders of the *escena de avanzada* that erupted in Chile in 1977 in response to the post-1973 status quo of repressive state institutions and public discourses. As Brito and Richard recall (both are participant witnesses of this period, Brito as a poet and literary critic active in the *avanzada* and Richard as a French emigré and art critic living in Chile since 1970, who reviewed the work of the writers): "In 1977, the 'avanzada' or 'new scene' emerged with its neo-avant-garde bent, bringing together writers (Raúl Zurita, Diamela Eltit, Gonzalo Muñoz, etc.), artists (Eugenio Dittborn, Carlos Leppe, Carlos Altamirano, Lotty Rosenfeld, etc.), critics (Adriana Valdés, Eugenia Brito, etc.), and philosophers (Ronald Kay, Patricio Marchant, Pablo Oyarzún, etc.)" (*Insubordination* 44). Created in 1979, the Colectivo de Acciones de Arte (CADA) formed a smaller group composed of "two writers (Raúl Zurita and Diamela Eltit), a sociologist (Fernando Balcells), and two visual artists (Lotty Rosenfeld and Juan Castillo)" (25). CADA's mission in particular was an uncompromising rejection of institutions, including art as an institution (museum art), and the reinsertion of art into public life. While the *avanzada* thus recuperated the program of the historical avant-garde, which sought to destroy art as an autonomous bourgeois institution and to "return art to the praxis of life,"[20] Richard insisted on retaining "the Spanish term *avanzada* to avoid confusion with the nostalgic connotations of the word 'avant-garde'" (*Margins* 21n1).

CADA realized its neo-avant-garde project of "*intervention in everyday life* by means of 'art actions'" (Richard, *Margins* 107) through two influential citywide performances, *Para no morir de hambre en el arte* (1979; So as not to die of hunger in the arts) and *¡Ay Sudamérica!* (1981; Oh, South America!).[21] *Para no morir* consisted of several simultaneous actions, among them the distribution of milk in a Santiago shantytown; the publication of a mini-manifesto in a newspaper that read, "Imagine this page completely blank/imagine this blank page as white as milk for daily consumption/imagine all corners of Chile deprived of milk for daily consumption as blank pages to be filled"; a parade of milk trucks through Santiago that terminated in front of the Art Museum of Chile; and the unfolding of a white canvas across the entrance of the museum, "metaphorically suggesting an act of institutional closure" (Richard, *Insubordination* 25). The neo-avant-garde fusion of unofficial urban practices (such as milk distribution) and writing (the published manifesto) is reinforced through the analogy forged between the whiteness of milk and the whiteness of the blank page to be filled with words.

Indeed, CADA's focus on the street and the urban represented a bid to reconquer the public space and the public sphere shut down by the dictatorship. Notably, the impulse that energized CADA's neo-avant-garde experimentalism was political—to negate official dictatorship institutions and discourses. To the official spectacle of the dictatorship in the Chilean capital and the mass media it opposed its unofficial urban counterspectacles. The most political of CADA's actions was the so-called "No +" initiative in 1983, the year of the tenth anniversary of Pinochet's regime. "No +" (no more of . . .) was a slogan artists wrote on the walls of the city. As Eltit recalls, "the idea was that people would fill in the missing word they would have come up with, No more political prisoners, no more hunger, no more dictatorship. And this was the slogan to put an end to the dictatorship" (Morales, *Conversaciones* 163).

Following on the heels of the military surgery on public language, the *avanzada*'s aesthetics of fragmentation and ellipsis (Richard, *Margins* and *Cultural Residues*) enacted a critical rearticulation of its shattered unity. The *avanzada* responded to the violent caesura of the military dictatorships by reproducing it *within* their art: "only by working with the fragmentary, or the ellipsis produced by the whole process of disunity, was it possible to account for the Chilean subject's sense of his own shattered and dislocated unity" (Richard, *Margins* 17). A project of rebuilding in the wasteland of cultural ruins, it produces allegorical assemblages of discontinuous fragments of subjectivity, language, and collective identity. Here we may note the kinship with Benjamin's critical project: the *avanzada* of postwar (or antiwar) reconstruction, as it were, takes place under the signs of catastrophe, ruin, defeat and loss. It is a project of thinking and writing from ruins and fragments, whose dominant mood is pessimism and melancholia, as critic Alberto Moreiras states in an influential essay: "In an extreme paradoxical manner, thinking in the post-dictatorship is to suffer more than to celebrate. Marked by the loss of the object, it thinks from depression."[22]

In the same vein, the dictatorships intensified the latent manicheanism in Latin American culture and arts, sharpening the lines dividing the spheres of the official state and its institutions from unofficial and counterinstitutional culture.[23] A wide chasm opened between center and margin, between what the regimes proclaimed in "official speak" via the censored media and what ordinary citizens experienced, as suggested in the title of Richard's study of post-1973 art in Chile—*Margins and Institutions.* The subject of Richard's and Brito's studies is the anti-institutional new arts scene of visual, textual, and performative work, an "*unofficial field* (which rejected the dictatorial paradigm)" (Richard, *Insubordination* 39) that was firmly opposed to the "*official field* (integrated into the military regime's double language of 'modernization-repression')" of the streamlined mass media (39). To remake official language, the antidictatorial "new scene" inside Chile, Brito explains, positioned itself firmly on the site of the margin and the anti-institutional: "The site from which the scene of Chilean writing develops is the site of the 'margin,' where it safeguards its dissidence and guarantees the possibility of re-creating, within this space, the signs that vacate the urban design of the codification imposed by the repressive order" (Brito 16).

Eltit's literary project in particular was formed by the logic of manicheanism: it was forged under and against the oppressive weight of the dictatorship, which she had to endure in her day job as a public employee and schoolteacher. To avoid conflating the marginal orientation of Eltit's writing with clichés in contemporary criticism, it is important to situate it within its proper sociohistorical conditions of authoritarianism that formed "[her] development as a writer [that] took place during those years of the military regime."[24] In an important essay, Eltit explains that she wrote the novel that would become her first, *Lumpérica,* to get even with power, "because it was the only way I could save . . . my own honor. When my freedom—I don't mean *freedom* in the literal sense but in its whole symbolic range—was threatened, then I took the liberty of writing freely. . . . I wrote four books under dictatorship, and social space is what I recovered for myself during that period" ("Errant" 5). It is often noted that Eltit's writing declares itself in solidarity with the social space of the marginal, the excluded, and the oppressed. Referring also to her lower middle-class background and her upbringing in a poor neighborhood by a single mother, Eltit affirms that "my greatest political solidarity—unrestricted, epic even—is with those spaces of neglect, and my aspiration is to a greater social stability and to flexibility in the power structure" (ibid. 9). The counterhegemonic space of the margin forms the existential site for Eltit to recover meaning among the shattered frameworks of intelligibility: "in appealing to instances of marginality I have been able to organize some structures of meaning" (ibid. 6). *Lumpérica* is paradigmatic in this respect: the title—a portmanteau word composed of three elements, "lumpen," "América," and the figure of woman—announces the novel's counterinstitutional site as a book about a "minoritarian and indigent 'america,'" a subaltern America, inhabiting the feminized space of the margin (Avelar, *Untimely* 171).

A significant part of Eltit's performative and literary work has been with and about beggars, prostitutes, and the mentally ill. After Eltit's 1980 performance of *Lumpérica* at a brothel, she produced two *testimonios,* a new hybrid, "as told to" documentary genre that emerged in Latin America in the 1960s and with the mission to empower previously silenced voices of the subaltern and marginalized. *El infarto del alma* (1994; Heart attack of the soul), a joint project with the photographer Paz Errázuriz, features the lives of mental patients in an asylum, in particular romantic couples and lovers.[25] In illustrating the subject of love through the bodies and lives of people excluded from the dominant logic of advertising images (emphasizing health, beauty, youth, and wealth), Eltit and Errázuriz make the marginal—the leftovers of humanity who are cast aside by the consumer society promoted by Pinochet—the center of their work. *El padre mío* (1989; My father) is a portrait of a schizophrenic urban vagabond who lived in a public square and whose prolific monologues Eltit tape-recorded in the mid-1980s.[26] The vagabond's narrative revolves around the emblematic figure of the patriarch (whom the vagabond calls "el padre mío," with uncanny echoes of Pinochet, dictator and "father of the nation"). It discusses figures of political and economic power and their illegal machinations, mentioning the names of Pinochet, Allende, and other Chilean public figures.

Eltit's informant claims to have been the target of an assassination attempt and talks of people whose business is extermination and assassination. The vagabond's delirious discourse is fascinating for its political paranoia and the symptomatic chasm between official power and the everyday. Oscillating between sense and nonsense, his incoherent speech comes to mirror the deep crisis of public language and meaning in Chile under dictatorship, as Eltit points out in an often quoted statement of these parallels between the delirious speech of this marginalized homeless schizophrenic and the psycholinguistic state of the Chilean nation: "This is Chile, I thought. Chile whole and in pieces in the sickness of this man; tatters of diaries, fragments of extermination, syllables of death, pauses that lie, commercial slogans, names of the dead. It is a profound crisis of language, an infection of memory, a disarticulation of all ideologies. It is a pity, I thought" (*El padre mío* 17). The margins give testimony to the catastrophic effects of authoritarianism on Chilean collective identity and public discourse: both are in a state of fragmentation and disintegration. As Richard notes, the psychotic speech of a marginalized individual comes to stand as an allegory of national identity (*Residues* 49).[27] The actual subaltern informant, of course, is not aware of these additional layers of significance. As in *Lumpérica,* Eltit's editorial method in this first *testimonio* is that of Benjamin's baroque allegorist: to extract material from its life context and reassemble it in her introduction to the documentary chapters (which are word-for-word reproductions of her informant's speech), assigning it new meanings that do not derive from its original source.

It is instructive to note the parallels between Eltit's comments on the schizophrenic disintegration of the Chilean language under dictatorship and Jameson's observations on the schizophrenic structure of postmodern discourse: "a new depthlessness" characteristic of a culture of the simulacrum and a "consequent weakening of historicity" (*Postmodernism* 6). Commenting that with "the breakdown of the signifying chain . . . the schizophrenic is reduced to an experience of pure material signifiers" (27), Jameson turns his attention to the semiotic games of contemporary U.S. art and literature, to diagnose "schizophrenic fragmentation as their fundamental aesthetic" (28). Clearly, Jameson and Eltit describe the same immaterial effects of late capitalism: the disintegration of the "centered subject" (Jameson) and the fragmentation of existing cultural master narratives and frameworks of intelligibility. In contrast to certain U.S. varieties of postmodernism, however, the variety of the Latin American postmodern discussed in this chapter is the cultural logic of the postdictatorship *as well as* that of late capitalism. Its affect is different, however: in place of a free-floating euphoria that uncritically accepts commodification (Jameson), there is a Benjaminian melancholia for the (high, unacceptable) social cost of capitalist restructuring. This melancholia appears in Eltit's afterthought in the passage above: "It is a pity, I thought." Without a doubt, here lies the key to the popularity of Eltit's work in U.S. academic circles: it offers an edge to the critique of late capitalism rarely found in the United States.

CADA's neo-avant-garde dissolution of the boundary between art and life explains its second programmatic feature, the interdisciplinarity and the interartistic nature of the artists' works. These works open up what performance theorist Diana Taylor calls the *archive* (written texts or documents) to the *repertoire* (embodied practice, such as speech, dance, sports, or music). This interdisciplinary impulse is essential to understanding Eltit's first novel: *Lumpérica* reads less like a novel and more like a script for a performance; it is narrative as much as a movie script. Indeed, Eltit made a point of reading *Lumpérica* in a site far removed from literary institutions, a brothel.

Apart from the *avanzada*, one major strategy of the post-Boom was to return to the documentary and social realism via the emergence of the collaborative genre of the *testimonio*. The *testimonio* continued to rely on a transparent language of communication to fulfill its antihegemonic purpose of giving voice to the silenced subaltern.[28] The *avanzada*, in contrast, rejected realism, opting instead for antirepresentationalism and a critique of the myth of language's transparency. As revealed in Zurita's aforementioned comment on the "appearance of the unstated," the vehicle of referential language could no longer be trusted. As might be expected, there were tensions throughout the *avanzada*'s tenure (between 1977 and its disintegration in the mid-1980s) with left groups remaining in Chile, who accused the *avanzada* of elitism and continued to adhere to the *testimonio* "for expressing solidarity with the popular struggle" (Richard, *Margins* 111). This debate on the politics of representation further illuminates the innovative quality of Eltit's *El padre mío,* which applies the experimental strategies of the *avanzada* to the *testimonio* genre (which is why it has been largely ignored by mainstream scholars of *testimonio*) (see Richard, *Residues* 52 and 183n5).

The *avanzada*'s deconstructive strategy of antirealism and artifice was shared by some (if not all) Chilean writers in exile, including José Donoso, who was living abroad on a fellowship at the time of the coup and who opted for exile until his return to Chile in the late 1980s.[29] Donoso explains that *Casa de campo* emerged from the crisis of representation caused by the Chilean political tragedy and his subsequent search for new strategies of writing: "In *Casa de campo* appears the tragedy, the necessity to speak about a Chilean issue. But facing the impossibility of doing this in my Chilean language, . . . *I had to invent a language,* as I had to invent a new country to be able to write about it. . . . I was consciously predisposed against magical realism, against the fantastic. I thought that the only thing that could serve to confront reality was not the fantastic but the artificial. I set myself the task to write this novel as an artifice, as a contestation of naturalism and realism."[30] A major Boom figure (outside the inner circle of the "fabulous four" of Julio Cortázar, Gabriel García Marquez, Mario Vargas Llosa, and Carlos Fuentes), Donoso is also the author of an influential memoir of the Boom, in which he argues that the Chilean 9/11 of the 1973 coup marks the emblematic event that ended the Boom.[31] Begun on September 18, 1973, and completed on June 19, 1978 (the dates are included in the Spanish edition only), *Casa de campo* marks Donoso's debut as a post-Boom writer for whom the dictatorships signal the need to replace magic realism's fictions of enchantment with a new literature of disenchantment. *Casa de campo* is an allegorical and antirealist historical novel that sets the dramatic events of the Allende years and the 1973 coup against the foil of Chile's traditional economic and social domination by a quasi-feudal oligarchy. Akin to *avanzada* strategies of disillusionment, *Casa de campo*'s resolute antinaturalism and artifice serve to demystify the false harmonies of the official self-representation of Pinochet's regime. Against Pinochet's rhetoric of continuity through economic progress and patriarchal social values, *Casa de campo* is organized around violent discontinuities assembled from the ruins of the post-1973 Chilean wasteland of culture.

Rather than juxtaposing antidictatorship texts from different countries—say, Argentina and Chile—in this chapter I compare two Chilean narratives of the interior and exile, respectively. My comparative discussion has two aims: first, to establish the significance of the neobaroque as a literary strategy that is employed across the division of post-Boom literatures of exile and of the interior, and second, building on this comparison, to tease out the distinct footprint the experience of living under the dictatorship has left on Eltit's antidictatorial texts. This dimension of living under the dictatorship is absent from Donoso's novel. Richard has identified one of the expressions emerging from living under the dictatorship as a "rhetoric of the [wounded] body" (*Margins* 65–73). Interactive with the performance arts, this work stages the destructive effects of the authoritarian regime on the body and its everyday practices, but brushed against the grain of power and turned against the official authorities of church and state. In contrast, the neobaroque dimension of Donoso's exile novel consists in a recovery of baroque forms of representation that remain squarely within the realm of the literary. In his Chilean historical novel that demystifies the propaganda of Pinochet's regime, Donoso avails himself of baroque illusionism, the distinctive baroque awareness of the kinship between appearance and reality, in which self-evident certainties are unmasked as fabrications and lies. Here the baroque's subjectivism becomes a critical tool in the project of emancipatory antirealism: because (to adapt Heinrich Wölfflin's famous observation) the baroque represents things "as they seem to be," in contrast to realism, which "represents things as they are," it can explore the disturbing proximity of truth and delusion and unmask the polished surfaces of normalizing national discourse.[32] As we shall see, both *Lumpérica* and *Casa de campo* give new life to Lezama Lima's thesis that the Latin American baroque is the "art of counterconquest."[33] Both works represent minoritarian baroques directed against the authoritarian state and its official self-representation.

Indeed, the seventeen-year Pinochet dictatorship created a deep chasm between Chilean literature at home and in exile. In her history of post-coup literature, Eugenia Brito draws a categorical line between Chilean literature at home and abroad: "I must clarify that I will never talk about the writers who reside outside of Chile" (14). She elaborates, "My work excludes texts written outside of Chile, or writers who have composed their works abroad. Future studies may offer an account of them. The literature of resistance is generated in Chile and has as its audience and authors Chileans who reside here, who lacked any institutional support or support from the mass media for the reception of their work" (21). In contrast to the domestic arts scene, Richard writes, Chilean exile art and literature

> did not feel the same urgency to question the systems which produce meaning as did the *avanzada,* who tried to "dissolve the boundaries between poetry, art, and politics." Overseas the exiled artists more or less remained faithful to the traditional techniques and genres, and did not attempt to deconstruct them. They appeared to respond to the trauma of separation, to the lost ties with history and biography by becoming fixated on repetition—as though the stability of forms would guarantee a continuity with the past, as though the reaffirmation of the duration of that past and its traditions would compensate for, or repair, their *loss of identity.* (*Margins* 112)

In part, the conflict between literature at home and in exile revolves around the question of which artistic strategy, the open protest characteristic of exiles such as Dorfman or the camouflaged protest of the interior, represents the most trenchant mode of opposition to the fascist regimes. More painfully, it revolves around accusations of co-optation by the official regime of the avant-garde work produced in the interior during the dictatorships. The exile Chilean writer Roberto Bolaño's savage caricature of the *avanzada* poet Zurita, the leading poet of the antidictatorship generation of Chileans residing in Chile, as a fascist bard and murderer in his detective novel *Estrella distante* (1996; *Distant Star*) is a recent and telling example.[34] It testifies to the gulf that divides exile from domestic Chilean literature of the Pinochet years. The historical Zurita is unrecognizable in Bolano's diabolical avant-garde poet Carlos Wieder, who rises to fame after the coup as Chile's new major writer. Eulogized (like Zurita) by conservative Christian critics in the pages of the regime's press, Wieder proclaims the revolution of Chilean poetry through the same interartistic performance poetry practiced by Zurita. With a Nazi Messerschmitt plane borrowed from the military, Wieder writes poems in the sky above Chile, in prophetic, biblical language that parodies the Christian rhetoric in Zurita's poem "La vida nueva" ("The New Life"), written in the sky above New York in 1982. But in the place of Zurita's self-mutilation, Wieder practices the persecution, mutilation, and murder of others—fellow poets from the Popular Unity years, which he also photographs. He then organizes a private exhibit of these photographs (for military and friends only) as "visual poetry." Bolaño's novel thus fires off a fierce polemic against the *avanzada*'s neo-avant-garde rhetoric of "making it new" in general, and the fusion of art and life in CADA's unofficial urban spectacles in particular, which is symptomatic of the exile-interior schism. Bolaño's first-person narrator plays the role of the detective, who retrospectively investigates the decades-old crimes of the poet-assassin Wieder. Yet Bolaño's Sherlock Holmes clearly adheres to a Chilean hermeneutic of exile that fails to understand the more complex codes of Chilean antidictatorship art of the interior.

Even though Eltit has not been the target of such attacks, the danger of co-optation looms over all art and literature produced under the dictatorship.[35] For antidictatorship works produced in the interior operate within a double-bind structured by the repressive conditions of public expression, in which censorship constitutes one pole and the goal of subverting it the other. Like a criminal or a con artist, the antidictatorship writer has to hide her subversive message under a mask—the disguise of authorized discourse—which by the very fact of its being authorized also runs the risk of co-optation and assimilation by official, authoritarian discourse. Publishing under the dictatorship is a treacherous terrain in which "zones of resistance" (Richard, *Margins* 27) and zones of acquiescence and conformity overlap within the same work, simply because an element of conformity—even if duplicitous—is the sine qua non for publication.

In an interview, Diamela Eltit recounts the anxieties surrounding the 1983 publication of *Lumpérica,* her first novel, which she feared would be banned, as she thought it "too subversive, too anti-dictatorial" (Morales, *Conversaciones* 148). And yet, when the time came to take the manuscript to the censorship office, it was approved instantly: "They approved it in a half hour. . . . The censor opened the novel surely and said, no, but he let it pass. . . . And I was certain . . . that I was not going to get past the censor. . . . But no. I did not have the slightest problem. Because, of course, maybe I didn't pick up on their signals. But how strange, I said, these people, that would approve this subversive novel. . . . How extraordinary . . . I thought" (149). Eltit's unspoken worries can be read between the lines: could a text as subversive as *Lumpérica* possibly be misread? If so, could this mean that the work is compromised after all, contrary to what the author had thought? In retrospect, Eltit's worries were unfounded, since the reception of *Lumpérica* in the main focused on the same transgression and marginality (of class, gender, power, genre) the author intended.[36] The main price Eltit paid for the orientation of her work was being ignored and dismissed as "incomprehensible." Eltit recalls that *Lumpérica*'s publication did not elicit an immediate response: "Three or four articles came out that were cautiously positive."[37]

I close this introduction to the antidictatorship neobaroque with some concluding remarks on the period framework of Eltit's and Donoso's works discussed here. It is no accident that both the Donoso and the Eltit neobaroque texts selected were published early in the era of the military dictatorships, during Pinochet's regime. In the 1990s, Chilean as well as Southern Cone postdictatorship literature entered a new phase (related to the rise of a new generation of writers, including Roberto Bolaño and McOndo writers such as Alberto Fuguet) whose poetics are neither neo-avant-garde nor neobaroque but instead engage in yet further post-Boom varieties of postmodernisms and new realisms. For example, Bolaño's *Historia de la literatura Nazi in América* (1996; *Nazi Literature in the Americas*) is a make-believe literary history of extreme right-wing writers (all invented) from Argentina to the United States and from the early to the late twentieth century.[38] Another narrative mode that has become more prominent is the Latin American *novela neopoliciaca* (detective fiction), which emerged earlier in the 1970s, appearing, for example, in Piglia's *Respiración artificial* (1981; *Artificial Respiration*), as well as in Bolaño's *Estrella distante*.[39] Sifting through evidence to reconstruct and solve a crime, the detective story brings to postdictatorship narrative a unifying impulse that puts scattered fragments of knowledge back together into a single coherent narrative. As the example of *Estrella distante* shows, detective fiction's assimilating impulse is antithetical to the neobaroque's fragmented constructions. Donoso's second antidictatorship novel, *La desesperanza* (1986; *Curfew*), a political-literary autobiographical fiction about the return of a Chilean exile, a famous protest singer, in the mid-1980s, is a neorealist narrative.[40] And while Eltit's neo-avant-garde work continues in the twenty-first century, she has turned away from the neobaroque strategies of *Lumpérica* and *El padre mío*. Her recent postdictatorship narratives, *Los vigilantes* (1994; *Custody of the Eyes*) and *Mano de obra* (2002; Manual labor), for example, which protest the commodification of social relations in free-market Chile, retain an allegorical abstraction in their plots and characters. But their language is too spare to be baroque; the exhuberant theatricality of *Lumpérica* is missing.[41]

This is not to say, however, that the neobaroque has faded with increasing temporal distance from the dictatorships. As demonstrated by the important 1996 collection of neobaroque Latin American poetry *Medusario*, the neobaroque represents a major paradigm of Latin American poetry since the 1960s that continues to gather force in the twenty-first century.[42] The chief aim of *Medusario* is precisely to offer evidence of the ongoing popularity of the neobaroque: it includes antidictatorship poets from Argentina (Perlongher) and Chile (Gonzalo Muñoz) but extends significantly beyond that era. As Jacobo Sefamí has shown, the neobaroque movement in poetry was influenced by, but ultimately continues independently of, the writers of the several (nationally focused) antidictatorships.[43] Nourished by several sources, including Lezama Lima's and Sarduy's essays and the work of the Brazilian concretists, in particular Haroldo de Campos's essays and his collection of poetry, *Galaxias* (1984), poets across the American hemisphere, from Argentina to Mexico to Latin American poets living in the United States (the Cuban José Kozer and the Uruguayan Eduardo Espina), specialize in the neobaroque poetics of extravagant play with the materiality of the signifier.

Baroque Allegory: Writing History from the Ruins with Benjamin

In my earlier discussion of Eliot's *Waste Land,* I referred in some detail to Benjamin's theory of baroque allegory. Here I want to take up Benjamin's theory again in greater depth, and present it in light of the related yet distinct problematic of the Latin American antidictatorship neobaroque. In *The Origin of German Tragic Drama,* Benjamin draws a categorical distinction between tragedy proper and the baroque *Trauerspiel,* or tragic drama: whereas tragedy interprets myth, the subject of baroque plays is (secular) history. It is this secular history—ancient and contemporary seventeenth-century history of religious and imperial warfare, regicide, and revolution—that the *Trauerspiel* authors (the Silesian Protestant playwrights Andreas Gryphius, Daniel Casper von Lohenstein, Johann Christian Hallmann, and others) present as ruin and decay: "In the ruin history has physically merged into the setting" (*Origin* 178).[44] Compared to Eliot's philosophical critique of dissociated modernity, for Latin American antidictatorship writers (as for Benjamin himself) this notion of history as ruin takes on a special urgency as it refers to contemporary political cataclysms of fascisms and dictatorships. In addition, the late capitalist free-market policies of the Latin American military regimes shed new light on Benjamin's analyses of allegory beyond the seventeenth-century baroque proper—the study of Baudelaire and the nineteenth-century culture of capitalist modernity in the unfinished *Arcades Project.*[45] In the development from the *Trauerspiel* study to the *Arcades Project,* the seventeenth-century problematic of allegory and melancholia is expanded into the triangular constellation of allegory, melancholia, and commodity that, according to Benjamin, is specific to Baudelaire's capitalist nineteenth century.[46]

According to Benjamin, allegory operates under the signature of the untimely. "Brush[ing] history against the grain" ("Theses" 257), it affords an insight into the transience of things that is antithetical to notions of history as progress and organic continuity.[47] The history that is presented on the baroque stage—and that "merges into the setting" (*Origin* 92)—is a wasteland of ruins, strewn with the rubble and the residues of the obsolete, shattered past. Two important ideas underpin Benjamin's proposition that "in allegory the observer is confronted with the *facies hippocratica* of history as a petrified, primordial landscape" from which all life has been extinguished (*Origins* 166). One is allegory's demystifying, critical function (in comparison to the "organic" symbol, and, more poignantly for our capitalist times, the fantastic aura of the commodity): by presenting objects in their late, exhausted stage—as discarded garbage rather than the latest fashion, as ruins and corpses instead of living nature—it exposes the destructive effect of time. By extirpating the semblance of beauty, allegory dismantles the illusion of organic continuity: "The majesty of allegorical intention: the destruction of life and the organic—the extinction of appearances."[48] Allegory's utility for antidictatorship art and literature is obvious: the anti-illusionist, demystifing nature of allegory makes it an ideal tool to destroy "the false unity constructed by the dictatorial process" (Brito 15), to shatter the false harmonies of the official culture of Pinochet's Chile. It also demolishes the aura of the commodity, which Pinochet's economic policy had prioritized above the lives of citizens, whose losses have in turn been assigned to official oblivion. Allegory demystifies what the symbol—and, more recently and urgently, the culture of late capitalism—falsely idealize. In her recent study of postdictatorial Chile of the 1990s, *Cultural Residues,* Richard's critical approach is explicitly Benjaminian. Richard enters the cultural field of Chilean late capitalism from the strategic site of the "residual" (the remnants of the past, repressed memories, disappeared bodies, broken cultural narratives) in order to expose the erasures and fabrications underpinning the official values of the present, the transition to democracy—"modernization, consensus, market, pluralism, etc." (*Residues* 4).

In addition to the critical strategy of writing history from the ruins, another key Benjaminian concept to be noted in this context is the notion of history as catastrophe. The baroque sense of history as decay contains an insight that proved revolutionary for Benjamin's subsequent development of a materialist and antiteleological philosophy of history. In his work on Baudelaire and nineteenth-century mass culture, he encountered the same shattering of the object world, but in contrast to baroque allegory, decay no longer is the natural result of life's transience but is engineered and accelerated by capitalist commodification. And just as allegory is a willful montage of image and intellectual meaning, so commodities are priced arbitrarily; there is no organic connection between objects and their exchange value. Hence, "emblems return as commodities" ("Zentralpark" 675). For Benjamin, allegory thus becomes a timely instrument for the writing of history, modern and baroque. In the 1940 essay "Theses on the Philosophy of History," Benjamin proposes his neobaroque theory of history as catastrophe, not progress. The historian's task is not to tell the past "the way it really was" (introducing a coherence that does not exist) but rather to "seize hold of a memory as it flashes up at a moment of danger" ("Theses" 255). Benjamin's famous "angel of history" understands what "we" (Benjamin's figure of a collective implied reader) don't: that history is not "a chain of events" but "one single catastrophe which keeps piling wreckage upon wreckage" (257). Looking back to the past, the angel of history "would like to stay, awaken the dead, and make whole what has been smashed" (257). But he cannot; the passage of time propels him "into the future . . . while the pile of debris before him grows skyward" (258). In this way, modernity's master narrative of progress—recently reissued in the neoliberal doctrines of the Chicago Boys—is demystified as a fiction: neither a single concept nor person, neither the supernatural savior-angel nor his self-styled secular counterpart, the dictator, can redeem the heap of trash and rubble that is history.

Benjamin's radical revision of the historical method was, in Susan Buck-Morss's words, to "search for truth in the 'garbage heap' of modern history, the 'rags, the trash,' the ruins of commodity production."[49] According to Benjamin, "The concept of progress must be founded in the idea of catastrophe. That things continue 'as they are' *is* the catastrophe" ("Zentralpark" 246). To write history from the ruins means to mourn the human and material cost of the so-called progress that official regimes want to erase and forget. There are strong parallels between Donoso's allegorical method of telling the history of Chile in *Casa de campo* and Benjamin's philosophy of history. Both employ a "construction of history that looks backward, rather than forward, at the destruction of material nature as it *has actually taken place,* [and that] provides dialectical contrast to the futurist myth of historical progress (which can only be sustained by forgetting what has happened)" (Buck-Morss 95). *Casa de campo* similarly exposes the discontinuity of Latin American history as the proverbial heap of rubble.

"Theses" also displays Benjamin's own allegorical critical method at work: the baroque inspired Benjamin's famous conceptual allegory of the angel of history, composed, in the manner of an emblem, as a textual commentary on an image (Paul Klee's painting *Angelus Novus*). The angel of history belongs to the related idiosyncratic Benjaminian genres of philosophical allegories, or *Denkbilder* (thought pictures), and what (after 1935 and in the context of the *Arcades Project*) he came to call dialectical images. Their internal structure, combining images and text, is borrowed from the early modern emblem.[50] Widely circulated between the sixteenth and eighteenth centuries, emblems are picture-poems composed of a montage of three clearly distinguished parts: an image, a title or interpretive motto placed above it (*inscriptio*), and a commentary or interpretive poem (*subscriptio*) placed below.[51] The very separation, in the emblem, of the two dimensions of the sign, presentation and representation, signifier (the picture) and signified (the text), exposes the artificiality and posteriority of meaning-making. The emblem illustrates the discontinuity of the abstract and the concrete unified in the Romantic symbol: there is an image that presents something, an idea or maxim or moral lesson, which the text makes explicit. For the early modern reader, part of the pleasure of reading emblems was to solve the puzzle posed by the icon and decoded by the text. An avid collector of emblems, Benjamin situates the emblem (along with allegory, without drawing a clear distinction between them) in the *Trauerspiel* study within the historical context of the baroque crisis and the disintegration of the medieval and Christian outlook.[52] In the emblem or allegorical sign, representation does not heal the ravages wrought by history and politics but *rearticulates them* at the level of (literary, artistic) expression—through decentered, broken wholes, compositions that Eco and de Campos would later come to call open works. This is the meaning of Benjamin's aphorism, "Allegories are, in the realm of thoughts, what ruins are in the realm of things" (*Origin* 178). As Theresa Kelley puts it, the emblem/allegory shows "how images might also be ruins, montage-like assemblages from the past" (255).

In contrast to the emblem, however, the Benjaminian *Denkbild* and the dialectical image do not include any visuals; instead, they explore the dialectic of abstraction and sensuous realism within language alone, as if to marry Pound's or Williams's imagism to its antithesis, conceptual discourse. But following the model of the emblem artist or allegorist, the meaning Benjamin ascribes to Klee's painting is not induced from it but projected onto it by way of a sovereign, arbitrary act. As Benjamin explains in the *Trauerspiel* study, the allegorist "must not conceal the fact that his activity is one of arranging," for the "principal impression . . . aimed at" in his work is "its obviously constructed quality" (*Origin* 179). Akin to Eliot's ideals of undissociated expression and metaphysical poetry, *Denkbilder* and dialectical images are critical conceits in which abstract thought is yoked to concrete images that are its sensuous equivalents. They are produced by extracting material from the falsifying, narcotic official master narratives of history and presenting it directly: "Method of this project: literary montage. I needn't *say* anything. Merely show" (*Arcades* 460). Benjamin's critical conceits intended nothing less than to remake and renovate philosophical and historical discourse. Along with the montage method of collating quotations and abstract reflection in the *Trauerspiel* study, these new forms demonstrate Benjamin's employment of allegory as a critical strategy of his own neobaroque cultural and literary criticism.

There are affinities with Eltit's and Donoso's emphasis on allegory and artifice, which I examine in the following sections. The concept of character in Donoso's *Casa de campo* is explicitly derived from the early modern emblem: "I make no appeal to my readers to 'believe' my characters: I would rather that they were taken as emblems" (Donoso, *House* 286). In *Casa de campo,* allegory works at the level of plot, character, and narration, without dismantling the genre of the novel as such. The same is the case in the grounding of Eliot's *Waste Land* in the genre of poetry: fragmentary strategies in both Donoso and Eliot stop short of disassembling the realm of the literary as such. The situation is different in Eltit's *Lumpérica.* Here, avant-garde poetics of fragmentation and montage position the work on the borderline between literature and the visual or performance arts. Throughout her work, Eltit rarely presents places (such as the house), the body, or characters as wholes—only fragments are seen. Benjamin's notion of allegory, and of the allegorical work as "consciously constructed ruins" (*Origin* 182), has often been related to avant-garde montage, although Benjamin never did so himself.[53] Nevertheless, Peter Bürger founds his *Theory of the Avant-garde* and its principal concept of the "nonorganic work of art" on Benjamin's notion of allegory. Bürger identifies the numerous correspondences in principles (antirealism and artifice) and procedures: the extraction of material from its original function (or life context); the combination and assemblage of discontinuous and dissimilar material into new, artificially constructed wholes; the arbitrary assignment of meaning regardless of original functions and contexts. "For avantgardistes," Bürger concludes, "material is just that, material. Their activity initially consists in nothing other than in killing the 'life' of the material, that is, in tearing it out of its functional context that gives it meaning" (70).

The Wounded Self and the Baroque Iconography of Sanctified Suffering in Diamela Eltit's *Lumpérica*

Diamela Eltit's neo-avant-garde postdictatorship narrative *Lumpérica* (1983) is deeply interactive with the visual and performance arts: a succession of ten scenes rather than a continuous plot, it reads like a film script or a script for a performance. Set on a single winter night in a public square in the Chilean capital Santiago, it has as one of its themes the visual panopticism of state power, embodied in a flashing neon sign (El Luminoso), whose cold electric light drenches the nightly residents of the square, the woman protagonist (L. Iluminada) and an anonymous urban crowd, the "pale people," or homeless who congregate in the square at night despite the curfew.[54] *Lumpérica* presents a succession of scenes in this complex triangulated relationship between the allegorical eye of state power and its citizen subjects, which are at once stages in the physical and spiritual torment of L. Iluminada and the urban homeless at the hands of sadistic power, but also stages in their symbolic redemption and liberation.

Like CADA's citywide performances, *Lumpérica* is set outdoors. Eltit's first novel emerges directly from CADA's neo-avant-garde emphasis on making art outside of institutions and enclosed spaces (the museum) and inserting it into everyday life. The fifth and sixth chapters of *Lumpérica* narrate the writing of graffiti in the square, recalling CADA's 1983 "No +" initiative of writing on the walls of the city. *Lumpérica*'s very setting announces its counterhegemonic program. Notably, its public space belongs to a residential neighborhood; it is not the central square (*plaza mayor*) of the Latin American city, site of government buildings and home of the political elite.[55] In a much-cited claim, Brito affirms that *Lumpérica* has done no less than restore the possibility of narrating the city in the post-1973 Chilean novel. After *Lumpérica*'s publication, "the literature of Resistance would see the city and its inhabitants appear in the literary space opened by Eltit"; henceforth, "the city would circulate more freely in Chilean literature" (Brito 111). Incorporating the military's destruction of the public sphere, previous narratives published in the interior had taken refuge in closed spaces (ibid. 111; "espacios cerrados").[56]

Eltit affirms what the French urbanist Henri Lefebvre calls "the right to the city" as the concrete, spatial condition of fundamental citizenship rights.[57] Civic freedoms (of expression, of congregation, and so forth) are linked to urban practices—of walking, gathering, meeting, talking. The "right to the city" reclaims urban space for the unofficial realm of the everyday, and the everyday practices of urban users. This unofficial city and its spontaneous urban practices have been marginalized by capitalism and the city of capitalist spectacle (Debord). Reduced almost totally to shopping, consumption, tourism, and other commercial activities, the late twentieth-century city must be recovered for symbolic and spatial practices and uses distinct from the circulation of commodities and the generation of profit. "The claim to nature, and the desire to enjoy it," writes Lefebvre, "displace the right to the city" (Lefebvre 158). However, to "flee the deteriorating and unrenovated city" (158) for nature is a false solution: what must be salvaged are not green spaces but public spaces and the city as the work (*oeuvre*) of citizens. The nightly activities depicted in *Lumpérica* follow the same impulse: to appropriate the space of a public city square for the uses of its citizens, in violation of the military curfew that prohibits them and that keeps watch over the violent imposition of the city of capitalist spectacle in Chile. In the police interrogation that is recorded in the second and seventh chapters, the interrogator keeps returning to the initial, ominous question that he poses to the unnamed detainee: "¿cuál es la utilidad de la plaza pública?" (What is the purpose of a city square?) (*Lumpérica* 47; *E. Luminata* 50). The counterhegemonic answer is given by the graffiti in the square and other insubordinate actions.

According to Brito, *Lumpérica* is situated at the crossroads of three paradigms that mark its marginality: lumpen, América, and the figure of woman (123). The first chapter is a series of film shots that establishes the basic parameters of power and resistance, official and unofficial city. It also establishes the metaphorics of power as vision: a flashing neon sign installed on top of a building in the square named "El Luminoso" (the luminous one) is the personification of the official power of the state in Chile. "L. Iluminada" (the illuminated one), the main protagonist, is the paradigmatic citizen-subject. From Plato to Descartes and beyond, as Martin Jay has shown, vision has been synonymous with truth in Western culture.[58]

Western discourses of philosophy, politics, and religion are pervaded with visual metaphors that exalt vision as the "noblest of the senses." *Lumpérica* takes up this visual metaphorics of knowledge as "enlightenment" (and darkness as irrationality, delusion, error, nature, the feminine) to structure its setting—the darkness of night, broken only by the artificial lighting of the neon sign and street lamps—and the hierarchy of power. Lying on her back in the center of the square and moving her limbs to the rhythm of the neon light in a mixture of pain and passion approximating ecstasy as portrayed by St. Teresa, L. Iluminada is metaphorically "enlightened" as she is physically lit up by the neon sign. The English translation (*E. Luminata*) also captures the meaning of the main protagonist's name: "the illuminated/enlightened one." It quickly becomes clear, though, that this name states an ideal rather than a fact, and that the rituals the protagonist undergoes from dusk to dawn, accompanied by the homeless lumpen, serve the purpose of attaining the authentic enlightenment that she is named for. This moment arrives at the end of the sixth chapter, whose last page is blank, except for these words: "Escribió:/iluminada entera, encendida" (She wrote:/illuminated entirely, turned on) (*Lumpérica* 144; *E. Luminata* 134). On the previous page, we find the content of the central insight:

Nuevas fundaciones
como llamado de atención para que los chilenos
descansen sus espaldas en esas máquinas que
alzarán en varios centímetros sus cerebros.
Nos contaron que en esas fundaciones hubo
vencedores y vencidos.
Yo digo que eso es verdad a medias: hubo
vencidos y muertos. Nada más.
(*Lumpérica* 143)

(New foundations
like a trumpet call to Chileans
so they rest their backs on those machines that
elevate their brains by several centimeters.
It's been told to us that on these foundations there were
conquerors and conquered.
I say that's a half truth: there were
conquered and corpses. Nothing else.)
(*E. Luminata* 133)

The utopian discourse ("new foundations") referred to is that of Pinochet's regime, which used to stage public spectacles to celebrate anniversaries of the coup in the 1970s. And the central insight is a Benjaminian one that questions the official history of the victors who claim progress for themselves. Alternatively, it finds truth by searching the wasteland for the victim's corpses left in the wake of the victor's progress.

As might be expected, L. Iluminada's authentic enlightenment has no relation to the artificial rays of the neon sign, which represents (to borrow Mary Louise Pratt's phrase) the "relentless drone" (resembling "martial music played on radio during a coup") that was the monolithic, homogeneous, and prescriptive discourse with which the regime showered Chilean citizens, through its early years in particular (Pratt 23). The fascist state interpellates its citizens and assigns them their "proper" identities. The opening scene is about this ritual of becoming-subject via the subjection to state ideology: "Porque el frío en esta plaza es el tiempo que se ha marcado para suponerse un nombre propio, donado por el letrero que se encenderá y se apagerá, rítmico y ritual, en el proceso que en definitiva les dará la vida: su identificación ciudadana" (Because the cold in this public square is the hour appointed for assuming a proper name, bestowed by the signboard that will turn on and off, rhythmic and ritual, in the process that will definitively give them life: their civic identity) (*Lumpérica* 9; *E. Luminata* 14). The signboard (and source of illumination) itself represents Althusser's ideological state apparatuses (ISAs), the state institutions (mass media, education, religion, etc.) that work to create obedient citizens by indoctrinating them with prescripted values.[59] In her education in the Department of Humanistic Studies at the University of Chile, Eltit and her collaborators read much French poststructuralist theory, including Foucault, Lacan, and Derrida, which became a formative influence in her writing.[60] No regime survives in the long term by relying on violent force alone, administered by repressive state apparatuses (RSAs), such as the military, the police, the prison system, etc. Even as Pinochet's RSAs laid brutal siege to Chile, he pursued the project of normalizing his regime by manufacturing consent through ISAs (a goal that, however, would elude him in the end). L. Iluminada's "assuming a proper name" and "civic identity" (*E. Luminata*) assigned to her by El Luminoso dramatizes the process Althusser describes: ideology "hails or interpellates concrete individuals as concrete subjects" (Althusser 117). For Althusser, ideology operates through a paradigmatic scene of greeting and recognition: ideology greets the individual ("Hey, you there! L. Iluminada"), when she answers the call she has assumed the identity (subjectivity) assigned to her.

Lumpérica's opening scene stages this process of the transmission of ideology through the realm of subjectivity theorized by Althusser (following Lacan). Ideology is not false consciousness but the "imaginary relationship of individuals to their real conditions of existence" (Althusser 109). The claustrophobic atmosphere derives from the panoptic presence of state institutions. There is no escape: public space is under His Eye. L. Iluminada is lying on her back because this posture allegorizes the individual's vulnerable posture before state institutions. For the same reason, Eltit depicts a night scene where lighting is artificial rather than natural: the state's address of citizens is not neutral or organic, but only masquerades as such. The opening paragraphs point out the difference between how brightly L. Iluminada's face shines in natural light and how "la luz eléctrica la maquilla fraccionando sus ángulos" (the electric light makes her up by splitting her angles) (*Lumpérica* 9; *E. Luminata* 14). Notice the following passage, which describes the process of interpellation by presenting it at once as baptism and as sexual intercourse. It highlights the blending of domination by social forces with the individual's own imagination and desire:

> L. Iluminada en el centro de la plaza empieza otra vez a convulsionarse. Los pálidos . . . fijan sus miradas en el bautizo, mientras el luminoso acomete directo en ella que, frenética, mueve las caderas bajo la luz: sus muslos se levantan del suelo y su cabeza colgante se golpea por tantas sacudidas contra el pavimiento.
>
> Le ratifica el nombre en dos colores paralelos, el luminoso ampliado sobre el cuerpo escribe L. Iluminada y rítmicamente va pasando la cantidad posible de apodos. (*Lumpérica* 10)

> (E. Luminata in the center of the square starts to convulse again. The pale people . . . rivet their gaze on the baptism, while the illuminated sign directly strikes her who, frenetic, moves her hips under the light: her thighs rise from the ground and her drooping head pounds from so much striking against the pavement.
>
> It confirms her name in two parallel colors, that lighted sign spread across her body writes E. Luminata and runs rhythmically through the possible gamut of aliases.) (*E. Luminata* 15)

During L. Iluminada's baptism the third party in the cast of characters enters. "Llegan los desharrapados de Santiago, pálidos y malolientes a buscar su área" (The ragged people of Santiago arrive, pale and stinking, in search of their space) (*Lumpérica* 9; *E. Luminata* 14). The homeless lumpen are also assigned their proper names, though of a generic type: "serán nombrados genéricamente pálidos como escalafón provisorio. . . . [El luminoso] sigue tirando la suma de nombres que los va a confirmar como existencia" (they will be generically named the pale people as a provisional ranking. . . . [El luminoso] goes on printing out the sum of names that will confirm their existence) (*Lumpérica* 9–10; *E. Luminata* 14). But the neon sign also assigns specific economic identities to the urban underclass: "el luminoso anuncia que se venden cuerpos. Sí, cuerpos se venden en la plaza" (the sign announces bodies for sale. That's right, bodies are sold in the square) (*Lumpérica* 13; *E. Luminata* 18). The indirect meaning is not hard to find—in the social inequality of the post-coup transition from state to market, which delivered Chilean workers as a cheap workforce to global markets and imposed extreme hardships on the poor. The lumpen's economic interpellation as a cheap labor force is equally answered by the lumpen's self-(mis)recognition: "Por puro deseo propietarios al venderse al luminoso como mercaderías. Esos son los que se esperan con ansias" (Proprietors out of sheer desire as they sell themselves to the sign like merchandise. These are the ones who wait eagerly) (*Lumpérica* 14; *E. Luminata* 19).

If the dictatorship's interpellation of Chilean citizens as uncritical, willing subjects of the regime marks *Lumpérica*'s starting point, its subsequent trajectory follows an antithetical quest for subversion. Imprinted with their official names and functions, L. Iluminada and the lumpen seek to undo and remake the official script that has been tattooed on their skins. In Pratt's fitting phrase, the object is "overwriting Pinochet," a quest for reappropriation that hinges on its performative nature. Michel de Certeau's notion of everyday practice and his distinction between strategies and tactics are helpful in explaining why and how. If (following Althusser and Foucault), de Certeau contends, the "grid of 'discipline' is everywhere becoming clearer and more extensive, it is all the more urgent to discover how an entire society resists being reduced to it."[61] Despite state institutions' and capitalism's best efforts to reduce people to passive consumers of official ideologies—compare how L. Iluminada and the lumpen are entranced by the light of Pinochet's ISA as the bearer of truth in the first scene—ideological hegemony is unstable. Within the space of the official city, there is the realm of the unplanned, unofficial city and its diverse practices belonging to urban users, who inhabit, and "make do" with, the urban spaces they do not control. These practices (such as walking, talking, or—to offer examples from *Lumpérica*—rubbing each other in the cold, neighing, and writing in the square) are mobile operations (tactics) that cannot count on a space of their own, an institutional location. "The place of tactic belongs to the other. A tactic insinuates itself into the other's place, fragmentarily, without taking it over in its entirety. . . . Whatever it wins, it does not keep" (de Certeau, *Practice* xix).

De Certeau's observations on everyday practice elucidate the nature and condition of the strange, frequently bizarre performances and rituals of the remainder of *Lumpérica*. There are no alternative spaces to escape to, and public space remains under the eye of El Luminoso. Yet even as the official system continues in its efforts to impose order and authority, the nightly inhabitants reappropriate and thereby resignify their identities (individual and collective), as well as public space. Nonetheless, by the time morning arrives, nothing remains of this varied repertoire of practice. It can only count on stealing time, not on permanently repossessing public space. The institutional archive (Taylor) remains in the hands of power. (To be sure, the performances of reappropriation have been recorded, since we can read about them between the covers of a book. But Eltit's published novel never entered any institutional settings in the dictatorship years.)

In particular, the second scene announces the beginning of the anti-institutional counterspectacle to El Luminoso's official spectacle of state interpellation: "Por eso lo que resta de este nuevo anochecer será el verdadero reencuentro para L. Iluminada y los pálidos" (That's why the remains of this new nightfall will be the true meeting of E. Luminata and the pale people) (*Lumpérica* 19; *E. Luminata* 24). To undo the official baptism, L. Iluminada embarks on an orgy of self-mutilation. First, "estrella su cabeza contra el árbol una y otra vez hasta que la sangre rebasa su piel" (she smashes her head against the tree again and again until the blood overflows the skin) (*Lumpérica* 19; *E. Luminata* 24) and walks around the square parading "el goce de su propia herida" (her pleasure in her own wound) (*Lumpérica* 19; *E. Luminata* 24). Next, she sticks her hand into the campfire that the lumpen have lit to warm themselves until the skin blisters and discolors. The self-inflicted wound makes a mark on the body that unwrites the tattoo of the official baptism: "Y así la quemada te dará nueva cicatriz que le forjará el cuerpo a voluntad" (And so the burned one will give her a new scar that will forge her body as she wills) (*Lumpérica* 37; *E. Luminata* 42). Throughout the process of her self-wounding, she repeatedly utters the words, "tengo sed" (I'm thirsty), which are Christ's words on the cross. A collective—epochal—symbolism underpins her self-injuring: "El nuevo daño se ha producido y por ella otros dañados comparecen. Se ha abierto un nuevo circuito en la literatura" (The new injury has been produced and because of it other injured make their appearance. A new circuit has been opened in literature) (*Lumpérica* 36; *E. Luminata* 42). In other words, L. Iluminada's self-mutilation remembers, and thereby redeems, the "other injured," the victims of state terror, who have been erased from memory by the official politics of oblivion.

At this point, we encounter one of *Lumpérica*'s core neobaroque strategies: Eltit's appropriation of the Passion of Christ and the iconography of hagiography so popular in the Counter-Reformation baroque. Like Barnes, Eltit is not religious. But the ten-step process of suffering depicted in her movielike novel recalls the stations of the cross, and L. Iluminada's communion with the urban beggars recalls Christ's self-sacrifice on behalf of fallen humanity. A postmodern (or neobaroque) female redeemer in the genealogy of Christ, L. Iluminada takes up the cross of physical martyrdom to mourn and redeem the victimization of the citizens of Chile under the dictatorship. Eltit (like Barnes) appropriates the baroque iconography of sanctified suffering to create a secular mythology of her personal agony as well as of the collective agony of the Chilean people under Pinochet. The holy martyrdom of Jesus and the saints is suffering in the service of *a cause* (the faith for which they were persecuted and died), suffering that is redemptive and heroic (rather than abject and meaningless). Baroque religious art and the cult of the saints enabled Eltit to create a glamorous, stylized representation of the psychological and physical torment Chileans endured under the dictatorship. It is from their agony that Eltit (like other neo-avant-garde Chilean writers of the time, such as Zurita) fashioned her resistant political art, which covertly pointed to a time and place beyond the dictatorship. In Eltit's case (as in Barnes's), it is also a specifically female art that investigates the gendering of torture, of the tormented body and heroic endurance. Eltit's strategy differs from that of Barnes in placing the emphasis not on the individual but on the symbolic ties that self-inflicted pain knits between the individual and the collective. As Richard explains, "Zurita and Eltit appeal to pain as a way of approaching the borderline between individual and collective experience. . . . The threshold of pain enables the mutilated subject to enter areas of collective identification, sharing in one's own flesh the same signs of social disadvantage as the other unfortunates" (*Margins* 66–68).

Chapter 8, titled "Ensayo General" (Dress Rehearsal), is prefaced by a photograph of L. Iluminada (embodied by Eltit herself) with her arms injured and bandaged, reminiscent of the dramatic images of Jesus's agony on the Via Dolorosa. In clinical detail, the text of chapter 8 describes how L. Iluminada inflicts the stigmata on her body by scarring her skin with a knife: "Horizontal sentido acusa la primera línea o corte del brazo izquierdo./Es solamente marca, signo o escritura que va a separar la mano que se libera mediante la línea que la antecede. Este es el corte con la mano" (Horizontal direction betrays the first line or cut on the left arm./It is solely a mark, sign or writing that is going to separate the hand that frees itself by means of the preceding line. This is the cut by the hand) (*Lumpérica* 165; *E. Luminata* 153) (fig. 6). The photograph, dating from Eltit's 1980 performance *Maipu* at a brothel, shows Eltit seated and facing the camera, with her bare arms stretched out before her and resting on her knees so as to present the wounds directly to the spectator. Her forearms are covered with bandages, under which patches of blood are visible. Eltit makes direct eye contact with the spectator; her gaze is serious and intense. Eltit's pose can be traced directly to a specific figure from the iconography of the Passion of Christ, the so-called Man of Sorrows.

The Man of Sorrows is a devotional image that depicts Christ bearing the stigmata (the five wounds) but that is also detached from a specific scene of any of the traditional fourteen stations of the cross (fig. 7). According to Gertrud Schiller, the Man of Sorrows is the Christ who has suffered and through his suffering brought Redemption, who lives and is the Redeemer present in his eternal suffering. This is the distinction between the Man of Sorrows and the figure of Christ in other devotional images centered on the Passion, which depict him in a specific situation at a specific moment before his Death (Christ bearing the Cross, Christ on the column of the Flagellation, *Herrgottsruh* [Repose of the Lord], Christ in Distress, or as a mourned corpse [Lamentation], *Pietà*). If some of the works depict stations on the way of the Passion that leads to the Crucifixion and others the mourning of

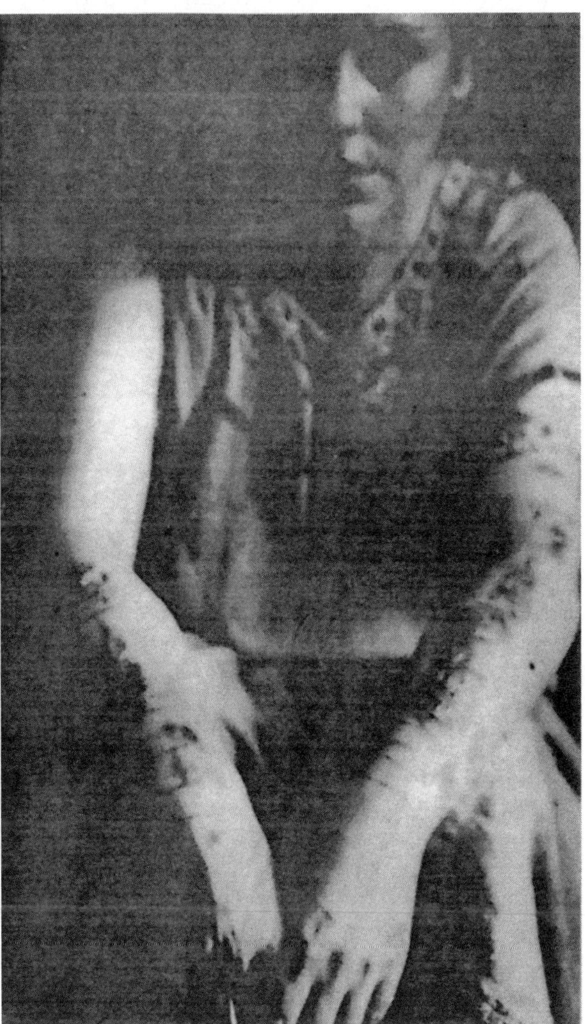

Fig. 6. Diamela Eltit as L. Iluminada (photographic portrait with self-inflicted cuts and burns from *Maipu* art action). (Reproduced by permission of the artist)

> the dead Christ, the Man of Sorrows is an image of the Redeemer who participates equally in life and death. The Man of Sorrows differs from the figures of Christ in the stations of the Passion in that he always bears the wounds . . . ; [he differs] from the dead Christ by his living posture (he may stand, sit, or kneel), his gestures, and often . . . by his open eyes.[62]

In short, the Man of Sorrows conveys an abstract statement of the spiritual significance of Christ's sacrifice—the redemption of sinful mankind. It is addressed to man: "See what I have suffered for thee." "Accept my sacrifice." Schiller elaborates: "The image of the Man of Sorrows, who is dead as man and living as God, . . . actualizes Christ's sacrificial Death as a divine

Fig. 7. *Man of Sorrows,* Church of Santo Domingo, Popayán, Colombia. (From Pál Kelemen, *Baroque and Rococo in Latin America,* Dover 1967, vol. 2, plate 14. Reproduced by permission of Dover Publications)

act of Redemption: 'Mors mea, vita tua' [My death is your life]. . . . New emotional qualities characterize the western Man of Sorrows; they are intimacy, compassion, exhortation and intercession. So direct is his confrontation with the spectator that the suffering Son of God and the sinful man seek one another in their love" (198).

Eltit's impersonation as L. Iluminada, "Woman of Sorrows," similarly interpellates the Chilean people with the Christian symbolism of redemptive self-sacrifice. At the level of the fictional events, L. Iluminada's Christ-like self-sacrifice binds her and the lumpen together in loving communion. The burns, cuts, and other wounds L. Iluminada inflicts on herself as part of the series of anti-institutional practices in the hours between dusk and dawn are visually presented in this neobaroque devotional image. Here they also fully assume their immaterial, "spiritual" significance: they are the stigmata of a clandestine, antidictatorial practice of redemption and collective solidarity. It is a clever recodification of official Christian iconography for minoritarian and insurgent purposes. According to Richard, this also explains the popularity of Zurita's and Eltit's work: "At a time when the real is forbidden, there is *a demand for the symbolic,* a demand which their Christian message is able to satisfy" (*Margins* 68). More to the point, the visual representation of the stigmatized body of this postmodern, secular woman messiah enacts the baroque aesthetic of direct sensual address of the believer through the holy image. The graphic staging of L. Iluminada's self-mutilation (in image and narrative) resignifies the Counter-Reformation baroque tradition of hypersensualistic religious art, which (as we saw in chapter 2) visualizes the invisible and naturalizes the supernatural, making the things of the spirit real and palpable to the senses. In the New World baroque, religious baroque art reached unique peaks of bloodthirstiness, something that derived from the colonial context in which Christianity flourished in the New World for more than three centuries. The symbols of official Christianity in the New World became overdetermined with the real-world suffering of indigenous converts. (I explore this subject further in chapter 5, on Latin American popular baroques and visual art.) A good example is the so-called *Cristos sangrantes* (bleeding Christs) of Mexico, wooden sculptures of Christ depicting a variety of stations of the Passion that display an extreme amount of bleeding wounds (fig. 8). According to Lois Parkinson Zamora, during "Holy Week, the *Cristos sangrantes* are removed from walls and placed in aisles or in front of altars, where their wounds can be touched" (*Inordinate Eye* 37). Indeed, the Colombian "Man of Sorrows" shown in figure 7 is also a *Cristo sangrante* who bears the wounds of "physical torture": blood is flowing down his shoulders and chest, and his knees and elbows are bleeding from falling under the weight of the cross.[63] In like fashion, L. Iluminada, "Woman of Sorrows," invites

Fig. 8. *Cristo sangrante,* Santa María Xoxoteca, Mexico. (Photograph: Lois Parkinson Zamora)

reader-spectators to contemplate her sacrifice (and the immaterial promise of the secular, counterinstitutional redemption that it references) through the physical and material presence of her injured body.

References to Catholic ritual are pervasive in *Lumpérica* and extend beyond the Passion. The "baptism" that occurs in the opening scene invokes the influence the Catholic Church still has as an "ISA" in Latin America, operating as a conduit for the transmission of dominant values. In the police interrogation in chapters 2 and 7, the unnamed male detainee echoes L. Iluminada's exclamation, "tengo sed" (I'm thirsty) (*Lumpérica* 53; *E. Luminata* 55)—a confirmation of the symbolic link between her self-sacrifice and his emblematic victimization by state terror. Briefly put, the interrogation revolves around what the anonymous man may have seen of the nightly events in the square. Specifically, it centers on what happened when L. Iluminada fell to the ground, and what she said to him and he said to her as he caught her in her fall and helped her up. Here the parallel is with Christ's falling three times on the road to Calvary and Simon of Cyrene helping him up and carrying the cross for him. The ninth chapter, "Escenas múltiples de caídas" ("Multiple Scenes of Falls"), amplifies this episode. The tenth and final chapter—a realist account of L. Iluminada sitting in the square, providing a retrospective look after the end of the performances as daybreak nears—offers a description of L. Iluminada's external appearance: her head is shaved, and she is dressed like a penitent or a pilgrim, wearing "un traje gris bastante más largo que el que está en uso. Un traje casi sin formas tomado a la cintura con un cordón también gris" (a grey dress rather longer than what is in fashion. An almost shapeless dress cinched at the waist by a cord, also grey) (*Lumpérica* 205; *E. Luminata* 190).

Lumpérica, like Eltit's work in general, has been read through the Deleuzian concept of minor literature, which refers to the insurgent rearticulation of a dominant language by its users: "A minor literature doesn't come from a minor language; it is rather that which a minority constructs within a major language."[64] As Juan Carlos Lértora contends, the subversive remaking of the codes of dominant institutional discourses is the major feature of Eltit's work.[65] Its minoritarian rearticulation of Christian ideology that "tears it away" from the religious ISA (as it were) adds *Lumpérica* to the corpus of works that Lezama Lima calls the *barroco de contraconquista,* the anti-institutional baroque of counterconquest. Eltit's insertion of a minoritarian messiah—the "Woman of Sorrows"—into a narrative of one night's goings-on in a public square also employs the allegorical technique of fragmentation and assemblage theorized by Benjamin.

In the crucial eighth chapter, which depicts L. Iluminada inflicting incisions on her skin with "surgical precision" (Avelar, *Untimely* 176), we find the following unexpected metafictional statement: "Así este quinto corte se incribe sobre (o bajo) la epidermis quemada, que se ha vuelto a ciencia cierta barro, barrosa, barroca, en su tramado" (So this fifth cut is inscribed over (or under) the burned epidermis, which has in all certainty become bog/barbered, barbaric, baroque in its weave) (*Lumpérica* 173; *E. Luminata* 161). Here the realist description of cutting the skin swerves to another dimension of the neobaroque in *Lumpérica,* the poststructuralist neobaroque celebration of makeup, masquerade, tattoo, and simulation characteristic of Sarduy's work. The Spanish original conveys Eltit's nod to Perlongher in the term "barrosa," which is lost in translation. Perlongher coined the term *neobarroso* for neobaroque poetry from Argentina and Uruguay, a punning formulation that blends *barroco* with *barro* (mud, alluding to the mud of the River Plate): "ese flujo escritural que embarroca o embarra las letras transplatinas" (this flow of writing that barroquizes or muddies literatures of the River Plate).[66] The *neobarroso,* or River Plate neobaroque, according to Perlongher "tends specifically towards the low, dirty and the sexual, dirtying literature and dragging classical tropes through the mud" (Bollig 169). Pelongher's neologism marks regional differences between the dominant New World baroque of Mexico and Peru and diverging developments in Argentina and Uruguay, which did not have comparable colonial baroque traditions. In addition to marking Southern Cone regionalism, *Lumpérica* likely references Perlongher's low-culture *neobarroso* to strengthen its alliance with the poor and the homeless marginalized in Pinochet's official Chile.

Suddenly, cutting the skin—the solemn work of stigmatizing the body—transforms into play with the proliferation of signifiers, an ornamental tattoo on the skin "baroque in its weave." Eltit often mentioned that she was influenced by Sarduy, and that the model for *Lumpérica* in particular was Sarduy's novel *Cobra* (1972), as well as the theater of the Spanish Siglo de Oro, the seventeenth-century baroque.[67] Eltit recalls, "Reading *Cobra* made me lose my fear, my insecurity, because it helped me understand that I could do what I want" (Morales, *Conversaciones* 37). Nonetheless, despite her extensive readings in poststructuralist theory, she "never renounced [her] Spanish Golden Age" (90). Eltit mentions that she also enjoyed reading Severo Sarduy's *Escrito sobre un cuerpo* (1969; *Written on a Body*), a much-discussed collection of critical essays on Spanish and Latin American literature, including Boom writers, Lezama Lima, and Góngora, which employs structuralist and Lacanian theory.[68] Eltit thus encourages us to think of *Lumpérica* as a combination of seventeenth-century baroque theater (another hint at the performative nature of Eltit's narrative) and Sarduy's neobaroque narrative and theory.

The slippage from Eltit's self-sacrificial "rhetoric of the body" (Richard) to an emphasis on the ornate baroque texture of the stigmatized skin in the passage quoted above mirrors Sarduy's concern with the materiality of the decorative, hyperabundant signifier and the artificiality of representation. Sarduy's antirealist literary theory and fiction shift from a "depth" model of identity and culture as essential being to a "surface" model of identity as stylized performance, bodily gestures, and masquerade. Sarduy's *Cobra* is illuminating in this regard: it is a novel about transvestites and transsexuals that begins in the "Lyrical Theater of Dolls" and closes with the "Indian Diary" (with quotations from Columbus's diary). The characters (who include a motorcycle gang of drug dealers and a sect of exiled Tibetan monks) wind up in the Tibetan region on their flight from the West to the Orient. Cobra is the name of the drag queen heroine, but it is also the object of many word games that yoke the heroine to COBRA, the anagram for a neo-avant-garde group of the 1950s and an allusion to an experimental poem by Octavio Paz. In Sarduy's novels, the continuities of character and plot dissolve, along with verisimilitude.[69]

The same is true for *Lumpérica,* which adopts the same discontinuous sequence of scenes in place of a plot. And like Sarduy's characters (to adapt González Echevarría's observation), Eltit's are totally flat and artificial: they have no inner depth.[70] Everything about them is externalized, either visible (external appearance and physical gestures) or audible (speech). *Lumpérica*'s lack of interiority is a baroque feature, comparable in principle to, if much more radical than, Barnes's *Nightwood.* Eltit rarely presents the thoughts of her protagonist or the lumpen; if she does, they are focalized externally, through the report of the authorial narrator. To offer an exemplary passage from the first chapter: "Ella está en el centro de la plaza, mientras sus pies se deslizan. Los cuerpos bullentes de los desharrapados que, por efectos de luz de un luminoso que cae desde un edificio cercano, produce en la piel un tinte ligeramente distorsionado y fantasmagórico" (She's there in the middle of the square, as her feet slip from under her. The ragged people's seething bodies that, with neon lighting effects falling from a nearby building, producing on their skin a slightly distorting, phantasmagoric tint) (*Lumpérica* 15; *E. Luminata* 20).

Also highly noticeable are the stagy visual effects. As expected in the histrionic baroque, characters' speeches, actions, and gestures are refracted and multiplied through an ever-changing kaleidoscope of masks and disguises. In the third chapter, the characters masquerade as animals: L. Iluminada is a mare or a cow galloping around the square, neighing and bellowing along with the lumpen. "Porque ni sus mugidos, ni la fuerza experta del relinchar han logrado diluir la fuerte marca de ese luminoso que le ha robado su única presencia ante los pálidos escudados tras sus letras" (But neither her moos nor the expert power of neighing have managed to dilute the strong mark of that luminous sign which had robbed her of her only presence before pale people shielded behind its letters) (*Lumpérica* 72; *E. Luminata* 70). In the fourth chapter, and the first to bear a title ("Para la formulación de una imagen en la literatura"; "Towards the Formulation of an Image in Literature"), the physical interaction between them becomes eroticized. At the same time, language becomes so experimental (including neologisms) as to lapse into hermetic inscrutability: "L'incesto actúa de indolora forma. Funda y precisa el continuo apellido, animal detestable que avala su hundida superficie, en el gris de su untada salivar especie./Suda sedimenta sala su entramado: la destetan a temprana hora, madre más impía su madona master para dejarla en el cemento de la plaza" (Thincest works painlessly. It founds and specifies the continuous name, loathsome animal that vouches for its sunken surface, in the gray of its smeared salival species./She sweats sediments salts her framework: they wean her early, mother more ungodly her madonna master for leaving her on the concrete in the square) (*Lumpérica* 98; *E. Luminata* 91). The chapter is a stylistic parody of Lezama Lima's neobaroque poetry, for whose notoriously hermetic theory of the poetic image and so-called "imaginative eras" it is named.[71] As the dedicatory poem reveals, L. Iluminada "piensa en Lezama" (thinks about Lezama) as the curtain to this fourth act rises (*Lumpérica* 83; *E. Luminata* 77). *Lumpérica*'s verbal and performative excess also returns us to the central paradox of baroque expression that Fuentes has baptized the language of abundance and insufficiency. Richard elaborates the subversive function of baroque decoration in *Lumpérica:* "Art of make-up, feminine practice of the *supplement:* this writing of devastation, born of the dispossessing violence of the dictatorship's seizure of power, knew how to take revenge against the punishment of deprivation, unleashing an *excess* of words that luxuriously (cosmetically) rename loss. Baroque hyperboles of lack regale the literary artifice of verbal excess with superfluous, redundant words."[72]

Lumpérica's very first sentence announces a baroque spectacle, ruled by artifice: "Lo que resta de este anochecer será un festín para L. Iluminada, ésa que se devuelve sobre su propio rostro, incesantemente recamada" (The remains of this evening will be a feast for E. Luminata, that woman who recrosses her own face, incessantly appliquéd) (*Lumpérica* 9; *E. Luminata* 14). As becomes clear, the baroque exteriorization of character into hyperbolic performance and masquerade ("acting" and "appearing" rather than "being") is compatible with *Lumpérica*'s goal of the reconquest of public space. *Lumpérica*'s baroque spectacle is a counterhegemonic urban festival, not unlike the happenings of the 1960s or the situationist urban festivals from which Lefevbre derived his inspiration.[73] As Eugenia Brito observes in regard to *Lumpérica*'s multiple features of marginality, "The city is a space semiotized in the feminine" (130). In the fifth and sixth chapters, L. Iluminada and the lumpen collaborate in writing graffiti in the square. L. Iluminada writes, "Quo vadis?" (another allusion to the Passion of Christ) in chalk on the ground at the center of the square. Arousing the lumpen's curiosity, her writing engages them in a feverish exchange: having recognized the subversion of her writing, the lumpen stand on the letters and erase them with their feet to protect her. "Por eso tapan el rayado. Han comprendido la agresión" (That's why they cover up the lines. They have understood the aggression) (*Lumpérica* 123; *E. Luminata* 114). The ritual is repeated; L. Iluminada draws the letters again, and the lumpen rub them out, until she achieves her goal—to get the lumpen to write for themselves:

> Este lumperío escribe y borra imaginario, se reparte las palabras, los fragmentos de letras, borran sus supuestos errores, ensayan sus caligrafías, endilgan el pulso, acceden a la imprenta.
>
> Se quedan quietos observando y como profesionales empiezan a tender su propio rayado en el centro. Es perfecto. Están enajenados en la pendiente de la letra, alfabetizados, corruptos por la impresión. (*Lumpérica* 124–25)

> (This lumpenpack pretend-writes and rubs out, parcels out the words, the fragments of letters, they rub out their supposed errors, try out their calligraphies, steady their shaking, agree to the printing.
>
> They stay still watching and like professionals begin to lay out their own lines in the center. It's perfect. They get carried away on the slope of the letter, made literate, corrupted by printing.) (*E. Luminata* 115–16)

As in previous scenes, this communion with chalk and graffiti is a minoritized Catholic ritual at the same time that it constitutes a counterhegemonic tactic in taking back the city. The sixth chapter reflects on the meaning of the graffiti in the square in short verses under headings such as "La escritura como proclama" (Writing as proclamation), "La escritura como desatino" (Writing as folly), "La escritura como evasión" (Writing as evasion). One entry begins:

La escritura como iluminación
En esta cuidad reconstituida / de opereta /
se realiza sólo la norma restringiendo
la imaginería . . .

(*Lumpérica* 140)

(Writing as illumination
In this city reconstituted / out of some operetta /
the norm is effected only by restricting
imagery . . .)

(*E. Luminata* 130)

Under the title "La escritura como erosión" (Writing as erosion), the final entry ends with L. Iluminada's central insight—a revelation of Chile as wasteland strewn with corpses—quoted at the beginning of this section.

Much has been written about Eltit's aesthetics of the fragment.[74] Eltit herself has repeatedly spoken about how she has been unable to write about anything in unified wholes, such as the body or the house: "It is always in pieces" (Morales, *Conversaciones* 143). In part, the fragmentary construction of Eltit's narratives derives from her neobaroque poetics of the open work, influenced by Sarduy and Benjamin, on whose theory of allegory Eltit recalls attending a university seminar (see Morales, *Conversaciones* 109). But unlike Sarduy, whose work radically dismantles the referential and communicative function of language to release the anarchic play of the signifier, Eltit uses neobaroque fragmentation to recapture the possibility of communication (though for liberating and anti-institutional purposes). The difference between Sarduy's apolitical and Eltit's counterhegemonic political stance is important to keep in mind when observing that the disobedient nightly practices of "making do" in the city under dictatorship portrayed in *Lumpérica* are fragmented and discontinuous. There is no heroic resistance because (as Richard notes and as the *avanzada* recognized) the heroic model of resistance has been contaminated by the military's official propaganda and disappeared among the opposite political spectrum. The disintegration of the subject, of the collective, and of language that takes place in *Lumpérica* is the result of the catastrophe of 1973 and an example of the far-reaching effects of the military's "iron surgery" in the immaterial spheres of subjectivity and narratives of collective identity. As Walter Benjamin proposes in "Theses," the authentic history of the victims is fragmented and discontinuous and avoids the false continuities of the history of the victors.

Allegories of History as Catastrophe in José Donoso's *Casa de campo*

Casa de campo hinges on an allegorical image of the contemporary Chilean nation and state as the eponymous country house, a hermetically sealed microcosm whose idyllic artificiality and orchestrated timelessness represent the escapism, neofeudalism, and baroque aesthetics of illusionism of the Chilean oligarchy. Known by the imaginary name of Marulanda, the country house is a contradictory construct of Arcadian idyll on the inside and ruthless exploitation on the outside, which emblematizes Chile's social inequality and residual internal colonialism persisting into the late twentieth century. Beginning with Luis Iñigo Madrigal's detailed deciphering of *Casa de Campo*'s political allegory, critics have recognized the novel's allegorical procedure of "speaking otherwise," whereby one story (the fictional history of Marulanda) alludes to another, hidden story, the history of Chile in particular and Latin America in general.[75] Divided into two parts, Donoso's novel sets the socialism of the Allende years (narrated in Part I) and the Pinochet coup (narrated in Part II) against the background of the residual colonial structures evoked through the setting, Marulanda's double-edged idyll.

A small number of central characters and events in *Casa de campo* translate more or less directly into the historical figures and events of Chile in the 1970s, such as Adriano, "the liberator" (Salvador Allende); the Mayordomo, "the dictator" (Pinochet); and Francisco de Asís, the martyred bard of the revolution (Víctor Jara). Even though allegorical representation in the novel is not completely reducible to a political satire or a linear roman à clef (as Madrigal points out), the inhabitants of the house and the natives of Marulanda correspond to a schematic social composition of Chile's population. The adults are the ruling oligarchy; the children, the middle classes; the Marulanda natives, the proletariat or lower classes (including actual indigenous peoples); and the servants most certainly are the armed forces (Madrigal 13). The allegorical correspondence between the fictional family house and the real nation-state is suggested, for example, by the fact that the children do not act or talk like children but like adults. Likewise, the majority of the characters are flat, without interiority, obviously created to embody abstract principles.

As they do every year, the Ventura clan, consisting of fourteen adults and thirty-five children, and accompanied by an "army" of servants hired anew each year, embark on an epic journey from the capital to vacation at their summer residence at Marulanda. They leave before the advent of the annual "thistlestorms" in the fall, a tempest of grass seeds that chokes all life on the beautiful plain. The trip, however, is more than a vacation, for Marulanda harbors the material base of the family's fabulous wealth—gold, which is mined and manufactured into laminate by local natives. The Venturas justify the colonization and enslavement of the natives as a civilizing mission (to eradicate the cannibalism of the natives, which the Venturas claim threatens to spring up again the moment the natives return to their natural state [*Casa* 43; *House* 18]). Yet no Ventura has ever had any personal contact with the "fierce" natives except for the doctor Adriano Gomara, who married into the family and whom the clan punishes by declaring him mad and locking him away in a remote tower. In the year narrated, the adults decide to embark on a picnic in a fabulous paradisiacal glade on their estate. Accompanied by the servants (for protection from the cannibal natives), they abandon the children in the house. Reacting to the power vacuum created by this departure, the children break into factions and undertake a variety of ventures: some, the conservative elite around Juvenal and Melania, struggle to uphold authority and prevent "lawlessness" by continuing to perform the play *La marquise est sortie à cinq heures* (The marquise left at five), a disciplinary tool designed to keep the children trapped in the fantasy world of a courtly masque and distract them from reality.

Others prepare the rebellion: Wenceslao, the son of the imprisoned Adriano Gomara, liberates his father. Tired of ceremonial make-believe, iconoclastic Mauro, the "Young Count" of the play *La marquise,* becomes the leader of one group of children who uproot the fence, erasing the barricade between the artificial interior and the unknown world outside. Another, materialistically minded group of children breaks into the cellars and makes off with the family gold. Fraternizing with the natives who have invaded the defenseless mansion, Adriano "the Liberator" subsequently assumes power and initiates a series of radical changes, abolishing the old class- and race-based hierarchy and installing a left revolutionary order in its place. However, Adriano's egalitarian regime is weakened by internal factionalization and economic collapse resulting from the breakdown of gold production and trade. Encountering evidence of the revolution on their way home from their outing, the adults dispatch the servants to restore the old order. Under the Mayordomo's command, the servants topple the revolutionary regime in an orgy of bloodshed and destruction, killing Adriano and his inner circle and torturing and executing children and natives. Under the ensuing dictatorship, the old reign of terror and discipline is reimposed in the war-ravaged mansion with double force to erase any memory of the recent past and its revolutionary changes.

An early draft of the novel ended with Marulanda in the grips of the Mayordomo's totalitarian regime while Wenceslao and a small circle of refugees escape through the underground labyrinth to freedom.[76] In the published version, Donoso brings the Ventura parents back to Marulanda, accompanied by English-speaking foreigners, to whom they intend to sell the decaying estate. In this episode, Donoso glosses the dictatorships' policies of neoliberal modernization and integration of national into global markets.[77] Accordingly, the oligarchy's own disempowerment is staged next, as the servants, conspiring with the foreigners, sideline the Venturas altogether in a third revolt. Hijacking the wagon train, the conspirators leave the Ventura adults and children in the ruined house to perish in the fall storms. Desperate, most of the adults crowd into a mule cart and escape across the plain at a crawling pace, to their certain deaths. The remaining Venturas seek shelter in the house, which also receives a stream of natives seeking refuge from the choking tempest. As the Venturas join the natives in their traditional survival technique of slow breathing to the rhythmic beat of a triangle, the novel ends with a tableau of an uncertain new dawn of yet another social order. The motley group hopes to weather the storm by living together in Marulanda "según las costumbres tradicionales que pueden enseñarnos los que conocen la región mejor que nosotros" (according to the traditional customs we can learn from those who know the land better than we do) (*Casa* 485; *House* 343), as Wenceslao explains.

In *Casa de campo,* as in the seventeenth-century German baroque plays analyzed by Benjamin, "history merges into the setting" (*Origin* 92): rather than being narrated sequentially, time is represented spatially and visually, in a series of static panoramas of the allegorical country house. In part, this is because history—that is, any possibility of revolutionary change—is considered a threat to the ruling social order. But, more important, the spatialization of history is a central strategy of Donoso's critical philosophy of history. Like Benjamin's angel, Donoso represents Latin American history as a sequence of social orders imposed violently, only to be overthrown each in its own turn, failing to achieve anything resembling organic development and progress while simply "piling wreckage upon wreckage" ("Theses" 257). *Casa de campo* similarly exposes the discontinuity of Latin American history as the proverbial heap of rubble. The historical orders narrated in *Casa de campo* (the conquest of the natives, the colonial order of the Ventura oligarchy, Adriano/Allende's revolution, the Mayordomo/Pinochet's dictatorship) each arise through the destruction of what precedes them and, in turn, collapse themselves, culminating in the final natural apocalypse of the thistlestorm. (The thistles are non-native plants introduced by the Venturas to the region; thus the annual thistlestorm is a natural catastrophe resulting from environmental engineering.) Each new regime pretends to construct a better world when in actuality it merely continues the work of destruction. History in Chile/Marulanda amounts to a sequence of static orders and their cataclysmic overthrow.

Spatialized History: The Marulanda Panoramas

Specifying his claim of the baroque spatialization of history, Benjamin explains, "*in the ruin* history has physically merged into the setting" (*Origin* 177–78; emphasis added). In the broken residues left over from the past, time has been transformed into space, petrified into fossils: "The term 'panoramic' has been coined," Benjamin adds, "to give an excellent description of the conception of history prevalent in the seventeenth century" (*Origin* 92). One can trace the periods of fictional Marulanda history in *Casa de campo* through a series of such static pictures or panoramas of the country house that emblematize the respective current stage of historical development. Thus, a description of the design of the park in the opening chapters portrays an artificial implant on the surrounding plain, carefully bounded and isolated from exterior nature: "El parque, enclavado en esa llanura sin un solo árbol que manchara su extensión, era como una esmeralda, su profundidad cuajada de fantásticos jardines de materia más dura que la materia del paisaje" (The park, embedded in that plain without a single tree to mar its expanse, was like an emerald, its depths crystal with fantastic gardens of harder material than the stuff of the countryside) (*Casa* 57; *House* 34). The hyperreal beauty of the location—"sus amplios céspedes por donde ambulaban los pavos reales, la diminuta isla de *rocaille* en el *laghetto*" (broad lawns where peacocks strolled, the miniature rocaille island in the *laghetto*) (*Casa* 57; *House* 34)—seems to lift Marulanda out of history and project a fantastic utopian reality. The perfect microcosm of the Venturas, "una joya" (a gem) (*Casa* 57; *House* 34), Marulanda is the antithesis of the indigenous world onto which it has been grafted: "el laberinto de boj, el rosedal, el teatro de verdura poblado de personajes bergamascos, las escalinatas, las ninfas de mármol, las ánforas, remedaban sólo los modelos más exaltados, desterrando toda nota que lo comprometiera con lo autóctono" (the boxwood maze, the rose garden, the leafy green theater peopled with commedia dell'arte figures; the garden steps, the marble nymphs, the amphoras—all copied only the noblest models, banishing any trace that might compromise it with the indigenous) (*Casa* 57; *House* 34). This first of four panoramas of Marulanda presents the colonial regime as social utopia, the transcendent European civilizatory order that it officially claims to embody. To be sure, this is a mythic image, not a historical one. The park's nonutilitarian beauty epitomizes the leisured and nonproductive lifestyle of the aristocratic

Venturas, whose social status rests on the productivity of the subjugated local natives.

But the novel is written—to echo Benjamin—to extinguish this false appearance of imported European civilization as progress and social perfection. Under Donoso's allegorical gaze, the Ventura home sheds its semblance of ideal beauty and, falling into history, becomes a ruin. As a first step in Marulanda's decay, the aura of perfection is replaced by an atmosphere of indeterminate danger following the departure of the adults and servants, that is to say, of the ruling oligarchy and the army. This is registered in a second Marulanda panorama:

> Cuando los niños se vieron solos . . . sintieron que . . . el parque familiar revestía un aire insólito, hostil, y la casa, hoy tan despoblada, era colosal, autónoma, semejante a un dragón de entrañas constituidas por pasadizos y salones dorados y alfombrados capaces de digerir a cualquiera, de tentáculos que eran los torreones que intentaban atrapar la nubes siempre en fuga. (*Casa* 94)
>
> (When the children found themselves alone . . . they felt that . . . the familiar park wore a strange hostile air, and the house, so deserted today, seemed colossal, alive, a dragon with innards of carpeted hallways and gilded salons to swallow them up, with tower tentacles lunging after the swift clouds.) (*House* 61)

The home, the familiar place of shelter and orientation in the world, becomes unfamiliar, strange, and threatening: in this passage and elsewhere, Donoso employs the uncanny (here, the house as dragon) as an instrument in his defamiliarizing allegory of Latin American history. The uncanny, which, according to Freud, expresses the eruption of fear and terror within the sphere of the familiar, announces early in the novel the violent upheavals that are to follow.[78]

A subsequent and third panorama of Marulanda at the end of the revolutionary period spatializes the historical changes introduced by Adriano's regime. This tableau is made on the eve of the Mayordomo's dictatorship as the caravan of armed servants is bearing down on the house and the overthrow of the revolution is imminent. At this historical juncture, the following image of the liberated, decolonized estate is offered:

> Borrado el límite de la reja—no quedaba más que la historiada cancela cerrada por su cadena y su candado entre dos pilastras de piedra, como a la deriva en medio de la llanura—las gramíneas habían logrado fundir la extensión del paisaje con lo que antes fuera el civilizado parque. Crecían ahora irreprimibles, fantásticas en medio de los senderos y los prados, y hasta en los intersticios de los aleros y techos de la ahora deteriorada arquitectura, de manera que la mansión, antes tan majestuosa, parecía una de esas pintorescas ruinas empenachadas de vegetación que aparecen en los cuadros de Hubert Robert o de Salvatore Rosa. Pero

mirando mejor, el que observara se podia dar cuenta de que los jardines habían cambiado hasta lo irreconocible, no sólo debido a esa invasión sino gracias a una serie de acequias que salían del *laghetto,* que ya no era un estanque decorativo, sino fuente de riego para las hortalizas que sustituían a los elegantes canteros de antaño. Grupos de nativos y niños trabajaban inclinados bajo el sol, levantando una compuerta para inundar cierto sector que necesitaba agua, o cosechando lechugas, frambuesas y zanahorias. (*Casa* 290–91)

(With the railing gone—nothing remained but the fanciful gate chained and padlocked between two stone columns, as if adrift in the middle of the plain—the grass had succeeded in flooding its vast landscape over what had once been the civilized park. It was sprouting wildly, fantastically, in the middle of walks and lawns, even from cracks in the eaves and gables of the deteriorated architecture, so that the mansion, formerly so majestic, now resembled one of those overgrown picturesque ruins to be found in paintings by Hubert Robert or Salvatore Rosa. But on closer inspection, an observer would have discovered that the grounds had been altered beyond recognition not only by that invasion, but by a series of ditches running from the *laghetto,* no longer a decorative pool but rather a source of irrigation for the garden plots that had replaced the once elegant flower beds. Groups of natives and children stood working with backs bent to the sun, raising a gate to flood one of the plots that needed water, or harvesting lettuce, raspberries, and carrots.) (*House* 204)

The altered landscape bears the marks of, to adapt Benjamin, revolutionary history that has merged into the setting. To begin with, the artificial park has become an agricultural field, tilled by both "natives and children," a transformation that allegorizes the abolition of the leisured aristocracy and the introduction of an egalitarian distribution of labor. More important, the fence separating Marulanda from the surrounding plain has been removed, terminating the Venturas' insularity and opening the house and park to the outside. The removal of the boundary fence emblematizes the ideal principles of the revolution—the eradication of the barricades of class and race in the formation of a new "horizontal" fraternity of children and natives. In other words, we are seeing the formation of a modern nation, defined—according to Benedict Anderson—as an imagined community "conceived as a deep, horizontal comradeship."[79]

I use Anderson's term deliberately here to signal that the revolutionary order introduces, for the first time in the history of Marulanda, a national community. For the Venturas' colonial regime is the antithesis of the "deep, horizontal comradeship" that Anderson posits as the quintessence of the nation. The Ventura oligarchy is tribal, not national: the Venturas are in the habit of marrying their cousins; their loyalties do not extend beyond their own class and age group—not even to their children, whom they distrust, betray, and abuse (through the officially sanctioned terror of the servants), not to mention the natives, whom they consider barbaric. For the Venturas' cliquish attitude, "treasurer" Hermógenes' exclusionary use of the pronoun "we/our" is symptomatic. Excluding the children from the "imagined community" of Marulanda's owners, Hermógenes declares that the gold "es nuestro. . . . Mío y de mis hermanos. Ustedes son sólo niños . . . indisciplinados como los sirvientes, perezosos como los nativos" (is ours. . . . Mine and my brothers' and sisters'. You're just children . . . as unruly as servants and lazy as natives) (*Casa* 199; *House* 137). In a memoir tracing the history of his family over four hundred years back to the arrival of the first Donoso in Chile, Donoso reveals similar attitudes in what he calls his own "tribe." His ancestors, a *criollo* clan of landowners, isolated themselves in their rural provincial estates and contracted endogamous marriages.[80]

In the third Marulanda panorama, it is telling that even Adriano's revolutionary regime is shown to be built on ruins—as indicated by the description of the abandoned former gate "como a la deriva en medio de la llanura" (as if adrift in the middle of the plain), the deteriorated architecture of the mansion, wild grasses flooding "lo que antes fuera el parque civilizado" (what had once been the civilized park) (*Casa* 290; *House* 204). The historical process as such is premised on a layering of rubble that no historical agents, not even idealistic and progressive regimes, can remedy. On the same picture plane, Donoso's freeze-frame of history presents the discarded remnants of the old colonial order side by side with the revolutionary reforms of the landscape (which are themselves about to be destroyed by the approaching army of servants). The past resists seamless incorporation into the present. As Theresa Kelley has remarked about Benjamin, "the past has no organic, natural connective to the present; is always 'other'" (255). Donoso's allegory of Marulanda history is an assemblage of fragments whose parts (elements of the past and present) resist fusion into an organic whole. This is in accordance with Benjamin's melancholic understanding of history as loss—"This storm is what we call progress" ("Theses" 258).

The effect of disjunctive accumulation is enhanced by the passage's art historical allusions. Processes of layering of obsolete objects occur not only at the fictional level but also at the metafictional level: the spatial image both depicts and is itself a collage of fragments. Donoso alludes to the ruin landscapes of the Italian baroque painter Salvatore Rosa (1615–1673) and the French landscape painter Hubert Robert (1733–1808)—one of the novel's many citations of European paintings. References to European painting come especially from the period of the rococo and from the arcadian genre; for the most part, they serve to satirize the aestheticist escapism of the Venturas.[81] Donoso confirms this reading: "in *Casa de campo* . . . there is Boucher, Fragonard, Watteau" ("Coloquio" 107). The French painters

Jean-Antoine Watteau (1684–1721), Jean-Honoré Fragonard (1732–1806), and François Boucher (1703–1770) were the main representatives of French rococo painting, a style that arose in the late baroque period and replaced baroque monumentalism with an emphasis on delicate forms and refined ornament.[82] Derived from the French term *rocaille* (referring to shell ornamentation in grottos and gardens), the rococo prefers idyllic and idealized themes. Donoso associates what he dubs a "rosy" distortion of reality with the Latin American bourgeoisie imitating the courtly culture of the past: "the rosy deformation, the bourgeois deformation also appears" in *Casa de campo* ("Coloquio" 107). In sum, *Casa de campo* summons rococo kitsch—"la diminuta isla de *rocaille* en el laghetto" (the miniature *rocaille* island in the laghetto) (*Casa* 57; *House* 34)—as well as the monumental baroque, both small-scale and large-scale manifestations of seventeenth-century art.

The fourth and final panorama of Marulanda, taken from the postdictatorship period, completes the novel's fictional history rendered through spatial images. As the servants go about their military reconquest of the country house, the atmosphere darkens into "un escenario repleto de desolación y de muerte: gritos, persecuciones y disparos en el parque incendiado y enfangado, y cadáveres de anónimos nativos flotando en el *laghetto*" (a scene steeped in desolation and death: screaming, running, and shooting in the charred and muddy park, and corpses of nameless natives floating in the *laghetto*) (*Casa* 310; *House* 218). The last vestiges of Marulanda's "rosy" rococo artifice, already ravaged by the revolutionary regime's agricultural projects, are laid to waste. This new historical phase after the return of the Ventura parents is spatialized in the following panoramic view:

> La casa había quedado como arrumbada en la llanura, un lujoso objeto desasosegante, descompuesto, los arriates y los rosedales arrasados, gran parte del parque quemado o talado por el hacha de los nativos que necesitaron leña. . . . La casa misma, sus balaustradas ruinosas, sus estatuas decrépitas, las escamas saltadas del *trencadís* del techo, acogía a las gramíneas que se apoderaban de su arquitectura para enraizar en cualquier grieta o hendija, y crecer, espigar y agostarse allí mísmo, dotando a la casa de unos curiosos copetes sumisos a los vaivenes del viento. (*Casa* 411–12)

> (The house stood as if shipwrecked on the plain, a magnificent rotting hulk, the flowered walks and rose gardens leveled, most of the park burned or cut down for firewood by the natives' axes. . . . The house itself, its ruined balustrades, its shattered statues, the tiles dislodged from the mosaics on the towers and rooftops, invited the marauding grasses to take root in every crack and crevice of its architecture, and to grow, ripen, and wither where they would, endowing the house with curious sprigs blown by the shifting winds.) (*House* 291)

At this final stage, the trajectory from utopian idyll to ruin is completed. The estate has been reduced to the proverbial Benjaminian "pile of debris." Considering the analogy between "house" and (Chilean) state (the passage also harks back to the political allegory, the "ship of state"), the consequences of Pinochet's dictatorship are catastrophic. Any official claims to national progress founded in economic modernization are not just dismissed outright: their rejection is powerfully amplified by Donoso's deconstructive neobaroque strategy of writing history that presents a concrete material record of destruction to make its case.

Marulanda's Culture of the Baroque

It is impossible to date those portions of the fictional Marulanda history narrated in the first chapters precisely. But as critics have noted, scattered clues (such as mention of the railways, allusions to the opera season in the capital and to the Chilean currency of the time, as well as the international trade with "foreigners" based in a café near the shipyards) point to a "diffuse nineteenth century" (Madrigal 10n17) as the setting of these chapters, which describe the traditional oligarchic order preceding the rapid changes of regimes. By suturing this traditional oligarchic order directly to the upheavals of the 1970s (at this historical juncture, the focus also narrows from the hemispheric to the national, from an unspecified Latin America to Chile), Donoso shows that the colonial neofeudalist order survives into contemporary times—a withering critique on Donoso's part of anachronistic forms of exploitation in Latin America. The coexistence of the colonial and the contemporary, rooted out belatedly by Adriano's regime, is promptly reinstated by the Mayordomo's restoration of the old Ventura order. Here lies yet another powerful critique of the dictatorship's official rhetoric of modernization.

This persistence of "obsolete" colonial social structures in Latin American modernity motivates Donoso's recycling of features of the conservative "culture of the Baroque" (Maravall) in the fictional portrait of Marulanda. As the historian Mariano Picón-Salas observed in his 1944 study of the colonial baroque in Latin America, the baroque "was one of the elements that remained rooted in our culture for a very long time. Indeed, in spite of nearly two centuries of rationalism and modern criticism, we Spanish Americans have not yet emerged fully from its labyrinth."[83] Like José Lezama Lima, Diamela Eltit, and many other Latin American writers across the twentieth century, Donoso resorts to a neobaroque poetics to portray what Irlemar Chiampi calls Latin America's "dissonant modernity," which is haunted by the endurance of the obsolete.[84] *Casa de campo* depicts the baroque as a reactionary and repressive force—as the ideological, pedagogical, and aesthetic instrument of the Hispanic elite oligarchy. But Donoso's novel also illustrates the claims of Carpentier and Lezama Lima, who show how this "culture of conquest" is gradually transformed into an insurgent minor American baroque, the decolonizing baroque of the counterconquest.

In *Casa de campo,* as in the imperial seventeenth-century Iberian baroque imported to the Americas, the baroque is the official style in which Church, state, and the ruling elite represent themselves. Donoso's novel underscores and illustrates Ángel Rama's stern reminder that the baroque on "the American continent became the experimental field for the formulation of a new baroque culture," where, unlike in Europe, the "methodical application of baroque ideas" could be carried out without compromise while "opposing all local expressions of particularity, imagination, or invention."[85] As in Rome or Madrid, baroque monumental architecture and large-scale urban and palace design at Marulanda are intended as dramatic displays of power. Like Versailles, Marulanda is a baroque palace, complete with trompe l'oeil frescos, a grand staircase, and ornamental palace grounds. Similarly, Ventura family culture is carefully modeled after court ritual and the rigid orthodoxy and authoritarianism of the seventeenth-century state baroque described by Maravall. According to Maravall, the baroque is the reaction of a "conservative culture" to the progressive forces unleashed by the Renaissance and Reformation. Citing Joyce G. Simpson, he writes, "The baroque is a glorification of the established powers. It is the art of authoritarian regimes . . . that dominates the awed spectator and carries him or her away so that one forgets to doubt and question."[86]

Casa de campo magnificently presents the theatricality of the baroque, which saw the world as its stage, a "world in which things are *appearances*" (Maravall 192).[87] Illustrating Maravall's claim that the seventeenth-century baroque constituted Europe's first mass culture and cultural industry, Marulanda is a microcosmic replica of the official baroque's society of spectacle, which interpellated the new urban masses of illiterate migrants. In this regard, *Casa de campo*'s title, which points to a domestic and private setting, is misleading: the eponymous country house represents a public space, what William Childers dubs "the Baroque public sphere," the stage of the elaborate urban festivities, processions, and spectacles organized by the Counter-Reformation Church and the absolutist state.

At Marulanda, intellectual dogmatism rules, whereas dissent, doubt, and the use of critical reason are prohibited. "Para los Ventura el primer mandamiento era que jamás nadie debía enfrentarse con nada" (For the Venturas the first commandment was that under no circumstances should anyone confront anything openly) (*Casa* 182; *House* 124). The Venturas' bizarre aversion to critical reasoning and their cultivation of secrecy and dissimulation to the point of foolishness and cruelty make sense once these are read as glossing the dogmatism and antimodernism of Maravall's culture of the baroque. To cite one eloquent example: curious about the lances that compose the boundary fence, Mauro remarks to his parents that the lances have gold points. Perversely, the parents not only deny this obvious truth but also order him to forget about the lances, on threat of punishment by the servants. This seemingly absurd quarrel is resolved in a typical way, by both parties resorting to dissimulation: "Mauro era experto en mantener la superficie de su conducta impoluta, como todos los Ventura. Y . . . sus padres, a su vez, eran expertos en correr un tupido velo sobre cualquier cosa que los incomodara" (Mauro, like all the Ventura, was an expert at maintaining a flawless behavior on the surface. And . . . his parents, in turn, were experts at dropping a dark curtain over whatever made them uncomfortable) (*Casa* 107; *House* 70). What is officially considered truth and reality is but a derivative of doctrine and revealed authority, not the product of critical inquiry or modern empirical methods of observation and experiment. Whereas the adults emblematize the Counter-Reformation's militant faith in dogma and revealed truth, as well as its absolute rejection of criticism and reasoning, the children, still open to doubt and tempted by curiosity, live under an Inquisition-like regime of surveillance and punishment.

Likewise, the Venturas' hostility to social change, their insistence that "el mundo . . . debía seguir" "como era" (the world . . . must go on unchanged) (*Casa* 262; *House* 183), epitomizes the baroque "tendency toward immobility"—in Maravall's words—"toward directing the progressive forces that the Renaissance had set underway" (Maravall 30). The official baroque's closure toward the future and its rejection of the new is satirized in the episode narrating the adults' return from their fateful excursion. On first hearing about the revolution at Marulanda on their way home, Hermógenes exclaims, "Nada ha cambiado. Cualquier cambio en Marulanda indicaría la perniciosa infiltración de los antropófagos" (Nothing has changed! Any change at Marulanda would indicate the pernicious influence of the cannibals!) (*Casa* 256; *House* 179). Hermógenes's rallying cry is later echoed by the Mayordomo, who concludes his successful military offensive with the proclamation, "Aquí no ha pasada nada. La vida seguirá igual que siempre" (Nothing has happened here! Life will go on as before!) (*Casa* 311; *House* 219). Ironically, the parents' excursion to the fabulous Edenic glade had come about in the first place because of a rumor invented by Adriano and circulated among the adults by Wenceslao. The oligarchy thus falls victim to their own rigid prohibition of critical questioning, "regla tácita no sorprenderse ante nada, no aceptar lo insólito" (an unspoken rule not to be surprised at anything, not to consider anything extraordinary) (*Casa* 133; *House* 89). Deception is a double-edged instrument that can be turned against its master: by infiltrating the official canon of received opinion, Marulanda's colonial subjects (the children and the natives) succeed in overthrowing the baroque culture of conquest and razing the barricade that freezes Marulanda in a stagnant existence outside time.

Inculcating dogmatism and closing the children's minds to new ideas and "dangerous doubts" (*House* 63) is the pedagogical goal of the play *La marquise est sortie à cinq heures,* supervised by the adolescent elite around Melanie and Juvenal. The point could not be made any clearer:

> Proporcionaban con esto . . . una huida hacia otro nivel para aguardar allí, en almácigo y sin tener que enjuiciar los dogmas, el momento en que ellos también fueran "grandes" y ascendiendo a esa clase superior dejar de ser vulnerables a las dudas que por su naturaleza de niños los asediaban, para transformarse ellos también en manipuladores y creadores de dogmas. (*Casa* 95–96)
>
> (It provided an escape . . . to another level where, without having to question family dogma, they could stand waiting in the wings for the moment when they too would be "grown-ups" and, ascending to that superior class, cease to be vulnerable to the doubts which, by their very nature as children, assailed them, for then they too would be creators and manipulators of dogma. (*House* 62)

The escapist sterility of this play is further illustrated by this grandiloquent baroque soliloquy of its heroine, "the Beloved Immortal," impersonated by Melanie: "Finjámonos monumentos mientras el estruendo huracanado de la crueldad retumba en el horno que recuece las ánforas, transformando la ternura globular, los miembros rencorosos, en ríos verticales y contradictorios, que al anularse mutuamente lo anulan todo como triángulos superpuestos" (Let us conjure the Pyramids while the cruel blast of the hurricane rumbles in the ovens where the amphoras are tempering, transforming the globular tenderness, the rancorous elements, into vertical rivers of contradiction, canceling each other and in so doing canceling everything else like superimposed triangles) (*Casa* 224; *House* 155). Melanie's hyper-ornate but vacuous discourse is a satire of the reactionary official Hispanic baroque, in which "content yields to form" (Picón-Salas 95). Or, as Maravall explains, the "irruption of outlandish elements in poetry, literature, and art compensated for the deprivation of novelty elsewhere" (Maravall 138). The absence of intellectual content in Melanie's outré baroque rhetoric is an inverse reflection of its stylistic hyperbole, whose effects are pushed past the point of exhaustion.

The neofeudal order at Marulanda is maintained by a dual strategy: physical repression and the baroque regime of illusionism. The monumental, labyrinthine mansion, together with the artificial park that surrounds it, constitutes a hyperreal, phantasmagoric world, decorated and furnished with baroque artwork that blurs the boundary between reality and dream. Like the electric light of the neon sign that relentlessly batters L. Iluminada and the lumpen, Marulanda is filled to the rafters with illusionistic devices that broadcast the Venturas' official ideology. "Somos Ventura," explains Melania, one chief spokesperson of the official regime of deception, "por lo tanto, nunca debemos olvidar que la apariencia es lo único que no engaña" (We're Venturas, . . . that means that we must never forget that appearance is the only thing that never lies) (*Casa* 16; *House* 5). On the opposing side are a group of freethinkers, skeptics, and progressives who champion critical reason and the emancipation from dogma and colonial repression. As Wenceslao neatly phrases it, "En nuestra vida aquí, todo parece una ópera" (Everything about our life here is like an opera) (*Casa* 15; *House* 4). Tellingly, Wenceslao's critical jibe at Marulanda's culture of spectacle mirrors L. Iluminada's parallel insight in *Lumpérica* unmasking the make-believe of Pinochet's propaganda: "this city reconstituted/out of some operetta" (*E. Luminata* 130). As might be expected, the Mayordomo considers Wenceslao "el más peligroso de todos los niños porque es el que discrimina, piensa, y critica" (the most dangerous of all the children because he can think, judge, and criticize) (*Casa* 295; *House* 207).

In a passage quoted in the first chapter, Michel Foucault identifies the "new kinship between resemblance and illusion" as the essence of the baroque:[88] "Games whose powers of enchantment grow out of the new kinship between resemblance and illusion; the chimeras of similitude loom up on all sides, but they are recognized as chimeras; it is the privileged age of *trompe-l'oeil* painting" (*Order of Things* 53). Likewise, at Marulanda, the baroque play of illusion and disillusionment, the slippage between appearance and truth, reality and artifice, serves as the key instrument in the official regime's culture of deception. Melania's slogan that appearances never lie epitomizes the baroque strategy of deception sustaining the Venturas' regime. Such deception works by insisting on the old kinship between appearances and truth in Foucault's order of similitude while utilizing the new (baroque) kinship between appearances and illusion to propagate received opinion, and denying the difference between them. The visual and spatial materialization of deception, trompe-l'oeil frescos cover the walls and ceilings of many of Marulanda's rooms, transforming whole rooms illusionistically. "The French term 'Trompe l'oeil' (eye-deceiver)," explains art historian Sybille Ebert-Schifferer, "is commonly used today to describe paintings that represent things in an especially deceptive way, so that the representation of a thing seems to *be* the thing itself."[89] In the baroque, artists developed the large-scale form of the architectural trompe-l'oeil known as *quadratura,* such as painted heavens in churches and palaces, in which the game of visual illusion jumps scale from a painting on the wall to the illusionistic transformation of whole interiors (Ebert-Schifferer 22) (fig. 9).

Fig. 9. Andrea Pozzo, *Allegory of the Missionary Work of the Jesuits (Triumph of Saint Ignatius of Loyola)*, ceiling fresco, 1691–94. (S. Ignazio, Rome, Italy. Photograph: Alinari/Art Resource, New York)

In painted heavens, for example, the ceiling pretends not to be a ceiling but open sky, and walls pretend not to be solid walls but broken spaces with windows offering vistas to the outside. Painted ceilings, according to the art historian Robert Harbison, "are among the strongest Baroque protests against the boundaries and closures of architecture, which are all founded on the fiction that the roof does not exist, allowing the space we are in to extend upward out of sight."[90] This baroque strategy of the illusionistic transformation of whole environments plays a central role in the Venturas' official spectacle. And this same strategy is in turn usurped by the rebellious children and natives in a counterspectacle that ends the colonial order and inaugurates the revolution.

In close analogy with the panoramic technique of spatializing history, critics have remarked that *Casa de campo* is designed "to a large part like a succession of *tableaux vivants,*" its very characters "turned into actors and spectators within the theater of the fiction."[91] One such theatrical tableau spatializes the moment of the revolution at the end of the first part of *Casa de campo*. It depicts how invading natives, armed with lances, dressed in their recuperated ritual garments and disguised with plains grasses, advance on Marulanda's South Terrace, where the children, under Juvenal's direction, are busy staging the climactic episode of *La Marquise*. It is getting dark and cold as the first day of the Venturas' departure draws to a close; the setting acquires a heightened drama expressed in the chiaroscuro contrasts between the brilliantly lit stage and the darkening scenery of the surrounding park. It is in this critical moment that, for the first time, history and change erupt into the timelessness of Marulanda's microscopic setting. Juvenal, the chief representative of authority, is losing control to Wenceslao, Arabella, and Mauro, the agents of change, who have liberated Adriano and uprooted the fence. As the old social order crumbles, everyday reality at Marulanda is glaringly exposed as a game, a shallow simulation, a cosmic trompe-l'oeil in which the Venturas are trapped, just as the children are prisoners within the fiction of *La marquise*.

The approaching warriors *appear to be* plains grasses invading the fenceless park. "Las gramíneas, más animadas que de costumbre," Juvenal reflects, "aprovechaban el aumento de la penumbra para transgredir el antiguo emplazamiento de la reja. . . . El espectáculo, no podía negarlo, era bello: a esta hora del crepúsculo, . . . se veía a las plumas tendidas como una espalda de oro vivo, ondulando de placer con la caricia del viento" (The grass, more restless than usual, took advantage of the lengthening shadows to cross the former line of the railing. . . . The spectacle, he had to admit, was breathtaking: at this twilight hour, . . . the plumes could be seen stretching like a pelt of living gold, rippling with pleasure at the wind's caress) (*Casa* 231; *House* 160). Enacting the baroque aesthetics of visual illusionism and dramatic naturalism, the inanimate (grasses) appears to be animate (moving), acquiring fantastic visual qualities (gold pelts). These developments illustrate Heinrich Wölfflin's description of how the baroque "dissolves the line and replaces it by the restless mass," thereby replacing Renaissance calm repose with perpetual mobility.[92] The advancing "grasses" exemplify baroque dynamism in their restless movement and in the unfolding of a chain of visual metamorphoses: "las gramíneas de acero no se agitaban, erizándose amenazadoras, en cambio, al pie mismo de la balaustrada. . . . Pero no. No eran las gramíneas que los cercaban. Eran las lanzas . . . que ahora los recluía[n] con la prolífica enumeración de gramíneas simulando lanzas siempre más y más próximas" (the iron stalks were no longer swaying, but instead reared tall and menacing at the very foot of the balustrade. . . . But no. It wasn't the grass that had them surrounded. It was the lances . . . which now walled them in with [their] wild profusion of tall stalks mimicking a creeping ring of lances) (*Casa* 233; *House* 161–62). The rapid succession of visual illusions and the slippage between identity and mimicry (are the lances pretending to be grasses or are the grasses pretending to be lances?) result in hallucinatory effects typical of baroque representation:

> Fue entonces cuando comenzó la verdadera invasión de plumas: la vegetación en realidad se movía. No, no sólo se movía, avanzaba, más aún, marchaba, penachos, plumas, lanzas, plantas, gramíneas, una lenta selva desplazándose desde la oscuridad hacia ellos, hacia el elenco de la Marquesa Salió A Las Cinco atrapado en la luz artificiosa del *tableau vivant.* (*Casa* 239)
>
> (It was then that the invasion of plumes began in earnest: the foliage was definitely moving. No, not just moving: advancing ever closer, marching, crests, plumes, lances, bushes, tufts of grass, a slow forest creeping out of the darkness toward them, toward the cast of *La Marquise Est Sortie à Cinq Heures* caught in the artificial glare of the tableau vivant.) (*House* 166)

As external reality irrupts into Marulanda's hermetic self-enclosure, its idealized artificiality is publicly unmasked as a fraud. The "ruidosa mascarada" (shrill masquerade) (*Casa* 238; *House* 165) of *La Marquise* on the South Terrace is interrupted by another spectacle:

> los fantásticos penachos que los habían venido cercando durante el transcurso de la tarde . . . ahora inundaron la terraza ocupada por un grupo de niños ineficazmente pintarrajeados y disfrazados de grandes con ropas que no les pertenecían. A los nativos, en cambio, sí les pertenecían los ropajes con que iban cubiertos: los atavíos de ricas pieles moteadas de animales ahora inexistentes, . . . el tintineo de cadenas y amuletos, los collares, los peplos, las casacas, las máscaras de oro. (*Casa* 240)
>
> (the fantastic plumage that had been closing around them throughout the afternoon . . . was now flooding the terrace and its cluster of clumsily painted children dressed as grown-ups in clothes that didn't belong to them. The robes that covered the natives, on the other hand, were theirs by right: the raiments of sleek spotted furs from now extinct animals, . . . the jingling chains and amulets, the necklaces, tunics, cloaks, and gold masks.) (*House* 166–67)

At this point, the official deception is ended, and an alternate reality, previously invisible, is seen. The revolutionary counterspectacle culminates in a ceremonial reunion between the leader of the natives, Francis of Assisi, and Adriano, "una figura resplandeciente, envuelta en largos hábitos" (a resplendent figure draped in long robes) (*Casa* 239; *House* 166), in "un abrazo fraterno que arrancó un alegre ulular de las interminables legiones oscuras que lo acompañaban, y un aplauso cerrado, consagratorio, de la mayoría de los niños" (a fraternal embrace which drew a joyful howl from the innumerable dark legions that accompanied him and awestruck muffled applause from most of the gaping children) (*Casa* 241; *House* 167). New protagonists (the natives and Adriano) occupy Marulanda's baroque stage of history and inaugurate a new chapter of events (the history of Marulanda's revolutionary regime). The static picture of Adriano's and Francis of Assisi's embrace on the South Terrace emblematizing the triumph of the revolution, and the earlier *tableau vivant* of Melania and Juvenal performing *La Marquise* allegorizing the moribund ancièn regime, which the former replaces, constitute additional pictures in the album of Marulanda's spatialized history considered in the previous section. Pertaining to the present discussion of baroque illusionism, what remains to be noted is that historical change and the unfamiliar reality outside the boundaries of Marulanda's artificial enclave make their appearance in disguise: social reality vanquishes baroque artifice by masking as artifice. It is for this reason that this pivotal episode midway through *Casa de campo* offers a fictional equivalent of Lezama Lima's notion of the anticolonial New World baroque, the art of the *contraconquista.*

The baroque questioning of the difference between appearance and truth would later be reanimated in the modern notion of the illusory nature of truth that would find its radical expression in Nietzsche's famous axiom that truth is an effect of rhetoric: "What, then, is truth? A mobile army of metaphors, metonymns, and anthropomorphisms. . . . Truths are illusions about which one has forgotten that this is what they are."[93] While Melania's dogmatic baroque declares that illusion *is* truth, Nietzsche's skeptical neobaroque counters that truth *is* illusion, simply by reversing the affirmation. It thus comes as no surprise that, as mentioned earlier, in his short sketch "On the Baroque," published in 1878, Nietzsche vindicated the baroque decades before the comprehensive reevaluation of the baroque spearheaded by Wölfflin. Artifice, and the baroque interplay of truth and fiction, illusion and disillusionment (*engaño/desengaño*), may serve very different political ends—in the case of the Ventura's colonial baroque, aesthetic escapism that supports political orthodoxy, and in the case of the insurgent group's decolonizing neobaroque, the contestation of the truth claims of official post-Pinochet Chilean history.

By enacting the great baroque theme of the slippage between truth and appearance, *Casa de campo* demonstrates that the baroque is not, as some critics would prefer, inherently reactionary. The ironic reversals in its plot that are driven by the baroque kinship between appearance and reality establish that, as I have been arguing throughout, we need to replace the notion of one singular baroque (seventeenth-century, official, authoritarian) with that of multiple baroques. Evidence furnished by *Casa de Campo* as well as *Lumpérica* confirms that baroque aesthetics is an open and contested field. Even though it may originally have been territorialized by conservative majoritarian ideology, it can subsequently be deterritorialized by antidictatorial minoritarian practices.

The Allegorical Sign: Images That Are Also Ruins

One of Benjamin's achievements was to have elaborated the affinity between allegorical representation and the experience of historical crisis. For Benjamin, in the baroque and the neobaroque, language, like the world, takes the form of the ruin (allegories/realm of thought; ruins/realm of things). The ravages wrought by history are reproduced at the level of representation in an allegorical, "nonorganic work of art" (Bürger) defined by fragmentation, montage, artifice, and antirealism. According to the *Trauerspiel* study, allegory's manufactured, "dry rebuses . . . contain an insight" that the harmonious symbol cannot convey—"the lack of freedom, the imperfection, the collapse of the physical, beautiful, nature" (*Origin* 176).

Without doubt, Donoso's rejection of fantastic modes of narration and magical realism in *Casa de campo* serves Benjaminian goals—to extinguish the "false appearance of totality" (*Origin* 176) in Chile under dictatorship. As indicated earlier, it signals a transition from Donoso's previous Boom novel, *El obsceno pájaro de la noche* (1970; *The Obscene Bird of Night*), a shift much commented on in Donoso criticism.[94] Among the archaic literary devices Donoso brings back in his antidictatorship novel—in addition to allegory and the recuperation of the historical culture of the baroque discussed in the previous sections—is the embodied authorial narrator of the early period novel. Donoso's extradiegetic narrator stands aloof from the tale he narrates, displaying traditional omniscience in personal commentary, interpreting events and characters and commenting on the principles of the novel's construction. Early on, he offers the following metafictional commentary:

> Quiero . . . proponer al público que acepte lo que escribo como un artificio. Al interponerme de vez en cuando en el relato sólo deseo recordarle al lector su distancia con el material de esta novela. . . . Si logro que el público acepte las manipulaciones del autor, reconocerá no sólo esta distancia, sino también que las viejas maquinarias narrativas, hoy en descrédito, quizás puedan dar resultados tan sustanciosos como los que dan las convenciones disimuladas por el "buen gusto" con su escondido arsenal de artificios. (*Casa* 53)

> (I want to . . . [propose] that the public accept what I write as an artifice. By intruding myself from time to time on the story I simply wish to remind the reader of his distance from the material of this novel. . . . If I succeed in getting the public to accept the author's manipulations, they will be acknowledging not only this distance, but the fact that such old-fashioned narrative machinery, now in discredit, may yet give results as substantial as those offered by more modern conventions which, with their secret arsenal of illusion, masquerade as "good taste.") (*House* 31)

If *Casa de campo*'s main compositional principle is artifice, staunch antirealism equally governs Donoso's concept of character:

> Si escribo, es para que los que son como él *no* se reconozcan . . . ni entiendan. El feísmo extremado de algunos de mi [sic] anteriores libros pudo ser absorbido por gente como los Ventura porque toda intención de ser "real," aunque caiga en lo desagradable, cae dentro de lo aprobado. . . . [Utilizo] en el presente relato un preciosismo también extremado . . . , ya que el preciosismo es pecado por ser inútil y por lo tanto inmoral, mientras que la esencia del realismo es su moralidad. (*Casa* 400–401)
>
> (I write as I do so that people like [Silvestre Ventura] *won't* recognize themselves . . . or understand what I'm saying about them. The exaggerated ugliness of some of my earlier books could have been readily grasped by people like the Venturas, because every attempt at "realism," however unpleasant or disturbing, always meets with official approval. . . . [I] employ in this present tale an equally exaggerated artificiality . . . , since artifice is a sin for being useless and immoral, whereas the essence of realism is its morality.) (*House* 283)

Donoso repeatedly signals that his characters are emblems, not "believable" characters (*Casa* 404; *House* 286). Consider, for example, Wenceslao's disillusionment with Adriano's policies: "Yo ya no encarno sus ideas. Ya no encarno más que la desesperación de no tener ideas que encarnar" (I don't embody his [my father's] ideas any more. I only embody the despair of having no ideas to embody) (*Casa* 293; *House* 206). Or consider the narrator's description of the native leader Francis of Assisi before his execution: "la historia encarnada en este personaje emblemático" "[quien] tenía la conciencia de representar a todos los que eran como él" (an emblematic figure in whom abstract History stood incarnate" "conscious of representing an entire race) (*Casa* 303; *House* 214). The many emblematic characters in *Casa de campo* exemplify Benjaminian allegorical images that are "consciously constructed ruins" (*Origin* 182): broken composites that patch together concrete presentation and abstract representation.

Take the Mayordomo, allegory of Pinochet. His attributes embody various dimensions of Donoso's satire of the Latin American dictator: two-dimensional and faceless like the other servants/soldiers who are replaced year by year, he is defined by his uniform (Pinochet became general of the Chilean armed forces after the previous incumbent, General Schneider, was assassinated because of his loyalty to the Chilean constitution). Thus, despite having absolute command over the servants/armed forces and the Ventura children during curfew hours at night, "the dictator" is only a servant who receives orders to command other servants and lower orders. His distinguishing features are quantitative: the size of his uniform—"lo que en verdad resultaba difícil era encontrar un candidato de talla suficiente para que no quedara suelta" (*Casa* 42) (what proved truly difficult was to find a candidate large enough so that it wouldn't hang loose on him) (*House* 23)—his greater cruelty, and a larger compensation that includes "la casita . . . en la capital . . . en un barrio semejante al barrio donde vivían los señores, pero plebeyo" (a cottage in the capital . . . in a neighborhood resembling the masters', only plebeian) (*Casa* 42; *House* 24). The chapter named for the Mayordomo (which narrates the restoration of the old order under his command) shows that all his measures are derivative, lacking imagination and originality. He is an imitator, so intent on returning to the way things were that he lacks the understanding that "un orden restablecido no es nunca verdadero orden sino un remedo de otros, siempre desfasado en el tiempo" (an order reestablished is never a true order but simply an imitation, always out of phase) (*Casa* 316; *House* 222). Donoso's allegorical dictator is trying to reinstate an old order that was obsolete and corrupt long before it was overthrown—a doomed enterprise.

In this futile effort, the Mayordomo transforms into a satanic double of Benjamin's "angel of history," emblem of the discontinuity and nonteleology of history. Looking back to the past, the angel "would like to stay, awaken the dead, and make whole what has been smashed" ("Theses" 257). In his effort to erase all traces of the revolution, the Mayordomo literally attempts to abolish time by having all calendars and clocks confiscated, and all windows of the house painted black:

> —¡Día y noche, terminaré con vosotros! ¡Quien se refiera a vuestra cíclica autoridad . . . cometerá delito y será castigado! ¡Ni pasado ni futuro, ni desarollo ni proceso . . . , ni luz ni sombra: sólo fábula y penumbra! . . . Harás clausurar todos los postigos y pintar de negro todos los vidrios para mantener luces inalterables en todas las habitaciones, de modo que quede anulada la diferencia entre día y noche y todo transcurra en el remanso de lo que permanece afuera de la historia, porque la historia no se reanudará hasta el regreso de los amos. (*Casa* 330)
>
> (Day and Night, I shall end with you! Whosoever refers to your cyclic authority . . . is guilty of a crime and will be punished! Neither past nor future, neither development nor process, . . . neither light nor darkness: only fable and shadow! . . . Seal up all shutters and paint all the windows black, leaving an unvarying light in every room, so that the difference between day and night shall be canceled. All will henceforth take place in the doldrums of History, for History shall not resume until the masters come home!) (*House* 232)

By completely sealing off the house and its inhabitants from the outside, even from natural rhythms (the dining hall remains open day and night, now indistinguishable), the Mayordomo entombs the children in a "prolongado presente" (endless present) without change (*Casa* 336; *House* 237). Amputating chronological time and boarding up all windows is the Mayordomo's crude attempt to restore the inward-looking microcosm, the baroque civilized ideal, represented in the first Marulanda panorama. The blackened house also summons the phenomenon of the *memoria clausurada* and the *política del olvido* of the Latin American dictatorships (von Koerber 163). This analogy is literal: to erase the memory of Allende and the Popular Unity government after his assassination, Pinochet walled in the door of the presidential palace La Moneda (Morandé 80) through which Allende's corpse was removed to be buried in an unmarked grave (Nelson 21). The blackening of the house is the Mayordomo's last, most desperate (and, as we know, unsuccessful) attempt to maintain this artificial enclave intact.

The passage of time, Benjamin declares, propels the angel of history "into the future . . . while the pile of debris before him grows skyward" ("Theses" 258). Clearly, Benjamin's angel is more insightful than the Mayordomo—unlike the latter, the former understands that history is nothing but "one single catastrophe which keeps piling wreckage upon wreckage" (257). *Casa de campo*'s and Benjamin's allegories offer identical insights: no totality, neither grand narrative (left revolutionary utopia or dictatorship dystopia) nor individual, neither dictator (Mayordomo-Pinochet) nor savior-angel (Adriano-Allende), can reintegrate the heap of rubble that is History. That is to say, beyond its critique of the historical naivete of the Pinochet dictatorship, Donoso's satire of the Mayordomo has implications for his portrait of Allende in Adriano Gomara that have not been fully recognized. Founded on social utopianism, Adriano's revolutionary order founders partly because of the violence of a conceptual idealism related in principle (though not in political practice) to the Mayordomo's counterposition.

Neither the Mayordomo nor Adriano recognizes what Wenceslao understands in his progressive disillusionment about being left without "ideas to embody." That is why Wenceslao is the only emblematic hero in this dark novel, not because he embodies the weak and unprincipled middle classes who bring the radical Adriano to power and then defect to Pinochet (Madrigal 15–16) but because he understands what Benjamin's angel knows: that the continuity and progress we see in history is nothing but a disguise for the "wreckage" wrought by "the storm we call progress" ("Theses" 258). Wenceslao sounds like a nihilist: nothing "lo [iba] a arrastrar a formular una ortodoxia más concreta que su propia desilusión" (would ever again persuade him to embrace any philosophy more concrete than his own disillusionment) (*Casa* 390; *House* 275).

But this is not how the novel ends. For, as Gilles Deleuze argues in *The Fold,* the baroque gives an alternative response to the modern threat of nihilism after the delegitimation of metanarratives, traditional and modern: to the Benjaminian challenge of "Theses," Deleuze offers a response that I had the occasion to visit earlier in the context of Eliot's critique of dissociationism: "The Baroque solution is the following: we shall multiply principles—we can always slip a new one out from under our cuffs—and in this way we will change their use. We will not have to ask what available object corresponds to a given luminous principle, but what hidden principle responds to whatever object is given, that is to say, to this or that 'perplexing case.' . . . A case being given, we shall invent its principle."[95] Faced with the impasse of nihilism (the loss of absolute principles), the baroque, Deleuze argues, offers an anti-objectivist, creationist solution: the baroque is "the splendid moment when Some Thing is kept rather than nothing, and where response to the world's misery is made through an excess of principles" (*Fold* 68). The difference between Benjamin's and Deleuze's baroques may be approximated in terms of a distinction made by Brian McHale between modernism and postmodernism, via their emphasis on different problematics or "dominants."[96] Focusing on questions of knowledge and its conditions and limits, modernism's dominant is epistemological. Conversely, surpassing modernism's investigation of what can be known, by whom, and to what degree of certainty, postmodernism considers the "imaginative projection" of different fictional worlds (McHale 10). For this reason, postmodernism's dominant is ontological, concerning questions of being. Paralleling the transition McHale identifies from modernism's quest for "reliable knowledge" to postmodernism's playful engagement with speculation and "possible worlds" (10), these alternative "dominants," I would submit, also underpin Benjamin's and Deleuze's investigations of the baroque.

Deleuze's suggestion that something provisional, and admittedly fictional, may fill the proverbial (intellectual, existential) void of the baroque describes the response of Wenceslao (and that of the other Venturas abandoned at Marulanda) to the apocalyptic ending, the annual fall thistlestorm, which chokes all life outside. The remaining Venturas settle into an uncertain new beginning of a post-postdictatorship social order at Marulanda: the Mayordomo's troops and the foreigners have departed for the capital with, it is understood, the prospect of dividing between themselves the gold trade in the future. This is Donoso's final allegorical image of Chile under the rule of neoliberalism and globalization: the nation's profits go to foreign investors. Devastated by their dispossession by global capital, the majority of the defeated Ventura adults succumb to suicidal panic and meet their deaths crossing the plain in one overcrowded cart during the thistlestorm. But "something rather than nothing," as Deleuze puts it, is affirmed in the ruined and abandoned country house itself that is now receiving refugees—former masters, former slaves (natives), and the Ventura children. Faced with lawlessness and the threat of death, this heterogeneous group of refugees forms a new community built on new principles—not the revolutionary ideals that inspired Adriano, which have failed, but principles invented, it seems, in the press of the exigencies of a specific case (as Deleuze says): the case of Marulanda in ruins, during the season of the thistlestorm. The invented principle is a collective ritual of survival, namely, practicing a method of slow rhythmic breathing developed by the natives, which is allegorized by a final *tableau vivant:* "en el salon de baile, quedaron tumbadas las figuras de grandes y niños y nativos confundidas, apoyadas unas en otras, en los almohadones, cubiertas por las mantas a rayas tejidas por las mujeres de los nativos, respirando apenas, con los ojos cerrados, con los labios juntos, viviendo apenas" (in the ballroom, the bodies of grown-ups and children and natives alike lay mingled, resting in each other's laps, on the pillows, muffled in striped blankets woven by native women, scarcely breathing, eyes shut, lips sealed, barely alive) (*Casa* 498; *House* 352). This postscript to the Marulanda panoramas speaks for itself: colonialism is here to stay, consolidating into globalized neocolonialism (the oligarchy has simply gone global). The losers of globalization are ordinary Chileans, who can hope to survive the apocalypse only if they invent new forms of solidarity and community and practice local, vernacular arts of social and economic knowledge and survival.

Antidictatorship Neobaroque Cinema

Raúl Ruiz's *Mémoire des apparences* and María Luisa Bemberg's *Yo, la peor de todas*

I am not an ideologue of the baroque. I am simply Latin American. I can't help but be baroque. Allegory for me is much more than a game or an element of style.

—Raúl Ruiz, Sydney, February 3, 1993, quoted in Laleen Jayamanne, "Life Is a Dream"

The artistic outlook of the baroque is, in a word, cinematic.

—Arnold Hauser, *The Social History of Art,* vol. 2, *Renaissance, Mannerism, Baroque*

Film and the Baroque are natural allies. They share a central aim: the creation of illusion.

—Stephen Calloway, *Baroque Baroque*

This chapter builds on the previous one for its delineation of the revival of baroque expression as a response to the dictatorships that engulfed Latin America in the seventies and beyond. The neobaroque turned out to be particularly useful for the purposes of the post-Boom literature of defeat and disillusionment that arose in the wake of the coups. Against the deceptive illusionism of the fascist state's official narratives of progress, neobaroque antidictatorship literature mobilizes a critical poetics of artifice and disillusionment. Neobaroque fragmented allegorical images thus come to haunt the simulacra of the authoritarian state: to unmask the dictatorships' official narratives, the antidictatorship neobaroque employs the Benjaminian strategy of brushing history against the grain and revisioning it under the sign of melancholia and the untimely, thereby exposing Latin American civilization under the dictatorships as a wasteland of ruins, strewn with the rubble of the discarded cultural residues of the violently destroyed past.

Here I focus on visual culture, and film in particular, in the contexts of political authoritarianism and the "memory battles" that have erupted in the wake of the Southern Cone dictatorships. This chapter discusses two neobaroque films that also belong to the antidictatorship context, the exile Chilean filmmaker Raúl Ruiz's *Mémoire des apparences* (1986; *Memory of Appearances,* also known as *Life Is a Dream*) and the Argentine feminist filmmaker María Luisa Bemberg's *Yo, la peor de todas* (1990; *I, the Worst of All*). Like Donoso's and Eltit's fictional narratives, Ruiz's and Bemberg's cinematic narratives portray the struggle against authoritarian regimes. In both cases, protest is made indirectly and allegorically, via adaptations of the literature and culture of the historical baroque: Ruiz's film is an adaptation of a masterpiece of the Spanish Golden Age, Pedro Calderón de la Barca's play *La vida es sueño* (1635; *Life Is a Dream*).[1] Bemberg's film is a cinematic biography of the celebrated seventeenth-century Mexican poet and nun, Sor Juana Inés de la Cruz (1648?–1695),[2] who was acclaimed as the Tenth Muse during her lifetime and was one of the foremost writers of the transatlantic Hispanic baroque. Ruiz's and Bemberg's films are excellent further examples of the revival of the historical baroque that is a characteristic of neobaroque literature and visual culture from Eliot and the Generation of '27 across the twentieth century and into the twenty-first. Indeed, Bemberg's film is part of an ongoing Sor Juana revival, which has yielded a burst of creative adaptations of the poet's life by Latin American and U.S. Latina (as well as non-Hispanic) writers, artists, and playwrights.

This chapter moves from neobaroque literature to film, and examines cinema, which—along with contemporary entertainment media—has eclipsed literature as the main medium of transmitting institutionalized and hegemonic discourses. Cinema's illusionism—its potential for simulating artificial realities that mask as natural and real—is much greater than that of the traditional visual arts and literature. Exploiting hyperbole across the board, the neobaroque sensibility maximizes all registers of cinema: employing spectacular mise-en-scène, it manipulates cinema's real-world material (what is staged before the camera—setting, lighting, acting, costume, etc.). It also flaunts the constructivist and expressive resources of cinematography (the manipulation of the film strip in the shooting and editing phase). Ruiz's and Bemberg's films combine a neobaroque aesthetics—hyperrealist mise-en-scène, lavish cinematography, and discontinuous or theatrically visible editing—with critical readings of the official, authoritarian culture of the baroque (Maravall). Released seven years after the end of military rule in Argentina, Bemberg's film constructs explicit analogies between Sor Juana's tribulations under the colonial state baroque and twentieth-century fascism. In parallel ways, Ruiz deploys Calderón's baroque play about kingship and tyranny to allegorize totalitarian repression in Chile under Pinochet, forging elaborate parallels between state terror in the seventeenth century and in the twentieth century. The theme of tyrannical rule and the oedipal struggle between a dictator-father and his disinherited, deceived, and imprisoned son in *La vida es sueño* comes to allegorize Chile under totalitarian rule. In particular, the trials of Segismundo, Calderón's protagonist and the tyrant Basilio's son, mirror the trials of Ignacio Vega, a Chilean dissident and the film's protagonist: both are the victims of human rights abuses of authoritarian regimes. Ruiz's film is a brilliant reminder that absolutism and the baroque controversy over royal sovereignty offer a timely framework for describing authoritarianism in the twentieth century.

Baroque Genealogies of the Modern Authoritarian State: Seventeenth-Century Absolutism and Twentieth-Century Dictatorships

As historical films that frame the authoritarian culture of the baroque as the antecedent of contemporary dictatorships in the Southern Cone, Ruiz's *Mémoire des apparences* and Bemberg's *Yo, la peor de todas* reconstruct a transhistorical genealogy of the repressive state baroque. As critiques of the baroque as the instrument of the authoritarian state and the Counter-Reformation, their work continues the lineage of the "minor," anti-institutional and decolonizing baroque theorized in the essays of Lezama Lima and Carpentier and later practiced in fiction by Eltit and Donoso. Indeed, in his *Trauerspiel* study, Walter Benjamin worked with those same parallels between seventeenth-century absolutist political theory and twentieth-century dictatorships that Ruiz and Bemberg provocatively deploy in their films. Benjamin founded his analysis of absolutism, the baroque theory of sovereignty, and the baroque prince on the early work of the legal theorist and political philosopher Carl Schmitt.[3] Schmitt, a sympathizer of the Nazi regime and an outspoken critic of the liberal democracy of the Weimar Republic that was defeated by fascism, developed his theory of state sovereignty in deliberate opposition to the liberal-democratic theory of sovereignty of the people. The first sentence of Schmitt's *Political Theology* (1922)—Benjamin's model—announces his political agenda: "Sovereign is he who decides on the exception [*Ausnahmezustand*]."[4] The cornerstone of Schmitt's modern political theory is the sovereign's absolute power to make decisions that are final and unanswerable to any other authority—in short, dictatorial powers. Invoking Schmitt, Benjamin similarly defines the baroque prince as a ruler destined to become a tyrant: "Whereas the modern concept of sovereignty amounts to a supreme executive power on the part of the prince, the baroque concept emerges from a discussion of the state of emergency, and makes it the most important function of the prince to avert this. The [baroque] ruler is designated from the outset as the holder of dictatorial power if war, revolt, or other catastrophes should lead to a state of emergency. This is typical of the Counter-Reformation" (*Origin* 65). A few pages later Benjamin continues, "The theory of sovereignty which takes as its example the special case in which dictatorial powers are unfolded, positively demands the completion of the image of the sovereign, as tyrant" (69).

Benjamin's discussion of the baroque ruler destined to become a dictator thus avails itself of an authoritarian tradition in European political theory in which Schmitt, the theorist of twentieth-century totalitarianism, recuperates Thomas Hobbes, the political theorist of baroque absolutism. According to Schmitt's editor, Schmitt was such an admirer of Hobbes that he "deserves to be called the Hobbes of the twentieth century."[5] More urgently, here we encounter another reminder that it is imperative to distinguish between specific instances of twentieth-century baroque revivals and ideological orientation, as I have done throughout this book: if the dialectics between institutional and anti-institutional, repressive and liberating, colonial and decolonizing use dates from the baroque's seventeenth-century beginnings, this ideological Janus face of baroque expression similarly survives in the neobaroque. Whereas Lezama Lima and Carpentier (and their followers) recuperate the decolonizing New World baroque, Schmitt recovers Hobbes. In short, the repressive state baroque produces its own cycles of transmission from the baroque to the neobaroque.

Schmitt's emphasis on the exception, on the need for a strong central authority—the sovereign—and on executive decisiveness to master crises, restore stability, and protect the physical safety of citizens is rooted in the tumultuous Weimar years (the German political reality also lived by the author of the *Trauerspiel* study), just as it also resonates with the political and religious crises of the seventeenth century that gave rise to Hobbes's *Leviathan* (1651), written during the English Civil War (1642–51). Hobbes's characteristically baroque view that nature is nothing, civilization everything—as expressed in his famous aphorism that life in the state of nature is "solitary, poor, nasty, brutish, and short"[6]—affirms the need for an authoritarian government that holds nature's destructive and blind forces in check. Hobbes's apology of absolutism, like Schmitt's neobaroque authoritarian political theory, is founded on a crisis mentality dominated by fear. Schmitt affirms: "The exception is more interesting than the rule. The rule proves nothing; the exception proves everything: It confirms not only the rule but also its existence, which derives only from the exception. In the exception the power of real life breaks through the crust of a mechanism that has become torpid by repetition" (*Political Theology* 15).

If Schmitt's focus on the exception and absolute executive authority makes him an advocate of the repressive state baroque, does Benjamin's debt to Schmitt cast a shadow on the *Trauerspiel* study, as offended critics have charged? It is true that in his analysis of tragic drama—*Trauerspiel*—Benjamin follows Schmitt in focusing on the absolutist ruler's management of the exception. He departs from Schmitt, however, by testing Schmitt's *doctrine* of sovereignty against the *practice* of rule by baroque princes as depicted in baroque drama, to discover striking disparities there. This insight prompts Benjamin to pronounce the failure of Schmitt's theory in political reality. A key source of dramatic conflict in the baroque *Trauerspiel,* according to Benjamin, is the "antithesis between the power of the ruler and his capacity to rule" (*Origin* 70). Nonetheless, "the prince, who is responsible for making the decision to proclaim the state of emergency, reveals, at the first opportunity, that he is almost *incapable* of making a decision" (71; my emphasis).

Among the principal sources of executive incompetence are indecisiveness, as exhibited by Hamlet, the melancholy prince, and a lack of judgment, the problem that afflicts Basilio, astrologer and king of Poland in Calderón's play, who makes a poor decision in disinheriting and imprisoning his son Segismundo at birth. His motive is an inauspicious horoscope predicting that Segismundo will grow up to be a tyrant who will overthrow his father and drive the kingdom into civil war. The horoscope is fulfilled to the letter, but for an unthought-of reason: civil war and Basilio's overthrow do occur, but as the direct consequence of the injustice Basilio commits against his son and legitimate heir to the throne to prevent them. To forestall tyranny and the violation of legitimate rule, Basilio in turn violates the natural order of the divine right of kings—a cornerstone of absolutist political theory—thereby becoming a tyrant himself.[7] One of the many allegories of kingship produced by seventeenth-century playwrights, Calderón's Golden Age drama centers on the most important function of the absolutist prince—executive power—and its tribulations. Benjamin argues that absolutism's concept of state sovereignty carries within itself a catastrophic seed that, far from safeguarding against tyranny and civil war, engenders tyranny and civil war.[8] In addition, absolute sovereignty's inevitable course toward war, terror, and violence also brings about the baroque prince's destruction, either by corrupting him as a tyrant or by killing him as a martyr: "In the baroque the tyrant and the martyr are but the two faces of the monarch" (*Origin* 69).

Benjamin thus puts his finger on a weakness of totalitarian political theory: the absolute sovereign's human shortcomings. If the "strong leader" proves incompetent, gets depressed, or commits an error of judgment, as Basilio does, the repercussions, as Calderón shows, reach cosmic dimensions. Drawing on Schmitt's notion of the sovereign's status as the exception to the juridical order he upholds, Giorgio Agamben has recently explored totalitarian tendencies in traditional Western political theory since Aristotle.[9] Agamben's (controversial) claim that the concentration camp is the hidden paradigm of modern political power in both totalitarian and democratic regimes has become newly topical since the post-9/11 U.S. regime in Guantánamo. Agamben outlines a genealogy of authoritarianism in Western states that is broadly related to Benjamin's, Ruiz's, and Bemberg's efforts.

Far from being co-opted by the ideas of his political adversary, then, Benjamin fashions Schmittian theory into a critical tool exposing the continuities between seventeenth-century absolutism and twentieth-century fascism. For confirmation, we may appeal to Benjamin's famous remark on fascism's aestheticization of politics at the end of his essay "The Work of Art in the Age of Mechanical Reproduction": "This is the situation of politics which Fascism renders aesthetic. Communism responds by politicizing art."[10] Preceding fascism's aestheticization of politics, it was the baroque that first perfected the link between art and state power. As José Antonio Maravall and Arnold Hauser elaborate, the seventeenth century is the period in which the modern, centralizing nation-state emerged in the form of absolutism, which sought to bring all independent regional, military, economic, intellectual, and artistic domains under its central, national command.[11] Maravall in particular points out that while the state baroque's political ideology (centralizing authoritarianism and the restriction of regional, individual, and other autonomies), as well as the political strategies employed to realize it, is doubtlessly repressive, it is also fundamentally modern. Absolutist states created modern (national and imperial) bureaucratic, military, and legal structures of state domination heretofore unknown. And they utilized modern strategies—populism and public relations—to manipulate the hearts and minds of their citizens, thereby producing Europe's first urban mass cultures and state-controlled culture industries, the state baroque.

In Madrid, Rome, Versailles, Vienna, and Prague, secular princes and princes of the Church alike availed themselves of the baroque "grand style" for their official self-representation, staging a display of their sovereignty in monuments, piazzas, palaces, and grand avenues, in processions and tournaments, fireworks and water festivals, in triumphal arches and princes' formal entries into the city, and, last but not least, in the theater itself, which, like the Spanish theater of the Golden Age, flourished as never before.[12] State and Church patronage of the arts and literature expanded, as also did direct state control via proliferating national academies. The "typically modern conflict, so familiar to us, between the conservative and the progressive factors in artistic life, . . . between an academic-official and a non-official free art," was born in the baroque (Hauser 199). The baroque deployed institutionalized, official arts and literature in its power struggle against antagonistic social forces. The quintessential theatricality of the baroque is captured in the conceit that, as in the Calderonian and Shakespearian maxim, "all the world's a stage" (*theatrum mundi*).[13] In Louis XIV's Paris, "the whole city was the stage" and "backdrop" on which the spectacle of the absolutist monarchy was performed in fixed daily and seasonal rituals.[14] In the Roman baroque and elsewhere in Italy, buildings were reconfigured as backdrops and continuous surfaces around piazzas, creating a stage for public festivals based on a new integration of inside and outside, building and surrounding space.[15] State-sponsored baroque spectacles and art are invariably political, and as such are the forebears of the Nazi aestheticization of politics critiqued by Benjamin. In many cases, fascist urban planning and architecture is an oversized adaptation of the baroque city. Baroque grand palaces, triumphal arches, and wide, straight avenues that served as parade grounds were blown up to an even more monumental scale in fascist architecture (as, for example, in Albert Speer's master plan for Berlin). In the seventeenth century, European national capitals were transformed to display the sovereignty of new, centralizing nation-states and their absolute monarchs. This imperial baroque style was appropriated by twentieth-century despots for its eloquent political symbolism.[16]

If Ruiz's film remakes Calderón's *Trauerspiel* into an allegory of Chile's ordeal under Pinochet, Bemberg similarly adapts her cinematic biography of Sor Juana to the contemporary postdictatorship Argentine condition. In an interview, Bemberg revealed that she designed her film's historical mise-en-scène to depict authoritarianism: "high angles and grand traveling shots of columns and cupolas, of that huge, hard, imposing proto-fascist baroque architecture whose bad taste only emphasizes the power to which it testifies. . . . I needed to emphasize power, opulence, force. That's why I thought of the association with fascism."[17] But whereas Ruiz's film employs a dual plot—and the device of the play-within-the-play (or film-within-the-film)—to construct explicit analogies between authoritarianism in the seventeenth century and in the twentieth century, Bemberg's narrative concentrates on the life of Sor Juana, suggesting analogies with the contemporary Latin American dictatorship only indirectly.

Yo, la peor de todas takes its title from several renunciations Sor Juana signed in 1694, with her own blood, in which she condemned her previous life and secular works and pledged herself to withdrawing into complete silence and seclusion, dedicated to the religious life appropriate to her vows. "Yo, la peor del mundo" (I, worst of all the world) was the epithet with which she referred to herself in one of these documents.[18] Born an illegitimate child, Sor Juana had enjoyed a stellar career as a prolific writer and intellectual, which began at the court of the Viceroy of New Spain in Mexico City and continued after she joined the convent of San Jerónimo. A rare woman *letrado* (a literate, educated person), she was a celebrated member of the tiny colonial elite that Ángel Rama calls "the lettered city," acquiring an international reputation and corresponding with intellectuals in the

Americas and in Europe. Around 1690, Sor Juana came under increasing pressure from the Church, which she resisted defiantly at first, penning *Respuesta a Sor Filotea* (1691; *Reply to Sor Filotea*), a famous autobiographical and feminist self-defense unique for her times, which asserts women's rights to use their minds just like men. Because of the lack of contemporary sources on her life beyond her own works in three volumes, which were published at the end of her lifetime (in 1689 and 1692) and posthumously (in 1700), the extraordinary reversals in her biography have long given rise to intense speculation over the motivation of key events of her life.

Indeed, the life of the seventeenth-century Mexican nun and poet has become the subject of a surge of recent adaptations in literature and the visual arts. The last decades have seen a steady output of Latina creative literature and art about Sor Juana from both Latin and North America. This Latina trend coincides with a much broader Sor Juana revival, which began at midcentury (after the tercentenary of her birth, celebrated in 1951, and with the publication of Sor Juana's collected works, edited by Alfonso Méndez Plancarte), and has gathered steam since the 1980s, after the publication of Octavio Paz's magisterial intellectual biography, *Sor Juana; or, The Traps of Faith* (first published in 1982, translated into English in 1988).[19] This revival took place in scholarly Sor Juana studies, as well as in literature and film adaptations. The breadth of interest in Sor Juana is quite striking: Sor Juana is the protagonist of two recent novels written in English, the Canadian Paul Anderson's 1,400-page novel *Hunger's Brides* (2004) and the Chicana writer Alicia Gaspar de Alba's 450-page novel *Sor Juana's Second Dream* (1999).[20] Sor Juana is also claimed by the contemporary Mexican state: the Mexican 200 peso bill features her portrait. At least three distinct groups can be identified as participants in this recovery process: Latin American intellectuals, artists, and writers, who spearheaded the recovery, as well as inaugurating early feminist approaches to Sor Juana's life and work; U.S. Chicana writers and artists, such as Amalia Mesa-Bains, whose recreation of Sor Juana's cell and library as part of her visual autobiography is discussed in the next chapter; and, finally, non-Hispanic creative writers.[21] Although many of the adaptations of Sor Juana's life are not neobaroque stylistically, they follow a primary feminist ethos of recovering a lost Latina precursor in the battle for women's rights, as well as an early modern woman genius.

In contrast, Bemberg's film, like Mesa-Bains's installation, combines neobaroque stylization with a feminist reading of Sor Juana's life, which recovers Sor Juana's gendered rebellion vis-à-vis the patriarchal and imperial society of New Spain in the Golden Age. Bemberg's film script is based on Paz's biography, which is also the main source of most subsequent Latina adaptations of Sor Juana's life. As the feminist Sor Juana scholar Stephanie Merrim acknowledges, Paz's meticulously researched study overthrew a long-standing critical tradition that domesticated Sor Juana and downplayed the force of her secular, intellectual quest for knowledge independent of religion, thus paving the way for more enlightened and feminist readings of Sor Juana.

Inevitably, the Sor Juana revival raises questions about the baroque in the New World. To what extent can her work be dissociated from the monumental, official state baroque of the Spanish Empire and the Church? To what extent does it contribute to new, insurgent practices of the alternative, decolonizing New World baroque? Intent on recovering a forgotten Latina feminist precursor, many twentieth-century Latina creative adaptations of Sor Juana's life disregard the Sor Juana who was a *letrado,* a member of the Hispanic elite class of intellectuals economically dependent on state and Church patronage.[22] Instead, they highlight this other, rebellious Sor Juana, whose work has led scholars of the baroque such as Paz and Irlemar Chiampi to discover the "(strange) modernity of the Mexican nun—a modernity avant la lettre—exercised vitally and spiritually *through* her experience with the baroque aesthetic, not outside or against it."[23] In the analogy with the contemporary dictatorship evoked by Bemberg, Sor Juana ended her life as a persecuted dissident and victim of the human rights abuses of the Counter-Reformation. Before her fall, however, she was a court poet who enjoyed the protection of the palace, which enabled her to follow her secular, literary, and intellectual pursuits and which depended on her active participation in the official spectacles of the colonial court and the Church, as well as on her political skills in respecting the core orthodoxies of baroque Counter-Reformation society.

Scholars of the early modern era, such as Maravall, John Beverley, and Anthony Cascardi, have outlined the emergence of the modern subject in the seventeenth century as what Cascardi dubs the "subject of control." They show how the modern and newly mobile subjectivity of self-regulation and self-mastery emerges from a new habitus produced by the internalization of the discipline of the rising absolutist state. According to Maravall, the repressive culture of the baroque sought to reproduce the status quo by channeling human energy into prescripted molds through a modern, rationalist method of systematic "guidance" and control.[24] As Cascardi points out (and as I discuss in more detail later on), Calderón's protagonist Segismundo exemplifies this process by which modern subjectivity arises from an anterior subjection to an external system of higher authority.[25] The "new" Segismundo, who agrees to discipline his passions during his process of education, in which he comes to incarnate the persona of the "virtuous prince," emblematizes this modern "subject of control," who has incorporated the discipline of the absolutist state. Thus, part of this chapter's argument revolves around the dialectics between Calderón's reformed Segismundo, the former victim of baroque authoritarianism who becomes its new dictator-ruler, and the historical Sor Juana, the woman genius who, against all odds, broke through the walls of the lettered city to steal into the inner sanctum of the patriarchal and colonial institutions of baroque New Spain, but who was expelled and punished at the end of her life for her transgression. To be sure, gender is key to Segismundo's and Sor Juana's opposite trajectories. Without a doubt, the defiant defense of intellectual pursuits by women that threads through Sor Juana's writings indicates that the simple fact of Sor Juana's gender placed her subjectivity in a permanent state of conflict (and thus outside of conformity and reproduction of the status quo) with the baroque social order of her day. The mere fact of a woman claiming the authority of authorship during the emergence of the modern "subject of control" seems to have stretched the boundaries of that subjectivity to the breaking point and laid bare the mechanisms of discipline underlying its formation. For this, Sor Juana's spectacular abdication and silencing at the end of her life offers eloquent evidence.

The Struggle for Memory and against Oblivion: Recuperating the Past after the Dictatorship

Raúl Ruiz's *Mémoire des apparences* centers on the problem of memory in authoritarian society. His protagonist is an exiled Chilean dissident and teacher of literature, Ignacio Vega, who is charged to commit to memory a network of anti-Pinochet dissidents in 1974. Arrested shortly after, he must forget everything. The film's plot begins ten years later, in 1984, after Vega has been recalled to his childhood city of Valparaíso by putative former political friends and charged to retrieve the list of the dissident network. Suspense arises from two sources: first, the drama of Vega's recovery of his lost memory, and second, Vega's betrayal and his discovery that he has fallen victim to an elaborate conspiracy engineered by his pro-Pinochet enemies, who have lured him back home to ensnare and eliminate him.

As its title suggests, Ruiz's film stages the question of memory within an elaborate baroque context, linking memory to illusionism and the quintessential baroque awareness of the kinship of appearance and deception. The baroque—to reiterate Heinrich Wölfflin's observation—self-consciously represents things "as they seem to be" rather than "as they are."[26] It is this baroque sensibility of an ironic slippage between truth and semblance that antidictatorship filmmakers like Ruiz (and writers like Donoso and Eltit) leverage to dismantle the falsehood that official dictatorship discourse passes off as the truth. Like the authors discussed in the previous chapter, Ruiz adapts the baroque play of illusion and disillusionment for emancipatory purposes. Paralleling *Casa de campo*, furthermore, *Mémoire des apparences* stages conflicting uses of illusionism—institutional versus anti-institutional, authoritarian versus anti-authoritarian, reactionary versus emancipatory. The oscillation between these polarities in Ruiz's film is further enriched by Ruiz's anti-authoritarian, ironic, and witty adaptation of Calderón. As its alternate title indicates, Ruiz's cinematic adaptation of Calderón's play turns on Calderón's central conceit, the hyperbolic baroque doubt that life is only a dream and that what seems to be real is nothing but an illusion. As Segismundo eloquently puts it at the end of his famed soliloquy in act 2 of *La vida es sueño,*

> ¿Qué es la vida? Un frenesí.
> ¿Qué es la vida? Una ilusión,
> una sombra, una ficción,
> y el mayor bien es pequeño;
> que toda la vida es sueño,
> y los sueños, sueños son.
>
> (What is life? A frenzy.
> What is life? An illusion,
> a shadow, a fiction,
> and our greatest good is but small;
> for, all of life is a dream,
> and even dreams are dreams.)
> (*La vida es sueño* 122–23)

Calderón stages doubt as a strategic ploy within a Christian moralist framework of educating the young prince's free will (*libre albedrío*) to choose correctly between virtuous and sinful conduct: the concerns of earthly life are vain; life must be lived facing death and the eternal afterlife. Good works and self-discipline are necessary for salvation. Calderón's Catholic, theological outlook, typical of the Spanish Golden Age, corresponds to the official, authoritarian positions of the Counter-Reformation and the absolutist state. In contrast, Ruiz's antidictatorship adaptation ingeniously turns Calderón's doctrinaire Counter-Reformation pedagogy on its head.

Like the seventeenth-century "guided culture" of the baroque, twentieth-century mass media under the censorship of the military are subject to an official politics of oblivion that subordinates historical fact to censorship. Both stage carefully orchestrated spectacles of entertainment as opiates for the people and offer blatantly partisan constructs of the past. As Elizabeth Jelin affirms, the authoritarian regimes in Chile, Argentina, Brazil, Paraguay, and Uruguay have invariably resulted in crises of collective memory.[27] In principle, all political transitions and transformations of the state involve revisions of established master narratives of the past, "a new foundational moment, with new readings and meanings given to the past" (Jelin 30).

However, periods of political repression, state terrorism, and wars trigger especially acute crises in established memory scripts, followed by battles over the representation of the dictatorship years in the symbolic realm that echo the actual political violence. Jelin's argument is corroborated by the work of the historian Steve Stern.[28] On the eve of Pinochet's unexpected arrest in London in 1998 and almost a decade after the return to democracy, Stern argues, Chile had reached a virtual "memory impasse" in which conflicting memories of the Pinochet years seemed irreconcilable. The political right and supporters of Pinochet continued to celebrate the coup as Chile's salvation from communism. Conversely, the human rights movement, including relatives of victims and survivors of state terror, persevered in protesting the catastrophic upheaval that led to human rights abuses that had never been punished. In the end, it took an external and unforeseen event—Pinochet's London arrest—to break the deadlock in Chile's national memory crisis, as well as Pinochet's stranglehold on the Chilean state after the return to democracy.

Ruiz's and Bemberg's historical films help mend the chain of memory broken by the Chilean and Argentine military regimes. At the same time, they are symptoms of the acute "memory fever" (Jelin) that afflicts postdictatorship societies. As Jelin suggests, modernity as such has given rise to a "culture of memory" that compensates for the ravages wrought by the modern acceleration of social and economic change in the domain of individual and group identities, for identity "is linked to a sense of permanence (of being oneself, of selfhood) through time and space" (Jelin 14). According to French historian Pierre Nora, organic *milieux de mémoire* (real environments of memory) have given way to artificial *lieux de mémoire* (sites of memory) as modern societies construct and manufacture sites of memory (commemorative festivals, museums, monuments) to replace lost spontaneous memory: "We speak so much of memory because there is so little of it left."[29] The spiral of accelerating modernization fuels the counterspiral of expanding artificial sites of memory: modern oblivion is combated with ever new and varied artificial modes of archiving and performing the past. Thus, it is only a superficial paradox that postmodern depthlessness and the weakening of historicity (as described by Fredric Jameson) prompted the production of simulated official national memory scripts in Pinochet's Chile and General Vidal's Argentina, run by the very same regimes whose neoliberal policies of accelerated modernization originally caused the capitalist disarticulation of national cultures and memory.

Ruiz's *Mémoire des apparences* focuses on memory as artifice contending with amnesia and oblivion, challenging the falsifications of history in Pinochet's Chile. But Ruiz's gesture also evokes the artificiality of modern memory as such, identified by Nora's notion of *lieux de mémoire*. As Ruiz's extra- and heterodiegetic narrator explains at the outset, “In early April 1974, literature teacher Ignacio Vega had to learn the names of 15,000 anti-junta resisters. It took him only a week.” A greenish, artificial color appears on screen, coloring luminous veils, under which a person is vaguely visible. The narrator continues, “He had found a mnemonic. He recalls having dared to learn Calderón’s *Life Is a Dream* in 3 days as a teenager. He decided that Calderón’s play would be his mnemonic device. Each line hid a militant’s name, each metaphor an address, each stanza a military operation. Caught shortly after, he had to forget everything.” With these words, the screen goes black, then the narrator continues: “Ten years have passed. And our story begins.” Ignacio Vega appears onscreen in long shot on a hotel bed, resting and thinking. “We find him, in summer ’84, at Hotel Paradise in Valparaíso registered under an alias. After three days he met his contact who asked him to reconstruct the network lost ten years ago. All night he vainly grapples to remember a single stanza, a line of *Life Is a Dream*. After an endless night, he decides to give up, and go to the movies instead, to the theater of his childhood, at the risk of meeting old foes.”

As Ruiz has pointed out in interviews, the mnemonic employed by Vega is the classical technique of artificial memory: “It is a film about the art of memory, classical memory. I was very fascinated by a book of Frances Yates [*The Art of Memory*], and I started reading a lot around the idea of the art of memory in the seventeenth century.”[30] Yates’s study traces the method of artificial memory from its sources in the oratory of antiquity through the Middle Ages to the Renaissance and, finally, to its application to new uses in the growth of modern science in the seventeenth century.[31] This method of memorizing hinges on visual imagination rather than language: the text to be remembered is attached to specific images deployed in an imaginary building (the so-called memory palace). Once deposited in a spatial order, memory can later be recovered by mentally visiting the images in turn and collecting their deposits. Or, as Ruiz explains, “In the art of memory, you need a place that you know perfectly: it can be your body, your house, your town with your church. Then you need to put a sign there, . . . particular and unforgettable images” (Martin, “Never One Space” 61). The classical arts of artificial memory enabled European cultures prior to print technology to store vast amounts of knowledge. Vega in turn appropriates the art of memory for his contemporary Chilean purposes of clandestine communication, using Calderón’s play as his mnemonic device to encrypt the dissident network: “Each line of the play hid a militant’s name, each metaphor an address, each stanza a military operation.”

The local cinema Vega goes to for distraction “showed the same movies as twenty years ago,” the narrator explains. It turns out that the films screened are all North American B movies: Flash Gordon, Captain Marvel, the "staple diet of Ruiz' childhood."[32] In a marvelous breakthrough, Vega suddenly recuperates his lost memory of Calderón's play (and of the militant network). The narrator announces this event by omniscient commentary: "He suddenly remembers the opening of the drama *La vie est un songe* [*Life Is a Dream*], linked with images of a pre-war British thriller." Simultaneously, the camera cuts to an extended scene from the thriller, set in a dimly lit train compartment; alternating shots show a man and a woman seated, with their eyes closed. These are external images of the film screened in the theater, witnessed by Vega. The voiceover then switches to a female voice beginning to recite Rosaura's opening soliloquy from Calderón's play (as adapted by Ruiz):[33]

> Violent hippogriff, vying with the wind, how can you ray without flame, bird without hue, fish without scales, beast without instinct, race, caper, gallop? Stay, be Phaeton to the beast on that mountain. And I, with no way but the laws of destiny, blind and desperate, will leave these chaotic heights already burnt by the sun. Hard host to a stranger, Poland, you mark his arrival in blood, drowning him in sorrows. So my fate foretold me: where was pity for the wretched?

Unlike the narrator's extradiegetic commentary, this voiceover is strictly internal, subjective: it is coming from Vega's reignited memory. We are hearing the lines from Calderón's play that surge in Vega's memory as he is watching the British thriller. To portray this momentous event of Vega's reawakening memory, Ruiz uses unmatched, nonsynchronous sound and visuals: while the images are external and derive from the movie then screening and being watched by Vega, the sound is internal and issues from his inner consciousness. Yet the situation becomes even more intricate: as Rosaura's soliloquy continues, extraneous images are intercut with the external images of the thriller. A close-up appears of gloved hands, which (as is revealed later) belong to Rosaura. As the pressure of Vega's internal, imaginary reality grows, it increasingly displaces external images and sounds. From the moment when Vega's memory starts to unravel, Ruiz begins to screen two parallel films: the external plot of events following Vega's return to Chile and the internal film, as it were, that has started to run in the theater—or cinema—of Vega's mind. Ruiz here portrays what psychologists dub psychocinema. Nonsynchronous sound and images are antirealist cinematic devices that signal the splitting of Vega's consciousness between external and internal reality, present and past, the returning exile's reality in 1985 and the reemerging memory lost in 1974.

Back in his hotel room, Vega realizes that to reconstruct the play he must go to the cinema every day. The remainder of *Mémoire des apparences* traces Vega's recovery of Calderón's play scene by scene, act by act, in shots intercut with shots from the external plot of Vega's tightening entrapment in the conspiracy plotted by his false childhood friends. Yet, we might ask, why doesn't Vega simply read the text of *Life Is a Dream* to remember the network?[34] But the text won't do, and Ruiz's point is that Calderón's play is no longer archived as a script in Vega's mind but rather as a visual sequence of scenes, as in a film. Otherwise put, the method of artificial memory used by Vega—Yates's "memory palace"—is image-based (like film) rather than text-based (like Ruiz's literary source). The paradigm shift from textual to visual narrative is crucial. For the textual continuity of the printed play is shattered and replaced by the new spatial and visual order of artificial memory, which corresponds to the visual logic of cinema, the disjunctive and combinatory process of montage.

That Vega's access to Calderón's play is restricted to the visual logic of the memory palace (appropriately rendered via cinema) also signals, at an abstract level, Ruiz's intervention into literature through film adaptation. For Ruiz's cinematic adaptation of Calderón's seventeenth-century masterpiece for the screen, like Bemberg's adaptation of Paz's biography of Sor Juana, is marked by a deliberate act of shattering the textual continuity of the literary original. It is completed by montage, the rearrangement and suturing of the fragments according to the unique visual logic of cinema. Ruiz's work illustrates Benjamin's influential cinematic aesthetics of fragmentation, which argues that the procedure through which a film is produced—shot by shot, as the editor splices together camera takes filmed at different times and in different places—has revolutionary potential because it destroys aura and authenticity (Benjamin, "Work of Art"). As Benjamin intended, Ruiz's montage style of discontinuous editing shatters the aura of the original artwork by flouting the constructed quality of cinematic narrative. By the same token, it also undermines the neo-auratic false harmonies and continuities of the Chilean national consensus fabricated by Pinochet. To explore these questions in greater depth, we now turn to a discussion of cinema as medium.[35] How does cinema signify? How is the neobaroque aesthetics articulated in cinema? What constitutes a neobaroque poetics of cinema?

Raúl Ruiz's Theory of a Neobaroque Cinema of Visual Excess

In the history of Latin American cinema, a development parallel to the aforementioned process in Latin American literature occurs in which the optimism and effervescence of the Boom of the 1960s give way to the sober post-Boom mood in the 1970s. The 1960s saw the emergence of the New Latin American Cinema, the cinematic equivalent of the Boom with regard to formal innovation and the spirit of cultural nationalism, which affirmed Latin America's independence in the cultural domain.[36] Analogous to the literary Boom, "new" cinemas developed across Latin America, such as Brazil's Cinema Novo,

Argentine filmmakers Fernando Solanas's and Octavio Getino's "Third Cinema," Fernando Birri's Argentine documentary school, and postrevolutionary Cuban cinema. The New Latin American Cinema had panhemispheric ambitions, intending to break the cultural hegemony of European and North American cinema in Latin America. Unlike the Boom in fiction, however, innovation in New Latin American Cinema emphasized documentary and related kinds of social realism. According to Ana López, the "films of the New Latin American Cinema were revolutionary, explicitly political, called for an end to underdevelopment, poverty, oppression, hunger, exploitation, illiteracy, and ignorance."[37] Nonetheless, the New Latin American Cinema, like the literary Boom, was disrupted by the dictatorships in the early 1970s. Many Chilean and Argentine cineastes—among them Raúl Ruiz, but not Bemberg—went into exile, where their work took new directions, and their trajectories diverged as they dispersed around the world. The flowering of postdictatorship Argentine cinema in the 1980s, and subsequently of Chilean cinema, took place in the wake of the rupture that the military regimes introduced into Latin American cultural production: the "conditions that gave rise to a militant cinema of the 1960s . . . no longer existed" (King, *Magical Reels* 93).

Ruiz's work is situated in a complex transnational context. One of the "Popular Unity" filmmakers who went into exile after the coup, Ruiz has worked out of exile since 1973. Like Donoso, but unlike Bemberg (as well as Eltit), his cinematic representation of the dictatorship is not based on personal experience. While Ruiz's early career unfolded in Chile in the 1960s and during the Popular Unity years, his work, according to Zuzana Pick, "was marginal to what was termed the *cinema of Allende*" (Pick, "Wanderings" 51). Although Ruiz was a Socialist Party militant, his early cinema in Chile went against the grain of the New Latin American Cinema and its documentary and social realism (King, *Magical Reels* 177). And even though Ruiz enrolled at the School of Social Documentary in Santa Fé, Argentina, under its director, Fernando Birri, he soon left because of disagreements with Birri's aesthetics (Pick, "Wanderings" 51). Indeed, some critics have situated Ruiz's entire oeuvre within the ambit of surrealist cinema, which seeks to destabilize the realist continuity principles underlying documentary and classical Hollywood cinemas. In an essay on surrealism and cinema, Adrian Martin singles out "the entire, prolific oeuvre of the Chilean exile Raúl Ruiz, whose films since the late 1960s have conjured up, as in a feverish dream, the images and obsessions of . . . surrealism."[38] One editing technique within the discontinuity system typically employed by surrealist cinema to dissolve narrative logic and rationality—and also used by Ruiz—is unmatched shots, "cutting from one shot to another so that there is no apparent continuity in action . . . [to create] disorientation in time and space."[39] (Here I recall, for example, Ruiz's allegorical montage of Calderón's play screening in Vega's head, and the main, external narrative of Vega's return to Chile.) After 1978, Ruiz's films became more French, as he started to film in French, with French crews and actors (Pick, "Dialectical Wanderings" 51). Critics generally agree that Ruiz developed a unique style marginal to both Chilean and French cinemas (ibid. 54).

Receiving "unprecedented recognition as an experimental filmmaker," Ruiz has seen his cinematic style called "modernist"; he has also been described as a "montage director."[40] More to the point, he has identified himself—and has been recognized—as a neobaroque filmmaker throughout his varied career.[41] Underscoring this point is his disarming revelation, voiced at an Australian film festival and recorded by Laleen Jayamanne: "I am not an ideologue of the baroque. I am simply Latin American. I can't help but be baroque. Allegory for me is much more than a game or an element of style."[42] Sustaining the argument of this study, Ruiz also stresses the distinction between multiple baroques, contrasting the imperial Hispanic state baroque to anti-institutional popular baroques in Latin America:

> National Chilean popular culture . . . is curiously very baroque because it started in the moment of the baroque. The poetical improvisation of the countryman, the peasant, in Chile comes directly from the seventeenth century, around the end of the 16th century. The themes they talk about are very seventeenth century. There are, for instance, the themes of "the siesta of the saints," "the reversed world," "the scattered body distributed around the world in pieces," "the disbursed feast in many places at the same time," "the feast of the birds," "the train which goes from heaven to hell," and "the marriers of blacks." I am simply fascinated by my own culture, Latin American culture, which has this particularity that started in the moment of the baroque in Spain. (Martin, "Never One Space" 58–59)

Elsewhere, Ruiz refers to discussions about the baroque as early as the 1960s in Chile.[43] The point at which Ruiz's baroque style and his several other denominations (experimental, surrealist, modernist) converge is his resolute antirealism, his penchant for flaunting the artificiality of the cinematic medium across all registers—through allegorical and nonlinear narration, spectacular mise-en-scène, and theatrically visible cinematography, including editing.

Indeed, this paradigmatic antirealist stance is the central concern of Ruiz's theoretical work on cinema, *Poetics of Cinema 1* (1995) and *Poetics of Cinema 2* (2007).[44] *Poetics of Cinema 1* is organized around a polemical critique of what Ruiz cryptically refers to as "central conflict theory," the actual target of which is the continuity system perfected by classical Hollywood cinema. "I recall the first statement of the theory," explains Ruiz, "a story begins when someone wants something and someone else doesn't want them to have it. From that point on, through various digressions, all the elements of the story are arranged around this central conflict" (*Poetics 1* 11). In the film critic David Bordwell's account, the script manual for classical Hollywood cinema's realist storyline, the implied target of Ruiz's parody, reads as follows:

> The classical Hollywood film presents psychologically defined individuals who struggle to solve a clear-cut problem or to attain specific goals. In the course of this struggle, the characters enter into conflict with others or with external circumstances. The story ends with a decisive victory or defeat, a resolution of the problem and a clear achievement or nonachievement of the goals. The principal causal agency is thus the character, a discriminated individual endowed with a consistent batch of evident traits, qualities, and behaviors.[45]

Classical Hollywood cinema creates the smooth, seamless illusion for which it has been so influential around the world through its continuity principles, which it applies across all dimensions of cinema—narration, mise-en-scène, and cinematography. Narration is linear, telling a story as a chain of cause and effect set in continuous time and space. Mise-en-scène is realist (while taking into account that standards of realism have changed with time). Finally, cinematography and editing are "invisible," subordinated to the fictional story: throughout, form follows function. Cinematic techniques are treated as mere vehicles to render the story "transparent" without calling attention to the cinematic medium (in other words, frequently the camera moves only when characters move, to keep the subject within the frame; visible jump cuts are forbidden) (Bordwell, "Classical Narration" 156–66). According to Bordwell, classical Hollywood's "voyeurism" (Tom Gunning's term for this style) results from the systematic cinematic adaptation of the paradigm of Renaissance classicism (the image as transparent window into space).[46]

Continuity editing (classical Hollywood cinema) and discontinuity editing (including theatrically visible editing) (the montage style of early Soviet directors such as Eisenstein or post–World War II art cinema directors such as Godard) are opposite approaches to this paradigmatic virtuality of cinematic space-time, or cinematic illusionism. Here the comparison with the theater, which influenced early cinema, is instructive. (Cinemas are still built like theaters, with spectators facing the screen instead of the stage.) In cinema, the *physical* extended space of the theater stage, in which characters are located and move, disappears, to give way to a *virtual* space whose space-time continuities are principally illusionary, inferred by the spectator as a result of manipulations of the camera in the shooting and editing phase. As demonstrated by the famous Kuleshov experiments in the 1920s, based on seeing a series of shots taken in disparate locations, spectators will infer a continuous spatial whole that has no counterpart in reality. Cinematic illusionism is the result of editing with its unique logic of cinema, which shatters the natural, physical unity of space and time and—in the developing phase in the laboratory—cuts its fragments into a new, artificial and virtual continuity. As Benjamin observes, in film "the camera [*Apparatur,* machine] is substituted for the public. . . . The equipment-free aspect of reality here has become the height of artifice; the sight of immediate reality has become an orchid [*blaue Blume,* blue flower] in the land of technology" (Benjamin, "Work of Art" 229, 233). More to the point, cinematic montage (discontinuous or visible editing) is the equivalent of baroque and neobaroque literary allegory. Not surprisingly, Benjamin figures as an influential theorist for both literary and cinematic kinds of montage. Differing only in medium, they are identical in technique (arbitrary arrangement of fragments and assignment of meaning), form (broken, artificial wholes), and outlook (antirealism and antiorganicism).

By concealing its technical production, Hollywood's continuity style masks cinema's paradigmatic illusionism, making its spectacle seem like reality. In contrast, the discontinuity styles of montage editors such as Eisenstein and Godard flaunt the director's sovereignty in manipulating the selective rearrangement and concatenation of shots, highlighting cinema's powerful illusionism. A prolific and experimental filmmaker, Ruiz absorbed the legacy of French New Wave cinema (alongside the modernist theater of Beckett, Ionesco, and Pinter) as a beginning filmmaker in Chile during the late 1950s and early 1960s, long before exiling himself to France in 1973 (Peters, "Annihilating" 18). New Wave cinema employs—as does Ruiz's *Mémoire des apparences*—vivid and expressive mise-en-scène, as well as the montage style of jump cuts made famous by Godard.

Bordwell's influential theory of mainstream Hollywood cinema between 1917 and 1960 as cinematic classicism, while not uncontroversial, is extremely helpful for our purposes.[47] According to Bordwell, Staiger, and Thompson, "the principles which Hollywood claims as its own rely on notions of decorum, proportion, formal harmony, respect for tradition, mimesis, self-effacing craftsmanship, and cool control of the perceiver's response—canons which critics in any medium usually call 'classical'" (*Classical Hollywood Cinema* 3–4). Bordwell attributes Hollywood's global hegemony primarily to the effectiveness of its narrative and visual style, said to offer an optimal interface with the hard-wired biological structures of human cognition (Hansen, "Mass Production" 339). Celebrating Hollywood cinema's modern, technological achievement of the classical ideal of art, Bordwell accordingly defines Hollywood cinema via Renaissance and eighteenth-century neoclassical models in the visual arts and drama—the use of closed, self-contained forms; the (notorious) three unities of time, space, and action; and the classicist rule that form follows function (Bordwell, "Classical Narration" 158).

In reducing Hollywood's global appeal to its stylistic classicism and universalism, Miriam Hansen asserts, Bordwell is mythologizing. Be that as it may, as Ruiz's adversarial response shows, Hollywood style, as the classical norm, has served as a touchstone for the articulation of anticlassical alternatives, such as neobaroque cinema. Indeed, many of Hollywood's classical cinematic techniques easily translate into the art historical principles proposed by Heinrich Wölfflin to distinguish the elusive, subjectivist baroque from objectivist classicism. First, its use of closed, self-contained forms rather than fragmentary open forms evokes Wölfflin's third pair of categories, "closed versus open form." In addition, the Wölfflinian distinction of "absolute versus relative clarity" elucidates Hollywood cinema's lighting techniques. Classical Hollywood cinema uses clear, evenly distributed ("invisible") lighting, such as three-point lighting (key, fill, and backlighting on figures), that achieves absolute clarity of vision.

Ruiz relates how, as a beginning filmmaker in the 1960s, he encountered the Hollywood model as a rigid and "immutable, almost universal system" (Peters, "Annihilating" 16). What Ruiz finds problematic about "central conflict theory"—his grand metaphor for the Hollywood continuity principles that he learned in "North and South American universities" (*Poetics 1* 11)—is precisely its exclusionary linear logic: it "forces us to eliminate all stories which do not include confrontation and to leave aside all those events which require only indifference or detached curiosity, like a landscape, a distant storm, or dinner with friends—unless such scenes punctuate two fights between the bad guys and the good guys" (11). In contrast, Ruiz proposes that "in narrative cinema—and all cinema is narrative to a certain degree—it is the type of image produced that determines the narrative, and not the reverse" (8). In short, he recasts the notion of (narrative) cinema by reversing priorities: whereas classical Hollywood valorizes character, causality, and conflict over the cinematic image, Ruiz places the cinematic image—and, by extension, the cinematic medium—at the center (Peters 16). In more general terms, Ruiz liberates cinematic form and style from service to function. It shouldn't escape anyone's notice how closely Ruiz's cinematic antirealism corresponds to Sarduy's theories of neobaroque "artificialization," which we had occasion to review in relation to Djuna Barnes's neobaroque attack on the realist claims of modern medical theories of homosexuality. Championing the "apotheosis of artifice" and "the mockery of nature," the baroque, according to Severo Sarduy, unmasks realist-mimetic representation as the fabrication that it actually is. Seconding Sarduy, Ruiz's cinematic neobaroque enacts a rebellion against functionalism and the functionalist subordination of language and style to reference—in particular, the reduction of the cinematic medium to an "invisible" vehicle of the message.

Along these lines, one entire chapter of *Poetics of Cinema 2,* "Shadows," is dedicated to attacking the Hollywood principle of evenly spread, "invisible" lighting. "In today's cinema," Ruiz affirms, "there is too much light. It is time to return to the shadows." "A lighting technician is above all a maker of shadows. Though nobody seems to notice" (*Poetics* 2 10, 23). "Shadows" is a plea for baroque dramatic lighting that heightens emotional tension, including effects such as the chiaroscuro style cultivated by Caravaggio and other baroque artists.[48] Ruiz's comments parallel Wölfflin's account of how, in preferring uneven, "irrational lighting" and the play of light and shadow, the baroque liberates color and light from the classical priorities of clarity and precision (Wölfflin 202). Furthermore, Ruiz offers a superb illustration of another major twentieth-century neobaroque theory of baroque visuality, Christine Buci-Glucksmann's "madness of vision." In her study *La folie du voir* (1986; Madness in vision), Buci-Glucksmann argues that baroque visuality contests the dominant visual regime of the modern era, the Cartesian model of vision, which posits a detached and disembodied spectator who observes and analyzes the world from afar.[49] The baroque "madness of vision" undermines the rationalist fiction of disembodied consciousness and its equation of the thinking "I" with the all-seeing but unseen "eye" in the modern, mathematical concept of perspective, elaborated by Renaissance artist Alberti in the visual arts and later established by Descartes in philosophy.

Influenced by phenomenology, Buci-Glucksmann's concept of "madness in vision" comes from Maurice Merleau-Ponty's late work.[50] In endeavoring to overcome modern dissociationism and its separation of mind and body, spectator and spectacle, phenomenology contends that all perception—including visual perception—is *embodied* perception. For Buci-Glucksmann, Merleau-Ponty's "madness in vision" captures the "enigma of visibility" of the human body, which is both visible and seeing, at once spectator *and* spectacle.[51] In the baroque's direct sensual address, the body returns to the visual field from which it has been expelled by rationalism—"to dethrone the disinterested gaze of the disincarnated Cartesian spectator" (Jay, "Scopic Regimes" 188). Thus, the same baroque impulse to "move and amaze," "stir and impress," that Maravall interprets as a cynical technique for manipulating the illiterate masses in the absolutist state baroque (Maravall 75) is vindicated by Buci-Glucksmann as an antihegemonic strategy from another perspective—the baroque and neobaroque critique of rationalist dissociationism, which we have discussed in detail with regard to the work of T. S. Eliot.

Not coincidentally, Buci-Glucksmann is also the author of a full-length study on Ruiz, as well as the coeditor of a collection of interviews with the director.[52] Ruiz, according to Buci-Glucksmann, establishes a "Baroque cogito," founded on vision and the spectacle of seeing and visibility, an alternative to the Cartesian disembodied cogito founded on reason alone: "Such is the Baroque cogito of Ruizian cinema: I see therefore I am in so far as I make the shadows, the ghosts and the living-dead visible, and as much as I practice a visual cannibalism of every possible form by establishing language as a trap or a 'language game'" (Buci-Glucksmann, "Baroque Eye" 38). As Buci-Glucksmann recognizes, Ruiz's clever quip about the cinematographer as a "maker of shadows" is part of the baroque rebellion against the modern dictatorship of reason and rationalism's reductive definition of the real.

Furthermore, Ruiz, like Sarduy, delights in the conspicuous wastefulness of baroque style. In his *Poetics of Cinema* series of cinematic manifestos, Ruiz makes the case for a neobaroque cinema that displays cinematic style at anarchic play, rather than at work in the service of an extraneous purpose (such as effective communication as constructed by mainstream media theory). Embracing "superabundance, brimming cornucopia, prodigality, and wastefulness," the baroque, asserts Sarduy, is "a mockery of all functionality, of all sobriety."[53] Ruiz offers a similar eulogy of redundancy in cinema, in which the cinematic signifier triumphs over the signified and throws off the yoke of machine age principles of efficiency—Hollywood's continuity system. The chapter "The Photographic Unconscious" distinguishes between two dimensions or levels of photographic (and cinematic) signifiers: intentional signifiers, which are necessary and central to the official meaning of the image, and "involuntary or uncontrolled signs," which have crept in by accident (*Poetics 1* 58). Every picture contains these accidental, unnecessary elements, which, Ruiz claims, "reorganize themselves forming an enigmatic corpus . . . that conspires against the ordinary reading of the picture, adding to it an element of uncanniness, of suspicion" (57). Borrowing a term from Benjamin, Ruiz names this reservoir of unofficial, hidden elements that disrupt the surface narrative "the photographic unconscious" (57).

Ruiz's fascination with cinema's loose ends—"the ghosts that hover around mechanically reproduced images" (65)—explains the long-standing passion he professes to have for B movies. He recounts a hilarious anecdote:

> For years, I watched the so-called Greco-Latin films (toga flicks, with early Christians devoured by lions, emperors in love, and so on). My only interest in those films was to catch sight of planes and helicopters in the background, to discover the eternal DC6 crossing the sky during Ben Hur's final race, Cleopatra's naval battle, or the *Quo Vadis* banquets. . . . For me all those films, the innumerable

> tales of Greco-Latinity, all partook of the single story of a DC6 flying discreetly from one film to the next. (60)

Indeed, Ruiz's witty scenario of the "eternal DC6" "flying discreetly" from one toga flick to the next is the cinematic equivalent of baroque excess.

In more general terms, as signaled in the DC-6 anecdote and the above discussion of Ruiz's dramatic, antiobjectivist lighting techniques, Ruiz's neobaroque poetics of cinema centers on his revision of cinematic spectatorship, in ways antithetical to Hollywood classicism. Paralleling the literary concept of the resistant reader—a reader who challenges the ideological premises of the text she is reading—Ruiz posits the figure of a resistant spectator whose viewing performance runs against the grain of the official narrative. This figure of a creative and imaginative spectator is modeled both in his cinematic poetics as well as in his films. Here we may recall Ruiz's montage of two parallel films in *Mémoire des apparences,* the external plot of Vega's entrapment in Chile and the psychocinema of his reawakening memory. Vega's imagination *resists* the actual movies—all North American B movies—that he is watching in the Valparaíso cinema, to the purpose of resurrecting the clandestine network of antidictatorship activists. Ruiz asks real spectators—us—to follow Vega's model and become active, creative spectators who similarly resist Hollywood cinema's seamless illusionism. Deriding the passive spectator of classical Hollywood cinema, Ruiz models a critical, resistant spectator, who—gifted with the quintessential baroque awareness of the kinship between appearance and deception—is a savvy, critical viewer, mindful of the fabrication of cinema's illusion. Ruiz's subversive viewing brings to light what hegemonic systems and official narratives attempt to conceal—such as cinema's mode of production, or the fabrication of modern ideologies of mass consumption transmitted by Hollywood's dream machine.

Ruiz has given Ignacio Vega, his protagonist in *Mémoire des apparences,* his own perverse enjoyment of U.S. B movies. As Adrian Martin explains (here framing Ruiz's neobaroque antirealism as surrealism), "Surrealists have always worshipped 'tacky,' cheaply made 'B' films whose tricks and bursting seams are completely evident. . . . 'B' films—particularly in popular genres such as fantasy, horror, *film noir,* science fiction and the musical—can reach the heights of dreamlike abstraction precisely *because* they are so blatantly artificial" (Martin, "Artificial Night" 193). According to Martin, the reassertion of marginal over central visual codes

> is a phenomenon that Ruiz has often described and celebrated: the triumph of *secondary* over *primary elements* in a film. Primary elements are the standard dominants: plot, character, subject, theme, semi-realistic atmosphere. And professionals of the old school (such as Howards Hawks) like to keep the secondary

> elements, the stylistic or expressive elements (such as colour, camera angle or editing rhythm), as invisible as possible, as mere support for the primary elements: the achievement of that *seamless flow* is what we call *classicism* in cinema. Yet when these secondary elements rear up and assert themselves, the classical economy of form-to-content is powerfully, sometimes ecstatically, overthrown.[54]

In *Mémoire des apparences,* there are many such digressive "loose ends"—intentionally staged rather than accidental, to break the cinematic illusion—that distract from the film's main story, complicating the already difficult storyline even further. For example, when Vega suddenly recuperates his memory, the camera cuts to images of a toy train running along the floor of the Valparaíso cinema—a major setting of the film—past discarded cigarette stubs. The toy train reappears later in a scene in the police station that Vega discovers behind the cinema but has no direct narrative function other than a vague evocation of childhood, memories of which feature marginally in Vega's reencounter with his Chilean past. However, the live (and crowing) chickens that also walk into the frame as the toy train appears for the first time are completely redundant. At times, birds are flying through the darkened cinema above the heads of Vega and scattered local moviegoers. Dialogue from Calderón's play is repeatedly intercut with an enigmatic subplot in an oriental setting, in which the Calderón actors wear Arabic costumes, and which turns out to be the Sinbad story. At one point, Vega and his Chilean companions retire to a futuristic nightclub, where the use of special goggles allows them to see people stark naked, but without nipples—another instance of subversive spectatorship. As Vega learns, the absence of nipples is due to the fact that the pro-Pinochet conspiracy leader (a police official) hates them. "He used to tear them off prisoners." As the (unnamed) policeman (earlier identified as a cop working in the police station behind the cinema, where detainees are being beaten during interrogation) comments, "That's censorship."

Throughout *Mémoire,* such marginalia are on the brink of running away with the main story. Clearly, Raúl Ruiz is another devotee of Lezama Lima's baroque maxim, "Only the difficult is stimulating."[55] Ruiz employs the same digressive structure in his two cinematic manifestos, where the main argument is constantly detoured toward elaborate parables and anecdotes that make the point indirectly rather than explicitly. *Poetics of Cinema 1* announces Ruiz's playfully nonlinear argument: "I have chosen a genre resembling what in sixteenth-century Spain were called *Miscelaneas,* theoretical/narrative discourses where the author's prowess is to turn verbal somersaults, with sudden shifts of focus and unexpected interpolations—in short, a hodgepodge, a farrago, 'everything but the kitchen sink'" (8). The baroque cues here include a montage of fragments, forged by wit, or *agudeza* ("verbal somersaults"), as the intellectual faculty needed to compose these manufactured conceits that perceive likeness in the dissimilar.

Ruiz's polemic against "central conflict theory" and his plea for a baroque cinema of stylistic excess that flaunts its illusionist tricks and loose ends ("the photographic unconscious") are supplemented by his notion of "shamanic cinema." "The cinema I find interesting," affirms Ruiz, "always involves a voyage to different worlds" (105). Shamanic cinema is the antithesis of Hollywood commercial cinema, whose silver-screen spectacles Ruiz likens to the "guided culture" of the baroque, designed to manufacture consent with the ruling political order (absolutism then, capitalism now): "Cinema in its industrial form is a predator. It is a machine for copying the visible world and a book for people who can't read" (73). In contrast to an "ordinary narrative movie," a shamanic film "would be more like a land mine":

> it explodes among these potential films and sometimes provokes chain reactions, allowing other events to come into being. In the same way, the shamanic sequence makes us believe we remember events which we have not experienced; and it puts these fabricated memories in touch with genuine memories which we never thought to see again, and which now rise up and march towards us like the living dead in a horror movie. This mechanism is the first step in a process which would permit us to pass from our own world into the animal, vegetable, and mineral kingdoms, even to the stars, before returning to humanity again. (79–80)

Ruiz's image of the shamanic journey for his nonlinear cinema of baroque multiplicity and excess is thought-provoking. In contrast to the ordinary journey of the realist action-adventure type, which crosses space horizontally, the shaman travels vertically, journeying from the human world into the underworld and the heavens. Unlike ordinary mortals, shamans are able to cross boundaries into nonhuman realms and journey across mutually exclusive worlds (of the living and the dead, of the realms of eternal and mortal beings).[56] The shaman's ecstatic crossing into mutually incompossible worlds recalls Deleuze's model of a nondualist, antidissociationist, inclusive baroque solution to modernity's epistemological upheavals, which we have had the occasion to refer to more than once: the baroque is the "splendid moment" where "response to the world's misery is made through an *excess* of principles" (my emphasis).[57] For Ruiz, baroque cinema—like Deleuze's mobile fold that expresses becoming and the creation of worlds, rather than static being—emancipates itself from the classicist and rationalist rejection of nonlinear logic. It enables a fantastic, imaginary journey across mutually exclusive worlds and realities: "The cinema would become the perfect instrument for the revelation of the possible worlds which coexist alongside our own" (*Poetics 1* 90).

I conclude this section with some general—if cautionary—reflections on the scope of neobaroque cinema: neobaroque cinema is difficult to define in the abstract, beyond the common rejection of cinematic classicisms and the corresponding endorsement of the principle of visual excess. To begin with, as scholarship on Ruiz's "surrealist" cinema shows, there are considerable overlaps between neobaroque cinema and other alternative cinemas that also employ anticlassical techniques. Furthermore, neobaroque tendencies appear in various, unrelated cinemas and directors (European, North American, and Latin American). For example, there are several European auteurs, such as Derek Jarman and Peter Greenaway, whose personal, idiosyncratic styles across a range of films have been recognizably neobaroque.[58] On the other hand, there is the problem of neobaroque tendencies in contemporary (post-1970s) Hollywood cinema. For Angela Ndalianis, the neobaroque is a late, self-reflexive style that mainstream Hollywood cinema has adopted after the end of its classical period in the 1960s, in which its own naturalized systems of representation become self-conscious artifices.[59] Even so, classical realist narrative paradigms (cause-and-effect narratives, goal-oriented characters) persist. For this reason, Ndalianis proposes the nonoppositional coexistence of "classical" and "baroque" in post-1970 mainstream Hollywood cinema: "the Baroque embraces the classical, integrating its features into its own complex system" (Ndalianis 5). As the differences between, say, Jarman and contemporary Hollywood indicate, and as differences between Ruiz's and Bemberg's neobaroque styles will further illustrate in the following sections, there is considerable variation in what cinematic excess (the principle of "more is not less" or "more is more") can mean in concrete terms. To be sure, it would be an error to generalize from Ruiz's position and reduce neobaroque cinema to antirealism: the neobaroque sensibility in cinema maximizes all registers of cinema, including realist and antirealist.

Raúl Ruiz's *Mémoire des apparences*

Mémoire des apparences approaches the Pinochet dictatorship from an explicitly antirealist angle. Indeed, Ruiz's distance from Chile in French exile is also inscribed into this film through its language of sound, which is French, not Spanish. As Ruiz explains in an interview, "I wanted to make a film about what happened in Chile without using Chilean elements. It was a case where allegories infected other systems and made everything else allegorical. The film is making a connection between at least two allegorical systems: one is the system of memory and the other is the system allowing *La vida es sueño* to stand for Latin America. By mixing both, the result is that Chile itself becomes an allegory for something else" (Martin, "Never One Space" 61). As might be expected, Ruiz expresses a profound interest in allegory. He continues: "This connecting aspect of allegory is one of the things that fascinated me the most in this moment. You make an allegory and this allegory touches an element of real life and makes this element become an allegory of something else, of some distant object, and when this object is touched it becomes another allegory and so on" (61). Thus far, we have observed the allegorical method at work in Eliot's *Waste Land,* where it produced a modernist long poem structured as a montage of quotations from millennia of Indo-European literature, as well as in Donoso's *Casa de campo,* where it generated an antirealist historical novel featuring emblem-like artificial characters, an intrusive narrator, and an allegorical plot punctured by emblematic panoramas picturing the fictional setting's cumulative ruin. In the fragmentary plot of Eltit's *Lumpérica,* allegorical flat characters perform a counterspectacle to the official political spectacles organized by the Chilean military regime.

But how does allegory translate from static artworks such as literature and painting to the moving picture? In *Mémoire des apparences,* allegory's aesthetic of fragmentary composition has produced a film that is the cinematic counterpart of the nonorganic artwork (Bürger) and the antithesis of the cinematic equivalent of the organic symbol (seamless whole)—the seamless flow of classical Hollywood. Ruiz's film combines—yokes together allegorically—two stories distant in time and space: Calderón's celebrated Golden Age play and the story of a contemporary dissident exile's return to Chile, his betrayal, and his assassination. We have already discussed the critical purpose of this transhistorical parallel: the illumination of hidden correspondences in state terror between seventeenth-century absolutism and twentieth-century Latin American dictatorships.

In more general terms, allegory is a nontraditional method of film adaptation in Ruiz's *Mémoire des apparences,* a method of adapting literature to the screen that reverses traditional priorities between original and copy. As discussed earlier, it involves the shattering of the textual continuity of Calderón's original and the sovereign rearrangement of the scattered fragments—translated into cinematic shots—into a new, artificial whole. In this way, Ruiz dismisses the "fidelity" debate that has haunted the critical literature on film adaptations of literary classics (Is the film faithful to the literary original?).[60] Attempts to bring literary masterpieces to the screen have been as frequent and persistent as has their censure as inferior versions that "betray" the original. Ruiz's allegorical approach to cinematic adaptation of literature establishes the paradigmatic difference that any transposition from one medium to another entails: Ruiz's film is more usefully viewed as a creative remaking of Calderón's baroque play. Nonetheless, the viewer has to know Calderón's original well, or else Ruiz's film will make little sense. By translating Calderón's story of tyranny and deception into the Chilean dictatorship present, Ruiz also succeeds in exposing Calderón's hidden endorsement of authoritarianism. The following discussion of Ruiz's film adaptation details the key analogies Ruiz constructs between Calderón's play and the Chilean situation, beginning with elements faithful to the Golden Age original before turning to Ruiz's key parodic departures. It is amplified by a formalist close reading of Ruiz's neobaroque cinematic style.

Calderón's melancholy baroque prince, Segismundo, becomes the counterpart of the exiled Chilean dissident Vega. Both are the victims of elaborate conspiracies: As King Basilio recounts in his expository soliloquy in act 1 introducing the background of Segismundo's imprisonment, and as the soldier liberating Segismundo later repeats, Basilio intends to rob Segismundo of his lawful claim and title and give them to a foreign prince, Astolfo the Moscovite. Similarly, the exiled dissident Vega has been led into a trap by his former pro-Pinochet enemies, who lured him back to Chile under false pretenses. In both cases, the perpetrators are state officials; both conspiracies involve state terror. Likewise, the tribulations of Calderón's protagonist come to prefigure the tribulations of Vega, the persecuted dissident. Like Segismundo, Vega struggles to integrate the fragments of his dislocated identity and distinguish truth from illusion, dream from wakefulness. When, after awakening in the palace dressed in royal robes, Segismundo wonders, "¡Válgame el cielo! ¿qué veo? . . . ¿Yo Segismundo no soy?" (Heaven help me! What's this I see? . . . Am I not Segismundo?) (*La vida es sueño* 70–71), his soliloquy also epitomizes Vega's mental disorientation, Vega's vacillation between lapses of amnesia and sudden recollections of forgotten events and people. Ruiz signals these thematic parallels by intercutting Segismundo's soliloquies with Vega's unraveling drama, including enigmatic shots allegorizing the confusion in Vega's mind, where veiled anonymous figures stumble through a space filled with cobwebs and drenched in surreal greenish light. The garishly artificial green in these shots is another instance of Ruiz's strategy of artificialization, or derealization. As Martin observes, Ruiz's films from the 1980s "use bargain basement special effects from cinema's earliest days: mirrors, split screens, optical toys, smoke, shadow, garishly colored filters" (Martin, "Magnificent" 10). Like Barnes's late works, Ruiz's postdictatorship film (following Calderón's original) thus examines a baroque melancholic self, a self constituted by suffering and loss. At the same time, the pathos of suffering is undercut by Ruiz's concerted attack on cinematic realism and its "central conflict" narrative.

In *Mémoire,* editing and distance of framing are highly idiosyncratic. The continuity principles of classical Hollywood cinema constructing a "realist" cinematic world are violated. One element in particular, spatial and temporal continuity, results from a routine editing sequence (so-called "analytical editing"), which begins with an establishing shot that orients the viewer to the visual content of the scene and is followed by close-ups of characters and objects in the scene, as well as iterations of shot patterns or reverse shot patterns for conversations between characters. There is a return to a reestablishing shot in case of any change in the scene (for example, when a new character appears). In contrast, instead of beginning scenes with establishing shots, *Mémoire* frequently delays them or avoids them completely. Cuts to new scenes often begin with a series of close-ups (sometimes extreme close-ups, at times medium shots) of characters and objects in the scene. Long shots that establish the spatial relations of the surrounding setting are rare and come late, if at all.

For example, when Vega leaves the restaurant where he meets his brother's friend for lunch at the beginning of the film and makes his way to the cinema of his childhood, one of the film's main settings, there is no establishing shot of the street scene. First we see a close-up of a foot pedaling and a section of a bicycle wheel. In the absence of an establishing shot, we can merely infer a figure riding a bicycle, whose identity remains unknown. Accompanying the extradiegetic narrator's commentary—"On the way to the cinema the streets are empty. Uniformed soldiers play Boulness, a mixture of cops and robbers and table hockey"—we then see youngsters in uniform with dirt-smeared faces playing soccer in the streets. Once again, only extreme close-ups and close-ups of the various players are presented before any medium shots and medium long shots that would give even a rough idea of the surroundings. Next, Ruiz cuts to a medium close-up of Vega in profile walking in the street, past passers-by who cannot be identified because of the close distance of framing. Someone greets Vega as he rushes past, saying, "I have my pew at the church." Vega returns the greeting, but again the passer-by cannot be identified because of the absence of establishing shots. Only later does a conversation identify this person as Vega's lunch companion.

Ruiz's discontinuous cinematographic and editing style results in a systematic disorientation of the viewer. Eschewing spatiotemporal continuity, the close-distance cinematography in *Mémoire des apparences* immerses the viewer in a wealth of visual and auditory detail while withholding complete contextual information the viewer needs to assign narrative meaning. In addition, unmatched shots, or jump cuts between close-ups without long shots that reestablish continuous spatial background, create enigmatic sequences of images. By undermining classical cinema's linear logic, *Mémoire des apparences* undermines realism. As a result, Ruiz's cinematic images approximate surreal, mysterious dream images. Indeed, the viewer is drawn into a dream world of chaotic images that mirrors the experience of the protagonist Vega, who slowly sinks into a quagmire of memories and paranoia that he increasingly fails to distinguish from external reality. Like Vega, then, the viewer experiences a kind of locked-in syndrome, where the viewer's vision is shrunk and restricted. By creating uncertainty about the "real" (external) status of visual detail processed by the eye, vision in *Mémoire des apparences* abandons realist cinema's firm grasp of external reality. In this way, Ruiz's cinematic technique enacts the film's theme of confusion between reality and appearance: life is a dream.

This overall effect of perceptual and cognitive subjectivity is enhanced by point-of-view shots and sound that predominate in Ruiz's film. Throughout, narration is restricted to the protagonist Ignacio Vega's viewpoint; the viewer rarely knows more than the protagonist. Visuals and narrative voiceover frequently plunge into Vega's mind, reporting his internal perceptions, thoughts, memories, and fantasies. A prime example is Vega's breakthrough to the recovery of his lost memory of the Calderón play and the dissident network discussed earlier.

Another neobaroque feature of Ruiz's cinematic style—partly running counter to his avoidance of establishing shots—is his preference for deep space mise-en-scène, sometimes (not always) accompanied by deep-focus cinematography. Technically, the cinematic image depends on the same spatial illusion as the still images of painting and photography: the image projected on the screen is two-dimensional and flat, but it represents a three-dimensional space in which the action takes place (see Bordwell and Thompson, *Film Art* 190–96). Renaissance artist Alberti formulated the conceit of the painting as "window on the world": the picture plane simulates a transparent window that opens out to an imaginary pictorial space behind it.[61] This pictorial space pretends to be three-dimensional like the viewer's space. Since there is no real space extending behind the screen, in cinema (as in painting and photography) "depth clues" are needed to suggest that the represented space "has both *volume* and several distinct *planes*" (ibid. 192). The cinematic spectrum runs from shallow-space to deep-space compositions, "in which a significant distance seems to separate planes" (195).

When not avoiding establishing shots to disorient the viewer, *Mémoire des Apparences* frequently employs deep-space mise-en-scène, staging scenes in deep space, that is, on several different planes separated by marked distances. According to cinematic "realism" debates, deep-space staging is a realist technique pertaining to the mise-en-scène, which is opposed to the montage style otherwise predominant in Ruiz. Carrying deep-space mise-en-scène to extremes, however, Ruiz makes it hyperbolic, in other words, baroque: at times—as Martin notes—the distances between foreground and background are grotesque (Martin, "Magnificent" 9). This technique also creates diagonal unbalanced compositions whose left and right halves are asymmetrical and where points of interest are in extreme and opposite edges of the frame. Furthermore, the term deep space applies "regardless of

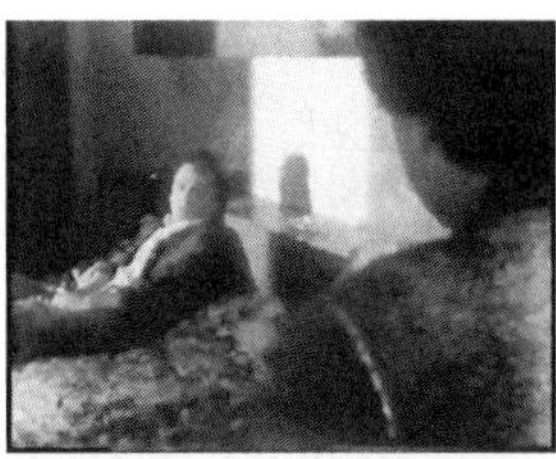

Fig. 10. Dialogue between police official and Vega in *Mémoire des apparences.*

Fig. 11. Dialogue between Vega and his false friend in *Mémoire des apparences.*

whether or not all of these planes are in focus" (Bordwell and Thompson, *Film Art* 220); if all planes of the image are in sharp focus, this practice is called deep-focus cinematography (a feature disseminated in Hollywood by the influence of *Citizen Kane*).[62] Ruiz does not always have all planes in focus, which calls even more attention to the distance between the planes on which action is taking place simultaneously.

Deep-space compositions (and the accompanying asymmetry of the frames) are an effective technique to emphasize conflict and hierarchical power relations between interlocutors. Ruiz employs this technique consistently in confrontations between enemies: first, in the first personal encounter and clash between King Basilio and his son, Segismundo, in the palace in act 2 of Calderón's play; second, in the first confrontation in Vega's hotel room between Vega and the policeman-leader of the Chilean conspiracy (following the latter's unauthorized intrusion into Vega's room) (fig. 10); third, in the conversation in the cinema between Vega and Vega's false friend (and lunch companion at the beginning of the film), during which the latter admits—for the first time—the plot against Vega, and his own betrayal (fig. 11). In each case, criminal and victim are separated from each other on distant planes: the tyrants and agents of state terror (Basilio, the Chilean pro-dictatorship conspirators) are in the foreground, whereas the victims (Segismundo, Vega) are in the distant background. In another scene, seen in the frontal planc and in medium shot, Basilio is facing front and holding forth rigidly, insensitive to the location of his interlocutor—a body expression calculated to be authoritarian and condescending. In contrast, Segismundo is placed in a distant background plane, where he moves around until he comes up behind Basilio, constantly glaring at his royal father while berating him from the back. The unmatched eyelines and the hierarchical positioning of Basilio and Segismundo in deep space express the hostile character of their exchange, as well as their uneven power relationship: Segismundo is unaware that he is a marionette in a scheme masterminded by his father.

In the confrontational deep-space composition set in Vega's hotel room (see fig. 10), the plainclothes cop is shown in profile and in medium close-up in front, addressing (and intimidating) Vega, who is shown in long shot in a distant plane resting on his bed. For the most part, the conversation is driven by the cop's mysterious (but nonetheless threatening) statements to Vega ("Anyone ever said you're heavy? Like a dead man!"). The real point of the conversation is the official's assertion of power over Vega, threatening that he has a key to his private room and that Vega is at the mercy of his old enemies working for the dictatorship. Finally, in the third scene that stands out for staging state terror against citizens in deep space, Vega's false friend is shot in three-quarters profile and extreme close-up, facing the camera while addressing Vega, who is sitting in a distant row of the interior of the Valparaíso cinema (see fig. 11). Not surprisingly, this scene (in which Vega's brother's old friend is exposed as a traitor) is the first time that this ex-friend is shot in a confrontational deep-space composition with Vega. In this scene, as in the hotel scene depicted in figure 10 (though to a greater degree), the tone is seriocomic rather than serious as in the Calderón scene of Basilio and Segismundo's first encounter, signaling the diverging trajectories of the Calderonian and Chilean conspiracies.

> *False friend:* Do you mind being caught so easily?
> *Vega:* Not at all.
> *False friend:* You expected it?
> *Vega:* I did.

Incidentally, the scene in figure 11 is closely intercut with a scene from Calderón (Segismundo's liberation from the tower by a popular army in act 3). The cross-cutting between the two plots, both of which are approaching their climax and conclusion at this point, serves to drive home the parallels between Calderón's fictional story and the Chilean real-life story of state tyranny and terror. From the spectator's perspective, Ruiz's jump cutting also breaks the cinematic illusion, producing a defamiliarization effect that heightens the spectator's awareness of these eloquent parallels. Furthermore, this scene furnishes proof that the Calderón play is invisible to Vega's enemies, screening only in the theater of Vega's mind—furnishing additional evidence of the dissident spectatorship modeled in *Mémoire*. When Vega asks, "What are you waiting for?," his ex-friend replies, "The film's ending. I'll kill you when they kiss. Love scenes bore me." Since Calderón's *Life Is a Dream* is not a romance in which kissing can be expected as an element of the ending, it is clear that only the spectator (but none of Ruiz's fictional

Fig. 12. Tintoretto, *The Last Supper,* 1592–94. (S. Giorgio Maggiore, Venice, Italy. Photograph: Scala/Art Resource, New York)

characters in the cinema with Vega) are privy to the unfolding drama of Segismundo's trials. The cross-cutting between the two conspiracies is restricted to Vega's inner consciousness, constituting subjective point-of-view shots.

Ruiz's preference for deep-space mise-en-scène finds strong legitimation in the theory of baroque visual culture. Deep space is how cinematic mise-en-scène emulates the stunning dynamic recessional compositions of seventeenth-century baroque painting (fig. 12). According to Wölfflin, the baroque treats linear perspective differently than the Renaissance, emphasizing spatial depth and restlessness: in contrast to the classical "plane type," which presents sequences of clearly delineated and static planes, in baroque recessional compositions "the eye relates objects essentially in the direction of forwards and backwards" (*Principles* 15). Wölfflin suggests that a diagonal movement in the disposition of figures in space is frequently employed to create this recessional effect of forward and backward movement across planes (75). The result is the exemplary baroque dynamism that sets painted (and cinematic) spaces in motion. Baroque recessional style can lead to extreme uses of foreshortening, as it famously does in Caravaggio's *The Conversion of St. Paul.* A parallel effect can be observed in Ruiz's *Les trois couronnes du matelot* (1982; *The Three Crowns of the Sailor*), a film about a sailor's travels on a ghost ship, which, like *Mémoires des apparences* (and several other of Ruiz's films) is based on the slippage between reality and fantasy or dream. A filmmaker with a deep interest in baroque themes and cinematic styles, Ruiz has staged several of his films in baroque deep space. In her study on Ruiz, Buci-Glucksmann interprets deep space as an aspect of what she terms the "baroque eye of the camera" in Ruiz's films: "The beginning of *Three Crowns of the Sailor,*" explains Buci-Glucksmann, is

> a veritable Welles remake. But unlike the Baroque of *Citizen Kane* or *The Lady from Shanghai* where depth of field theatricalizes bodies and beings, unifying all the shots in a movement either tunnelling, diagonal or spiralling (which the seventeenth century painting of Tintoretto and Rubens had already explored), here the same procedure evokes only an empty, rundown theatre, reduced to ceilings and close-ups of faces: pure *trompe l'oeil* and even *trompe l'esprit,* deceiving the mind. ("Baroque Eye" 33)

If Ruiz's re-creation and critical revision of Calderón's original is operative throughout, it moves center stage at the conclusion of *Mémoire des apparences.* Ruiz's film departs dramatically from Calderón's ending, which is happy, whereas Ruiz's is tragic—at least in terms of the bare facts of Vega's assassination by his enemies, if not in terms of mood. The elegant resolution of Calderón's play, which defeats the conspiracy against Segismundo and restores him to the throne while averting civil war, is made possible by Segismundo's psychological and moral conversion. Segismundo agrees to control his aggressive and libidinal passions, submitting to the principles of self-discipline, humility, prudence, and benevolence, and thus adopting the persona of the "virtuous prince" (Cascardi, "Subject" 243). Upon being rescued from the tower by a popular uprising against Basilio, Segismundo proves his intrinsic nobility by pardoning, and prostrating himself before, his royal father, whose tyrannical decision to raise Segismundo in captivity was the original cause of his lifelong suffering. According to the official message of Calderón's play, the legitimate heir, though unjustly deprived of his birthright by his own father, is restored to the Polish throne only after he has proved himself a virtuous prince worthy of his office. For it takes Segismundo's magnanimous pardon to undo his father's foundational act of violence, which, as Anthony Cascardi observes, had "engendered disorder in the natural world."[63]

In this way, the rehabilitation of Segismundo comes to depend on the restoration of patriarchal authority, and is thus intricately bound up with the restoration of the authority of the absolutist monarch and state. Just as Segismundo's moral reform is nothing but his rebirth as the "subject of control" who willingly "submit[s] to the State's political force" (Cascardi, "Subject" 239), the resolution of Calderón's play affirms absolutism's repressive political order. Indeed, individual justice for Segismundo is tied up with a brutal act of injustice he commits immediately after ascending to the throne: his act of clemency toward his father is directly followed by his unjust imprisonment of the same rebel soldier to whom he owes his liberty and rehabilitation—the righting of his father's wrong. Nonetheless, Segismundo throws the soldier into the dungeon:

> La torre; y porque no salgas
> de ella nunca hasta morir,
> has de estar allí con guardas,
> que el traidor no es menester
> siendo la traición pasada.
>
> (The tower! And, so that you never
> leave it until you die,
> you shall be kept under guard there,
> because a traitor is no longer needed
> once the treason is over)
> (*La vida es sueño* 184–85)

To be sure, Segismundo would have languished in the tower for the rest of his life after Basilio returned him there had he not been freed by a popular uprising. Nevertheless, in the instant the liberated baroque prince and legitimate dynastic heir ascends the throne, he becomes a tyrant like his father. *La vida es sueño* furnishes evidence for Benjamin's aphorism in the *Trauerspiel* study that the baroque ruler is destined to become a tyrant. In fact, Benjamin observes that "nowhere but in Calderón could the perfect form of the baroque *Trauerspiel* be studied" (*Origin* 81).

As Anthony Cascardi has argued, *La vida es sueño* is a double-edged allegory of power: while explicitly affirming absolute rule and delegitimizing individual (Segismundo) and popular rebellion (the uprising), Calderón's play nevertheless exposes the "inability of absolute power to conceal its violent origins" ("Allegories" 24). The disinherited son learns that he must endure his father's violence, for any expression of righteous anger is used against him to justify his father's original injustice. The father has abused the son with impunity; nonetheless, the victim's pardon of the royal perpetrator is the condition for the restitution of his rights. Finally, Segismundo's liberator is thrown into the dungeon—by his own beneficiary. Only royal sovereignty and the authority of the state are sacrosanct: rebellion is never justified, even if the sovereign is a tyrant. In Calderón's play, then, Segismundo's dungeon-tower stands out as a harsh reminder of the Realpolitik of authoritarian rule. As the tower receives its second political prisoner at the conclusion of the play that celebrates the restoration of the established order, the message is plain: political prisons are the dark underside of the absolutist state.

Fig. 13. Still of miniature of mountaintop tower-prison from *Mémoire des apparences.*

In its justification of political prisons, *La vida es sueño* exposes its uncritical support of authoritarianism. Calderón's play is an apology for the dictatorial state, and the echoes with twentieth-century dictatorships are loud. How does Ruiz respond to them? First, Ruiz highlights the Calderonian image of a mountaintop tower-prison throughout the film: the mise-en-scène of one of the B movies (a thriller) Vega watches at the beginning is a tower on a craggy mountaintop. Furthermore, this image becomes a nomadic image floating through Ruiz's film, illustrating the "photographic unconscious" he theorizes in *Poetics of Cinema 1* (fig. 13). Constructed from a miniature model—one of Ruiz's obviously artificial "bargain basement" special effects (Martin)—the mountaintop tower-prison constitutes one of the digressive marginalia that seem to detour the main line of the narrative. From our present concern, however, it becomes a key emblem that allegorizes the repressive ideological core of Calderón's play, as well as Ruiz's critical re-vision. An image that tells the story that it encapsulates, it represents an instance of the cinematic allegorical image in Ruiz's work. As he explains, "I have aimed, above all, to play with the idea of restoring to the image its natural ability to engender stories" (*Poetics 2* 18).

Ruiz offers an ironic, playful, and profoundly subversive response to Calderón's double-edged ending, which purchases Segismundo's rehabilitation with his co-optation by the institutional reason of the dictatorship state. Ruiz's film ends with a shootout in the cinema in which the right-wing Chilean group kills Vega as well as each other. The screen goes white, then cuts to shots of the group, including Vega, on a beach, their faces covered in streaming blood. It turns out that everyone has woken up in a paradisiacal afterlife—dead, but alive—where they continue the diverting conversations they were having in the cinema as if nothing had happened. In a comical twist on the theme of Calderonian skepticism—"life is a dream"—Vega, dead, exclaims, "I dreamed that I was alive." At first it appears that the Calderón adaptation is not carried through to the end but cut off after the soldier's speech announcing Segismundo's liberation. The obvious reason would be that the parallels between the trajectories of Segismundo and Ruiz, the two victims of state terror, end with Vega's assassination.

Nevertheless, at this point we encounter a major new development of Calderón's theme of deception-as-reality: First, taken literally, life really turns out to have been a dream for Vega, now that he has awoken from it in the afterlife, shot dead by his Chilean enemies. (Segismundo, by contrast, continues alive, dreaming, in Calderón's original conceit.) To be sure, Vega's act-by-act, scene-by-scene procedure of the recovery of his lost memory (and Calderón's play) has officially ended. But as if by way of a perverse compensation for the loss of *Mémoire*'s dual structure of external and internal films, the Calderonian metaphor of reality as fantasy has jumped scale and fully invaded the main plot centered on Vega. Furthermore, Ruiz's closing scene of awakening in the eternal afterlife is a joke about Calderón's theological outlook that underwrites the play's theme of life as dream (in the Christian sense of *memento mori* that exposes the vanity and deceit of this world): Calderón's Segismundo is reformed, converted to self-control and the domination of his passionate nature, because he knows he must die and thus prepare himself for the eternal life of his soul by being virtuous and doing good ("acudamos a lo eterno," let us look to eternity) (*La vida es sueño* 166–67). If Segismundo consents to self-discipline for fear of death, or of awakening from the dream of life, Ruiz, by setting his closing scene in the afterlife of "eternity," has called Calderón's bluff, as it were. State terror in Ruiz has an—if only nominal—tragic ending, which it does not in Calderón: Vega makes his final speeches from the tomb, so to speak, an experience Segismundo is spared when he is liberated from his tower, where he was leading a captive life "siendo un animado muerto" (like an animated corpse) (*La vida es sueño* 14–15), "as if" buried in a tomb.

However, Vega's tragic murder is redeemed by a happy conviviality between him and his assassins in the afterlife, where their souls roam on a beach as ghosts. In other words, *Mémoire*'s afterlife, where Vega is now a "living corpse" or a "soul without body"—even as it literalizes Calderón's Christian denial of earthly life for eternity, as well as the related metaphor Segismundo uses for his life in the tower—is a travesty of repressive, somber Counter-Reformation ideology. Ruiz's afterlife is a paradise where earthly desires are fulfilled: First, Vega gets his girl. ("Vega: Can I kiss you? Bonitas: With what lips? Vega: The soul's lips.")[64] Second, he is reconciled with his assassins: they are friends now, the persecution is finished. Paradoxically, then, the afterlife in Vega's tomb is more liberated than Segismundo's freed life as the puppet of—the subject engendered by his subjection to—the absolutist state.

Finally, *Mémoire*'s afterlife-as-beach-vacation scene also completes the Calderonian adaptation after all, although in Vega's posthumous present rather than through his recovery of memory when alive. The camera cuts to a medium shot of Segismundo, framed in profile against the ocean as background, speaking his final soliloquy from act 3, in his new persona of "virtuous prince" and Poland's rightful sovereign, which culminates in his pardon of his father. "Illustrious Court of Poland, witness to such wonders: hear your prince is speaking." Ruiz, however, excerpts only the beginning of Segismundo's speech, in which he rebukes Basilio and eloquently exposes the magnitude of Basilio's violation of his son's human rights: "To exorcise my wild nature, my father, present here, turned me into a beast. Even with my fair nobility, my courage, my valor, were I born meek and gentle, such upbringing would still have led to a beast's ways." The camera then cuts to the beautiful sunset panorama, and Segismundo's last words (and the final words spoken in *Mémoire*) are voiced from off-screen: "May this spectacle be a lesson, this horror, this prodigy." In short, Ruiz's Calderón adaptation ends on the vantage point of the "eternal afterlife" where the final scene of Vega's via dolorosa is set.

How to assess Ruiz's bold manipulation? First, we note that Segismundo's final dialogue takes place in Vega's posthumous afterlife, not in the separate fictional space-time of memory unfolding in the theater of Vega's mind. Vega dies before he can finish recovering the play, as he points out to his false friend before the first shots ring out:

Vega: Pity, I'd nearly learned the play.
False friend: I'm here to make you forget.

The process of Vega's recuperation of memory has clearly ended, and Segismundo is now standing on the same beach as Vega. In other words, the Calderonian and Chilean figures inhabit the same reality. The border between the parallel worlds of Vega's external reality and his internal memory has collapsed, and the Calderonian fiction has invaded the contemporary Chilean "reality," as noted above with regard to Calderón's Christian dialectic of life and afterlife. In this way, Ruiz concludes his film with an ingenious performance of the mise-en-abîme, a popular baroque framing structure (a play-within-the-play) that incorporates its own picture into the body of its representation.[65] Ruiz's interpolation of Calderón's baroque play and the contemporary fiction set in Pinochet's Chile in a mirror play of brilliant reflections and contrasts culminates in the conflation of the film-within-the-film into one single film.

In point of fact, and to offer a final instance of Ruiz's Lezamian love of the difficult, during the last scene set during "life," the shootout in the Valparaíso cinema, the actor cast as Segismundo newly impersonates Vega's biological brother, whom Vega had believed dead. As is now revealed, in reality he had been working with the Pinochet camp to entrap Vega. Ruiz's conflation of fantasy and reality thus thickens further before all differences evaporate in the complete externalization of Calderón's fiction within the contemporary Chilean world. Thus, the figure who is speaking Segismundo's final monologue in the persona of the "reformed prince" is a composite of Calderón's protagonist and Vega's brother, a pro-Pinochet traitor. As such, he lectures his audience (the court of Poland, and the allegorical immensity of the ocean) on not inflicting tyranny and terror, lest they *bring about* the evils they seek to forestall. In this way, Ruiz's film ends with an antidictatorship speech after all, spoken into the ocean and the setting sun, from the epistemological vantage point of "eternity." Ruiz could not possibly have found a more powerful mise-en-scène for this final antidictatorship lecture, as he posts Calderón's lesson as the moral that also concludes Vega's contemporary Chilean story. After Segismundo ceases speaking, the camera cuts to a close-up of ocean waves, colored blood red. The final frame is occupied by the nomadic image of Segismundo's mountaintop tower-prison, also colored blood red.

María Luisa Bemberg's *Yo, la peor de todas*

Like Ruiz's adaptation of Calderón within the context of the recent Pinochet dictatorship, Bemberg's cinematic adaptation of Paz's biography of Sor Juana is driven by the contemporary experience of authoritarianism. Indeed, *Yo, la peor de todas* (1990) is the second of two critical historical films in which Bemberg allegorizes the recent Latin American dictatorships.[66] The earlier feature, *Camila* (1984), is set during the dictatorship of the legendary *caudillo* Juan Manuel de Rosas (1829–52) in the early years of Argentine independence. The heroines of both films are unconventional, assertive women who rebel against the authoritarian regimes of their times: *Camila* portrays the life of Camila O'Gorman, an upper-class woman who elopes with a priest and who at Rosas's special behest is executed in 1848 by a firing squad at the side of her lover, despite her pregnancy and in violation of existing law.[67] Both *Camila* and *Yo, la peor de todas* narrate their rebellious heroines' struggles and ultimate tragic defeat, while exposing the authoritarian social structures that destroy them. In contrast to *Yo la peor de todas,* the anti-authoritarian melodrama *Camila* frames a specifically Argentine history of political despotism: *Camila* was released closely after the demise of the Argentine military regime, during the first year of Raúl Alfonsín's newly elected democratic government. It became "the first and biggest box office success of the new regime," as well as an international success, including a nomination for an Oscar for best foreign film.[68] Its success was due in part to its "allegory of the recent political terror" (King, "María Luisa Bemberg" 23), as the human rights violations during Rosas's nineteenth-century dictatorship were seen to foreshadow those of the contemporary Argentine military regime. As John King notes, this reading was encouraged by "posters for the film which showed the final execution scene" under a headline reading “Núnca más” (Never again), an explicit allusion to the Truth Commission set up under Alfonsín (24).

In the 1970s, Bemberg did not go into exile as did many other established Argentine directors who received death threats from right-wing death squads—Octavio Getino, Fernando Solanas, and others (King, “María Luisa Bemberg” 19). This is likely because at that time her career had yet to begin in earnest; until 1980, when Bemberg’s first feature was released, she had made only two short films and worked as screenwriter. However, the beginning of her career as a director in the late 1970s and the 1980s was tensely conditioned by Argentina’s political climate, first the dictatorship (1976–83), then the return to democracy in 1984. In the late 1970s, her script of what would become her second feature film, *Señora de nadie* (1982; *Nobody’s Wife*), the story of an upper-class woman’s divorce from her husband and her development as an autonomous person, was turned down by the censors on the grounds that it set “a very bad example for Argentine mothers” as it featured adultery and also included a homosexual character.[69] With the loosening of the military’s censorship at the beginning of the 1980s, the film was finally approved and screened, although Bemberg still felt obliged to offer two versions, including one alternate with a less controversial ending (King, “María Lusia Bemberg” 21). Bemberg’s career as a feminist filmmaker thus flourished in Argentina’s postdictatorship climate of the 1980s and early 1990s; it was cut short by her early death in 1995.

Argentine cinema in the immediate postdictatorship period, from 1983 until the economic crisis of 1989, was distinguished by an explosion of film production, in part sponsored by the newly elected democratic government (through the Instituto Argentino de Cinematográfica) in its effort to promote “redemocratization and the analysis of recent Argentine history” (Foster, *Contemporary Argentine Cinema* 2). The result was a renaissance of technically high-quality Argentine cinema that also critically confronted social conflicts, and whose achievements were recognized by international awards, including Oscars (King, *Magical Reels* 92). “In Argentina in the first years of the newly restored democratic government of Alfonsín, the state provided film funding which allowed the traumas of the recent past to be explored through cinema” (ibid. 278). According to King, along with Luis Puenzo and Fernando Solanas, Bemberg ranks among the three most important directors of the 1980s who witnessed Argentina’s return to democracy (96). Bemberg’s historical feature films from the 1980s, which were produced independently, cast a critical eye on authoritarianism in Latin America from a feminist viewpoint.[70] It is noteworthy that Bemberg’s critical examination of Argentine (and hemispheric Latin American) history and society coincided with a period of critical nationalism in Argentina, in which the new and fragile democracy subsidized "new, redemocratized Argentine filmmaking" (Foster, *Contemporary Argentine Cinema* 153).[71]

In *Yo, la peor de todas,* Bemberg opted to go in a direction opposite the historicizing bent of *Camila,* which was filmed on location in Argentina. As Bemberg recalls, "I was determined to emphasize the universal over the local" (Pick, "Interview" 80). Abandoning her original plans to film in real cloisters on location in Mexico, Bemberg shot the film entirely on "an abstract film set" in a studio in Buenos Aires.[72] The studio set helped her realize her intention to universalize Sor Juana's story, including broadening it from the Mexican to a hemispheric Latin American scale, as well as telescoping it in time to make the link with twentieth-century fascism and authoritarianism. In the interview with Zuzana M. Pick, quoted earlier, that reviews her explicit gloss of fascism through "high angles" and "grand traveling shots" of a "huge, hard, imposing proto-fascist architecture," Bemberg defends her cinematic strategy of spatial and temporal abstraction: "I chose to deemphasize that national context, in part because Mexico at the time Sor Juana lived was not a nation in the modern sense, but rather New Spain, a loyal colony of the mother country, so Sor Juana's world was not confined to Mexico but rather extended to the entire Spanish-speaking, Catholic world. . . . Sor Juana was a product of colonialism. I think the impact of colonialism is very palpable in the film—the power of the viceroys, their paternalism, and how very unprotected Sor Juana finds herself when the viceroys depart" (Pick, "Interview" 81). Bemberg elaborates, "I needed to create in the viewer the sensation that we are 300 years removed in time. But that we could also be here, today" (80).

Bemberg's mise-en-scène—the setting and lighting in particular—is thus essential to her cinematic reinvention of the life of one of the most celebrated authors of the Hispanic baroque. I will focus on the mise-en-scène before I discuss the details of Bemberg's feminist, antidictatorship adaptation of Paz's biography of Sor Juana, on which she relies in most major points for her portrayal of historical events and participant characters.[73] If early cinema (1890s–c. 1910) was influenced by the theater and theatrical techniques from which it soon emancipated itself, Bemberg recovers some of early cinema's theatrical techniques by way of a deliberate anachronism. As Denise Miller notes, in *Yo, la peor de todas* Bemberg borrows from early cinema what film historians call a "tableau construction" (Miller 158)—a mise-en-scène in box form, resembling the theater stage. According to Ben Brewster and Lea Jacobs, cinematic tableau construction refers to "the centered axial long shot, looking at an interior as if at a box set on stage from the centre of the theatre stalls. Many early films consist largely of such shots, linked by intertitles."[74] Bemberg's mise-en-scène—which includes many stunning deep space compositions, as in Ruiz—consists of a succession of such stage-like tableaux. Each scene—except for a few scenes constituted by cross-cutting between two distant events—is staged on its own tableau set. More to the point, each scene is *identical with* a tableau: when the camera cuts to a new tableau, the scene has ended. In other words, the temporal limits of the scene correspond to the spatial limits of the cinematic stage tableau.

Rather than being narrated sequentially, time is represented spatially and visually, in a series of static panoramas that shatter the narrative conventions of commercial film at the same time as they transpose the temporal art of Paz's textual telling into cinematic showing. More than a technical effect of transposition into cinematic medium, the stage tableau in Bemberg's film also recalls the spatialized images of history that Benjamin notes are an essential element of the *Trauerspiel.* In the baroque, "history merges into the setting," and the "image of the setting . . . becomes the key to historical understanding" (*Origin* 92). We have seen how Donoso constructed the fictional history of Marulanda through a series of such static pictures or allegorical panoramas. Bemberg's tableaus, borrowed from stage-influenced early cinema, are the cinematic equivalent of Donoso's novelistic panoramas. Both are instances of neobaroque spatial images that, as Benjamin puts it, present "the disconsolate chronicle of world-history" (*Origin* 92) as it slouches toward catastrophe.

In any of these tableau scenes, distinct camera takes break down, or add up to, a near-complete picture of the stage tableau. Bemberg alternates establishing shots and close-ups, frequently reversing sight lines by 180 degrees to reveal the spatial continuity that exists in the actual studio set staged *before* the camera (rather than emerging as the virtual effect of editing). Frequently, editing follows a mirroring pattern across deep space: what used to be in the (distant) background appears in the foreground, and vice versa. For example, in the stage tableau at the beginning of the film showing the performance of Sor Juana's play *Los empeños de una casa* (*The Trials of a Noble House*) in the convent patio of San Jerónimo, the camera first tracks along the side of the patio to outline the continuous space containing both the stage and the audience. It then cuts to a frontal view of the audience from the stage, and next reverses the view to show the audience's view of the stage. Two strategies are used to delineate each tableau: first, the montage of variable-distance frames, amplified by shot/reverse shot patterns (as in classical Hollywood analytical editing), composes a mosaic of the tableau, which permits glimpses of natural spatial continuities through background detail. Second, Bemberg's camera also travels, panning, tilting, tracking, and craning to reveal the natural unity of the tableau more explicitly. For example, the convent performance scene begins with shot/reverse shot sequences alternating between frontal shots of the actors performing onstage and of

Sor Juana prompting them from an unidentified hidden location nearby. After the end of the play, a traveling shot follows Sor Juana as she steps forward onto the stage to join the actors bowing to the audience downstage. By revealing that her "prompter's box" had been directly behind the stage, the traveling camera adds this location to the organic spatial unity of the performance tableau in the convent patio. Using continuous movement of the camera, Bemberg takes great pains to stage all parts of the dramatic action of each scene on one single, continuous cinematic stage tableau.

Bemberg frequently introduces new tableaus with a moving camera, tracking or panning to outline the extension of the tableau along its entire length. She then switches to alternating static establishing shots and close-ups that focus on various protagonists. In establishing shots, the camera often occupies a central position that creates centered frames whose left and right halves are symmetrical, at times in perfect symmetry—the "centered axial long shot" of early cinema's tableau (Brewster and Jacobs). This is the case in the often described opening scene (set in 1680, the year of the arrival of the new viceroy, the Marquis de la Laguna, in Mexico City), which pictures Archbishop Aguiar y Seijas (Sor Juana's nemesis) and the viceroy (Sor Juana's protector) seated at a table across from each other, sharing a toast to celebrate the occasion of their respective assumptions of office. The camera portrays their encounter in profile, occupying the left and right halves of the screen, respectively, first in close-up, then in long shot. The precise symmetry of the shot's composition allegorizes the dual power structure of colonial New Spain, shared between Church and state (which is also the topic of the conversation between the two officials) (fig. 14).

Fig. 14. Final toast of the viceroy and the archbishop in the opening scene of *Yo, la peor de todas.*

With the exception of some flashbacks to Sor Juana's youth, Bemberg's film narrates the last fifteen years of Sor Juana's life, the period between 1680 and Sor Juana's renunciation of literature in 1694 (a year before her death). It includes the time (November 1680–April 1688) that the Marquis and Marquise de la Laguna—great personal friends of Sor Juana and supporters of her work—lived in Mexico City as the rulers of New Spain, and which also saw the production of Sor Juana's mature work (such as her philosophical poem *Primero Sueño* [*First Dream*]). This period, according to Paz, was "the richest and fullest" in Sor Juana's life (*Sor Juana* 138). After the departure of the de la Lagunas—and even as the Marquise oversaw the publication (in 1689 and 1692, respectively) of the first and second volumes of Sor Juana's works in Spain—the austere and misogynistic Aguiar y Seijas began to cast his shadow over Sor Juana, and finally succeeded in terminating her literary career when Sor Juana was at the height of her abilities and fame. Bemberg's film traces Sor Juana's trajectory from literary triumph and public acclaim to her silencing and formal self-denunciation before a private (noninquisitorial) Church tribunal. The initial meeting between Viceroy de la Laguna and Archbishop Aguiar y Seijas is invented; Aguiar y Seijas was appointed in 1683, three years after the Marquis' formal assumption of office.[75] Clearly, Bemberg here seeks to gloss the conflicting external forces that shaped Sor Juana's world—the generous viceroy, whose reign allowed her to flourish, and the hostile archbishop, whose rule destroyed the world she had built for herself. I disagree with Deborah Shaw's thesis that Bemberg downplays the viceregal couple's role as "representatives of the colonial world" by focusing on their personal friendship with Sor Juana (Shaw 125). To the contrary, the opening scene serves as a prologue that identifies the imperial powers who make and unmake Sor Juana and her world. It establishes an abstract, institutional frame around the personal story that follows.

The split mise-en-scène in the encounter between archbishop and viceroy foreshadows their growing division over Sor Juana's privileges and fame. Another symmetrical long shot occurs in the chapter meeting of the sisters of San Jerónimo, where the camera repeatedly returns to a central vantage point in the middle of an aisle separating opposite rows facing each other, where the nuns are seated. The divided seating arrangement in the convent chapter meeting (evoking debating clubs or the British Parliament) similarly foreshadows the eruption of internal divisions within the convent between liberal and conservative factions, allied with the viceregal couple (and supporters of Sor Juana) and the archbishop (and enemies of Sor Juana in the Church) respectively. In montage sequences of variable-distance frames, Bemberg's camera frequently returns to occupying identical static positions (as in the two scenes just described). As Miller notes, "Bemberg actually keeps her camera still, rendering her tableau effect even more pronounced" (Miller 158).

There is a second (and strong) sense of tableau style that is conditional on such stillness—the freezing of the action, and (generally) the stilling of camera movement. The tableau in this strong sense refers to a highly charged moment when the action stops while all the characters remain more or less motionless within the frame, which allows the meaning of the situation to emerge: According to Brewster and Jacobs, "the tableau represents a moment of suspended action, a moment chosen so that the grouping of figures epitomizes the forces arrayed in conflict. It arrests the flow of the narrative so as to produce a heightened sense of its significance" (41). In contrast to the stage tableaus that constitute the building bricks of Bemberg's mise-en-scène, I will refer to this tableau—a visual still or freeze frame generated by a static camera, arising from cinematography—as an "allegorical" tableau. A third type of tableau is the *tableau vivant,* which also plays a role in neobaroque cinema more generally. It likewise appears in *Yo, la peor de todas,* as well as in Ruiz's work (although not in *Mémoire*).[76] "The precise reproduction by living but motionless people of celebrated and universally familiar pictures or sculptural groups" (Brewster and Jacobs 38), the *tableau vivant* reenacts the scenes depicted in historical paintings. Bemberg explores the *tableau vivant* via a series of scenes that "drew their inspiration from baroque painting" (King, "María Luisa Bemberg" 27).

As Miller suggests, Bemberg uses the allegorical tableau effectively at the end of the confrontation between the archbishop and Sor Juana in the convent locutory (Miller 157–58). After the archbishop has left, Sor Juana is shown in a "long visual still" (158) standing motionless behind the grille of her locutory, while clutching the bars above her head with both hands (fig. 15). The significance presented through the suspension of the action is an allegory of imprisonment that likens Sor Juana to a captive, even an "animal in a cage" (Bergmann 243). On previous occasions, during Sor Juana's salon in the locutory, the bars had never been an obstacle for Sor Juana, as she asserts in response to the vicereine's request to remove the bars that disturb her, "I no longer see them." However, when the political situation turns against Sor Juana, the bars that used to be invisible to her at the height of her success assert their material presence, and she consequently seizes them.

The scene of the conservative nuns' conspiratorial meeting with the archbishop in his residence, staged in stark chiaroscuro lighting, offers another memorable example of Bemberg's use of these two types of tableau, the allegorical tableau and the cinematic stage tableau. After the meeting ends, the veiled nuns turn and leave in the direction they had come from. As the

Fig. 15. Sor Juana behind the bars of her locutory in *Yo, la peor de todas.*

camera tracks their steps in profile, it follows them through an arcade in almost complete darkness, contrasting with the brightly illuminated floor, until they reach the sound of keys turning at the entrance gate, which a shadowy guardian opens for them. After the nuns' exit, the camera freezes for a moment on a visual still of the deserted entrance. Then the archbishop's secretary enters the stilled frame, spreading holy incense behind the closed gate and casting smoke illuminated by fabulous blue-white light all the way from the entrance to the site of the meeting, as he walks backward, retracing the steps the nuns have just taken. The incense serves to erase the womanly scent of the nuns in the archbishop's palace, an allusion to Aguiar y Seijas's infamous quasi-hysterical horror of women, which made the presence of women, especially their physical sight, scent, and touch, intolerable for him (see Paz, *Sor Juana* 408). As the camera tracks first the nuns' pathway of exit from the archbishop's residence from left to right, then the secretary's subsequent symbolic "erasure" of the nuns' physical presence in the opposite direction, Bemberg's cinematography once again reveals the setting of the entire scene as the organic, continuous space of a cinematic stage tableau. In contrast, the interpolated allegorical still of the deserted entrance gate in turn epitomizes the chilling secrecy of the conspiracy against Sor Juana, as well as the intended outcome of the plot—the aim to silence Sor Juana and to erase her public presence, burying her in invisibility.

Bemberg's use of the allegorical tableau, as well as the cinematic stage tableau, inserts her film within a complex history of the tableau in nineteenth-century theater and early cinema. According to Brewster and Jacobs, the appearance of the tableau in early cinema

> signals a set of functions performed by the stage picture: to punctuate the action, to stress or prolong a dramatic situation, and to give a scene an abstract or quasi-allegorical significance. Filmmakers still felt that certain dramatic situations called for this constellation of functions, to the point that they still used the term "tableau" as shorthand for what occurred at these points, even recommended "tableaux" to others. . . . The tableau thus provides an example of a theatrical device which, while not being adopted into film in any straightforward way, still affected how filmmakers conceived their practice. (35)

Significantly, however, cinematographic techniques (such as camera movements) introduced discontinuity and dynamism into the cinematic tableau that were absent in its stage predecessor. For a "major difference between theatrical tableaux and their use in early cinema was that even if the characters remained still within the frame, cinematic movements could and usually did render the tableau dynamic" (Miller 158).

As discussed earlier, editing and montage invariably fragment the *natural* space-time unity of the mise-en-scène staged before the camera, replacing it with a *virtual* space whose continuities are principally illusionary. Cinematic style in *Yo, la peor de todas* straddles the paradigmatic opposition between the actual theater stage and the illusionist space-time of cinema, combining realist techniques that preserve the actual, unified space of the tableaux (such as traveling shots, deep-space compositions, and deep-focus photography) and antirealist montage techniques that cut it up and recombine the fragments into new, artificial continuities. Compared with *Mémoire des apparences,* however, *Yo, la peor de todas* leans much farther toward mise-en-scène-oriented hyperrealism than Ruiz's film. Although the interior of the Valparaíso cinema functions as something like a tableau in *Mémoire,* and while Ruiz's camera frequently tracks along the aisles and across the rows of the cinema's auditorium, this is mainly to follow Vega as he enters and moves around in this space. Among realist cinematic registers, deep space compositions are the primary feature that Ruiz systematically develops to hyperbolic, neobaroque excess. Bemberg, in contrast, often utilizes traveling shots that are not motivated by figure movement to introduce her mise-en-scène directly to the viewer. In this way, the actual spaces of Bemberg's tableaus—indeed, the complete mise-en-scène, including lighting, costumes, and figural gestures—are singled out as independent foci of attention. In short, the neobaroque style of *Yo, la peor de todas* arises predominantly from the hypernaturalism of its mise-en-scène, that is to say, its cinematic stage tableaus, its allegorical tableaus, and (as we will examine shortly) is *tableaux vivants.* Through these three types of tableaus, Bemberg's mise-en-scène acquires baroque qualities of opulence and drama, surpassing the control and restraint of classical realism in cinema.

Bemberg has called attention to the "magical, glacial light" provided by her cinematographer, Felix Monti (Pick, "Interview" 81). These qualities are particularly pronounced in the many scenes shot in dramatic chiaroscuro lighting that immerses entire sections of the frame in darkness while sharply illuminating some details and parts of the figures, such as the face and hands. Monti recalls Bemberg asking him to "remember Zurbarán's light."[77] Francisco Zurbarán (1598–1664), one of the masters of Spanish baroque painting, was influenced by Caravaggio's brand of extreme chiaroscuro lighting (tenebrism), which isolates figures, causing lit areas within the frame to come forward and the darkened spaces in the background to recede.[78] In using polarizing dark-light contrasts, Bemberg is quoting Caravaggio—or rather the Caravaggism of his followers, such as Zurbarán and Georges de la Tour. She is also joining a neo-Caravaggism in contemporary art recently analyzed by Mieke Bal.[79] Furthermore, tenebrism is also particularly effective in creating eerie contrasts between the nuns' white robes and black veils. In her use of extreme light-dark contrasts, Bemberg visits the "madness of vision" topos that Buci-Glucksmann identifies with the baroque, as well as seconding Ruiz's observation that the cinematographer is a maker of shadows. In more general terms, Bemberg also uses lighting symbolically: chiaroscuro lighting (and nighttime settings) are employed for many scenes portraying the activities of the forces of "obscurantism" (the archbishop and his allies), to borrow Deborah Shaw's distinction, whereas scenes depicting the forces of "enlightenment" are usually shot in brighter light and set during daytime.

Tellingly, many of the tableaus in the archbishop's residence and the censorship office of the Inquisition are staged in chiaroscuro. So too is the celebration of the conservative Sor Ursula's victory at the convent polls over the liberal Abbess Mother Leonor, which takes the form of a procession in the convent with Sor Ursula crowned as the new abbess. The same is true of most scenes after the departure of the viceregal couple from Mexico and the ascendancy of the archbishop: the light seems to have gone out in Sor Juana's world. This second half of the film is also dominated by the deaths of people close to Sor Juana, which are narrated in scenes shot in chiaroscuro: the death of Sor Juana's mother; the wake of Mother Leonor, the former liberal abbess; and the meeting in Spain in 1692 between the former vicereine, María Luisa, dressed in mourning because of the sudden death of her husband, and Sor Juana's friend, the Mexican writer Sigüenza y Góngora. When Sigüenza returns from Spain to hand Sor Juana a copy of her works just published, thanks to the efforts of María Luisa, the convent locutory he steps into is almost completely dark.[80]

In her account of Sor Juana's final years, Bemberg conflates the epidemic that broke out in San Jerónimo in April 1695 (killing Sor Juana the same month, as well as 90 percent of those who fell ill) with the social crisis of 1692. In 1691–92, apocalyptic rains inundated Mexico City, causing a food shortage that in 1692 triggered the most serious popular riots in Mexico City during the colonial era (Paz, *Sor Juana* 443–44). The crisis was mismanaged by the new viceroy, the Count de Galve, strengthening the hand of Aguiar y Seijas. In *Yo, la peor de todas* rain is seen pouring down in streams in front of convent windows and flooding the patio as the camera tracks around the beds in the chiaroscuro convent infirmary, registering the suffering of the sick sisters and the labor of the healthy to look after them and remove the dead. The Church organized prayers, processions, and public flagellations to stop the rain and the hunger, which were seen as God's punishment (ibid. 438ff.).

The film's representation of these earthly calamities and the Counter-Reformation Church's retrograde, authoritarian response to them features Bemberg's most memorable protofascist mise-en-scènes, achieved through the combined effect of the studio set's monumental architecture, chiaroscuro lighting, "totalitarian" high angles, and a geometric choreography of figure arrangement and movement. The camera cuts to a long shot of an interminable, dark convent hallway filled with moisture and illuminated in chiaroscuro, tilts down to a high-angle shot of the ground, then tracks back to capture the bodies of dead nuns lying on the floor in orderly rows. Several tableaus show processions of nuns doing penance by praying, chanting, or scourging their backs. One high-angle static shot shows a darkened convent hallway illuminated by torchlight to the offscreen sound of chanting nuns; as the dark silhouettes of a procession of nuns in single file enter the frame in the foreground and slowly pass to the distant background, it becomes clear that they are lashing their own backs, and that their habits and flesh are covered in blood. The orderly file begins to break up as the some sisters stagger from exhaustion and the last one collapses to the ground.

The wake for Mother Leonor, the ex-abbess, lying in state in the convent's chapter hall that was also the site of the chapter meeting discussed earlier, constitutes another of the film's most impressive protofascist tableaus. Shot in complete diegetic silence (somber nondiegetic music is the only sound), the scene lasts one minute and is composed of two long traveling shots. The camera cuts to a close-up of the bare feet of the corpse by candlelight and pans along the length of the gowned body to Mother Leonor's head, adorned with a floral crown in the manner of baroque portraits of "crowned nuns." It continues tracking past Mother Leonor's head to the seated audience, pausing on a medium long shot of Sor Juana in mourning, framed by her sisters. The second traveling shot begins with a static shot, a symmetrical extreme long shot of the assembly of nuns in the chapter hall seated in rows facing each other, with everyone facing the corpse lying in state in the center aisle. The camera then slowly cranes upward to an extreme high angle from its precise center position, revealing the geometric disposition of figures in space more clearly from its aerial perspective, as well as Mother Ursula, seated on the elevated podium at the head of the hall, who in turn is dwarfed by a massive floor-to-ceiling cross on the wall behind her. This tableau allegorizes the absolute power of church institutions over the women at San Jerónimo.

In contrast, the early scenes of entertainment in the viceregal palace during the reign of the Marquis de la Laguna are staged in bright light; the frames contain hardly any shadows. At least two scenes from that period are set outdoors, before an enormous artificial blue sky as backdrop. Similarly, the early scenes of Sor Juana's salon in the locutory are lit in warmer colors. Sor Juana is debating mythology and other intellectual questions with learned men—even as in frontal shots Sor Juana always appears from the point of view of her visitors, behind bars. One scene underlines the extraordinary achievement of her public career in the conservative, patriarchal, and misogynist world of the Hispanic Golden Age in which, Sor Juana declares, "Knowledge is always a transgression. All the more so for a woman." This scene culminates in Sor Juana crowning herself with a headdress of brilliant quetzal plumes (like that worn by Aztec rulers), striking a theatrical posture, and exclaiming, "Montezuma lies prostrate at the Conqueror's feet!," to laughter and applause from her visitors. A gift from the vicereine, the brilliant blue-green feathers emblematize the varied secular activities she was able to pursue despite her cloistered existence. Yet even in some daylight scenes, especially in the convent, the glacial lighting tones down colors to a gray-blue scale so that Bemberg's color movie seems to approximate a black-and-white film.

Another notable feature of the mise-en-scène of *Yo, la peor de todas* is its allusions to baroque painting via *tableaux vivants*. The cinematic portrait of the deceased Madre Leonor wearing a floral crown is one such example (fig. 16). Depictions of "'crowned nuns,' both living and dead, are a characteristic manifestation of baroque painting in New Spain" (fig. 17).[81] In particular, "floral crowns, a symbol of the virtuous soul, were also used in portraits of dead nuns, with the implication that at her death, the nun should be even more richly clothed for her final meeting with her divine spouse than on her entry into the convent and her spiritual marriage to Christ" (Rishel and Stratton 385). This specific art historical citation in Bemberg's film is particularly impressive for the iconographic accuracy with which it re-creates the regional baroque culture of New Spain.

A different *tableau vivant* early in the film, following the convent vote that sweeps the conservative faction to power, depicts Sor Juana seated at a table in melancholic meditation, her head resting pensively on her upstage

Fig. 16. Madre Leonor lying in state in *Yo, la peor de todas.*

Fig. 17. Sister Elvira de San José, eighteenth century, Mexico. (Museo Nacional del Virreinato, Tepotzotlán/Consejo Nacional para la Cultura y las Artes (CONACULTA), Mexico/ Instituto Nacional de Antropología e Historia, Mexico)

Fig. 18. Sor Juana in melancholic meditation by candlelight from *Yo, la peor de todas.*

hand, the downstage hand mechanically holding a skull (fig. 18). Her brooding stare is fixed on the candlelight, which produces a stark chiaroscuro illumination accenting her face and hands and some nearby objects while leaving the remainder of the room in impenetrable darkness. This composition alludes to Georges de la Tour's painting of Mary Magdalen, *Mary Magdalen Meditating,* a study famous for the contrasting chiaroscuro effect provided by a candlelight source. The repentant Magdalen in Georges de la Tour's painting "sits staring hypnotically at the lamp-flame, oblivious of the skull that she holds in her lap and of the books, scourge and cross lying on the table. The enclosing darkness, the silence, and the utter stillness transmit with extraordinary clarity the state of mind of the penitent sinner" (Martin 80). Bemberg's tableau of Sor Juana echoes de la Tour's polarized lighting, Magdalen's dejected stare into the candlelight, and her pensive gesture of supporting her head by her hand. Sor Juana's black veil falling over her shoulders parallels the black hair cascading over Magdalen's shoulders. Or, to risk a Borgesian reading of de la Tour's painting as the successor influencing her precursor: Bemberg's cinematic adaptation of this baroque portrait shows how much de la Tour's converted Magdalen actually looks like a nun who has already taken the veil.

Like the wake of Mother Leonor, this *tableau vivant* is shot in diegetic silence. Sor Juana's offscreen voice is heard reciting the first four lines of her sonnet 146, wherein she defends her secular intellectual pursuits: "En perseguirme, mundo, ¿qué interesas?" (World, in hounding me, what do you gain?) (*Sor Juana Anthology* 94–95). Narrating Sor Juana's silent thought, the poem makes the case that Sor Juana's intellectual pursuits are compatible with her religious vows, since they espouse an asceticism of the mind that is the secular equivalent of monastic asceticism. The final tercet reads, "teniendo por mejor, en mis verdades,/consumir vanidades de la vida/que consumir la vida en vanidades" (Mine is the better and the truer way:/to leave the vanities of life aside,/not throw my life away on vanity) (*Sor Juana Anthology* 96–97).

Bemberg's portrait of Sor Juana as an intellectual ascetic is reinforced by Sor Juana's earlier comment justifying her renunciation of motherhood: "I call my body abstract" (an allusion to one of her poems—romance 48—which makes this claim). The Countess de Paredes later also reflects on Sor Juana's detachment from her womanhood: "I never met a woman like you. More poet than nun, more nun than woman." Romance 48 brings up the charged issue of gender for Sor Juana: the poem is a reply to "un caballero del Perú, que le envió unos barros diciéndole que se volviese hombre" (a gentleman from Peru who had sent her some small clay vessels, telling her she should become a man) (*Sor Juana Anthology* 27).[82] The often quoted verses claiming the genderless neutrality of her body read: "y sólo sé que mi cuerpo,/sin que a uno u otro se incline,/es neutro, o abstracto, cuanto/sólo el alma deposite" (Of one thing I am sure: that my body/disinclined to this man or that,/serves only to house the soul—/you might call it neuter or abstract) (*Sor Juana Anthology* 30–31). Because of her virginal state owing to her religious vocation, Sor Juana asserts, her body transcends the duality of sex. She also avails herself of Roman Catholic theology, which claims that the soul is undifferentiated in regard to sex (or race)—a theme, Paz notes, that "is the motif of innumerable variations in *romances, décimas, glosas,* and sonnets" (*Sor Juana* 221). As *sorjuanistas* have commented, Sor Juana's universalizing claim to a genderless soul (and intellect) served to deflect the misogyny of her times that denied her access to learning for being a woman.

Sor Juana's strategic use of monastic asceticism for the feminist purpose of liberating herself from the burden of her sex in New Spain's colonial, patriarchal society is an important motif in the film. As the child Sor Juana explains in a subjective flashback in which Sor Juana, at her mother's deathbed, recalls her plan to attend university dressed as a man, "Since I couldn't dress as a man I dressed as a nun!" This strategic asceticism also overcodes Bemberg's tableau of Sor Juana in the pose of de la Tour's Magdalen. The "inward illumination" that "has brought the sinner to a state of penitence" in de la Tour's portrait (Martin 240) is also present in Bemberg's Sor Juana. There, however—despite Sor Juana's wearing the veil as the outward token of her religious life, and as the offscreen citation of sonnet 146 suggests—such inner light is the light of secular, intellectual illumination. Once again, we witness Bemberg's critical reinvention of a European baroque masterpiece.

Indeed, more than the converted penitent who has renounced the vanity of all earthly pursuits, the pensive Sor Juana recalls the figure of the melancholic genius in Dürer's *Melencolia I* (1514) (see fig. 5, p. 113). Tellingly, Bemberg's feminist appropriation of the iconography of Renaissance melancholia (the scholar lapsed into a state of brooding inaction, head resting on her hand, sitting passively among the instruments and tools of learning, which are littered around her) parallels that of Djuna Barnes. To be sure, if any woman before 1800 could lay claim to the heroic figure of the melancholic creative genius, it would have to be Sor Juana. Like the Renaissance melancholic, in sonnet 146 (as in her 1691 autobiographical self-defense, *La Respuesta*) Sor Juana is hypereloquent in articulating her suffering and arguing with her detractors. In short, far from allegorizing a crisis of conscience that leads to her rebirth as a "new Juana" (paralleling de la Tour's "new Magdalen")—a development absent until the show trials of her final years—the torment represented in this tableau stems from her persecution by the forces of obscurantism, who have just won the upper hand in the convent.

If the previous *tableau vivant* quotes Georges de la Tour, another one, depicting Sor Juana at rest in her cell during the epidemic in San Jerónimo, quotes both Dutch genre painting (Vermeer) and Caravaggio at once. The interior of the cell is in almost impenetrable darkness. A long shot shows Sor Juana in semiprofile standing at, and looking out of, the arched window in the background toward the left half of the frame, through which pouring rain is seen. She turns to full profile, takes off her apron, and slowly sits down. Several offscreen light sources—in the manner of Caravaggio—throw some detail into stark relief: the strings of rain visible outside, Sor Juana's face and figure, a cross in the right background, and books and a skull on a nearby table. Most strikingly, the thick window frame is illuminated in white light from an aerial position outside, contrasting violently with the shadowy interior. A second shot of the tableau, intercut with the arrival of Sigüenza from Spain, shows Sor Juana in the middle plane facing front and cleansing her hands with liquid from a flask as she is preparing to make her way to the meeting in the locutory, while a shaft of light from offscreen right articulates the folds of her habit.

The interior of this tableau is Vermeer's, but the lighting belongs to Caravaggio, since Vermeer did not work with starkly polarizing tenebrist lighting. Bemberg's composition recalls Vermeer's shallow space compositions typical of the Dutch baroque,[83] in particular genre painting depicting scenes from daily life in the household, such as *The Music Lesson*. Iconographic elements borrowed from Vermeer include the "window on the left-hand side through which bright light pours into the room" and "spacious interiors in which the figures . . . have plenty of surrounding room and freedom of movement."[84] The comparative shallow-space composition of this tableau, portraying Sor Juana performing simple, domestic tasks in the manner of Dutch genre paintings, contrasts pointedly with the deep space mise-en-scène dominating much of Bemberg's film, especially in scenes narrating the activities of the despotic faction. What is the point of this tableau, which in some ways—and despite the tenebrist lighting—undercuts the paranoid mood of this closing part of the film? As adjacent scenes show, at this moment, Sor Juana is wearing the coarse habit of a scullery maid, she is sweaty and dirty. On the one hand, this "Vermeer Sor Juana" tableau allegorizes the domestic drudgery to which the entire convent, including Sor Juana, has been reduced as a result of the epidemic. It shows how San Jerónimo, one of the richest convents in Mexico City, has been diminished, degraded to a daily routine of sheer creatural suffering, labor, and exhaustion—far from the civilized religious and secular life the nuns are shown to enjoy at the outset. This tableau depicts the simple, domestic woman Sor Juana has become on the eve of her submission to the discipline of the Church as a result of unforeseen natural disasters, an issue we will now examine.

As critics have noted, Bemberg departs from Paz in her interpretation of the riddle of Sor Juana's last years, which has long puzzled her biographers: what motivated Sor Juana's renunciation of literature and secular learning when she was at the height of her fame and mature artistry? Was it a genuine religious conversion, brought about by the loving guidance of her confessor, Father Antonio Núñez de Miranda, as Sor Juana's first biographer, Father Diego Calleja, claimed?[85] Twentieth-century research overturned what Paz calls the "pious lies" of Sor Juana's clerical biographers and critics after Calleja, to pave the way for a critical biography of Sor Juana.[86]

Bemberg narrates the basic facts. In November 1690, the *Carta atenagórica* (Athenagoric letter), a critique by Sor Juana of the theology of an eminent Portuguese Jesuit, Vieyra, was published under the imprimatur of the bishop of Puebla, Manuel Fernández de Santa Cruz y Sahagún. The political avalanche that it set off appears to have little connection with the occasion or the content: the text in question was a sermon Vieyra had delivered in Lisbon forty years earlier on the question of which of Christ's expressions of love (*finezas*) was his greatest; Vieyra refuted the Church fathers on this issue, whereas Sor Juana defended them, in turn critiquing Vieyra. Most ironically, Vieyra, living in Brazil, never learned of Sor Juana's critique (see *Sor Juana* 389–91). But Vieyra was much admired by the archbishop of Mexico, Aguiar y Seijas, another member of the Jesuit order, all-powerful in New Spain at the time, who had overseen the publication of Vieyra's sermons in Mexico (Schons, "Some Obscure Points" 157). Sor Juana's refutation was prefaced by a stern letter (signed with a pseudonym, Sor Filotea de la Cruz, an obvious mask of the bishop) admonishing Sor Juana to give up her intellectual and secular pursuits. The following year, in March 1691, Sor Juana composed her famous autobiographical self-defense *Respuesta a Sor Filotea,* in which she affirms women's right to education, secular learning, and access to authorship and a public voice. As Bemberg shows (following Paz), the real motive behind the publication of Sor Juana's critique—which would eventually trigger Sor Juana's downfall—was to launch a veiled attack on Aguiar y Seijas. Aguiar y Seijas was an old rival of the bishop of Puebla and thus a common antagonist of both Sor Juana and the bishop.

Why did Sor Juana, who had always been an adept and cautious politician, dare to provoke the wrath of her powerful superior and confirmed enemy, Aguiar y Seijas? Had the bishop of Puebla published this document with or without Sor Juana's consent? Paz contends that Sor Juana knowingly intervened into the public debate between the powerful princes of the Church, and that she was fully aware of the risk involved in producing a critique of Vieyra's sermon. To defend her own access to the unstable "Baroque public sphere" (to recall William Childers's notion) on which her literary career depended, and which the current archbishop threatened to cut off, Sor Juana willingly took a big risk. Bemberg, in contrast, presents Sor Juana as the bishop's victim, an involuntary pawn in a political cabal plotted by the bishop of Puebla and the new viceroy, the Count de Galve. In an inspired instance of unmatched sound and visuals, Sor Juana's voice reciting her *Carta Atenagórica* is heard offscreen while the camera pauses on a close-up of the bishop reflecting silently, then cuts in mid-sentence from the secret meeting in the viceregal palace to Sor Juana in the locutory continuing the reading from the manuscript of her theological critique to her visitor, the bishop. In other words, Sor Juana's essay begins as the bishop's private thought, and is then externalized as objective reality. In this conspiratorial meeting, Sor Juana expresses her pleasure at the chance to "get back at the archbishop," but cautions the bishop that she "wants no trouble with the Inquisition." The bishop, framed in extreme close-up to convey the intimacy of their agreement, assures her in response that no one is going to publish the manuscript and that it will only circulate among a small group of readers.

Childers's observations on the baroque public sphere help illuminate the sensitive details here. Childers argues that in the baroque, a "full-fledged public sphere takes shape, in which individuals and groups attain political agency without the transparency of rational debate or any pretense of equal participation."[87] Unlike the Enlightenment public sphere theorized by Habermas, however, the baroque public sphere is a hybrid formation, based on the theatricalized performance of identity and the epistemology of rumor. The printing press "did not simply displace the manuscript"; rather, manuscripts "could still be preferred as a way to get around censorship or to avoid legal responsibility"; conversely, printed texts "circulated freely in a transparent space, yet they were 'shadowed' by manuscripts whose circulation was clandestine" (167). According to Childers, this "duplicitous structure" is characteristic of the baroque public sphere in general (167). In contrast to the bourgeois public sphere of the eighteenth century, grounded "in a distinction between public and private, in the baroque, the opposite of 'public' is 'secret'" (167). More to the point, "since what is 'public' is only the tip of the iceberg, and there is no way any one individual can know how much more is 'secret,' the game of public interaction in the baroque is always played under the sign of an uncertainty arising from not knowing how much the other person might be hiding, or how much of what one knows it might be prudent to reveal" (168). Seen in this way, and according to Bemberg, then, Sor Juana agreed to pen a clandestine manuscript at the bishop's orders, intending to circulate it secretly. By publishing the *Carta Atenagórica,* the bishop betrays Sor Juana by forcing it from the secret onto the public plane.

The final tableaus of Sor Juana's confession are shot in polarized angles of framing, suggesting the imbalance of power between the persecuted individual and the official of the church. Miranda always appears in low angle, "looking down" on Sor Juana, physically expressing his newly gained dominance and control over her. Sor Juana, in turn, always appears in high angle, "looking up to" her confessor, suggesting dependence and helplessness. One particularly striking instance is their first reunion after Miranda (who had abandoned her after her clash with the archbishop) returns as Sor Juana's confessor on Sor Juana's request. To send for Miranda, Paz argues, was "equivalent to a tacit renunciation" (*Sor Juana* 449), the decisive step that Sor Juana knew implicated her subsequent punishment. Bemberg follows Paz in depicting Sor Juana taking this decisive step out of fear and as a result of her isolation. Sor Juana is kneeling and scrubbing the floor in the convent infirmary as the camera cuts to a low angle of Miranda standing above her and saying: "This is the Juana I've hoped to see for over twenty years. Self-sacrificing, devoted to the services of God." Before, the world was at her feet; now, Sor Juana is kneeling at her confessor's feet. Earlier, crowned with Montezuma's feathers, she playfully enacted Montezuma's prostration before Cortes; now abjection has jumped scale from leisurely make-believe to Sor Juana's existential condition. Sor Juana's submissive and subdued posture epitomizes the place the Church wants her to occupy, which is women's archetypal place in a patriarchy.

Bemberg also goes farther than Paz in investigating the gendered nature of Sor Juana's transgression, and of her persecution by the Counter-Reformation church. Bemberg suggests that Sor Juana "threatened the church as a woman and not least as one who was in love with another" (Miller 138).

One of the most discussed aspects of *Yo, la peor de todas* is Bemberg's hypothesis—contra Paz—that there was a lesbian, though chaste, love relationship between Sor Juana and the vicereine, María Luisa.[88] Bemberg's María Luisa lays the foundation of their close friendship by comparing their lot, defining it as women's imprisonment in patriarchal society: "You wear a veil. I wear a crown. You are locked up in the convent. Do you think I can escape from the Palace?" For aristocratic Spanish women like María Luisa, and poor *criollo* women like Sor Juana who want to protect their reputation, the only avenues open are the varieties of genteel incarceration offered by marriage and the convent.[89] Paz dedicates an entire chapter to making the case that Sor Juana's poems dedicated to the Vicereine were nothing but the "homage of a professional poet to the poet's lord" (*Traps of Faith* 201) employing the language of courtly love and patrimonialism. According to Paz, it was more appropriate for a woman poet to address her lady (the vicereine) in these terms than her lord (the viceroy), and the "daring expressions" Sor Juana slipped in would not have been understood as saying anything different (200). Against Paz, Bemberg bases her queer reading of the relationship between the two women on Sor Juana's poems to María Luisa. Curiously, however, Bemberg does not include any of these poems in her script, but instead other love poems to unnamed addressees (Bergmann, "Abjection" 234). Among them are *redondilla* 84, "Este amoroso tormento/que en mi corazón se ve" (That my heart is suffering/from love pangs is plain) (*Sor Juana Anthology* 78–79) and sonnet 164, "Esta tarde, mi bien, cuando te hablaba" (Speaking to you, belovèd, this afternoon) (*Sor Juana Anthology* 80–81). In *Yo, la peor de todas,* one entire session of Sor Juana's final confession is dedicated to the review of her relationship with the vicereine. Miranda's censure rests on the ecclesiastic argument that "for a nun to love a worldly object is infidelity to her Divine Spouse" (Paz, *Sor Juana* 460). As a token of renouncing her love for the vicereine, Sor Juana surrenders the medallion, a portrait of María Luisa, that she has been wearing around her neck.

The final tableaus representing Sor Juana's confession and public renunciation depict Sor Juana's rebirth as the "modern subject of control" (Cascardi) who has internalized the discipline of the Counter-Reformation Church. The language with which Father Miranda interpellates Sor Juana and the disciplinary techniques he uses in his interrogation eerily recall Segismundo's conversion, in the course of which Segismundo consents to disciplining his rebellious and amorous passions and comes to impersonate the "model prince." Miranda declares: "God wants a different Juana." Like the "new Segismundo," the "new Juana" who is born during the extended confession with Miranda is an obedient subject who comes "willingly to submit" to the absolute power of the Church (Cascardi, "Subject" 229).

Miranda's review of Sor Juana's sinful previous life is exhaustive; nothing is left unexamined. But unlike Calderón, Bemberg exposes the disciplinary methods—in short, the human rights violations—that produce this new, docile subjectivity. Her subjection to institutional authority borders on her annihilation, as Sor Juana cleverly suggests:

Miranda: [God wants] another Juana.
Sor Juana: Or none?

The same point is made in the moving tableau of Sor Juana's formal renunciation before an assembly of her fellow nuns chaired by the abbess and Father Miranda, which depicts her reciting publicly, then signing with her own blood, a declaration that is a composite of the three documents Sor Juana signed in February and March 1694 and that constitutes her public abjuration (*Traps of Faith* 469). To draw blood for her signature, Sor Juana breaks her reading glasses with her bare hands, destroying the instrument that had aided her studies. The final tableau is an inventory of Sor Juana's empty cell. The camera slowly scans across empty bookshelves and passes over tables cleaned of all but a cross and a candle, until it stops on the figure of Sor Juana, silent and unmoving, sitting on the steps in front of her arched window.

Since the publication of Paz's biography and the release of Bemberg's film, new archival research has turned up several major finds that confirm that Sor Juana's renunciation was the result of a "secret inquisitorial trial that the Archbishop brought against the nun in 1693" and not, as clerical *sorjuanistas* had long claimed, a genuine conversion (Scott, "Controversy" 196).[90] Bemberg's final "empty cell" tableau must also be considered obsolete: the inventory of Sor Juana's cell on her death has been found, which lists as the most important objects "a bookcase with one hundred eighty volumes of selected works and fifteen bundles of writings, mystic and secular poetry" (197). These findings confirm earlier research by Dorothy Schons, who studied documents of a lawsuit San Jerónimo brought against the heirs of Aguiar y Seijas after the archbishop's death in 1698 to recover portions of money and jewels confiscated from Sor Juana's cell *after* her death (Paz, *Sor Juana* 468–69). During the critical years of 1692 and 1693, and likely in anticipation of the outcome of her travails, Sor Juana also made several "substantial investments with a rich banker without the permission of the Archbishop," a strategy indicating that "far from capitulating, she was looking toward the future" (Scott 196). In short, the story of Sor Juana's life is a lesson about the weapons of the weak in the intricate struggle between authoritarianism and resistance, even if at the end of her life she could no longer afford to resist openly. True to the theatricality of the baroque—a "world in which things are appearances" (Maravall 192)—according to which the world was a stage and identity an unstable and ever-shifting performance, the Counter-Reformation Church staged an operatic conversion featuring Sor Juana as repentant sinner and pious heroine striving for sainthood. But as in much such official make-believe, the institutionalized deception underpinning the hagiographic script of Sor Juana's life was eventually exposed. Recent archival research has recuperated a "secret," resilient Sor Juana, a figure whose behavior belies the official script of Sor Juana's public identity as the docile "subject of control" she was forced to endorse in the baroque public sphere—"Yo, la peor del mundo." This secret Juana is a woman who looked after her future economic survival during the worst times of her persecution, who began to rebuild her library after her official humiliation and dispossession, and who continued to write.

Hemispheric Genealogies of the New World Baroque

Early Modern New World Baroque and Diasporic Baroques in Contemporary U.S. Latino/a Art and Culture

> During the early years of the Cold War, big American cars functioned like the Baroque Cathedrals of the Counter-Reformation. . . . Today, lowrider cars combine and exacerbate old and modern Baroque sensibilities, transforming American cars into sexualized moving altars of the American dream gone amok.
>
> —Rubén Ortiz Torres, "Cathedrals on Wheels"

> Hip-hop might be a contemporary Baroque. . . . Think about it: the jewelry, the shiny clothing, the elaborately painted fingernails, all of the gold and platinum—it is fundamentally about excess and about an appetite for Baroqueness.
>
> —Luis Gispert, in *Luis Gispert: Loud Image*

Mexican novelist Carlos Fuentes's novel *La frontera de cristal* (1995; *The Crystal Frontier*), which is set on the U.S.-Mexico border, begins with the impressions of a young, aristocratic *criolla* from Mexico City on her first visit to the border region of northern Mexico.[1] Prepared by her Blue Guide tour book, which tells her that "there is absolutely nothing of interest" (*Crystal Frontier* 3) to be found in *el norte,* Michelina indeed sees nothing but the absence of the elite Hispanic architecture of the Mexican capital she calls her home: "She could see nothing. Her gaze was captured by a mirage: the distant river and, beyond it, golden domes, glass towers, highway cloverleafs like huge stone bows. But that was on the other side of the crystal frontier. Over here, below—the guidebook was right—there was nothing" (4). A study in contrasts, Fuentes's novel highlights (to the point of stereotype) familiar differences between the United States' and Mexico's adjacent border region, on the one hand—modern, wealthy, and successful, but cultureless, faceless, and without history—and the "deep" Mexico further south, on the other—poorer and less developed, but rich in national identity and cultural heritage. *El norte*'s deficiency is summed up in an architectural image. The emblems of modernity and progress, the glass towers of modern U.S. skyscrapers, are contrasted with the colonial baroque cathedrals of central Mexico, the monuments of the New World baroque. In Tamaulipas, Michelina observes, "the Baroque came this far, to the very edge of the desert—to this point and no farther" (9).

This chapter aims to prove Michelina (and, by extension, her real-world counterparts among baroque scholars) wrong. For the baroque has indeed traveled far into North America, migrating north from Latin America and the Caribbean. It has entered the United States through the cultural memories and aesthetic sensibilities of migrants from Mexico, Cuba, and other Latin American countries, who imported the Catholic baroque into alien territory, the domain of Anglo-American Protestantism. But where in the nation founded by Protestants who built churches with bare white walls does the ornate Latino neobaroque manifest itself? As this chapter will establish, a neobaroque sensibility is present across contemporary U.S. Latino/a art. More generally, it permeates U.S. Latino/a popular visual culture, underpinning folk art phenomena such as Mexican American folk shrines, including home altars and yard shrines, as well as Chicano lowrider culture. The Mexican cultural critic Carlos Monsivaís and the Chicano scholar Tomás Ybarra-Frausto have identified baroque currents in twentieth-century Mexican popular arts and handicrafts (*artesanías*) and Chicano vernacular styles (*rasquachismo*), respectively.[2] The art historian Lynette M. F. Bosch affirms that Cuban American exiles have trafficked the Latin American baroque across the Straits of Florida, thereby expanding "the permeable borders of *Barroquismo.*"[3] I propose to deepen these scholars' insights into a diasporic Latino baroque sensibility now visible in the United States more than ever. It is found especially in Mexican and Mexican American folk arts favoring flamboyant display, gaudy colors, and delirious ornamentation, which, according to Monsivaís, "recall the Churrigueresque's ultraelaborate church facades and altarpieces" (182).

Expanding the frame of analysis from ethnic and national to pan-Latino and hemispheric scales, this chapter discusses popular baroques in U.S. Latino/a visual culture and art by placing them within their proper context, the genealogy of the New World baroque. It presents a transhistorical and transhemispheric exhibit in the form of a triptych, juxtaposing the historical New World baroque with close readings of two sets of contemporary U.S. Latino baroques: first, the flamboyant folk baroque manifested in Chicano lowriders, as well as the lowrider-oriented videos of the Mexican-born, California-based artist Rubén Ortiz Torres; and second, the neobaroque installations of Mexican American artist Amalia Mesa-Bains, inspired by home altars, and the hip-hop baroque art of Cuban American Luis Gispert. Building on New World baroque theory, I hope to demonstrate that, like the historical New World baroque, neobaroques in U.S. Latino art tend to constitute insurgent, anti-institutional baroques arising from the rebellious consumption of state-sponsored, institutionalized, or hegemonic art and culture. Self-consciously working out of this popular baroque tradition, contemporary U.S.-based Latino artists have reanimated the New World baroque and further expanded its domain, giving it a new and impressive scope extending into twenty-first-century North America.

As premised earlier, the baroque originated as the repressive tool of European absolutism and the Counter-Reformation; its arrival in the Americas owed to European expansionism. The key question, therefore, concerns the nature of the "new" American baroques that grew up in Spain's and Portugal's overseas colonies: were they nothing but reactionary instruments furthering the transatlantic spread of European empires? The Cuban intellectuals Alejo Carpentier and José Lezama Lima popularized the notion that in Latin America, the official imperial European baroque was adapted and transformed at the hands of indigenous and non-European artisans, whose labor created most of the monuments of baroque art in the Iberian colonies in the Americas in the seventeenth and eighteenth centuries. The rebellious remaking of the European baroque at the hands of Spain's and Portugal's colonial subjects gave rise to "new," mestizo American baroques that subverted European colonial ideologies. The liberating irony of the New World baroque, as César Salgado and Lois Parkinson Zamora both contend, is "the survival of Otherness piggybacking on the unsuspecting signs of Empire."[4] The art of the Counter-Reformation, Lezama affirms, became "arte de la contraconquista," the art of counterconquest. At stake is the rebellious consumption of the European baroque against the grain of its origins: the repressive Iberian state baroque, instrument and symbol of the Counter-Reformation, absolutism, and empire, is transformed into an anti-institutional vehicle of the popular expression of the conquered. In more general terms, the baroque is an instance of what James Clifford calls "traveling cultures"; it likewise exemplifies the ironic reversals of social function and meaning that occur with the displacement of cultures from their origins.[5] Clifford argues that "such cultures of displacement and transplantation are often inseparable from specific, often violent, histories of economic, political, and cultural interaction—histories that generate what might be called *discrepant cosmopolitanisms*" (36). The task of this chapter is to investigate such discrepancies between the baroque's roots and its subsequent routes.

My particular aim throughout is to make visible the hemispheric and transhistorical continuities of the New World baroque, with special emphasis on its diasporic expansion into North America. My intention is to show how truly visionary and apt the term New World baroque (originally an English translation of the term *barroco de indias,* or "baroque of the Indies," coined by Venezuelan critic Mariano Picón-Salas in the 1940s) has proved to be, beyond even Alejo Carpentier's and José Lezama Lima's boldest dreams. For neither of them anticipated or demonstrated awareness of the dissemination of the Latin American mestizo baroque in popular U.S. Latino/a visual culture and contemporary U.S. Latino/a visual art. Existing scholarship on either end of the continuum (New World baroque theory and U.S. Latino visual culture and art, respectively) does not connect except all too rarely. My contribution is to strengthen this connection and to trace the descent of neobaroque U.S. Latino/a expression from within the genealogy of the New World baroque.

Stepping back from Latin America for a moment, it is noteworthy that the (re)turn to the baroque in the contemporary visual arts is not exclusive to U.S. Latino and Latin American art. Indeed, a series of exhibition catalogs and critical studies from the 1990s on documents a broad neobaroque trend among North American and European artists, encompassing such figures as Frank Stella, Cindy Sherman, Jeff Koons, Andres Serrano, Kehinde Wiley, Nicola Verlato, and George Deem.[6] As is widely recognized, contemporary art has been moving toward the baroque for several decades. In the broadest of terms, the contemporary baroque is framed as an escape from the "impasse" of the "absolute, ahistorical style that modernism reached in abstract expressionism." The contemporary baroque constitutes a "return to figuration after abstract expressionism," in which artists reconnect with the past, especially with the baroque.[7] Visually expressive, this neobaroque art breaks with "three decades of postmodernist aesthetics mainly based on the grid, minimalist restraint and predominantly conceptual approaches to artmaking" (Giovannotti and Korotkin 19). Frequently, in these generalist studies neobaroque U.S. Latino and Latin American artists figure side by side with other North American and European artists, as is the case with Ana Mendieta and Andres Serrano in Mieke Bal's study *Quoting Caravaggio.* For Bal, who insists on speaking of a "contemporary Baroque" rather than the neobaroque, contemporary artists engage in acts of appropriation of the historical baroque, acts of "quotation" that result in unsettling the temporal hierarchy between past and present: "Quoting Caravaggio changes his work forever" (Bal 1). In envisioning creation as re-creation, Bal's investigation of the baroque nature of contemporary art recalls the Borgesian unsettling of the difference between original and copy. More generally, her analysis of the baroque in contemporary art as a technique of secondhand creation underscores Haroldo de Campos's claim, raised in the introduction, that the baroque strategy of "critical devouring of universal cultural heritage" has become definitive of our contemporary cultural condition.[8]

However, the neobaroque also needs to be recognized as a distinct development in twentieth-century U.S. Latino and Latin American art, considered separately. The Latin American neobaroque comprises artists as diverse as the Mexicans Alberto Gironella (1929–1999), whose re-creations of Velázquez's royal portraits are parodies of colonialism, and Frida Kahlo (1907–1954), whose self-portraits incorporate folk baroque expression such as popular ex-votos (religious offerings in the form of personalized thank-you paintings for miraculous favors received); the Brazilians Adriana Varejão (1964–), who produces "wounded" canvases and tilework where trompe l'oeil guts spill from cracks, similarly suggesting colonial violence, and Cildo Meireles (1948–), whose neo-concretist installations focus on the perceptual aspect of experience, maximizing color and materiality; and the Colombian Fernando Botero (1932–), renowned for figures of extravagant plumpness that recuperate the European baroque (Rubens) as well as the New World baroque.

As demonstrated in several recent exhibition catalogs, the neobaroque unfolds in a unique trajectory in the art of the Latino United States and of Latin America, the region that, according to Alejo Carpentier's influential claim, has always been "the chosen territory" of the baroque.[9] The most comprehensive and articulate overview is the 2000 catalog *Ultrabaroque: Aspects of Post-Latin American Art*.[10] Curator-editors Elizabeth Armstrong and Victor Zamudio-Taylor take up Carpentier's notion of the mestizo New World baroque, following his argument that *mestizaje*—defining the makeup of mainstream Latin American culture after the European conquest—found its culminating expression in the baroque: "All symbiosis, all *mestizaje*, engenders the Baroque" (Carpentier, "Baroque" 100). According to Armstrong and Zamudio-Taylor, twentieth-century U.S. Latino and Latin American artists opt for the neobaroque because of the ever-increasing displacement and global circulation of cultures and people, which first engendered the mestizo New World baroque: "hybridity and *mestizaje* is one of the defining characteristics of the work in *Ultrabaroque*." Furthermore, because the historical baroque coincides with the inception of globalization—colonial urban centers such as Mexico City were the first global cities—it paved "the way for a mestizo global culture" that today encompasses "nearly every . . . aspect of daily life." By inventing a hybrid, differential art made by cannibalizing preexisting art, the cultures of present-day Latin America bequeathed the world a hybrid model of expression for the global future. "Curatorially, we suggest that the baroque is a model by which to understand and analyze the process of transculturation and hybridity that globalization has highlighted and set into motion."[11] For the same reason, the twentieth-century neobaroque from Latin America is really "post-Latin American": the mestizo blend it displays registers the contemporary planetary scope of transnational, transcultural flows. Its emblematic illustration is Rubén Ortiz Torres's *Bart Sánchez* (1991), a portrait of a cross-eyed, Mexicanized Bart Simpson sporting a sombrero (Armstrong and Zamudio-Taylor 122).

Rubén Ortiz Torres, a Mexican-born artist active in the California Latino arts scene since the 1990s, is also my first representative *barrocotraficante.* I begin with Torres's brilliant discussion of Chicano lowriders as neobaroque "cathedrals on wheels":

> During the early years of the Cold War, big American cars functioned like the Baroque Cathedrals of the Counter-Reformation. They were meant to seduce and convert people from Puritan morality and the austerity of social justice to the excesses of individual freedom and the market economy. They required an inordinate amount of gas and parking space, and they may not have been as easy to fix as the German Volkswagen Beetle (literally the car of the people), but who cares about practical earthly matters when you can drive a big rocket-looking conveyor with space-age tail fins that launches you to heaven? . . . Style is a function of politics. . . . Today, lowrider cars combine and exacerbate old and modern Baroque sensibilities, transforming American cars into sexualized moving altars of an American dream gone amok.[12]

Educated at the Academy of San Carlos in Mexico City and currently a faculty member in the Department of Visual Arts at the University of California–San Diego, Torres is thoroughly familiar with New World baroque theory:

> The Americas conquered by the Catholic kings were the perfect laboratory to test this Baroque ideology. Mexico and Peru had large amounts of souls who (in the eyes of the Church) needed to be saved, and skillful artisans to do the work. A "New World" was to be created. The indigenous artisans who worked in the new cathedrals were able to indulge in all sorts of exquisite extreme ornamentation in order to offer a glimpse of the gates of the kingdom of heaven in an otherwise temporary and painful terrestrial life. European architectural styles were adapted to local needs and sensibilities. (Torres 26)

In fashioning elaborate correspondences between baroque cathedrals and contemporary Chicano lowriders as "cathedrals on wheels," Torres has also produced an ingenious neobaroque conceit of his own. The truth expressed through such comparison can be summarized as follows: what Indians did to the imperial Spanish baroque in the seventeenth century, Chicanos are doing to the American car today. Then as now, power deploys style and art as propaganda. Over time, however, official culture and art are mongrelized by the people who are subjected to it.

The Mestizo New World Baroque

This section annotates Torres's bold analogy between New World baroque cathedrals and Chicano lowriders by examining the New World baroque in the light of twentieth-century New World baroque theory. Figures 19 and 20 present the Church of Santa María in Tonantzintla, a rural parish church and

Fig. 19. Side altar, Church of Santa María, Tonantzintla, 1690–1730, state of Puebla, Mexico.

a prime example of Mexican *poblano* (from the state of Puebla) style. Along with the Andean mestizo style of Peru, Ecuador, and Bolivia, the Puebla baroque is one of the most famous regional manifestations of the popular, transculturated New World baroque, which blends Catholic and indigenous iconographies. It was not until the mid-twentieth century that Latin American art historians acknowledged the popular *mestizaje* that existed in colonial baroque art and architecture, in the work of revisionist art historians Ángel Guido, Pál Kelemen, George Kubler, and Manuel Toussaint, publishing (except for Guido) in the wake of World War II (Salgado, "Hybridity" 320).[13] Kelemen's assessment is paradigmatic:

> Colonial art in Spanish America is far from being a mere transplantation of Spanish forms into a new world; it grew out of the union of two civilizations which in many ways were the antithesis of each other. Non-European factors were at work also. Thus it incorporated the Indian's preferences, his characteristic sense of form and color, the power of his own heritage, all of which, as overtones, modulated the imported style. . . . The Baroque style lent itself amazingly well to the fusion of these influences. A full-blooded Baroque spread to even the less

Fig. 20. Detail of interior wall, Church of Santa María, Tonantzintla. (Photograph: Lois Parkinson Zamora)

> accessible regions of Latin America and with its vast register of variations developed such regional expressions as the "Andean mestizo" and the "Mexican *poblano*" style. (Kelemen 1:22)

In contrast to the Roman baroque, the Spanish baroque and (especially) the Spanish American baroque are "decorative rather than . . . structural."[14] Walls do not undulate and bend as they do in the architecture of Borromini and Bernini, where baroque dynamism works to set the solid structures of buildings in motion as if they were made of putty rather than stone. Instead, the delirious baroque effect is achieved by letting ornamentation run riot on interior walls, retablos, and facades (Bottineau 85). Meanwhile, buildings and plans remain simple in structure. It is for this reason that the Churrigueresque, an eighteenth-century late baroque style of heavy decoration named after José Beníto de Churriguera (1665–1725) and his family of artists, "became a characteristic expression of Mexico; for here was a style which could endow a simple structure with a highly alive and ostentatious elegant air" (Kelemen 1:89). Characteristic of the Churrigueresque is the *estípite,* a pilaster narrower at the bottom than at the top (like an inverted pyramid), which is often broken into sections.[15] The conversion of structural elements into pure ornament, as in the *estípite,* a column with nothing to support, made the ultrabaroque Churrigueresque the epitome (or, as its detractors had it, the ultimate folly) of baroque artifice and antifunctionalism. However, the Churrigueresque is not to be confused with mestizo American styles such as the Puebla baroque. The most famous example of the Mexican Churrigueresque, the facade of the Sagrario Metropolitano, the parish church belonging and adjacent to the Mexico City cathedral, like several other Churrigueresque churches in Mexico, such as the Church of San Francisco in Tepotzotlán, does not display any indigenous elements (fig. 21). More to the point, the colonial baroque of central Mexico displays a fluid spectrum, from the very orthodox and official Hispanic baroque to the most hybrid folk baroque. Rural parish churches like that in Tonantzintla (built by local architects, many of them amateurs) generally display uniquely regional styles, many of which derive from indigenous traditions. In contrast, metropolitan cathedrals (like the Sagrario), tied more closely to European norms and usually designed by European architects (the Sagrario's architect was the Andalusian Lorenzo Rodríguez), may display regional variations, but hardly any indigenous influence (see Bailey 275). "New World baroque" is generally used as an umbrella term to refer to all baroque expression in literature and the visual arts produced in the American hemisphere. However, the degree of American idiosyncracies varies greatly, for example, the use of local materials and designers in architecture, and, more crucially, the influence of pre-Columbian iconography.

In telescoping back in time to the historical New World baroque, my purpose in this section is twofold: first, to present key arguments from representative theories of the New World baroque, and second, to illustrate these claims by presenting vivid artistic examples of the New World baroque's rebellious consumption of the European baroque. In placing emphasis on the

Fig. 21. Lorenzo Rodriguez, facade, Sagrario Metropolitano, 1749–68, Mexico City, Mexico.

New World baroque's foundational place at the beginning of a hemispheric and transhistorical genealogy of alternative, anti-institutional baroques, I want to underline its present appeal beyond the merely archival. Likewise, I urge the recognition of the New World baroque's vitality to anti- and postcolonial studies more generally.

The European conquest and colonialism (and its legacy) were the crucible in which the New World baroque was forged. The New World baroque is first and foremost a contestatory baroque, the instrument of what Lezama Lima calls a popular *contraconquista* (counterconquest) of foreign European art and culture. For this reason, the raw materials of anti-institutional baroques always come from the dominant culture. It is the icons and symbols of the dominant civilization (the Iberian state baroque, the American car) that constitute its semantic building blocks, which are appropriated—stolen—and transformed in ways that negate the dominant and repressive ideologies for which they originally stood (Christianity, imperialism, capitalism, Anglo hegemony). In the New World baroque, to create is always to re-create the alien, European image; to write is to rewrite the alien, colonial text. Hence the internal (structural) antagonism of anti-institutional baroques, which yoke together warring—foreign versus native—artistic sensibilities and ideologies. It follows that the decolonizing American baroque is not a unified autochthonous, non-Western expression but a distorting refraction of the colonial European model. Nonetheless, as the contemporary example of flamboyant Chicano lowriders demonstrates, it would be erroneous to decry such secondhand cultural creation as derivative, as a passive imitation of the dominant standard.

In the broadest of terms, the artistic archive and the theories of the New World baroque belong to a type of decolonizing expression that departs from radically non-Western, subaltern voices. The New World baroque is a hybrid, mongrelized expression built on a European base, but in such a way that this base is overwritten with pre-Hispanic and other non-Western symbols and meanings. In this way, the "unsuspecting signs of Empire" (Salgado 324) become the vehicles of what Lezama Lima dubs counterconquest. In postcolonial practice and theory, these two types of decolonizing expression—the pure expression of the non-Western Other and decolonizing hybridity—have been implicated in long debates over scope and effectiveness. (An example is the debate between Ngũgĩ wa Thiong'o and Chinua Achebe over the use of African languages versus English.)[16] It is no accident that certain Latin American regions that are famous for their hybridized cultures (such as the Caribbean and Brazil) have also been cradles of New World baroque theory. Caribbean and Brazilian postcolonial theorists and writers (Édouard Glissant, Carpentier, Lezama Lima, Haroldo de Campos) challenged binary, essentialist models of postcolonial expression, each articulating New World baroque theory via alternative cross-cultural anticolonial models of creolization, *mestizaje,* and critical anthropophagy, respectively.[17]

Together, these theorists affirm that the New World baroque is not about being-Other (fixed essence, finished product) but about the process of *becoming*-Other (processes of transformation and transculturation). Carpentier, Lezama Lima, Glissant, de Campos, and affiliated theorists seize on the baroque not as a mimetic mode of representation but rather as a device for the creation of new worlds, new cultures, new collective identities, and new forms of expression. Indeed, the New World baroque is a salient example of what Deleuze and Guattari describe as the becoming-minor of a "major" (official, institutionalized) expressive form: the metamorphosis of a dominant culture at the hands of "strangers" or "aliens" living within its domain, who labor (intellectually and artistically) to make it their own.[18] According to Deleuze and Guattari, "major" and "minor" don't refer to "two kinds of languages but two possible treatments of the same language. Either the variables are treated in such a way as to extract from them constants and constant relations or in such a way as to place them in continuous variation" (*A Thousand Plateaus* 103). In more general terms, "a minor literature doesn't come from a minor language; it is rather that which a minority constructs within a major language" (Deleuze and Guattari, *Kafka* 16). Minor literature is the literature of minorities, if (as Ronald Bogue points out) "not in the usual sense of that word."[19] Deleuze and Guattari's neologism makes a distinction between being a minority artist and the mode in which minority artists create: only those works that subvert and unsettle the privileged majoritarian standard, not those that perpetuate it, are examples of minor literature.

The anticolonial New World baroque, discovered after World War II by Latin American and Caribbean intellectuals, should be framed within processes of creative appropriation and rearticulation. As might be expected, New World baroque theory runs up against skeptical questions, such as: Why choose the baroque, a European formation, to talk about anticolonial expression? How does a term borrowed from European art history help one understand what the colonized were doing? One response is the notion of reorigination: expressive forms do not continue to have the social meanings they had at their origins. All cultural expression and discursive formations are subject to continuing cycles of appropriation, rearticulation, hegemonic co-optation, and popular subversion. In addition to the concept of the minor, Stuart Hall's and Ernesto Laclau's theories of articulation offer further assistance in explaining how the baroque came to be used against the grain of its origins in the institutionalized, authoritarian European state baroque.[20] An articulation is a historically and socially contingent connection between unrelated phenomena that is temporarily forged and broken over time and across cultures. Hall cites the example of "an 'articulated' lorry," a cab and trailer that "can, but need not necessarily, be connected to one another" (Hall, "On Postmodernism" 141). Discussing Rastafarians in Jamaica, Hall outlines wayward processes of decolonizing cultural transformation by way of rebellious appropriations, which recode (biblical) texts and symbols "that did not belong to them" in the sense of an essential, inner truth. Nonetheless, such processes enabled Jamaican Rastafarians to emerge as "new political subjects": "they *became* what they are" (143). Likewise, the baroque has been extracted from its original social setting as the instrument of absolutism and the Counter-Reformation. The Iberian state baroque in its turn provided the building blocks for new articulations that hybridized the norms of the imperial baroque.

With this noted, there is also something about the European baroque's quintessential excess and dynamism—its anticlassical impulse to spill beyond set limits, to project to infinity, to open enclosed forms, to make the familiar strange—that made it the ideal medium for transculturation. As Roberto González Echevarría explains, "The new American sensibility found in the Baroque an avenue for the different, the strange, that is to say, the American. . . . The Baroque allowed for a break with the Greco-Latin tradition by allowing the fringes, the frills, as it were, to proliferate, upsetting the balance of symmetry, displacing the centrality of Renaissance aesthetics, and occupying an important position."[21] The baroque was born in the practice of breaking the classical rules of art; today, New World baroque scholars acknowledge that these heretic origins of the European baroque facilitated further (if unpremeditated) cultural heresies in the baroque's transatlantic and transhistorical migrations.

Alongside Lezama Lima, Alejo Carpentier was long recognized as the first to argue strenuously that, in the Americas, the baroque represented a new beginning, and that the baroque signaled the emergence of a new, authentically American culture in the wake of the European conquest. In his 1975 essay "The Baroque and the Marvelous Real," Carpentier summarizes his proposition of an insurgent, decolonizing baroque originally formulated in essays published in 1964:[22] "And why is Latin America the chosen territory of the baroque? Because all symbiosis, all *mestizaje*, engenders the baroque. The American Baroque develops along with *criollo* culture, . . . with the self-awareness of the American man, be he the son of a white European, the son of a black African or an Indian born on the continent . . . : the awareness of being Other, of being new, of being symbiotic, of being a *criollo;* and the *criollo* spirit is itself a baroque spirit" (100). Throughout his work, Carpentier associates the New World baroque with Latin America's sociohistory of *mestizaje*. In drawing the critical difference from Spain and the Spanish baroque, Carpentier systematically includes *criollos,* American-born whites, in this process of cultural *mestizaje,* and treats *criollo* as synonymous with mestizo. (This is an idiosyncrasy that is partly rooted in the particularities of Cuban cross-racial nationalism, but it also reflects the *criollo* identification with mestizo difference that is typical of certain decolonial Latin American discourses.)

Carpentier builds on the typological baroque theory of the Catalan art historian Eugenio d'Ors, who occupies a key role as disseminator of German baroque theories in the Hispanic world in the early twentieth century. As discussed in more detail in chapter 1, in *Lo barroco* (1935), d'Ors argues that the baroque was not a period style but a timeless spirit occurring in all places and cultures. As Carpentier's dependence on d'Ors shows, while dubious from an art historical viewpoint, d'Ors's abstraction of the baroque from its original setting in seventeenth-century Europe cleared the way for the subsequent recognition of how far the baroque's American routes would carry it away from its European roots. For Carpentier, the baroque displays "a creative impulse that recurs cyclically throughout history in artistic forms, be they literary or visual, architectural or musical" ("Baroque" 90). Just as there is "an eternal return to the imperial spirit," there is an "eternal return of the baroque in art through the ages" (91). Tweaking d'Ors's and Wölfflin's antithetical terms of baroque versus classical, Carpentier posits a "creative" baroque that destratifies (or decolonizes) an "imperial" classical. In a complete negation and reversal of the baroque's seventeenth-century ideological origins, Carpentier thereby articulates the baroque to a new, anti-imperial ideology, which Lezama Lima calls counterconquest.

The Cuban poet, prose writer, and essayist José Lezama Lima puts forward an Americanist poetics of creation as re-creation complementary to Carpentier's, elaborating his own theory of the New World baroque independently but in close parallel to his compatriot. Lezama Lima's ideas about the reinvention of the baroque in the Americas are scattered across various essays written in the late 1940s and 1950s, as well as in his neobaroque novel *Paradiso* (1966).[23] However, the most important work by far is "La curiosidad barroca" ("Baroque Curiosity"), an essay about the colonial baroque in Latin America across literature and the fine arts. It constitutes the second chapter—and intellectual center—of *La expresión americana* (1957; American expression), a collection of essays about the distinctiveness of (mainly Latin) American art and literature from the conquest to the twentieth century. Lezama Lima begins this essay by drawing a categorical distinction between the European and American baroques through arcane poetic and geological metaphors. Whereas the European baroque is "accumulation without tension, asymmetry without plutonism," the American baroque possesses what it lacks: "First, there is tension in the Baroque; second, there is plutonism, an originary fire that breaks the fragments and unifies them."[24] Plutonism (from Pluto, Greek God of the Underworld) and its "originary fire" may refer to an eighteenth-century geological theory by James Hutton that traced the rocks on the earth's surface to volcanic origin.[25] Whether or not Lezama had Hutton specifically in mind, it is clear that his image of solid substances—such as rocks—undergoing transformation by melting and plutonic fire is a powerful evocation of metamorphosis and morphogenesis, the process of rebellious re-creation also described by Carpentier. Such is Lezama Lima's image of the baroque becoming-minor in the crucible of the Latin American *mestizaje*.

Like Carpentier, Lezama Lima believes that one can say something radically new by refashioning old forms. Ironically for our purposes, Lezama begins *La expresión americana* with an attack on a fellow American modern poet-critic who allegedly disputes the possibility of creation in modern times—none other than T. S. Eliot. Eliot's notion of the "mythic method," Lezama Lima insists, demonstrates that he is fundamentally "a pessimistic critic of the crepuscular era," for Eliot believes that "only the ancients were truly creative and that we contemporaries are left with nothing but the play of combinations."[26] Even though Lezama misreads Eliot (see the discussion in chapter 1), his critique is nevertheless instructive for underscoring what, for Lezama Lima, is axiomatic: the possibility of creating not only against the burden of the past (Eliot's criterion) but also against the legacy of colonialism.

While also discovering in the New World baroque what Carpentier calls an anti-imperial "creative spirit," Lezama Lima arrives at his concept of a Plutonic baroque poesis by way of his own idiosyncratic poetic theory, baroque in its own right for its labyrinthine complexity. Briefly put, Lezama Lima envisions the history of cultures as the history of so-called "imaginary eras," periods that attain authentic expression through the poetic image.[27] Lezama Lima regards poetry as a form of knowledge: all deep knowledge is poetic, and poetic "gnosis" takes precedence over reason. Indeed, he puts his own theory of plutonism into practice by drawing on an eclectic selection of sources, including the romantic and symbolist traditions; the philosophers of history Giambattista Vico, Georg Wilhelm Friedrich Hegel, and Oswald Spengler; and his own Catholic faith. Replacing imageless, secular history, "imaginary eras" appear on the world historical stage through the intervention of so-called "metaphorical subjects" (artists and poets), the creators of their respective eras' images, who invariably are rebellious outsiders to established authority. Poets and artists accomplish this task by mediating between place and history in a negotiation that also forges cultural correspondences across race and class divides. Indeed, the "metaphorical subject" is named for the source of its creativity—the expression of correspondences and the creation of relations. More to the point, according to Irlemar Chiampi, *La expresión americana* "develop[s] the concept of the destiny of America as an imaginary era in which the baroque becomes the shaping paradigm and authentic beginning of a truly American reality" (Chiampi, "Baroque" 512). "What we have called 'the American era of the image,'" Lezama Lima argues elsewhere, "has its most evident expressions in the new meanings of the chronicler of the Indies, the baroque dominion, the rebellion of romanticism."[28]

The baroque is historically rooted in Latin America, where it performed the formative role occupied by the Enlightenment in Europe and North America. The baroque, as Irlemar Chiampi, the editor of *Expresión americana*'s annotated Mexican edition, has persuasively argued, constitutes Latin America's alternative modernity. According to Chiampi, the baroque "function[s] to redefine the terms according to which Latin America enters into the orbit of Euro-American modernity" ("Baroque" 508). "It is no accident, then, that the Baroque—pre-Enlightenment, premodern, prebourgeois, pre-Hegelian—should be reappropriated from this periphery (which enjoyed only the leftovers of modernization) as a strategy for subverting the historicist canon of the modern" (ibid. 522). Chiampi's comments illuminate Lezama's project in *La expresión americana:* to investigate a modernizing American baroque that was critical rather than obscurantist and that emerged, to adopt Walter Mignolo's phrase, "out of the *colonial difference.*"[29] As Lezama Lima affirms, "This Baroque of ours, which we situate toward the late seventeenth and through the entire eighteenth century, is closely related to the Enlightenment" ("Baroque Curiosity" 216).

Lezama Lima's main piece of evidence is the work of the poet Sor Juana Inés de la Cruz and her philosophical poem and masterpiece *Primero sueño* (1692; *First Dream*), in particular. Stylistically modeled on Góngorine *culteranismo* in its use of latinisms, syntactical inversions, and *culto* vocabulary, and honoring Góngora in its title (which alludes to Góngora's *Soledad primera* [1612; *First Solitude*]), *Primero sueño* nevertheless turns Gongorine language to new, intellectual uses. It narrates a purported autobiographical account of a philosophical dream in which the soul, desiring to understand the universe, ascends to the peak of creation, only to recoil, failing to achieve its vision. Nonetheless, as Octavio Paz suggests, *First Dream* is "not a poem about knowledge as a vain dream, but a poem about the act of knowing"; it is an "act of faith: not in learning, but in the desire to learn."[30] A "poem of absolute originality," *First Dream* is unprecedented in Spanish baroque literature, a late "baroque poem that negates the baroque," prefiguring the Enlightenment and "modern poetry that centers in the paradox at the heart of her poem: the revelation of nonrevelation" (Paz, *Sor Juana* 381). A repository of humanist learning unique in Hispanic letters for turning science into poetry, *Primero sueño*'s originality is also marked by its distance from Góngora's *Solitudes*. For the latter is a "poem of disillusion" that affirms neither the desire for knowledge nor faith, but that "responds to the horror of the world and to the nothingness of the beyond with a language beyond language, that is, with words that have ceased to be communication to become spectacle" (380). Although, as Christopher Johnson argues, there may be good reasons for unsettling such a "critical abyss dividing Góngora's use of hyperbole to create aesthetic beauty and glorify an agrarian ideal from Sor Juana's use of hyperbole to explore the limits of reason and imagination," no one would want to question *Primero sueño*'s status as an outstanding instance of what both Lezama Lima and Chiampi champion as the alternative modernity of the Latin American baroque.[31]

In the simplest of terms, Latin America's "dissonant modernity" (Chiampi) presupposes that in Latin America, the baroque's tenure lasted throughout the eighteenth century, in some regions into the nineteenth. In point of fact, the two most emblematic New World baroque artists both flourished in the eighteenth century: José Kondori, the Quechua Indian sculptor of the facade of the Church of San Lorenzo, Potosí, and Antônio Francisco Lisboa (c. 1738–1814), known as "O Aleijadinho" (the little cripple), a Brazilian mulatto architect and sculptor, whose work represents the culmination of Brazilian colonial art.[32] In the long-standing debate over the baroque and the Enlightenment in Portugal's and Spain's colonies in the New World, recent scholarship is unsettling older Eurocentric diagnoses of deficiency. Nonetheless, these older diagnoses strangely resurface at the beginning of the same intellectual biography of Sor Juana by Octavio Paz that Chiampi applauds for its recognition of "the (strange) modernity of the Mexican nun" as well as its "restoration of Sor Juana to her world [that] implies as well *our* [Latin American] restoration to the Baroque" (Chiampi, "Baroque" 524, 525). "From the perspective of modern Western history," Paz declares, Latin American history "has been ex-centric. We have had no age of critical philosophy, no bourgeois revolution, no political democracy: no Kant, no Robbespierre, no Hume, no Jefferson" (*Sor Juana* 16). Notwithstanding the lack of a Latin American Kant, as historian Jorge Cañizares-Esguerra has recently shown, the eighteenth century in Latin America saw developments toward "radical renewal" and "aggressive modernity" coming from *within* the colonial baroque system.[33]

Lezama Lima proclaims the decolonizing American baroque by way of a pun that invokes—and inverts—Werner Weisbach's definition of the baroque as the art of the Counter-Reformation: "Repeating Weisbach's phrase and adapting it to America, we can say that for us the Baroque was an art of counterconquest" ("Baroque Curiosity" 213). The claim to counterconquest is literal: citing the work of Kondori and Aleijadinho, Lezama

Lima establishes a close parallel between artistic rebellion in the baroque arts and political rebellion against European colonial power. "In eighteenth-century America, the Baroque style has already created a family pact with the Indian Kondori and the prodigiously triumphant Aleijadinho, who pave the way for the next century's rebellion and offer proof that the continent has matured and is ready for a rupture" (ibid. 237).

Analyzing José Kondori's work on the facade of San Lorenzo (fig. 22), Lezama Lima observes that into the Christian iconography of the facade,

> the Indian Kondori succeeds in inserting the Inca symbols of the sun and the moon, abstractly rendered, and Inca mermaids, oversized angels whose Indian faces reflect the desolation of their exploitation in the mines. . . . The supports of his columns flaunt a powerful abstraction of Inca suns, whose opulent energy cascades over the plaintive face of a *mitayo* mermaid playing a native guitar. . . . Even today we may take pleasure in guessing the reaction of the Jesuit fathers. . . . How did they view the unsought bonus that equated American leaves with Greek trefoils, the Inca half-moon with the acanthus foliage of Corinthian capstones, and the music of the *charangos* [a native musical instrument] with the sound of Doric instruments and the Renaissance viola da gamba? (ibid. 236)

One of "the masterpiece[s] of the Andean mestizo style," Kondori's facade of the Church of San Lorenzo is an outstanding example of the transculturation of the colonial baroque "from below" in so-called *tequitqui* (Nahuatl for tributary) art, created by usually anonymous indigenous and mestizo artisans who built, sculpted, and painted the monuments of the New World baroque.[34] Indeed, the bare mention of Kondori's name as its creator alone (documentation seems to be missing, as well as any unequivocal identification of Kondorí's ethnicity) separates San Lorenzo from such anonymous artistic production.[35]

Tequitqui art is a wonderful example of Deleuze and Guattari's notion of the becoming-minor of a majoritarian expression that sets the frozen standard of the dominant culture into variation. Perhaps the most stunning instance of the transposition of the imported European baroque into the hybrid American is a phenomenon that Lezama Lima describes as an indiatid (*indiátide*):

> In the wonderful works of the Indian Kondori, from whose creative fire contemporary architects have much to learn, we may observe an audacious and amazing addition, the *indiatid.* In the doorway of San Lorenzo Potosí, in the midst of rotund larval angels, hanging stone leaves, keys that sail on carved, stonelike galleons, an Incan princess emerges, sumptuous and hieratic, with all her attributes of power and disdain. In the closed world of theology, still bound by the medieval furor of the divine, that figure, that audacity of stone obliged to choose

its symbols, sets all the elements ablaze, permitting the Indian princess to parade amid an entourage of praise and reverences. ("Baroque Curiosity" 216)

Lezama Lima borrows the term *indiátide,* a permutation of the European term caryatid, as well as the intellectual content of his analysis, from a now-forgotten study, the Argentine art historian Ángel Guido's magisterial

Fig. 22. José Kondori, facade, Church of San Lorenzo, 1728–44, Potosí, Bolivia.

illustrated history of Latin American art, *Redescubrimiento de América en el arte* (1940).[36] Guido's coinage refers to the anthropomorphic columns in San Lorenzo's portal, which are made to represent indigenous (rather than European) women. To illustrate his argument, Guido included an annotated close-up photograph of Kondori's *indiátide* (fig. 23). These two female figures "with arms akimbo and exotically costumed with a flounced skirt" (Kelemen 1:190) are found in the upper portion of the outer sets of columns, above the twisted Salomonic columns where Indian masks protrude from

Fig. 23. José Kondori, detail illustrating *intiátide* (here an Incan princess), Church of San Lorenzo, Potosí. (Reproduced by permission of the heirs of Ángel Guido)

Fig. 24. Erechtheion, view of caryatid porch, c. 421–405 BCE, Acropolis, Athens. (Photograph: Scala/Art Resource, New York)

among the carved foliage. A second set of mestizo caryatids, or *indiátides,* adorns the inner set of columns framing the doorway.

Ángel Guido's (1896–1960) analysis of Kondori's *indiátide* in the fourth chapter of *Redescubrimiento,* titled "El espiritú de la emancipación en dos artistas americanos" (The spirit of emancipation in two American artists), originally a conference paper presented in 1931, makes this Argentine architect, sculptor, poet, and art historian the very first scholar to shed light on the hidden mechanism of the mestizo re-creation of the Iberian baroque. Rather than passively imitating the European anthropomorphic column, Guido claims, Kondori adapted the caryatid for his Andean setting by sculpting it after the model of an Indian princess. As is well known, Greek caryatids represent the women of Caryae, "doomed to hard labour" for siding with the defeated Persian aggressors of Greece (fig. 24).[37] Kondori borrowed this meaning of abject servitude and forced labor, already featured in the original Greek caryatid, and powerfully re-created it within his own contemporary social context of the Spanish Empire erected on the ruins of Tawantinsuyo, the ancient Inca territory in the Andes. There it acquires new political meanings in the context of the cruel *mita* draft labor system imposed on Andean peasants to extract the silver from the mines at Potosí. In the *indiátide,* Guido affirms, "Kondori sculpted in living stone the image of the subjected Indian, the symbolic effigy of the *mita* laborer"

(*Redescubrimiento* 144). Guido explicates the analogy between Greek caryatids and Kondori's *indiátides,* in which art memorializes the suffering of the slave:

> One Indian woman each supports for an eternity one of the two stony cornices, as if their constant weight were the legacy that the white man had bequeathed to the American Indian. But if the Greek caryatids were those enslaved female prisoners that the artist transfigured into Attic beauty in the Erechtheum [on the Acropolis in Athens], so the Quechua Kondori transforms into *criollo* beauty all his own human bitterness, all his suffocated anguish of rebellion, facing the bloody slavery of the Indian slave worker, his brother in blood and in spirit. (ibid. 144)

In Deleuze and Guattari's terms, Kondori's *indiátide* constitutes a "deterritorialized language, appropriated for strange and minor uses" (Deleuze and Guattari, *Kafka* 17). For Kondori's indiatid evokes two centers of reference: the original caryatid and the Indian "stranger" who, working within the foreign language of the European baroque, deforms and transposes the European model into a new expression. The same is true of the other mestizo elements in San Lorenzo identified by Guido and Lezama Lima. Particularly noteworthy are the two Indian mermaids with the "plaintive faces" of *mitayos* playing the *charango* (the native guitar), each hovering on the background of the arched recess into which the facade is set, up high along the sides of the second order. Above their heads Kondori sculpted "the skies of Inca astrology" (*Redescubrimiento* 140): the Inca sun appears above the head of one Indian mermaid, the moon above that of the other, and the remaining space is filled with stars. Furthermore, these mestizo configurations are much more than mere "signifiers" or allegories. That is to say, they don't merely reference social facts, such as the oppression of Indians in tribute slavery or perhaps Inca pride and the composition of the Inca cosmos. They generate a whole new world of "sense" in terms of creating a new regime of meaning, thereby allowing corporeal and material change—the inauguration of New World mestizo identities. Or, with Deleuze, the New World baroque is not a mimetic mode of representation but rather a device for the creation of new (mestizo) worlds, new collective identities, and new forms of expression.

The influence Guido exerted on Lezama Lima's essay "La curiosidad barroca" is largely ignored, but it was decisive, and can be traced to near-verbatim echoes. In addition to the analysis of *indiátides* and the close reading of San Lorenzo in general, Guido is also the source of Lezama Lima's pairing of Kondori and Aleijadinho as the two emblematic heroes of mestizo New World baroque art. Furthermore, Lezama Lima's denomination of the New World baroque as the *barroco de contraconquista* (baroque of the counterconquest) is not simply, as most critics (including Lezama

Lima's editor Chiampi) assume, a permutation of Weisbach's proposition of the European baroque as the art of the Counter-Reformation. It is also an adaptation of Guido's notion of an anticolonial reconquest (*reconquista*) of the arts in Latin America in the seventeenth and eighteenth centuries.[38]

In *Redescubrimiento,* Guido narrates Latin American art history from the conquest to the present, employing a nonlinear and antiteleological temporality—history is a spiral, meandering through circuitous turns. Guido posits two cycles of European "conquest" and Latin American anticolonial "reconquest," in society as well as in the arts. In each case, a period of European conquest is followed by another period of American reconquest, in which Latin Americans put forward a decolonial antithesis to the imperial thesis. The first conquest begins in 1492, and Guido argues that a reconquest was achieved in the seventeenth and eighteenth centuries through the transculturated New World baroque. Ironically, the second cycle of conquest occurs in the nineteenth century, the century of Latin American independence, when Latin America was newly conquered by the European positivist ideologies adopted by the *criollo* political elites in their efforts to modernize their new nations. Finally, in Guido's own time, the first decades of the twentieth century, a second American reconquest is again taking shape, represented by the work of Diego Rivera and the North American architects Frank Lloyd Wright and Louis Sullivan. The intellectual climate that formed Guido was the new mestizo nationalisms and *indigenismos* that emerged in Latin America in the early twentieth century. These "anti-racist counter-orthodoxies" that overturned nineteenth-century orthodoxies of evolutionary racism are not themselves unproblematic, as the Mexican anthropologist Guillermo Bonfil Batalla and the critics Alan Knight and Joshua Lund have charged.[39] Yet they stand within a transhistorical impulse, originating in the seventeenth century and resurfacing in the twentieth, of challenging the monopoly of whiteness and recognizing the social reality of Latin America as a place of mongrel nations.

I gloss Guido's historical schema because it so aptly expresses the genealogy of what Chiampi calls Latin America's alternative baroque modernity. The seventeenth and twentieth centuries—baroque and neobaroque—are linked as periods of the first and second American "reconquest"; conversely, Enlightenment modernity and its nineteenth-century corollaries are denounced as equivalents of Europe's invasion of the Americas in the fifteenth and sixteenth centuries. Guido's nonlinear neobaroque historical schema exposes what postcolonial Latin Americanists Aníbal Quijano, Enrique Dussel, and Walter Mignolo decry as the coloniality of modernity in Latin America.[40] The European model of modernity as linear progress does not work in Latin America and wherever else modernization was uneven or racially discriminatory. Rethinking modernity from the colonial difference

(Mignolo), Guido demonstrates that such reorientation entails revising the basic construct of historical emplotment (Hayden White)—deforming the plot of history as progress and bending it into baroque turns, folds, or spirals.

For the sake of variety, I examine another example of *tequitqui* art from Mexico, and from the Puebla baroque in particular. The Church of Santa María in Tonantzintla near Cholula (see figs. 19–20), according to Carlos Fuentes's review of this renowned folk baroque church,

> is one of the most startling confirmations of syncretism as the dynamic basis of postconquest culture. What happened there happened throughout Latin America. The Indian artisans were given engravings of the saints and other religious motifs by the Christian evangelizers and asked to reproduce them inside the churches. But the artisans and masons of the temples had something more than a copy in mind. They wished to celebrate their old gods as well as the new ones, but they had to mask this intention by blending a praise of nature with a praise of heaven and making them indistinguishable. Tonantzintla is in effect a re-creation of the Indian paradise. White and gold, it overflows with plenty as all the fruits and the flowers of the tropics climb up to its dome, a dream of infinite abundance. Religious syncretism triumphed as, somehow, the conquerors were conquered.[41]

The profuse ornamentation that covers Santa María Tonantzintla's interior walls depicts a syncretic cosmos in which Christian saints associate with Indians (see fig. 19). Tropical fruit and vegetation carved in stucco, gilded, and colored in polychrome climb up all the way to the apex of the cupola, setting the stage for the appearance of the images of Counter-Reformation worship—the cult of Mary, of saints and martyrs, and so forth. Everywhere Indian faces and bodies peer out from among the carved forest of thick local vegetation; many are shown feeding on the fruits of the land (see fig. 20). Contemplating this exuberant spectacle blending images holy and profane, Christian and indigenous, of the eternal life and of local life, the observer cannot help feeling that, as Robert Harbison put it, "Christian imagery has been swamped by something else."[42] As these images demonstrate, Santa María Tonantzintla also teems with *indiátides*. Everywhere on the interior wall decoration, Indian boys with dark hair are found at the top (or the bottom) of pilasters, symbolically holding up the weight of the capital (or the entire pilaster) with their upturned bare hands (fig. 25).

In Santa María Tonantzintla's ornamental tropical forest, which harbors both an Indian paradise and the Christian heaven, there appears an image of a falling child, seemingly in the midst of a vertical dive.[43] With his head down and his feet floating above him, hands stretched out in front, he lifts his face and gazes directly at the observer (fig. 26). According to Antonio Rubial García, the official Christian meaning of this figure is the infant Jesus

Fig. 25. Detail of interior wall illustrating *indiátide* (here young boys holding up the weight of the capital), Church of Santa María, Tonantzintla. (Photograph: Lois Parkinson Zamora)

descending from heaven "to nest in the womb of the Virgin Mary."[44] But this is a baby Jesus like no other. Who has ever seen Jesus's bottom like that? Granted, the official gloss goes some way toward explaining the infant Jesus's odd diving posture. If children are born head first, surely the Immaculate Conception could also be imagined in this position? Nevertheless, and given the pre-Hispanic cosmology underpinning Tonantzintla's mestizo baroque interior, there is sufficient reason to believe that the inspiration for this descending infant Jesus is, in fact, an indigenous deity, *el diós descendiente*, a "diving god" or, more precisely, a "god in diving position" (fig. 27). My illustration of the pre-Hispanic *diós descendiente* comes from the postclassic period of the Mayan Yucatan Peninsula. But there was in fact extensive trading, cultural, and religious contact between the Yucatan and central Mexico, especially in the postclassic period, named for the period following

Fig. 26. Detail of interior wall (the infant Jesus in an unusual presentation), Church of Santa María, Tonantzintla.

the fall of the great ceremonial centers at Teotihuacan (central Mexico) and Palenque and Tikal (Maya). Thus, in the Puebla area, diving god images can be found in the Ocotelulco murals in Tlaxcala, dating from the same post-classic period immediately preceding the Spanish conquest. The Ocotelulco structures include an altar with polychrome murals representing a series of diving figures with snakelike bodies, representations of *Xiuhcoatl,* or the fire serpent.[45] Nevertheless, I am including the Maya image here because it is a three-dimensional sculpture and the visual parallels with the Tonantzintla baby Jesus figure are stronger than with the two-dimensional Ocotelulco mural.

As in Kondori's transposition of the Greek caryatid into an *indiátide,* the Tonantzintla infant Jesus constitutes another synthesis of pre-Hispanic and Christian religious motifs. And like the portal of San Lorenzo, this figure invokes a dual frame of reference: the official framework of Christian theology, as well as the unofficial grid of pre-Hispanic religion. By superimposing the physical posture of the indigenous diving god on the infant Jesus, the *tequitqui* artist appropriates the institutionalized European religious image and resignifies it from below. As in a secret code, the hidden subtext below the surface text of this idiosyncratic "infant Jesus" can only be retrieved by those Indian worshippers already (or rather still) familiar with this particular pre-Hispanic religious icon. The reference to the *diós descendiente* interpellates a limited insider group of Indian initiates while excluding the dominant Christian observer. Likewise, it could also elude the censorship of the Inquisition's Holy Office, which throughout the colonial period oversaw the production of religious images in Mexico.[46] As Bonfil Batalla has argued, a "popular Catholicism" that mixes "Christian elements with those

Fig. 27. Incense holder representing the god of maize in his diving god persona; Maya, ceramic, late postclassic period, 1250–1550 CE, Dzibanché, Quintana Roo, Mexico. (National Museum of Anthropology, Mexico City/Consejo Nacional para la Cultura y las Artes (CONACULTA), Mexico/Instituto Nacional de Antropología e História, Mexico)

of diverse, but basically Mesoamerican, origins" has been one of the paths of Indian survival in Mexico since the fifteenth century: "Diverse Indian societies have taken the signs, symbols, and practices of the imposed religion and made them their own by reorganizing and reinterpreting them within the core of their own religious beliefs. . . . They have been subordinated within a framework that is not Christian and that has its origins in Mesoamerican religion" (*México Profundo* 136).

On the other hand, there is no question that such popular syncretisms owe their existence in good measure to official tolerance, in particular motivated by the method of syncretism developed by the Jesuits in their global project of conversion. Aiming for the "unification of diverse civilizations and cultures . . . under the sign of Rome," the Jesuits "attempted to reconcile non-Christian religions with Roman Catholicism" (Paz, *Sor Juana* 39, 38). Overturning the tabula rasa policy of conversion of the missionary orders (especially the Franciscans) that first arrived in Mexico, the Jesuits, who soon became all-powerful in New Spain, sought to establish a bridge of communication by foregrounding similarities between native and Christian rites and beliefs. It is crucial to keep in mind that the new Jesuit syncretism, "in contrast to the popular syncretism of the Indians, proposed not to Indianize Christianity but, rather, to seek prefigurations and signs of Christianity in paganism" (35). Nevertheless, the Jesuit policy of subordinate inclusion did end up conceding a measure of acceptance to these "pagan" beliefs. Underpinning mestizo images such as the Tonantzintla infant Jesus, therefore, are two kinds of syncretisms articulated from distinct—and very distant—locations in the colonial social pyramid—"from below" and "from above," respectively. These happened to look alike and at times operated in concert, as in the genesis of Mexico's most spectacular mestizo icon, the cult of Tonantzin–Virgin of Guadalupe, but they actually served diametrically opposite ideological projects.[47]

The Ecuadorian philosopher Bolívar Echeverría's recent study, *La modernidad de lo barroco,* sheds further light on this issue. Echeverría examines a historical strategy of adaptation to dominant Spanish culture that he calls the baroque ethos (*ethos barroco*).[48] Inspiring the popular, indigenous syncretism from below that sets out to Indianize Christianity, the baroque ethos is a minor strategy of deformation and appropriation that fulfils the task of living *within* the belly of the beast, as it were, of making the official colonial culture habitable for the conquered. It is important that the baroque is *not* a revolutionary solution. "A strategy of radical resistance, the baroque *ethos* is, however, not a revolutionary *ethos* in and of itself: its utopia is not in the 'beyond' of an economic and social transformation, in a possible future, but rather in the imaginary 'beyond' of a intolerable *hic et nunc* theatrically transfigured" (Echeverría 16). Like all the aforementioned intellectuals, Echeverría argues that such decolonizing aspects of the New World baroque constitute subversive modifications of the official colonial system, limited to the realm of everyday use and unofficial practices. Given the futility of armed rebellion (in view of Spain's military superiority), this was an effort to re-create the dominant European civilization, which came from "the most abject social strata of the colonial social pyramid" (181):

> It is the *criollos* of the lower strata, mestizos of Indian and African heritage, those who, without knowing it, would end up doing what Bernini had done to the classical canons: *they would re-make the most viable, the dominant civilization, the European.* They would awaken and later reproduce its original vitality. In so doing, in nourishing the European codes with the ruins of the pre-Hispanic code (and with the residues of African codes of the slaves that had been violently imported), they would soon construct something different from what they had planned; they would create a Europe that never existed before them, a different, "Latin American" Europe. (Echeverría 82; my emphasis)

I conclude with some general observations on the New World baroque. Although, in the broadest of terms, the New World baroque includes all cultural expression produced in the Iberian colonies in the Americas, there are important differences between the extremes of official (for example, vice-regal court spectacles) and unofficial art (for example, the folk baroque). Likewise, parallel asymmetries divide *culto* literature from the popular visual arts. Scholars agree that the driving engine of popular *mestizaje* was in the visual arts, where the ordinary practices of countless anonymous artisans submerged the imperial baroque within a new, mongrel expression. The popular classes, especially nonwhites and the mixed-race *castas*, were excluded from colonial baroque literature, which was tied to the state-sponsored conservative arts and associated with the elite circles of colonial society. With some well-publicized exceptions, *criollo* literature was limited to a small group of urban intellectuals (*letrados*) dependent on state sponsorship, such as Sor Juana. For this reason, in investigating the mestizo originality of the New World baroque, an earlier generation of cultural historians immediately preceding Lezama and Carpentier, the so-called *barroco de Indias* historians—Picón-Salas, the Dominican intellectual Pedro Henríquez Ureña, and the Mexican critic Alfonso Reyes—privileged the visual arts over literature.[49] In contrast, Lezama Lima and Carpentier work with a "more interdisciplinary and fluid notion of culture" (Salgado, "Hybridity" 320) that allows them to appreciate transculturating practices in *criollo* baroque literature. Thus, parallel to Sor Juana's aforementioned philosophical amplification of baroque poetry, Lezama Lima also retrieves neglected mestizo aspects in Sor Juana's literary work, such as Sor Juana's use of Nahuatl and black voices in her *villancicos* (Christmas carols) that foreshadow the ethnolinguistic experiments in Afro-Antillean modernism, for example in Nicolás Guillén's *son* poetry.[50] Historian James Lafaye confirms Sor Juana's key role in the formation of the mestizo discourse and identity that came to form the basis of Mexican nationalism directed against Spanish rule: because of "the role that she assigns to the Indians, the mestizos, the blacks, and to the Nahuatl language, Sor Juana is a Mexican, in the largest sense of the word, and her work represents an essential link in the progressive formation of the Mexican national consciousness" (Lafaye 74).[51] While Sor Juana's elite *criollo* syncretism is articulated from above and Kondori's popular, indigenous syncretism from below, Sor Juana's *villancicos* and Kondori's transformation of caryatids into *indiátides* are allied to the extent that they are both rebellious syncretisms directed against colonial social hierarchies.

Chicano Lowriders and Rubén Ortiz Torres's Lowrider-Based Video Art

Figures 28 and 29 depict two lowriders customized by the Luna Brothers of the Viejitos Car Club in Los Angeles, George (known as "Crazy George" in lowrider circles) and Robert. Both cars were on display in the 2000 exhibition *Arte y estilo: The Lowriding Tradition* at the Petersen Automotive Museum in Los Angeles, the first of two lowrider exhibitions put on by this respected car museum located in Southern California, the cradle of lowriding, in a landmark event that marked the recognition of the Chicano lowrider

Fig. 28. Robert Luna, *El Maldito,* 1939 Chevrolet. (Photograph: Petersen Automotive Museum)

Fig. 29. George Luna, *Midnight Illusions,* 1947 Chevrolet Sedan Delivery. (Photograph: Petersen Automotive Museum)

tradition in mainstream American car culture.[52] Ironically and sadly, mainstream acceptance and recognition (also manifest in the Smithsonian's Virtual Exhibition of lowriders) came long after lowrider cruising was banned almost entirely from public streets in Southern California (and elsewhere in the United States) in the late 1970s and early 1980s, "at least in part because of police intolerance."[53] Venues for public display of lowriders today are designated car shows and car club picnics, many of which are organized by (and advertised in) *Lowrider Magazine,* the popular monthly magazine that originated in Los Angeles in 1977 and today enjoys a circulation of over 400,000 in thirty countries. As Luis Plascencia has shown, *Lowrider Magazine* played a key role in the commercialization of lowriding, as well as in its national and international dissemination, which brought lowriding to African Americans, Asian Americans, and whites and has won lowriding new *aficionados* in Japan and Europe.[54] Originally, however, lowriding arose in Mexican American barrios among oppressive social conditions—poverty and racial discrimination against Mexican Americans and immigrants. It is on lowriding as a popular Chicano practice of social protest and display of ethnic pride and defiance that this discussion is focused.

Gaudy-colored, flamboyantly stylized, and often hyperornate folk artworks on wheels, Chicano lowriders are customized cars that stand in the same provocative and subversive relation to the American car—the all-American fetish of post–World War II affluence and materialism—as the New World baroque does to the Spanish baroque. In both cases, the icons of the dominant culture are appropriated by common folk through strategies of inversion, partial negation, and resignification. In Spain's and Portugal's American colonies, indigenous peoples, stripped of their native faiths and forced to accept the European civilization of the colonizers, found a way to smuggle the signs of their forbidden faiths and cultures into the Western art and culture they were ordered to copy as artisans. Twentieth-century immigrants to the United States from Mexico were faced with a parallel situation. Ever since the U.S. annexation of Mexico's northern territories from California to Texas in 1848 and the beginning of Chicano history under the sign of conquest by outsiders—"Occupied America" (Rudolfo Acuña)—Mexican Americans have been struggling against systematic race-based oppression. Chicano scholars in the 1960s and 1970s defined this condition as internal colonialism, a domestic form of colonialism. Chicanos were a colonized minority, which explains their pervasive poverty, spatial segregation in substandard housing and professional segregation in inferior employment, low levels of education, low voting participation, and frequent harassment by the police in areas of concentrated population such as Los Angeles.[55] Prevented from assimilating to first-class U.S. citizenship, new immigrants from Mexico coming to the purported land of freedom were forced into institutionalized social spaces of de facto subordinate status. The practice of lowriding emerged between the 1930s and 1950s as a defiant protest against lingering colonial-racial types of oppression in which Mexicans were cast as unassimilable Others within a dominant U.S. system. Samuel Huntington's diatribe against Mexican immigrants as unassimilable aliens in his 2004 book, *Who Are We? Challenges to American Identity,* shows how very alive these ideas remain today.[56]

The term lowrider "refers to any automobile, van, pickup truck, motorcycle, or bicycle lowered to within a few inches of the road. It refers as well to any individual or club associated with the style and the 'ride' characterized as 'low and slow, mean and clean.' These are lovingly customized vehicles—with heavy-duty hydraulic suspension systems ('juice'), costly lacquer paint jobs, stylized murals, etched glass logos, plush interiors, and a proliferation of luxury 'extras.'"[57] In the words of George Luna, the owner of *Midnight Illusions* (see fig. 29), "*Manejar bajo* [to drive low] is for the pride. And *despacio* [slow] is because we want to be seen" (quoted in Torres, "Cathedrals" 31). First and foremost, lowriding is about social visibility and recognition and the reconquest of public space. Indeed, it was about taking back the city and the streets of L.A.'s Chicano *barrios:* by driving slowly, lowriders undermined the official function of roads as instruments for transportation and efficient circulation. During lowriding's heyday in the 1960s and 1970s, on Whittier Boulevard in East L.A., San Diego County's Highland Avenue, and other cruising strips in Southern California, a caravan of lowriders, crawling along bumper to bumper on Friday and

Saturday nights, turned California roads into parade (and party) grounds for *la raza,* displaying their sovereign rule, in style, on their home turf, Aztlán. Naturally, as one journalist noted, this brought them into conflict with the police, "who tend to regard city streets as thoroughfares, not concourses for displaying flashy slope-roof Buicks with hand-painted murals of half-naked women riding pterodactyls on the trunk, no door handles, six speakers going full blast, the front end jumping up and down, sparks flying from under the car, and the whole package going three miles per hour with a young man at the wheel so laid back you have to hold a mirror to his face to make sure he is breathing."[58] Driving and speed, as Baudrillard states, are a "form of amnesia," intent on obliterating space.[59] Chicano lowriders reject speed for slowness and individual driving for communal cruising in groups, to occupy space, to see and be seen in this alternative Chicano public space that lowriding as a social practice was magically opening up on America's roads, every weekend night until early in the morning, year after year, for as long as this rebellious ritual lasted. In the words of one *veterano* of the cruising scene, Roberto Rodriguez, cruising "was the Chicano alternative to Disneyland. It brought Raza together from all parts of Southern California. It was unequalled entertainment for a minimal price."[60]

The car symbolizes the contemporary American way of life, particularly in Los Angeles, the automobile metropolis. Indeed, lowrider culture cannot be separated from the post–World War II explosion of American car culture in the 1950s, which saw the construction of interstate freeways and the birth of customization fads such as drag racing and other car sports. The "surge of lowriding must also be seen in light of a diversity of car-related pursuits that grew rapidly after the war: hot rodding, stock-car and drag racing, demolition derbies, cars shows, and motorcycling. Lowriding thus represents one of the many genres of American car culture" (Stone 96).[61] As such, lowriding is a "uniquely American mode of cultural expression" (ibid. 87). Yet lowriding emerged as "a conscious rebellion against the stereotypical hot rodder of the middle-class Anglo American youth of the 1940s and 1950s. . . . The hot rodder 'jacks up' his car, replaces his stock tires with oversized 'mags,' and races recklessly about town at breakneck speed."[62] In contrast, Chicanos found an ingenious way of adapting, and leaving their signature on, the mainstream American craze over automobile technology and speed. Chicano youth opted for a cool, low-to-the-ground, flamboyant style that deemphasized performance to prioritize aesthetics and style: by driving "low and slow" rather than racing fast, by opting for recycling used cars rather than purchasing new cars they could not afford, and by taking a utilitarian, mass-produced product of advanced technology and converting it into a unique work of art. It is instructive that originally, lowriders were made from secondhand American, domestically manufactured cars (although this has changed since the 1980s, when Japanese trucks became popular, in part for drawing fewer citations for vehicle violations).[63] According to Dick DeLoach of *Lowrider Magazine,* the "'traditional' low-rider is considered to be a vintage car from the 1930s through the 1960s. The 1962 to 1964 Chevy Impalas are perhaps the most coveted lowrider cars."[64] In short, Chicano lowriders are "customized hybrids" (C. Ondine Chavoya) that affirm the bicultural identity of Mexican Americans, "Mexican by heritage and American by destiny" (Stone 86–87).[65] "We [Chicanos] have taken a Detroit machine and we have personalized it. We chicano-ized it," observes artist Gilbert "Magu" Lujan (Sandoval and Polk 20).

To detour performance toward style and artifice is a quintessentially baroque gesture, all the more so when the object in question is the automobile, an actual machine, one of the trophies of machine age technology. Engineering values—efficiency, economy, functionalism—are negated and rejected: the functionalist ideal "less is more" is jilted for its opposite, "more is not less," the baroque principle of abundance and excess. While lowriders deemphasize engine technology for decorative features, there is, however, "one performance aspect of the lowrider sport that has nothing to do with engine performance: hydraulics" (DeLoach 14). Hydraulic suspension systems allow the car to be lowered and raised at the flip of a switch, and to "hop," bouncing their wheels off the ground in intricate rhythms that, in the "hopping" contests that emerged in the 1970s, became choreographed dancing, as vehicles learned to jump side to side and front to back. Developed in the 1960s for a pragmatic purpose (to be able to raise the chassis to street-legal height when police were around), hydraulic lifts were adapted from aircraft technology (they were used to "power wing flaps" [Bright 106]). Here is another imaginative technology transfer testifying to the ingenuity of Chicano technicians, who retooled mainstream technology against the grain of its origins: they invented an ostentatious, anti-utilitarian baroque mode of locomotion for lowriders that countered money and speed with "juiced" cars that preferred hopping and bouncing to racing.

As Torres observes, Chicano lowriders are stylistically related to baroque churches through a second dimension—proliferating, inordinate ornamentation. Lowriders "fix their cars in the most incredible, excessive baroque way ever imagined. Metal flake illustrated paint jobs, gold-plated engines and brakes, velvet upholstery, disco lights, video systems and deafening stereos are some of the features that transform Chevies and other makes into shrines to be admired on the streets" (fig. 30).[66] The Luna Brothers' *El Maldito* (see fig. 28) is hyperornate, with car murals and graffiti filling every available blank space on the chassis in an imaginative reenactment of the baroque principle of *horror vacui.* The effort to fill all empty spaces is similarly operative in the thick decoration of the New World baroque,

Fig. 30. *Twilight Zone,* 1962 Chevrolet Impala SS, interior with custom-tailored velour upholstery, swivel chairs, wet bar, and decorative skulls. (Photograph: Petersen Automotive Museum)

such as the interior walls of the Church of Santa María Tonantzintla (see figs. 19–20) or the Sagrario's Churrigueresque (see fig. 21). Splendor, sensory overload, and stylish extravagance rule in lowriders, as they did in the gold-plated, flamboyantly decorated altarpieces of the Churrigueresque. As Torres glosses the chasm between extravagance in Latino popular baroques and minimalism, which achieved new dominance through modern European design, "lowrider cars are Montezuma's revenge against Mondrian" ("Cathedrals" 30). More urgently, the conversion of performance components into style in lowriders recalls the Churrigueresque's playful transformation of structure into ornament: just as the load-bearing column evolved into the decorative *estípite,* so the car evolved into an artwork whose most elaborate specimens, show cars, are as incapable of driving as *estípites* are incapable of supporting ceilings.

Like hip-hop bling, whose baroqueness is explored in the work of Luis Gispert (as we shall see shortly), lowriders embody a lowbrow counterculture of exotic and fashionable excess. Torres argues that the recent "marriage between hip hop and lowriding" testifies to the kinship between these two aesthetics of conspicuous display that have each emerged from nonwhite urban subcultures in the "'hoods and the barrios" (Torres, "Cathedrals" 27).[67] Wealth clashes with poverty in both cases, and wealth makes

Fig. 31. Lowrider, gold-plated wire wheels. (Photograph: Jack Parsons)

poverty disappear temporarily in the manner of a baroque festival, as in the carnival of Rio de Janeiro. Installing accessories such as gold-plated wire wheels and chrome-plated engines in lowrider show cars is like poor carnival revelers putting on extravagant jewelry and makeup (fig. 31). It is true that not every lowrider is laden with ornamental car murals and other costly accessories. But the underlying principle that distinguishes lowriders from noncustomized cars (and connects them with the baroque) is an inordinate emphasis on style over function.

In Mexican American urban youth culture of the 1950s, lowriders succeeded the zoot suit and pachuco subcultures of the 1930s and 1940s. As some observers affirm, "Lowriders today are the modern Zoot Suiters" (quoted in Plascencia 146). The development is logical: just like lowriders, the flamboyant drapes of the zoot suiter—high-waisted trousers, wide-brimmed hats, and long, gold link watch chains—are in-your-face symbols of Mexican American pride and the defiant self-assertion against dominant Euro-American culture.[68] Both are spectacular "styles of refusal" (Cosgrove) to submit to mainstream tastes; both are connected to collective urban practices such as strolling on sidewalks and cruising urban boulevards aiming to take back the city by being hypervisible and looking outrageously different. It is only natural that at the birth of the U.S. mass car culture in the 1950s, Chicanos would shift the focus of subversive appropriation from clothing to cars in order to transform this emergent American icon into a symbol of their own. Indeed, the mythical origin of lowriders is in so-called "pachuco cars": some "directly link the origin of lowriding to the pachucos and the vehicles they drove in the 1940s" (Sandoval and Polk 20). Before the invention of hydraulics in the 1960s, cars were lowered by cutting suspension coils, or simply by placing heavy objects in the trunk of the car, such as sandbags, bricks, or cement bags.[69] Likewise, some of the words from Chicano slang (*caló*) used for lowriders, such as *ramfla* or *ranfla* (jalopy), "came from the pachucos, or zoot-suiters, of the forties and fifties."[70] In point of fact, lowriders "frequently incorporate images of pachucos into the decoration of their cars and occasionally dress in zoot suits for special events" (Sandoval and Polk 21). For example, Robert Luna's *El Maldito* features a car mural depicting his brother George and himself as zoot suiters (fig. 32). Finally, lowriding also harks back to a traditional Mexican urban custom: the Sunday *paseo* (walk) around the central plaza. According to Torres, "Lowriders organize in car clubs and go cruising on weekends in specific boulevards, updating the old Mexican practice of walking around the town plaza on Sundays in order to socialize and flirt with the girls" ("Cathedrals" 28).

Lowriders are folk artists. "In the hands of the dedicated lowrider, the automobile becomes a work of folk or popular art" (Gradante 71). And like other Chicano folk art, such as home altars or folk shrines, each lowrider

Fig. 32. Detail showing mural of the Luna brothers, *El Maldito*. (Photograph: Petersen Automotive Museum)

is unique to the person who creates it, reflecting his or her personal tastes, faith, history, and identity (Bright, "Remappings" 106). The personal names given to many lowrider cars testify to such unique identity into which customizing has transformed a mass-produced commodity like the car. Likewise, the lowrider stories that are attached to many such vehicles, telling the history of their loving creation over the years, amplify the lowrider's expression of self and connectedness to people, places, and history. One outstanding example is *Dave's Dream,* a New Mexico lowrider originally owned by Dave Jaramillo (and recently purchased by the Smithsonian). *Dave's Dream* is the product of several generations of one family, symbolizing their aspirations and also commemorating two family members, David Jaramillo Jr. and Sr., who worked on the car and died while it was still unfinished.[71]

But the originality of lowrider art, as of home or yard shrines and folk shrines in general, is of a singular nature, not to be confused with newness. As many of the materials are secondhand and old, it is less a creation than a re-creation by recycling. Lowrider production is an instance of the secondhand mode of production from existing materials that is characteristic of the poor and the underprivileged, which Chicano critic Tomás Ybarra-Frausto dubs *rasquachismo.* In his influential essay "*Rasquachismo:* A Chicano Sensibility," Ybarra-Frausto stresses the deliberate contrast to the capitalist consumer ethos: "*rasquachismo* is an underdog perspective—a view from *los de abajo*" (156). A "Chicano vernacular" idiom of "verbal-visual" expression, or an "alternative aesthetic," the *rasquache* is "brash and hybrid," a "sort of good taste of bad taste" (155–56). Drawing on the "tattered, shattered, broken" as its raw materials, *rasquachismo* uses "whatever is at hand" (157). In the production of Chicano lowriders from old cars and folk altars from a bricolage of used objects, things "are not thrown away, they are saved and recycled" (157). The seeming contradiction to the baroque preference for ostentatious display and extravagant ornamentation is but superficial: "high value is placed on making do, hacer rendir las cosas [making things yield their maximum]. . . . The visual distinctiveness of the barrio unites the improvisational attitude of making do with what's at hand to a traditional and highly evolved decorative sense" (157).

Ybarra-Frausto broadly associates the Chicano *rasquache* baroque with the domain of the everyday and its myriad activities—such as storytelling, walking, praying, gardening, and singing, as well as customizing and cruising lowriders—that is also the subject of Michel de Certeau's *The Practice of Everyday Life.*[72] De Certeau argues that everyday practice—that is, how users make do with the structures they must inhabit but cannot shape or control—is the realm of antidiscipline. Ordinary culture, de Certeau contends, is a "*practical science of the singular*" (de Certeau 2:256). Endlessly creative, cunning, and resilient, everyday practice, he insists, resists being forced into the mold of capitalism. It finds ways of asserting itself within official structures and systems that seek to dominate and discipline practice. In chapter 3 we observed how Eltit's *Lumpérica* makes precisely this case within the contemporary Chilean dictatorship setting. According to de Certeau, practice is "dispersed, but it insinuates itself everywhere, silently and almost invisibly, because it does not manifest itself through its own products but rather through its *ways of using* the products imposed by a dominant economic order" (de Certeau 1:xii–xiii). The history of discipline investigated by Foucault and Bourdieu is only half the story: de Certeau insists that no matter how efficient the strategies by which modern institutions seek to colonize the everyday or how extensive their reach, the realm of use remains "*other* within the very colonization that outwardly assimilates them" (1:xiii). In short, only the study of specific local, unofficial practices—such as lowriding—of how real people actually get by within the ready-made official world can determine their nature and meaning.

Like de Certeau's everyday practice, *rasquachismo* is a mobile tactic of resistance that cannot count on a "proper," "institutional localization" (de Certeau 1:xix) and that must therefore operate within the space of the dominant Other. As Ybarra-Frausto suggests, "In an environment always on the edge of coming apart (the car, the job, the toilet), things are held together with spit, grit, and movidas. Movidas are the coping strategies you use to gain time, to make options, to retain hope. *Rasquachismo* is a compendium of all the movidas deployed in an immediate, day-to-day living" (156). As the police backlash against lowriding that banned cruising from American streets demonstrates (and as do the 1943 zoot suit riots, when U.S. servicemen ambushed and ritually stripped pachucos of their zoot suits), the Chicano reconquest of public space and the city was an uneven battle between Chicano everyday practices and official U.S. institutions.

In the broadest of terms, the anticolonial baroque of the New World baroque theorists Carpentier and Lezama Lima and Chicano *rasquachismo* converge in what de Certeau dubs everyday practice, which exists in all periods and places. Such ordinary and spontaneous ways of operating are also what underpins Carpentier's questionable concept of the baroque as a transhistorical type—a human spirit that recurs throughout history—which, as we have seen, was inspired by d'Ors. The baroque "creative spirit" manifest in all cultures, forever battling its natural antagonist, classicism's "imperial spirit," is nothing but the ever-present realm of practice asserting itself within and against institutional structures (Carpentier, "Baroque" 90–91). In the *rasquache* baroque of Chicano lowriders and visual culture, the creativity of such anti-institutional, popular use and recycling looms so large precisely because of the antimonumental nature of the simple materials it works on—not grand public works like cathedrals but everyday objects such as used cars, or home altars. According to Bonfil Batalla, strategies of appropriation that take "as [their] own cultural elements that were foreign and that come from the imposed, dominant culture" in part account for the survival of Indian peoples through five centuries of Spanish colonization (135). Indeed, Chicanos inherited the *rasquache* strategy from Mexico's indigenous campesinos, who invented the creative recycling of industrial products, such as turning automobile tires into the famous huaraches (sandals) (Bonfil Batalla 138).

And how do mass-produced commodities such as cars become baroque art? With this question, we turn to Rubén Ortiz Torres's work as a practicing artist. Torres's own artwork amplifies the transhistorical continuities he establishes between seventeenth-century New World baroque cathedrals and twentieth-century lowriders as "cathedrals on wheels." It opens up new dimensions of the problem of re-creating commodity culture as art, by linking lowrider customizing's hyperbolic stylization to related projects of the historical avant-garde, and to Marcel Duchamp's invention of the ready-made in particular. Educated first at a conservative Mexican art academy, the Academy of San Carlos (one of the oldest art schools in the Americas), and later at the experimental California Institute of the Arts in Valencia, California, Torres has been trying to "find a balance" between fine art and popular culture, as well as Latin American and U.S. cultures.[73] His work was featured in *Ultrabaroque*, where it is introduced as paradigmatically hybrid and transgeneric, dealing "with issues revolving around processes of transculturation" (Armstrong and Zamudio-Taylor, *Ultrabaroque* 75–79, 75). Torres works across a wide range of media, including sculpture, painting, photography, video, film, and "a series of customized commercial products from baseball caps to a Nissan pickup truck that challenge the traditional division between the reified art object and the degraded curios of popular culture" (Chavoya 141).

After his relocation to California, Torres adopted customizing as his artistic method. "As an aesthetic strategy," states Torres, "what I've learned and what I'm really interested in, here in California, is the whole process of customizing. The development of art and culture has been a development of cultural exchange. . . . [A] lowrider is not producing a new car, he is participating in this process of dialogue and negotiation . . . a lot like what hip-hop culture does" (Kelley, "Interview"). Modeling his practice as a professional artist on lowrider customizing, Torres refuses to create from scratch, opting instead to recycle and customize commercial products, thereby artistically adopting everyday methods of making do within the ready-made world of capitalist production. Torres's art situates itself within the condition of ordinary users who appropriate things and spaces they did not design but must nonetheless consume and inhabit (indigenous and mestizo artists in the "guided culture" of colonial New Spain; consumers today). His "neobaroque pop" or "multicultural pop" art showcases consumption as improvised, rebellious re-creation (Chavoya 145)

Below I focus on Torres's lowrider-based video art, in particular the following three videos: *Custom Mambo* (1992), *Alien Toy: La Ranfla Cósmica (Unidentified Cruising Object)* (1997), and *The Garden of Earthly Delights* (1999).[74] *Custom Mambo*—the first video Torres made on the subject of lowriders—begins with a traveling shot of long lines of cars waiting to cross the U.S.-Mexico border at night. Soundover superimposes the voice of George Luna ("Crazy George") from the Viejitos Car Club—the owner of *Midnight Illusions* (see fig. 29)—expounding lowriding's articles of faith in eloquent Spanglish:

> First of all, *manejar bajo es un* [driving low is a] pride. *Es un orgullo* [It's a pride]. And slow—*despacio—es el estilo* [slow—is the style] from the car, and the lifestyle. See, that's how you distinguish a lowrider from a different car. Every time you see a lowrider he is driving low and slow, or it's not a one hundred percent lowrider! . . . And if you ride too fast, people won't be able to check 'em out! So you have to ride low and slow, *para que la gente mire lo que traes* [so that people see what you've got]! And you can be proud of what you're driving!

Luna's speech continues as visuals switch to one of the ubiquitous signs north of the border warning motorists to slow down because of undocumented migrants running across freeways. By intercutting images, Torres connects lowriding to the theme of undocumented migration, as well as to other U.S. stereotypes of Mexico, such as Speedy González. The intention is to convey the stigma attached to lowriders and lowriding on the part of mainstream American culture. On the other hand, in an ironic twist—and a stab at the mainstream obsession with speed—lowriders are presented as model law-abiding motorists who save lives by not speeding.

Custom Mambo's soundtrack mixes music clips from Pérez Prado (the king of mambo) with sounds of clanging machines, thereby illustrating the hybrid nature of lowrider customizing that turns technology into art by teaching cars how to dance. Several shots feature lowrider hopping spectacles. In one acrobatic performance the front of a lowrider jumps several feet into the air, while the camera stores the successive arcs of these jumps in a single frame, so that the hopping lowrider comes to resemble an enormous stylus drawing waves on its own photograph as if on a drawing board (fig. 33). In another shot accompanied by one of Pérez Prado's mambos, one lowrider dances by alternating hops on its right front and left back tire, so that the car sways diagonally. This shot is intercut with the sensuous dance of a trio of scantily clad lowrider women, simulating the lowrider courting them. Both the lowrider and the women seem to be gyrating their "bodies" in unison to the hypnotic beat of the same "custom" mambo, obliterating the difference between machine and human.

Originally presented at the Southern California art show *InSITE97,* the main protagonist of *Alien Toy*—its off-Hollywood star, as it were—is an award-winning lowrider named *Wicked Bed.* Departing from the classic models built from American-made brands, *Wicked Bed* is a pickup truck customized by an artist from Mexico, Salvador "Chava" Muñoz. Torres explains,

> As an outsider to the lowrider community, [Muñoz] was able to free himself from the classicism of the Chevy Impala. A self-taught iconoclast, he transformed a 1973 Nissan pickup truck into *Wicked Bed.* The bed of the truck rises and spins in two directions while it opens up into four independent parts. The doors fly out and spin around while the hood jumps off and twirls as well. The front of the truck separates itself from the back and drives around independently, while the rest of the car dances. Like some sort of Doctor Frankenstein, this showman has given

Fig. 33. Rubén Ortiz Torres, still from *Custom Mambo,* 1992. (Reproduced by permission of Rubén Ortiz Torres)

Fig. 34. Rubén Ortiz Torres, stills from *Alien Toy: La Ranfla Cósmica* (*Unidentified Cruising Object*), 1997. (Reproduced by permission of Rubén Ortiz Torres)

> new life to an aggressive, irrational machine. The future is happening now, out of control, like a mutated virus. (Torres, "Cathedrals" 30)

Here, lowrider hydraulics and hopping have been taken to radical extremes (fig. 34). Surpassing the tropicalized car dances in *Custom Mambo,* the "juiced" pickup in *Alien Toy* enacts a progressive auto-disintegration of the entire vehicle into independent spinning parts. It thereby transforms itself—our familiar automobile—into the bizarre "alien toy" announced in the video title. Neobaroque defamiliarization—lowriding's negation of technology's functionalism and its stylization as artifice—is here exceeding established limits. What better emblem of the baroque art of excess—"Montezuma's revenge against Mondrian"—than this "cubist pickup" (ibid. 30) resembling a schizophrenic rotating sculpture, or a mechanical bird flapping its wings?

An additional source of provocation in *Alien Toy* is found in Muñoz's choice of car make and paint finish. Nissan pickups are among the car models used by the U.S. Border Patrol, and *Wicked Bed* has been stylized as a parody of a Border Patrol vehicle. Painted solid white with one thick horizontal stripe across the length of the chassis, which is adorned with a logo in the shape of a round medallion, *Wicked Bed* resembles an ordinary Border Patrol vehicle in its inactive mode and seen from a distance. On closer inspection, however, it becomes clear that the words "U.S. Border Patrol" in the official logo have been replaced by "Alien Toy," and the circumference of the medallion reads "Unidentified Cruising Object." Muñoz's gesture of overwriting the official Border Patrol logo, thereby creating a lowrider "dark twin" of the Border Patrol car, is a brazen political joke. Indeed, *Wicked Bed*'s performance as the Border Patrol vehicle's enemy double, the "toy" of undocumented immigrants and other aliens, constitutes the narrative thread of Torres's video. Connecting U.S. nativist propaganda against illegal aliens with the science fiction plot of alien invasions, Torres stages a marvelous transformation of a Border Patrol truck into an unidentifiable "cruising object" against the foil of a dystopian plot of an alien invasion of earth. The opening shot shows a UFO in the sky tracked by spectators; the footage of *Wicked Bed*'s cubist dance is intercut with tabloid news reports of alien sightings. Torres has even worked in the legendary monster Chupacabra, a vampire-like phantom allegedly drifting about Latin America, infamous for its signature mangling of the necks of its animal victims.

Torres also draws on the history of modern art. The provocation in Muñoz's retitling of the official U.S. Border Patrol logo—as well as the magical transformation of a police truck into the aliens' "toy"—harks back to Duchamp's invention of the readymade. Torres explicitly situates his method and aesthetics of customizing consumer objects within the lineage of Duchamp's readymade, describing it as a "permutation that incorporates the teachings of the first Marcel" ("Yepa" 59). Duchamp famously selected random commodity objects (a urinal, a bicycle wheel), signed them, and sent them to art exhibits. This gesture, as Peter Bürger observes, erases the difference between the spheres of mass culture and art. The artist's signature marks an object as a work of art, a creation that is "both individual and unique."[75] By affixing his signature to a mass-produced urinal, Duchamp negated both the concept and the social institution of art developed since the Renaissance (Bürger 56). During the scandal provoked by his most famous readymade, *Fountain by R. Mutt* (1917), Duchamp wrote the following statement in defense of *Fountain* as a unique work distinct from the industrial product of the urinal: "Whether Mr. Mutt with his own hands made the fountain or not has no importance. He CHOSE it. He took an ordinary article of life, placed it so that its useful significance disappeared under the new title and point of view—created a new thought for that object."[76] According to Marjorie Perloff, the avant-garde legacy of Duchamp that has been "central to [American] arts" is this "notion that art can be made from everyday objects and materials," and that "the artist is not so much a talented draftsman or painter but simply the person *who chose it*" (209). To translate Duchamp's and Perloff's observations into de Certeau's terms, the readymade is a *practiced* consumer object, a commodity re-created in the crucible of everyday use.

Torres updates the American avant-garde project of breaking down the barriers between everyday life and art. For Torres as for Duchamp, the "utilization of [mass-produced] objects is a path towards questioning systems of validation."[77] Torres views his customized art as a new generation of readymades for an age in which "any banal ready-made can be permuted into a valuable commodity, and the avant-garde has become institutionalized."[78] Duchamp's once provocative readymades have been accepted as art and have lost their edge, while art as a bourgeois institution has prevailed. Consequently, new strategies of protest and provocation are needed to continue the avant-garde project of "forcing" mass-produced products into the realm of art (Bürger). Far from mocking claims to individual creativity altogether, Torres's customized neo-readymades recast the notion of individual creativity and originality in ways outlined above, as a secondhand mode of production. Creation lives on, but as re-creation, the conceptual and artistic recycling of the detritus of industrial consumer culture.

In *The Garden of Earthly Delights,* Torres trains customizing on a new and different mass-produced "found" object, the lawn mower. The video and its related sculpture series, *Power Tools/Herramientas de Alto Poder* (1999), arose in the context of a controversy over gasoline-powered gardening tools (leaf blowers) that erupted in Los Angeles in 1998.[79] Complaints about noise and pollution on the part of suburban homeowners had led to a citywide ban against gasoline-powered leaf blowers in residential neighborhoods. The consequences of this ban threatened the livelihood of L.A.'s predominantly Mexican-descent gardeners, who operated small businesses that employed these industrial tools. The mechanization of gardening (lawn mowers, leaf blowers, weed whackers) had freed them from the drudgery of garden labor (brooms, rakes). It had transformed—in Torres's apt phrase—"former feudal peasants into space-age garden warriors."[80] As Torres explains in an essay outlining the topical context of his *Power Tools* sculpture series, without the leaf blower "gardeners, most of whom work for themselves, have to do twice the work for the same pay, because their customers are reluctant to pay more. Given the new law, a decent salary and even one's job are threatened by an endless pool of unskilled cheap labor who will broom for almost no pay" ("Power Tools" 30). L.A. Gardeners' protests culminated in a hunger strike, which attracted international media coverage. This standoff inspired a Salvadoran immigrant and L.A. resident,

Gody Sánchez, an "air force mechanic trained by Americans and Israelis" (31), to improvise a new leaf blower prototype with less noise and pollution. The first customized leaf blower Sánchez presented at L.A. City Hall "used a car battery to turn a gasoline-powered motor into an electrical one" (31). A second model "adopt[ed] the silencer of an automatic weapon into the exhaust pipe of a filtered gasoline-powered leaf blower, and produce[d] a quieter, lighter, and more powerful machine" (31). Sánchez's ingenuity convinced lawmakers that industrial leafblower design could be improved on; a compromise was reached, and the hunger strike was ended. For Torres, this anecdote reveals the creativity of the customizing approach to (in this case, faulty) industrial technology. "Gody has proven the feasibility of an interactive nonlinear creative process, a kind of futurism where technology is not a goal in itself, but—through customization—a way to access a more democratic future for everyone" (31). It also consolidates the place of Chicano *rasquache* tactics in the annals of innovation.

The Garden of Earthly Delights centers on such *rasquache* futurism of customized gardening tools. In the opening shots, and to the sound of bird calls, the camera travels over nicely cropped front lawns and beautiful L.A. backyard lawns lined by palm trees with distant views of downtown. This first Edenic phase ends with a cut to two baseball-capped Mexican gardeners, who break the quiet by starting their tools, a lawn mower and a weed whacker. Rapid intercutting between the two tools in operation, underlined by cascading volumes of noise, quickly produces an infernal audiovisual environment, illustrating the motive for residents' complaints that led to the 1998 ban. Next, however, the noise suddenly stops, and the screen goes black. A Spanish-speaking voice (clearly belonging to one of the gardeners) interjects from offscreen, "Tengo otra, no?" (I have another one, no?). The camera then cuts to a profile shot of a customized four-wheel minitractor lawn mower flaunting a gold-plated chain-link steering wheel (a "fat man" steering wheel, in lowrider parlance), hot pink custom paint, and elaborate hydraulics. A brown hand in close-up is shown picking up the controls. Instantly, the vehicle begins to dance, and its various parts—the hood, the trunk, the seat—lift and twirl in the air to the sound of techno and hip-hop music. As in the previous video, we see a familiar industrial product—a tractor, in this case—(d)evolve into a part monstrous, part wondrous "alien toy."

In Wölfflin's terms—as well as those of Umberto Eco and Haroldo de Campos bearing on the open work of art—customizing enables the vehicle to move from a classic phase of closed composition (self-contained, finite whole) toward a baroque phase of open form.[81] Both *Alien Toy* and *The Garden of Earthly Delights* stage the disintegration of vehicles into fragmented assemblages, with all parts frantically fleeing the center. *Wicked Bed* and this customized gardening tractor are car culture's answer to the avant-garde, or, if you will, Eliot's *Waste Land*—they are nonorganic works of art, hyperstylized artifices that flaunt the seams of their construction. And as in *Alien Toy*, the viewer's disorientation is enhanced by Torres's extravagant cinematography: extreme high and low camera angles on the spinning vehicle, extreme close-ups of twirling parts, and superfast editing that barely allows the viewer time to understand the movements she is watching. The dystopian scenario of noisy gardening machines at work has given way to the Dionysian dance of a customized lawn mower at play. The mass-produced commodity refuses service, launching into an ecstatic artistic performance. Again, here is the Sarduyan point of baroque anti-utilitarianism: the "mockery of all functionality" and the playful squandering of resources, consuming advanced technology such as hydraulics in exuberant stylization.[82] Or, in the terms of *The Garden of Earthly Delights*' allegorical title, we are witnessing the *rasquache* technology of Chicano futurism give a taste of the alternative Edenic delights of its counterinstitutional spectacles. To conclude: the *rasquache* baroque of Chicano lowriders and Torres's lowrider-based video art showcase the insurgent creativity of everyday practice, which does not produce originals but remakes existing materials. In this way, official systems of value and art are bypassed and temporarily suspended. Users and consumers assert themselves as independent makers within the ready-made official world by turning commodities into readymades.

Contemporary U.S. Latino/a Neobaroque Visual Art, with Amalia Mesa-Bains and Luis Gispert

This final section deepens the discussion of the U.S. Latino/a neobaroque, opening out from lowrider-based neobaroques and Ortiz Torres's video art to a broader assessment. In tracing the hemispheric and transhistorical routes of the New World baroque, the tension between elite *culto* literature and the popular visual arts that we noted in the historical New World baroque is reproduced (in modified fashion) in contemporary neobaroque expression by U.S. Latinos. Overall, it is difficult to find neobaroque literature by U.S.-based Latinos who have not been educated outside the United States. The dominant stratum of mestizo baroque expression by Latinos in the United States (especially Chicanos) is the popular baroque in visual culture and the visual arts, which is the domain that produced Chicano lowriders. In contrast, twentieth-century Chicano and Nuyorican literature in particular has tended toward varieties of realist expression that eschew the hyperbolic artifice and flamboyant expenditure of verbal material so characteristic of the neobaroque. It is not too difficult to see why this is the case; the ensuing brief discussion of the U.S. Latino literary neobaroque offers some reflections on this issue.

In large part, the cultural origins of Hispanic expression in the United States are in the popular classes. Among the three historical U.S. Latino communities, this is especially true for Chicanos and Nuyoricans (and, more generally, Puerto Rican migrants to East Coast metropoles), less so for Cuban Americans. Chicano literature, for example, as Ramón Saldívar has argued, has its "folk base" in the *mexicano* oral tradition.[83] For all three groups, book-length publications were rare in the nineteenth century and the early twentieth century, and newspapers, especially the Spanish-language press, were the primary publishing outlets for Hispanic literature in the United States before 1950.[84] As the Puerto Rican critic Juan Flores has observed, a Latino community exists within the United States today in part because "portions of Latin America have been incorporated into what has become the United States."[85] Flores's point is that twentieth-century Latino mass migration to the United States is a symptom of Latin America's drift into the orbit of economic dependency on the United States. With the exception of nineteenth-century Cuban and Puerto Rican intellectuals exiled to the United States, contemporary Cuban exiles fleeing the Cuban Revolution, and the upper-class elite among the first generations of Mexican Americans after the U.S. annexation of the borderlands in 1848, Latin Americans and hispanophone Caribbeans have largely come to the mainland United States to find work, and they have predominantly been working class. Furthermore, because of the colonial-racial type of subordinate incorporation of Mexicans and Puerto Ricans in the wake of 1848 and 1898, these Latino minorities stayed working class for generations after their arrival, whether they came as migrants in the twentieth century or descended from the original native residents of the Mexican American borderlands. Writing about social problems has been a primary concern for authors emerging from these groups. And while some writers have accomplished this goal while going beyond realism and employing a range of modernist and postmodernist styles, such as decentered narrative (Tomás Rivera, Rolando Hinojosa, Sandra Cisneros), cyberpunk (Alejandro Morales), or historiographic metafiction (Junot Díaz), they have for the most part avoided the baroque's notorious rhetorical hyperbolism.

José Kozer, a Cuban exile poet of Jewish descent who has been living in the United States since 1960 and who writes exclusively in Spanish and is nourished by Latin American (not U.S.) literary traditions, illustrates my point.[86] The coeditor (with Roberto Echevarrén and Jacobo Sefamí) of the 1996 landmark collection of neobaroque Latin American poetry *Medusario*, Kozer writes poetry that is a cornucopia of linguistic games. Neobaroque in "abhor[ring] a vacuum,"[87] Kozer's poetry avoids abstractions, depicting a world in microscopic detail. Statements give way to amplifications and digressions in parentheses without ever terminating conclusively, creating a rupturing "cubist" effect. Kozer's poetic speaker is a voracious chameleon who consumes and recycles verbal material; as Kozer points out in one of his poetic self-portraits, "He has one ambition: the entire vocabulary."[88] In both poetry and essays, Kozer affirms that the neobaroque is a kind of poetry "where language is both king and queen"[89]: "The truth is I only care about words, not every word (I don't care for the word word, if truth be told) snow isn't a word I care for (I don't care to be cold, and snow—I mean to say lyric snow—has become so commonplace) one less word now: and for the letter n there are others. A multitude. Nabob, an exotic word" ("Last Will & Testament," in *Stet* 121). Or, as he explains in critical prose:

> A summary of Neobaroque poetry would include notions such as dispersion, the re-appropriation of former styles, styles that move in barbaric landscapes, where ruins are put together; a writing where the *trobar clus* and the hermetic proliferates, where there is great turbulence, unnatural mixtures, the joy of combining languages, the dissolving of a unidirectional sense, no praising of the Self or the Ego or the I; polyphony, polyvalence and versatility, utilization of former styles in order to deconstruct them, creating a true explosion of different forms of writing, a soiling of materials, a signature towards the ugly, the sordid, the recyclable. ("Neobaroque" 19–20)

In the United States, the literary neobaroque for the most part tends to be found among recent immigrant writers from Latin America, such as Kozer and Eduardo Espina (from Uruguay). Although an expanding phenomenon, the baroque tradition in U.S. Latino literature seems largely a recent import. The Nuyorican writer Nicholasa Mohr, for example, adopts an outspoken anti-baroque stance, which voices familiar objections. In a 1987 essay defending the autonomy and distinctive voice of Nuyorican literature vis-à-vis the authority of Puerto Rican literature from the island, Mohr charges that "the commonly used baroque style of writing in Spanish seems to act as filler rather than substance."[90] Fending off island-based claims of cultural and linguistic superiority and purity and corresponding blame that Nuyorican literature and culture is tainted by Americanization, Mohr asks whether the "use of baroque Spanish might not be a way for some [Puerto Rican] intellectuals to attempt to safeguard their privilege and power against the strong North American influence which presently permeates Puerto Rico" (92). Mohr identifies as a "daughter of the Puerto Rican diaspora" in the United States, while qualifying this by stating that she is "not an avid reader of the literature published in Puerto Rico" (88, 90). Mohr's shift as a Nuyorican writer from Spanish to English (or bilingual Spanglish) thus appears to have cut her off from the Latin American baroque.

At least in part, Kozer's and Mohr's opposing positions on the baroque relate to their respective acceptance or denial of Spanish-language literary traditions for the U.S. Latino diaspora. Yet, as might be expected, it is possible to adopt other stances on this question. I conclude these brief reflections on the neobaroque and U.S. Latino literature with the Chicano novelist Rolando Hinojosa's endorsement of what he dubs the "Hispano-American Baroque."[91] Descended from the original eighteenth-century Mexican colonists of the Rio Grande Valley (in what is today South Texas) on his father's side of the family, Hinojosa is the prize-winning author of the bilingual *Klail City Death Trip* series and one of the pioneers of contemporary Chicano literature.[92] Many of Hinojosa's novels use the decentered narrative form of the chronicle, which records conversations and documents local history and customs: they are "not held together by the . . . plot as much as by *what* the people who populate the stories say and *how* they say it."[93] In a short essay, Hinojosa argues that the baroque deformation and "refraction" of classical aesthetic norms is a useful tool for understanding the hybrid Chicano experience in the U.S.-Mexico borderlands. More to the point, he proposes a Chicano baroque variety of the DuBoisian concepts of double consciousness and "second sight": Chicano "dual belonging" relates to duality as "an important element in the Baroque" (Hinojosa, "Hispano-American Baroque" 25). Second sight is manifested in the act of deciphering inscriptions on gravestones in historical cemeteries in the Rio Grande corridor, the site of popular nineteenth- and early twentieth-century *mexicano* rebellions against U.S. rule as well as their brutal repression. Hinojosa explains: "Outsider's eyes would [simply] . . . see flat surfaces with names. . . . We would see lines crossing and crisscrossing across the years and across the wars that would cause the flat surfaces to show us another reality which I learned later on was refraction, one of the chief attributes of the Baroque" (24). In other words, just as the baroque deforms the classical "straight line," bicultural, bilingual Chicano identity demands the disfigurement of Anglo norms (23). Hinojosa's point recalls González Echevarría's observation that the European baroque's taste for difference and transgression made it the ideal medium for New World transculturations.

In contrast to such rare instances of the literary neobaroque, the baroque has had a long-standing presence in Mexican American visual culture, undergirding the Chicano folk arts since the very beginning of Chicano history in the nineteenth century. Indeed, it is fascinating to realize that the delirious ornamentation and flamboyant display of Chicano home altars, folk shrines, and more recently lowriders derives from the genealogy of the popular mestizo baroque originating in Tonantzintla and elsewhere in colonial Mexico and was transmitted to *el norte* via everyday practice and migration. "All along the Rio Grande, the custom of having folk shrines—called *grutas* (grottoes) or *nichos* (niches) . . . —still flourishes."[94] North of the border, flower pots and other objects of daily use are made out of cans and car tires, as in Mexico. A contemporary home altar to the Mexican folk saint El Niño Fidencio from San Antonio, Texas, perfectly illustrates this *rasquache* Chicano baroque that "favor[s] the elaborate over the simple, the flamboyant over the severe" (Ybarra-Frausto 158) (fig. 35). One of the

Fig. 35. *Tronito* (throne), a special kind of Mexican home altar in honor of El Niño Fidencio, San Antonio, Texas. (Photograph: Kay Turner)

images illustrating Ybarra-Frausto's essay on *rasquachismo,* its hyperbolic decoration and idiosyncratic assemblage of personal, religious, and commodity objects reflects traditional Mexican religious expression. "Home altars, often placed on a table or the top of a chest in a bedroom, contain collections of sacred images, crucifixes, candles (often in glass jars depicting an image of a holy figure), incense, *medallitas* (saints' medals), flowers, family photographs, and other personal items arranged on an altar cloth. . . . Each altar is unique to the person who created it, usually a woman, and is the center of the family's spiritual life."[95] As Pat Jasper and Kay Turner explain, "What is at work in the folk arts of Mexican-American San Antonio is an aesthetic of bold display; images, objects, and ornamentation are not absorbed into environments, but, rather, they are pushed forward to catch the eye and to carry meaning."[96]

Indeed, the Latin American folk baroque sensibility of ostentatious display, gaudy colors, and ornamentation run riot appears in a broad range of contemporary U.S. Latino visual culture, including some well-known Chicano artists such as Luis Jiménez and Amalia Mesa-Bains and Cuban American artists such as Luis Gispert. Born into a family of Mexican American craftsmen in El Paso, Luis Jiménez (1940–2006) was apprenticed by his father, a neon-sign maker, before he went to art school. He soon began to work with "low culture" materials such as fiberglass, drawing on lowrider art and pop culture.[97] Jiménez became famous for his large, heroic figures depicting Mexican and Chicano themes, such as *vaqueros,* horses, and Aztec warriors. Several of his sculptures, including *Vaquero* (1980/1990), are now on view at the Smithsonian (fig. 36). Depicting a pistol-brandishing Mexican *vaquero* on his bucking horse, this dynamic composition transforms the ordinary into the mythic. The horse's intense, artificial blue coloring, its thick reddish mane that summons the image of flames running down its neck, and the *vaquero*'s gold trousers flapping in the wind turn horse and rider into one single fused supernatural being visiting earth, as in a miracle or the apparition of a saint. On the one hand, Jiménez's bright pop sculpture clearly parodies "pompous equestrian statues of military heroes found in parks all over the Western world" (Mitchell, "Baroque Populism" 104). On the other hand, it also corrects an ingrained Anglo-American stereotype, which claims that the cowboy was an invention of the American frontier. To the contrary, as Mitchell points out, Jiménez reminds viewers that the American cowboy was a remake of Mexican *vaquero* culture already in place in Mexico's northern provinces prior to their becoming the American West (ibid. 104).

This Mexican baroque visual tradition also sheds fresh light on Richard Rodriguez's analysis of the gay remodeling of Victorian townhouses in San Francisco's Castro District. In a chapter titled "Late Victorians" in his second book of autobiographical essays, *Days of Obligation: An Argument with My Mexican Father* (1992), Rodriguez investigates the "renovation of Victorian San Francisco into dollhouses for libertines" by highlighting the neobaroque strategy of "artificialization" (Sarduy) that animates such endeavor[98]: "Homosexuals have made a covenant against nature. Homosexual

Fig. 36. Luis Jiménez, *Vaquero*, modeled 1980/cast 1990. Acrylic urethane, fiberglass, steel armature. (Estate of Luis A. Jiménez, Jr./Artists Rights Society [ARS], New York. Photograph: Smithsonian American Art Museum, Washington, DC/Art Resource, New York)

survival lay in artifice, in plumage, in lampshades, sonnets, musical comedy, couture, syntax, religious ceremony, opera, laquer, irony" (Rodriguez 32). "Late Victorians" intervenes between two essays about Mexico and Mexican American culture in which Rodriguez reclaims his Mexican heritage, the Catholicism of his immigrant parents, and above all his brownness, his belonging to the mestizo race that he had disavowed earlier in his best-selling autobiography *Hunger of Memory* (1982).

When a decade later in *Days of Obligation* he reveals his homosexuality, along with laying claim to his Mexican heritage, Rodriguez notably switches codes to discuss architecture, art, and home decoration. The language of artistic design serves as a vehicle for the expression of gay identity. "Late Victorians" hinges on an elaborate conceit that yokes together the remote themes of architecture and homosexuality. Indeed, the very title enacts the Gongorine strategy of metonymic displacement (or what Sarduy dubs "radial reading"), in which the eponymous late Victorians come to substitute for the elided referent, gay men. Gay men, Rodriguez observes, don't "need decorators. They were born knowing how" (32). In rehearsing familiar observations on gay taste and aptitude for design, Rodriguez blends the latter with the Mexican baroque sensibility. The gay community has refashioned the multigenerational family homes of a bygone age in the same way that the baroque refracts the classical, and the New World baroque in turn re-creates the European baroque: "The impulse is not to create but to re-create, to sham, to convert, to sauce, to rouge, to fragrance, to prettify. No effect is too small or too ephemeral to be snatched away from nature, to be ushered toward the perfection of artificiality. *We'll bring out the highlights here.* The homosexual has marshaled the architecture of the straight world to the very gates of Versailles—the great Vatican of fairyland" (33).

Amalia Mesa-Bains's 1994 installation *The Library of Sor Juana Inés de la Cruz,* a re-creation of Sor Juana's cell and library, raises the question of the transculturation of the official state baroque by insurgent New World practices that rearticulate and resignify it. This installation was presented at Williams College, where it is now housed, and it was also displayed in the 1995 exhibition *Going for Baroque* at the Contemporary and Walters Museum in Baltimore.[99] Mesa-Bains's visual art is part of the ongoing Sor Juana revival that began in the mid-twentieth century and accelerated in the 1990s, and that includes María Luisa Bemberg's cinematic biogaphy of Sor Juana, *Yo, la peor de todas,* discussed in the previous chapter. Like Bemberg, Mesa-Bains combines the feminist impulse inherent in the Sor Juana revival with the use of neobaroque aesthetics.

The Library of Sor Juana belongs to the second installment of Mesa-Bains's three-volume visual autobiography, *Venus Envy.* Its full title, *Venus Envy Chapter Two: The Harem and Other Enclosures; The Library of Sor*

Fig. 37. Amalia Mesa-Bains, *The Library of Sor Juana Inés de la Cruz* (from the installation *Venus Envy Chapter Two: The Harem and Other Enclosures,* Williams College Museum of Art, Williamstown, MA, July 9–December 31, 1994). (Photograph: Williams College Museum of Art)

Juana Inés de la Cruz, names the artist's choice of setting, the traditional feminine space of the domestic interior. Through this domestic space, Mesa-Bains explores the double-sidedness of Sor Juana's choice of the convent as the site of her intellectual and creative life—both protective retreat and prison. *The Library of Sor Juana* is an installation consisting of one room with several large objects: a large "examination table" (Corrin), which displays objects of Sor Juana's intellectual pursuits next to articles from contemporary Chicano culture; a baroque mirror urging the deceptiveness of appearances placed above a bench covered with books; a gashed chair across the room, flanked by candelabra; a reading area with stool and table. The walls are decorated with images and inscribed with excerpts from Sor Juana's works. The installation further includes another gashed chair behind the examination table, a collector's cabinet, and additional furniture, much of it covered with books (fig. 37).

The display on the examination table is a carefully composed assemblage uniting objects of disparate kinds and origins (fig. 38): there are articles referring to Sor Juana's intellectual and artistic pursuits—forceps, a magnifying glass, a microscope, a globe, pre-Columbian pottery, beakers and distillation devices, and a handmade book containing her writings. Other objects reinforce the vanitas theme of life's transience that underpins the installation—a skull, an hourglass, candles, and photographs, as well as a strand of severed hair referencing Sor Juana's tragic renunciation and silencing shortly before her death. While all of these are indices of Sor Juana's historical world, the table also holds articles from contemporary popular Chicano and Chicana culture (holy cards, lotería cards, a milagro heart, herbs) (fig. 39). One might point out that Mesa-Bains's underlying method is postmodern, employing historical citations, or that it harks back to the baroque cabinet of curiosities that was the modern museum's predecessor,

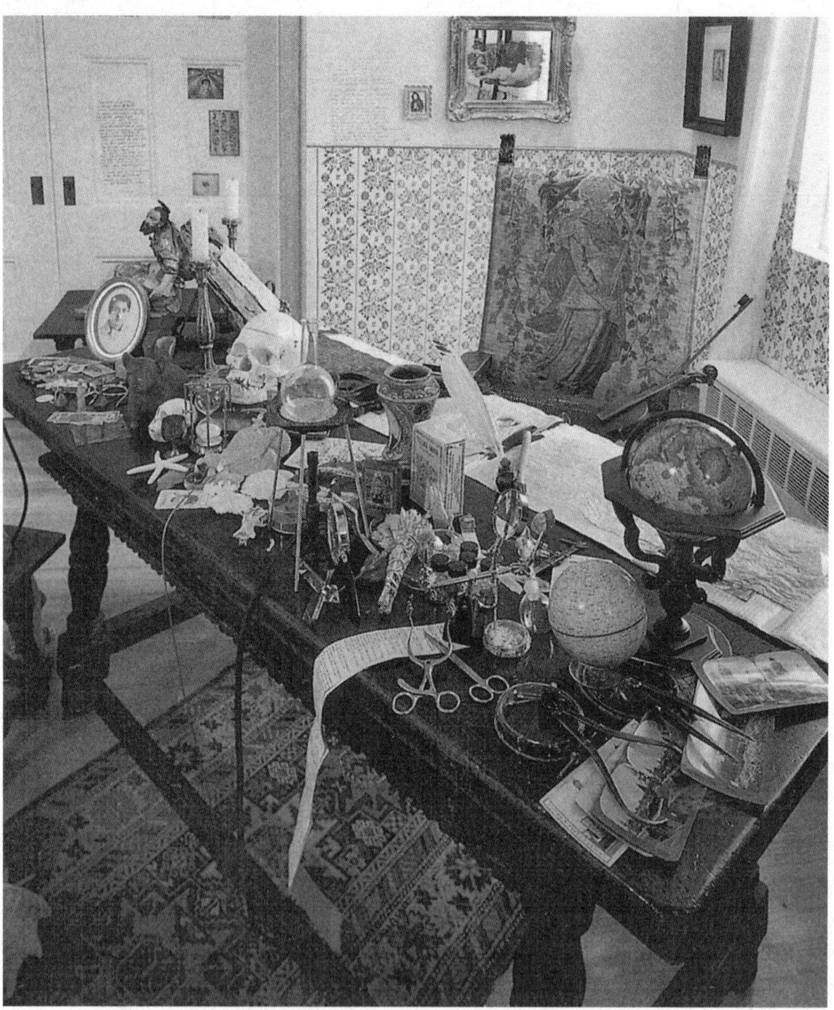

Fig. 38. Amalia Mesa-Bains, *Library of Sor Juana,* detail, examination table. (Photograph: Williams College Museum of Art)

Fig. 39. Amalia Mesa-Bains, *Library of Sor Juana,* detail, close-up of examination table. (Photograph: Williams College Museum of Art)

where collectibles were displayed for their exotic appeal for European tastes as much as according to contemporaneous scientific principles.

Mesa-Bains, however, names another source of inspiration: the Sor Juana installation developed out of her interest in Mexican and Chicano home altars, domestic shrines presenting a collection of sacred and personal objects. In this Mexican vernacular tradition, each home altar, the living document of everyday use, is an idiosyncratic expression of the person who creates it. As Mesa-Bains explains in her essay "'Domesticana': The Sensibility of Chicana *Rasquache,*" home altars express the sensibility of *rasquachismo* characteristic of Chicano culture, inflected by a Chicana feminist viewpoint: "Chicana *rasquache* (*domesticana*), like its male counterpart, has grown out of not only a defiance of an imposed Anglo-American cultural identity but from defiance of restrictive gender identity within Chicano culture. *Domesticana* is presented as a spirit of Chicana emancipation grounded in collective struggle, women's family practices, and the domestic setting."[100] Like Ybarra-Frausto, Mesa-Bains celebrates the working-class *rasquache* aesthetic of recycling rooted in "the everyday reality of Chicano cultural practices," which makes art out of trash: "Aesthetic expression comes from discards, fragments, even recycled everyday materials such as tires, broken plates, plastic containers, which are recombined with elaborate and bold display in yard shrines (*capillas*), domestic décor (*altares*), and even embellishment of the car" ("Domesticana" 157–58). Somehow, making "the most out of the least" magically yields excess, creating quintessential baroque effects.

In Mesa-Bains's previous work, her interest in domestic altars and her feminist *rasquache* aesthetic had taken the form of altar installations in homage of famous Mexican women, such as her *Ofrenda for Dolores del Río,* a composition centered on photographs of the Mexican film star's career.[101] The re-creation of Sor Juana's library similarly celebrates the creative recycling of ordinary objects in altars for everyday use in the traditionally feminine domestic setting. As in ordinary yard shrines and home altars, the juxtaposition of dissimilar objects on the examination table creates an open-form artwork whose composition is a montage of fragments rather than an organic whole, a work that flaunts its artifice and constructedness. Furthermore, neobaroque elaborate decoration and bold display characterize the examination table, densely scattered with objects so as to fill all empty spaces (*horror vacui*). More urgently still, Mesa-Bains emulates the mongrel syncretism of the New World baroque, thereby creating a heterogeneous composition. Just as Christian saints were rendered strange by their vicinity to indigenous symbols in San Lorenzo or Tonantzintla, the objects depicting Sor Juana's New World baroque world in Mesa-Bains's exhibit are resignified by their mixture with popular Chicano articles. Across the obvious chasm of history and class, the underlying assimilative acts are the same: continuing the New World baroque genealogy of critical anthropophagy, Mesa-Bains feeds on Sor Juana as a precursor for the contemporary Chicana struggle, just as colonial *tequitqui* artists had consumed the European baroque for their own purposes.

The second major object in the installation is a mirror in the form of a triptych (fig. 40). A frequent element (along with skulls, candles, and hourglasses) of the allegorical vanitas still-life paintings so popular in the baroque, the mirror reinforces the vanitas theme of Mesa-Bains's composition. The *Going for Baroque* exhibition frames Mesa-Bains's installation as a citation of vanitas still lifes. Indeed, there are good reasons to interpret *The Library of Sor Juana* as a re-creation of baroque vanitas still lifes memorializing the futility of earthly life and the inevitability of death. Mesa-Bains offers numerous clues: the mirror is accompanied by one of Sor Juana's sonnets on the baroque themes of the vanity of earthly things and of appearance as delusion, "Éste, que ves, engaño colorido." Transcribed in Mesa-Bains's own hand, the Spanish original is on the left side of the mirror, the English translation on the right ("This that you gaze on, colorful deceit").[102] As Paz observes, "Sor Juana's poetry is filled with mirrors and the companions to mirrors, portraits" (*Sor Juana* 84), a symptom of the baroque obsession with visuality and its traps and tricks. One of Sor Juana's loveliest poems, this sonnet takes as its subject a portrait of herself, and Mesa-Bains has placed a reproduction of the earliest extant portrait of Sor Juana (the famous portrait painted by Juan de Miranda during Sor Juana's lifetime, in the 1680s) on the central mirror panel. Each of the mirror's three panels bears an image of a woman, but the middle panel is cracked in the very place where de Miranda's portrait of Sor Juana is affixed.

An ekphrastic poem, Sor Juana's sonnet reflects on the vanity of the portrait's attempt to vanquish mortality:

Éste, que ves, engaño colorido,
que del arte ostentando los primores,
con falsos silogismos de colores
es cauteloso engaño del sentido;

Fig. 40. Amalia Mesa-Bains, *Library of Sor Juana,* detail, mirror. (Photograph: Nicholas Whitman)

éste, en quien la lisonja ha pretendido
excusar de los años los horrores,
y venciendo del tiempo los rigores
triunfar de la vejez y del olvido,
es un vano artificio del cuidado,
es una flor al viento delicada,
es un resguardo inútil para el hado:
es una necia diligencia errada,
es un afán caduco y, bien mirado,
es cadáver, es polvo, es sombra, es nada.

(This that you gaze at, colorful deceit,
that so immodestly displays art's favors,
with its fallacious arguments of colors
is to the senses cunning counterfeit;
this on which kindness practiced to delete
from cruel years accumulated horrors,
constraining time to mitigate its rigors,
and thus oblivion and age defeat,
is but an artifice, a sop to vanity,
is but a flower by the breezes bowed,
is but a ploy to counter destiny,
is but a foolish labor, ill-employed,
is but a fancy, and, as all may see,
is but a cadaver, ashes, shadow, void.)[103]

Layering conceit over conceit, the poem systematically deconstructs the lifelike appearance in the portrait and reduces it to nothing. In so doing, it emulates the way age and mortality will decompose its original—the flesh-and-blood body and face of Sor Juana—to "cadaver, ashes, shadow, void." That the portrait, a likeness, is an actual falsehood is a favorite baroque theme, related to the kinship of visuality and deception underlying the trompe l'oeil and other baroque visual games. Engaging the baroque slippage between appearance and truth, Sor Juana plays off words against images, unmasking the visual illusion of her portrait by way of her word-based poem.

Mesa-Bains's multimedia installation, in turn, restages Sor Juana's play on dueling media—the lying visual image versus the truth-telling word. By placing a reproduction of Miranda's portrait on the central mirror panel (just under the top of the frame, above eye level), Mesa-Bains reconstructs the scene of the poem's creation—in a manner reminiscent of the *tableau vivant*—for Sor Juana must have composed her sonnet while contemplating her portrait. But by placing the portrait on a mirror, Mesa-Bains creates a second level of representation interpellating us, the contemporary spectator, through Mesa-Bains's own neobaroque game of appearance and disillusionment. For as we gaze into the mirror, it reflects back to us our own likeness below Sor Juana's portrait, hovering above the reflection of our face. As we begin to read the poem, we cannot help but take the poem's direct address, "This that you gaze on," as a reference to our own mirror image, which we see in front of us. Mesa-Bains's mischievous visual trick will draw in spectators blessed with a vivid imagination, who will no doubt see their bodies crumbing to baroque dust in their mind's eyes. To be sure, the crack in the mirror echoes the gashes in the chairs across the room and behind the examination table. These breakages summon many ideas, including the fragility of life, the Benjaminian notion of history as catastrophe and ruin, and the duplicity of representation, to say nothing of the deep cultural divide that ran through the colonial society of Sor Juana's Mexico, separating Westernized and Hispanicized colonial subjects such as Sor Juana from the indigenous communities, traditional campesinos, and subordinate urban groups.[104] In this way, Mesa-Bains avoids erasing the colonial wound that Sor Juana's world was built on and that could not be but present as a haunting absence in her marvelous work, despite its substantial challenges to the colonial civilization in which she flourished.

I conclude this section by turning to a neobaroque visual artist from the broader U.S. Latino community outside the Chicano constituency, the Cuban American Luis Gispert (1972–). Born in Jersey City, New Jersey, raised in Miami, and now living in Brooklyn, Luis Gispert belongs to a younger generation of U.S.-born Cuban Americans who have challenged established paradigms of Cuban American art. Inspired as much by U.S. youth and popular culture as by his Cuban heritage, Gispert "mixes a dizzying array of sources that include Hip Hop and Miami Bass culture, Renaissance and Baroque painting, and early modern furniture and design."[105] Gispert's blend of lowbrow subculture, pop culture, and "high" art historical allusions in his glossy photography, sculpture, and video art results in hybrid works that bring out "the Baroque and Byzantine in bling, the operatic ethos in gangsta ethics."[106] In this way, Gispert produces new twenty-first-century versions of the hypersensuous, hypnotic baroque of artists such as Bernini (see fig. 3, p. 85).

Perhaps the best example of Gispert's mongrel highbrow-lowbrow art is his *Cheerleader Series,* which is featured centrally in the catalog of his 2004 solo exhibition at the Hood Museum of Art at Dartmouth College, *Luis Gispert: Loud Image.*[107] The individual images in the series, which comprises two videos and eleven photographs, all portray young women dressed in identical cheerleader uniforms. Many are heavily made up, with inch-long, garishly painted artificial nails, and laden with gold jewelry on their arms, hands, and necks. They are photographed in carefully scripted and staged poses, mostly in group settings, in the manner of *tableaux vivants* and the cinematic tableau discussed in the previous chapter. To recall: a technique characteristic of early film, the tableau represents "a moment of suspended action, a moment chosen so that the grouping of figures epitomizes the forces arrayed in conflict."[108] In the cinematic tableau, the flow of action is suspended to produce a moment of heightened significance, like an allegorical still or picture that abstracts the deeper meaning of the cinematic narrative. Indeed, film is an important point of reference for Gispert, who came to art though film, which he absorbed early, during his education at a magnet high school for film and video in Miami (see Tejada, *Luis Gispert* 21). He consciously borrows techniques from film: "Getting ready to take a photograph is, for me, a lot like writing a film script."[109] Gispert photographed the images in the *Cheerleader Series* against a monochrome green background, "a film technique that allows any kind of fake setting to be put in later" and whose monotony, he notes, served to stress "the highly symbolic activity being performed by these actors" (Cartwright, "Subwoofers" 27). In this way, Gispert prepares an ideal stage to present his extravagant neobaroque live sculptures.

Several distinct cultural ingredients enter into Gispert's U.S.-Latino iconographic stew. The first is the figure of the American cheerleader, the all-American icon of popular culture. Gispert takes the cliché of the "heroic, blonde" (26) cheerleader and sets it into variation by celebrating cheerleaders of color along with whites—blacks, Latinas, and Asian Americans. This is no trivial matter: ethnic discrimination in high school cheerleader elections was one of the events that triggered the Chicano movement in the 1960s. In South Texas, student protests against the exclusion of Chicanas from high school cheerleader positions contributed to the founding of the Raza Unida Party, one of the landmark organizations of the *movimiento*. Another element is the hip-hop subculture, especially its counterculture of luxury, epitomized by bling, or bling-bling, a term coined by rap artists to refer to the expensive, flashy jewelry and accessories they wear (gold-plated necklaces and wristwatches, jeweled dental grills).[110] A neologism of the 1990s, bling captures a sound effect suggesting the reflection of light on shiny surfaces such as gold and diamonds, and it evokes hip-hop's alternative culture of conspicuous consumption and fashionable excess. The Latina cheerleader in *Untitled (Chain Mouth)* is among those wearing heavier bling (fig. 41).[111]

A third element is, of course, the iconography of baroque art, especially religious art. In Gispert's photographs, brown, black, and light-skinned cheerleaders transform into Madonnas and levitating saints. As Roberto Tejada has observed, a number of Gispert's cheerleader images "evoke all manners of baroque bodily gesture and composition, as in *Untitled (Three*

Fig. 41. Luis Gispert, *Untitled (Chain Mouth, a.k.a. Muse Ho)*, 2001. (Copyright by Luis Gispert. Courtesy of Mary Boone Gallery, New York)

Asian Cheerleaders) (2001), an arrangement that coalesces what appear to be an angelic apparition and the descent from the Cross" (fig. 42).[112] Amplifying Tejada, I would suggest that the three Asian American cheerleaders in this image are posing in a composition that reenacts at least three distinct Catholic devotional images—the Pietà, Christ's deposition (the removal of Christ's body from the cross), and Marian apparitions. The two cheerleaders reposing on the floor on the right are restaging the Pietà, as the seated woman emulates Mary cradling the body of Christ in her lap. Airborne with the help of suspension wires, the floating cheerleader on the left reincarnates Christ's deposition, one of the Stations of the Cross depicting the moment when Christ's lifeless body is taken down from the cross, sliding into the arms of Joseph and others lending a hand.[113] In addition, she echoes the miraculous apparition of the Virgin that occurred in Catholic regions in Europe and across the world, which also inspired the cult of the "brown Virgins" of the Americas, such as Mexico's Virgin of Guadalupe. As in popular Catholic depictions of the Virgin Mary on holy cards, Mary is opening her arms with upturned palms in a gesture of benediction.

In addition to obvious European sources, one of Gispert's possible American allusions in this image is to Cuba's mulatto Virgin, the Virgen de la Caridad del Cobre, patron saint of Cuba. In close analogy with the pattern of Marian apparitions to humble Indians and blacks across the Americas

Fig. 42. Luis Gispert, *Untitled (Three Asian Cheerleaders)*, 2001. (Copyright by Luis Gispert. Courtesy of Mary Boone Gallery, New York)

(as in the apparition of the Virgin of Guadalupe to the Indian Juan Diego in 1531), in 1608 the Virgin of Charity appeared to two black slaves and an Indian in the copper-mining town of El Cobre, near Santiago de Cuba. Mariolatry and the cult of the charitable coppery virgin became a core identity of the slaves of this region in Santería, the Cuban syncretic religion that links Catholic saints to African orishas. (The Virgin de la Caridad del Cobre's African counterpart is Ochún, goddess of rivers and freshwater and one of the most venerated orishas in Cuban Santería.)[114]

Gispert's hip-hop baroque seems to demonstrate Carpentier's dictum that all syncretism and *mestizaje* engenders the baroque. As Tejada notes, "Gispert's Baroque impulse functions not unlike colonial art of the Americas, . . . which fused traits or cultural criteria made available by the various ethnic groups that came together in the new world" ("Gispert" 17). In analogy with the blend of pre-Columbian and Christian iconography in the mestizo New World baroque, Gispert's neobaroque adds a contemporaneous ingredient to the baroque mélange: the symbols of hip-hop counterculture. Gispert explains how this particular medley occurred to him when sketching compositions of cheerleaders of various ethnicities: "By putting them together in a tableau that was inspired by my study of Italian Baroque painting, I started to imagine connections to hip-hop, which also has a strong Baroque quality to it. . . . Think about it: the jewelry, the shiny clothing, the elaborately painted fingernails, all of the gold and platinum—it is fundamentally about excess and about an appetite for Baroqueness" (qtd. in Cartwright, "Subwoofers" 27).

This is a clever insight. To be sure, Gispert's observation connects to the century-long vogue of the baroque in fashion, stage, and screen design that Stephen Calloway documents in his beautifully illustrated study *Baroque Baroque: The Culture of Excess*. According to Calloway, the "association of the Baroque with the world of fashion and *haute couture* is an obvious one, and one that has been perennially renewed; for fashion, . . . [must] always be an expression of conspicuous consumption and belong to the culture of excess. Inevitably designers return again and again to the richness of the Baroque for inspiration" (19). Calloway's neobaroque in twentieth-century fashion and design encompasses the "Wrenaissance" of the Edwardian Era in England; Hollywood sets from the 1910s and 1920s; the baroque revival inspired by the Sitwell siblings in lifestyle and books such as Sacheverell Sitwell's *Southern Baroque Art* (1924); the Ballets Russes; Cecil Beaton's fashion photography; Helena Rubinstein's and Coco Chanel's lifestyles; and the films of Federico Fellini, Derek Jarman, and Peter Greenaway, to offer an incomplete selection. It is instructive to juxtapose the hip-hop fetish for expensive jewelry, such as gold and diamonds, to Calloway's archive, as a rare example of a cult of ostentations wealth and materialism that emerged from outside the gated community of upper-class society. Hip-hop's and lowriding's aesthetic of sensory overload share these same working-class cultural roots. In point of fact, Gispert's work is not an isolated instance of the hip-hop baroque, which is also found in the work of the African American visual artist Kehinde Wiley. As Krista Thompson argues, Wiley and Gispert both appropriate the European baroque to "visualize another history of art, one that brings the black body (and other ethnicities, in Gispert's case), literally and figuratively to the surface."[115]

A third composition in the *Cheerleader Series, Untitled (Girls with Ball)* (2000) offers a witty comment on the multiple sources of the baroque cult of excess in contemporary culture beyond hip-hop bling—such as professional sports (fig. 43). In this image, two cheerleaders are portrayed leaping into the air toward a ball floating between them just above their fingertips, as one would see from above two volleyball or basketball players rising together in competition. A second glance, however, reveals that the ball is not a volleyball or a basketball but a heavy bowling ball. Gispert explains that because the picture was taken against a monochrome green background, no one can "actually tell if they are falling or ascending in this picture. Baroque ceiling paintings in chapels by Tiepolo and the image derived from NBA 'basket-cams' were thus brought together. I had the bowling ball custom-made so that in the place of the logo, it says 'BLING'" (quoted in Cartwright, "Subwoofers" 27). The cheerleaders' levitation in this image, according to

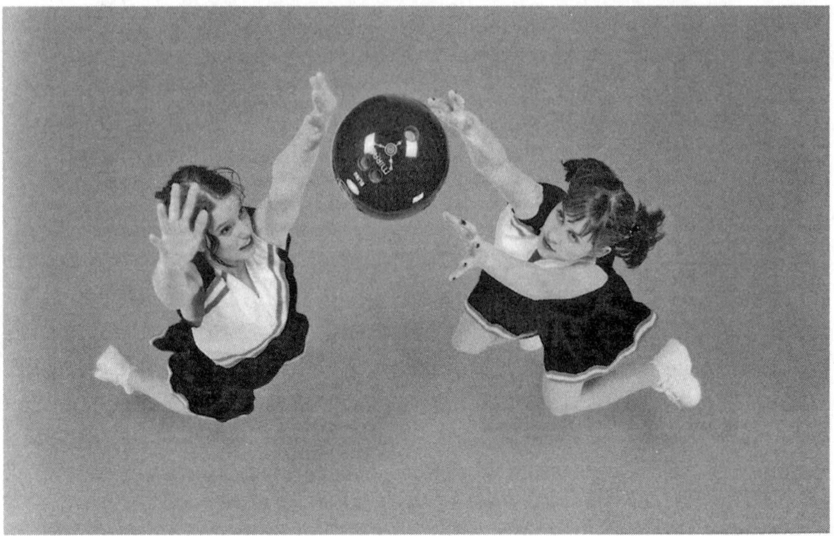

Fig. 43. Luis Gispert, *Untitled (Girls with Ball),* 2000. (Copyright by Luis Gispert. Courtesy of Mary Boone Gallery, New York)

Gispert, cite not only Marian apparitions but also contemporary athletes: their superhuman feats, showcased in slow-motion sports footage, have acquired near-mythic dimensions that recall the miraculous levitations of saints. Just as saints magically rising up in the air made the power of their faith manifest, so in contemporary times the marvelous is made real by athletes like "Michael Jordan who actually seemed to fly" (27).

Lynette Bosch distinguishes two generations of Cuban American artists, an older generation of Cuban-born artists (*la vieja guardia*) who arrived in Miami in the 1960s and 1970s as mature artists and a younger generation trained in the United States in the 1970s (157). She argues that it was the younger generation—such as Gispert, although he is not featured in her study—who introduced quotations of the baroque into Cuban American art to represent their bicultural (U.S. and Cuban) experience: younger Cuban-American artists "have recontextualized the figurative vocabulary of the Renaissance and the Baroque to give expression and form in their work to their experience as bicultural exiles. In so doing, they have introduced Cuban *Barroquismo* as a significant movement into contemporary art in the United States" (166). In this way, Cuban American art, contends Bosch, has been connected not only with the Cuban neobaroque of Carpentier, Lezama Lima, and Sarduy but also with the broader transnational trend of the Latin American neobaroque—"the Cuban and Latin American cultural movement called *Barroquismo*" (163). Put differently, a new generation of artists has trafficked the *neobarroco* into U.S. territory, expanding its reach and in turn hybridizing U.S. art. "Cuban artists brought *Barroquismo*'s diversity to a new arena, where they incorporated contemporary American art and culture into the permeable borders of *Barroquismo*" (164). In this way, Gispert is taking us full circle, by reconnecting us to the transhistorical genealogy of the New World baroque that has been the subject of this chapter. Latino/a expression in the United States is a rapidly expanding phenomenon, and we look forward to future developments in the ever-growing empire of the baroque.

NOTES

Introduction

All unacknowledged translations are mine.

1. See Margaret Miles, "Vision and Sixteenth-Century Protestant and Roman Catholic Reforms," in *Image as Insight,* 95–125. Sources on the baroque, the New World baroque, and the neobaroque, as well as sources cited in more than one chapter, are collected in a selected bibliography, to which the reader should refer for complete citations.

2. Greene, "Baroque and Neobaroque," 151.

3. I borrow this language from Ross Posnock, "Planetary Circles: Philip Roth, Emerson, Kundera," in *Shades of the Planet: American Literature as World Literature* (Princeton, NJ: Princeton University Press, 2007), 141–68, 144.

4. See Braider, *Baroque Self-Invention and Historical Truth,* 7. On the history of "baroque," see Hauser, "The Concept of the Baroque," in *The Social History of Art,* vol. 2, *Renaissance, Mannerism, Baroque,* 172–82 (hereafter *Renaissance, Mannerism, Baroque*); Hoffmeister, "Zur Begriffsgeschichte von 'Barock,'" in *Deutsche und europäische Barockliteratur,* 1–9; Martin, "The Question of Style," in *Baroque,* 19–39; Migliorini, "Etymologie und Geschichte des Terminus 'Barock,'"; Moser, "The Concept of Baroque"; Niefanger, "Barockbegriff," in *Barock,* 8–12; Panofsky, "What Is Baroque?"; Pauly, "Zur Geschichte des Begriffs *neobarroco,*" in *Neobarroco,* 13–36; Warnke, "Terms and Concepts," in *Versions of Baroque,* 1–20; and Wellek, "The Concept of Baroque."

5. Unlike romanticism or the Enlightenment, as Moser points out, the baroque is a "historically exogenous concept," "invented after the fact": "Nobody in the seventeenth century had the slightest idea that theirs was going to be named and conceptualized as the Baroque by historians and critics of the late nineteenth and twentieth centuries" (31).

6. For example, this formula for the baroque (the nonclassicist or unclassical use of classical forms) appears in *The Oxford Companion to English Literature,* ed. Margaret Drabble, 5th ed. (Oxford: Oxford University Press, 1985), s.v. "Baroque."

7. See Hauser, "The Baroque of the Catholic Courts" and "The Baroque of the Protestant Bourgeoisie," in *Renaissance, Mannerism, Baroque,* 182–207, 207–25. "The baroque of courtly and Catholic circles is . . . wholly different from that of middle-class and Protestant communities, the art of a Bernini and a Rubens . . . depicts a different inner and outer world from that of a Rembrandt and a van Goyen" (172). The study that rediscovered the French baroque was Rousset, *La littérature de l'âge Baroque en France.* On differences between Catholic and Northern European Protestant baroque, see also Jay, "Scopic Regimes of Modernity," and Alpers, *The Art of Describing.*

On the etymology of *baroque,* see Wellek, Panofsky, Hoffmeister, Migliorini, and ger. The most exhaustive discussion is offered by Migliorini, whom I follow here. eister, Migliorini, and Niefanger prefer the irregular pearl thesis, Panofsky and the scholastic syllogism.

9. For a while, it seemed that "baroque," "Renaissance," and related terms had been replaced with the umbrella term "early modern." Still, new studies continue to be published on the baroque, as only recently, Braider, *Baroque Self-Invention and Historical Truth,* and Johnson, *Hyperboles.*

10. Clifford, "Traveling Cultures," in *Routes,* 17–39.

11. Carpentier, "The Baroque and the Marvelous Real," 100. The problematic of the French baroque also translates to France's New World colonies. Both are outside the scope of this study. For further reference, see La Bossière, "Past and Present: The Neobaroque Novel in French Canada," and Dorothy Baker, "Baroque Self-Fashioning in Seventeenth-Century New France," in Zamora and Kaup, *Baroque New Worlds,* 450–66.

12. Rama, *The Lettered City,* 10.

13. Salgado, "Hybridity in New World Baroque Theory," 324.

14. Chiampi, "The Baroque at the Twilight of Modernity" and *Barroco y modernidad;* Celorio, "From the Baroque to the Neobaroque"; Echeverría, *La modernidad de lo barroco;* Lange-Churión, "Neobaroque: Latin America's Postmodernity?"

15. See Dipesh Chakrabarty, *Provincializing Europe: Postcolonial Thought and Historical Difference* (Princeton, NJ: Princeton University Press, 2000) and *Habitations of Modernity: Essays in the Wake of Subaltern Studies* (Chicago: University of Chicago Press, 2002); Arjun Appadurai, *Modernity at Large: Cultural Dimensions of Globalization* (Minneapolis: University of Minnesota Press, 1996); Dilip Parameshwar Gaonkar, ed., *Alternative Modernities* (Durham, NC: Duke University Press, 2001); Charles Taylor, "Two Theories of Modernity," in Gaonkar, *Alternative Modernities,* 172–96; Paul Gilroy, *The Black Atlantic: Modernity and Double Consciousness* (Cambridge, MA: Harvard University Press, 1993); and Néstor García Canclini, *Hybrid Cultures: Strategies for Leaving and Entering Modernity* (Minneapolis: University of Minnesota Press, 1995).

16. See Dussel, "World-System and 'Trans'-Modernity."

17. On Wölfflin, see Hauser, "The Concept of the Baroque," and Brown, "The Classic Is the Baroque."

18. Spengler, *The Decline of the West* (1920–22); Worringer, *Form in Gothic* (1911); d'Ors, *Lo barroco* (1935); and Focillon, *The Life of Forms in Art* (1934). On the influence of Germanic typological theories of the baroque on Latin American thinkers, see also Pauly, *Neobarroco,* 13–36, and González Echevarría, "Góngora's and Lezama's Appetites."

19. Eco, "The Poetics of the Open Work"; Barth, "The Literature of Exhaustion" and "The Literature of Replenishment"; Foucault, *The Order of Things;* Buci-Glucksmann, *Baroque Reason* and *La folie du voir;* Barthes, *Sade, Fourier, Loyola;* Deleuze, *The Fold.*

20. Gustavo Pérez Firmat, "Cheek to Cheek," introduction to *Do the Americas Have a Common Literature?,* ed. Gustavo Pérez Firmat (Durham, NC: Duke University Press, 1990), 1–5.

21. See Armstrong and Zamudio-Taylor, *Ultrabaroque;* Calabrese, *Neo-Baroque;* Calloway, *Baroque Baroque;* Chiampi, *Barroco y modernidad;* González Echevarría, *Celestina's Brood;* Harbison, *Reflections on Baroque;* Lambert, *The Return of the Baroque in Modern Culture;* Ndalianis, *Neo-baroque Aesthetics and Contemporary Entertain-*

ment; Murray, *Digital Baroque;* Pauly, *Neobarroco;* Spadaccini and Martín-Estudio, *Hispanic Baroques;* and Zamora, *The Inordinate Eye.* I limit this list to full-length studies.

22. Weisbach, *Barock als Kunst der Gegenreformation* (1921); Maravall, *Culture of the Baroque.* Another proponent of the baroque as an imperial hispanicizing culture is Acosta. For recent studies on the Counter-Reformation baroque, see Levy, *Propaganda and the Jesuit Baroque,* and Sebastián, *Contrareforma y barroco.*

23. Picón-Salas, "Baroque of the Indies," 85. See Irving Leonard's parallel 1959 verdict that "the Baroque spirit sought to reconcile a bold modernism in form with an extreme oldness in content" (Leonard, *Baroque Times in Old Mexico* 223).

24. See Robbins, *The Challenges of Uncertainty,* 43.

25. Eco, "The Poetics of the Open Work"; de Campos, "The Open Work of Art" (1955), in *Novas,* 220–22.

26. Braider here echoes the findings of Wilfried Barner, who similarly points to a discrepancy between "classicist-traditional rhetorical theory and baroque practice": "most theoreticians of the baroque differ from classical tradition only by slight variations and nuances; decisive shifts occur only towards the end of the era" (Barner, *Barockrhetorik* 59, 56–57). Discussing Balthasar Gracián's theory of wit, *Agudeza y arte de ingenio* (1642), Christopher Johnson, on the other hand, disagrees with this assessment. Gracián celebrates the poet's ingenious ability to express difficult truths—the more difficult such truths are, "the more pleasant" (Johnson 116). Johnson observes that "valuing difficulty in this way ignores conventional classical and Renaissance notions of poetic decorum" (120).

27. Benjamin, *The Origin of German Tragic Drama;* Bürger, *Theory of the Avant-garde.*

28. On baroque strategies of "hyperbolic doubt" in Descartes, see Copleston, *A History of Philosophy,* vol. 4, *Modern Philosophy: Descartes to Leibniz,* 100ff. (hereafter *Modern Philosophy: Descartes to Leibniz*), and Johnson, *Hyperboles,* 365–414.

29. In every age, the structure of artistic forms registers contemporary scientific and cultural constructions of reality (Eco 13). On this subject, see also Nicolson, *The Breaking of the Circle.*

30. Sarduy, *Barroco* (1974), in *Obra Completa,* 2:1195–1261. See also Sarduy's definition in the interview "El Barroco après la lettre."

31. See Norberg-Schulz, *Baroque Architecture,* and Michael J. Crowe, "Kepler's 'War with Mars,'" in *Theories of the World from Antiquity to the Copernican Revolution,* 2nd rev. ed. (Mineola, NY: Dover, 1990), 152–54.

32. Sarduy, "The Baroque and the Neobaroque," 289.

33. See Sarduy, *Barroco,* in *Obra completa,* 2:1245–46.

34. Borges, "Preface to the 1954 edition of *A Universal History of Iniquity,*" in *Collected Fictions,* 4–5.

35. Nietzsche, "On the Baroque," 44.

36. On the Borgesian variety of neobaroque, see Zamora, "Borges' Neobaroque Illusionism," in *The Inordinate Eye,* 233–84, and Lambert, "The Baroque Detective: Borges as Precursor," in *The Non-Philosophy of Gilles Deleuze,* 73–89.

37. De Campos, "Anthropophagous Reason," 159.

38. Reinhart Koselleck, *Futures Past: On the Semantics of Historical Time* (Cambridge, MA: MIT Press, 1985).

39. Pollard, *New World Modernisms,* 15.

40. Braider, *Baroque Self-Invention and Historical Truth,* 7; Wellek, "The Concept of Baroque," 113; Sypher, *Four Stages of Renaissance Style;* Praz, "Baroque in England,"

"The Flaming Heart" (1925), and *Studies in Seventeenth-Century Imagery* (1964). See also comparativist studies by Warnke, *Versions of Baroque;* Segel, *The Baroque Poem;* and Nelson, *Baroque Lyric Poetry.*

41. Davidson, *The Universal Baroque,* 65.

1. Neobaroque Eliot

1. Eliot, preface to *For Lancelot Andrewes: Essays on Style and Order* (Garden City, NY: Doubleday, 1929), vii–viii, vii.

2. See Jewel Spears Brooker, "Eliot Studies: A Review and a Select Booklist," in *The Cambridge Companion to T. S. Eliot,* ed. David Moody (Cambridge: Cambridge University Press, 1994), 236–50, 239–40, for an overview of research trends in Eliot studies and recent progress in publication of unpublished Eliot writings.

3. Pollard, *New World Modernisms.* See also Peter Kalliney, "Metropolitan Modernism and Its West Indian Interlocutors: 1950s London and the Emergence of Postcolonial Literature," *PMLA* 122, no. 1 (2007): 89–104.

4. Eliot, *The Varieties of Metaphysical Poetry: The Clark Lectures at Trinity College, Cambridge, 1926, and the Turnbull Lectures at The Johns Hopkins University, 1933,* ed. Ronald Schuchard. The American edition came out in 1994, a year after the British edition by Faber in 1993. Subsequent references appear parenthetically in the text. For the sake of clarity, I differentiate between the Clark Lectures and the Turnbull Lectures, using separate short titles (Clark Lectures, Turnbull Lectures), although the lectures are collected in the same volume.

5. Schuchard, "Editor's Introduction to the Clark Lectures," in Eliot, *The Varieties of Metaphysical Poetry,* 1–36, 1 (hereafter "Clark Introduction").

6. See Schuchard, "Clark Introduction," 23, and "Editor's Introduction to the Turnbull Lectures," 231–44, 244 (hereafter "Turnbull Introduction"). In an essay written to honor the 1931 tercentenary of John Donne's death, Eliot is explicit about abandoning his long-delayed publication project for good: "I know that by 1926, when I gave some lectures on Donne, the subject was already popular, almost topical; and I know that by 1931 the subject has been so fully treated that there appears to me no possible justification of turning my lectures into a book" ("Donne in Our Time" [1931], in Spenser, *A Garland for John Donne* 1–19, 4). I am indebted to Schuchard's introductions to both lectures and his detailed editorial notes throughout this discussion.

7. "Dissociation of sensibility" and the "insistence on impersonality" are often identified as the two most influential of Eliot's doctrines. See Charles Altieri, "Eliot's Impact on Twentieth-Century Anglo-American Poetry," in Moody, *The Cambridge Companion to T. S. Eliot,* 189–209, 192.

8. Eliot, "The Metaphysical Poets" (1921), in *Selected Prose of T. S. Eliot, 59–67.*

9. Whereas the early Eliot adopted a narrower and harsher stance, famously blaming specific writers (Milton, Dryden) and limiting his analysis to England, the later Eliot modified his earlier claims by retracting the specific attacks on Milton and Dryden and opening his analysis to a European perspective. See Eliot, from "Milton II" (1947), in *Selected Prose of T. S. Eliot,* 265–74, 266.

10. Schuchard tracks Eliot's "nascent theory of metaphysical poetry" to reviews from 1917 to 1920, where he begins to formulate the idea of the "dissociation of object, feeling, and thought." See "Clark Introduction," 2.

11. Davidson, *The Universal Baroque,* 65.

12. Egginton, "Of Baroque Holes and Baroque Folds," 56–57.

13. See Copleston, *Modern Philosophy: Descartes to Leibniz,* 23.

14. This statement recurs in various writings. I quote from the "Discourse on Metaphysics" (1686), Leibniz's earliest systematic presentation of his metaphysics, where he transfers his unique style of developing mathematical and logical ideas to metaphysics. The passage quoted is presented as evidence for Leibniz's sixth thesis ("That God does nothing which is not orderly, and that it is not even possible to conceive of events which are not regular"): "Thus we may say that in whatever manner God might have created the world, it would always have been regular and in a certain order. God, however, has chosen the most perfect, that is to say the one which is at the same time the simplest in hypotheses and the richest in phenomena, as might be the case with a geometric line, whose construction was easy, but whose properties and effects were extremely remarkable and of great significance" ("Discourse on Metaphysics," in *Leibniz: Selections,* ed. Philip P. Wiener [New York: Charles Scribner, 1951], 290–345, § 6, 297).

15. Nicholas Jolley, introduction to Jolley, *The Cambridge Companion to Leibniz,* 1–18, 1. Leibniz is not alone in asserting the existence of God as part of his rationalist philosophical system, as a certainty proven by the new, mathematical method of philosophy. So did Descartes, as well as Spinoza. It testifies to Descartes's influence on eighteenth-century Enlightenment thinkers that Descartes was not singled out for mockery as Leibniz was.

16. See note 14 above and Rescher, *The Philosophy of Leibniz,* 19.

17. Here I am thinking of Cixous's famous list of binaries, including activity/passivity and culture/nature, and concluding with male/female. See Hélène Cixous and Catherine Clément, *The Newly Born Woman,* trans. Betsy Wing (Minneapolis: University of Minnesota Press, 1986), 63–64.

18. Deleuze, *The Fold,* 67 (first ellipses in original). Among the vast literature on Deleuze, one of the studies I have found helpful is Lambert, *The Non-Philosophy of Gilles Deleuze.*

19. See, for example, Robert McRae, "The Theory of Knowledge," in Jolley, *The Cambridge Companion to Leibniz,* 176–98, 181.

20. Conley, "Folds and Folding," 177.

21. See Rémy de Gourmont, "Góngora y le Gongorisme" (1911), in *Promenades Littéraires,* 7 vols., *Souvenirs du Symbolisme et autres études* (Paris: Mercure de France, 1927), 4:299–310.

> *Culteranismo,* originally a satiric term implying literary heresy (like *luteranismo,* Lutheranism) and used to attack the new style of poetry of Luis de Góngora y Argote (1561–1627), or gongorism, is best understood in relation to *conceptismo* or conceptism. In Spanish literary history, *culteranismo* traditionally describes a poetic style in which learned words, Hispanicized from Latin and Greek, are prominent. *Conceptismo,* on the other hand, is a style in poetry or prose characterized by ingenious or 'precious' ideas. In other words, according to this view, *culteranismo* concerns poetic vocabulary, while *conceptismo* concerns the expression of thought. (Alex Preminger and T. V. F. Brogan, eds., *The New Princeton Encyclopedia of Poetry and Poetics* [Princeton, NJ: Princeton University Press, 1993], s.v. "Culteranismo," 261–62, 261)

See also a new bilingual edition of Góngora, *Selected Poems of Luis de Góngora.*

22. Chiampi, "The Baroque at the Twilight of Modernity," 510.

23. The discussion of Eliot's work as neosymbolist, dating from Eliot's self-identification with Jules Laforgue and other French symbolist poets, is long established and threads through all periods of Eliot criticism, positive and negative. For a rehabilitation of Eliot's neosymbolism, see Charles Altieri, "'Preludes' as Prelude: In Defence of Eliot as Symboliste," in *T. S. Eliot: A Voice Descanting; Centenary Essays,* ed. Shyamal Bagchee (London: Macmillan, 1990), 1–27.

24. According to Jean-Michel Rabaté, dissociation

> for de Gourmont is a method of analysis, "analogous to what is called analysis in chemistry"—the dissociation of a material into its various elements "in order to prepare for a new synthesis." His idea is that the critic in his constant care for the language must similarly "dissociate" the usual commonplaces that pass for deep truths. But Eliot used the term quite differently, to signify the disintegration of a unified tradition, as when he blamed Milton and Dryden for ending a period in which feeling and thinking made up a single process. "Dissociation" was thus shifted from a technique of analysis to the name given to a cultural disaster. Instead of being a technique by which sensibility refines itself, it refers to a historical splitting of the communal consciousness. ("Tradition and T. S. Eliot," in Moody, *The Cambridge Companion to T. S. Eliot,* 210–22, 216)

See Rémy de Gourmont, "The Cultivation of Ideas" (1900), in *Rémy de Gourmont: Selections from All His Works,* ed. and trans. Richard Aldington, 2 vols. (New York: Covici-Friede, 1929), 2:373–95, 373. This passage from Gourmont, cited by Rabaté, has been known as Eliot's source for some time. See Frank Kermode, "'Dissociation of Sensibility': Modern Symbolist Readings of Literary History," in *Romantic Image* (New York: Macmillan, 1957), 138–61, 150.

25. Preminger and Brogan, *The New Princeton Encyclopedia of Poetry and Poetics,* s.v. "Symbolism," 1256–59, 1256.

26. See Eliot, "Hamlet," in *Selected Prose of T. S. Eliot,* 45–49, 48.

27. On Hispanic *modernismo* and differences between Hispanic (Spanish as well as Latin American) and German, English, and French traditions of modern poetry, see Paz, *Children of the Mire,* 78–101.

28. John Beverley breaks down the vanguardist revival of the baroque by political orientation: "In the decade of the 20s this revision is joined to the emergent problematic of the avant-garde, in its divergent variations: fascist (Spengler, d'Ors), liberal (Ortega y la Generación del 27 en España), and Marxist (Walter Benjamin)" (Beverley, *Una modernidad obsoleta* 16).

29. See Oropesa, *The Contemporáneos Group,* 2.

30. Borges's early collections of essays, *Inquisiciones* (1925), *El tamaño de mi esperanza* (1926), and *El idioma de los argentinos* (1928), are now available together in *Textos recobrados, 1919–1929.* See also the useful anthology of manifestos of Latin American avant-gardes edited by Hugo Verani, *Las vanguardias literarias in Hispanoamérica: Manifiestos, proclamas y otros escritos* (Mexico City: Fondo de Cultura Económica, 2003). All of Lezama Lima's poetry falls in this category. Born in 1910 and too young to belong to the avant-garde, Lezama Lima develops his own neobaroque poetics from the 1930s, in poetry at first, later also in Latin American cultural theory (the landmark essay "Baroque Curiosity" in *La expresión americana* [1957]) and fiction (his neobaroque novel *Paradiso* [1966]). See Bejel, *José Lezama Lima.* According to Chiampi, Lezama Lima's

> poetry, beginning with *Muerte de Narciso* (*Death of Narcissus,* 1937), followed by *Enemigo Rumor* (*Hostile Rumor,* 1941) and *La fijeza* (*Fixity,* 1949), illustrates the recovery of the "trademark" of Baroque poetics, obscurity, which he inscribes in a modern version of the inaccessibility of meaning. . . . In Lezama's poetics, the Baroque metaphor is transformed through unpredictable analogies, creating an extension of the imaginary in the verbal material, in quest of the mysterious sound of the invisible world. (Chiampi, "Baroque" 510–11)

Like Lezama Lima, Octavio Paz is a key twentieth-century neobaroque practitioner across genres—the author of landmark experimentalist neobaroque poetry, such as "Himno entre ruinas" (1948; "Hymn among the Ruins"), dedicated to Góngora, and "Homenaje y Profanaciones" (1960; "Homage and Desecrations"), dedicated to Quevedo, as well as criticism, most recently his magisterial study of the life and work of the seventeenth-century Mexican poet Sor Juana Inés de la Cruz, *Sor Juana; or, The Traps of Faith*. For parallels between Paz and Eliot, see Cecilia Enjuto Rangel, "Cities in Ruins."

31. For a detailed history of German baroque enthusiasm of the 1920s, see Wellek, "The Concept of Baroque."

32. Croce, *Storia della età barocca in Italia* (1929).

33. These include Góngora, *Las soledades*, ed. Dámaso Alonso; Alonso, *Estudios y ensayos gongorinos;* García Lorca, "La imagen poética de Don Luis de Góngora"; and Diego, *Antología poética en honor de Góngora* (1927). The Mexican critic Alfonso Reyes (*Cuestiones gongorinas;* "Sabor de Góngora") collaborated with Alonso and Diego, but his efforts to rehabilitate Góngora also predated those of the Generation of '27. On the Góngora revival of the Generation of '27, see Gumbrecht, "Warum gerade Góngora?: Poetologie und historisches Bewusstsein in Spanien zwischen Jahrhundertwende und Bürgerkrieg," some of whose observations I summarize here.

34. Alonso, "Claridad y belleza de las *Soledades*" (1927), in *Estudios y ensayos gongorinos*, 66–91.

35. Friedrich, *The Structure of Modern Poetry*, 15.

36. For one landmark attack on the genetic continuity underlying Friedrich's study, see Paul de Man, "Lyric and Modernity," in *Blindness and Insight: Essays in the Rhetoric of Contemporary Criticism* (New York: Oxford University Press, 1971), 166–86, 171ff.

37. See Friedrich, *The Structure of Modern Poetry*, 83, 88–90, 92, 110–14.

38. See Martin Puchner, *Poetry of the Revolution: Marx, Manifestos, and the Avant-garde* (Princeton, NJ: Princeton University Press, 2006), for a history of literary vanguards through the lens of a history of the manifesto as an interdisciplinary (political and artistic) and transnational genre.

39. García Lorca, "La imagen poética de Don Luis de Góngora," 62. "More than Cervantes, one could call Góngora the father of our [Castilian] language" (77).

40. See Kermode, "Dissociation of Sensibility," in *Romantic Image*.

41. Foucault reads *Las Meninas* as an allegory of classical representation "and the definition of space it opens up to us," which hinges on the painting's famous overlapping of two empty subject positions. These are, first, the (transitory) viewer and, second, the absent presence of the Spanish king and queen, Felipe IV and Mariana of Austria, the invisible subjects represented in the hidden painting within the painting. For Foucault, the elision "of the person it resembles [that is, the monarchs] and the person in whose eyes it is only a resemblance" clears the way for the foregrounding of "representation in its pure form" (16).

42. See Michel Foucault, *Madness and Civilization: A History of Insanity in the Age of Reason*, trans. Richard Howard (New York: Pantheon Books, 1965).

43. Robbins, *The Challenges of Uncertainty*, 10.

44. Jameson, *A Singular Modernity*, 68.

45. Octavio Paz, "La tradición de la ruptura," in *Los hijos del limo: Del romanticismo a la vanguardia* (Barcelona: Seix Barral, 1974), 15–35, 15. The English translation of Paz's term, "A Tradition against Itself" (*Children of the Mire* 1–18), unnecessarily suppresses the paradox that Paz intends.

46. On the slipperiness of period concepts such as "Renaissance" and "Middle Ages"

and the supposed break between them, see also Hauser, "The Concept of the Renaissance," in *Renaissance, Mannerism, Baroque,* 3–16.

47. Jameson's four maxims read: "1. One cannot not periodize. 2. Modernity is not a concept but rather a narrative category. 3. The one way not to narrate it is via subjectivity (thesis: subjectivity is unrepresentable). Only situations of modernity can be narrated. 4. No 'theory' of modernity makes sense today unless it comes to terms with the hypothesis of a postmodern break with the modern" (*Singular Modernity* 94).

48. Grierson, introduction to *Metaphysical Lyrics and Poems of the Seventeenth Century,* 13–58.

49. Laura Doyle, *Freedom's Empire: Race and the Rise of the Novel in Atlantic Modernity, 1640–1940* (Durham, NC: Duke University Press, 2008).

50. Eliot, "*Ulysses,* Order, and Myth" (1923), in *Selected Prose of T. S. Eliot,* 175–78, 177.

51. On the vagaries of Eliot's objectivist doctrine, see Richard Shusterman, "Eliot and the Mutations of Objectivity," in Bagchee, *T. S. Eliot: A Voice Descanting,* 195–225. Tracing its transformations in Eliot's prolific output following his generative 1919 essay, Shusterman concludes that because Eliot "could find no philosophically adequate solution" to the "complex problem of objectivity," he "came increasingly to affirm and emphasise the subjective and personal" (220).

52. Eliot, "Tradition and the Individual Talent" (1919), in *Selected Prose of T. S. Eliot,* 37–44, 43.

53. Sanford Schwartz, "T. S. Eliot," in *Prospects for the Study of American Literature: A Guide for Scholars and Students,* ed. Richard Kopley (New York: New York University Press, 1997), 241–65, 245.

54. There are many variants of the chemical analogy for metaphysical poetry in the Clark and Turnbull lectures. For example, John Donne and Richard Crashaw are "the two great innovators: the transmuters, the alchemists, of thought into feeling, or of feeling into thought" (Clark Lectures 225–26). In contrast, Alexander Pope is not a metaphysical but a discursive poet because the "fusion is less perfect, or made at a lower temperature" (Turnbull Lectures 252; see also Clark Lectures 50).

55. For the arrogant stance, see "The Function of Criticism" (1923), where Eliot recalls, "At one time I was inclined to take the extreme position that the *only* critics worth reading were the critics who practised, and practised well, the art of which they wrote. But I had to stretch this frame to make some important inclusions" (*Selected Prose* 68–76, 74). In a humbler vein, Eliot concedes that his "attitude is that of a craftsman who has attempted for eighteen years to make English verses, studying the work of dead artisans who have made better verses" (Clark Lectures 44).

56. A short list of Eliot's poetic heroes and demons might look something like this: Milton, Dryden, Wordsworth, Keats, Shelley, and Shakespeare's *Hamlet* are out, whereas Donne, Marvell, Herbert, Chapman, Webster, and Shakespeare's *Macbeth* are in. Critics often comment on how Eliot's aggressive critical stance when younger gave way to a more accepting one when older, when, as Timothy Materer points out, he no longer had to "make a place for his own revolutionary poems" ("T. S. Eliot's Critical Program," in Moody, *The Cambridge Companion to Eliot,* 48–59, 49). Like many others, Charles Pollard affirms that "it was primarily his New Critical successors who hermetically sealed this list [of Eliot's preferences] as *the* canon in Anglo-American universities" (Pollard 43).

57. Marjorie Perloff's "Avant-Garde Eliot" (in *21st-Century Modernism: The "New" Poetics* [Oxford: Blackwell, 2002], 7–43) responds in part to the first edition of Eliot's unpublished early poems, *Inventions of the March Hare: Poems 1909–1917,* ed. Christopher

Ricks (London: Faber & Faber, 1996); see the section titled "The Meticulous Metic" in Jean-Michel Rabaté, "Tradition and T. S. Eliot," in Moody, *The Cambridge Companion to T. S. Eliot,* 210–22, 211–14.

58. Peter Nicholls, *Modernisms: A Literary Guide,* 2nd ed. (New York: Palgrave Macmillan, 2009), 164.

59. I thank my colleague Brian Reed for drawing my attention to this point.

60. Borges, "Pierre Menard, Author of the *Quixote*" (1944), in *Collected Fictions,* 88–95.

61. In the section titled "Neglect and Misinterpretation of Baroque Tragedy" in the Epistemo-Critical Prologue to *The Origin of German Tragic Drama,* Benjamin writes, "The *Trauerspiel* of the German Baroque appeared to be a caricature of classical tragedy" (50).

62. Commenting on the absence of metaphysical writers from "the English Parnassus," Mario Praz notes that not even Marvell's masterpiece, "To His Coy Mistress," was included in "the widespread nineteenth-century anthology, Palgrave's *Golden Treasury*" ("Baroque in England" 173).

63. Argument and analysis in the Clark Lectures are frequently meandering; the lectures do not always fully explain their own points. It is certainly true that Eliot's definitions of metaphysical poetry and his characterizations of its major proponents through the centuries (Dante, Donne, Crashaw, Cowley, Laforgue, Corbière) are restated repeatedly—often enough to become refrains for his lecture audience. But Eliot's key innovation, the shift in meaning and the departure from a period study, is not clear enough. References to the Grierson anthology prefaced by Eliot's 1921 essay *Metaphysical Lyrics and Poems of the Seventeenth Century,* which the audience was asked to use as a "course reader" of sorts, would have added to the confusion, as these obscured the difference between the orthodox period meaning of "metaphysical" and Eliot's reinvention of the term. Eliot may have learned from this and decided to make revisions accordingly, for the point is not to be missed in the Turnbull Lectures. In the first Turnbull Lecture, Eliot's unorthodox approach is the first item of discussion: "What we have to do, in the end, is to impose a meaning" (Turnbull Lectures 249); "I think, however, that by its long association with the excellent society of Donne and others, the adjective is now entitled to a *tertiary* meaning, and that we propose to discover or invent" (253).

64. D'Ors, "The Debate on the Baroque," 88.

65. For the reader's convenience, d'Ors lists the twenty-two baroques in a table accompanying his narrative (see d'Ors, *Lo barroco* 93).

66. Wellek, "The Concept of Baroque," 92.

67. Praz, "Baroque in England," 173, 174.

68. The essays were published in Spenser, *A Garland for John Donne.*

69. See Praz, *Secentismo e marinismo in Inghilterra* (1925). The essay on Crashaw has been translated ("The Flaming Heart: Richard Crashaw and the Baroque") and reprinted in *The Flaming Heart,* 204–63.

70. See Schuchard, "Clark Introduction," 19–21. Schuchard writes that Praz's "main concern was whether Eliot would be able to illustrate his theory about the disintegration of the intellect with sufficient detail and forcefulness" (19).

71. See Praz, "Donne and the Poetry of His Time," in Spenser, *A Garland for John Donne,* 51–71, 58–59.

72. In 1960, Praz concurred on this important point, stressing the formative impact of the metaphysical revival for modern poetry and criticism. See Praz, "Baroque in England," 173.

73. For this point, see especially Pollard's chapter "Not Borrowers, But Bearers of a Tradition" in *New World Modernisms,* 41–78.

74. Carpentier, "The Baroque and the Marvelous Real," 98.

75. See Schuchard, "Clark Introduction," 3.

76. See de Campos's 1981 manifesto "Anthropophagous Reason," which recuperates Brazilian vanguardism's polemical anthropophagy and frames it within the neobaroque.

77. Eliot, quoted in Perloff, "Avant-Garde Eliot," 15.

78. See Jewel Spears Brooker, "T. S. Eliot and the Revolt against Dualism: His Dissertation on F. H. Bradley in Its Intellectual Context," in *Mastery and Escape: T. S. Eliot and the Dialectic of Modernism* (Amherst: University of Massachusetts Press, 1994), 172–90.

79. M. A. R. Habib, *The Early T. S. Eliot and Western Philosophy* (Cambridge: Cambridge University Press, 1999). Habib writes,

> At the core of Eliot's thinking . . . was his antipathy to the entire thrust of modern liberal thought as archetypally expressed since the Enlightenment in the various forms of rationalism, empiricism, pragmatism and utilitarianism. . . . These notions are: the primacy of reason, the viewing of the human being as an autonomous, stable, and free agent, an epistemological dualism of subject and object, an emphasis on pluralism and the reality of particulars rather than universals, the exaltation of science, commitment to an ethic of work rather than contemplation, and an exclusive pragmatic focus on the present which parenthesises the past. (3)

80. The specter of periodization raises its head again here: Dante is claimed as both a medieval and a Renaissance poet.

81. Preminger and Brogan, *The New Princeton Encyclopedia of Poetry and Poetics,* s.v. "Conceit," 231–32, 231.

82. See Wellek, "Concept of Baroque," 113, 121, and Gerhart Hoffmeister, "Englischer Barock" (Baroque in England), *Deutsche und europäische Barockliteratur,* 32–40.

83. Preminger and Brogan, *The New Princeton Encyclopedia of Poetry and Poetics,* s.v. "Symbol," 1250–54, 1253.

84. Eco, "The Poetics of the Open Work"; de Campos, "The Open Work of Art" (1955), in *Novas,* 220–22.

85. This was the case with Praz, for example, who in his initial critique praised the last of the Clark Lectures most because of the light they shed on Eliot's poetry. See Schuchard, "Clark Introduction," 19–20.

86. Quotations from Eliot's poem in the text are from Michael North's Norton Critical Edition of *The Waste Land* (New York: W. W. Norton, 2001). Among the immense literature on *The Waste Land,* I have found helpful the following: Jewel Spears Brooker and Joseph Bentley, *Reading "The Waste Land": Modernism and the Limits of Interpretation* (Amherst: University of Massachusetts Press, 1990); Marianne Thormählen, *"The Waste Land": A Fragmentary Wholeness* (Lund: C. W. K. Gleerup, 1978); Ronald Bush, "'Unknown Terror and Mystery': *The Waste Land,*" in *T. S. Eliot: A Study in Character and Style* (New York: Oxford University Press, 1983), 53–78; as well as older studies by Hugh Kenner, *"The Waste Land,"* in *The Invisible Poet: T. S. Eliot* (New York: Ivan Obolensky, 1959), 145–82, and Cleanth Brooks, "*The Waste Land:* An Analysis," *Southern Review* 3, no. 2 (1937): 106–36. For a recent account of the poem's publication history, see Lawrence Rainey, "The Price of Modernism: Publishing *The Waste Land,*" in *Revisiting "The Waste Land"* (New Haven, CT: Yale University Press, 2005), 71–101.

87. Eliot's Harvard doctoral thesis was published during his lifetime, in 1964. See Richard Shusterman, "Eliot as Philosopher," in Moody, *The Cambridge Companion to*

T. S. Eliot, 31–47; Brooker, "T. S. Eliot and the Revolt Against Dualism"; Habib, *The Early T. S. Eliot and Western Philosophy.* According to Brooker, the *locus classicus* of earlier neglect of Eliot's philosophical training is Kenner's dismissal of Bradley in his Eliot study: "Bradley has an attractive mind, though he has perhaps nothing to tell us" (*Invisible Poet* 63).

88. Spengler's *Decline of the West* (1922) is not mentioned in Eliot's *Waste Land* notes. But Spengler's analysis of the exhaustion of Western civilization held powerful sway over the immediate postwar period. The publication of Spengler's book was delayed by the outbreak of World War I, but when the first edition came out in 1918, it seemed to define the apocalyptic mood of the moment. See Jewel Spear Brooker, "Mastery and Escape: T. S. Eliot and the Dialectic of Modernism," in *Mastery and Escape,* 1–20, 6, and Thormählen, *"The Waste Land,"* 136–40, for a discussion of Spengler's impact on Eliot and other modernists.

89. See Cleanth Brooks's description of the process in *"The Waste Land,"* 117, as well as a recent return to the topic in James Longenbach, "'Mature Poets Steal': Eliot's Allusive Practice," in Moody, *The Cambridge Companion to T. S. Eliot,* 176–188.

90. See Michael North's editorial notes (7n1 and 22nn5–6) in the Norton edition of *The Waste Land* and Brooker and Bentley, *Reading "The Waste Land,"* 83.

91. Eliot's depersonalization of the lyric speaker is much commented upon; see, for example, Brooks, *"The Waste Land,"* 134.

92. Celorio, "From the Baroque to the Neobaroque," 501–2.

93. This realization triggered William Carlos Williams's famous denunciation of Eliot has having "sold out to Europe," even though Williams's own long poem, *Paterson,* would itself be influenced by *The Waste Land,* using the same montage method of juxtaposing fragments. See J. Hillis Miller, "William Carlos Williams and Wallace Stevens," in *Columbia Literary History of the United States,* ed. Emory Elliott (New York: Columbia University Press, 1988), 972–92, 974.

94. De Campos, "Anthropophagous Reason," 175.

95. Eliot, from "Philip Massinger" (1920), in *Selected Prose of T. S. Eliot,* 153–60, 153.

96. See Brooker and Bentley's reading of this movement (154–171).

97. Qtd. in Witte, *Walter Benjamin—Der Intellektuelle als Kritiker,* 125. See also ibid., 125–32, and Witte, *Walter Benjamin: Mit Selbstzeugnissen und Bilddokumenten,* 60.

98. Steinhagen, "Zu Walter Benjamins Begriff der Allegorie," 674.

99. Preminger and Brogan, *The New Princeton Encyclopedia of Poetry and Poetics,* s.v. "Symbol," 1250, and s.v. "Allegory," 31–36, 31.

100. Benjamin, "Zentralpark," in *Illuminationen,* 230–50, 245.

101. Kelley, *Reinventing Allegory,* 255.

102. In her study of the organization of Eliot's poem, which responds to the 1971 facsimile edition of the *Waste Land* manuscripts, Thormählen concurs that "it is not possible to pinpoint any one readily recognisable unifying factor in *The Waste Land*" (204). Persistent attempts by early critics of the poem to "search for a unifier" have taken many forms, but none is satisfactory—the composition history shows that the Weston material, for example, did not become available to Eliot before most of the material "was already on paper" (199). Thormählen suggests that the only unifying factor is that which the act of reading constructs (205). See also Nicholas Halmi's essay, "Walter Benjamin's Unacknowledged Romanticism," *Lingua Humanitatis: Journal of the International Association for Humanistic Studies in Language* 2, no. 2 (2002): 163–82.

103. Bürger, *Theory of the Avant-garde,* 68.

104. Brooks writes, "Eliot's theme is the rehabilitation of a system of beliefs, known but now discredited. Dante did not have to 'prove' his statement; he could assume it and move within it about a poet's business. Eliot does not care, like Spenser, to force the didacticism. He prefers to stick to the poet's business. But, unlike Dante, he can not assume acceptance of the statement. A direct approach is calculated to elicit powerful 'stock responses' which will prevent the poem's being *read* at all. Consequently, the only method is to work by indirection. The 'Christian' material is at the center, but the poet never deals with it directly. The theme of resurrection is made on the surface in terms of the fertility rites; the words which the thunder speaks are Sanscrit words" (*"The Waste Land"* 135–36).

105. T. S. Eliot, *After Strange Gods* (New York: Harcourt Brace, 1934).

106. See Eliot's notes and the editor's notes to *The Waste Land,* 19–20, 25–26.

107. In addition to traditional approaches, see recent psychoanalytic readings of waste as abjection by Maud Ellman, *The Poetics of Impersonality: T. S. Eliot and Ezra Pound* (Cambridge, MA: Harvard University Press, 1987), and Tim Armstrong, *Modernism, Technology, and the Body: A Cultural Study* (Cambridge: Cambridge University Press, 1998), 68–74.

108. See Kenner, *The Invisible Poet,* 157.

109. See Witte, *Walter Benjamin—Der Intellektuelle als Kritiker,* 133.

2. The Neobaroque in Djuna Barnes

1. In the introduction to the 1944 collection *The Wedge,* Williams writes, "A poem is a small (or large) machine made of words. . . . There can be no part, as in any other machine, that is redundant" (*The Collected Later Poems of William Carlos Williams* [New York: New Directions, 1963], 4).

2. Le Corbusier, *Towards a New Architecture* (1923), trans. Frederick Etchells (New York: Dover, 1986), 4.

3. I have found helpful the following three important studies examining intersections between modernist literature and technology: Cecelia Tichi, *Shifting Gears: Technology, Literature, Culture in Modernist America* (Chapel Hill: University of North Carolina Press, 1987); Miles Orvell, *The Real Thing: Imitation and Authenticity in American Culture, 1880–1940* (Chapel Hill: University of North Carolina Press, 1989); and Tim Armstrong, *Modernism, Technology, and the Body: A Cultural Study* (Cambridge: Cambridge University Press, 1998).

4. Burton, *The Anatomy of Melancholy* (1621), ed. Jackson.

5. Joseph Frank, "Spatial Form in Modern Literature" (1945), in *The Widening Gyre: Crisis and Mastery in Modern Literature* (Bloomington: Indiana University Press, 1963), 3–62.

6. T. S. Eliot, introduction to Barnes, *Nightwood,* xi–xvi, xvi.

7. "But to find anything approaching their combination of ironic wit and religious humility, their emotional subtlety and profound human simplicity, their pathos, their terror, and their sophisticated self-consciousness, one has to go back to the religious sonnets of John Donne" (Frank 43).

8. Phillip Herring, *Djuna: The Life and Work of Djuna Barnes* (New York: Penguin, 1995), 262, 264. Djuna Barnes, *The Antiphon* (1958) (Los Angeles: Green Integer, 2000). Compare also "Barnes wrote her late play *The Antiphon* in a style informed by the Restoration drama" (Herring 99).

9. I regret having to forgo a discussion of *The Antiphon* for reasons of space. Benjamin discusses the plays of the Protestant German baroque as "unclassical tragedies"—

unclassical because the tragic is expressed in a noisy and demonstrative clamor that is antithetical to the silences of Greek tragedy. "The relationship between mourning and ostentation," Benjamin writes, "is . . . brilliantly displayed in the language of the baroque" (*Origin* 140). Like the lamentations of baroque drama, lamentation in *Nightwood* is theatrical and directed at an audience; it is extroverted rather than introverted grief, a public display that shifts the emphasis from the tragic suffering itself (objectivism) to its expression and articulation (subjectivism and emotional appeal). In *Nightwood* and *The Antiphon,* as in the baroque plays analyzed by Benjamin, suffering is a spectacle.

10. Mary Lynn Broe, introduction to *Silence and Power: A Reevaluation of Djuna Barnes,* ed. Mary Lynn Broe (Carbondale: Southern Illinois University Press, 1991), 3–23, 7.

11. Caroline Rupprecht's reference to "Barnes' idiosyncratic, baroque language" is representative of this tendency of the baroque to surface by way of casual definitions of Barnes's style, only to be dropped without further exploration ("Between Birth and Death: The Image of the Other in Djuna Barnes' *Nightwood,*" in *Subject to Delusions: Narcissism, Modernism, Gender* [Evanston, IL: Northwestern University Press, 2006], 93).

12. Louis F. Kannenstine, *The Art of Djuna Barnes: Duality and Damnation* (New York: New York University Press, 1977), 104.

13. Dianne Chisholm, "Obscene Modernism: *Eros Noir* and the Profane Illumination of Djuna Barnes," *American Literature* 69, no. 1 (1997): 167–206, 176.

14. Herring mentions not one but two baroque studies as Barnes's favorites: "her two lifelong favorites Robert Burton's *The Anatomy of Melancholy* (1621) and Sir Robert Browne's *Religio Medici* (1643)" (Herring 219).

15. Klibansky, Panofsky, and Saxl, *Saturn and Melancholy: Studies in the History of Natural Philosophy, Religion, and Art.* First published in 1964, this work is the result of decades of research by the famous faculty of the Warburg Institute, going back in its earliest version to Panofsky and Saxl's study of Albrecht Dürer's influential engraving *Melencolia I* (1514), *Dürers 'Melencolia I': Eine quellen- und typengeschichtliche Untersuchung* (Leipzig: B. G. Teubner, 1923). A landmark portrait of the Renaissance melancholic intellectual, Dürer's *Melencolia I* was also a key source for Benjamin's theory of the baroque in his *Trauerspiel* study (see Burkhardt Lindner, "Allegorie," in Opitz and Wizisla, *Benjamins Begriffe,* 1:50–94, 57–58).

16. Jennifer Radden, "Introduction: From Melancholic States to Clinical Depression," in Radden, *The Nature of Melancholy,* 3–51, 12. The Renaissance revision of melancholia was notably based on the authority of Aristotle, who had linked melancholia to genius.

17. Indeed, Klibansky, Panofsky, and Saxl note that Burton's learned compendium "could only have been written in England" (233n49) because it was in England and Spain, during the baroque period, that the reconfigured melancholy produced the richest yield in art and culture. Their comments on parallels between England and Spain are valuable clues toward recovering Anglo-Protestant parallels to the continental baroque.

> This dynamic liberation first occurred in the Baroque period. Significantly enough, it achieved its fullest and most profound results in the countries where the tension which was to bear fruit in artistic achievement was at its most acute—in Cervantes's Spain, where the Baroque developed under the pressure of a particularly harsh Catholicism, and still more in Shakespeare's and Donne's England, where it asserted itself in the teeth of a proudly stressed Protestantism. Both countries were and remained the true

domain of this specifically modern, consciously cultivated melancholy—for a long time the "melancholy Spaniard" was as proverbial as the "splenetic Englishman." (233–34)

18. Juliana Schiesari, *The Gendering of Melancholia: Feminism, Psychoanalysis, and the Symbolics of Loss in Renaissance Literature* (Ithaca, NY: Cornell University Press, 1992), 3.

19. Victoria L. Smith, "A Story beside(s) Itself: The Language of Loss in Djuna Barnes's *Nightwood*," *PMLA* 114, no. 2 (1999): 194–206, 201.

20. Deborah Parsons, "Djuna Barnes: Melancholic Modernism," in *The Cambridge Companion to the Modernist Novel* (Cambridge: Cambridge University Press, 2007), 165–77, and Esther Sánchez-Pardo, "Melancholia Reborn: Djuna Barnes' Styles of Grief," in *Cultures of the Death Drive: Melanie Klein and Modernist Melancholia* (Durham, NC: Duke University Press, 2003), 306–42. See also Gary Sherbert, "'Hieroglyphics of Sleep and Pain': Djuna Barnes's Anatomy of Melancholy," *Canadian Review of Comparative Literature* 30, no. 1 (2003): 117–44. Less useful than Parsons and Smith, Sherbert offers a very narrow psychoanalytic reading of the "grandmother incest" theme in *Nightwood* informed by the Kleinian theorists Nicolas Abraham and Maria Torok. Related issues (Barnes's style and transhistorical links to Burton) are ignored. Sánchez-Pardo's reading of melancholia in *Ryder* is similarly tilted toward the complexities of Kleinian theory, exploring melancholia at an abstract cultural level related to anxieties around reproduction that are symptomatic of "modernist cultures of the death drive."

21. In a 1971 interview, Barnes praised Frank's interpretation of *Nightwood* while also criticizing Eliot's introduction (quoted in Herring 233). Frank writes, "Modern literature, as exemplified by such writers as T. S. Eliot, Ezra Pound, Marcel Proust, and James Joyce, is moving in the direction of spatial form; and this tendency receives an original development in Djuna Barnes' remarkable book *Nightwood.*" Modernist writers "ideally intend the reader to apprehend their work spatially, in a moment of time, rather than as a sequence" (Frank 8–9). A section dedicated to *Nightwood* (25–49) presents Barnes's novel as the paradigm of the simultaneous "space-logic" of poetry that modern novelists introduce into the sequential "time-logic" of narrative (13). *Nightwood* thus epitomizes a modernism as defined by the experimental formalism championed by the New Critics. Frank's theory of modernism's spatial form triggered a decades-long debate, one of whose key participants was Frank Kermode, who advocated for a different, plot-centered approach to controlling temporality in fiction in *The Sense of an Ending* (1967). See W. J. T. Mitchell, "Spatial Form in Literature: Toward a General Theory," *Critical Inquiry* 6, no. 3 (1980): 539–67, and Jeffrey R. Smitten and Ann Daghistany, eds., *Spatial Form in Narrative* (Ithaca, NY: Cornell University Press, 1981).

22. For compendia of feminist Barnes criticism, see Shari Benstock, *Women of the Left Bank: Paris, 1900–1940* (Austin: University of Texas Press, 1986); Mary Lynn Broe, ed., *Silence and Power: A Reevaluation of Djuna Barnes;* and the 1993 special issue of the *Review of Contemporary Fiction* 13, no. 3 (Fall 1993). For an essay on style by a feminist critic, see Carolyn Allen, "'Dressing the Unknowable in the Garments of the Known': The Style of Djuna Barnes' *Nightwood,*" in *Women's Language and Style,* ed. Douglas Butturff and Edmund L. Epstein (Akron, OH: University of Akron Press, 1978), 106–18. While feminist readings of Barnes's modernism continued in the 1990s (see Bonnie Kime Scott, *Refiguring Modernism,* vol. 2, *Postmodern Feminist Readings of Woolf, West, and Barnes* [Bloomington: Indiana University Press, 1995]), the 1990s also saw an intensification of new historicist readings. See especially Dianne Chisholm, "Obscene Modernism," and Dana Seitler, "Down on All Fours: Atavistic Perversions and the Science of Desire

from Frank Norris to Djuna Barnes," *American Literature* 73, no. 3 (2001): 525–62. For LGBT approaches to Barnes, see notes 38 and 64 below.

23. Djuna Barnes, *Ryder* (1928; Normal, IL: Dalkey Archive, 1990); *The Book of Repulsive Women and Other Poems,* ed. Rebecca Loncraine (New York: Routledge, 2003); *Collected Stories,* ed. Phillip Herring (Los Angeles: Sun & Moon Press, 1997); *Interviews by Djuna Barnes,* ed. Alyce Barry (College Park, MD: Sun & Moon Press, 1985); *New York,* ed. Alyce Barry (Los Angeles: Sun & Moon Press, 1989); *Creatures in an Alphabet* (New York: Dial Press, 1982).

24. See, for example, Tyrus Miller, "Beyond Rescue: Djuna Barnes," in *Late Modernism: Politics, Fiction, and the Arts between the World Wars* (Berkeley: University of California Press, 1999), 121–68. Miller remarks that the most consistent and notable trait of Barnes's major works is the "rich stylization of sentence and the luxuriant proliferations of trope" (148).

25. See, for instance, ibid., 136, and Benstock's comment that Barnes's writings "divided themselves along lines of sexual orientation" (245).

26. Barnes, "The Walking-Mort" (1971), in *The Book of Repulsive Women and Other Poems,* 60.

27. See Friedrich, *The Structure of Modern Poetry,* 83 and 89, on differences between the soluble obscurity of baroque poetry and the insoluble obscurity of its modern (neobaroque) counterpart.

28. My account of Barnes's biography is indebted to Phillip Herring's excellent and engagingly written intellectual biography, *Djuna.* See also Deborah Parson's recent *Djuna Barnes* (Tavistock, UK: Northcote House, 2003), for a very useful introductory discussion to Barnes's works and life.

29. At one point, the girl Julie in *Ryder* (the Djuna figure) actually rejects her grandmother Sophia's (Zadel) profession of love, accusing her instead, "You have betrayed me" (*Ryder* 169).

30. Marjorie Perloff, "The Avant-garde Phase of American Modernism," in *The Cambridge Companion to American Modernism,* ed. Walter Kalaidjian (Cambridge: Cambridge University Press, 2005), 195–217.

31. See Herring's chapter, "Greenwich Village as It Was," in *Djuna,* 103–29.

32. See Barnes's reflection in 1936 about Thelma Wood during a period when she was meeting her as a friend: "I have *had* my great love, there will never be another" (quoted in Herring 166). The "Paris Stories" consist of "Aller et Retour" and a cluster of stories ("Cassation," "Le Grande Malade," and "Dusie") called "little girl" stories for their narrator. See Parsons, *Djuna Barnes,* 23–27. For a reading of their covert lesbian psychodynamics, linked to the mother-daughter relation, and of the light they shed on the incest component of the relationship between Nora and Robin in *Nightwood,* see Carolyn Allen, "Sexual Narrative in the Fiction of Djuna Barnes," in *Sexual Practice/Textual Theory: Lesbian Cultural Criticism,* ed. Susan J. Wolfe and Julia Penelope (Cambridge: Blackwell, 1993), 184–98.

33. This is testified independently by Radden ("Introduction" 45 and 282) and Schiesari (33). Sigmund Freud, "Mourning and Melancholia" (1917), in *The Standard Edition of the Complete Psychological Works of Sigmund Freud,* ed. and trans. James Strachey, 24 vols. (London: Hogarth, 1953–74), 14:239–58.

34. Jean-Paul Sartre, "On *The Sound and the Fury:* Time in the Work of Faulkner," in *Literary Essays* (New York: Philosophical Library, 1957), 79–87, 85.

35. James Strachey, editor's note to Freud, "Mourning and Melancholia," in *Standard Edition,* 14:239–42, 241.

36. Radden, editor's note to Freud, in *The Nature of Melancholy,* 282–83, 283.

37. Sigmund Freud, *The Ego and the Id* (1923), trans. James Strachey (New York: Norton, 1961), 43 (additions in the original).

38. See, for example, Jane Marcus: "Nora is the archetypal Dora or female hysteric, and Dr. Freud is brilliantly parodied in the figure of Dr. Matthew-Mighty-grain-of-salt-Dante-O'Connor." Twisting medical power relations, "the patient asks the questions and the doctor answers" ("Laughing at Leviticus: *Nightwood* as Woman's Circus Epic," in Broe, *Silence and Power,* 221–50, 233). Andrea L. Harris reads O'Connor as a parody of the sexologists Krafft-Ebing and Havelock Ellis ("the theoretician of sex as bearded lady") in "The Third Sex: Figures of Inversion in Djuna Barnes' *Nightwood,*" in *Eroticism and Containment: Notes from the Flood Plain,* ed. Carol Siegel and Ann Kibbey (New York: New York University Press, 1994), 233–59. Carolyn Allen's psychoanalytic discussion of *Nightwood,* focusing not on the Doctor but on the Nora-Robin relation, is probably the most detailed ("Djuna Barnes: The Erotics of Nurture," in *Following Djuna: Women Lovers and the Erotics of Loss* [Bloomington: Indiana University Press, 1996], 22–37). See Rita Felski, *The Gender of Modernity* (Cambridge, MA: Harvard University Press, 1995), for a discussion of alternative accounts of the liberating rather than repressive effects of the rise of sexology as "ultimately enabling for women in acknowledging their status as desiring subjects" (181).

39. Barnes's two biographies, by Herring and Andrew Field (Field, *The Life and Times of Djuna Barnes* [New York: Putnam, 1983]), yield no information on this topic. The same is true for Benstock's intellectual portraits of Barnes's female modernist circle. Parsons is more affirmative:

> The intellectual consciousness of Barnes' Greenwich Village milieu in the 1910s and 1920s was extremely receptive to the new social-scientific and psycho-medical discourses, principally to the work of Freud, which was widely translated and popularized. . . . Barnes' writing indicates that she was well versed in Freudian concepts, and notably the understanding of sexuality as rooted in the struggle between the desires of the unconscious and the demands of modern civilization, but there is little evidence that she approached psychoanalysis with anything other than ambivalence, regarding it as just one of a history of reductive disciplinary systems of identity. (*Djuna Barnes* 68)

40. See, for example, Alan Bullock's assessment: "No single man, probably, has exercised a greater influence on the ideas, literature and art of the twentieth century than Freud" ("The Double Image," in *Modernism: A Guide to European Literature, 1890–1930,* ed. Malcolm Bradbury and James McFarlane [London: Penguin, 1991], 58–70, 67).

41. Michel Foucault, *The History of Sexuality,* vol. 1, *An Introduction,* trans. Robert Hurley (New York: Random House, 1990).

42. To underline the continuities between baroque and neobaroque conceits, I cite the reprint of Quevedo's poem, in Spanish and English translation, as part of Octavio Paz's poem in honor of Quevedo, "Homenaje y profanaciones" (1960; "Homage and Desecrations"), in *The Collected Poems of Octavio Paz, 1957–87,* 82–91, 82–83.

43. According to Herring, it was on this 1931 trip with her then lover Charles Henri Ford to Munich, Vienna, and Budapest that Barnes began taking notes for the background of *Nightwood* (178).

44. Zamora, *The Inordinate Eye,* 182. Her discussion of "Frida Kahlo's New World Hagiography" is found on pp. 182–99.

45. Georgette Fleischer, "Djuna Barnes and T. S. Eliot: The Politics and Poetics of *Nightwood*," *Studies in the Novel* 30, no. 3 (1998): 405–37, 406. There are exceptions to Fleischer's claim; see, for example, Jane Marcus's essay "Laughing at Leviticus."

46. Hauser, "The Baroque of the Protestant Bourgeoisie," in *Renaissance, Mannerism, Baroque,* 207–25, 212.

47. Miles, *Image as Insight,* 95ff. See especially the chapter "Vision and the Sixteenth-Century Protestant and Roman Catholic Reforms," 95–125.

48. There are important exceptions to the equation between Protestantism and iconoclasm. For example, the reformed Church of Beatae Mariae Virginis (1608–) in Wolfenbüttel in Lower Saxony near Hannover, Germany, features a full-fledged baroque altar that was specifically commissioned by the local Lutheran congregation for this church, and whose iconography corresponds to Lutheran reformed doctrine.

49. See Norberg-Schulz, *Baroque Architecture,* 10.

50. See Martin, "Sacred Art and Naturalism," in *Baroque,* 54–59.

51. Here I follow Christopher Warnes's definition in "Naturalizing the Supernatural: Faith, Irreverence and Magical Realism," *Literature Compass* 2 (2005): 1–16.

52. Lacan, "On the Baroque." Lacan's essay on the baroque reads "the exhibition of the body evoking *jouissance*" in Bernini's St. Teresa into the framework of the self's subjection to the discourse of the Other: "The Baroque is the regulating of the soul by corporal radioscopy" (113, 116).

53. See Martin, "Martyrdom," in *Baroque,* 108–112, 112.

54. For a brief introduction to Galen's contribution to the genealogy of melancholia, see Radden, *The Nature of Melancholy,* 61–68. According to Galen, "the spleen or the atrabiliary glands were the organs associated with black bile" (Radden 62).

55. Sarduy, "The Baroque and the Neobaroque," 272.

56. This point is also made by Smith.

57. Fuentes, "The Novel as Tragedy," 543.

58. Again, the austere visual classicism of Protestant religious interiors results from the *linguistic* focus of Protestant worship and the elimination of distracting other media, especially visuals. See Miles, *Image as Insight,* 100–108 and 113–18.

59. Braider, *Baroque Self-Invention and Historical Truth,* 9–10.

60. Like Fuentes, the Caribbean writers Gabriel García Márquez and Édouard Glissant have claimed Faulkner as a Caribbean and hemispheric American writer. In turn, Faulkner's work has become one of the centerpieces in the remapping of U.S. Southern studies within the framework of hemispheric American studies. See George B. Handley, *Postslavery Literatures in the Americas: Family Portraits in Black and White* (Charlottesville: University of Virginia Press, 2000); Deborah N. Cohn, *History and Memory in the Two Souths: Recent Southern and Spanish American Fiction* (Nashville, TN: Vanderbilt University Press, 1999); and Jon Smith and Deborah Cohn, eds, *Look Away! The U.S. South in New World Studies* (Durham, NC: Duke University Press, 2004).

61. Schiesari, *The Gendering of Melancholia,* 18. Her fascinating account of the suppression of women's public mourning as a symptom of the "defeminization of the public sphere" is found in chapter 3 of that work, "Appropriating the Work of Women's Mourning: From Petrarch to Gaspara Stampa, and from Isabella di Morra to Tasso," 160–90. She notes that the same humanists, Petrarch and Ficino, who created the masculine subject of melancholic genius by reviving classical sources were among the most vocal opponents of women's rituals of public mourning.

62. On *Ladies Almanack* as biographical roman à clef, see the essays collected in Broe, *Silence and Power,* particularly those by Karla Jay ("The Outsider among the

Expatriates: Djuna Barnes' Satire on the Ladies of the *Almanack,*" 184–93), Frann Michel ("All Women Are Not Women All: *Ladies Almanack* and Feminine Writing," 170–82), and especially Susan Sniader Lanser ("Speaking in Tongues: *Ladies Almanack* and the Discourse of Desire," 156–68) See also Benstock for a description of the culture and many of the writers who figure in *Ladies Almanack.*

63. Barnes had firsthand experience with obscenity laws and trials through the publication of her own novel *Ryder,* the American edition of which was expurgated against her will. Furthermore, Barnes was familiar with the trials of the lesbian novel *The Well of Loneliness,* for the author, Radclyffe Hall, was a member of Natalie Barney's circle, as well as of *Ulysses,* as she knew Joyce as a personal friend.

64. Susan Lanser and Karla Jay discuss another reason for self-censorship, Barnes's discomfort with being identified as a member of Barney's lesbian circle and her ambivalence about identifying herself as lesbian. While Jay argues that Barnes's reluctance to do the latter is expressed in a "reductionist vision of lesbianism" in *Ladies Almanack* (193), Lanser proposes that the rhetorical stance that matters is the book's "inside stance" (165), independent of the author's well-publicized disclaimer decades later, "I'm not a lesbian; I just loved Thelma." From the neobaroque perspective adopted here, the realist grounding of the lesbian text in the lesbian life of the author is not the central issue, given—following the Cuban theorist Sarduy—the baroque focus on artificialization and denaturalization, which includes the text's reference to the author's life.

65. Esther Newton, "The Mythic Mannish Lesbian: Radclyffe Hall and the New Woman," *Signs* 9 (1984): 557–75, 566. See the collection *Sexology and Culture: Labeling Bodies and Desires,* ed. Lucy Bland and Laura Doan (Chicago: University of Chicago Press, 1998), on the dissemination of sexology's medical concepts in late nineteenth- and early twentieth-century culture and literature. Important analyses of modern discourses of sexuality in Barnes's work are Harris, "The Third Sex," and Leigh Gilmore, "Obscenity, Modernity, Identity: Legalizing *The Well of Loneliness* and *Nightwood,*" *Journal of the History of Sexuality* 4 (1994): 603–24.

66. *Encyclopedia of Homosexuality,* ed. Wayne R. Dynes et al. (New York: Garland, 1990), s.v. "Inversion," 1:610–11.

67. Ellis wrote a famous and supportive preface to *The Well of Loneliness.* Other early twentieth-century writers who adopted important aspects of the figure of the "third sex" are Gertrude Stein and Vita Sackville-West. See Newton, "The Mythic Mannish Lesbian," 568, and Suzanne Raitt, "Sex, Love and the Homosexual Body in Early Sexology," in Bland and Doan, *Sexology and Culture,* 150–64.

68. See, for example, Parsons, "Sapphic Satire: *Ladies Almanack,*" in *Djuna Barnes,* 44–59, 45–46 and 55–56.

69. The parallel between Wendell Ryder and Dame Evangeline Musset has been noted by several critics; see, for example, Parsons, "Sapphic Satire," 49. Like Wendell, Evangeline rides a horse astride, "like any Yeoman," and "was made, hour by hour, less womanly" (*Ladies Almanack* 7), in a scene that also evokes, only to mock, the psychoanalytic theory of women's supposed castration.

70. Regarding the debate over the measure of the unnamed narrator's satirical and critical distance from the lesbian community portrayed (see also note 65), I would suggest that it is mild and affectionate. It consists of Patience Scalpel's criticism of her lesbian friends, whom she never abandons ("January" and "August"), Evangeline's complaint (in "May") that lesbianism has become fashionable, and the narrator's critique of runaway romantic clichés in lesbian love letters (in "July") as well as demonstrative, indiscreet

behavior in public (in "August"). If Barnes distanced herself from this text later in life, excluding it from the 1962 edition of her *Selected Works* (see Lanser 164), this only shows the importance of distinguishing between the real, biographical author, whose outlook changes during life, and the implied author, a construct inferred from the total design of the text (Shlomith Rimmon-Kenan, *Narrative Fiction: Contemporary Poetics* [London: Routledge, 1983], 87).

71. Lanser makes this point when she notes that "many of *Ladies Almanack*'s terms for the female body—furrow, nook, path, keyhole, whorl, crevice, conch shell . . . —are clearly designed to counteract emerging Freudian notions of phallic supremacy and clitoral insufficiency" (162).

72. See Kuhnheim, "Sensual Excess," 116. See Roman Jakobson, "Linguistics and Poetics," in *Language in Literature,* ed. Krystyna Pomorska and Stephen Rudy (Cambridge, MA: Harvard University Press, 1987), 62–94.

73. *Encyclopedia of Homosexuality,* "Inversion," 1:611.

74. In fact, Barnes here parodies an early modern scientific theory called "preformativism," the theory that life develops from very tiny beings that are already as they will be in all but size. In the words of the eighteenth-century naturalist the Comte de Buffon: "It . . . appears very probable that there really exists in nature an infinity of small organized beings, similar in every respect to the large organized bodies that appear in the world, that these small organized beings are composed of living organic parts which are common to animals and vegetables; that these organic parts are primitive and incorruptible; that the assemblage of these parts forms what in our eyes are organized beings" (quoted in Marjorie Grene and David Depew, *The Philosophy of Biology: An Episodic History* [New York: Cambridge University Press, 2004], 85). Grene and Depew elaborate: "On the performativist family of views, the cause of an organism's coming-to-be is presumed to lie entirely in a pre-existing germ (whether sperm or egg) that already contains the whole differentiated organism in miniature, which merely unfolds or rolls out. . . . For his part, Leibniz had no trouble with preformationism in this sense. . . . Leibniz showed marked enthusiasm for the notion of an infinity of infinitely small systems organized into functionally differentiated parts" (95).

75. See Stephen Wilson, introduction to *Saints and Their Cults: Studies in Religious Sociology, Folklore and History,* ed. Stephen Wilson (Cambridge: Cambridge University Press, 1983), 1–53. My discussion of hagiography and saint's cults is indebted to Wilson and to David Hugh Farmer, ed., *The Oxford Dictionary of Saints* (Oxford: Clarendon Press, 1978).

76. To be sure, the parallel has been recognized: for example, Lanser notes that *Ladies Almanack* "uses or parodies the saint's life, the ode, the prayer, the lullaby, the allegory, the myth, as well as specific works from the Bible to *Finnegans Wake*" (157). What has been neglected is the structural function of hagiography, both in regards to the plot and, especially, in relation to the epistemological challenge to sexology's scientific discourse.

77. Daniela Caselli, "Novitiates, Saints, and Priestesses: The Unreadable Pleasures of *Ladies Almanack,*" *Textual Practice* 20, no. 3 (2006): 463–89. See Barnes, foreword to *Ladies Almanack* (New York: Harper & Row, 1972), n. pag.

78. David Hugh Farmer, introduction to *The Oxford Dictionary of Saints,* vii–xx, vii. Farmer notes that despite the Reformation's opposition of the cult of saints, saint's days were retained in the Book of Common Prayer of the Church of England (xiii).

79. A glance at entries in Farmer's *Oxford Dictionary of Saints* will confirm this.

80. Wilson recounts that a "number of modern Marian apparitions—La Salette, Fátima, Garabandal—have been used to criticize papal policy, while La Salette, in particular, has been the focus of dissident and schismatic groups" (Introduction 35).

81. For recent studies of the Mexican scholar Carlos de Sigüenza y Góngora in the context of the seventeenth-century intellectual background, see Ross, *The Baroque Narrative of Carlos de Sigüenza y Góngora,* as well as Buscaglia-Salgado, "The Creole in His Labyrinth."

82. See Warnes, "Naturalizing the Supernatural."

83. Reading for the biographical allegory in *Ladies Almanack,* Karla Jay critiques this description of Natalie Barney as "insulting," considering that Barney "considered herself to be completely feminine," not at all a "pseudo-man" (187, 186). In contrast, I contend that the denaturalization of modern scientific myths of sexuality, not biographical realism, is Barnes's main concern in this text.

84. Karla Jay reports that it "is a direct reference to Barney's love affair in 1898–1899 with Liane de Pougy, who was the most famous courtesan of her day, and whom Barney did succeed in seducing" (187). Many of the biographical allusions are so obscure, however, that not even Barney was able to name all the characters and episodes in *Almanack* (191). Barnes obviously took pains to obscure allegorical references to her writer friends' lives, diluting the book's referential function even in its dimension as a closet biography.

85. See "Teresa von Avila," in Rosa Giorgi, *Die Heiligen: Geschichte und Legende,* trans. Suzanne Fischer and Karl Pichler (Milan: Electa, 2002), 340–42.

86. These wrong charges were in part based on factual errors in Andrew Field's 1983 first biography of Barnes. For example, Field mistakenly claimed that Eliot had suggested the title *Nightwood.* It wasn't until Herring's biography of Barnes came out in 1995 that many of these errors were corrected. (On the editorial relationship between Barnes and Eliot, see Herring's chapters "Emily and Tom: The Practical Cats" and "Prussic Acid in Dramatic Form: *The Antiphon*" in *Djuna,* 218–41, 259–81). To appreciate the change in the assessment of the Barnes-Eliot relationship, compare Miriam Fuchs, "Djuna Barnes and T. S. Eliot: Authority, Resistance, and Acquiescence," *Tulsa Studies in Women's Literature* 12, no. 2 (1993): 288–313, and Fleischer, "Djuna Barnes and T. S. Eliot."

87. Maud Ellman, *The Poetics of Impersonality: T. S. Eliot and Ezra Pound* (Cambridge, MA: Harvard University Press, 1987), 93.

88. *"Le Prince d'Aquitaine à la tour abolie"* ("The Prince of Aquitaine in his ruined tower") (*Waste Land* l. 429). Julia Kristeva, *Black Sun: Depression and Melancholy* (New York: Columbia University Press, 1989).

89. As Smith notes, there "is perhaps a concatenation of losses. Robin's loss activates, and is contiguous with, larger losses." This and her subsequent comment that "the loss of [Robin] allows other losses to surface" evokes Sarduy's model of the proliferation of signifiers around an empty center, occupied (but not fully occupied) by Robin (202–3).

90. In fact, there are two passages in which Nora's grandmother appears (*Nightwood* 62–63 and 148–49). The first contains a brief recollection of the grandmother "of her childhood . . . who, for some unknown reason, was dressed as a man, wearing a billycock and a corked moustache, ridiculous and plump in tight trousers and a red waistcoat, her arms spread saying with a leer of love, 'My little sweetheart!'" (63). The childhood wound that Robin reopened may have been incest, as suggested here. But, given Djuna's many disappointments with maternal protector figures in her childhood, it may also have been the loss of the "good" maternal object more abstractly, which, following Freud, the child can only endure through the process of introjection and identification discussed earlier. Although there may have been extended passages on Nora's

grandmother in earlier drafts that were cut, there are no cuts in *Nightwood* that Barnes did not agree to. As Cheryl Plumb's publication of the remaining drafts of *Nightwood* shows, Barnes did successfully preempt cuts she deemed unacceptable, such as restoring the term "obscene" in the phrase "obscene and touching" in the crucial closing scene. (See *Nightwood: The Original Version and Related Drafts,* ed. Cheryl Plumb [Normal, Il: Dalkey Archive Press, 1995], 210.)

91. For an explanation of the narratologic concept of focalization, see Rimmon-Kenan, "Text: Focalization," in *Narrative Fiction,* 71–85.

92. My use of narratological terms follows Rimmon-Kenan, *Narrative Fiction,* throughout.

93. See, for example, Bonnie Kime Scott, "Barnes' Beasts Turning Human," in *Refiguring Modernism,* 2: 70–122. On Wendell Ryder as a precursor of Robin, see Parsons, *Djuna Barnes,* 40–43.

94. See Jane Marcus ("Laughing at Leviticus") for a Bakhtinian reading of Barnes, and Bonnie Kime Scott for an investigation of Barnes's refiguration of the association of woman with nature (221). See also Carolyn Allen's reading of *Nightwood* as a lesbian novel in "Sexual Narrative in the Fiction of Djuna Barnes."

95. See, for example, Gilmour's discussion of *Nightwood* as the "non-case" of a novel that successfully evaded the censors in "Obscenity, Modernity, Identity."

96. See Harris, "The Third Sex," 238, and Marcus, "Laughing at Leviticus."

97. Erwin Panofsky, *The Life and Art of Albrecht Dürer* (1943; Princeton, NJ: Princeton University Press, 1971), 156–57. A revised and expanded version of Panofsky's influential reading of *Melencolia I* as the fusion of two distinct iconographic traditions, creating the figure of "a thinking being in perplexity" (163), is also found in Klibansky, Panofsky, and Saxl, *Saturn and Melancholy.*

98. See, for example, Allen, "Dressing the Unknowable."

99. Lezama Lima, "Baroque Curiosity," 216.

100. Even though I agree with the principal orientation of Chisholm's claim that Barnes is "the artificer of an obscene resistance, laboring in tacit solidarity with her Surrealist contemporaries" (195), I find her analogy with surrealism problematic for the reasons stated here. *Nightwood* conducts its critique of rationality and scientific realism not in the surrealist manner, by abandoning consciousness and intellect, but rather by dismantling representation as an instrument of scientific communication. I borrow the notion of "intellectual night" from Octavio Paz's discussion of Sor Juana's philosophical poem *Primero Sueño* (*First Dream*) in *Sor Juana; or, The Traps of Faith.*

101. Incidentally, it was precisely these activities that Luther sought to eliminate from Christian worship as distractions from the word of God. See Miles, *Image as Insight,* 106.

102. Eliot, "*Ulysses,* Order and Myth," in *Selected Prose of T. S. Eliot,* 175–78, 177.

103. Ernest Hemingway, *The Sun Also Rises* (New York: Macmillan, 1986). On technology and Hemingway, see Tichi, *Shifting Gears,* and "Technology and the Novel," in *The Columbia History of the American Novel,* ed. Emory Elliott (New York: Columbia University Press, 1991), 465–84.

104. My discussion of *The Sun Also Rises* is indebted to the new gender criticism on Hemingway. For an exploration of gender (and race) trouble in Hemingway, see Wolfgang E. H. Rudat, "Hemingway's *The Sun Also Rises:* Masculinity, Feminism, and Gender-Role Reversal," *American Imago* 47, no. 1 (1990): 43–68; J. Gerald Kennedy, "Hemingway's Gender Trouble," *American Literature* 63 (1991): 187–207; Nancy R. Comley and Robert Scholes, *Hemingway's Genders: Rereading the Hemingway Text*

(New Haven, CT: Yale University Press, 1994); Walter Benn Michaels, *Our America: Nativism, Modernism, and Pluralism* (Durham, NC: Duke University Press, 1995); and James Nagel, "Brett and the Other Women in *The Sun Also Rises,*" in *The Cambridge Companion to Hemingway,* ed. Scott Donaldson (Cambridge: Cambridge University Press, 1996), 87–108.

3. The Latin American Antidictatorship Neobaroque

1. Williamson, *The Penguin History of Latin America,* 372.

2. On the post-Boom, see Philip Swanson, "The Post-Boom Novel," in *The Cambridge Companion to the Latin American Novel,* ed. Efraín Kristal (New York: Cambridge University Press, 2005), 81–101; Stephen M. Hart, "Some Postmodern Developments," in *A Companion to Spanish-American Literature* (London: Tamesis, 1999), 144–65; and Donald Shaw, *The Post-Boom in Spanish American Fiction* (Saratoga Springs, NY: State University of New York Press, 1997). Critics agree that the post-Boom shifts away from high literary experimentalism to various neorealisms and the incorporation of popular mass culture, and approaches literary experimentation from new, self-critical perspectives.

3. On the neobaroque in twentieth-century Latin American fiction, see the following important studies: Ortega, *La estética neobarroca en la narrativa hispanoamericana;* Guerrero, *La estrategia neobarroca;* Méndez Rodenas, *Severo Sarduy;* González Echevarría, *Celestina's Brood;* DuPont, "Baroque Ambiguities"; González, "Baroque Endings"; Zamora, *The Inordinate Eye;* Márquez Rodríguez, *El barroco literario en Hispanoamérica* and *Lo barroco y lo real-maravilloso en la obra de Alejo Carpentier;* Salgado, *From Modernism to Neobaroque;* Pauly, *Neobarroco;* Schumm, *Barrocos y modernos;* Figueroa Sánchez, *Barroco y neobarroco en la narrativa hispanoamericana;* Abeyta, "Ostentatious Offerings"; and Thomas, "Historiographic Metafiction and the Neobaroque in Fernando del Paso's *Noticias del imperio.*"

4. Perlongher, "Cadáveres," in *Poemas completos,* 119–31. Perlongher's essays on the neobaroque are collected in *Prosa plebeya: Ensayos 1980–92.* On Perlongher, see Adrián Cangi and Paula Siganevich, eds., *Lúmpenes peregrinaciones: Ensayos sobre Néstor Perlongher* (Rosario, Argentina: Beatriz Viterbo, 1996); Kuhnheim, "Sensual Excess," esp. 118–24; and Bollig, "Tie Me Up, Tie Me Down."

5. Benjamin, *The Origin of German Tragic Drama,* 219.

6. Benjamin, "Theses on the Philosophy of History," in *Illuminations,* 253–67, 255.

7. See Nelly Richard, *Cultural Residues; Margins and Institutions: Art in Chile since 1973* (Melbourne: Art and Text, 1986); and *The Insubordination of Signs: Political Change, Cultural Transformation, and the Poetics of the Crisis,* trans. Alice A. Nelson and Silvia R. Tandeciarz (Durham, NC: Duke University Press, 2004); Eugenia Brito, *Campos minados: Literatura post-golpe en Chile* (Santiago: Cuarto Propio, 1990); and Idelber Avelar, *The Untimely Present* and *The Letter of Violence: Essays on Narrative, Ethics, and Politics* (New York: Palgrave, 2004).

8. Eltit, *Lumpérica* (1983), English trans. *E. Luminata* (1997); Donoso, *Casa de campo* (1978), English trans. *A House in the Country* (1984).

9. See Leonidas Morales T., *Conversaciones con Diamela Eltit* (Santiago: Editorial Cuarto Propio, 1998), 58.

10. See also Alice A. Nelson's study of post-coup Chilean literature, which similarly straddles the divide between the dictatorship years and the 1990s: *Political Bodies: Gender, History, and the Struggle for Narrative Power in Recent Chilean Literature* (Lewisburg, PA: Bucknell University Press, 2002).

11. Jameson, *A Singular Modernity,* 29.

12. Francine Masiello, *The Art of Transition: Latin American Culture and Neoliberal Crisis* (Durham, NC: Duke University Press, 2001); Nelly Richard and Alberto Moreiras, eds., *Pensar en/la postdictadura* (Santiago: Editorial Cuarto Propio, 2001); Willy Thayer, *El fragmento repetido: Escritos en estado de excepción* (Santiago: Metales Pesados, 2006). For an assessment of the ongoing impact of the 1973 coup on Chilean society in the years of the democracy, see Silvia Nagy-Zegmi and Fernando Leiva, eds., *Democracy in Chile: The Legacy of September 11, 1973* (Brighton, UK, and Portland, OR: Sussex Academic Press, 2005).

13. The Peruvian dictatorship constitutes an exception, indeed, a diametrical contrast to the Southern Cone dictatorships. Appalled by the abject poverty the Peruvian generals had witnessed among Indian peasantry when they were called in to put down a guerilla insurrection in the Andes in the early 1960s, "the army in Peru launched a coup and chose, uniquely, to adopt the radical nationalist policies of the revolutionary left" (Williamson 351).

14. Mary Louise Pratt, "Overwriting Pinochet: Undoing the Culture of Fear in Chile," in *The Places of History: Regionalism Revisited in Latin America* (Durham, NC: Duke University Press, 1999), 21–33, 26. Pratt's quotation is from Hernán Vidal.

15. Fredric Jameson, *Postmodernism; or, The Cultural Logic of Late Capitalism* (Durham, NC: Duke University Press, 1991).

16. Jill Kuhnheim, *Gender, Politics, and Poetry in Twentieth-Century Argentina* (Gainesville: University Press of Florida, 1996), 103.

17. Ricardo Piglia, *La cuidad ausente* (Buenos Aires: Sudamericana, 1992), trans. by Sergio Waisman as *The Absent City* (Durham, NC: Duke University Press, 2000).

18. See Avelar, *The Untimely Present,* 44–48; Pratt, "Overwriting Pinochet," 26; and Amanda Holmes, "Scripting the City: Diamela Eltit's *Lumpérica* and *Vaca Sagrada,*" in *City Fictions: Language, Body, and Spanish American Urban Space* (Lewisburg, PA: Bucknell University Press, 2007), 117–41, 117.

19. Raúl Zurita, "Chile: Literatura, lenguaje y sociedad (1973–1983)," in *Fascismo y experiencia literaria: Reflexiones para una recanonización,* ed. Hernán Vidal (Minneapolis, MN: Institute for the Study of Ideologies and Literature, 1985), 299–331, 301.

20. Bürger, *Theory of the Avant-garde,* 58.

21. On CADA's urban performances, see especially the following analyses by Nelly Richard: "The Dimension of Social Exteriority in the Production of Art," in *Margins and Institutions,* 53–62, and "A Border Citation: Between Neo- and Post-Avant-Garde," in *The Insubordination of Signs,* 23–36. Eltit's recollections in "Acciones de arte, video, fotografía," in Morales, *Conversaciones con Diamela Eltit,* also offer excellent background information on the projects of the CADA art collective (157–78).

22. Alberto Moreiras, "Postdictadura y reforma del pensamiento," *Revista de crítica cultural* 7 (1993): 26–35, 26.

23. See Pamela Constable and Arturo Valenzuela's *A Nation of Enemies: Chile under Pinochet* (New York: Norton, 1991), which captures the nation's extreme polarization along ideological lines into "two Chiles"—right and left, rich and poor. More recently, the historian Steve Stern's studies on memory of the Pinochet years in Chile confirm these ongoing antagonisms in their discussion of the coexistence of irreconcilable "memory scripts" that had become entrenched during the dictatorship. By 1998, Stern observes, Chile had reached a de facto "memory impasse" as a result of the unresolved rivalry between these various scripts, which—to mention the two most at odds—remembered the coup either as Chile's "salvation" from socialism or as an unresolved catastrophe,

respectively. See Steve J. Stern, *Remembering Pinochet's Chile: On the Eve of London, 1998* (Durham, NC: Duke University Press, 2004).

24. This statement comes from Diamela Eltit, "Errante, Errática," in *Una poética de literatura menor: La narrativa de Diamela Eltit,* ed. Juan Carlos Lértora (Santiago, Chile: Cuarto Propio, 1993), 17–25. I cite a translation by Ronald Christ that appears in the English translation of *Lumpérica,* "Errant, Erratic," in *E. Luminata,* 4–12, 5. The equivalent passage is missing from the Spanish-language version printed in Lértora.

25. Diamela Eltit and Paz Errázuriz, *El infarto del alma* (Santiago: Zegers, 1994). On *El infarto del alma,* see Richard, "For Love of Art: Critical Ruptures and Flights of Fancy," in *Cultural Residues,* 159–76, and Mary Beth Tierney-Tello, "Testimony, Ethics, and the Aesthetic in Diamela Eltit," *PMLA* 114, no. 1 (1999): 78–96.

26. On *El padre mío,* see Richard, "Neobaroque Debris: Scabs and Decorations," in *Cultural Residues,* 49–58, and Michael J. Lazzara, "The Poetics of Impossibility (Diamela Eltit's *El Padre Mío*)," in *Chile in Transition: The Poetics and Politics of Memory* (Gainesville: University Press of Florida, 2006), 38–63.

27. Lazzara seconds Eltit's and Richard's allegorical reading of the madman's discontinuous discourse: it "is precisely the nonsensical nature of the madman's speech that refers us, metaphorically, to the general state of social paranoia that has invaded his psyche and to the overarching 'crisis of intelligibility' (Richard) originated by the dictatorship" (50).

28. John Beverley, "The Margin at the Center: On *Testimonio,*" in *The Real Thing: Testimonial Discourse and Latin America,* ed. Georg Gugelberger (Durham, NC: Duke University Press, 1996), 23–41.

29. See Juan Andres Piña, "José Donoso," in *Conversaciones con la narrativa chilena* (Santiago: Los Andes, 1991), 43–73, 64.

30. José Donoso, "La obra literaria del novelista José Donoso: Coloquio con el autor," in *Literatura y sociedad en América latina,* ed. Valentín Tascón and Fernando Soría (Salamanca: San Esteban, 1981), 103–16, 112, 108.

31. José Donoso, *The "Boom" in Spanish American Literature: A Personal History,* trans. Gregory Kolovakos (New York: Columbia University Press, 1977).

32. Wölfflin, *Principles of Art History,* 20.

33. Lezama Lima, "Baroque Curiosity," 213.

34. Roberto Bolaño, *Estrella distante* (Barcelona: Anagrama, 1996), trans. by Chris Andrews as *Distant Star* (New York: New Directions, 2004).

35. Throughout its existence, the Chilean *avanzada* was the target of counterinsurgent interpretations (as it were) on the part of official regime critics, the art critic Waldemar Sommer and the literary critic Valente, in the pages of *El Mercurio* (Richard, *Margins* 26). In turn, antidictatorship artists and writers were hyperaware of (and constantly struggling against) "the risk of being embraced by institutions and tailored to the needs of authority" (29).

36. See the early collection of criticism edited by Lértora in Chile, *Una poética de literatura menor.* Several of the essays included cite reviews of Eltit's work published in Chile in the 1980s. María Inés Lagos, for example, reports that Valente and other Chilean reviewers in the 1980s discussed Eltit's experimental narrative technique but avoided situating her work within its historical condition of publication, the Pinochet dictatorship ("Reflexiones sobre la representación del sujeto en dos textos de Diamela Eltit: *Lumpérica* y *El cuarto mundo,*" in Lértora, *Una poética de literatura menor,* 127–40, 127–28, 139n3).

37. Juan Andres Piña, "Diamela Eltit," in *Conversaciones con la narrativa chilena* (Santiago: Los Andes, 1991), 225–54, 236.

38. Roberto Bolaño, *Historia de la literatura Nazi en América* (Barcelona: Anagrama, 1996).

39. For a good introduction to representative primary and critical sources on the Hispanic *novela neopoliciaca,* see Persephone Braham, *Crimes against the State, Crimes against Persons: Detective Fiction in Cuba and Mexico* (Minneapolis: University of Minnesota Press, 2004), and the review essay by Claire Fox, "La novela neopoliciaca at the Crossroads," *A Contracorriente* 3, no. 1 (Fall 2005): 165–77, http://www.ncsu.edu/project/acontracorriente.

40. José Donoso, *La desesperanza* (Barcelona: Seix Barral, 1986). *La desesperanza* portrays the autobiographical protagonist's first person experience of the stifling climate in Chile under military siege and his confrontation with the broken texture of his Chilean past. Donoso's return to realism appears to be motivated by his focus on the clash between the two Chilean worlds of exile and interior.

41. Diamela Eltit, *Los vigilantes* (Santiago: Sudamericana, 1994) and *Mano de obra* (Santiago: Planeta, 2002). See also Avelar's comparison of *Lumpérica* and *Los vigilantes* in *Untimely Present,* 164–85.

42. Echevarrén, Kozer, and Sefamí, *Medusario.*

43. Sefamí, "El llamado de los deseosos."

44. On the historical sources for the baroque *Trauerspiele,* see Niefanger, "Schlesisches Trauerspiel," in *Barock,* 142–58. Among the royal and noble protagonists of baroque tragedies are Catherine of Georgia, Charles I of England, Maria Stuart, and Cromwell (early modern figures), and the Byzantine emperor Leo, Cleopatra, and the Numidian queen Sophonisbe (late antiquity).

45. Walter Benjamin, *The Arcades Project,* trans. Howard Eiland and Kevin McLaughlin (Cambridge, MA: Belknap Press of Harvard University Press, 1999).

46. See Burkhardt Lindner, "Allegorie," in Opitz and Wizisla, *Benjamins Begriffe,* 1:50–94. My observation is indebted to Lindner's comment on "the highly artificial poetry of Baudelaire in its specific constellation of allegory, melancholy, and commodity" (52).

47. On Benjamin's concept of allegory, see Lindner, "Allegorie"; Steinhagen, "Zu Walter Benjamins Begriff der Allegorie"; Buck-Morss, "Historical Nature: Ruin," in *The Dialectics of Seeing,* 159–201; and Kelley, "Conclusion," in *Reinventing Allegory,* 249–311.

48. Benjamin, "Zentralpark," in *Illuminationen,* 230–50, 238. "Zentralpark" is a selection of excerpts extracted from the *Arcades Project* and published independently.

49. Buck-Morss, *The Dialectics of Seeing,* 217–18.

50. On Benjamin's philosophical allegories, or the *Denkbild,* see Lindner, "Allegorie," 81–94, and Theodor W. Adorno, "Benjamin's Einbahnstrasse," in *Über Walter Benjamin,* ed. Theodor W. Adorno (Frankfurt am Main: Suhrkamp, 1968), 55–61. On the dialectical image, see Buck-Morss and Ansgar Hillach, "Dialektisches Bild," in Opitz and Wizisla, *Benjamins Begriffe,* 1:186–229.

51. On emblems, see the editors' introduction in Henkel and Schöne, *Emblemata: Handbuch zur Sinnbildkunst des XVI. und XVII. Jahrhunderts,* a magisterial handbook of emblems that collects and translates a total of 3,713 emblems from forty-seven emblem books published between Alciati's 1531 *Emblematum liber* and the last specimen published in the eighteenth century. On the emblem in the baroque, see also Schöne, *Emblematik und Drama im Zeitalter des Barock.*

52. Benjamin's conflation of allegory and emblem departs from standard readings in German literary history. Albrecht Schöne gives the following definition of their differences: emblematic icons are "found," whereas allegorical images are "invented," which is

to say emblems begin with the concrete picture, copying their icons from classical sources and thus reinterpreting an inherited stock of images. Allegory, in contrast, begins with an abstract idea, for instance justice, to which a concrete image is added to embody its various attributes. Thus, the female figure with the blindfold, scales, and sword is obviously an artificial image that has been constructed to transmit the meaning of the idea of justice (Schöne, *Emblematik* 261).

53. Lindner suggests that Benjamin wanted to avoid the danger of "reducing the notion of allegory to a formal principle of aesthetic modernity." See Lindner, "Allegorie," 52.

54. Even though I provide the text of the English translation along with the Spanish original, I will refer to main protagonists by their proper names in the Spanish original throughout.

55. Eltit confirms Morales's claim that "the plaza . . . in *Lumpérica* is a neighborhood plaza, not the central square" (Morales, *Conversaciones* 141).

56. On the city as a continuous setting in Eltit's work, see also Amanda Holmes, "Scripting the City," and Gwen Kirkpatrick, "El 'hambre de cuidad' de Diamela Eltit: Forjando un lenguaje del sur," in *Letras y proclamas: La estética literaria de Diamela Eltit,* ed. Bernadita Llanos M. (Santiago: Cuarto Propio, 2006), 33–68.

57. Henri Lefebvre, "The Right to the City," in *Writings on Cities,* ed. and trans. Eleonore Kofman and Elizabeth Lebas (Oxford: Blackwell, 1996), 147–59.

58. Jay, *Downcast Eyes.*

59. Louis Althusser, "Ideology and Ideological State Apparatuses," in *Lenin and Philosophy and Other Essays,* trans. Ben Brewster (New York: Monthly Review Press, 2001), 85–126.

60. See Eltit's comment on her university education in theory in Morales, *Conversaciones con Diamela Eltit,* 89.

61. De Certeau, *The Practice of Everyday Life,* 1:xiv.

62. Schiller, *Iconography of Christian Art,* vol. 2, *The Passion of Jesus Christ,* 198.

63. See Kelemen, *Baroque and Rococo in Latin America,* 1:51.

64. Deleuze and Guattari, *Kafka,* 16.

65. Lértora, "Diamela Eltit," in Lértora, *Una poética de literatura menor,* 27–36.

66. Perlongher, "Caribe transplatino," in *Prosa plebeya,* 93–102, 99. On Perlongher, see note 4 above.

67. Severo Sarduy, *Cobra* and *Maitreya,* trans. Suzanne Jill Levine (Normal, IL: Dalkey Press, 1995).

68. On the use of Lacan in Sarduy's work, see Gallo, "Sarduy avec Lacan."

69. See González Echevarría's work on Sarduy, which repeatedly makes this point: *La ruta de Severo Sarduy,* and "Plain Song: Sarduy's *Cobra,*" in *Celestina's Brood,* 212–37.

70. See González Echevarría, "Plain Song," 235.

71. José Lezama Lima, *Las eras imaginarias* (Madrid: Fundamentos, 1971).

72. Richard, "Tres funciones de escritura: Deconstrucción, simulación, hibridación," in Lértora, *Poética de literatura menor,* 37–51, 45–46.

73. On Lefebvre and the situationists, see Andrew Merrifield, *Henri Lefebvre: A Critical Introduction* (New York: Routledge, 2006), 34ff.

74. See, for example, Richard, "Tres funciones de escritura," 39.

75. Luis Iñigo Madrigal, "Alegoría, historia, novela: A propósito de *Casa de Campo,*" *Hispamérica* 9, nos. 25–26 (1980): 5–31. On this aspect, see also Ricardo Gutiérrez Mouat, *José Donoso, impostura e impostación: La modelización lúdica y carnavalesca de una producción literaria* (Gaithersburg, MD: Ediciones Hispamérica, 1983); Marie Murphy, *Authorizing Fictions: José Donoso's "Casa de Campo"* (London:

Tamesis, 1992); Flora González Mandri, "*Casa de campo:* Chile's History from Opera to Melodrama," in *José Donoso's House of Fiction: A Dramatic Construction of Time and Place* (Detroit, MI: Wayne State University Press, 1995), 86–108; and Irene-Maria von Koerber, *Raumkonfigurationen im Erzaehlwerk von José Donoso* (Geneva: Librairie Droz S.A., 1996).

76. The authorial narrator comments, "In an earlier version of this novel, Wenceslao, Agapito, and Arabela . . . vanished into the plain, heading vaguely for the blue mountains dotting the horizon, never to be seen again" (Donoso, *House* 275).

77. See Carlos Cerda, *José Donoso: Originales y metáforas* (Santiago: Editorial Planeta, 1988), 116.

78. Sigmund Freud, "The Uncanny," in *The Standard Edition of the Complete Psychological Works of Sigmund Freud,* ed. and trans. James Strachey (London: Hogarth Press, 1955), 17:218–52.

79. Benedict Anderson, *Imagined Communities: Reflections on the Origin and Spread of Nationalism* (London: Verso, 1991), 7.

80. Donoso, *Conjeturas sobre la memoria de mi tribu* (Buenos Aires: Alfaguara, 1996), 30.

81. See von Koerber, *Raumkonfigurationen im Erzaehlwerk von José Donoso,* 138–139 and 91–92. Other paintings featured are Nicolas Poussin's two paintings titled *Et in Arcadia Ego* (dated during the 1630s and cited as a frame of reference in a description of the refugee Wenceslao and his friends on the plain; *House* 263) and Antoine Watteau's *Embarkation for Cythera,* which Celeste points out is hanging on the walls of the mansion (*House* 9).

82. See Burbaum, *Kunst-Epochen: Barock,* 13–14.

83. Picón-Salas, "The Baroque of the Indies," 87.

84. Chiampi, "The Baroque at the Twilight of Modernity," 508.

85. Rama, *The Lettered City,* 10.

86. Maravall, *Culture of the Baroque,* 143. (Maravall is here quoting another scholar, Joyce G. Simpson.)

87. On the theater as baroque metaphor, see Egginton, *How the World Became a Stage.*

88. Foucault, *The Order of Things,* 51.

89. Sybille Ebert-Schifferer, "*Trompe l'Oeil:* The Underestimated Trick," in *Deceptions and Illusions: Five Centuries of Trompe l'Oeil Painting,* ed. Sybille Ebert-Schifferer (Washington, DC: National Gallery of Art, 2002), 17–37.

90. Harbison, *Reflections on Baroque,* 24.

91. Ricardo Gutiérrez Mouat, "*Casa de Campo:* la carnevalización del discurso alegórico," in *José Donoso, impostura e impostación,* 197–248, 225. Von Koerber (*Raumkonfigurationen im Erzaehlwerk von José Donoso*) also uses the term *tableaux vivants.*

92. Wölfflin, *Principles of Art History,* 16.

93. Nietzsche, "On Truth and Lie in an Extra-Moral Sense," in *The Portable Nietzsche,* ed. and trans. Walter Kaufmann (Harmondsworth: Penguin, 1959), 42–47, 46–47.

94. See von Koerber, *Raumkonfigurationen im Erzaehlwerk von José Donoso,* 85–86. Murphy places the novel "beyond the nostalgic and epic seriousness of the boom, exemplifying the postmodern pastiche and self-consciousness of the 70s and 80s" (17).

95. Deleuze, *The Fold,* 67.

96. Brian McHale, *Postmodernist Fiction* (London: Methuen, 1987), 9–10.

4. Antidictatorship Neobaroque Cinema

Thanks are due to Eric Ames and James Tweedie for many helpful suggestions, and to Eric Ames for his thoughtful reading of an earlier version of this chapter.

1. No manuscript of *La vida es sueño* survives, and there is considerable variation among early published versions of Calderón's play. To simplify the coordination of the quotation of excerpts in Spanish and English, I cite from the Dover bilingual version of Calderón de la Barca, *La vida es sueño.* Whereas all editions are divided into the standard three acts of the Spanish *comedia,* there is little consistency in further subdivision into scenes, which were added in later editions. Following "the sparse indications in the first edition," the Dover bilingual edition refrains from any formal subdivision of acts into scenes, even in the case of a change of setting (such as from Segismundo's prison-tower to the royal palace) (*La vida es sueño* xviii).

2. See Deborah Shaw, "Representing Inequalities: *The Voyage* by Fernando Solanas and *I, the Worst of All* by María Luisa Bemberg," in *Contemporary Cinema of Latin America: Ten Key Films* (New York: Continuum Press, 2003), 105–41, 120. Sor Juana's birth date is disputed; new research has corrected the year that used to be given, 1651, to 1648. See Paz, *Sor Juana,* 63ff.

3. Benjamin, *The Origin of German Tragic Drama.* On Benjamin's debt to Schmitt, see Witte, *Walter Benjamin,* 58–59, and *Walter Benjamin: Der Intellektuelle as Kritiker,* 130. This controversial relationship is reexamined in Lutz P. Koepnick, "The Spectacle, the *Trauerspiel,* and the Politics of Resolution: Benjamin Reading the Baroque Reading Weimar," *Critical Inquiry* 22, no. 2 (Winter 1996): 268–91.

4. Carl Schmitt, *Political Theology: Four Chapters on the Concept of Sovereignty,* trans. George Schwab (Cambridge, MA: MIT Press, 1985). The German *"Ausnahmezustand,"* literally "exception," refers to what is commonly known as a state of emergency in English. Schwab offers a literal translation to broaden the meaning, arguing that in Schmitt's work, "a state of exception includes any kind of severe economic or political disturbance that requires the application of extraordinary measures. Whereas an exception presupposes a constitutional order that provides guidelines on how to confront crises in order to reestablish order and stability, a state of emergency need not have an existing order as a reference point because *necessitas non habet legem*" (Schmitt 2n1).

5. George Schwab, introduction to *Political Theology,* by Carl Schmitt, xi–xxvi, xxvi.

6. Thomas Hobbes, *Leviathan,* ed. C. B. Macpherson (Harmondsworth: Penguin, 1968), 186.

7. I am setting aside internal differences within absolutist political theory for the sake of this argument. In the "Hobbesian or 'liberal' version of Absolutism" (Cascardi, "Allegories of Power" 22), civil society and government by sovereign authority are based on a social contract: sovereignty is founded on the originary decision *of the subjects* to cede their natural rights of self-government to the sovereign for their own protection. Although Hobbes was a royalist who favored monarchy over democracy, Hobbes's theory undermines the divine right of kings that underpinned the Catholic monarchy of Spain (see Copleston, *A History of Philosophy,* vol. 5, *Modern Philosophy: The British Philosophers,* part I, *Hobbes to Paley,* 40–41).

8. For a cautionary note on Benjamin's equation of absolute rule and tyranny, see Skrine, *The Baroque,* 92.

9. Giorgio Agamben, *Homo Sacer: Sovereign Power and Bare Life,* trans. Daniel Heller-Roazen (1995; Stanford, CA: Stanford University Press, 1998).

10. Benjamin, "The Work of Art in the Age of Mechanical Reproduction," in *Illuminations,* 217–51, 242.

11. Maravall, *Culture of the Baroque;* Hauser, *The Social History of Art,* vol. 2, *Renaissance, Mannerism, Baroque* (hereafter Hauser, *Renaissance, Mannerism, Baroque*).

12. See Hauser, *Renaissance, Mannerism, Baroque,* 172ff.; Jay, *Downcast Eyes,* 45ff.; Mumford, "The Baroque City"; Skrine, "All the World's a Stage," in *The Baroque,* 1–24; Norman, *The Theatrical Baroque.*

13. The metaphor of world as stage (*theatrum mundi*) originated in pagan antiquity and Christian writers, who mingled in late antiquity before they reached medieval Europe. "The profound thought, which Plato once threw out . . . undergoes a brilliant rebirth in seventeenth-century Catholic Spain" (Ernst Robert Curtius, *European Literature and the Latin Middle Ages,* trans. Willard R. Trask [Princeton, NJ: Princeton University Press, 1963], 142).

14. See Toman, "Setting the Stage for the Sun King," in *Baroque,* 138–39, 139.

15. See Norberg-Schulz, *Baroque Architecture,* 26–27 and 62ff.

16. See Iain Boyd White, "National Socialism and Modernism: Architecture," in *Art and Power: Europe under the Dictators, 1930–45,* ed. Dawn Ades (London: Thames and Hudson, 1995), 258–69. Speer's master plan for Berlin, with its giant north-south and east-west axes, may be viewed as a reprise of Pope Pius V's plan for Rome: in each case, the hierarchical centralization of the city symbolized the unifying power of the state.

17. Zuzana M. Pick, "An Interview with María Luisa Bemberg," *Journal of Film and Video* 44, nos. 3–4 (1992–93): 76–82, 80.

18. The text in question is a note in the Hieronymite Convent's Book of Professions. See "A todas pido perdón por amor de Dios y de su Madre. Yo, la peor del mundo. Juana Inés de la Cruz" (Sor Juana, "Documentos en el libro de profesiones del Convento de San Jerónimo," in Sor Juana, *Obras completas,* ed. Monterde, 1026–27, 1027). Compare also Paz's translation and discussion of this note, "Of them I ask forgiveness, for the love of God and his Mother. I, the worst of all the world, Juana Inés de la Cruz" (*Sor Juana* 464–65).

19. Sor Juana, *Obras completas,* ed. Méndez Plancarte, 4 vols. (1951–57). To facilitate the coordination of Spanish and English versions, quotations from Sor Juana's work are taken from Trueblood, *A Sor Juana Anthology.* My numbering of the poems also follows Trueblood's example.

20. Alicia Gaspar de Alba, *Sor Juana's Second Dream* (Albuquerque: University of New Mexico Press, 1999); Paul Anderson, *Hunger's Brides: A Novel of the Baroque* (New York: Carroll & Graf, 2004).

21. Merrim's collection, *Feminist Perspectives on Sor Juana Inés de la Cruz,* gathers twentieth-century Latin American feminist approaches to Sor Juana in translation. The proceedings of the international congress held in Mexico City (at the Universidad del Claustro de Sor Juana, which now occupies the space of Sor Juana's former convent) on the occasion of the tercentenary of Sor Juana's death on 1995 include several important new essays. See López-Portillo, *Sor Juana y su mundo.* See also Bergmann and Schlau, *Approaches to Teaching the Works of Sor Juana Inés de la Cruz.*

In addition to Gaspar de Alba's novel, works by U.S. Chicana writers and artists include Jovita González's short story, "Shades of the Tenth Muses" (c. 1930), which stages an encounter between two seventeenth-century women poets, Sor Juana and Ann Bradstreet, also celebrated as the Tenth Muse in her time, in *The Woman Who Lost Her Soul and Other Stories,* ed. Sergio Reyna (Houston: Arte Público, 2000), 108–15; Estela Portillo Trambley's play *Sor Juana* (written in the late 1970s), in *Sor Juana and Other*

Plays (Tempe, AZ: Bilingual Press, 1983), 143–95; María de los Angeles Romero's recent multimedia play *Sueño de un caracol,* written and performed by Angeles Romero, directed by Johannes Birringer and Jennifer Schlueter (Espiral Productions, 2nd ed., 2006), CD-ROM, www.angelesromero.com.

22. See Rama, *The Lettered City.* For a discussion of the *letrado* as "the organic intellectual of Hapsburg imperialism," tied to a polemic against the institution of literature for its roots in the baroque state-sponsored conservative arts, see Beverley, "On the Spanish Literary Baroque."

23. Chiampi, "The Baroque at the Twilight of Modernity," 524–25.

24. See Maravall, "A Guided Culture," in *Culture of the Baroque,* 57–78.

25. Cascardi, "The Subject of Control," 240.

26. Wölfflin, *Principles of Art History,* 20.

27. Elizabeth Jelin, *State Repression and the Labors of Memory,* trans. Judy Rein and Marcial Godoy-Anativia (Minneapolis: University of Minnesota Press, 2003). While the main focus of Jelin's study is on the Southern Cone, she also draws on examples from the Jewish Holocaust, Japan, and the Spanish Civil War.

28. Stern's project is a trilogy of studies on how Chileans remember September 11, 1973, and its aftermath, including *Remembering Pinochet's Chile: On the Eve of London, 1998* (Durham, NC: Duke University Press, 2004) and *Battling for Hearts and Minds: Memory Struggles in Pinochet's Chile, 1973–1988* (Durham, NC: Duke University Press, 2006).

29. For a concise statement of Pierre Nora's ideas inspiring his multivolume research project on modern memory, see "Between Memory and History: *Les Lieux de Mémoire,*" in *History and Memory in African-American Culture,* ed. Geneviève Fabre and Robert O'Meally (New York: Oxford University Press, 1994), 284–300, 284.

30. Adrian Martin, "Never One Space: An Interview with Raúl Ruiz," *Cinema Papers* 91 (January 1993): 30–62, 61. See also Lesley Stern, "Life Is a Dream: Written on the Wind," in *The Scorsese Connection* (Bloomington: Indiana University Press, 1995), 161–66, 162.

31. Frances Yates, *The Art of Memory* (Chicago: University of Chicago Press, 1966).

32. John King, *Magical Reels: A History of Cinema in Latin America,* 2nd ed. (London: Verso, 2000), 181.

33. I quote Ruiz's English subtitles throughout, though lamentably they are frequently rough and unidiomatic.

34. Alice Craven makes this point in "Literary History Is a Dream; or, How I Stopped Worrying and Learned to Love Film," *Discours Social/Social Discourse* 2, no.4 (Winter 1989): 161–74, 171.

35. My discussion of cinematic techniques and differences between the styles of classic Hollywood and other cinemas (such as Soviet montage cinema and the French New Wave) throughout this essay is informed by David Bordwell and Kristin Thompson, *Film Art: An Introduction,* 5th ed. (New York: McGraw-Hill, 1997); David Bordwell, *Narration in the Fiction Film* (Madison: University of Wisconsin Press, 1985); and Louis D. Giannetti, *Understanding Movies* (Englewood Cliffs, NJ: Prentice-Hall, 1976).

36. The best history of Latin American cinema is King, *Magical Reels.* Directors' manifestos by Solanas, Glauber Rocha, Birri, and Tomás Gutiérrez Alea and analyses of the New Latin American cinema are collected in Michael T. Martin, ed., *New Latin American Cinema,* vol. 1, *Theory, Practices and Transcontinental Articulations,* vol. 2, *Studies of National Cinemas* (Detroit, MI: Wayne State University Press, 1997). See also Zuzana M. Pick, "The Dialectical Wanderings of Exile," *Screen* 30, no. 4 (Autumn 1989):

48–64; John King and Nissa Torrents, eds., *The Garden of Forking Paths: Argentine Cinema* (London: British Film Institute, 1988); and David William Foster, *Contemporary Argentine Cinema* (Columbia: University of Missouri Press, 1992).

37. Ana M. López, "An 'Other' History: The New Latin American Cinema," in Martin, *New Latin American Cinema,* 1:135–56, 150.

38. Adrian Martin, "The Artificial Night: Surrealism and Cinema," in *Surrealism: Revolution by Night* (Canberra: National Gallery of Australia, 1993), 190–95, 191. See also Laleen Jayamanne, "Life Is a Dream." The critical literature on Ruiz is small but expanding. One recent collection I reference frequently is Bandis, Martin, and McDonald, *Raúl Ruiz.*

39. Susan Hayward, *Cinema Studies: The Key Concepts* (London: Routledge, 2006), 480.

40. Zuzana M. Pick, "Chilean Cinema in Exile, 1973–1986," in Martin, *New Latin American Cinema,* 2:423–42, 437; Adrian Martin, "Displacements," in Bandis, Martin, and McDonald, *Raúl Ruiz,* 45–53, 45.

41. Waldo Rojas, "Images of Passage," in Bandis, Martin, and McDonald, *Raúl Ruiz,* 7–14, 13.

42. Laleen Jayamanne, "'Life Is a Dream': Raúl Ruiz Was a Surrealist in Sydney; A Capillary Memory of a Cultural Event," in *Kiss Me Deadly: Feminism and Cinema for the Moment,* ed. Laleen Jayamanne (Sydney: Power Institute of Fine Arts, 1995), 221–51, 221.

43. See Benoît Peters, "Annihilating the Script: A Discussion with Raúl Ruiz," in Bandis, Martin, and McDonald, *Raúl Ruiz,* 15–30, 20.

44. Ruiz, *Poetics of Cinema 1* and *Poetics of Cinema 2.* The key document is *Poetics of Cinema 1,* which is a programmatic exposition of Ruiz's cinematic style and principles. *Poetics of Cinema 2* revisits and clarifies these principles.

45. See Bordwell, "Classical Narration: The Hollywood Example," in *Narration in the Fiction Film,* 156–204, 157.

46. Tom Gunning, "The Cinema of Attractions: Early Film, Its Spectator and the Avant-Garde," in *Early Cinema: Space, Frame, Narrative,* ed. Tomas Elsaesser and Adam Barker (London: British Film Institute, 1990), 56–62.

47. See David Bordwell, Janet Staiger, and Kristin Thompson, *The Classical Hollywood Cinema: Film Style & Mode of Production to 1960* (New York: Columbia University Press, 1985). For an alternative approach to Hollywood cinema that restores its historicity, see Miriam Bratu Hansen, "The Mass Production of the Senses: Classical Cinema as Vernacular Modernism," in *Reinventing Film Studies,* ed. Christine Gledhill and Linda Williams (New York: Oxford University Press, 2000), 332–50.

48. On baroque lighting and the vogue of tenebrism (extreme chiaroscuro) following Caravaggio, see Martin, *Baroque,* 223–47.

49. On Buci-Glucksmann, see Jay, *Downcast Eyes,* 47–48, and "Scopic Regimes of Modernity."

50. Maurice Merleau-Ponty, "Eye and Mind" (1961), in *The Primacy of Perception and Other Essays on Phenomenological Psychology, the Philosophy of Art, History and Politics,* ed. James M. Edie (Evanston, IL: Northwestern University Press, 1964), 159–90; *The Visible and the Invisible,* ed. Claude Lefort, trans. Alphonso Lingis (1964; Evanston: Northwestern University Press, 1968). See also de Certeau, "The Madness of Vision."

51. Buci-Glucksmann, "The Work of the Gaze," 145.

52. Christine Buci-Glucksmann, *Raoul Ruiz* (Paris: Dis Voir, 1987) and *Conversaciones con Raúl Ruiz,* ed. Christine Buci-Glucksmann and Eduardo Sabrovsky (Santiago:

Universidad Diego Portales, 2003). An abbreviated version of the first section of *Raoul Ruiz* is available in English: Buci-Glucksmann, "The Baroque Eye of the Camera," in Bandis, Martin, and McDonald, *Raúl Ruiz,* 31–44.

53. Sarduy, "The Baroque and the Neobaroque," 281.

54. Adrian Martin, "Raúl Ruiz' Magnificent Obsessions," chap. 12 of "Towards A Synthetic Analysis of Film Style," PhD diss., Monash University, Australia, 2006, 342–388, 348.

55. Lezama Lima, *La expresión americana,* 49.

56. See Mircea Eliade, *Shamanism: Archaic Techniques of Ecstasy,* trans. Willard R. Trask (Princeton, NJ: Princeton University Press, 1972).

57. Deleuze, *The Fold,* 68.

58. See, for example, Tweedie, "Caliban's Books" and "The Suspended Spectacle of History," and Gruzinski, "From the Baroque to the Neo-Baroque." Timothy Murray's *Digital Baroque* combines the study of the baroque in directors such as Greenaway with an investigation of digital media as baroque form.

59. Ndalianis, *Neo-Baroque Aesthetics and Contemporary Entertainment.*

60. See, for example, Deborah Cartmell and Imelda Whelehan, eds., *The Cambridge Companion to Literature on Screen* (Cambridge: Cambridge University Press, 2007).

61. On Renaissance artificial perspective, see Alberto Pérez-Gómez and Louise Pelletier, *Architectural Representation and the Perspective Hinge* (Cambridge, MA: MIT Press, 1997), 18–29. See also Martin Jay's helpful summary of the Albertian notion of the transparent window into space in *Downcast Eyes,* 54ff.

62. Deep focus photography was made possible through the invention of a new lens. Prior to this time, most lenses could photograph only one plane in focus, making other planes in the foreground or background blurred (Bordwell and Thompson, *Film Art* 220–21).

63. Anthony J. Cascardi, "Allegories of Power," 23.

64. Vega's love interest, a member of the Chilean group that assassinates him, is played by the actress also cast as Calderón's Rosaura. Her name is Bonitas, but at times she is also called Rosaura. This multiple casting of actors in the different subplots of Ruiz's film—Bonitas-Rosaura is not the only instance—intensifies the intertextuality between Calderón's play and the contemporary Chilean conspiracy.

65. See Braider, *Baroque Self-Invention and Historical Truth,* 8.

66. There is a growing body of critical literature on Bemberg, as well as on *Yo, la peor de todas,* as attested by a recent book-length study: King, Whitaker, and Bosch, *An Argentine Passion.*

67. On *Camila,* see Alan Pauls, "On *Camila:* The Red, the Black, and the White," in King, Whitaker, and Bosch, *An Argentine Passion,* 110–21, and Claire Taylor, "María Luisa Bemberg Winks at the Audience: Performativity and Citation in *Camila* and *Yo, la peor de todas,*" in *Latin American Cinema: Essays on Modernity, Gender and National Identity,* ed. Lisa Shaw and Stephanie Dennison (Jefferson, NC: McFarland, 2005), 110–24.

68. John King, "María Luisa Bemberg and Argentine Culture," in King, Whitaker, and Bosch, *An Argentine Passion,* 1–32, 23.

69. Sheila Whitaker, "Interview with María Luisa Bemberg," in King and Torrents, *The Garden of Forking Paths,* 115–21, 116. Bemberg adds, the "colonel said that he would rather have a son who had cancer than one who was homosexual, so I couldn't do it."

70. Bemberg cofounded her own production company, GEA Cinematográfica, with producer Lita Stantic, who produced her first five feature films (King, "María Luisa Bemberg" 20).

71. According to King, the critical self-reflection on state terror in Argentine cinema came to an end in the early 1990s. Amnesty and other laws halting ongoing prosecutions of military human rights abuses were passed in the late 1980s and early 1990s to allay threats of new military coups. As in the new, fragile democracy in Chile of the early 1990s, in Argentina amnesia and amnesty began to prevail as a political necessity (King, *Magical Reels* 265–67).

72. Denise Miller, "María Luisa Bemberg's Interpretation of Octavio Paz' *Sor Juana,*" in King, Whitaker, and Bosch, *An Argentine Passion,* 137–73, 140. See also Nina M. Scott, "Sor Juana and Her World," *Latin American Research Review* 29, no. 1 (1994): 143–54, 152.

73. Bemberg's allegory of contemporary Latin American totalitarianism in *Yo, la peor de todas* has been noted by several critics. For example: "Bemberg makes a generalized historical link between the values of Sor Juana's society and and 20th-century fascism and totalitarianism, so relevant to Argentina's recent history" (Shaw, "Representing Inequalities" 127).

74. Brewster and Jacobs, *Theatre to Cinema,* 38.

75. See Nina M. Scott, "Sor Juana Inés de la Cruz: Three Hundred Years of Controversy and Counting," in Bergmann and Schlau, *Approaches to Teaching the Works of Sor Juana Inés de la Cruz,* 193–200, 200. See also Paz's discussion of the intrigue that won Aguiar y Seijas the office of archbishop over his rival, the Bishop of Puebla (*Sor Juana* 400–03).

76. Ruiz mentions the *tableau vivant* in *Poetics of Cinema 1,* in the context of a discussion of another of his neobaroque films, *L'Hypothèse du tableau volé* (1978; *Hypothesis of the Stolen Painting*), which is based on this popular nineteenth-century entertainment form, which flourished on an off-theater stage (*Poetics 1* 51ff.). For Ruiz, the reincarnating impulse underlying the *tableau vivant* signals an excess of verisimilitude that "can distort an original work" and engender the hyperrealist baroque (44). See also Tweedie's discussion of Derek Jarman's use of the *tableau vivant* in *Caravaggio* in "The Suspended Spectacle of History."

77. Lita Stantic, Jorge Goldenberg, Félix Monti, et al., "Working with María Luisa Bemberg," in King, Whitaker, and Bosch, *An Argentine Passion,* 33–72, 48.

78. See Karin Hellwig, "Painting in Italy, Spain, and France in the Seventeenth Century," in Toman, *Baroque,* 372–427, 413.

79. Bal, *Quoting Caravaggio.*

80. Bemberg changes the chronology of the first edition of Sor Juana's works, overseen by Sor Juana's aristocratic friend María Luisa Manrique de Lara y Gonzaga, Countess de Paredes and Marquise de la Laguna. The first volume was published in 1689, the second in 1692 (see Paz, *Sor Juana* 509). Bemberg has the first volume appear in the year of the Marquis de la Laguna's death, 1692, likely for reasons of economy, as she has compressed several other events during Sor Juana's final years.

81. Joseph J. Rishel and Suzanne L. Stratton, eds., *The Arts in Latin America, 1482–1820* (Philadelphia: Philadelphia Museum of Art, 2006), 385.

82. See Paz's comments on this poem (*Sor Juana* 221). As critics have noted, romance 48 is "related to *Primero Sueño* (*First Dream*), in which Sor Juana defines the soul as a non-gendered, neutral entity who seeks the paths to knowledge" (Rocío Quispe-Agnoli, "'Guileful Deception of Sense': Semantic Fields and Sor Juana's Baroque Poetry," in Bergmann and Schlau, *Approaches to Teaching the Works of Sor Juana Inés de la Cruz,* 119–26, 126).

83. On differences between the iconography of the Roman baroque and that of Northern Europe, see Jay, "Scopic Regimes of Modernity," 184–86, and *Downcast Eyes,*

60ff.; and Alpers, *The Art of Describing*. Compositions of the Dutch baroque, according to Alpers, deemphasize linear perspective's illusionist abilities to suggest deep, even limitless, space.

84. Kira van Lil, "Painting in the Netherlands, Germany, and England in the Seventeenth Century," in Toman, *Baroque,* 430–80, 463, 462.

85. There is no contemporary biography of Sor Juana. Calleja's narrative was published as a preface to the third volume of her works, which appeared in 1700.

86. See Paz, *Sor Juana,* 503ff.; Stephanie Merrim, "Toward a Feminist Reading of Sor Juana Inés de la Cruz: Past, Present, and Future Directions in Sor Juana Criticism," in Stephanie Merrim, *Feminist Perspectives on Sor Juana Inés de la Cruz,* 11–37; and Schons, "Some Obscure Points in the Life of Sor Juana Inés de la Cruz" and "Some Bibliographical Notes on Sor Juana Inés de la Cruz."

87. Childers, "The Baroque Public Sphere," 166.

88. See Emilie Bergmann, "Abjection and Ambiguity: Lesbian Desire in Bemberg's *Yo, la peor de todas,*" in *Hispanisms and Homosexualities,* ed. Sylvia Molloy and Robert McKee Irwin (Durham, NC: Duke University Press, 1998), 229–47; Bruce Williams, "A Mirror of Desire: Looking Lesbian in María Luisa Bemberg's *I, the Worst of All,*" *Quarterly Review of Film and Video* 19, no. 2 (2002): 133–43; and María Claudia André, "Empowering the Feminine/Feminist/Lesbian Subject through the Lens: The Representation of Women in María Luisa Bemberg's *Yo, la peor de todas,*" in *Tortilleras: Hispanic and U.S. Latina Lesbian Expression,* ed. Lourdes Torres and Inmaculada Pertusa (Philadelphia: Temple University Press, 2003), 159–75.

89. Poor women without means such as Sor Juana could not enter a convent without a rich sponsor who would pay their dowries (Paz, *Sor Juana* 118). The life of the poor in New Spain, as well as of mestizo and indigenous ethnic groups, is outside the purview of *Yo, la peor de todas.*

90. Scott's "Sor Juana Inés de la Cruz: Three Hundred Years of Controversy and Counting" summarizes the research of Elías Trabulse and Teresa Castelló de Yturbide. See Elías Trabulse, "Los años finales de Sor Juana: Una interpretación (1688–1695)," in López-Portillo, *Sor Juana y su mundo,* 25–33.

5. Hemispheric Genealogies of the New World Baroque

1. Carlos Fuentes, *La frontera de cristal* (Mexico City: Alfaguara, 1995); *The Crystal Frontier,* trans. Alfred MacAdam (New York: Harcourt Brace, 1997).

2. Ybarra-Frausto, "*Rasquachismo:* A Chicano Sensibility"; Monsivaís, "The Neobaroque and Popular Culture" (first published in 1994 as "Neobarroco y cultura popular," in Echeverría, *Modernidad, mestizaje cultural, ethos barroco,* 299–309).

3. Bosch, *Cuban-American Art in Miami,* 164.

4. Salgado, "Hybridity in New World Baroque Theory," 324. Lois Parkinson Zamora observes, "So we arrive at one of the few satisfying ironies of the Spanish colonization of Latin America: the form most associated with the cultural repression of the monological Spanish Counter-Reformation in Latin America—the Baroque—provides the very structure with which to subvert that expression" ("Magical Ruins/Magical Realism" 81).

5. Clifford, "Traveling Cultures," in *Routes,* 17–39.

6. See Corrin, *Going for Baroque* (1995); Bal, *Quoting Caravaggio* (1999); Giovannotti and Krokotkin, *Neo-Baroque!* (2006); Wacker, *Baroque Tendencies in Contemporary Art* (2007); and Martineau et al., *Peculiar Culture* (2009).

7. Iving Lavin, "Why Baroque," in Corrin, *Going for Baroque,* 5–8, 7, 8.

8. De Campos, "Anthropophagous Reason," 159.

9. Carpentier, "The Baroque and the Marvelous Real," 100.

10. Armstrong and Zamudio-Taylor, *Ultrabaroque.* On twentieth-century neobaroque in Latin America, see also the exhibition catalog *El Corazón Sangrante/The Bleeding Heart* (1991), edited by Oliver Debroise, Elizabeth Sussman, and Matthew Teitelbaum, which focuses on the "appeal of the bleeding heart" in colonial and contemporary Mexican art, a mestizo symbol nourished both by Catholic and pre-Columbian cultures, and which stunningly documents its ongoing ubiquity in contemporary (and especially gay) neobaroque Mexican art (*Corazón* 7); Bailey, "Epilogue," in *Art of Colonial Latin America,* 375–411; Sillevis, *The Baroque World of Fernando Botero.*

11. Elizabeth Armstrong, "Impure Beauty," in Armstrong and Zamudio-Taylor, *Ultrabaroque,* 1–18, 15, 3.

12. Torres, "Cathedrals on Wheels," 26.

13. Original publication dates are: Guido, *Redescubrimiento de América en el arte* (1940); Toussaint, *Colonial Art in Mexico* (1948); Kelemen, *Baroque and Rococo in Latin America* (1951); Kubler and Soria, *Art and Architecture in Spain and Portugal and Their American Dominions, 1500–1800* (1959). Bolivian scholars Gisbert's and Mesa's first contributions on the Andean mestizo baroque were published in the fifties; among their numerous essays and books see Gisbert, *Iconografía y mitos indígenas en le arte,* and Gisbert and Mesa, *Arquitectura Andina: 1530–1830.* See also Kelemen and de Sandoval, *Folk Baroque in Mexico;* Mather, *Baroque to Folk;* and Sebastián, *El barroco iberoamericano.*

14. Bottineau, *Iberian-American Baroque,* 85.

15. See Bottineau, *Iberian-American Baroque,* 87–88; Kelemen, *Baroque and Rococo in Latin America,* 1:88–89.

16. See, for example, Bill Ashcroft, Gareth Griffiths, and Helen Tiffin, *The Empire Writes Back: Theory and Practice in Post-Colonial Literatures* (London: Routledge, 1989).

17. See Glissant, *Caribbean Discourse* and *Poetics of Relation;* de Campos, "Anthropophagous Reason." On Caribbean neobaroque writers such as Carpentier and Glissant, see Chancé, *Poétique baroque de la Caraïbe.*

18. See Deleuze and Guattari, *Kafka;* Deleuze and Guattari, "November 20, 1923: Postulates of Linguistics," in *A Thousand Plateaus,* 75–110. On the New World baroque, see also Egginton, "The Corporeal Baroque and the New World Baroque," and Moraña, "Baroque/Neobaroque/Ultrabaroque."

19. Ronald Bogue, "The Minor," in *Gilles Deleuze: Key Concepts,* ed. Charles J. Stivale (Chesham, UK: Acumen, 2005), 110–20, 113.

20. See Laclau, *Politics and Ideology in Marxist Theory;* Hall, "Race, Articulation and Societies Structured in Dominance" and "On Postmodernism and Articulation."

21. González Echevarría, *Celestina's Brood,* 198.

22. See the collection of Carpentier essays *Tientos y diferencias* (1964), in *Obras completas,* vol. 13, *Ensayos* (Mexico City: Siglo Veintiuno, 1990), 11–127, and English translations "The City of Columns" and an excerpt from "Questions Concerning the Contemporary Latin American Novel."

23. See especially "Sierpe de Don Luis de Góngora" (The serpent of Don Luis de Góngora), in Lezama Lima, *Esferaimagen.*

24. Lezama Lima, "Baroque Curiosity," 213.

25. *Encyclopedia Britannica Online,* s.v. "James Hutton." Without naming sources, Irlemar Chiampi points in this general direction by referring to "the Plutonic as the igneous magma from which the earth's crust is formed" (Chiampi, "The Baroque at the Twilight of Modernity" 512).

26. Lezama Lima, *La expresión americana,* 57.

27. My discussion of Lezama Lima's poetic theory is informed by Bejel, *José Lezama Lima,* and González Echevarría, "Apetitos de Góngora y Lezama."

28. Lezama Lima, "Image of Latin America," 326.

29. Walter Mignolo, *The Idea of Latin America* (Oxford: Blackwell, 2005), 62.

30. Paz, *Sor Juana,* 380.

31. Johnson, *Hyperboles,* 145.

32. Aleijadinho is a Brazilian national hero. A symptom of this status, he is singled out as the only Brazilian baroque artist to whom a section as an individual artist is dedicated in the 2001 catalog of the exhibition, *Brazil: Body and Soul,* ed. Sullivan, 238–53.

33. Cañizares-Esguerra, *How to Write the History of the New World,* 9, 320.

34. Kelemen, *Baroque and Rococo in Latin America,* 1:190. George Kubler and Martin Soria call San Lorenzo "the masterpiece of the Potosí style" (*Art and Architecture* 97).

35. Kelemen writes that the section of Potosí where San Lorenzo is located has "always been an Indian quarter, and there can be little doubt that the carver was a mestizo if not an Indian" (Kelemen 1:191). Most sources identify Kondorí as a Quechua Indian; Bailey cautions that the architect of San Lorenzo cannot be named with certainty because of lack of documentation (*Andean Hybrid Baroque* 281).

36. Guido, *Redescubrimiento de América en el arte* (1940). I quote from a published translation of Guido's first chapter, "America's Relation to Europe in the Arts," and an unpublished translation of the fourth chapter, "El espíritu de la emancipación en dos artistas americanos" (121–47; The spirit of emancipation in two American artists) by Anke Birkenmaier. Bailey documents how Guido's pioneering insights into the mestizo syncretism of the Andean baroque were later buried due to a scholarly schism over the nature and interpretation of that syncretism (*Andean Hybrid Baroque* 15–44).

37. *Encyclopedia Britannica Online,* s.v. "Caryatid." The most celebrated example of the caryatid is "the caryatid porch of the Erechtheum with six figures (421–405 B.C.), on the Acropolis of Athens."

38. Very few critics mention, even in passing, the link between Lezama Lima's thesis of the *arte de contraconquista* and Guido's thesis of the baroque as a *reconquista de América en el arte.* See Pauly, *Neobarroco,* 95, and Gimbernat de González, "La curiosidad barroca." Another essay that mentions Guido (but without the Lezama Lima connection) is Morales Benítez, "El mestizo y el barroco."

39. See Guillermo Bonfil Batalla, *México Profundo: Reclaiming a Civilization,* trans. Philip A. Dennis (Austin: University of Texas Press, 1996), 108–28; Alan Knight, "Racism, Revolution, and *Indigenismo, 1880–1930,*" in *The Idea of Race in Latin America, 1870–1940,* ed. Richard Graham (Austin: University of Texas Press, 1990), 71–113; and Joshua Lund, *The Impure Imagination: Toward a Critical Hybridity in Latin American Writing* (Minneapolis: University of Minnesota Press, 2006). The term "anti-racist counter-orthodoxies" is Lund's.

40. Aníbal Quijano, "Colonialidad del poder, cultura y conocimiento en América Latina," *Anuario Mariateguiano* 9, no. 9 (1997): 113–21; Dussel, "World-System and 'Trans'-Modernity"; Mignolo, *The Idea of Latin America.* Quijano, in fact, proposes a spiraling historical schema much like Guido's, linking the sixteenth and nineteenth centuries as periods (re)imposing what he calls the "coloniality of power," and the seventeenth and twentieth centuries as periods of subversion. Like Guido, he mentions Aleijadinho and Kondori as twin agents of anticolonial cultural subversion. Did Quijano read Guido, and is his well-known essay another reincarnation of the neobaroque genealogy of Latin American modernity?

41. Fuentes, *The Buried Mirror,* 146–47.

42. Harbison, *Reflections on Baroque,* 172.

43. I thank Lois Parkinson Zamora for her help with researching and interpreting this image.

44. Rubial García, *Santa María Tonantzintla,* 72.

45. On the Ocotelulco murals in Tlaxcala, see José Eduardo Contreras Martínez, "Los murales y cerámica policromos de la zona arqueológica de Ocotelulco," in *Mixteca-Puebla: Discoveries and Research in Mesoamerican Art and Archaeology,* ed. H. B. Nicholson and Eloise Quiñones Keber (Culver City, CA: Labyrinthos, 1994), 7–24.

46. See Gruzinski, "The Admirable Effects of the Baroque Image," 152–59.

47. On Guadalupe, see Lafaye, *Quetzalcoatl and Guadalupe,* and Gruzinski, "The Admirable Effects of the Baroque Image."

48. Echeverría, *La modernidad de lo barroco.*

49. This is particularly the case for Picón-Salas, "The Baroque of the Indies." For more recent assessments of the *barroco de Indias,* see Moraña, *Viaje al silencio, Relecturas del barroco de Indias,* and "The Baroque and Transculturation."

50. On these parallels, see González Echevarría, "Guillén as Baroque: Meaning in *Motivos de son,*" in *Celestina's Brood,* 194–211.

51. Lafaye here translates an observation by Robert Ricard.

52. See the beautiful exhibition catalog *Arte y estilo,* edited by Denise Sandoval and Patrick A. Polk, which features *Midnight Illusions* but not *El Maldito.* The Petersen's second exhibition, *La Vida Lowrider: Cruising the City of Angels,* took place from October 2007 to June 2008.

53. See James Sterngold, "Making the Jalopy an Ethnic Banner," *New York Times,* February 19, 2000, B9–11, B9. The Smithsonian's Virtual Exhibition is titled *Lowrider: An American Cultural Tradition* and can be accessed at http://latino.si.edu/virtualgallery/Lowrider/Lowrider.htm.

54. Luis F. B. Plascencia, "Low Riding in the Southwest: Cultural Symbols in the Mexican Community," in *History, Culture, and Society: Chicano Studies in the 1980s,* ed. Mario T. García, Francisco Lomelí, Mario Barrera et al. (Ypsilanti, MI: Bilingual Press, 1983), 141–75.

55. Important studies that employ the theory of internal colonialism are Rodolfo Acuña, *Occupied America: The Chicano's Struggle toward Liberation* (San Francisco, CA: Canfield Press, 1972). and Mario Barrera, *Race and Class in the Southwest: A Theory of Racial Inequality* (Notre Dame, IN: University of Notre Dame Press, 1979). For an assessment of internal colonialism from its highest popularity during the Chicano movement to its subsequent critique and effective abandonment "for more accommodationist politics and ideas" in the 1980s, see Ramón A. Gutiérrez, "Internal Colonialism: An American Theory of Race," *Du Bois Review* 1, no. 2 (2004): 281–95, 281.

56. Samuel Huntington, "Mexican Immigration and Hispanization," in *Who Are We? The Challenges to America's National Identity* (New York: Simon & Schuster, 2004), 221–56.

57. Michael Stone, "*Bajito y suavecito:* Low Riding and the 'Class' of Class," *Studies in Latin American Popular Culture* 9 (1990): 85–126.

58. Wayne King, "Low Riders Are Becoming Legion among Chicanos," *New York Times,* May 9, 1981, 8.

59. Jean Baudrillard, *America,* trans. Chris Turner (London: Verso, 1988), 9.

60. Quoted in Brenda Jo Bright, "Remappings: Los Angeles Lowriders," in *Looking High and Low: Art and Cultural Identity* (Tucson: University of Arizona Press, 1985),

87–123, 99. For memories of the "golden age" of lowrider cruising, see also Sandoval and Polk, *Arte y estilo,* 21.

61. See also Plascencia, "Low Riding in the Southwest," 155ff.

62. Bill Gradante, "Art among the Lowriders," in *Folk Art in Texas,* ed. Francis Edward Abernethy (Dallas: Southern Methodist University Press, 1985), 71–77, 76.

63. See Mike Apan, "Lowriders: They've Shifted from Old Cars to Customized Trucks," *Los Angeles Times,* October 20, 1986, A1, A3.

64. Dick DeLoach, "What Is Lowriding?," in Sandoval and Polk, *Arte y estilo,* 12–15, 14.

65. See C. Ondine Chavoya, "Customized Hybrids: The Art of Rubén Ortiz Torres and Lowriding in Southern California," *CR: The New Centennial Review* 4, no. 2 (Fall 2004): 141–84. This judgment reflects the critical consensus: "The lowrider look, originally superimposed (in the fifties) on domestically manufactured cars like Chevys and Fords, represents the hybridization of a principal icon of the American Dream. . . . The fact that lowriders originated as American cars (now almost collector's items) affirms the 'native' nature of the lowriding experience. Indeed, lowriders are 'born and [made] in the U.S.A.'" (Alicia Gaspar de Alba, *Chicano Art Inside/Outside the Master's House: Cultural Politics and the CARA Exhibition* [Austin: University of Texas Press, 1998], 60).

66. Rubén Ortiz Torres, "For the Record: Rants about Art and Culture across Borders in a Post Colonial Era," http://rubenortiztorres.org/for_the_record/.

67. Hip-hop artists have recently begun to feature lowrider vehicles in their music videos.

68. See Stuart Cosgrove, "The Zoot Suit and Style Warfare," in *Zoot Suits and Second-Hand Dresses: An Anthology of Fashion and Music,* ed. Angela McRobbie (Basingstoke: Macmillan, 1989), 3–22. Plascencia and other critics note that *Lowrider Magazine* has played a significant part in keeping the memory of pachuco styles alive among lowriders. "*Lowrider* reinforced the linkage between the pachuco and lowriding primarily through three forms: the development of a section in the magazine titled 'Lowriders Pasados' (Old Lowriders); the extensive usage of pachuco dialect or *caló* throughout the magazine; and the interchangeable use of the terms 'pachuco' and 'lowrider' in the magazine" (Plascencia 148).

69. See Denise Sandoval, "Bajito y suavecito: The Lowriding Tradition," http://latino.si.edu/virtualgallery/Lowrider/LR_SandovalEssay.htm, 1–49, 4.

70. Jack Parsons, Carmella Padilla, and Juan Estevan Arellano, *Low 'n Slow: Lowriding in New Mexico* (Santa Fe: Museum of New Mexico Press, 1999), 27. *The Dictionary of Chicano Spanish,* ed. Roberto A. Galván, 2nd ed. (Chicago: National Textbook Company, 1995), s.v. "'Ramfla' (slang) jalopy, old battered-up car."

71. On the history of *Dave's Dream,* see Brenda Jo Bright, "'Heart Like a Car': Hispano/Chicano Culture in Northern New Mexico," *American Ethnologist* 25, no. 4 (1998): 583–609, 594. See also the Smithsonian's online description of "Dave's Dream" (now on display in the National Museum of American History's former Road Transportation Hall) at http://americanhistory.si.edu/onthemove/collection/object_1187.html.

72. Michel de Certeau, *The Practice of Everyday Life,* vol. 1 and vol. 2, *Living and Cooking.*

73. Bill Kelley, Jr., "Interview with Rubén Ortiz Torres," *LatinArt.com* (2000), http://www.latinart.com/faview.cfm?id=8.

74. All three videos have been posted on YouTube by the artist and are readily available for viewing. *Custom Mambo,* 5 min. 13 sec., ChiL.A.ngo Productions, CalArts,

Valencia, California, 1992; *Alien Toy: La Ranfla Cósmica (Unidentified Cruising Object),* 3/4″ SP, 8 min, Raza Cósmica Productions, Los Angeles, 1997. I have not been able to obtain production information for *The Garden of Earthly Delights.*

75. Bürger, *Theory of the Avant-garde,* 56.

76. Quoted in Marjorie Perloff, "The Avant-Garde Phase of American Modernism," in *The Cambridge Companion to American Modernism,* ed. Walter Kalaidjian (Cambridge: Cambridge University Press, 2005), 195–217, 209.

77. Tyler Stallings, "Cross-Cultural Customizer/*Adaptor Transcultural,*" in *Rubén Ortiz Torres: Desmothernismo,* ed. Tyler Stallings (Santa Monica, CA: Small Art Press and Huntington Beach Art Center, 1998), 8–29, 10.

78. Rubén Ortiz Torres, "Yepa, Yepa, Yepa," in Stallings, *Rubén Ortiz Torres,* 46–59, 58.

79. On the sculpture series, see Chavoya, "Customized Hybrids," 162–71.

80. Rubén Ortiz Torres, "Holy Power Tools, Batman! A Los Angeles Tale," *Art Issues* 57 (March–April 1990): 30–31, 30.

81. Eco, "The Poetics of the Open Work" and de Campos, "The Open Work of Art," in *Novas,* 220–22.

82. Sarduy, "The Baroque and the Neobaroque," 281.

83. Ramón Saldívar, *Chicano Narrative: The Dialectics of Difference* (Madison: University of Wisconsin Press, 1990), 26ff.

84. For an overview of the literary heritage of U.S. Hispanics and the key role played by periodicals, see *Herencia: The Anthology of Hispanic Literature in the United States,* ed. Nicolás Kanellos, Kenya Dworkin y Méndez, José B. Fernández et al. (Oxford: Oxford University Press, 2002), and *Hispanic Periodicals in the United States, Origins to 1960: A Brief and Comprehensive Bibliography,* ed. Nicholás Kanellos and Helvetia Martell (Houston: Arte Público Press, 2000).

85. Juan Flores, *From Bomba to Hip-Hop: Puerto Rican Culture and Latino Identity* (New York: Columbia University Press 2000), 192.

86. José Kozer's first book of selected poems, *Stet: Selected Poems,* with bilingual Spanish-English versions, was published in 2006. A useful and broader recent anthology is Kozer, *No buscan reflejarse.* On Kozer, see Sefamí, *La voracidad grafómana.*

87. Gustavo Pérez Firmat, *Life on the Hyphen: The Cuban-American Way* (Austin: University of Texas Press, 1994), 162.

88. Kozer, "Noción de José Kozer," in *No buscan reflejarse,* 20.

89. Kozer, "The Neobaroque," 17.

90. Nicholasa Mohr, "Puerto Rican Writers in the United States, Puerto Rican Writers in Puerto Rico: A Separation Beyond Language," *Americas Review* 15, no. 2 (1987): 87–92, 90.

91. Hinojosa, "The Baroque in the Life and Literature of the Hispano-American," 22–27.

92. Hinojosa's *Klail City Death Trip* series contains more than ten narratives, not counting his own recreations of novels originally published in Spanish and English in the respective other language. On Hinojosa, see *The Rolando Hinojosa Reader: Essays Historical and Critical,* ed. José David Saldívar (Houston: Arte Público, 1985).

93. Rolando Hinojosa, "The Sense of Place," in Saldívar, *Rolando Hinojosa Reader,* 18–24, 21.

94. John O. West, "*Grutas* in the Spanish Southwest," in *Hecho en Tejas: Texas-Mexican Folk Arts and Crafts,* ed. Joe Graham (Denton: University of North Texas Press, 1991), 263–77, 264.

95. Helen Simons and Roni Morales, "Churches, Chapels, and Shrines: Expressions of Hispanic Catholicism in Texas," in *Hispanic Texas: A Historical Guide,* ed. Helen Simons and Cathryn A. Hoyt (Austin: University of Texas Press, 1992), 107–120, 117. On Mexican home altars, see also Ramón A. Gutiérrez, ed., *Home Altars of Mexico* (Albuquerque: University of New Mexico Press, 1997).

96. Pat Jasper and Kay Turner, "Art Among Us/*Arte entre nosotros:* Mexican-American Folk Art in San Antonio," in Graham, *Hecho en Tejas,* 48–61, 52. See also the catalog of the exhibition curated by Pat Jasper and Kay Turner, *Art among Us/Arte entre nosotros: Mexican American Folk Art of San Antonio, San Antonio Museum of Art, 27 April-15 June 1986* (San Antonio: San Antonio Museum Association, 1986), where the photograph of the altar to El Niño Fidencio originally appeared.

97. On Luis Jiménez, see Katherine Manthorne, "Luis Jiménez' *Vaquero* and the Trojan Horse," *American Art* 20, no. 2 (Summer 2006): 28–31; Charles Dee Mitchell, "A Baroque Populism," *Art in America* 87, no. 3 (March 1999): 100–105; and Rudolfo Anaya and Luis Jiménez, eds., *Man on Fire: Luis Jiménez/El hombre en llamas* (Albuquerque: The Albuquerque Museum, 1994).

98. Richard Rodriguez, *Days of Obligation: An Argument with My Mexican Father* (New York: Penguin, 1992), 26–47, 31.

99. See Amalia Mesa-Bains, *Memory, Cultural Identity and the Social Imaginary: Art of the Chicano/a Community,* ed. María Chacón (Stanford: Stanford Center for Chicano Research, Stanford University, 1996). For a description of Mesa-Bains's installation, see Corrin, *Going for Baroque,* 26–27. Bal also discusses this installation in *Quoting Caravaggio,* 217–30, 247–48.

100. Amalia Mesa-Bains, "'Domesticana': The Sensibility of Chicana *Rasquache,*" *Aztlán* 24, no. 2 (Fall 1999): 157–67, 161. I quote an earlier version of this passage found in Mesa-Bains's "Curatorial Statement" for the exhibition catalog, *Ceremony of Spirit: Nature and Memory in Contemporary Latino Art* (San Francisco: Mexican Museum, 1993), 9–18, 12.

101. On Mesa-Bains's previous work in the context of the *CARA* (*Chicano Art: Resistance and Affirmation*) exhibit, see Alicia Gaspar de Alba, *Chicano Art: Inside/Outside the Master's House; Cultural Politics and the CARA Exhibition* (Austin: University of Texas Press, 1998), 76 and passim. A photograph of the *Ofrenda for Dolores del Río* can be found in *Chicano Art: Resistance and Affirmation, 1965–1985,* ed. Richard Griswold del Castillo, Teresa McKenna, and Yvonne Yarbro-Bejarano (Los Angeles: Wight Art Gallery, University of Los Angeles, 1991), 63.

102. The sonnet is identified in Mesa-Bains, *Memory, Cultural Identity and the Social Imaginary,* 4, and Bal, *Quoting Caravaggio,* 247–48.

103. See *A Sor Juana Anthology,* trans. Alan S. Trueblood, 94, for the original. I cite the English version from Bal's transcription of the text on the installation (Bal, *Quoting Caravaggio,* 248) (Mesa-Bains did not use the translation by Trueblood).

104. Max Benavides quotes an unpublished manuscript by Mesa-Bains in which she states that the gashed chairs are a "reference to the colonial trauma of 1492" ("Chicano Montage: Art and Cultural Crisis," 1–8, 4, http://zonezero.com/magazine/essays/distant/zmonta2.html).

105. "Luis Gispert," *Review: Literature and Arts of the Americas* 37, no. 1 (2004): 96–100, 96.

106. Ana Finel Honigman, "Interview with Luis Gispert," http://www.saatchi-gallery.co.uk/blogon/2006/08/luis_gispert_interviewed_by_an.php.

107. Tejada, *Luis Gispert.*

108. Brewster and Jacobs, *Theatre to Cinema,* 41.

109. Gispert quoted in Derrick R. Cartwright, "Subwoofers, Subcultures, Subversions: An Interview with Luis Gispert," in Tejada, *Luis Gispert,* 20–34, 26.

110. *Oxford English Dictionary Online,* s.v. "'bling,' *n.* and *adj.* A. *n.* (A piece of) ostentatious jewellery. Hence: wealth; conspicuous consumption. B. *adj.* Ostentatious, flashy; designating flamboyant jewellery or dress. Also: that glorifies conspicuous consumption; materialistic."

111. This beautiful composition is a recreation of a photograph by Bruce Nauman entitled *Self-Portrait as Fountain* (1970), in which the artist poses ejecting a jet of water from his mouth that falls in an arc as in a water fountain. See Cartwright, "Subwoofers, Subcultures, Subversions," 21.

112. Roberto Tejada, "Luis Gispert: Radical Feedback," in Tejada, *Luis Gispert,* 14–19, 17.

113. On iconographic conventions of the Pietà and the Deposition, see Schiller, *Iconography of Christian Art,* vol. 2, *The Passion of Jesus Christ,* 169ff. and 164ff.

114. On the place of the Virgen de la Caridad del Cobre in the *santería* pantheon, see Miguel Barnet, *Afro-Cuban Religions,* trans. Christine Ayorinde (Princeton, NJ: Markus Wiener, 2001), 57 and passim. On the royal slaves of El Cobre who engendered the cult of what would later become Cuba's national saint, see also María Elena Díaz, *The Virgin, the King, and the Royal Slaves of El Cobre: Negotiating Freedom in Colonial Cuba, 1670–1780* (Stanford: Stanford University Press, 2001).

115. Thompson, "The Sound of Light," 482.

SELECTED BIBLIOGRAPHY

Abeyta, Michael. "Ostentatious Offerings: The Neobaroque Economies of Carlos Fuentes's *Terra Nostra*." *Confluencia* 18 (Fall 2002): 103–17.

Acosta, Leonardo. "El barroco de Indias y la ideología colonialista." In *El barroco de indias y otros ensayos*. Havana: Casa de las Américas, 1984. 9–52.

Alonso, Dámaso. *Estudios y ensayos gongorinos*. Madrid: Gredos, 1955.

Alpers, Svetlana. *The Art of Describing: Dutch Art in the Seventeenth Century*. Chicago: University of Chicago Press, 1983.

Armstrong, Elizabeth, and Victor Zamudio-Taylor, eds. *Ultrabaroque: Aspects of Post–Latin American Art*. La Jolla, CA: Museum of Contemporary Art, 2000.

Avelar, Idelber. *The Untimely Present: Postdictatorial Latin American Fiction and the Task of Mourning*. Durham, NC: Duke University Press, 1999.

Bailey, Gauvin Alexander. *Art of Colonial Latin America*. London: Phaidon, 2005.

———. *The Andean Hybrid Baroque: Convergent Cultures in the Churches of Colonial Peru*. Notre Dame, IN: University of Notre Dame Press, 2010.

Bal, Mieke. *Quoting Caravaggio: Contemporary Art, Preposterous History*. Chicago: University of Chicago Press 1999.

Bandis, Helen, Adrian Martin, and Grant McDonald, eds. *Raúl Ruiz: Images of Passage*. Australia: Rouge Press, 2004.

Barner, Wilfried. *Barockrhetorik: Untersuchungen zu ihren geschichtlichen Grundlagen*. 2nd. ed. Tübingen: Max Niemeyer, 2000.

———, ed. *Der literarische Barockbegriff*. Darmstadt: Wissenschaftliche Buchgesellschaft, 1975.

Barnes, Djuna. *Ladies Almanack*. 1928. Normal, IL: Dalkey Archive Press, 1982.

———. *Nightwood*. 1936. New York: New Directions, 1961.

Barth, John. 1984. "The Literature of Exhaustion" (1967) and "The Literature of Replenishment: Postmodernist Fiction" (1979). In *The Friday Book: Essays and Other Nonfiction*. New York: Putnam, 1984. 62–76, 193–206.

Barthes, Roland. *Sade, Fourier, Loyola*. Trans. Richard Miller. New York: Hill and Wang, 1976.

Bejel, Emilio. *José Lezama Lima: Poet of the Image*. Gainesville: University of Florida Press, 1990.

Bemberg, María Luisa, dir. *Yo, la peor de todas*. Produced by Lila Stantic. Argentina, 1990. Spanish, with English subtitles. Color. 105 min.

Benjamin, Walter. *Illuminationen: Ausgewählte Schriften*. Vol. 1. Frankfurt am Main: Suhrkamp, 1974.

———. *Illuminations: Essays and Reflections*. Ed. Hannah Arendt. New York: Schocken, 1969.

———. *The Origin of German Tragic Drama*. 1928. Trans. John Osborne. London: Verso, 1985.

Bergmann, Emilie L., and Stacey Schlau, eds. *Approaches to Teaching the Works of Sor Juana Inés de la Cruz*. New York: Modern Language Association of America, 2007.

Beverley, John. "On the Spanish Literary Baroque." In *Against Literature,* 47–65. Minneapolis: University of Minnesota Press, 1993.

———. *Una modernidad obsoleta: Estudios sobre el barroco*. Los Teques, Venezuela: Fondo Editorial A.L.E.M., 1997.

Bollig, Ben. "Tie Me Up, Tie Me Down: On the *Neobarroco,* Masochist Suspension and Class Tension in the Work of Néstor Perlongher." *Romance Studies* 22, no. 2 (July 2004): 165–82.

Borges, Jorge Luis. *Collected Fictions*. Trans. Andrew Hurley. New York: Penguin Books, 1999.

———. *Textos recobrados, 1919–1929*. Ed. Sara Luisa del Carril. Buenos Aires: Emecé, 1997.

Bornhofen, Patricia Lynn. "Cosmography and Chaography: Baroque to Neobaroque." PhD diss., University of Wisconsin, Madison, 1995.

Bosch, Lynette M. F. *Cuban-American Art in Miami: Exile, Identity, and the Neo-Baroque*. Burlington, VT: Lund Humphries, 2004.

Bottineau, Yves. *Iberian-American Baroque*. Trans. Kenneth Martin Leake. Lausanne: Benedikt Taschen, 1990.

Braider, Christopher. *Baroque Self-Invention and Historical Truth: Hercules at the Crossroads*. Burlington, VT: Ashgate, 2004.

Brewster, Ben, and Lea Jacobs. *Theatre to Cinema: Stage Pictorialism and the Early Feature Film*. Oxford: Oxford University Press, 1997.

Brown, Marshall. "The Classic Is the Baroque: On the Principle of Wölfflin's Art History." *Critical Inquiry* 9, no. 2 (1982): 379–404.

Buci-Glucksmann, Christine. *Baroque Reason: The Aesthetics of Modernity.* Trans. Patrick Camiller. London: Sage, 1994.

———. *La folie du voir: De l'estétique baroque*. Paris: Galilée, 1986.

———. "The Work of the Gaze." Trans. Dorothy Z. Baker. In Zamora and Kaup, *Baroque New Worlds,* 140–57.

Buck-Morss, Susan. *The Dialectics of Seeing: Walter Benjamin and the Arcades Project*. Cambridge, MA: MIT Press, 1989.

Bürger, Peter. *Theory of the Avant-garde*. Trans. Michael Shaw. Minneapolis: University of Minnesota Press, 1984.

Burbaum, Sabine. *Kunst-Epochen: Barock*. Stuttgart: Reclam, 2003.

Burton, Robert. *The Anatomy of Melancholy.* 1621. Ed Holbrook Jackson. New York: New York Review of Books, 2001.

Buscaglia-Salgado, José F. "The Creole in His Labyrinth." In *Undoing Empire: Race and Nation in the Mulatto Caribbean*. Minneapolis: University of Minnesota Press, 2003. 128–82.

Calabrese, Omar. *Neo-Baroque: A Sign of the Times*. Trans. Charles Lambert. Princeton, NJ: Princeton University Press, 1992.

Calderón de la Barca, Pedro. *La vida es sueño/Life Is a Dream*. Ed. and trans. Stanley Appelbaum. Mineola, NY: Dover, 2002.

Calloway, Stephen. *Baroque Baroque: The Culture of Excess*. London: Phaidon, 1994.

Cañizares-Esguerra, Jorge. *How to Write the History of the New World: Histories, Epistemologies, and Identities in the Eighteenth-Century Atlantic World.* Stanford, CA: Stanford University Press, 2001.

Carpentier, Alejo. "The Baroque and the Marvelous Real." Trans. Tanya Huntington and Lois Parkinson Zamora. In *Magical Realism: Theory, History, Community.* Ed. Lois Parkinson Zamora and Wendy B. Faris. Durham, NC: Duke University Press, 1995.

———. "The City of Columns." Trans. Michael Schuessler. In Zamora and Kaup, *Baroque New Worlds.* 244–58.

———. "Questions Concerning the Contemporary Latin American Novel" (excerpts). Trans. Michael Schuessler. In Zamora and Kaup, *Baroque New Worlds.* 259–64.

Cascardi, Anthony J. "Allegories of Power." In *The Prince in the Tower: Perceptions of "La vida es sueño."* Ed. Frederick A. de Armas. Lewisburg, PA: Bucknell University Press, 1993. 15–26.

———. "The Subject of Control." In *Culture and Control in Counter-Reformation Spain.* Ed. Anne J. Cruz and Mary Elizabeth Perry. Minneapolis: University of Minnesota Press, 1992. 231–54.

Castillo, David R., and Massimo Lollini, eds. *Reason and Its Others: Italy, Spain, and the New World.* Nashville, TN: Vanderbilt University Press, 2006.

Celorio, Gonzalo. "From the Baroque to the Neobaroque." Trans. Maarten van Delden. In Zamora and Kaup, *Baroque New Worlds.* 487–507.

Chancé, Dominique. *Poétique baroque de la Caraïbe.* Paris: Karthala, 2001.

Chiampi, Irlemar. *Barroco y modernidad.* Mexico City: Fondo de Cultura Económica, 2000.

———. "The Baroque at the Twilight of Modernity." Trans. William Childers. In Zamora and Kaup, *Baroque New Worlds.* 508–28.

Childers, William. "The Baroque Public Sphere." In Castillo and Lollini, *Reason and Its Others.* 165–85.

Clifford, James. *Routes: Travel and Translation in the Late Twentieth Century.* Cambridge, MA: Harvard University Press, 1997.

Conley, Tom. "Folds and Folding." In *Gilles Deleuze: Key Concepts.* Ed. Charles Stivale. Chesham: Acumen, 2005. 170–81.

Copleston, Frederick. *A History of Philosophy.* Vol. 4, *Modern Philosophy: Descartes to Leibniz.* Garden City, NY: Image Books, 1994.

———. *A History of Philosophy.* Vol. 5, *Modern Philosophy: The British Philosophers;* part I, *Hobbes to Paley.* New York: Doubleday, 1994.

Corrin, Lisa G., ed. *Going for Baroque: Eighteen Contemporary Artists Fascinated with the Baroque and Rococo.* Baltimore, MD: Contemporary and Walters Galleries, 1995.

Croce, Benedetto. *Storia della età barocca in Italia.* Bari: G. Laterza, 1929.

Cuperman, Pedro. *American Baroque: December 1988, Holly Solomon Gallery.* New York: Holly Solomon Gallery, 1988.

Davidson, Peter. *The Universal Baroque.* Manchester: Manchester University Press, 2007.

Debroise, Oliver, Elizabeth Sussman, and Matthew Teitelbaum, eds. *El corazón sangrante/The Bleeding Heart.* Boston: Institute of Contemporary Art, 1991.

de Campos, Haroldo. "Anthropophagous Reason: Dialogue and Difference in Brazilian Culture." Trans. Odile Cisneros. In *Novas,* 157–77.

———. *Novas: Selected Writings.* Ed. Antonio Sergio Bessa and Odile Cisneros. Evanston, IL: Northwestern University Press, 2007.

de Certeau, Michel. "The Madness of Vision." *Enclitic* 7, no. 1 (1983): 24–31.

———. *The Practice of Everyday Life*. Vol. 1. Trans. Stephen Rendall. Berkeley: University of California Press, 1984.

———. *The Practice of Everyday Life*. Vol. 2, *Living and Cooking*, trans. Timothy J. Tomasik. Minneapolis: University of Minnesota Press, 1998.

de la Cruz, Juana Inés. *A Sor Juana Anthology*. Ed. and trans. Alan S. Trueblood. Cambridge, MA: Harvard University Press, 1988.

———. *Obras completas*. Ed. Alfonso Méndez Plancarte. 4 vols. Mexico City: Fondo de Cultura Económica, 1951–57.

———. *Obras completas*. Ed. Francisco Monterde. Mexico City: Porrúa, 1969.

Deleuze, Gilles. *The Fold: Leibniz and the Baroque*. 1988. Trans. Tom Conley. Minneapolis: University of Minnesota Press, 1993.

Deleuze, Gilles, and Félix Guattari. *A Thousand Plateaus: Capitalism and Schizophrenia*. Trans. Brian Massumi. Minneapolis: University of Minnesota Press, 1987.

———. *Kafka: Toward a Minor Literature*. Trans. Dana Polan. Minneapolis: University of Minnesota Press, 1986.

Diego, Gerardo, ed. *Antología poética en honor de Góngora: Desde Lope de Vega a Rubén Darío*. 1927. Madrid: Alianza, 1979.

Donoso, José. *Casa de campo*. Barcelona: Seix Barral, 1978.

———. *A House in the Country*. Trans. David Pritchard, with Suzanne Jill Levine. New York: Random House, 1984.

d'Ors, Eugenio. *Lo barroco*. 1935. Ed. Ángel d'Ors and Alicia García Navarra de d'Ors. Madrid: Tecnos, 2002.

———. "The Debate on the Baroque in Pontigny" (excerpt). Trans. Wendy B. Faris. In Zamora and Kaup, *Baroque New Worlds*. 78–92.

DuPont, Denise. "Baroque Ambiguities: The Figure of the Author in *Terra nostra*." *Latin American Literary Review* 30, no. 59 (2002): 5–19.

Dussel, Enrique. "World System and 'Trans'-Modernity." *Nepantla* 3, no. 2 (2002): 221–44.

Echevarrén, Roberto, José Kozer, and Jacobo Sefamí, eds. *Medusario: Muestra de poesía latinoamericana*. Mexico City: Fondo de Cultura Económica, 1996.

Echeverría, Bolívar. *La modernidad de lo barroco*. Mexico City: Ediciones Era, 1998.

———, ed. *Modernidad, mestizaje cultural, ethos barroco*. Mexico City: Universidad Nacional Autónoma de México: El Equilibrista, 1994.

Eco, Umberto. "The Poetics of the Open Work." 1962. In *The Open Work*. Trans. Anna Cancogni. Cambridge, MA: Harvard University Press, 1989. 1–23.

Egginton, William. "The Corporeal Baroque and the New World Baroque." *South Atlantic Quarterly* 106, no. 1 (Winter 2007): 107–27.

———. *How the World Became a Stage: Presence, Theatricality, and the Question of Modernity*. Albany: State University of New York Press, 2003.

———. "Of Baroque Holes and Baroque Folds." In Spadaccini and Martín-Estudillo, *Hispanic Baroques*. 55–71.

———. "Reason's Baroque House (Cervantes, Master Architect)." In Castillo and Lollini, *Reason and Its Others*. 186–203.

Eliot, T. S. *Selected Prose of T. S. Eliot*. Ed. Frank Kermode. New York: Farrar, Straus and Giroux, 1975.

———. *The Varieties of Metaphysical Poetry: The Clark Lectures at Trinity College, Cambridge, 1926, and the Turnbull Lectures at the Johns Hopkins University, 1933*. Ed. and introd. by Ronald Schuchard. New York: Harcourt Brace, 1994.

Eltit, Diamela. *El padre mío*. Santiago: Zegers, 1989.

———. *E. Luminata*. Trans. Ronald Christ. Santa Fe, NM: Lumen, 1997.

———. *Lumpérica*. 1983. Santiago: Seix Barral, 1998.

Figueroa Sánchez, Cristo Rafael. *Barroco y neobarroco en la narrativa hispanoamericana: Cartografías literarias de la segunda mitad del siglo xx*. Bogotá: Editorial Pontificia Universidad Javeriana; Editorial Universidad de Antioquia, 2008.

Focillon, Henri. *The Life of Forms in Art*. 1934. Trans. Charles B. Hogan and George Kubler. New York: Zone Books, 1992.

Foucault, Michel. *The Order of Things: An Archeology of the Human Sciences*. New York: Vintage, 1973.

Friedrich, Hugo. *The Structure of Modern Poetry: From the Mid-Nineteenth to the Mid-Twentieth Century*. Trans. Joachim Neugroschel. Evanston, IL: Northwestern University Press, 1974.

Fuentes, Carlos. *The Buried Mirror: Reflections on Spain and the New World*. Boston: Houghton Mifflin, 1992.

———. "The Novel as Tragedy: William Faulkner." 1970. Trans. John Ochoa. In Zamora and Kaup, *Baroque New Worlds*. 531–53.

Gallo, Rubén. "Sarduy avec Lacan: The Portrayal of French Psychoanalysis in *Cobra* and *La simulación*." *Revista Hispánica Moderna* 60, no. 1 (2007): 35–60.

García Lorca, Federico. "La imagen poética de Don Luis de Góngora." In *Obras completas*. Ed. Arturo del Hoyo. Madrid: Aguilar, 1972. 62–85.

Gimbernat de González, Ester. "La curiosidad barroca." In *Coloquio internacional sobre la obra de José Lezama Lima*. 2 vols. Poitiers: Centro de Investigaciones Latinoamericanas, University of Poitiers, 1982. 2:59–64.

Giovannotti, Micaela, and Joyce B. Korotkin, eds. *Neo-Baroque! Petah Coyne, Ann Craven, Angelo Filomeno, Robert Longo, Emilio Perez, Alexis Rockman, Takagi Masakatsu & Saeko Takagi, Fred Tomaselli, Nicola Verlato, Kehinde Wiley*. Milan: Charta, 2006.

Gisbert, Teresa. *Iconografía y mitos indígenas en el arte*. La Paz, Bolivia: Gisbert, 1980.

Gisbert, Teresa, and José de Mesa. *Arquitectura Andina: 1530–1830*. 2nd ed. La Paz, Bolivia: Embajada de España en Bolivia, 1997.

Glissant, Édouard. *Caribbean Discourse: Selected Essays*. Trans. J. Michael Dash. Charlottesville: University of Virginia Press, 1989.

———. *Poetics of Relation*. Trans. Betsy Wing. Ann Arbor: University of Michigan Press, 1997. 77–79.

Góngora, Luis de. *Las soledades*. Ed. Dámaso Alonso. 3rd ed. Madrid: Sociedad de Estudios y Publicaciones, 1956.

———. *Selected Poems of Luis de Góngora*. Ed. and trans. John Dent-Young. Chicago: University of Chicago Press, 2007.

González Echevarría, Roberto. *Celestina's Brood: Continuities of the Baroque in Spanish and Latin American Literature*. Durham, NC: Duke University Press, 1993.

———. "Góngora's and Lezama's Appetites." Trans. Maarten van Delden. In Zamora and Kaup, *Baroque New Worlds*. 554–70.

———. *La ruta de Severo Sarduy*. Hanover, NH: Ediciones del Norte, 1987.

González, Eduardo. "Baroque Endings: Carpentier, Sarduy and Some Textual Contingencies." *Modern Language Notes* 92, no. 2 (1977): 269–295.

Greene, Roland. "Baroque and Neobaroque: Making Thistory." *PMLA* 124, no. 1 (2009): 150–55.

Grierson, Herbert J., ed. *Metaphysical Lyrics and Poems of the Seventeenth Century: Donne to Butler*. 1921. London: Oxford University Press, 1965.

Gruzinski, Serge. "The Admirable Effects of the Baroque Image." In *Images at War: Mexico from Columbus to "Blade Runner" (1492–2019)*. Trans. Heather MacLean. Durham, NC: Duke University Press, 2001. 96–160.

———. "From the Baroque to the Neo-Baroque: The Colonial Sources of the Postmodern Era (The Mexican Case)." In Deboise, Sussman, and Teitelbaum, *El corazón sangrante/The Bleeding Heart*. 62–89.

Guerrero, Gustavo. *La estrategia neobarroca: Estudio sobre el resurgimiento de la poética barroca en la obra narrativa de Severo Sarduy*. Barcelona: Ediciones del Mall, 1987.

Guido, Ángel. "America's Relation to Europe in the Arts." Trans. Patrick Blaine. In Zamora and Kaup, *Baroque New Worlds*. 183–97.

———. *Redescubrimiento de América en el arte*. Rosario: Republica Argentina, 1940. (Reissued: Rosario: Imprenta de la Universidad del Litoral, 1941; Buenos Aires: Editorial El Ateneo, 1944.)

Gumbrecht, Hans Ulrich. "Warum gerade Góngora? Poetologie und historisches Bewusstsein in Spanien zwischen Jahrhundertwende und Bürgerkrieg." In *Lyrik und Malerei der Avantgarde*. Ed. Rainer Warning and Winfried Wehle. Munich: Wilhelm Fink, 1982. 145–91.

Hall, Stuart. "On Postmodernism and Articulation: An Interview with Stuart Hall." In *Stuart Hall: Critical Dialogues in Cultural Studies*. Ed. David Morley and Kuan-Hsing Chen. London: Routledge, 1996. 131–50.

———. "Race, Articulation and Societies Structured in Dominance." In *Sociological Theories: Race and Colonialism*. Paris: Unesco, 1980. 305–45.

Harbison, Robert. *Reflections on Baroque*. Chicago: University of Chicago Press, 2000.

Hauser, Arnold. *The Social History of Art*. Vol. 2, *Renaissance, Mannerism, Baroque*. New York: Vintage, 1985.

Henkel, Arthur, and Albrecht Schöne, eds. *Emblemata: Handbuch zur Sinnbildkunst des XVI. und XVII. Jahrhunderts*. Stuttgart: Metzler, 1996.

Hinojosa, Rolando. "The Baroque in the Life and Literature of the Hispano-American." *Point of Contact* 3, no. 3 (April 1993): 22–27.

Hoffmeister, Gerhart. *Deutsche und europäische Barockliteratur*. Stuttgart: Metzler, 1987.

Jameson, Fredric. *A Singular Modernity: Essay on the Ontology of the Present*. London: Verso, 2002.

Jay, Martin. *Downcast Eyes: The Denigration of Vision in Twentieth-Century French Thought*. Berkeley: University of California Press, 1993.

———. "Scopic Regimes of Modernity." In *Modernity and Identity*. Ed. Scott Lash and Jonathan Friedman. Oxford: Blackwell, 1992. 178–95.

Johnson, Christopher D. *Hyperboles: The Rhetoric of Excess in Baroque Literature and Thought*. Cambridge, MA: Harvard University Press, 2010.

Jolley, Nicholas, ed. *The Cambridge Companion to Leibniz*. Cambridge: Cambridge University Press, 1995.

Kaup, Monika. "Becoming-Baroque: Folding European Forms into the New World Baroque with Alejo Carpentier." *CR: The New Centennial Review* 5, no. 2 (2005): 107–49.

———. "'The Future Is Entirely Fabulous': The Baroque Genealogy of Latin America's Modernity." *MLQ* 68, no. 2 (2007): 221–41.

———. "The Neobaroque in Djuna Barnes." *Modernism/Modernity* 12, no. 1 (2005): 85–110.

———. "Neobaroque: Latin America's Alternative Modernity." *Comparative Literature* 58, no. 2 (2006): 128–52.

———. "Postdictatorship Allegory and Neobaroque Disillusionment in José Donoso's *Casa de campo*." *Chasqui* 34, no. 2 (November 2005): 92–112.

———. "'¡Vaya Papaya!': Cuban Baroque and Visual Culture in Alejo Carpentier, Ricardo Porro, and Ramón Alejandro." *PMLA* 124, no. 1 (2009): 156–71.

Kelemen, Pál. *Baroque and Rococo in Latin America.* 1951. 2 vols. New York: Dover, 1967.

Kelemen, Pál, and Judith Hancock de Sandoval. *Folk Baroque in Mexico: Mestizo Architecture through the Centuries.* Orlando, FL: Brewton Co., 1974.

Kelley, Theresa. *Reinventing Allegory.* Cambridge: Cambridge University Press, 1997.

King, Jon, Sheila Whitaker, and Rosa Bosch, eds. *An Argentine Passion: María Luisa Bemberg and Her Films.* London: Verso, 2000.

Klibansky, Raymond, Erwin Panofsky, and Fritz Saxl. *Saturn and Melancholy: Studies in the History of Natural Philosophy, Religion, and Art.* London: Nelson, 1964.

Kozer, José. "The Neobaroque: A Converging in Latin American Poetry." *S/N: New World Poetics* 1, no. 1 (2010): 14–20.

———. *No buscan reflejarse: Antología poética.* Ed. Jorge Luis Arcos. Havana: Letras Cubanas, 2001.

———. *Stet: Selected Poems.* Trans. Mark Weiss. New York: Junction Press, 2006.

Kubler, George, and Martin Soria. *Art and Architecture in Spain and Portugal and Their American Dominions, 1500–1800.* Baltimore, MD: Penguin, 1959.

Kuhnheim, Jill. "Sensual Excess: The Neobaroque." In *Spanish American Poetry at the End of the Twentieth Century.* Austin: University of Texas Press, 2004. 115–44.

La Bossière, Camille. "Past and Present: The Neobaroque Novel in French Canada." In *Studies on Canadian Literature: Introductory and Critical Essays.* Ed. Arnold Davidson. New York: Modern Language Association of America, 1990. 193–206.

Lacan, Jacques. "On the Baroque." In *The Seminar of Jacques Lacan.* Vol. 20, *On Feminine Sexuality. The Limits of Love and Knowledge.* Ed. Jacques-Alain Miller, trans. Bruce Fink. New York: Norton, 1998. 104–17.

Laclau, Ernesto. *Politics and Ideology in Marxist Theory: Capitalism, Fascism, Populism.* London: Verso, 1977.

Lafaye, James. *Quetzalcoatl and Guadalupe: The Formation of Mexican National Consciousness, 1531–1813.* Trans. Benjamin Keen. Chicago: University of Chicago Press, 1976.

Lambert, Gregg. *The Non-Philosophy of Gilles Deleuze.* New York: Continuum, 2002.

———. *The Return of the Baroque in Modern Culture.* New York: Continuum, 2004.

Lange-Churión, Pedro. "Neobaroque: Latin America's Postmodernity?" In *Latin America and Postmodernity: A Contemporary Reader.* Ed. Lange-Churión and Eduardo Mendieta. Amherst, NY: Humanity Books, 2001. 253–73.

Leonard, Irving A. *Baroque Times in Old Mexico: Seventeenth-Century Persons, Places, and Practices.* Ann Arbor: University of Michigan Press, 1959.

Levy, Evonne. *Propaganda and the Jesuit Baroque.* Berkeley: University of California Press, 2004.

Lezama Lima, José. "Baroque Curiosity." Trans. María Pérez and Anke Birkenmaier. In Zamora and Kaup, *Baroque New Worlds.* 212–40.

———. *Esferaimagen: Sierpe de Don Luis de Góngora; Las imágenes posibles.* Barcelona: Tusquets, 1970.

———. "Image of Latin America." In *Latin America in Its Literature*. Ed. César Fernández Moreno et al. Trans. Mary Berg. New York: Holmes and Meier, 1980. 321–27.

———. *La expresión americana*. 1957. Ed. Irlemar Chiampi. Mexico City: Fondo de Cultura Económica, 1993.

López-Portillo, Carmen Beatriz, ed. *Sor Juana y su mundo: Una mirada actual*. Mexico City: Fondo de Cultura Económica, 1998.

Maravall, José Antonio. *Culture of the Baroque: Analysis of a Historical Structure*. Trans. Terry Cochran. Minneapolis: University of Minnesota Press, 1986.

Márquez Rodríguez, Alexis. *El barroco literario en Hispanoamérica: Ensayos de teoría y crítica*. Bogotá, Colombia: Tercer Mundo Editores, 1991.

———. *Lo barroco y lo real-maravilloso en la obra de Alejo Carpentier*. Mexico City: Siglo Veintiuno, 1982.

Martin, John Rupert. *Baroque*. New York: Harper & Row, 1977.

Martineau, Luanne, Lisa Baldissera, Jake Chapman, Dinos Chapman, and Lee Henderson, eds. *Peculiar Culture: The Contemporary Baroque*. Victoria, BC: Art Gallery of Greater Victoria, 2009.

Mather, Christine. *Baroque to Folk: De lo barroco a lo popular*. Santa Fe: Museum of New Mexico Press, 1980.

Méndez Rodenas, Adriana. *Severo Sarduy: El neobarroco de la transgresión*. Mexico City: Universidad Nacional Autónoma de México, 1983.

Merrim, Stephanie, ed. *Feminist Perspectives on Sor Juana Inés de la Cruz*. Detroit, MI: Wayne State University Press, 1991.

Mesa-Bains, Amalia. *The Library of Sor Juana Inés de la Cruz*. From the installation *Venus Envy Chapter Two: The Harem and Other Enclosures*. 1994. Mixed media installation. Williams College Museum of Art.

Migliorini, Bruno. "Etymologie und Geschichte des Terminus 'Barock.'" Trans. Lili Sertorius. In Barner, *Der literarische Barockbegriff*. 402–19.

Miles, Margaret. *Image as Insight: Visual Understanding in Western Christianity and Secular Culture*. Boston: Beacon Press, 1985.

Monsivaís, Carlos. "The Neobaroque and Popular Culture." Trans. James Ramey. *PMLA* 124, no. 1 (2009): 180–88.

Morales Benítez, Otto. "El mestizo y el barroco." In *América Latina: Integración por la cultura*. Ed. Mariano J. Garreta. Buenos Aires: Fernando García Cambeiro, 1977. 29–50.

Moraña, Mabel. "Baroque/Neobaroque/Ultrabaroque: Disruptive Readings of Modernity." In Spadaccini and Martín-Estudillo, *Hispanic Baroques*. 241–81.

———. "The Baroque and Transculturation." In *Literary Cultures of Latin America: A Comparative History*. 3 vols. Ed. Mario J. Valdés and Djelal Kadir. Vol. 3, *Latin American Literary Culture: Subject to History*. New York: Oxford University Press, 2004. 180–90.

———. *Viaje al silencio: Exploraciones del discurso barroco*. Mexico City: Fondo de Cultura Económica, 1998.

———, ed. *Relecturas del Barroco de Indias*. Hanover, NH: Ediciones del Norte, 1994.

Moser, Walter. "The Concept of Baroque." *Revista canadiense de estudios hispánicos* 33, no. 1 (2008): 11–37.

Mumford, Lewis. "The Baroque City." In *The Lewis Mumford Reader*. Ed. Donald Miller. New York: Pantheon Books, 1986. 127–47.

Murray, Timothy. *Digital Baroque: New Media Art and Cinematic Folds*. Minneapolis: University of Minnesota Press, 2008.

Ndalianis, Angela. *Neo-Baroque Aesthetics and Contemporary Entertainment.* Cambridge, MA: MIT Press, 2004.

Nelson, Lowry. *Baroque Lyric Poetry.* New Haven, CT: Yale University Press, 1961.

Nicolson, Marjorie Hope. *The Breaking of the Circle: The Effect of the "New Science" upon Seventeenth-Century Poetry.* New York: Columbia University Press, 1960.

Niefanger, Dirk. *Barock.* Stuttgart: Metzler, 2000.

Nietzsche, Friedrich. "On the Baroque." 1878. Trans. Monika Kaup. In Zamora and Kaup, *Baroque New Worlds.* 44–45.

Norberg-Schulz, Christian. *Baroque Architecture.* New York: Rizzoli, 1986.

Norman, Larry, ed. *The Theatrical Baroque.* Chicago: David and Alfred Smart Museum of Art, University of Chicago, 2001.

Opitz, Michael, and Erdmut Wizisla, eds. *Benjamins Begriffe.* 2 vols. Frankfurt am Main: Suhrkamp, 2000.

Oropesa, Salvador A. *The Contemporáneos Group: Rewriting Mexico in the Thirties and Forties.* Austin: University of Texas Press, 2003.

Ortega, José. *La estética neobarroca en la narrativa hispanoamericana.* Madrid: José Porrúa Turanzas, 1984.

Panofsky, Erwin. "What Is Baroque?" 1934. In *Three Essays on Style.* Ed. Irving Lavin. Cambridge, MA: MIT Press, 1995. 19–88.

Pauly, Arabella. *Neobarroco: Zur Wesensbestimmung Lateinamerikas und seiner Literatur.* Frankfurt am Main: Peter Lang, 1993.

Paz, Octavio. *Children of the Mire: Modern Poetry from Romanticism to the Avant-Garde.* Trans. Rachel Phillips. Cambridge, MA: Harvard University Press, 1991.

———. *The Collected Poems of Octavio Paz, 1957–87.* Ed. and trans. Eliot Weinberger. New York: New Directions, 1987.

———. *Sor Juana; or, The Traps of Faith.* 1982. Trans. Margaret Sayers Peden. Cambridge, MA: Harvard University Press, 1988.

Perlongher, Néstor. *Poemas completos: 1980–1992.* Ed. Roberto Echevarrén. Buenos Aires: Seix Barral, 2003.

———. *Prosa plebeya: Ensayos 1980–92.* Ed. Christian Ferrer and Osvaldo Baigorria. Buenos Aires: Colihue, 1997.

Picón-Salas, Mariano. "The Baroque of the Indies." In *A Cultural History of Spanish America: From Conquest to Independence.* 1944. Trans. Irving A. Leonard. Berkeley: University of California Press, 1962. 85–105.

Pollard, Charles W. *New World Modernisms: T. S. Eliot, Derek Walcott, and Kamau Brathwaite.* Charlottesville: University of Virginia Press, 2004.

Praz, Mario. "Baroque in England." 1960. Trans. in *Modern Philology* 61, no. 3 (1964): 169–79.

———. "The Flaming Heart: Richard Crashaw and the Baroque." 1925. In *The Flaming Heart: Essays on Crashaw, Machiavelli, and Other Studies in the Relations between Italian and English Literature from Chaucer to T.S. Eliot.* Garden City, NY: Doubleday, 1958. 204–63.

———. *Secentismo e marinismo in Inghilterra: John Donne–Richard Crashaw.* Florence: "La Voce," 1925.

———. *Studies in Seventeenth-Century Imagery.* Rome: Edizioni de Storia e Letteratura, 1964.

Radden, Jennifer, ed. *The Nature of Melancholy: From Aristotle to Kristeva.* Oxford: Oxford University Press, 2000.

Rama, Ángel. *The Lettered City.* Trans. John Charles Chasteen. Durham, NC: Duke University Press, 1996.

Rangel, Cecilia Enjuto. "Cities in Ruins: The Recuperation of the Baroque in T. S. Eliot and Octavio Paz." In *How Far Is America from Here? Selected Proceedings of the First World Congress of the International American Studies Association, 22–24 May 2003.* Ed. Theo D'Haen et al. Amsterdam: Rodopi, 2005. 283–96.

Rescher, Nicholas. *The Philosophy of Leibniz.* Englewood Cliffs, NJ: Prentice-Hall, 1967.

Reyes, Alfonso. *Cuestiones gongorinas.* 1927. In *Obras completas.* Vol. 7. Ed. Ernesto Mejía Sánchez. Mexico City: Fondo de Cultura Económica, 1958. 10–167.

———. "Sabor de Góngora." 1928. In *Obras completas.* Vol. 7. Ed. Ernesto Mejía Sánchez. Mexico City: Fondo de Cultura Económica, 1958. 117–98.

Richard, Nelly. *Cultural Residues: Chile in Transition.* Trans. Alan West-Durán and Theodore Quester. Minneapolis: University of Minnesota Press, 2004.

Robbins, Jeremy. *The Challenges of Uncertainty: An Introduction to Seventeenth-Century Spanish Literature.* Lanham, MD: Rowman & Littlefield, 1998.

Rodríguez, Paul A. Schroeder. "La fase neobarroca del nuevo cine latinoamericano." *Revista de crítica literaria latinoamericana* 37, no. 73 (2011): 15–35.

Ross, Kathleen. *The Baroque Narrative of Carlos de Sigüenza y Góngora: A New World Paradise.* Cambridge: Cambridge University Press, 1993.

Rousset, Jean. *La littérature de l'âge Baroque en France.* Paris: J. Corti, 1954.

Rubial García, Antonio. *Santa María Tonantzintla: Un pueblo, un templo.* Álvaro Obregón, Mexico: Universidad Iberoamericana, 1991.

Ruiz, Raúl. *Poetics of Cinema 1: Miscellanies.* Trans. Brian Holmes. Paris: Dis Voir, 1995.

———. *Poetics of Cinema 2.* Trans. Carlos Morreo. Paris: Dis Voir, 2007.

———, dir. *Mémoire des apparences* (*Memory of Appearances;* also known as *Life Is a Dream*). France, 1986. French, with English subtitles. Color. 100 min.

Sáenz, Pilar. *The Life and Works of Eugenio d'Ors.* Troy, MI: International Book Publishers, 1983.

Salgado, César Augusto. *From Modernism to Neobaroque: Joyce and Lezama Lima.* Lewisburg, PA: Bucknell University Press, 2001.

———. "Hybridity in New World Baroque Theory." *Journal of American Folklore* 112, no. 445 (1999): 316–31.

Sandoval, Denise, and Patrick A. Polk. *Arte y estilo: The Lowriding Tradition.* Los Angeles: Petersen Automotive Museum, 2000.

Sarduy, Severo. "The Baroque and the Neobaroque." 1972. Trans. Christopher Leland Winks. In Zamora and Kaup, *Baroque New Worlds.* 270–91.

———. "Baroque Cosmology: Kepler." 1974. Trans. Christopher Leland Winks. In Zamora and Kaup, *Baroque New Worlds.* 292–315.

———. "El Barroco après la lettre: Entrevista con Alberto Cardín y Biel Mesquida." *Diwan* (Zaragoza) 5–6 (September 1979): 87–109.

———. *From Cuba with a Song.* 1967. Trans. Suzanne Jill Levine. Los Angeles: Sun & Moon Press, 1994.

———. *Obra completa.* 2 vols. Ed. Gustavo Guerrero and François Wahl. Madrid: Galaxia Gutenberg; Nanterre, France: ALLCA XX, 1999.

———. *Written on a Body.* 1969. Trans. Carol Maier. New York: Lumen, 1989.

Schiller, Gertrud. *Iconography of Christian Art.* Vol. 2, *The Passion of Jesus Christ.* Trans. Janet Seligman. Greenwich, CT: New York Graphic Society, 1971.

Schöne, Albrecht. *Emblematik und Drama im Zeitalter des Barock.* Munich: Beck, 1993.

Schons, Dorothy. "Some Bibliographical Notes on Sor Juana Inés de la Cruz," *University of Texas Bulletin* 2526 (July 8, 1925): 5–30.

———. "Some Obscure Points in the Life of Sor Juana Inés de la Cruz." *Modern Philology* 24, no. 2 (1926): 141–62.

Schumm, Petra, ed. *Barrocos y modernos: Nuevos caminos en la investigacion del Barroco Iberoamericano.* Madrid: Iberoamericana, 1998.

Sebastián, Santiago. *El barroco iberoamericano: Mensaje iconográfico.* Madrid: Encuentro Ediciones, 1990.

———. *Contrareforma y barroco: Lecturas iconográficas e iconológicas.* Madrid: Alianza Editorial, 1981.

Sefamí, Jacobo. "El llamado de los deseosos: Poesía neobarroca latinoamericana." *Siglo XX/20th Century* 12, nos. 1–2 (1994): 219–37.

———, ed. *La voracidad grafómana: José Kozer.* Mexico City: Facultad de Filosofía y Letras, Universidad Autónoma Nacional de México, 2002.

Segel, Harold B. *The Baroque Poem: A Comparative Survey.* New York: E. P. Dutton, 1974.

XVII Congreso del Instituto Internacional de Literatura Iberoamericana: Sesión de Madrid. 3 vols. Vol. 1, *El Barroco en América.* Ed. Centro Iberoamericano de Cooperación. Madrid: Ediciones Cultura Hispánica del Centro Iberoamericano de Cooperación, 1978.

Sillevis, John, with contributions by David Elliott and Edward J. Sullivan. *The Baroque World of Fernando Botero.* Alexandria, VA: Art Services International, 2006.

Skrine, Peter N. *The Baroque: Literature and Culture in Seventeenth-Century Europe.* London: Methuen, 1978.

Spadaccini, Nicholas, and Luis Martín-Estudillo, eds. *Hispanic Baroques: Reading Cultures in Context.* Nashville, TN: Vanderbilt University Press, 2005.

Spengler, Oswald. *The Decline of the West. 1920–22.* Trans. Charles Francis Atkinson. 2 vols. New York: Knopf, 1980.

Spenser, Theodore, ed. *A Garland for John Donne, 1631–1931.* Gloucester, MA: Peter Smith, 1958.

Steinhagen, Harald. "Zu Walter Benjamins Begriff der Allegorie." In *Formen und Funktionen der Allegorie.* Ed. Walter Haug. Stuttgart: Metzler, 1979. 666–85.

Sullivan, Edward J., ed. *Brazil: Body and Soul.* New York: Guggenheim, 2001.

Sypher, Wylie. *Four Stages of Renaissance Style: Transformations in Art and Literature. 1400–1700.* Garden City, NY: Doubleday, 1955.

Tejada, Roberto, ed. *Luis Gispert: Loud Image.* Dartmouth, NH: Hood Museum of Art, 2004.

Thomas, Peter N. "Historiographic Metafiction and the Neobaroque in Fernando del Paso's *Noticias del imperio.*" *Indiana Journal of Hispanic Literature* 6–7 (1995): 169–84.

Thompson, Krista. "The Sound of Light: Reflections on Art History in the Visual Culture of Hip-Hop." *Art Bulletin* 91, no. 4 (2009): 481–505.

Toman, Rolf, ed. *Baroque: Architecture, Sculpture, Painting.* Cologne: Könemann, 1998.

Torres, Rubén Ortiz. "Cathedrals on Wheels." *Art Issues* 54 (September/October 1998): 26–31.

———, dir. *Alien Toy: La Ranfla Cósmica (Unidentified Cruising Object).* 3/4″ SP. 8 min. Raza Cósmica Productions, Los Angeles, 1997.

———, dir. *Custom Mambo.* 5 min. 13 sec. ChiL.A.ngo Productions. CalArts, Valencia, California, 1992.

Toussaint, Manuel. *Colonial Art in Mexico.* 1948. Trans. and ed. Elizabeth Wilder Weismann. Austin: University of Texas Press, 1967.

Tweedie, James. "Caliban's Books: The Hybrid Text in Peter Greenaway's *Prospero's Books.*" *Cinema Journal* 40, no. 1 (Fall 2000): 104–26.

———. "The Suspended Spectacle of History: The Tableau Vivant in Derek Jarman's *Caravaggio.*" *Screen* 44, no. 4 (2003): 379–403.

Wacker, Kelly A., ed. *Baroque Tendencies in Contemporary Art.* Newcastle, UK: Cambridge Scholars, 2007.

Warnke, Frank J. *Versions of Baroque: European Literature in the Seventeenth Century.* New Haven, CT: Yale University Press, 1972.

Weisbach, Werner. *Der Barock als Kunst der Gegenreformation.* Berlin: P. Cassirer, 1921.

———. *El barroco, arte de la contrareforma.* Trans. Enrique Lafuente Ferrari. Madrid: Espasa-Calpe, 1942.

Wellek, René. "The Concept of Baroque in Literary Scholarship." 1945, updated 1962. In *Concepts of Criticism.* Ed. Stephen G. Nichols, Jr. New Haven, CT: Yale University Press, 1963. 69–129.

Williamson, Edwin. *The Penguin History of Latin America.* London: Penguin, 1992.

Witte, Bernd. *Walter Benjamin—Der Intellektuelle as Kritiker: Untersuchungen zu seinem Frühwerk.* Stuttgart: Metzler, 1976.

———. *Walter Benjamin: Mit Selbstzeugnissen und Bilddokumenten.* Reinbek: Rowohlt, 1985.

Wölfflin, Heinrich. *Principles of Art History: The Problem of the Development of Style in Later Art.* 1915. Trans. M. D. Hottinger. New York: Dover, 1950.

———. *Renaissance and Baroque.* 1888. Trans. Kathrin Simon. Ithaca, NY: Cornell University Press, 1967.

Worringer, Wilhelm. *Form in Gothic.* 1911. Trans. Herbert Read. London: Alec Tiranti, 1957.

Ybarra-Frausto, Tomás. "*Rasquachismo:* A Chicano Sensibility." In *Chicano Art: Resistance and Affirmation, 1965–1985.* Los Angeles: Wight Art Gallery, University of California, Los Angeles, 1990. 155–62.

Zamora, Lois Parkinson. "Magical Ruins/Magical Realism: Alejo Carpentier, François de Nomé, and the New World Baroque." In *Poetics of the Americas: Race, Founding, and Textuality.* Ed. Bainard Cowan and Jefferson Humphries. Baton Rouge: Louisiana State University Press, 1997. 63–103.

———. *The Inordinate Eye: New World Baroque and Latin American Fiction.* Chicago: University of Chicago Press, 2006.

Zamora, Lois Parkinson, and Monika Kaup, eds. *Baroque New Worlds: Representation, Transculturation, Counterconquest.* Durham, NC: Duke University Press, 2010.

Zurita, Raúl. *Anteparadise: A Bilingual Edition.* Trans. Jack Schmitt. Berkeley: University of California Press, 1986.

———. *Purgatorio.* 1979. Trans. Jeremy Jacobson. Pittsburgh, PA: Latin American Literary Review Press, 1985.

INDEX

Page numbers in italics indicate figures.